PERSONAL ACCIDENT, LIFE AND OTHER INSURANCES

BUTTERWORTHS INSURANCE LIBRARY

PERSONAL ACCIDENT, LIFE AND OTHER INSURANCES

By

E. R. HARDY IVAMY, LL.B., Ph.D., LL.D.

of the Middle Temple, Barrister
Professor of Law in the University of London

OLD EDITION

LONDON
BUTTERWORTHS
1973

ENGLAND:	BUTTERWORTH & CO. (PUBLISHERS) LTD. LONDON: 88 KINGSWAY, W.C.2B 6AB
AUSTRALIA:	BUTTERWORTHS PTY. LTD. SYDNEY: 586 PACIFIC HIGHWAY, CHATSWOOD, NSW 2067 MELBOURNE: 343 LITTLE COLLINS STREET, 3000 BRISBANE: 240 QUEEN STREET, 4000
CANADA:	BUTTERWORTH & CO. (CANADA) LTD. TORONTO: 14 CURITY AVENUE, 374
NEW ZEALAND:	BUTTERWORTHS OF NEW ZEALAND LTD. WELLINGTON; 26/28 WARING TAYLOR STREET, 1
SOUTH AFRICA:	BUTTERWORTH & CO. (SOUTH AFRICA) (PTY.) LTD. DURBAN: 152/154 GALE STREET

ISBN 0 406 25290 4

Printed and bound in Great Britain by R. J. Acford Ltd., Industrial Estate, Chichester, Sussex

PREFACE

This is the fourth and final volume in the Butterworths Insurance Library, which began with the publication in 1966 of "General Principles of Insurance Law" (Second Edition 1970). This was followed in 1968 by "Fire and Motor Insurance" (Second Edition 1973) and in 1969 by "Marine Insurance".

The present book surveys all the remaining aspects of the law of insurance, and incorporates some of the material to be found in Welford's "Accident Insurance" (Second Edition 1932), a work which is still of considerable relevance. It is to be emphasized, however, that the reader should still refer to "General Principles of Insurance Law" on certain matters common to all branches of insurance, e.g. non-disclosure of material facts, conditions, exceptions, premium, the employment of agents, etc.

The first Part of this book relates to "Personal Accident Insurance", particular attention being given to the event insured against and the application of the doctrine of proximate cause.

In Part II "Life Insurance" is considered with special reference to non-disclosure and misrepresentation of material facts and the persons to whom payment under the policy may be made.

Part III discusses "Industrial Assurance" and sets out the rights of owners of this kind of policy.

The subject of Part IV is "Property Insurance" and covers a wide variety of different types of insurance, e.g. burglary, all risks, transit, livestock, aviation and war risks insurance.

"Liability Insurance" forms Part V and includes public liability, pollution by oil, professional indemnity, and employers' liability insurance.

Part VI concerns "Guarantee Insurance", and "Reinsurance" is to be found in Part VII.

A number of cases are reported only in Lloyd's Law Reports, and no book on insurance would be complete without liberal references to the decisions in that series of law reports. I am greatly indebted to Mr. G. M. Hall, the Editor, and to Mr. E. S. Mathers, the Consulting Editor, of these reports.

I should like to thank the staff of Butterworths for undertaking the arduous job of preparing the Index and the Table of Cases and Statutes, and for seeing the book through the press.

E. R. Hardy Ivamy

University College London.

May 1973.

TABLE OF CONTENTS

PAGE

PART II—LIFE INSURANCE

PART III—INDUSTRIAL ASSURANCE

TABLE OF STATUTES

References in this Table to "*Statutes*" are to Halsbury's Statutes of England (Third Edition) showing the volume and page at which the annotated text of the Act will be found. Page references printed in bold type indicate where the Act is set out in part or in full.

TABLE OF CASES

In the following Table references are given where applicable to the English
and Empire Digest where a digest of the case will be found.

A

Table of Cases

xli

PART I

PERSONAL ACCIDENT INSURANCE

I

INTRODUCTION

Personal accident insurance is intended to secure to the insured or his representatives the payment of a sum of money in the event of disablement or death by accident.[1] It may also be extended to protect the insured against the consequences of certain specified diseases. It resembles life insurance in that it is not a contract of indemnity,[2] but merely a contract to pay a sum of money in a certain contingency.[3]

A personal accident policy does not, however, cease to be a contract of personal accident insurance, and become a contract of life insurance, because it purports to cover death by accident.[4] A life insurance policy is a contract to pay a sum of money on an event which must happen i.e. the death of the life insured, the only element of uncertainty being the date at which the death will take place.[5] In the case of a personal accident policy, on the

---

[1] In Part II of the Companies Act 1967 "personal accident insurance business" means "the business of effecting and carrying out contracts of insurance against risks of the persons insured sustaining injury as the result of an accident or of an accident of a specified class or dying as the result of an accident of a specified class or becoming incapacitated in consequence of disease or disease of a specified class, not being contracts falling within [s. 59 (6) (b)] above": Companies Act 1967, s. 59 (8). Contracts falling within s. 59 (6) (b) are those "against risks of the persons insured sustaining injury as the result of an accident or of an accident of a specified class or dying as the result of an accident or of a specified class or becoming incapacitated in consequence of disease or of a specified class, being contracts that are expressed to be in effect for a period of not less than five years or without limit of time and either are not expressed to be terminable by the insurer before the expiration of five years from the taking effect thereof, or are expressed to be so terminable before the expiration of that period only in special circumstances therein mentioned". Such contracts come within the expression "ordinary long-term insurance business" used in s. 33 (6). See further Ivamy, *General Principles of Insurance Law*, 2nd Edn., 1970, pp. 31–32.

[2] *Theobald* v. *Railway Passengers Assurance Co.* (1854), 10 Exch. 45, *per* ALDERSON, B., at p. 53.,

[3] *Bradburn* v. *Great Western Rail. Co.* (1874), L.R. 10 Exch. 1, *per* BRAMWELL, B. at p. 2, applying *Dalby* v. *India and London Life Assurance Co.* (1854), 15 C.B. 365 (life insurance); see also *Jebsen* v. *East and West India Dock Co.* (1875), L.R. 10 C.P. 300 (breach of contract) *per* DENMAN, J., at p. 305.

[4] *General Accident Assurance Corporation* v. *Inland Revenue Commissioners* 1906, 8 F. (Ct. of Sess.) 477, where a policy containing a stipulation for return of half the premium in the event of the assured attaining 65 or of his previous death, if the policy remained in force, was held to be a personal accident policy and not a life policy. Hence, the existence of a personal accident policy need not be disclosed in answer to a question as to other insurance in a life insurance proposal: *Montreal Coal and Towing Co.* v. *Metropolitan Life Insurance Co.* (1904), 24 Q.R.S.C. 399 (life insurance). In *Re Turcan* (1888), 40 Ch.D. 5, C.A., a personal accident policy was assumed to be a life policy and, as such, subject to the Policies of Assurance Act 1867, which is in terms limited to policies of life insurance.

[5] *Prudential Insurance Co.* v. *Inland Revenue Commissioners*, [1904] 2 K.B. 658 (life insurance) *per* CHANNELL, J., at p. 663.

3

other hand, the event on which the money will become payable is one which may never happen.[1] The death of the insured, if it in fact happens, is not the event insured against; the event insured against is the happening of an accident,[2] and the death of the insured is only the consequence of the accident. There are thus two elements of uncertainty involved, i.e. whether an accident will ever happen or not, and whether, if the accident does happen, it will result in death.

The contract of personal accident insurance is, as a rule, made in the usual way by means of a proposal[3] and policy. But it may be made by means of a coupon.[4]

The policy describes the event insured against e.g. the event of bodily injury caused by violent, external and visible means resulting in the insured's death or disablement.[5]

The policy contains various exceptions.[6] Of particular importance in personal accident insurance policies is the application of the doctrine of proximate cause.[7]

There are special provisions in the policy as to the making of a claim.[8]

Although the Life Insurance Act 1774 applies to personal accident insurance policies,[9] the question of insurable interest is in such policies of comparative unimportance. A policy of personal accident insurance is, in practice, usually effected by the insured in respect of his own bodily safety. In such a case, although the insured clearly has an insurable interest, it is not a pecuniary interest, and an insurance based upon it is not within the mischief of the Act of 1774. There is therefore no limit on the amount for which he may insure, provided he effects the policy for his own benefit.

Where, however, the insured insures a third person against accident, the Act of 1774 applies.[10] The insured must, therefore, have an insurable interest in the safety of the person insured i.e. he must be in such a position that he will suffer pecuniary loss in the event of an accident to the person insured. Thus, where the insured has entered into a contract, which on the part of the third person, must necessarily be performed in person, and the non-performance of which by the third person will involve the insured in pecuniary loss e.g. where an actor is engaged to appear in public, the insured has a sufficient interest in the safety of the third person to entitle him to insure against the consequences of non-performance caused by an accident to the third person.[11] He cannot, however, recover more than the value of

---

[1] *Prudential Insurance Co.* v. *Inland Revenue Commissioners*, [1904] 2 K.B. 658 (life insurance) *per* CHANNELL, J., at p. 663.

[2] *General Accident Assurance Corporation* v. *Inland Revenue Commissioners* 1906, 8 F. (Ct. of Sess.) 477; cf. *Lancashire Insurance Co.* v. *Inland Revenue Commissioners*, [1899] 1 Q.B. 353 (employers' liability insurance) *per* BRUCE, J., at p. 359.

[3] See Chapter 2, *post.*

[4] See Chapter 8, *post.*

[5] See Chapter 4, *post.*

[6] See Chapter 5, *post.*

[7] See Chapter 6, *post.*

[8] See Chapter 7, *post.*

[9] *Shilling* v. *Accidental Death Insurance Co.* (1857), 2 H. & N. 42.

[10] *Ibid.*

[11] *Blascheck* v. *Bussell* (1916), 33 T.L.R. 51, where, however, the insurable interest was not disputed.

his interest,[1] which, as the policy is in this case a contract of indemnity, is limited to the actual loss which he has sustained.[2]

The insurance may be intended, not for the benefit of the insured, but for the benefit of a third person. The actual name[3] of the person for whose benefit the insurance is effected must appear in the policy; otherwise the insurance is void.[4]

The existence of a personal accident insurance policy or the fact that payment has been received under it does not affect the right of the insured or of his personal representatives to recover damages from any person responsible for the accident in respect of which a claim may arise or a payment may be made under the policy. It is immaterial whether the accident resulted in the disablement or death of the insured.

Moreover the damages recovered in such an action enure for the benefit of the insured or his personal representatives, and not for the benefit of the insurers, since the contract of personal accident insurance is not a contract of indemnity, and the insurers, therefore, are not subrogated,[5] on payment of the sum due under the policy, to the rights of the insured or of his personal representatives against third persons.

---

[1] Life Assurance Act 1774, s. 3.
[2] *Blascheck* v. *Bussell* (*supra*), where an actress was engaged for a tour, and a policy was effected against her inability to appear through accident or sickness.
[3] A policy purporting to cover any "relative or friend" of the insured does not comply with the Act of 1774: *Williams* v. *Baltic Insurance Association*, [1924] 2 K.B. 282 (motor insurance) *per* ROCHE, J., at p. 290.
[4] Life Assurance Act 1774, s. 2; *Shilling* v. *Accidental Death Insurance Co.* (*supra*).
[5] As to subrogation, see Ivamy, *General Principles of Insurance Law*, 2nd Edn., 1970, pp. 415–430.

2

THE PROPOSAL FORM

The principal matters with which the proposal form deals are:
1 The nature of the risk.
2 Circumstances affecting the risk.
3 Previous history of the proposed insured.
4 Circumstances rendering him peculiarly liable to accident or disease.

1 Nature of Risk

In personal accident insurance the insured himself is the subject-matter of insurance. A detailed description of the proposed insured is, therefore, necessary, not so much for the purpose of identification, for which the personal particulars usually required in other classes of insurance would be sufficient, as for the purpose of placing before the insurers full information as to the nature of the proposed risk.[1]

The proposed insured is, therefore, required to answer questions relating to the following matters:

a His age,[2] and date of birth.[3]
b His weight and height.[4]
c The existence of any physical defects, e.g. whether his sight[5] or hearing is affected.

2 Circumstances Affecting Risk

The proposed insured is usually obliged to answer questions relating to the following matters:

---

[1] Even the usual personal particulars e.g. the description of the insured's occupation, may be material to the risk: *Biggar* v. *Rock Life Assurance Co.*, [1902] 1 K.B. 516; *Equitable Life Assurance Society* v. *General Accident Assurance Corporation* 1904, 12 S.L.T. 348; cf. *Perrins* v. *Marine General Travellers' Insurance Society* (1859), 2 E. & E. 317; *Woodall* v. *Pearl Assurance Co.*, [1919] 1 K.B. 593, C.A.; *Morran* v. *Railway Passengers Assurance Co. of London, England* (1919), 43 O.L.R. 561, in which cases the misdescription was held not to be material; and see *Ayrey* v. *British Legal and United Provident Assurance Co.*, [1918] 1 K.B. 136, where there was a waiver.

[2] *Westropp* v. *Bruce*, (1826) Batty 155 (life insurance), where it was held that a warranty as to age could not be dispensed with by an agent; *Hemmings* v. *Sceptre Life Association, Ltd.*, [1905] 1 Ch. 365 (life insurance), where the insurers were estopped by their conduct from relying on a mis-statement of the age of the insured; *Connors* v. *London and Provincial Assurance Co.*, [1913] W.C. & Ins. Rep. 408 (life insurance), where the agent of the insurers, in filling up the proposal, mis-stated the age of the life insured; see also *Joel* v. *Law Union and Crown Insurance Co.*, [1908] 2 K.B. 863, C.A. (life insurance) *per* FLETCHER MOULTON, L.J., at p. 885.

[3] *Keeling* v. *Pearl Assurance Co., Ltd.* (1923), 129 L.T. 573 (life insurance), where the date of birth was inconsistent with the age stated.

[4] *Levy* v. *Scottish Employers' Insurance Co.* (1901), 17 T.L.R. 229, where the height was overstated and the weight was understated.

[5] In *Bawden* v. *London, Edinburgh & Glasgow Assurance Co.*, [1892] 2 Q.B. 534, C.A., no specific question was asked on this point.

a   *His State of Health at the Time of Insuring*[1]

In addition to a general question as to whether he is perfectly well and in sound health, he may be asked whether he is suffering from certain specified diseases,[2] or whether he has been exposed to any infectious disease within a specified period.

b   *Pursuits and Habits*[3]

He is usually asked to state specifically whether he engages in certain sports, and whether he is and always has been of strictly sober and temperate habits.[4]   He may also be asked whether he has any intention of travelling outside the United Kingdom.[5]

---

[1] *Fidelity and Casualty Co. of New York* v. *Mitchell*, [1917] A.C. 592, P.C., where the fact that tuberculosis was latent was held not to constitute a breach of a warranty that the insured was in sound condition mentally and physically, as he had no apparent disease and would have been passed as sound by any doctor who might have examined him; *Ross* v. *Bradshaw* (1761), 1 Wm. Bl. 312 (life insurance), where the fact concealed was not material; *Armstrong* v. *Turquand* (1858), 9 I.C.L.R. 32 (life insurance), where the insured did not disclose the fact that he was paralysed.   If there is a change in health after the proposal is filled up, it is the duty of the insured to inform the insurers: *Morrison* v. *Muspratt* (1827), 4 Bing. 60 (life insurance); *British Equitable Insurance Co.* v. *Great Western Rail. Co.* (1869), 38 L.J. Ch. 314 (life insurance); cf. *Canning* v. *Farquhar* (1886), 16 Q.B.D. 727, C.A. (life insurance).

[2] *Watson* v. *Mainwaring* (1813), 4 Taunt. 763 (life insurance), where the question referred to "disorders tending to shorten life", and it was held that a disorder, not generally having a tendency to shorten life, was not within the question, even though the insured in fact died of it; *Joel* v. *Law Union and Crown Insurance Co.*, [1908] 2 K.B. 863, C.A. (life insurance) *per* FLETCHER MOULTON, L.J., at p. 885.

[3] *Forbes & Co.* v. *Edinburgh Life Assurance Co.* 1832, 10 Sh. (Ct. of Sess.) 451 (life insurance), where the fact that the life insured was an opium eater was not disclosed.

[4] *Thomson* v. *Weems* (1884), 9 App. Cas. 671 (life insurance) *per* Lord BLACKBURN at p. 684: "The object of the insurance company was to know that the life to be insured was not merely not rendered already diseased by drinking, but that his habits were so temperate that there was no unusual risk that he should become a drunkard . . . I think, therefore, that . . . we must take into account the normal habits in the class and in the locality where the person assured lives.   I think gentlemen in the last century drank habitually a great deal more than they do now, and I do not think a gentleman then would properly have been held to be of intemperate habits (within the meaning of such a policy) though he drank so much habitually that, if a gentleman now did so, the insurers would reasonably dread that he might drink more; and then he would not be held of temperate habits within the meaning of such a policy.   And I think it is fair, so far as the evidence enables us, to take into account the normal habits of the town councillors of Johnstone; the evidence does not satisfy me that they, as a general rule, drank as freely as the assured did."; and *per* Lord WATSON, at p. 695: "I believe it to be useless to attempt a precise definition of what constitutes 'temperate habits' or 'temperance', in the sense in which these expressions are ordinarily employed.   Men differ so much in their capacity for imbibing strong drink that quantity affords no test; what one man might take without exceeding the bounds of moderation another could not take without committing excess.   In judging of a man's sobriety, his position in life, and the habits of the class, to which he belongs must, in my opinion, always be taken into account, because it is the custom of men engaged in certain lines of business to take what is called refreshment without any imputation of excess, at times when a similar indulgence on the part of men not so engaged would be, to say the least, suspicious.   But I do not think that the habits of a particular locality ought to be taken into account, or that a man who would be generally regarded as of intemperate habits, ought to escape from that imputation because he is no worse than his neighbours." The words relate only to the use or abuse of alcohol, and are inappropriate to drug habits: *Yorke* v. *Yorkshire Insurance Co.*, [1918] 1 K.B. 662 (life insurance).   In determining whether an answer is true, it is important to consider the exact phrasing of the question: *Connecticut Mutual Life Insurance Co. of Hertford* v. *Moore* (1881), 6 App. Cas. 644, 648, P.C. (life insurance).

[5] Unless the policy otherwise provides, the phrase "the United Kingdom" includes the Channel Islands: *Stoneham* v. *Ocean Railway & General Accident Insurance Co.* (1887), 19 Q.B.D. 237.

3 Previous History of the Proposed Insured

The proposed insured is usually asked whether he has suffered from any illness or accident within a specified period.[1] He may, further, be required to answer a specific question as to whther he has ever suffered[2] from certain named diseases;[3] and a similar question may be put as to his near relatives.[4]

Thus, in *Lee* v. *British Law Insurance Co., Ltd.*[5] the insured, who suffered from myopia, wished to effect a policy of personal accident and sickness insurance, and was asked the following question in a proposal form: "Has the person to be insured sustained any accidents or illnesses during the past five years?"

He completed the form on September 12, 1968, and answered "No" to this question, and also signed a declaration that he was in "good health and had no physical or mental defect or infirmity". In December 1968 his eyesight became worse, and he was found to have a cataract in each eye. He claimed under the policy, but the insurers repudiated liability on the policy on the ground that he had failed to disclose facts which were relevant for them to know *viz.* that in 1958 an eye specialist had sent him for pathological tests, that a condition of cataract had been discovered in both eyes in May 1968, and that although he was not told of his condition, he had been advised to have further tests at a hospital.[6] The Court of Appeal[7] gave judgment for the insurers. KARMINSKI, L.J., observed:[8]

"The [insured] was guilty of carelessness rather than bad faith. What is important is that he failed to make a full disclosure. In the case of eye illness this is as

---

[1] A question of this kind is of a somewhat embarrassing character and cannot be reasonably expected to be answered with strict and literal truth. It must be read with some limitation and qualification to render it reasonable. The insured cannot be expected to recollect and disclose every illness, however slight, or every personal injury, consisting of a contusion, or a cut, or a blow, which he may have suffered in the course of his life. Personal injury therefore, must be interpreted as one of a somewhat severe or serious character: *Connecticut Mutual Life Insurance Co. of Hertford* v. *Moore* (*supra*) (life insurance) at p. 648; see also *Joel* v. *Law Union & Crown Insurance Co.*, [1908] 2 K.B. 863, C.A. (life insurance) *per* FLETCHER MOULTON, L.J., at p. 844; *Yorke* v. *Yorkshire Insurance Co.* (*supra*) (life insurance); *I.O.F.* v. *Turmelle* (1910), 10 Q.R.K.B. 261 (life insurance), where the word "disease" was held to mean diseases of similar character to those specifically mentioned.

[2] This does not apply to isolated symptoms not due to disease: *Chattock* v. *Shawe* (1835), 1 Mood. & R. 498 (life insurance), where the insured had had a fit in consequence of an accident. Cf. *Geach* v. *Ingall* (1845), 14 M. & W. 95 (life insurance), where the insured had spat blood, not through having a tooth extracted, but from internal weakness.

[3] For cases in which the insured was unaware that he had suffered from a specified disease, see *Swete* v. *Fairlie* (1833), 6 C. & P. 1 (life insurance); *Jones* v. *Provincial Insurance Co.* (1857), 3 C.B.N.S. 65 (life insurance); *Fowkes* v. *Manchester and London Life Insurance Co.* (1862), 3 F. & F. 440 (life insurance); *Thomson* v. *Weems* (1884), 9 App. Cas. 671 (life insurance) *per* Lord WATSON at p. 693, explaining *Hutchison* v. *National Loan Fund Life Assurance Co.* 1845, 7 Dunl. (Ct. of Sess.) 467 (life insurance), and *Life Association of Scotland* v. *Foster* (1873), 11 Macph. (Ct. of Sess.) 351 (life insurance); *Joel* v. *Law Union and Crown Insurance Co.*, [1908] 2 K.B. 863, C.A. (life insurance); and cf. *British Equitable Insurance Co.* v. *Musgrave* (1887), 3 T.L.R. 630 (life insurance), where there was wilful concealment; *Smith* v. *Grand Orange Lodge of British America* (1903), 6 O.L.R. 588 (life insurance).

[4] *Anderson* v. *Fitzgerald* (1853), 4 H.L. Cas. 484 (life insurance); *Joel* v. *Law Union and Crown Insurance Co.* (*supra*) *per* FLETCHER MOULTON, L.J., at p. 885.

[5] [1972] 2 Lloyd's Rep. 49, C.A.

[6] The evidence is set out *ibid.*, at pp. 54–57.

[7] DAVIES, KARMINSKI and STEPHENSON, L.JJ.

[8] [1972] 2 Lloyd's Rep. at p. 57. See also the judgment of STEPHENSON, L.J., *ibid.*, at p. 57, where he said that he did not think that the case really turned on the answers in the proposal form, and that the failure of the insured to disclose facts which he must have known were relevant for the insurers to know.

important to disclose as in any other form or illness or ill health. Myopia . . . by itself need not probably be disclosed; but in this case there is ample evidence that there was more than mere myopia. The special importance of cataract in relation to a contract of this kind is that it may be, and often is, associated with other illnesses, for example, diabetes''.

The names and addresses of his usual[1] medical attendant and of any other medical man consulted by him within a specified period[2] are usually required to be given.[3]

The words "medical attendant" mean the person who has actually attended the insured, not a medical practitioner who attends the family and happens to be acquainted with the insured.[4] The person last in attendance ought, as a rule, to be named, not the person previously attending the insured.[5] But there may be circumstances in which, not the last person consulted, but the previous medical attendant is the "usual medical attendant" within the meaning of the question.

In the words of Lord ABINGER, C.B.:

"The terms and nature of the question proved that it was designed to extract from the person, who is the medical attendant best able to give an account of her constitution at that time; and if she has no usual medical attendant in the precise grammatical sense of the question, it appears to me that she is bound to mention who is the medical attendant who could give that information."[6]

Though a hypodermic injection is not a "surgical operation", within the meaning of a question in the proposal form, the medical man giving it is a "physician who has prescribed for or treated or been consulted by" the insured.[7]

4 Circumstances Rendering Him Peculiarly Liable to Accident or Disease

The proposal form may contain a general question requiring the proposed insured to state whether there are any circumstances connected with his occupation, health, pursuits, or habits of life, rendering him peculiarly liable to accident or disease.[8]

---

[1] The word "usual" implies having attended more than once: *Huckamn* v. *Fernie* (1838), 3 M. & W. 505 (life insurance) *per* Lord ABINGER, C.B., at p. 520; *Scamlan* v. *Sceales* (1849), 13 I.L.R. 71 (life insurance).

[2] *Cazenove* v. *British Equitable Assurance Co.* (1860), 29 L.J.C.P. 160, Ex. Ch. (life insurance); *Joel* v. *Law Union & Crown Insurance Co.*, [1908] 2 K.B. 863, C.A. (life insurance), where the jury found that the assured had foolishly, but not fraudulently, failed to disclose the fact of consulting a particular medical man; *Smith* v. *Grand Orange Lodge of British America (supra)*, where the concealment was fraudulent.

[3] *See Connecticut Mutual Life Insurance Co. of Hertford* v. *Moore* (1881), 6 App. Cas. 644, P.C. (life insurance), at p. 648.

[4] *Everett* v. *Desborough* (1829), 5 Bing. 503 (life insurance); *Huckman* v. *Fernie (supra)*; cf. *Hutton* v. *Waterloo Life Assurance Co.* (1859), 1 F. & F. 735 (life insurance).

[5] *Morrison* v. *Muspratt* (1827), 4 Bing. 60 (life insurance).

[6] *Huckman* v. *Fernie (supra)* at p. 519. Cf. also *Cazenove* v. *British Equitable Insurance Co.* (1860), 29 L.J.C.P. 160, Ex.Ch. (life insurance).

[7] *Mutual Life Insurance Co. of New York* v. *Ontario Metal Products Co.*, [1925] A.C. 344, P.C. (life insurance).

[8] *Bawden* v. *London, Edinburgh and Glasgow Assurance Co.*, [1892] 2 Q.B. 534, C.A., where the agent, who filled up the proposal, omitted to state that the insured had only one eye; *Cruikshank* v. *Northern Accident Insurance Co., Ltd.* 1895, 23 R. (Ct. of Sess.) 147, where the insured, who had been very lame from childhood, stated, on the agent's dictation, that he had a slight lameness from birth. Cf. *Australian Widows' Fund Life Assurance Society, Ltd.* v. *National Mutual Life Association of Australasia, Ltd.*, [1914] A.C. 634, P.C.

3

THE CONTENTS OF THE POLICY

The principal contents of a personal accident insurance policy concern:

1 The event insured against.
2 The exceptions.
3 The conditions.
4 The schedule.

Event Insured Against[1]

A typical personal accident insurance policy states that the insurers will pay the insured or his personal representatives a sum stated in the Schedule if he suffers bodily injury resulting from accident caused by violent, external and visible means which directly and independently of any other cause, results within a stated period e.g. 12 months, in death, loss or disablement.

Exceptions[2]

An exception often states that the insurers will not be liable for bodily injury or death if the insured wilfully exposes himself to any needless peril, or if such injury or death is consequent upon medical or surgical treatment.

Further exceptions from liability are if the injury or death is sustained whilst the insured is under the influence of drink, or is engaged in dangerous sports e.g. motor cycling and mountaineering, or is travelling in an aircraft in a non-scheduled flight.

Conditions[3]

A condition usually requires the insured to give notice to the insurers as soon as practicable of any event which may give rise to a claim. He is required to submit any information and evidence to them.

Schedule

The Schedule sets out the name and address of the insured, the period of insurance, the premium payable, the amount of compensation payable,[4] and the definition of the terms used in the policy.

---

[1] See Chapter 4, *post.*
[2] See Chapter 5, *post.*
[3] See pp. 55–58, *post.*
[4] See pp. 59–60, *post.*

4

THE EVENT INSURED AGAINST

The undertaking of the insurers under a personal accident policy is, in the words of a form in common use,

> "to insure the insured against the event of bodily injury caused by violent, accidental, external and visible means, which injury shall, solely and independently of any other cause, cause his death or disablement."

Many other forms of expression are in use, differing in effect, especially with regard to the qualifications imposed upon the general undertaking of the insurers. It is, therefore, necessary, more perhaps in personal accident insurance than in any other branch of insurance, to consider carefully the exact words used in a particular policy to express the event insured against.[1]

Complications are introduced by the fact that there are at least two chains of causation involved:

1 The death or disablement must be caused by bodily injury; and
2 The bodily injury must be caused by accident.

In addition, it may be necessary to take into consideration the cause of the accident.

The policy may, if the party so desires, extend to cover death or disablement by certain specified diseases. In this case no difficulty as to causation arises, the only question being whether the disease which causes the death or disablement is one of the diseases specified in the policy.

Sometimes the policy expressly covers any injury that might possibly be sustained. Thus, in *Woolford* v. *Liverpool County Council; Surrey County Council; and Inner London Education Authority*[2] the plaintiff took part in a venture course in North Wales which was organised by the defendants. The application form for the course stated "The [defendants] take out a special insurance policy[3] to cover any injury that might possibly be sustained during the course." No insurance policy was taken out by the defendants. The plaintiff was injured on the course while rock climbing and claimed £1,750 from them. They maintained that their liability was limited to a sum which

---

[1] Cf. *Smith* v. *Accident Insurance Co.* (1870), L.R. 5 Exch. 302, where death from erysipelas set up by an accidental injury was not held not to be covered by the policy, with *Mardorf* v. *Accident Insurance Co.*, [1903] 1 K.B. 584, where death from erysipelas in similar circumstances was held to be covered. See p. 50, *post*.

[2] [1968] 2 Lloyd's Rep. 256, Q.B.D.

[3] His Lordship said that he was content to assume that the words "a special insurance policy" meant an insurance policy specially taken out for this particular course which was being carried out between April 16 and April 25, 1965; *ibid.*, at p. 258.

would have been payable to the plaintiff if they had taken out a personal accident policy such as might reasonably have been effected in the circumstances.

ROSKILL, J., held that the action succeeded. He said[1] that what the defendants were obliged to do was to provide a special policy which had it been obtained would have covered any injury which might possibly have been sustained. It might be that such a policy would have been different from the ordinary run of personal accident policies. Further, it might have been a difficult policy to obtain, and it might have been more expensive to obtain than the ordinary run of personal accident policies. But the question was not one of cost. On the language which they had seen fit to use they obliged themselves to provide a policy unrestricted in amount covering any injury that might possibly be sustained by any young person upon the course.

Further, his Lordship said[2] that when one saw that the words "to cover any injury" were followed by the words "that might possibly be sustained during the course", the use of the adverb "possibly" in the context[3] suggested that the intention was not only to provide reassurance to parents, but also to provide a cover of considerable width.

"BODILY INJURY"

There are certain cases in which the existence of bodily injury is obvious, e.g. when the insured's leg or skull is fractured, or his finger crushed, or where he is stabbed or otherwise wounded.

It is not, however, necessary that there should be any fracture or lesion, or that the injury should manifest itself by outward and physical signs.[4]

Thus, immediate death, without the intervention of external injury, whether by drowning[5] or by suffocation caused by smoke[6] or gas,[7] or by a fall from the top of a house,[8] is caused by bodily injury, within the meaning of the policy.

Moreover, an internal injury, such as a rupture[9] or a strained muscle or tendon,[10] is sufficient. Even disease or bodily infirmity of any kind amounts to bodily injury within the meaning of the policy, if caused by accident and not merely developed within the system by natural causes.[11] In particular,

---

[1] His Lordship said that he was content to assume that the words "a special insurance policy" meant an insurance policy specially taken out for this particular course which was being carried out between April 16 and April 25, 1965; *ibid.*, at p. 259.

[2] *Ibid.*, at p. 258.

[3] *Ibid.*, at p. 258.

[4] *Trew* v. *Railway Passengers Assurance Co.* (1861), 6 H. & N. 839, Ex.Ch., *per* COCKBURN, C.J., at p. 844; *Hamlyn* v. *Crown Accidental Insurance Co., Ltd.*, [1893] 1 Q.B. 750, C.A.; *Re Etherington and Lancashire and Yorkshire Accident Insurance Co.*, [1909] 1 K.B. 591, C.A.

[5] *Trew* v. *Railway Passengers Assurance Co.* (*supra*); *Winspear* v. *Accident Insurance Co.* (1880), 6 Q.B.D. 42.

[6] *Trew* v. *Railway Passengers Assurance Co.* (*supra*) *per* COCKBURN, C.J., at p. 844.

[7] Cf. *Re United London and Scottish Insurance Co., Ltd., Brown's Claim*, [1915] 2 Ch. 167, C.A., where it was assumed that, but for an exception, the cause of death would have been within the policy.

[8] *Trew* v. *Railway Passengers Assurance Co.* (*supra*), *per* COCKBURN, C.J., at p. 844.

[9] *Fitton* v. *Accidental Death Insurance Co.* (1864), 17 C.N.B.S. 122.

[10] *Hooper* v. *Accidental Death Insurance Co.* (1860), 5 H. & N. 546, Ex. Ch.; *Hamlyn* v. *Crown Accidental Insurance Co., Ltd.*, [1893] 1 Q.B. 750, C.A.; cf. *Re Scarr and General Accident Assurance Corporation*, [1905] 1 K.B. 387, *per* BRAY, J., at p. 393.

[11] *Mardorf* v. *Accident Insurance Co.*, [1903] 1 K.B. 584; *Re Etherington and Lancashire and Yorkshire Accident Insurance Co.*, [1909] 1 K.B. 591, C.A.; *Youlden* v. *London Guarantee and Accident Co.* (1913), 28 O.L.R. 161.

the following diseases, when caused by accident, have been held to fall within the scope of a personal accident policy:- hernia,[1] erysipelas,[2] and pneumonia.[3]

Mere mental pain or grief or shock does not constitute bodily injury, unless manifesting itself by operating upon the person of the insured and producing physical disease.[4]

"Accident"

The word "accident" involves the idea of something fortuitous and unexpected.

> "It is difficult to define the term 'accident' as used in a policy of this nature, so as to draw with perfect accuracy a boundary line between injury or death from accident, and injury or death from natural causes; such as shall be of universal application. At the same time, we may safely assume that, in the term 'accident' as so used, some violence, casualty or *vis major*, is necessarily involved. We cannot think disease produced by the action of a known cause can be considered as accidental."[5]

The term is opposed to something proceeding from natural causes;[6] and injury caused by accident is to be regarded as the antithesis to bodily infirmity caused by disease in the ordinary course of events.[7]

An injury is caused by "accident" in the following cases:

1 Where the injury is the natural result of a fortuitous and unexpected cause.

2 Where the injury is the fortuitous and unexpected result of a natural cause.

3 Where the injury is caused by the act of a third person.

4 Where the injury is caused by the act of the insured himself.

1 Natural Result of Fortuitous and Unexpected Cause

In this case the element of accident manifests itself in the cause of the injury. Examples are: where the insured is run over by a train,[8] or thrown from his horse while hunting,[9] or injured by a fall, whether through slipping

---

[1] *Fitton* v. *Accidental Death Insurance Co.* (*supra*).

[2] *Mardorf* v. *Accident Insurance Co.* (*supra*), where erysipelas was followed by septicaemia and septic pneumonia resulting in death, and the policy was held to apply; *Accident Insurance Co. of North America* v. *Young* (1892), 20 S.C.R. 280; cf. *Smith* v. *Accident Insurance Co.* (1870), L.R. 5 Ex. 302, where the majority of the Court held that the supervening erysipelas fell within an exception.

[3] *Isitt* v. *Railway Passengers Assurance Co.* (1889), 22 Q.B.D. 504; *Mardorf* v. *Accident Insurance Co.* (*supra*); *Re Etherington and Lancashire and Yorkshire Accident Insurance Co.* (*supra*).

[4] *Pugh* v. *London, Brighton and South Coast Rail. Co.*, [1896] 2 Q.B. 248, C.A.

[5] *Sinclair* v. *Maritime Passengers' Assurance Co.* (1861), 3 E. & E. 478 *per* Cockburn, C.J., at p. 485. See further, *Reynolds* v. *Accidental Insurance Co.* (1870), 22 L.T. 820 *per* Willes, J., at p. 821: "I think that the fact of the deceased falling into the water from sudden insensibility was an accident"; *Re Scarr and General Accident Assurance Corporation* (*supra*), *per* Bray, J., at p. 393: "The evidence shows that there was no intervening fortuitous cause."; *Pugh* v. *London, Brighton and South Coast Rail. Co.* (*supra*), *per* A. L. Smith, L.J., at p. 253.

[6] *Re Scarr and General Accident Assurance Corporation* (*supra*), *per* Bray, J., at p. 393.

[7] *Sinclair* v. *Maritime Passengers' Insurance Co.* (*supra*), *per* Cockburn, C.J., at p. 485.

[8] *Lawrence* v. *Accidental Insurance Co., Ltd.* (1881), 7 Q.B.D. 216; *Cornish* v. *Accident Insurance Co.* (1889), 23 Q.B.D. 453; *Wallace* v. *Employers' Liability Assurance Co.* (1912), 21 O.W.R. 249; cf. *Pugh* v. *London, Brighton and South Coast Rail. Co.*, [1896] 2 Q.B. 248, C.A., where the injury was caused by apprehension of a collision.

[9] *Re Etherington and Lancashire and Yorkshire Accident Insurance Co.*, [1909] 1 K.B. 591, C.A.

on a step[1] or otherwise;[2] or where the insured drinks poison by mistake;[3] or is suffocated by the smoke of a house on fire[4] or by an escape of gas,[5] or is drowned whilst bathing,[6] or dies from a bite of a poisonous insect,[7] or from a fall out of bed,[8] or from carbon monoxide poisoning when a car is stuck in a snowdrift and the insured was trying to free it by rocking it back and forth under power and carbon monoxide was caused by snow piling up at the rear of the vehicle.[9]

In *Pugh* v. *London Brighton and South Coast Railway Co.*[10] the employers of a signalman working on their railway issued him with a personal accident insurance policy, which stated that they would pay him a specified weekly sum in case of "his being incapacitated from employment by reason of accident sustained in the discharge of his duty in the company's service". The insured was on duty at a signal box near East Croydon station when he saw fire and dust coming from underneath a Pullman car of the Brighton express.[11] He leaned out of the window, and by waving a red flag succeeded in stopping the train. The result of the excitement of the moment was a severe shock to the insured's nerves which incapacitated him from any employment. He claimed under the policy, but the employers would not pay the sum insured on the ground that the insured had suffered no "accident" within the meaning of the policy. The Court of Appeal[12] gave judgment for the insured, for what had happened was an "accident". KAY, L.J., observed:[13]

> "But it is said this is not within the policy because he was not touched by the train, or injured by any impact of air occasioned by an explosion, or by anything accidentally happening in connection with the passage of the train. All he suffered from was the shock to the nerves occasioned by the excitement, and the tremendous responsibility which was suddenly thrown upon him, and that, it is said, was not an accident. Now, I confess that I am not able to follow that argument. It seems to me that it was an accident which occasioned his incapacity quite as much as if he had been struck down by the train in passing. I might

---

[1] *Theobald* v. *Railway Passengers Assurance Co.* (1854), 10 Exch. 45; *Powis* v. *Ontario Accident Insurance Co.* (1901), 1 O.L.R. 54.

[2] *Fitton* v. *Accidental Death Insurance Co.* (1864), 17 C.B.N.S. 122; *Isitt* v. *Railway Passengers Assurance Co.* (1889), 22 Q.B.D. 504; *Accident Insurance Co. of North America* v. *Young* (1892), 20 S.C.R. 280.

[3] *Cole* v. *Accident Insurance Co., Ltd.* (1889), 61 L.T. 227.

[4] *Trew* v. *Railway Passengers Assurance Co.* (1861), 6 H. & N. 839, Ex. Ch., *per* COCKBURN, C.J., at p. 844.

[5] *Re United London and Scottish Insurance Co., Ltd., Brown's Claim*, [1915] 2 Ch. 167, C.A.

[6] *Trew* v. *Railway Passengers Assurance Co.* (*supra*); *Young* v. *Maryland Casualty Co.* (1909), 10 W.L.R. 8; *Haines* v. *Canadian Railway Accident Insurance Co.* (1910), 15 W.L.R. 300; *Ferland* v. *Prudential Insurance Co.*, [1938] 4 D.L.R. 813; *MacDonald* v. *Refuge Assurance Co.* 1890, 17 R. (Ct. of Sess.) 955; *Reynolds* v. *Accidental Insurance Co.* (1870), 22 L.T. 820.

[7] *Castle's Estate* v. *Southern Life Association* (1906), 23 S.C. 338.

[8] *Little* v. *London and Lancashire Guarantee and Accident Co. of Canada*, [1941] 1 D.L.R. 187.

[9] *Sklar* v. *Saskatchewan Government Insurance Office* (1965), 52 W.W.R. 264. Cf. *Smith* v. *British Pacific Life Insurance Co.*, [1965] S.C.R. 434, where the insured suffered a heart attack whilst in a car stuck in a snowdrift and it was held that his death had not been caused by "accident", for although he was operating the vehicle by driving it alternately forward and in reverse, the facts did not show any unintended happening which in itself could be deemed accidental and the cause of death.

[10] (1896), 74 L.T. 724.

[11] The cause of the fire and dust was that a wheel had broken up and left the rails: *ibid.*, at p. 725.

[12] Lord ESHER, KAY and SMITH, L.JJ.

[13] (1896), 74 L.T. at p. 726. See also the judgment of Lord ESHER, M.R., *ibid.*, at p. 725, and that of SMITH, L.J., *ibid.*, at p. 726.

put a hundred instances. What occurred to me was this. Suppose the man had been on the line in the four-foot way in the discharge of his duty, and had suddenly seen the train coming upon him and had hurried to get out of the way, and by the tremendous effort he made to get out of the four-foot way before the train came upon him had sustained such a shock to his nervous system that he never recovered from it, or even had died. Could it possibly be said that that was not an accident occurring to him in the discharge of his duty? I confess I should be unable to agree to that."

Again, in *Trew* v. *Railway Passengers Assurance Co.*[1]

The insured had taken out a personal accident insurance policy, by the terms of which the insurers would pay the sum insured if "he sustained any injury caused by accident or violence and should die within 3 months". He left his lodgings at Brighton, and six weeks later his body was washed ashore on the Essex coast. His personal representatives claimed that the insurers were liable under the policy.
Held, by the Court of Exchequer Chamber[2], that assuming that he died from "drowning", it was death by "accident" within the meaning of the policy, and the personal representatives were entitled to the sum insured.

COCKBURN, C.J., said:[3]

"It is said that, assuming the deceased died by drowning, drowning is not one of the cases comprehended in this policy of assurance. [Counsel] ingeniously argued that the policy only applies to cases where from accident or violence some injury occurs from which death may or may not ensue; and if it ensues within three months, the sum assured is payable. But he contended, in effect, that where the cause of death produces immediate death without the inter- vention of any external injury, the policy does not apply; and whereas from the action of the water there is no external injury, death by the action of the water is not within the meaning of this policy. That argument, if carried to its extreme length, would apply to every case where death was immediate. If a man fell from the top of a house, or overboard from a ship, and was killed; or if a man was suffocated by the smoke of a house on fire, such cases would be excluded from the policy, and the effect would be that policies of this kind, in many cases where death resulted from accident, would afford no protection whatever to the assured. We ought not to give to those policies a construction which will defeat the protection of the assured in a large class of cases. We are therefore of opinion that, if there was evidence for the jury that the deceased died by drown- ing, that was a death by accident within the terms of this policy."

In *Reynolds* v. *Accidental Insurance Co.*[4] a clause in a personal accident insurance policy stated that

"No claim shall be payable . . . under the policy in respect of death or injury by accident or violence unless such death or injury shall be occasioned by some external and material cause operating upon the person of the . . . insured . . .".

The insured while on a visit to Hastings went into the sea to bathe. While in a pool about 1 ft. deep he became insensible from some unexplained internal cause, and fell into the water with his face downwards. A few minutes afterwards he was found lying dead, and water escaped from his lungs in such a manner as to prove that he had breathed after falling into

---

[1] (1861), 6 H. & N. 839.
[2] The court ordered a new trial in order that it might be established whether in fact the insured had died from drowning: *ibid.*, at p. 845.
[3] *Ibid.*, at p. 844.
[4] (1870), 22 L.T. 820.

the water. The immediate cause of death was by suffocation by the water, but the pool being shallow, suffocation would not have taken place if the insured had not been incapable of helping himself. His personal representative claimed from the insurers the sum insured under the policy. WILLES, J., held that the claim succeeded, and said:[1]

> "In this case the death resulted from the action of the water on the lungs, and from the consequent interference with respiration. I think that the fact of the deceased falling in the water from sudden insensibility was an accident, and consequently that our judgment must be for the plaintiff."

2   Fortuitous and Unexpected Result of Natural Cause

In this case the element of accident manifests itself, not in the cause, but in its result. Instances are where a person lifts a heavy burden in the ordinary course of business and injures his spine,[2] or stoops down to pick up a marble and tears a ligament in his knee,[3] or ruptures himself whilst playing golf.[4]

In *Hamlyn* v. *Crown Accidental Insurance Co.*[5] the insurers issued a personal accident insurance policy to the insured against bodily injuries "caused by violent, accidental external and visible means". The insured was a shopkeeper. A child, who was with a customer in the shop, dropped a marble on the floor. The insured stooped down and reached to pick it up, but could not do so. When he rose, he found that his knee was stiff and would not straighten. The medical evidence showed that he suffered from dislocation of the semi-lunar cartilage i.e. the slipping out of the cartilage from between the femur and the tibia. He had not stepped on anything nor had he hit his knee or leg against anything. When he claimed under the policy, the insurers repudiated liability on the ground that he had not suffered an "accident" within the meaning of the policy. The Court of Appeal[6] held that the claim succeeded, Lord ESHER, M.R., saying:[7]

> "I cannot feel any doubt but that this was an accident; the man did not intend to wrench his knee, and a wrench would not be the ordinary result of what he did. The wrench was an accident. Then was it 'violent?' We must construe that word broadly, and I think it was clearly violent. Was it 'external?' That is really the word which we have to construe in this policy. After having exhausted all argument as to the meaning of that word, I feel certain that the word 'external' in this policy and in the place in which it is used, and when we look at the subsequent proviso, bears a meaning which is the antithesis of 'internal'. I think that the meaning of the policy is, that if the cause is internal, such as a clot of blood or inherent weakness, the case is not within the policy, but that if

---

[1] (1870), 22 L.T. at p. 821.
[2] *Martin* v. *Travellers' Insurance Co.* (1859), 1 F. & F. 505; cf. *Youlden* v. *London Guarantee and Accident Co.* (1913), 28 O.L.R. 161; *Horsfall* v. *Pacific Mutual Insurance Co.* (1903), 98 Am. St. Rep. 846, distinguished in *Re Scarr and General Accident Assurance Corporation*, [1905] 1 K.B. 387. See also *Semkow* v. *Merchants' Casualty Insurance Co.*, [1937] 2 W.W.R. 669, where the insured tried to lift a heavy iron jack from the ground and strained his back in doing so.
[3] *Hamlyn* v. *Crown Accidental Insurance Co.*, [1893] 1 Q.B. 750, C.A.
[4] *Claxton* v. *Travellers' Insurance Co. of Hartford* (1917), Q.R. 52 S.C. 239. But in *Long* v. *Colonial Mutual Life Assurance Society, Ltd.*, [1931] N.Z.L.R. 528, where the insured was in normal health, and severely sprained his shoulder while throwing up a tennis ball, he failed in his claim that the bodily injury had been caused solely and directly by accidental violent external and visible means because the evidence did not warrant that the injury was other than the natural result of his voluntary act.
[5] (1893), 68 L.T. 701.
[6] Lord ESHER, M.R., LOPES and SMITH, L.JJ.
[7] (1893), 68 L.T. at p. 702.

the cause is not internal, it is external, and the case is within the policy. I am clearly of opinion that 'external' is meant to be the opposite of 'internal.' Here there was no internal cause, and therefore it was an external cause. Everything that happened was the opposite of internal, and was therefore external, and, if external, was visible; the stooping and reaching were all visible. What happened in this case was within the terms of the policy, and the plaintiff was entitled to succeed."

LOPES, L.J., agreeing, said[1] that the word "accidental" meant "unexpected, unforeseen, casual", and what happened in this case was all three, and was "accidental". It did not arise from natural causes nor inherent weakness, but from stooping and reaching after the marble. The cause was "external" and visible. SMITH, L.J., delivered a concurring judgment.[2]

In *Weyerhaeuser* v. *Evans*[3] the insured had effected a personal accident insurance policy which insured him against "any bodily injury by accident which shall . . . directly cause the death of the assured". During the currency of the policy a pimple formed in the insured's left nostril, and according to the claim put forward by his personal representatives, a friend of his squeezed and jabbed the pimple, and thus caused a break in the tissues by which bacteria reached the blood stream and by which the insured died of septicaemia. The personal representatives contended that the insured died as the result of an "accident", but this was denied by the underwriter, who repudiated liability.

ROCHE, J., held that there was no evidence showing that there was any accident or accidental injury causing the pimple.[4] It had not been established that the friend treated the pimple in the manner alleged,[5] and even if such fact were proved, it had not been shown that the treatment had caused the infection.[6] The personal representatives had not discharged the burden of proving that the death was due to accident.[7]

In *Martin* v. *Travellers' Insurance Co.*[8] the plaintiff was insured under a personal accident insurance policy against bodily injury "arising from any accident or violence provided that the injury shall be occasioned by any external or material cause operating on the person of the insured". In the course of his business he lifted a heavy weight and injured the muscles of his back. On a claim being made by the insured WIGHTMAN, J., in directing the jury said:[9] "The question is whether the injury really and substantially

---

[1] (1893), 68 L.T. at p. 702.
[2] *Ibid.*, at p. 703.
[3] (1932), 43 Ll. L. Rep. 62, K.B.D.
[4] *Ibid.*, at p. 66.
[5] *Ibid.*, at p. 66.
[6] *Ibid.*, at p. 67.
[7] *Ibid.*, at p. 68. His Lordship left open the point as to whether the friend's action was covered by an exception in the policy which stated: "This policy does not cover death directly caused or contributed to by . . . disease or natural causes . . . nor does it cover death directly or indirectly resulting from medical or surgical treatment", and observed (*ibid.*, at p. 68): "It is said that treatment by a nurse or an osteopath, if it is directed and purports to be medical or surgical treatment, is as much medical or surgical treatment as if it is administered by a doctor or a surgeon. Against that [counsel for the plaintiffs] puts the direct negative in argument; he says that if a person takes too much Eno's fruit salts of his own motion or on the prescription of a friend, that is not medical or surgical treatment. Again, that is a nice question on which a lengthy and powerful argument can be adduced. All I can say about it is that it is unnecessary for me to decide it . . .".
[8] (1859), 1 F. & F. 505, Surrey Spring Assizes.
[9] *Ibid.*, at p. 507.

arose from the accident; if it did not, find for the [insurers]; if it did, find for the [insured]". The jury gave their verdict for the plaintiff for the full sum insured under the policy.

On the other hand, an injury is not caused by accident if it is the natural result of a natural cause,[1] e.g. where a person is exposed in the ordinary course of his business to the heat of a tropical sun and in consequence suffers from sunstroke,[2] or where a person with a weak heart injures it by running to catch a train,[3] or by some other intentional act involving violent physical exertion,[4] or through a blister caused by the insured wearing light shoes, which had been worn only a few times, while walking over rough country.[5]

In this case the element of accident is broadly speaking absent since the cause is one which comes into operation in the ordinary course of events, and is calculated, within the ordinary experience of mankind, to produce the result which it has in fact produced.[6]

Thus, in *Sinclair* v. *Maritime Passengers' Assurance Co.*[7]

> The master of a vessel was insured under a personal accident insurance policy by the terms of which the insurers agreed to pay the sum insured if he sustained "any personal injury or death from or by reason of any accident which should happen to him on any ocean, sea, river or lake". Whilst acting as master of the vessel in the River Cochin in south-west India, he was struck down by sunstroke and died. His personal representatives claimed the sum insured.
>
> *Held*, by the Court of King's Bench[8], that the insurers were not liable because the death of the insured had not arisen from "accident" within the meaning of the policy.

COCKBURN, C.J., said:[9]

> "The question is whether, under such circumstances, the death of the deceased can be said to have arisen from accident, within the meaning of the policy. We are of opinion that it cannot, and that our judgment must be for the defendants.
>
> It is difficult to define the term 'accident', as used in a policy of this nature, so as to draw with perfect accuracy a boundary line between injury or death from accident, and injury or death from natural causes; such as shall be of universal application. At the same time we think we may safely assume that, in the term 'accident' as so used, some violence, casualty, or *vis major*, is necessarily involved.

---

[1] It is immaterial that the result is not foreseen: *Re Scarr and General Accident Assurance Corporation* (*supra*), *per* BRAY, J., at p. 393.

[2] *Sinclair* v. *Maritime Passengers' Assurance Co.* (1861), 3 E. & E. 478; *Wyman* v. *Dominion of Canada General Insurance Co.*, [1936] 2 D.L.R. 268. Cf. *North West Commercial Travellers' Association* v. *London Guarantee and Accident Co.* (1895), 10 Man. L.R. 537, where the insured was caught in a blizzard.

[3] *Re Scarr and General Accident Assurance Corporation* (*supra*), *per* BRAY, J., at p. 394.

[4] *Ibid.*, where the insured, who was employed by a publican, strained his heart while attempting to eject a drunken man from his master's premises; *Appel* v. *Aetna Life Assurance Corporation* (1903), 86 App. Div. Rep. S.C.N.Y. 83, where the insured whilst riding a bicycle injured his appendix, one of the muscles used in riding having necessarily rubbed against it; approved in *Re Scarr and General Accident Assurance Corporation* (*supra*); *Columbia Cellulose Co.* v. *Continental Casualty Co.* (1963), 40 D.L.R. (2d) 297, where the insured over-exerted himself and suffered a haemorrhage which resulted in death.

[5] *Solboda* v. *Continental Casualty Co.*, [1938] 2 W.W.R. 237.

[6] *Sinclair* v. *Maritime Passengers' Insurance Co.* (*supra*), *per* COCKBURN, C.J., at p. 485. See further, *Re Scarr and General Accident Assurance Corporation*, [1905] 1 K.B. 387, *per* BRAY, J., at pp. 392, 394.

[7] (1861), 3 E. & E. 478.

[8] COCKBURN, C.J., and HILL, J.

[9] (1861) 3 E. & E. at p. 485.

We cannot think disease produced by the action of a known cause can be considered as accidental. Thus, disease or death engendered by exposure to heat, cold, damp, the vicissitudes of climate, or atmospheric influences, cannot, we think, properly be said to be accidental; unless at all events, the exposure is itself brought about by circumstances which may give it the character of accident. Thus (by way of illustration), if, from the effects of ordinary exposure to the elements, such as is common in the course of navigation, a mariner should catch cold and die, such death would not be accidental; although if, being obliged by shipwreck or other disasters to quit the ship and take to the sea in an open boat, he remained exposed to wet and cold for some time, and death ensued therefrom, the death might properly be held to be the result of accident. It is true that, in one sense, disease or death through the direct effect of a known natural cause, such as we have referred to, may be said to be accidental, inasmuch as it is uncertain beforehand whether the effect will ensue in any particular case. Exposed to the same malaria or infection, one man escapes, another succumbs. Yet diseases thus arising have always been considered, not as accidental, but as proceeding from natural causes.

In the present instance, the disease called sunstroke, although the name would at first seem to imply something of external violence is, so far as we are informed, an inflammatory disease of the brain, brought on by exposure to the too intense heat of the sun's rays. It is a disease to which persons exposing themselves to the sun in a tropical climate are more or less liable, just as persons exposed to the other natural causes to which we have referred are liable to disastrous consequences therefrom. The deceased, in the discharge of his ordinary duties about his ship, became thus affected and so died.

We think, for the reasons we have given, that his death must be considered as having arisen from a 'natural cause', and not from 'accident' within the meaning of this policy."

In considering whether an injury is caused by accident, it is necessary to take into consideration the circumstances in which the injury is received. Similar natural causes may produce similar physical effects in two different persons. Yet the element of accident may be present in one case and absent in the other. Thus, in the case of a sailor on duty on the bridge of a ship, though he may suffer serious bodily injury or even death through exposure to the violence of a winter gale, yet the injury or death is not caused by accident within the meaning of the policy. If, on the other hand, the sailor is shipwrecked and is afterwards exposed in an open boat to the inclemency of the weather, the element of accident intervenes, and the result of the exposure, whether injury or death, falls within the policy.[1]

3   Injury Caused by Act of Third Person

There is clearly an accident where the third person, in the course of doing a lawful act in a lawful manner, happens, without any default on his part, by pure misfortune to injure the insured,[2] e.g. where, through some latent defect which no reasonable examination would have detected, the axle of a railway carriage wheel breaks or the head of a hammer flies off, and the insured in consequence suffers injury.

---

[1] *Sinclair* v. *Maritime Passengers' Assurance Co.* (1861), 3 E. & E. 478, *per* COCKBURN, C.J., at p. 485; *North West Commercial Travellers' Association* v. *London Guarantee and Accident Co.* (1895), 10 Man. L.R. 537, where the vehicle which the insured was driving broke down, in consequence of which he was overtaken by a blizzard and frozen to death, and it was held that his death was caused by accident within the meaning of the policy.

[2] So, where the insured, whilst on active service, is injured owing to the premature bursting of a British gun, there is an injury by "accident" within the meaning of the policy: *Howard* v. *City Mutual Life Assurance Society* (1919), 13 Q.J.P.R. 4.

There is equally an accident where the third person, through lack of skill or want of care, does something which he ought not to have done or omits to do what he ought to have done, and, in consequence, injures the insured. Negligence, whether in acts or omissions, is the most fruitful source of accident. Any injury, therefore caused by a third person, whether by misfortune or through negligence, is an injury by "accident" within the meaning of the policy;[1] and it is immaterial that the injury results in death, or that, in the circumstances, the third person is guilty of the manslaughter of the insured. It has never been suggested that, if the insured is killed in a railway accident, the fact that the accident is due to the criminal negligence of a signalman or engine driver, who is subsequently convicted of manslaughter, precludes a claim under a policy.

A difficulty arises where the act of the third person is not, so far as the third person is concerned, accidental, and the injury to the insured caused thereby is not fortuitous or unexpected. On the contrary, the act may be done by design, and the third person may foresee, intend, and expect the consequences which the act in fact produces.

Thus, the third person may deliberately drive into the insured for the purpose of injuring him. He may even kill the insured with malice aforethought. It is submitted, however, that it is unnecessary to take into account the third person's state of mind, and that, for the purpose of ascertaining whether the element of accident is present in any given circumstances, the insured is the only person to be considered, and the construction to be placed upon the circumstances must be determined from his standpoint.[2]

The commission of a wilful, wrongful act is not an event which can reasonably be said to be capable of being foreseen and expected in the same sense as an event in the ordinary course of nature. Any injury resulting from such an act, done against the insured without his consent, is, so far as he is concerned, fortuitous and unexpected, and such injury is to be regarded as caused by "accident" within the meaning of the policy.[3] If this is so, the

---

[1] Thus, a marine policy covers a loss by collision, whether the other vessel is at fault or not, since, in either case, there is a loss by a peril of the sea; and if a ship strikes a rock and is lost, it is immaterial whether the rock is uncharted, or whether the light which should have warned the mariner against it had become extinguished owing to the negligence of the person in charge: *Wilson, Sons & Co.* v. *Xantho (Cargo Owners)* (1887), 12 App. Cas. 503 (bill of lading), *per* Lord HERSCHELL, at pp. 511, 512, approved in *Trim Joint District School Board of Management* v. *Kelly*, [1914] A.C. 667 (workman's compensation), *per* Viscount HALDANE, L.C., at p. 674. Similarly, a fire policy attaches where the fire is caused by the negligence of a third person, see further Ivamy, *Fire and Motor Insurance*, 2nd Edn., 1973, pp. 12–13.

[2] See the discussion of the popular meaning of the word "accident" in *Trim Joint District School Board of Management* v. *Kelly*, [1914] A.C. 667 (workmen's compensation), *per* Lord SHAW OF DUNFERMLINE, at pp. 707, *et seq.*; and cf. *Sadler* v. *South Staffordshire and Birmingham District Steam Tramways Co.* (1889), 23 Q.B.D. 17, C.A. (trespass), where Lord ESHER, M.R., at p. 21, uses the word "accident" as applying to the act of a miscreant.

[3] *Morran* v. *Railway Passengers Assurance Co.* (1919), 43 O.L.R. 561, where a person injured in a fight in which he was not the aggressor was held to have been injured by accidental means; *Grant* v. *Southern Cross Assurance Co., Ltd.*, [1928] W.A.L.R. 65, where during a family dispute the insured was threatening his brother, and his father intentionally shot the insured in the leg which had to be amputated in consequence, and it was held that the injury was an "accident". But the insured's claim under the policy failed because the injury was the result of a "provoked assault", which was excepted by the terms of the policy; *Istvan* v. *Merchants Casualty Insurance Co.*, [1940] 2 W.W.R. 462, where the insured was shot when he answered the door at 3 a.m. by a person with whom he had previously had controversies and fights, and it was held that the injury to the insured was an

quality of the act is immaterial; the policy equally applies whether the act is tortious or criminal, or whether, if the death of the insured is caused thereby, it amounts to murder.[1]

On the other hand, the injury is not caused by accident where the insured consents to the action which causes it, e.g. where he is killed or wounded in a duel,[2] or where he pursues a course of conduct which naturally results in the intervention of third persons, as where he commits a crime and dies at the hand of the executioner.[3]

In these cases, the third person's act cannot be regarded separately. It is a consequence resulting from the insured's wrongful conduct which he ought reasonably to have foreseen and expected, and there is, therefore, so far as he is concerned, nothing accidental about it. There is, however, clearly an accident where the injury is not the natural consequence of the act to which the insured consented or which he brought about by his conduct, but is caused by the intervention of some fortuitous or unexpected circumstances, e.g. where he is killed in a fencing bout owing to the button coming off his adversary's foil, or, being a prisoner, is hanged by mistake or killed by an accident in the prison quarry.

Special considerations apply to surgical operations.[4] If, in the circumstances of the particular case it becomes advisable to perform an operation upon the insured and he dies under it, the operation, though the immediate cause of death, is to be disregarded and the death of the insured is to be attributed to the circumstances which rendered the operation advisable.[5] If

---

"accident", and that there was no reason for him to anticipate what took place. Cf. *Travellers Insurance Co.* v. *Elder*, [1940] 2 D.L.R. 444, where the insured wrongfully helped himself to some pickles in a restaurant and abused the custodian of the pickles who threw a glass at him, and it was held that the injury sustained was not the result of an "accident".

[1] In *Letts* v. *Excess Insurance Co.* (1916), 32 T.L.R. 361 it was assumed that the sinking of the *Lusitania* by a German submarine was an accident within the meaning of the policy, the only question being whether an exception applied. This appears to be the only reported case in personal accident insurance, in which the act causing the death was a wilful, criminal act. It may be pointed out, however, that scuttling a ship is "barratry" within the meaning of a marine policy (*Ionides* v. *Pender* (1872), 27 L.T. 244 (marine insurance)); that it is no defence under a life policy that the life insured was murdered (*Cleaver* v. *Mutual Reserve Fund Life Association*, [1892] 1 Q.B. 147, C.A. (life insurance)); or under a fire policy, that the fire was caused by arson (*Midland Insurance Co.* v. *Smith* (1881), 6 Q.B.D. 561 (fire insurance)), unless the person claiming the benefit of the insurance is party or privy to the crime. Further, under the Workmen's Compensation Act 1925, which was to be regarded, in a sense, as providing a statutory insurance for workmen, the word "accident" was construed to include the deliberate criminal act of violence, such as murder (*Trim Joint District School Board of Management* v. *Kelly* (supra), approving *Nisbet* v. *Rayne*, [1910] 2 K.B. 689, C.A. (workmen's compensation)) or assault (*Anderson* v. *Balfour*, [1910] 2 I.R. 497, C.A. (workmen's compensation)); and under the Fatal Accidents Act, 1846, it has never been suggested that relief could not be given because the act causing the death was wilful, intentional, or deliberate (*Trim Joint District School Board of Management* v. *Kelly* (supra), per Lord SHAW OF DUNFERMLINE)).

[2] Cf. *Midland Insurance Co.* v. *Smith* (supra), per WATKIN WILLIAMS, J., at p. 568, pointing out that under a fire policy, the assured cannot, in the case of arson, recover, if he is privy to it. The position is different where the insured is killed or wounded in self-defence: *Morran* v. *Railway Passengers Assurance Co.* (supra).

[3] Cf. *Amicable Society* v. *Bolland* (1830), 2 Dow. & Cl. 1 (life insurance), where the insured was executed.

[4] Surgical operations are usually the subject of an express exception. See p. 40, *post*.

[5] Cf. *Shirt* v. *Calico Printers' Association*, [1909] 2 K.B. 51, C.A. (workmen's compensation), where death under an operation which was reasonable in the circumstances was held to be caused by the accident which necessitated it; *Thomson* v. *Mutter, Howey & Co.*, 1913 S.C. 619 (workmen's compensation) where, in the course of an operation for hernia, the

therefore, the insured was suffering from disease, his death under the operation is a death from disease and not from accident.[1]   If, on the other hand,
the operation is performed in the hope of alleviating the consequences of
accidental injury, his death is a death from "accident" within the meaning
of the policy, notwithstanding his consent to the operation or his knowledge
that the operation was a dangerous one.[2]

4 Injury Caused by Insured's Own Act

An injury may be caused by "accident" within the meaning of the policy,
although it is caused by the act of the insured.[3]

But an injury which is the intended expected consequence of an act
deliberately done is not caused by "accident". Thus, no claim is maintainable
under the policy where the insured, for the purpose of making a claim against
the insurers, places his leg across a railway line and allows it to be cut off
by a passing train.[4]   Further, an injury which is the natural and direct
consequence of an act deliberately done by the insured is not caused by
"accident". A man must be taken to intend the ordinary consequences of
his acts, and the fact that he did not foresee the particular consequence, or
expect the particular injury, does not make the injury accidental if, in the
circumstances, it was the natural and direct consequence of what he did,
without the intervention of any fortuitous cause. Thus, in one case Lord ADAM
said:

> "The question, in the sense of this policy, is not whether death was the result of
> accident in the sense that it was a death which was not foreseen and anticipated
> . . . The question is, in the words of the policy, whether the means by which the
> injury was caused were accidental means. The death being accidental in the
> sense which I have mentioned, and the means which lead to the death as
> accidental, are to my mind, two quite different things. A man may do certain
> acts, the result of which acts may produce unforeseeable consequences, and may
> produce what is commonly called accidental death, but the means are exactly
> what the man intended to use, and did use, and was prepared to use. The means
> were not accidental, but the result might be accidental."[5]

Thus, if physical exertion, deliberately intended, such as e.g. running to
catch a train,[6] throws a strain upon his heart at a time when it is in a weak
and unhealthy condition, in consequence of which the insured dies, his

---

workman was found to be suffering from another hernia of long standing, and the operation was extended to both. See also *Charles* v. *Walker, Ltd.* (1909), 25 T.L.R. 609, C.A. (workmen's compensation), where, after the operation necessitated by the accident was finished,
the workman was kept under the anaesthetic for the purpose of removing a tooth.
[1] Presumably, if the death was due, not in any way to the effects of the operation, but to the
negligence of the surgeon operating, a fresh cause would intervene, and the death would
be due to accident.
[2] *Fitton* v. *Accidental Death Insurance Co.* (1864), 17 C.B.N.S. 122, where the operation was
necessary to relieve the assured from strangulated hernia caused by a fall; *Isitt* v. *Railway
Passengers Assurance Co.* (1889), 22 Q.B.D. 504, where it was admitted by the insurers that
they would clearly be liable if the accident rendered amputation of the limb necessary
and the insured died under the operation.
[3] *Clidero* v. *Scottish Accident Insurance Co.* 1892, 19 R. (Ct. of Sess.) 355, *per* Lord MACLAREN
at p. 363.
[4] Cf. *Shaw* v. *Robberds* (1837), 6 Ad. & El. 75 (fire insurance), *per* Lord DENMAN, C.J., at
p. 84; *Thompson* v. *Hopper* (1858), E.B. & E. 1038, Ex. Ch. (marine insurance), *per* BRAM-
WELL, B., at p. 1045.
[5] *Clidero* v. *Scottish Accident Insurance Co.* 1892, 19 R. (Ct. of Sess.) 355 at p. 362. See also
Re Scarr and General Accident Assurance Corporation, [1905] 1 K.B. 387, *per* BRAY, J., at p. 393.
[6] *Re Scarr and General Accident Assurance Corporation* (*supra*), *per* BRAY, J., at p. 395.

death is not to be regarded as accidental merely because the insured did not know his condition and therefore did not foresee the effect, provided that it was the natural and direct consequence of a strain being put upon a heart in that condition.

Similarly, where the insured whilst pulling on his stockings, felt something give way inside, and subsequently died of heart failure through pressure on the heart caused by the distension of the colon which had become obstructed, his death was held not to be due to "accident".[1]

Again, in *Re an Arbitration between Scarr and General Accident Assurance Corporation*[2]

> A personal accident insurance policy stated that the sum insured would be payable "if the assured shall sustain any bodily injury caused by violent, accidental, external and visible means . . . and such injury shall be the sole and immediate cause of death". The insured was a maltster's manager. He attempted to eject a drunken man from the premises, and used some physical exertion in doing so. This made a greater demand than usual on his heart, which was in a weak condition. He complained of a pain in the chest, and died a month later. When his personal representatives claimed under the policy, the insurers repudiated liability on the ground that the insured's death was not caused by accident.
>
> *Held*, by the King's Bench Division, that the claim failed, for there had been no "accident".

In giving judgment BRAY, J., said:[3]

> "It seems to me that there was nothing accidental in the pushing and pulling of the drunken man, or the exercise of physical exertion in so doing. Scarr intended to do this. The drunken man offered only passive resistance. There was no blow. Then was the effect on the heart accidental? The demand or strain on the heart was the natural and direct consequence of the physical exertion, which I have necessarily assumed to be violent physical exertion. Then was the effect of this demand or strain on the heart accidental? It is true that Scarr did not foresee the effect; but this, in my opinion, cannot make it accidental if it was the natural and direct consequence of a demand or strain on a heart in the condition described. The evidence shows that there was no intervening fortuitous cause. The injury to the heart, which I assume to be bodily injury, seems to me to have been caused by the violent exertion, and the violent exertion was intended and not accidental. There was no slip or fall or blow. He intended to push and pull, and he pushed and pulled. . . . Here, as I have said, Scarr intended to violently exert himself, and the injury to the heart followed as the natural consequence. He never got into any position which he did not intend. It seems to me very like the case of a man with a weak heart injuring it by running to catch a train. He intends to run. Nobody would call such an event an accident. No one would describe him as meeting with an accident. Nor would anyone in the present case speak of Scarr as having met with an accident."

On the other hand, an injury which is the consequence of an act deliberately done is caused by accident where the act is done with the intention of averting imminent danger and of preventing an accident from happening. The act, in this case, is a mere link in the chain of causation leading from the accident to the injury. It is immaterial that the expected accident does not in fact happen and that, but for the fact, the insured would have sustained no injury, provided that in the circumstances he acted reasonably in doing what he did. This is clearly the case if the injury is sustained whilst the insured is attempting to save himself from danger e.g. where he jumps

---

[1] *Clidero* v. *Scottish Accident Insurance Co.* (*supra*).
[2] (1905), 92 L.T. 128.
[3] *Ibid.*, at p. 131.

from a runaway carriage,[1] or from a window of a burning house.[2] Probably the injury is equally to be regarded as accidental if it is sustained in an attempt to save others from danger,[3] e.g. where the insured attempts to stop a runaway horse or rushes into the burning house for the purpose of saving the life of his child.[4]

An injury which is the direct and natural consequence of an act deliberately done by reason of its being done negatively is caused by "accident", since it is not the consequence of the act itself, but of the insured's negligence.[5] Thus, if the insured carelessly crosses a railway in front of a train whose approach he fails to observe,[6] or drinks poison instead of medicine owing to his failure to make certain that he had used the right bottle,[7] his death is caused by accident.[8]

An injury which is the unforeseen and unexpected consequence of an act deliberately done is caused by accident, provided that the act is not one calculated in the ordinary course of things to produce the consequences which it, in fact, produces. Thus, if the insured is drowned whilst bathing,[9] or crossing a stream,[10] or stumbles in walking and sprains his ankle,[11] or

---

[1] Cf. *Jones* v. *Boyce* (1816), 1 Stark. (N.T.) 493 (negligence), where a passenger in a coach reasonably apprehending that, owing to the negligence of the defendant, an accident was imminent, leapt from it and broke his leg, and it was held that he was entitled to recover, though no accident to the coach in fact happened.

[2] See *Machenan* v. *Segar*, [1917] 2 K.B. 325 (negligence).

[3] Cf. *Brandon* v. *Osborne, Garrett & Co.*, [1924] 1 K.B. 548 (negligence), where the plaintiff was injured in attempting to save her husband from a danger caused by the defendant's negligence and was held entitled to recover.

[4] The last example in the text was put as a question as to counsel in *Trew* v. *Railway Passengers Assurance Co.* (1861), 6 H. & N. 839, Ex. Ch., *per* COCKBURN, C.J., at p. 842, but no answer was given by the Court. In *Pugh* v. *London, Brighton and South Coast Rail. Co.*, [1896] 2 Q.B. 248, C.A., approved in *Clover, Clayton & Co.* v. *Hughes*, [1910] A.C. 242 (workmen's compensation), *per* Lord MACNAGHTEN, at pp. 249, 250, the insured, a railway signalman, after successfully preventing an accident to a train, was incapacitated from following his employment through nervous shock caused by his excitement, and fright arising from the danger to the train, and it was held that he was entitled to recover under a policy insuring him "against accidents occurring in the fair and ordinary discharge of his duty." It is true that by virtue of his employment, it was part of his duty to his employers who were also the insurers, to prevent accidents, and, consequently, in attempting to prevent the accident to the train, he was not assuming a risk or voluntarily exposing himself to danger in the same sense, as if it had been no part of his legal duty to prevent the accident. It is submitted, however, that the existence of a moral duty is sufficient; the attempt to save life cannot be regarded as an act of independent volition, since it is inspired by the impulsive desire to save human life when in peril, which has been called one of the most beneficial instincts of humanity: *Scaramanga* v. *Stamp* (1880), 5 C.P.D. 295, C.A. (marine insurance), *per* COCKBURN, C.J., at p. 304. Any injury sustained by the insured in the attempt to save life is, therefore, the natural result of the peril which led to the attempt being made, and as such, is caused by accident within the meaning of the policy. In practice, this point is frequently dealt with by an express provision.

[5] *Trinder, Anderson & Co.* v. *Thames and Mersey Marine Insurance Co.*, [1898] 2 Q.B. 114, C.A. (marine insurance), *per* A. L. SMITH, L.J., at p. 124; *Shaw* v. *Robberds* (1837), 6 Ad. & El. 75 (fire insurance), *per* Lord DENMAN, C.J., at p. 84; *Jameson* v. *Royal Insurance Co.* (1873), I.R. 7 C.L. 126 (fire insurance).

[6] *Cornish* v. *Accident Insurance Co.* (1889), 23 Q.B.D. 453, C.A., *per* LINDLEY, L.J., at p. 455.

[7] *Cole* v. *Accident Insurance Co.* (1889), 61 L.T. 227, where, however, an exception applied.

[8] The policy frequently contains an exception in case of exposure to obvious danger. See pp. 38–40, *post*.

[9] *Trew* v. *Railway Passengers Assurance Co.* (*supra*); *Reynolds* v. *Accidental Insurance Co.* (1870), 22 L.T. 820.

[10] *Winspear* v. *Accident Insurance Co.* (1880), 6 Q.B.D. 42; *Ballantine* v. *Employers' Insurance Co. of Great Britain* 1893, 21 R. (Ct. of Sess.) 305.

[11] *Re Scarr and General Accident Assurance Corporation*, [1905] 1 K.B. 387, *per* BRAY, J., at p. 394.

strains the internal cartilage of his knee-joint in stooping to pick up a marble,[1] or ruptures himself whilst playing golf,[2] his death injury is caused by accident. The death or injury though, in a sense, the consequence of an intentional act on his part, seeing that, if he had not put himself in a certain position, there would have been no death or injury, is not a consequence which could reasonably be expected to follow in the ordinary course from the act, and is, therefore, an accidental and not a natural consequence.

Again, an injury which is the direct and natural consequence of an involuntary and unintentional act is caused by accident, seeing that the act itself is unforeseen and unexpected.

In *Winspear* v. *Accident Insurance Co.*[3] a personal accident insurance policy stated that the insurers would pay the sum insured if the insured

"shall sustain any personal injury caused by accidental, external and visible means . . . and the direct effect of such injury shall occasion the death of the insured within 3 calendar months from the happening of such injury."

The policy contained a proviso which stated:

"Provided further that . . . this insurance shall not extend to death by suicide . . . or to any injury caused by or arising from natural disease or weakness or exhaustion consequent upon disease . . ."

The insured while crossing and fording a stream was seized with an epileptic fit, and fell into the water and was drowned. His personal representative claimed the sum insured, and the Court of Appeal[4] held that it was payable, for the insured's death was occasioned by an injury covered by the policy, and the proviso set out above did not apply. Lord COLERIDGE, C.J., observed:[5]

"I am therefore of opinion that the injury by which the assured died comes within the risks which the defendants have undertaken. Then the only question is, whether the case comes within the proviso contained in the policy so as to exempt the defendants from liability. That clause provides that no claim shall be made for any injury from accident, 'unless such injury shall be caused by some outward and visible means,' etc. The remarks I have already made apply to these words, and therefore the case is clearly not within the first part of the proviso. Then it goes on to provide that the 'insurance shall not extend . . . to any injury caused by or arising from natural disease, or weakness or exhaustion consequent upon disease . . . or to any death arising from disease, although such death may have been accelerated by accident.' Here the injury was caused by an accident—that is, drowning—and therefore I think that this clause has no application. It seems to me that the words of the policy must mean what they say, and in such a case as this the injury is what really causes death. Therefore the defendants are clearly liable."

Winspear v. *Accident Insurance Co.*[6] was followed in *Lawrence* v. *Accident Insurance Co., Ltd.*[7] where a personal accident insurance policy stated:

"This policy insures payment only in cases of injuries accidentally occurring from material and external causes operating upon the person of the insured

---

[1] *Hamlyn* v. *Crown Accidental Insurance Co.*, [1893] 1 Q.B. 750, C.A., distinguished in *Re Scarr and General Accident Assurance Corporation* (*supra*).
[2] *Claxton* v. *Travellers' Insurance Co. of Hartford* (1917), Q.R. 52 S.C. 239.
[3] (1880), 43 L.T. 459.
[4] Lord COLERIDGE, C.J., BAGGALLAY and BRETT, L.JJ.
[5] (1880), 43 L.T. at p. 460.
[6] *Supra*.
[7] (1881), 45 L.T. 29.

where such accidental injury is the direct and sole cause of death to the insured, but it does not insure in case of death arising from fits . . . or any disease whatsoever arising before, or at the time, or following such accidental injury (whether consequent upon such accidental injury or not, and whether causing such death or disability directly or jointly with such accidental injury)."

The insured whilst standing on a railway platform was suddenly seized with a fit, and an engine and some empty carriages passing through the station passed over his neck and body and killed him instantly. The Queen's Bench Division[1] held that his death arose from "accident" and not from the fit, and that the insurance company was liable to pay the sum insured under the policy. DENMAN, J., said:[2]

"The question here is whether the fit was one of the several events which occasioned his death, or, whether it was, within the meaning of this proviso, a thing which would prevent the policy from attaching. In *Winspear's* case[3] where a man who was fording a stream was seized with a fit and fell into it and was drowned whilst suffering from the fit, it was decided that the fit was not the cause of death within the meaning of the policy. That case, although not quite identical, is very like the present one. The policy here is somewhat different to the policy in that case, and the words which appeared to me to be strongly in favour of the defendants in this case are, 'Causing such death or disability, directly or jointly with such accidental injury.' If the words had simply been that 'this policy shall not attach in cases where death was caused by an accident jointly with the fit,' I should have thought that it was a case in which the defendants would have had a defence to this action. But these words are in a parenthesis, and are put in to explain the class of cases in which the three previous lines of the proviso will apply, that is where disease is one of the things which has caused the death itself, directly or jointly with the accidental injury. The words 'arising from fits . . . or any disease whatsoever,' which are defining words, have received a judicial interpretation in *Winspear's* case[4] and, so far as that part of the present case is concerned, are identical with those in *Winspear's* case,[5] where it was held that the death arose not from the fit, but from the drowning. So here the death arose from the accident of the engine passing over the man and so destroying him, and not from the fit having caused him to fall on to the rail."

WILLIAMS, J., agreed, and said:[6]

"It seems to me that the first maxim of Lord BACON is directly in point, in which it is said that 'it were infinite for the law to judge the causes of causes, and their impulsions one of another; therefore it contenteth itself with the immediate cause, and judgeth of acts by that, without looking to any further degree.' Applying that maxim to the words of this proviso, we must look to the immediate and proximate cause of death, and that would be the injury caused by the engine passing over the deceased. I think that the true meaning of this proviso is that if the death arose from a fit, then the company would not be liable, but it is essential to that construction that it must be made out that the fit was the immediate and proximate cause of death. I put my decision on the broad ground that death in this case did not arise from the fit, but from that which happened afterwards, and the plaintiff is therefore entitled to our judgment."

"VIOLENT, EXTERNAL AND VISIBLE MEANS"

For the purpose of describing the peril insured against various words and

---

[1] DENMAN and WILLIAMS, JJ.
[2] (1881), 45 L.T. at p. 30.
[3] *Supra.*
[4] *Supra.*
[5] *Supra.*
[6] (1881) 45 L.T., at p. 31.

phrases are used in the policy, a typical example being the phrase in common use by which the injury is required to be caused by "violent, accidental, external and visible means".[1]

So far as the effect of the policy is concerned, these words probably add nothing to the idea conveyed by the word "accident", since they merely give expression to the essential features of an accident. At the same time they serve a useful purpose in making clear the distinction between accidental and natural causes, and thus help to define with greater precision the scope of the insurance.[2]

1 "Violent"

In most cases of accidental injury the element of violence is obvious. Thus, there is clearly violence where the insured is knocked down by a train[3] or bitten by a dog,[4] or where he slips against the step of a railway carriage[5] or falls down.[6]

The degree of violence is, however, immaterial. The word "violence" means the contrary of "without any violence at all",[7] and merely expresses that the injury is due to other than purely natural causes, such as bodily weakness or disease.[8]

In particular, there is violence where the injury is caused by the use of any extra exertion or any extra physical force on the part of the insured. Thus, if the insured, in stooping to pick a marble up, dislocates the internal cartilage of his knee-joint[9] or if, by bodily exertion, he strains his heart,[10] the injury is caused by "violence".

Further, where the injury is caused by the direct physical act of a third person, it will be considered "violent" seeing that, unless the act is justifiable or excusable, an action of trespass to the person lies; the existence of justification or excuse does not alter the quality of the act, but only justifies or excuses its commission.[11]

Again, where the injury is caused by some external impersonal cause, such a cause must necessarily operate with violence, since otherwise the body

---

[1] Or in other words, the injury must be the result of a violent, accidental, external, and visible cause: *Hamlyn* v. *Crown Accidental Insurance Co., Ltd.,* [1893] 1 Q.B. 750, C.A., *per* Lord ESHER, M.R., at p. 753. A stipulation that death must be attributable to accidental, external, and visible injury bears the same meaning: *Burridge & Son* v. *Haines & Sons, Ltd.* (1918), 118 L.T. 681 (livestock insurance), where no importance was attached to the fact that other stipulations in the policy were phrased as in the text.

[2] The phrase was, however, adversely criticised in *Re United London and Scottish Insurance Co., Ltd., Brown's Claim,* [1915] 2 Ch. 167, C.A.

[3] *Lawrence* v. *Accidental Insurance Co., Ltd.* (1881), 7 Q.B.D. 216; *Cornish* v. *Accident Insurance Co.* (1889), 23 Q.B.D. 453, C.A.

[4] *Mardorf* v. *Accident Insurance Co.,* [1903] 1 K.B. 584, *per* WRIGHT, J., at p. 588.

[5] *Theobald* v. *Railway Passengers Assurance Co.* (1854), 10 Exch. 45.

[6] *Hooper* v. *Accidental Death Insurance Co.* (1860), 5 H. & N. 557, Ex. Ch.

[7] *Hamlyn* v. *Crown Accidental Insurance Co.,* [1893] 1 Q.B. 750, C.A., *per* Lord ESHER, M.R., at p. 752.

[8] Cf. *Sinclair* v. *Maritime Passengers' Assurance Co.* (1861), 3 E. & E. 478, *per* COCKBURN, C.J., at p. 485.

[9] *Hamlyn* v. *Crown Accidental Insurance Co.* (*supra*), *per* LOPES, L.J., at p. 754; "In stooping to pick up the marble the plaintiff used some extra exertion and some extra physical force, and I think that the expression 'violence' is satisfied by the facts which attended the injury." Cf. *Clidero* v. *Scottish Accident Insurance Co.* 1892, 19 R. (Ct. of Sess.) 355, where there was no evidence that extra exertion was used.

[10] *Re Scarr and General Accident Assurance Corporation,* [1905] 1 K.B. 387, *per* BRAY, J., at p. 393.

[11] *Holmes* v. *Mather* (1875), L.R. 10 Exch. Ch. 261 (trespass).

of the insured would not be affected.[1]   Thus, if the insured is drowned,[2] his death is caused by violence, and it is immaterial that he struck his head against a stone in diving,[3] or was seized in the water with a fit[4] or with cramp[5] or that he fell asleep on the beach and was overwhelmed by the tide before he could wake.[6]

If the element of violence is otherwise present, actual physical impact is not necessary, and the injury may be caused by shock, provided that the injury is proximately caused by the violence.[7]

2 "External"[8]

The word "external" is, as a rule, used as the antithesis of "internal", and if the cause of the injury is not internal, it must be external.[9]

Unless the policy so provides, it is not necessary that the injury itself should be external.[10] On the contrary, it may be wholly internal without there being anything on the surface of the body to disclose its existence.[11] Nevertheless, the cause of injury must be external; it must not arise within the body of the insured. Thus, if the spine is injured through lifting a heavy weight,[12] or if the internal cartilage of the knee-joint is dislocated through stooping to pick up a marble,[13] the cause of the injury is external, though the injury itself is internal. It, therefore, follows that the same kind of injury, such as hernia, may fall within or outside the scope of the policy according as it is the effect of some external cause or a mere disease arising within the system.[14]

If the actual cause of death is external, it is immaterial that it was brought into operation by some internal cause. Thus, if the insured is drowned through becoming insensible from a fit, his death is caused by an external cause i.e. the water, and not by the fit.[15]

---

[1] In *Re United London and Scottish Insurance Co., Ltd., Brown's Claim*, [1915] 2 Ch. 167, C.A., where an exception was held to apply, it was assumed that the inhaling of gas came within the phrase "violent, accidental, external, and visible means".

[2] Death may occur in the water from natural causes, such as apoplexy or cramp in the heart; but in such a case the insured would die, not from the action of the water causing asphyxia, but from natural causes: *Trew* v. *Railway Passengers Assurance Co.* (1861), 6 H. & N. 839, Ex. Ch., *per* COCKBURN, C.J., at p. 845.

[3] *Trew* v. *Railway Passengers Assurance Co.*, as reported (1860), 5 H. &. N. 211, *per* MARTIN, B , at p 217

[4] *Reynolds* v. *Accidental Insurance Co.* (1870), 22 L.T. 820.

[5] *Trew* v. *Railway Passengers Assurance Co.* (*supra*), *per* CROMPTON, J., at p. 841.

[6] Cf. *Winspear* v. *Accident Insurance Co.* (1880), 6 Q.B.D. 42, C.A.

[7] *Pugh* v. *London, Brighton and South Coast Rail. Co.*, [1896] 2 Q.B. 248, C.A.

[8] Or "outward".

[9] *Hamlyn* v. *Crown Accidental Insurance Co.* (*supra*), *per* Lord ESHER, M.R., at p. 753.

[10] *Trew* v. *Railway Passengers Assurance Co.* (1861), 6 H. & N. 839, Ex. Ch., *per* COCKBURN, C.J. at p. 844.

[11] *Hamlyn* v. *Crown Accidental Insurance Co., Ltd.*, [1893] 1 Q.B. 750, C.A., followed in *Burridge & Son, Ltd.* v. *Haines & Sons, Ltd.* (1918), 118 L.T. 681 (livestock insurance), where a van fell upon a horse and suffocated it, and it was held that the death of the horse was "solely attributable to accidental, external, and visible injury."

[12] *Martin* v. *Travellers' Insurance Co.* (1859), 1 F. & F. 505.

[13] *Hamlyn* v. *Crown Accidental Insurance Co., Ltd.* (*supra*).

[14] *Fitton* v. *Accidental Death Insurance Co.* (1864), 17 C.B.N.S. 122. The same principle applies in the case of a disease, such as pneumonia or erysipelas.

[15] *Winspear* v. *Accident Insurance Co.* (1880), 6 Q.B.D. 42, followed in *Lawrence* v. *Accidental Insurance Co., Ltd.* (1881), 7 Q.B.D. 216, where the insured fell in a fit in front of a train and was run over.

3 "Visible"

Any external cause must be "visible" within the meaning of the policy,[1] and it is therefore difficult to see what further precision in the definition of the peril insured against is gained by using the word. It may, however, serve the purpose of bringing out more clearly the fact that disease is excluded from the scope of the insurance. Disease from the medical point of view may be regarded as, in a sense, a consequence of an external cause, seeing that for the most part disease is due to the introduction of the microbe into the system. The cause of the disease, however, is not visible, though it may be discernible by a medical man.

Limitation of Insurance to Accidents of Particular Kind

The insurance may, by the terms of the policy, be limited to accident of a particular kind, e.g. railway accidents, or bus or coach accidents.[2]

An insurance against a railway or similar accident does not imply that there must be an accident to the train or other vehicle in which the insured is travelling. Thus, ALDERSON, B., said in one case:

> "As to railway accidents, my notion of a railway accident is an accident occurring in the course of travelling by a railway, and arising out of the fact of the journey. It does not necessarily depend upon any accident to the railway or machinery connected with it."[3]

There is a railway or similar accident within the meaning of the policy if the accident is attributable to the fact that he is a passenger and arises out of an act immediately connected with his being a passenger.

In *Theobald* v. *Railway Passengers Assurance Co.*[4] the insured took out an accident policy which stated that £1,000 would be payable

> "in the event of death happening to [him] from railway accident in any class carriage on any line of railway in Great Britain or Ireland; or a proportionate part of the £1,000 will be paid . . . in the event of his sustaining any personal injury by reason of such accident."

The insured in stepping out of the railway carriage in which he was travelling slipped off the iron step, and fell between the platform and the carriage and seriously injured his legs. He claimed under the policy, and one of the issues which arose was whether the injury had been sustained in a "railway accident". The Court of Exchequer held[5] that it was.

---

[1] *Hamlyn* v. *Crown Accidental Insurance Co., Ltd.* (*supra*), *per* LOPES, L.J., at p. 754: "Once admit that there is an external cause, it is plain that it was a visible one, and that condition also of the policy is satisfied." See also *Burridge & Son* v. *Haines & Sons, Ltd.* (*supra*).

[2] The insurance may be expressed in general terms and cover the insured whilst a passenger on a public conveyance. (*Fidelity and Casualty Co. of New York* v. *Mitchell*, [1917] A.C. 592, P.C., where the words of the policy were "while in or on a public conveyance (including the platform, steps and running board thereof) provided by a common carrier for passenger service"; *Powis* v. *Ontario Accident Insurance Co.* (1901), 1 O.L.R. 54, *Wallace* v. *Employers' Liability Assurance Co.* (1912), 26 O.L.R. 10), or whilst travelling by land or water: *Transit Insurance Co.* v. *Plamodon* (1903), Q.R. 13 K.B. 223. Insurances of this kind are frequently effected by means of coupons. See pp. 64–65, *post.*

[3] *Theobald* v. *Railway Passengers Assurance Co.* (*supra*), at p. 58. See also *Powis* v. *Ontario Accident Insurance Co.* (*supra*); *Wallace* v. *Employers' Liability Assurance Co.* (*supra*).

[4] (1854), 10 Exch. 45.

[5] POLLOCK, C.B., and ALDERSON, B.

POLLOCK, C.B., observed:[1]

"The first question is, whether this is a railway accident within the meaning of the policy. We are of opinion that it is. However much the company may desire that we should lay down a general rule as to what is a railway accident, I do not know that we are called on, or should be doing our duty, were we to lay down any rule beyond what is necessary to decide the actual case before us. Considering the great number of particulars that may enter into the decision of questions of this nature, and the very complicated character they may assume under circumstances that at present we may not anticipate, I think (and I believe the rest of the Court concur with me in thinking), that in the single instance brought before us under certain circumstances, some of which are not of a general nature, it would be assuming too much to lay down a rule to govern all cases. On the present occasion, it is quite plain that the plaintiff was a traveller on the railway; it is quite plain, that though at the time of the accident his journey had in one sense terminated, by the carriage having stopped, he had not ceased to be connected with the carriage, for he was still on it. The accident also happened without negligence on his part, and while doing an act which as a passenger he must necessarily have done, for a passenger must get into the carriage, and get out of it when the journey is at an end, and cannot be considered as disconnected with the carriage and railway, and with the machinery of motion, until the time he has, as it were, safely landed from the carriage, and got upon the platform. The accident is attributable to his being a passenger on the railway, and it arises out of an act immediately connected with his being such passenger."

ALDERSON, B., said:[2]

"As to railway accidents, my notion of a railway accident is an accident occurring in the course of travelling by a railway, and arising out of the fact of the journey. It does not necessarily depend on any accident to the railway or machinery connected with it."

The accident may happen during the transit.[3] This, however, is not necessary; the policy applies equally to accidents happening whilst the insured is in the act of entering[4] or leaving[5] the vehicle, at the beginning or end of the journey, e.g. where he accidentally slips upon the steps and is injured. If, however, the journey has ended and the insured has left the vehicle, the protection conferred by the policy ceases, and does not revive though the insured steps back upon the vehicle, if he does so, not for the purpose of resuming his journey as a passenger, but for some other purpose, e.g. to avoid a passing car.[6]

In some cases the policy may limit the insurance to accidents to the train or vehicle.

In the case of motor insurance, which frequently includes a personal accident insurance, the extent of the personal accident insurance depends on the particular policy. The insured may be protected only whilst driving the insured vehicle.[7] More usually, wider protection is given, and the personal

---

[1] (1854), 10 Exch. at p. 56.
[2] *Ibid.*, at p. 58.
[3] *Fidelity and Casualty Co. of New York* v. *Mitchell*, [1917] A.C. 592, P.C., where the accident happened whilst the train was in motion, the insured being thrown out of a sleeping berth.
[4] *Powis* v. *Ontario Accident Insurance Co.* (*supra*).
[5] *Theobald* v. *Railway Passengers Assurance Co.* (*supra*).
[6] *Wallace* v. *Employers' Liability Assurance Co.* (*supra*); cf. *Transit Insurance Co.* v. *Plamodon* (1903), Q.R. 13 K.B. 223, where the insured was injured at home.
[7] *African Guarantee and Indemnity Corporation* v. *Myles*, [1921] Cape P.D. 314, where the policy was expressed to cover either the insured or M., "whoever happens to be driving the car at the time of the accident", and it was held that M. could not recover for injuries sustained in an accident happening whilst the insured was driving.

accident insurance covers two classes of accidents:

1 Accidents happening in connection with the insured vehicle.

2 Accidents happening in connection with other vehicles.

In the first case protection is given not only to the insured, but also, to a limited extent, to other occupants of the vehicle. In the second case, the protection is confined to the insured. It may be given to him only whilst driving the other vehicle, or it may extend to all accidents happening whilst he is travelling in[1] the other vehicle. The other vehicle must, generally speaking, be a private vehicle.

DEATH OR DISABLEMENT

To give rise to a claim under the policy, the insured must die or be disabled. A policy which is not intended to cover accidental death only, usually describes the particular form of disablement to which it is intended to apply, and specifies the amount of compensation payable in respect of each. Thus, compensation may be payable for the loss of sight, in one eye or in both, and for the loss by severance of one or more members.

A statement that "permanent partial disablement implies the loss of one foot, or the complete and irrecoverable loss of sight" has been held to be ambiguous, the insured being entitled to recover for permanent partial disablement, though he had lost neither hand nor foot nor sight.[2]

There is no total loss of sight, if the evidence is that the eye can distinguish daylight from darkness[3] even though the eye is useless for the purpose of the insured's occupation.[4]

Loss of sight in both eyes means that the insured must be rendered totally blind by the accident.[5] If, therefore, the insurers accept a proposal from a one-eyed man, knowing that he had only one eye, they must, in the event of his losing his remaining eye, compensate him, not on the footing that he has lost one eye, but as having completely lost his sight.[6]

The loss of two fingers, does not entitle the insured to recover for permanent partial disablement in the case of injury causing the "loss by physical separation of one hand".[7]

Where no special provision is made for the payment of any particular sum except in the case of death, the insured is entitled to recover compensation,

---

[1] Including entering or dismounting from the other car.

[2] *Scott* v. *Scottish Accident Insurance Co.* 1889, 16 R. (Ct. of Sess.) 630.

[3] *MacDonald* v. *Mutual Life and Citizens' Assurance Co.* (1910), 29 N.Z.L.R. 478, 1073.

[4] *Copeland* v. *Locomotive Engineers' Insurance Association* (1910), 16 O.W.R. 739, but see *Shaw* v. *Globe Indemnity Co.*, [1921] 1 W.W.R. 674, where the insured was held to have irrecoverably lost the entire sight of one eye when he had lost all useful sight of the eye, although he was still able to distinguish light from darkness and to see a shadow if an object was placed close to the eye. But in *Long* v. *Graham*, [1967] N.Z.L.R. 1030 it was held that loss of vision was not the same thing as loss of sight, and if the sight was still there, but was masked by a cataract, there was no "loss of sight" within the meaning of the policy.

[5] *Bawden* v. *London, Edinburgh and Glasgow Assurance Co.*, [1892] 2 Q.B. 534, C.A., *per* Lord ESHER, M.R., at p. 540.

[6] *Ibid.*, where knowledge of the fact that the insured had only one eye was imputed to the insurers: but see *Newsholme Brothers* v. *Road Transport and General Insurance Co., Ltd.*, [1929] 2 K.B. 356, C.A. (motor insurance), *per* SCRUTTON, L.J., at p. 369. See further, Ivamy, *General Principles of Insurance Law*, 2nd Edn., 1970, pp. 493–498.

[7] *Cooke* v. *Southern Life Association* (1894), 15 Natal L.R. (N.S.) 127.

to be assessed by the Court, not exceeding the amount payable on death, for his pain and suffering and for the expenses which he has incurred. But he is not entitled to recover compensation for loss of time or business by reason of his being disabled from following his occupation, such compensation being, in effect, compensation for consequential loss and thus falling outside the policy.[1] In practice, however, the policy usually provides for payment of such compensation by way of a weekly or other periodical payments during disablement, the amount varying according as the disablement is total or partial. The rate of compensation may also vary according to the nature of the accident.

What amounts to total disablement depends to some extent on the exact phrasing of the policy. Thus, where the compensation is made payable whilst the insured is confined to the house through illness, it has been held that he is entitled to leave the house for the purpose of taking fresh air in accordance with medical advice.[2] But it is probably a question of fact what degree of disablement falls within the scope of the policy.[3] The policy may make the compensation payable in the event of the insured being wholly disabled from following his usual business or occupation, from engaging in or giving attention to his business or occupation, from attending to business of any kind, or from resuming his normal occupation.

a Inability to Follow Usual Business or Occupation

The phrase "usual business or occupation" includes the whole scope and compass of his mode of getting his livelihood.[4]

The disablement need not supervene at once; so long as it is caused by accident it may arise at any time.[5] Where the policy states that compensation is payable where the insured is unable to follow his usual business or occupation, the same kind of injury may give rise to compensation in one case and not in another. Thus, where an ankle is sprained, the insured, if a dancing master, is, whilst the sprain continues, wholly disabled within the meaning of the policy;[6] but, if he is a teacher of mathematics whose business it is to give lessons to pupils in his room, he is not necessarily, in similar circumstances, wholly disabled.[7]

It is not, however, necessary that the insured should be wholly disabled from following business in the sense that he is unable to attend to any part

---

[1] *Theobald* v. *Railway Passengers Assurance Co.* (1854), 10 Exch. 45.

[2] *Guay* v. *Provident Accident and Guarantee Co.* (1916), Q.R. 51 S.C. 328.

[3] *Hooper* v. *Accidental Death Insurance Co.* (1860), 5 H. & N. 546, Ex. Ch., *per* BLACKBURN, J., at p. 558. Cf. *Fidelity and Casualty Co. of New York* v. *Mitchell*, [1917] A.C. 592, 595, P.C. See further, *McGinn* v. *Fidelity and Casualty Co. of New York*, [1928] 3 D.L.R. 814; *Tucker* v. *South British Insurance Co.*, [1916] N.Z.L.R. 1142.

[4] *Hooper* v. *Accidental Death Insurance Co.* (*supra*), *per* POLLOCK, C.B., at p. 556.

[5] *Shera* v. *Ocean Accident and Guarantee Corporation* (1900), 32 O.R. 411, where the disablement did not arise for three weeks, and it was held to be covered, the word "immediately" in the policy being held to refer to causation, not to time, followed in *Claxton* v. *Travellers' Insurance Co. of Hartford* (1917), Q.R. 52 S.C. 239. But in *Matthews* v. *Continental Casualty Co.*, [1932] 4 D.L.R. 667, where the policy stated that the insured was covered where he was "at once and continuously disabled from working", it did not apply where the insured was returning to work and was subsequently disabled by the original injury.

[6] *Hooper* v. *Accidental Death Insurance Co.* (*supra*), *per* POLLOCK, C.B., at p. 556.

[7] *Ibid.*, *per* WIGHTMAN, J., at p. 558.

of his business. It is sufficient that he is unable to perform any substantial part of his business. Thus, WILDE, B., said in one case:

> "Surely 'wholly disabled' is equivalent to quite disabled, and a man is so unless he can do what he is called upon to do in the ordinary course of his business. It is not the same thing as 'unable to do any part of his business.' "[1]

In *Hooper* v. *Accidental Death Insurance Co.*[2] a solicitor, who was also a registrar of a county court, effected a personal accident insurance policy which stated that the insurers would pay him £5 per week during the continuance of any bodily injury of so serious nature as wholly "to disable him from following his usual business, occupation or pursuits". The insured while riding on horseback severely sprained his right ankle. He was confined to his bedroom and was unable to get downstairs. He claimed the sum payable under the policy, and the Court of Exchequer Chamber[3] held that he was entitled to it.

WIGHTMAN, J., said:[4]

> "We are all of opinion that the plaintiff, having received such an injury that he was obliged to lie on a sofa in his room, and being unable to put his foot to the ground or come down stairs, had received an injury which 'wholly disabled him from following his usual business or employment.' Great stress has been laid on the word 'wholly' as applicable to the word 'disabled.' In order to ascertain its meaning we must look at the other words in the sentence. From what is he to be wholly disabled? From following his usual occupation. When, as shown in this case, he was confined to his room and unable to see his clients, surely it is a reasonable construction to say that he was 'wholly disabled' from following his usual occupation."

In *Fidelity and Casualty Co. of New York* v. *Mitchell*[5] the insured under a personal accident insurance policy was an eye, ear, nose and throat specialist. The policy stated that in the event of "total disability that prevents the assured from performing any and every kind of duty pertaining to his occupation", he was to be paid Can. $150 weekly for as long as he lived. His hand became totally disabled when he was thrown out of a berth in a railway sleeping car to the floor. The Judicial Committee of the Privy Council[6] held[7] that this prevented him in any fair sense from performing any and every kind of duty pertaining to his occupation, and the insured sum was payable.

b Inability to Give Attention to his Business or Occupation

Where the policy states that compensation is to be payable if the insured is disabled from engaging in or giving attention to his business or occupation, nothing is payable where he is able to do any part of his business.

---

[1] *Hooper* v. *Accidental Death Insurance Co.*, (*supra*), *per* POLLOCK, C.B., at p. 554. See also *ibid.*, *per* POLLOCK, C.B., at p. 557. In *Tucker* v. *South British Insurance Co.*, [1916] N.Z.L.R. 1142, where the policy covered inability to pursue the insured's occupation or to attend to business, compensation was held payable for the whole period of the insured's inability to pursue his ordinary occupation, although he was only completely unable to attend to any business affairs whatever for part of such period.

[2] (1860), 5 H. & N. 546.

[3] WIGHTMAN, WILLIAMS, CROMPTON, WILLES, BYLES, KEATING and BLACKBURN, JJ.

[4] (1860), 5 H. & N. at p. 559.

[5] (1917), 117 L.T. 494.

[6] Viscount HALDANE, Lord DUNEDIN, Lord SHAW and Sir Arthur CHANNELL.

[7] (1917), 117 L.T. at p. 495. Another issue in the case was whether the injury suffered by the insured had resulted "directly, independently and exclusively of all other causes." As to this point, see p. 45, post.

Thus, in one case,[1] where "permanent partial disablement" was defined *inter alia* as the "complete and irrecoverable loss of the sight of an eye", it was held that the insured, whose eye was so injured that it was completely useless in his vocation, was not entitled to recover, since he was in fact able to follow his vocation by using the other eye.[2]

c Inability to Attend to Business of Any Kind

Where the policy makes compensation payable in the event of the insured being wholly disabled from attending to business of any kind, he is not entitled to recover merely because he is disabled from attending to his usual business. The incapacity for business must be absolute.[3]

But in *Pocock* v. *Century Insurance Co. Ltd.*[4]

> the insured was the manager of a grocery business, the character of which was described as that of a jobbing buyer. His practice was to drive all over the country buying job lots of grocery and then disposing of it cheaply at markets. The personal accident policy under which he was insured provided cover in respect of "temporary total disablement from attending to business of any and every kind." He was injured in a motor accident, and later was capable of making an appreciable contribution to business effort (not necessarily one for which he would be paid) e.g. making entries in books and acting as a part-time storeman.
>
> *Held*, that he had suffered "temporary total disablement" within the meaning of the policy.

Mr. Commissioner MOLONY, Q.C., said:[5]

> "I think . . . that the phrase must be looked at as a whole and in its context; and that what attention is directed to is attending to business of any sort, which might be that of a wholesale grocer doing the business nominated in this case or might be some substituted business to which that person might turn; and in order to bring the clause into operation, the question is whether a man is fit to go to business, to use a vernacular expression. Is he able to attend to a business

---

[1] *Hooper* v. *Accidental Death Insurance Co. (supra)*, *per* WILDE, B., at p. 554, and *per* POLLOCK, C.B., at p. 555.

[2] *MacDonald* v. *Mutual Life and Citizens' Assurance Co.* (1910), 29 N.Z.L.R. 1073. See also *Cathay Pacific Airways, Ltd.* v. *Nation Life and General Assurance Co., Ltd.*, [1966] 2 Lloyd's Rep. 179, Q.B.D. (Commercial Court) (aircrew disablement insurance), where "permanent total disablement" was defined as "any disablement due to personal injury to or illness, disease or disability including natural deterioration of the person insured which entirely prevents him from attending to the occupation and which appears beyond reasonable doubt to be of a permanent nature", and the insurers were held liable when a pilot was assessed by a medical board as unfit due to a diabetic condition. For the evidence leading to that conclusion, see *ibid.*, pp. 183–187.

[3] *Dodds* v. *Canadian Mutual Aid Association* (1890), 19 O.R. 70. Cf. *Copeland* v. *Locomotive Engineers' Insurance Association* (1910), 16 O.W.R. 739, where, on a policy covering total and permanent loss of sight, it was held not to be sufficient to show that the insured's sight had been so seriously affected that he could no longer follow his previous occupation. See also *Blackstone* v. *Mutual Life Insurance Co.*, [1945] 1 D.L.R. 165, where a professional musician was held to be suffering from a total and permanent disability "which continuously renders it impossible for the insured to follow a gainful occupation". The evidence showed that he suffered from a heart ailment which precluded him from engaging in concert work or teaching, that he could now do no work requiring physical exertion, and that his sole training and lifetime work had been music. The words of the policy did not require that the insured should be incapable of doing anything, but meant that the disability must be of such a character as to prevent the insured from engaging in such livelihood as he might fairly be expected to follow in view of his station, circumstances, and physical and mental capabilities.

[4] [1960] 2 Lloyd's Rep. 150 (Leeds Assizes).

[5] *Ibid.*, at p. 154.

of the nominated or substituted type? My view is that a person cannot be said to attend the business in that sense simply because he is capable of doing—perhaps rather badly—some minor part of the work involved in that or any other sort of business."

He then went on to observe:[1]

"The broad test that I think must be applied in order to understand the application of this clause is to ask oneself: Is a man fit to go to business? It does not mean that he has got to be fit to spend the whole day there; it does not mean that he has got to be fit to carry on all the activities which that business normally involves. The question is: Is he fit to attend there and play a worthwhile part in the conduct of it? If the answer is 'No', then . . . the [insured] was disabled from attending to 'business of any and every kind'."

d Inability to Resume Normal Calling

In *Williams* v. *Lloyd's Underwriters*[2]

a steel worker was insured under a personal accident policy covering him against "permanent total disablement". This term was defined in the policy as meaning: "The inability . . . to resume his . . . normal calling or occupation of any kind within 12 months from the date of receiving injury . . . and at the end of 12 months being so permanently . . . incapacitated as to render it impossible for him . . . to resume any such calling or occupation". The insured was injured in a motor accident and was permanently disabled from resuming his work as a steel worker, but had been able to secure employment as a night watchman.

Held, he had sustained "permanent total disablement" within the meaning of the policy.

Lord GODDARD, C.J., observed:[3]

"The learned arbitrator has held that the words in the first line[4] which mention resuming 'normal calling or occupation' refer to the man's pre-accident work or calling which in this case was that of a steel worker . . . Then, says the learned arbitrator, where it says 'resume any such calling or occupation', that must again refer to his normal calling or occupation . . . I agree with the learned arbitrator . . . . I must say that I attach perhaps more considerable importance to the fact that this is dealing with his *resumption* of a 'normal calling', or a resumption of an 'occupation of any kind'. I think it is distinguishing here between a man who has a normal calling and a man who may have an occupation which cannot be said to be his normal calling."[5]

---

[1] [1960] 2 Lloyd's Rep. 154 (Leeds Assizes).
[2] [1957] 1 Lloyd's Rep. 118, Q.B.
[3] *Ibid.*, at p. 120.
[4] Of the clause in the policy set out above.
[5] See, further, *Lang* v. *Metropolitan Life Insurance Co.*, [1937] 2 W.W.R. 453, where a trainman suffered from tuberculosis and the medical evidence showed that his disability prevented him from performing the work on which he had been formerly employed, and rendered him unfit except for very light work, and it was held that the fact that he could obtain a position involving the doing of practically no work did not disentitle him from claiming that he was "permanently disabled" within the meaning of the policy.

5

THE EXCEPTIONS IN THE POLICY

Apart from the cases in which the policy is, by its terms, limited to insurance against the consequences of a particular kind of accident only, various causes of death or disablement are, in practice, usually excepted from the scope of the policy. The exceptions[1] in use relate to the following matters:

1 The conduct of the insured.
2 The physical condition of the insured.
3 Other causes.

1 CONDUCT OF THE INSURED

Exceptions of this kind may exclude death or disablement due to certain specified causes only, or they may suspend the operation of the policy whilst the insured pursues a certain line of conduct. The conduct of the insured may fall within the scope of an exception and disentitle him to recover in the following cases:

a Employment in Hazardous Occupations

E.g. where he is employed in certain hazardous occupations[2] e.g. in actual service in the Armed Forces, or in the police or in a mine, a quarry or a gunpowder factory.

In this case, the cause of the accident is immaterial unless the exception is restricted to accidents arising out of and in the course of the employment.[3]

---

[1] As to exception clauses generally, see Ivamy, *General Principles of Insurance Law*, 2nd Edn., 1970, pp. 221–225.

[2] An exception of this kind appears to contemplate something in the nature of a regular occupation, and not isolated acts falling outside the regular occupation: *McNevin* v. *Canadian Railway Accident Insurance Co.* (1902), 32 S.C.R. 194, where a railway porter, who occasionally assisted in coupling railway carriages together, was killed whilst so engaged, and it was held that an exception in engaging in a more hazardous occupation did not apply. The exception may, however, extend to isolated acts: *Stanford* v. *Imperial Guarantee and Accident Insurance Co. of Canada* (1908), 18 O.L.R. 562, where the phrase was "temporarily or permanently engaged", and the insured was killed on a trial trip on which he acted as brakesman, his intention being to secure a permanent engagement; *Dominion of Canada Guarantee and Accident Insurance Co.* v. *Mahoney*, [1930] S.C.R. 123; *Cramer* v. *Ocean Accident and Guarantee Corporation*, [1942] 4 D.L.R. 625, where a salesman who performed travelling duties went into an elevator pit to look at an elevator floor at the request of his manager, and it was held that he was not engaged in "another occupation" within the meaning of a policy.

[3] In *Coxe* v. *Employers' Liability Assurance Corporation, Ltd.*, [1916] 2 K.B. 629, where the exception excluded death "directly or indirectly" caused by war, the insured, who was an Army officer, was killed by a train whilst engaged in the course of his military duties, and it was held that the exception applied. *See* p. 41, *post.* Cf. *Graham* v. *London Guarantee and Accident Co.* (1924), 56 O.L.R. 494, where the insured who was a truck driver was involved in a motor accident on his way home in the truck after finishing his work, and it was held to be an ordinary street accident and not a "hazard" of his occupation.

b Engaging in Hazardous Pursuit

E.g. mountaineering or steeple-chasing, or flying in an aircraft otherwise than as a passenger.[1]

c Under the Influence of Intoxicating Liquor

The exception does not apply unless he has taken sufficient liquor to disturb the quiet and equable exercise of his intellectual faculties.[2]

The exception applies only if the insured is under the influence of intoxicating liquor at the time of the accident.[3] The fact that the insured was not under such influence at the time of his death, if this occurs subsequently, is immaterial.

The burden of proving such an exception lies on the insurers.[4] Thus, in one case, where an insured, who disappeared and was ultimately found drowned, was still intoxicated when he was last seen, though earlier in the day he had been more intoxicated, it was held that the insurers had not discharged the burden of proof.[5]

d Engaged in Committing Breach of the Law

E.g. where the accident occurs whilst the insured is speeding,[6] or driving without lights,[7] or violating traffic bye laws,[8] or flying an aircraft in breach of air regulations,[9] or illegally poaching deer and illegally firing at a truck, which he thinks contains another poacher, to scare him off,[10] or shooting duck out of season.[11]

---

[1] *McAvoy* v. *North American Life Assurance Co.* (1968), 67 W.W.R. 200 (life insurance), where the insurers were liable only to repay the premiums and interest if the insured died "as a direct or indirect result of travel or flight in any kind of aircraft undertaken by [him] in any capacity other than solely as a passenger who has no duties to perform while in the aircraft . . .", and the insured was last seen piloting an aircraft, and it was held that a claim by his personal representatives fell within the exception.

[2] *Mair* v. *Railway Passengers Assurance Co.* (1877), 37 L.T. 356; *Louden* v. *British Merchants Insurance Co., Ltd.*, [1961] 1 All E.R. 705. For the facts of the case, see Ivamy, *Fire and Motor Insurance*, 2nd. Edn., 1973, p. 249, *Givens* v. *Baloise Marine Insurance Co.* (1959), 17 D.L.R. (2d) 7.

[3] *MacRobbie* v. *Accident Insurance Co.* (1886), 23 Sc.L.R. 391.

[4] *Haines* v. *Canadian Railway Accident Insurance Co.* (1910), 13 W.L.R. 709; *Earnshaw* v. *Dominion of Canada General Insurance Co.*, [1943] 3 D.L.R. 163, where it was held that where the circumstances of the death were such that if the insured were intoxicated, he was guilty of a criminal offence, the insurer had to satisfy the Court not only that the circumstances were consistent with the commission of an offence, but also that they were such as to be inconsistent with any other rational conclusion.

[5] *Haines* v. *Canadian Railway Accident Insurance Co.* (*supra*).

[6] *Ingles* v. *Sun Life Assurance Co.*, [1938] 3 D.L.R. 80.

[7] *Absalom* v. *United Insurance Co., Ltd.*, [1932] V.L.R. 494

[8] *Crown Life Insurance Co.* v. *Milligan*, [1939] 1 D.L.R. 737.

[9] *Shepherd* v. *Royal Insurance Co.*, [1952] 2 D.L.R. 55. See also *Bjorkman and Toronto Flying Club, Ltd.* v. *British Aviation Insurance Co., Ltd.*, [1956] S.C.R. 363, where the insured was not flying in accordance with the rules of a flying club.

[10] *Turner* v. *Northern Life Assurance Co.*, [1953] 1 D.L.R. 427.

[11] *Western Finance Corporation, Ltd.* v. *London and Lancashire Guarantee and Accident Co. of Canada*, [1928] 3 D.L.R. 592, where, however, the insured, who had been duck shooting out of season, was entitled to claim under the policy because at the time of the accident he had abandoned sport for the day, and was therefore not engaged in anything illegal at the time.

e Engaged in Duel

E.g. where he is killed or wounded in a duel[1] or prizefight, or dies at the hands of justice.[2]

f Suicide or Intentional Self-Injury

The scope of this exception refers to the insured dying by his own hand[3] or committing suicide.[4] In this form the exception covers all cases of self-destruction, and it is immaterial that the insured was insane at the time and unable to distinguish right from wrong, provided that he understood the physical nature and consequences of his act.[5]

The exception in this form does not, however, cover self-killing by accident, e.g.[6] where the insured drinks poison by mistake,[7] or unintentional self-destruction,[8] e.g. where the insured is delirious and throws himself out of a window.[9]

g Exposure to Obvious Risk of Injury

An exception of this kind must be construed literally.

It does not apply to a case where there is no negligence e.g. where the insured is killed or injured whilst crossing a street,[10] or where being a skilled swimmer and accustomed to bathe in cold water, he goes out for a swim on a chilly night,[11] or where the risk is one which the insured is, to the knowledge

---

[1] The insured is within the exception even though he never intended killing his opponent and fired in the air: *Clift* v. *Schwabe* (1846), 3 C.B. 437 Ex. Ch. (life insurance), *per* PATTESON, J., at p. 466, or although he was insane at the time: *Borradaile* v. *Hunter* (1843), 5 Man. & G. 639 (life insurance), *per* ERSKINE, J., at p. 662; *Clift* v. *Schwabe* (*supra*), *per* ALDERSON, B., at p. 468.

[2] The exception applies even though the insured is in fact innocent of the crime for which he is executed: *Clift* v. *Schwabe* (*supra*), *per* PATTESON, J., at p. 657.

[3] *Borradaile* v. *Hunter* (*supra*); *White* v. *British Empire Mutual Life Assurance Co.* (1868), L.R. 7 Eq. 394 (life insurance). The phrase is, of course, not to be taken literally so as to exclude self-destruction otherwise than by the hands of the insured: *Borradaile* v. *Hunter* (*supra*), *per* ERSKINE, J., at p. 657.

[4] *Clift* v. *Schwabe* (*supra*); *Ellinger & Co.* v. *Mutual Life Insurance Co. of New York*, [1905] 1 K.B. 31, C.A. (life insurance), where the exception was in the form of a warranty. The two phrases are equivalent: *Clift* v. *Schwabe* (*supra*), *per* PARKE, B., at p. 471; *Dufaur* v. *Professional Life Assurance Co.* (1858), 25 Beav. 599 (life insurance).

[5] *Clift* v. *Schwabe* (*supra*), *per* ROLFE, B. at p. 464: "In my opinion, every act of self-destruction is, in common language, described by the word suicide, provided it be the intentional act of a party knowing the probable consequence of what he is about". See also *Borradaile* v. *Hunter* (*supra*), *per* ERSKINE, J., at pp. 657–659.

[6] *Borradaile* v. *Hunter* (*supra*), *per* MAULE, J., at p. 662; *Clift* v. *Schwabe* (*supra*), *per* PATTESON, J., at p. 465. But the policy may contain another exception applicable to such a case: *Cole* v. *Accident Insurance Co., Ltd.* (1889), 61 L.T. 227. For the facts of this case, see p. 42, *post*; *Re United London and Scottish Insurance Co., Ltd., Brown's Claim*, [1915] 2 Ch. 167, C.A. For the facts of the case see p. 42, *post*.

[7] *Borradaile* v. *Hunter* (*supra*), *per* COLTMAN, J., at p. 662. Cf. *Cole* v. *Accident Insurance Co., Ltd.*, (*supra*), where there was an express exception against death caused by poison.

[8] *Borradaile* v. *Hunter* (*supra*), *per* MAULE, J., at p. 654; *Clift* v. *Schwabe* (*supra*), *per* PATTESON, J., at p. 465.

[9] *Stormont* v. *Waterloo Life and Casualty Assurance Co.* (1858), 1 F. & F. 22 (life insurance).

[10] *Cornish* v. *Accident Insurance Co., Ltd.* (1889), 23 Q.B.D. 453, C.A., *per* LINDLEY, L.J., at p. 456. For the facts of the case, *see* p. 39, *post*; *Shilling* v. *Accidental Death Insurance Co.* (1858), 1 F. & F. 116, where the insured was being taken for a drive. Cf. *Neill* v. *Travellers' Insurance Co.* (1881), 7 O.A.R. 570, where the Court was equally divided.

[11] *Sangster's Trustees* v. *General Accident Assurance Corporation, Ltd.* 1896, 24 R. (Ct. of Sess.) 56.

of the insurers, required to take in the ordinary performance of his duties.[1]

Nor does the exception apply to all cases of negligence, since one of the objects of insurance is to protect the insured against the consequences of his own negligence, and such a construction would render the policy little better than a snare to the insured.[2]

There are, however, degrees of negligence; and although it may be difficult to define with precision all the cases which fall within the exception, the exception plainly excludes from the scope of the policy all accidents in which the risk of injury to which the insured exposes himself is obvious to him[3] at the time when he exposes himself to it,[4] or would be obvious to him if he was paying reasonable attention to what he was doing.[5]

In *Cornish* v. *Accident Insurance Co., Ltd.*[6] a personal accident insurance policy contained an exception stating that the insurance company would not be liable if death or disability arose from "exposure of the insured to obvious risk of injury". The insured was run over and killed by a train whilst attempting to cross a main railway line in broad daylight from one part of his farm to another. At the place where he crossed there was no proper crossing, and no obstruction to prevent a person from seeing an approaching train. There was no evidence that the insured was short-sighted or deaf. His personal representative claimed the sum insured under the policy, but the insurance company repudiated liability on the ground that the case fell within the terms of the exception set out above. The Court of Appeal[7] accepted this contention, and held that the claim failed, for the insured had exposed himself to "obvious risk of injury".

LINDLEY, L.J., said:[8]

"We accept the view of the jury that this accident may be called an ordinary misadventure, but the question is whether the policy covers it. We think not. We are not prepared to say that injuries occasioned by the negligence of the insured are in all cases excepted. Such a construction would render the policy little better than a snare to the insured. But there are degrees of negligence, and we are unable to read this policy as protecting a man against the consequences of running risks which would be obvious enough to him if he paid the slightest attention to what he was doing. In the present case the deceased did in fact expose himself to risk of imminent death: that is quite clear. If he looked

---

[1] *Accident Insurance Co. of North America* v. *McFee* (1891), 7 M.L.Q.B. 255, where the exception further included getting on and off trains in motion, and it was held that, as the insured was expressly insured as a railway servant, and as his duties required him to get on and off trains in motion, the exception did not apply although he was killed whilst getting on a train in motion. Cf. *McNevin* v. *Canadian Railway Accident Insurance Co.* (1902), 32 S.C.R. 194.
[2] *Cornish* v. *Accident Insurance Co., Ltd.* (*supra*), per LINDLEY, J., at p. 457.
[3] I.e. evident to his senses: *ibid.*, per BOWEN, L.J., at p. 413. Hence the exception does not apply where the insured, being delayed by the breakdown of a waggon which he is driving, is caught by a blizzard and frozen to death: *North-West Commercial Travellers Association* v. *London Guarantee and Accident Co.* (1895), 10 Man. L.R. 537. In *McNevin* v. *Canadian Railway Accident Insurance Co.* (*supra*), where the exception related to "voluntary exposure to unnecessary danger", the Court took the view that the exception did not apply to a dangerous act e.g. the coupling of railway carriages, which the insured was accustomed to do and which he would not regard as dangerous.
[4] *Cornish* v. *Accident Insurance Co., Ltd.* (*supra*), per LINDLEY, L.J. at p. 456.
[5] *Ibid.*, following *Lovell* v. *Accident Insurance Co.* (1874), unreported.
[6] (1889), 23 Q.B.D. 453, C.A.
[7] LINDLEY and BOWEN, L.JJ.
[8] (1889), 23 Q.B.D. at p. 457.

and saw the train coming, the risk to which he exposed himself must have been obvious to him at the time. If the risk to which he exposed himself was not then obvious to him, that circumstance can only be accounted for on the supposition that he was not attending to what he was doing, i.e. not looking to see if a train was coming, and was near. We cannot construe the policy as covering a risk so run."

BOWEN, L.J., agreed, and said:[1]

"I concur in the judgment just delivered. I should be disposed to go even further, and to say that the risk the insured incurred was obvious as being evident to his senses. This was a main line of railway which could not be crossed like a street, and to cross it in such a place without looking whether a train was coming was to incur an obvious risk of imminent death. I think that a person who takes such a risk incurs risk evident to himself."

In the same way the exception applies where the insured takes a short cut along a railway line and is killed by a train,[2] or where he falls over a cliff through going too near the edge whilst gathering wild flowers.[3]

2 PHYSICAL CONDITION OF THE INSURED

For the purpose of making it clear that the policy is intended to apply in cases of accident only, an exception is usually inserted excluding liability for death or disablement from disease or, except in the case of a surgical operation rendered necessary by an "accident" within the meaning of the policy, from the consequences of surgical or medical treatment.[4]

Where, although at first sight there appears to have been an accident, it turns out that the insured's death or disablement is due solely to natural causes, the exception applies and the insurers are not liable.[5] Thus, where the insured's body is found in the sea, the natural assumption is that he has been drowned. If, however, the medical evidence shows that he died in the water from a apoplectic seizure or cramp in the heart and not by drowning, his death is not accidental, and therefore falls within the exception.[6]

Where, although there is an accident, the accident merely coincides with the disease to which the insured's death or disablement is due, and there is no causal link between them, the exception applies and the insurers are not liable.[7] Thus, where the insured dies shortly after he has been thrown out of a cart and injured, but the cause of death is kidney disease, which is not proved to have been caused by the accident, his death is not caused by accident but by disease.[8]

Where there is a causal link between the accident and the disease, the effect of the exception depends partly upon the terms of the exception and

---

[1] (1889), 23 Q.B.D. at p. 457.
[2] *Lovell* v. *Accident Insurance Co.* (1874), unreported.
[3] *Walker* v. *Railway Passengers Assurance Co.* (1910), 129 L.T. Jo. 64.
[4] See p. 21, *ante*.
[5] *Re Scarr and General Accident Assurance Corporation*, [1905] 1 K.B. 387.
[6] *Trew* v. *Railway Passengers Assurance Co.* (1861), 6 H. & N. 839, Ex. Ch., *per* COCKBURN, C.J., at p. 845. Cf. *Ballantine* v. *Employers' Insurance Co. of Great Britain* 1893, 21 R. (Ct. of Sess.) 305.
[7] *McKechnie's Trustees* v. *Scottish Accident Insurance Co.* 1889, 17 R. (Ct. of Sess.) 6. Cf. *Burnett* v. *British Columbia Accident and Employers' Liability Co.* (1914), 28 W.L.R. 425.
[8] *McKechnie's Trustees* v. *Scottish Accident Insurance Co.* (*supra*).

partly upon the application of the doctrine of proximate cause to the circumstances of the particular case.[1]

3 OTHER CAUSES

An exception of this kind excludes any other causes which the insurers may think fit to exclude e.g. death or disablement caused by:

a War or invasion.

b Poison.

c Inhalation.

a War or Invasion[2]

An exception of this kind applies, as a general rule, only where the death or disablement is proximately caused by war or invasion. It has no application where the war or invasion is only the remote cause.[3] Thus, where the insured, who has been injured by the bursting of a shell, is afterwards killed by a passing vehicle because he cannot get out of the way fast enough because of his crippled condition, war cannot be regarded as the proximate cause of his death.[4] Similarly, if he is killed by a bus whilst crossing a dimly lighted street, the fact that the street is darkened in anticipation of an air raid does not bring his death within the exception. The proximate cause is the street accident, and the darkening consequent on war is only the remote cause.[5]

The exception may, however, be framed in terms sufficiently wide to exclude the doctrine of proximate cause, and to extend to cases in which war is only the remote cause e.g. where the exception excludes death directly or indirectly caused by war.[6]

In *Coxe* v. *Employers' Liability Assurance Corporation Ltd.*[7] a personal accident insurance policy contained an exception which stated:

> "This policy does not insure against death or disablement, directly or indirectly caused by, arising from, or traceable to any of the following: self-injury or suicide, intoxicating liquors, war, invasion or civil commotion."

The insured was an Army officer who was walking alongside a railway line for the purpose of visiting guards and sentries who were guarding it in war time. He was killed by a train. The place where the accident happened was dark. Normally it would have been illuminated by the lights of a signal box, but they had been obscured in compliance with regulations made under

---

[1] See Chapter 6, *post*.

[2] See generally Ivamy, *General Principles of Insurance Law*, 2nd Edn., 1970, pp. 222–225; Ivamy, *Fire and Motor Insurance* (2nd Edn., 1973), pp. 82–85.

[3] See *Ionides* v. *Universal Marine Insurance Co.* (1863), 14 C.B.N.S. 259 (marine insurance). Cf. *Hahn* v. *Corbett* (1824), 2 Bing. 205 (marine insurance).

[4] *Leyland Shipping Co.* v. *Norwich Union Fire Insurance Society*, [1917] 1 K.B. 873, C.A. (marine insurance) (affirmed, [1918] A.C. 350), *per* SCRUTTON, L.J., at p. 897; *Crozier* v. *Thompson* (1922), 12 Ll.L. Rep. 291, where a car ran into a trench dug across a road by Sinn Feiners. See Ivamy, *Fire and Motor Insurance*, 2nd Edn.,1973, p. 264.

[5] *Coxe* v. *Employers' Liability Assurance Corporation, Ltd.*, [1916] 2 K.B. 629, where, but for the exception which included war as a remote cause, the insurers would have been held liable. For the facts of the case, see *infra*.

[6] *Coxe* v. *Employers' Liability Assurance Corporation (supra)*; *Letts* v. *Excess Insurance Co.* (1916), 32 T.L.R. 361, where, however, no question of causation arose.

[7] (1916), 114 L.T. 1180, K.B.D.

the Defence of the Realm Act 1914. The insured's personal representatives claimed under the policy. SCRUTTON, J., affirming the award of an arbitrator to whom the matter had been referred, held that the action failed, for the exception set out above applied. The insured's death was indirectly caused by war because he was walking near the railway line in pursuance of his military duties, which exposed him to special risks. His Lordship said:[1]

> "If it was merely that war put the man in a position, not specially exposed to any danger, in which a particular danger not connected with war, struck him, I think it would be most probable in that case that the matter would not come within the condition. To take the case which I put during the argument. Supposing, in connection with war, death by lightning, or that the assured had gone to a military camp, not in any way specially exposed to lightning, where lightning had struck him, I should be disposed to think that the war was so remote from the death that, in that case, you could not say that the death was undoubtedly caused by the war; but if the war has put the man in a position specially exposed to danger, as in a place especially exposed to be struck by lightning, if you can conceive such a place, and there lightning has struck him, it appears to be a question of fact, not a question of construction, whether the death is indirectly caused by war.
>
> The arbitrator has found here as a fact that this man's death was indirectly traceable to war; and the facts are that the deceased was put in a position of special danger, namely, where he had to be about the railway line in the dark, and with the lights turned out because of war, doing his military duties, and, while doing his military duties in that position of special danger, he is killed by the special danger which prevails at that particular place to which he is exposed by reason of his military duties.
>
> I am unable to say that the arbitrator cannot reasonably find, as a matter of fact, in that case that the death was indirectly caused by war. It is a matter for him to find, in my view, and not for me, and I can only interfere with him if the facts are such that, upon the true construction of the condition, he could not find the result that he has found."

b Poison

An exception of this kind applies although the insured drank by mistake the poison which caused his death.

In *Cole* v. *Accident Insurance Co., Ltd.*[2] the insured had taken out a personal accident insurance policy which excluded the liability of the insurance company "if his death or injury to him were caused by poison". He took a poisonous mixture instead of medicine and died three hours later. His personal representative claimed under the policy. The Court of Appeal[3] held that the claim failed, for the insured had died from "poison", even though it had been taken accidentally, and the exception accordingly applied.

c Inhalation

An exception of this kind is not, in the absence of express words, limited to voluntary inhalation. It applies wherever the insured inhales anything in consequence of which he dies, whether he did so intentionally or otherwise.

In *Re United London and Scottish Insurance Co., Ltd., Brown's Claim*[4] a personal accident insurance policy contained an exception which stated:

---

[1] (1916), 114 L.T. at p. 1181, K.B.D.
[2] (1889), 5 T.L.R. 736, C.A.
[3] Lord ESHER, M.R., LINDLEY and BOWEN, L.JJ.
[4] (1915), 113 L.T. 397, C.A.

"This policy does not insure against death or disablement by accident directly or indirectly caused to any extent by medical or surgical treatment, or fighting, ballooning, self-injury, or suicide or anything swallowed, or administered or inhaled."

The insured was found dead in his house. The gas was turned on but unlighted. A doctor certified that the cause of death was "suffocation from gas poisoning". The insured's personal representative claimed against the insurance company which was in liquidation. The Court of Appeal[1] held that the claim failed, for the insured had died from "anything inhaled" within the meaning of the exception. There was nothing to show that the words meant "voluntarily inhaled", as the personal representative had contended.

WARRINGTON, L.J., observed:[2]

"Was this death occasioned directly or indirectly to any extent by 'anything inhaled'? Unquestionably it was. The death was caused by noxious gas inhaled. But it is said that we are not to read this clause in the policy literally; we are to import from the context into it this limitation—that it is confined to death occasioned by something voluntarily inhaled or something inhaled under circumstances which show that the assured voluntarily exposed himself to the danger of inhaling. I think that it only requires to be stated to show how impossible it is to import any such limitation into the words of the condition. Directly you depart from the literal meaning of the words you embark upon a sea of difficulties and speculations which ought, I think, if possible, to be avoided.

In my opinion, the death in this case was occasioned by something inhaled. It is therefore within the limitation expressed in the condition, and accordingly not an accident recoverable for by the policy."

---

[1] Lord ESHER, M.R., PICKFORD and WARRINGTON, L.JJ.
[2] (1915), 113 L.T. at p. 400. See also the judgment of Lord ESHER, M.R., *ibid.*, at p. 399, and that of PICKFORD, L.J., *ibid.*, at p. 399.

6

THE APPLICATION OF THE DOCTRINE OF PROXIMATE CAUSE

The accident, the injury and the death or disablement may be so closely connected with each other and stand so clearly apart from all other circumstances that no reasonable doubt on the question of it can exist. Thus, death or disablement is obviously caused by accident where the insured, being of sound mind and body, is killed by a car while crossing the street or slips from a railway platform on to the line and breaks his leg, in consequence of which he is confined to his room until the fracture is healed.

The difficulty is that many of the cases arising under a personal accident insurance policy cannot be stated so simply. The insured, being human, is liable to suffer from disease; he may be suffering from disease at the time of the accident, or he may suffer from disease afterwards; and the disease from which he suffers may have some connection with the accident or may be independent of it.

Moreover, the policy is intended to protect the insured against the consequences of accident only and not against the consequences of natural causes, and this intention may be brought out by an exception referring in express terms to the particular disease from which the insured has suffered or framed in terms wide enough to cover it. The part played by the disease in the causation of the insured's death or disablement and its consequent effect upon the validity of any claim under the policy must, therefore, be taken into account.

For this purpose, the doctrine of proximate cause[1] is to be applied to the facts of the particular case.[2] It may also be necessary to consider whether its application is excluded or in any way modified by the language of the particular policy.[3]

---

[1] The word "direct", when used alone, is equivalent to "proximate"; *Fitton* v. *Accidental Death Insurance Co.* (1864), 17 C.B.N.S. 122; *Lawrence* v. *Accidental Insurance Co.* (1881), 7 Q.B.D. 216; *Mardorf* v. *Accident Insurance Co.*, [1903] 1 K.B. 584; cf. *Winspear* v. *Accident Insurance Co.* (1880), 6 Q.B.D. 42, C.A.; when used alone with "proximate", as in the phrase "direct or proximate cause", it is superfluous, unless it means something different, in which case it is a difficult question what it exactly does mean: *Re Etherington and Lancashire and Yorkshire Accident Insurance Co.*, [1909] 1 K.B. 591, C.A., *per* KENNEDY, L.J., at p. 602. The use of the word "indirect" on the other hand, makes it necessary to take into consideration even the remote cause: *Coxe* v. *Employers' Liability Assurance Corporation*, [1916] 2 K.B. 629. See further Ivamy, *General Principles of Insurance Law*, 2nd Edn., 1970, pp. 334–347.

[2] Cf. *Thom* (*or Simpson*) v. *Sinclair*, [1917] A.C. 127 (workmen's compensation), *per* Lord HALDANE, at p. 136.

[3] *Re Etherington and Lancashire and Yorkshire Accident Insurance Co.* (*supra*), *per* KENNEDY, L.J., at p. 602.

WHERE THE DISEASE PRECEDES THE ACCIDENT

Where the disease precedes the accident in point of time,[1] the disease and the accident are to be regarded as separate and independent causes, so far as the natural consequences of each are concerned.

Where the disease and the accident may throughout operate upon the insured independently of each other, and the death or disablement of the insured may be due entirely to the operation of the one without the intervention of the other, there is no connection whatsoever between the disease and the accident. They are merely contemporaneous in point of time, and, though there may be some difficulty in ascertaining the facts, there is no difficulty, once the facts are ascertained, in attributing the death or disablement to its proper cause.[2]

If, therefore, the death or disablement is caused by the accident, the policy applies; otherwise it does not.[3]

Thus, where the insured, whilst suffering from some disease which does not prevent him from attending to business, is killed by an accident to the train in which he is travelling to business, his death is merely caused by accident, and the existence of the disease is to be disregarded.[4]

Where the effect of the accident may be to make manifest the existence of the disease, but the death or disablement is nevertheless solely caused by the disease, there is equally no connection between the disease and the accident. The accident merely leads to an examination of the insured and an investigation into his physical condition, and the death or disablement, being caused by the disease, is not covered by the policy.[5]

Thus, where, after an accident, the insured claims under the policy on the ground that the accident has resulted in a rupture, and it is established that the insured had sustained no injury from the accident, but that he was suffering from congenital hernia, the claim must fail.[6]

If, on the other hand, there is, prior to the accident, nothing more than a pre-disposition to the particular disease,[7] or if the disease is then latent in the system, but the effect of the accident is that the disease becomes active, the death or disablement caused by the disease is the consequence of the accident and falls within the policy.

In *Fidelity and Casualty Co. of New York* v. *Mitchell*[8] the insured had taken out a personal accident insurance policy under which a certain sum would be paid to him in the case of "bodily injury sustained through accidental

---

[1] The shortness of the time intervening between the disease and the accident is immaterial: *Lawrence* v. *Accidental Insurance Co.* (*supra*), *per* WATKIN WILLIAMS, J., at p. 222.

[2] See *McKechnie's Trustees* v. *Scottish Accident Insurance Co.* 1889, 17 R. (Ct. of Sess.) 6, where the insured was thrown out of a cart and afterwards died of kidney disease, and it was held in the Court below that his death was due to disease accelerated by accident, but on appeal, that, on the facts, the death was not proved to have been caused by accident.

[3] *Fitton* v. *Accidental Death Insurance Co.* (*supra*) where the Court, having held that an exception against death arising from hernia did not apply where the hernia was caused by accident, allowed the pleadings to be amended so as to raise the question whether the hernia was occasioned by natural causes.

[4] See *Smith* v. *Accident Insurance Co.* (1870), L.R. 5 Exch. 302, *per* KELLY, C.B. at p. 311; *Hope's Trustees* v. *Scottish Accident Insurance Co.* 1896, 3 S.L.T. 252.

[5] *Fitton* v. *Accidental Death Insurance Co.* (*supra*).

[6] *Burnett* v. *British Columbia Accident and Employers' Liability Co.* (1914), 28 W.L.R. 425.

[7] *Claxton* v. *Travellers' Insurance Co. of Hartford* (1917), Q.R. 52 S.C. 239, where there was merely a pre-disposition to hernia, and the hernia was in fact caused by accident.

[8] (1917), 117 L.T. 494.

means . . . and resulting directly, independently and exclusively of all other causes". Whilst travelling in a railway sleeping car he was thrown from his berth on to the floor and severely sprained his wrist. It did not get any better, and was found to be in a tuberculous condition. Some years before the policy was issued he had suffered from a slight tuberculous affection of the left lung which had caused a lesion which had not healed. The disease then became latent, and probably would have remained so except for the accident. When the insured claimed under the policy, the insurers repudiated liability on the ground that the injury had not arisen "directly, independently and exclusively of all other causes".

It was held by the Judicial Committee of the Privy Council[1] that the insured was entitled to recover under the policy, for the tubercular condition of the wrist was not a fresh intervening cause, and the injury had been caused by the accident.[2]

Lord DUNEDIN said:[3]

> "But then comes the third condition, which is the critical point. This bodily injury, sustained through accidental means, and resulting in disability, must so result 'directly, independently, and exclusively of all other causes.' Now, the expression 'other' causes postulates a cause already specified. The word 'cause' has not, so far, been used in the sentence, and it must therefore be found in the words 'accidental means.' Therefore there must be independency between cause 1—the accident—and cause 2, whatever that may be. But in this case, on the view of the facts taken by both courts[4]—with which their Lordships agree, and which in any case they would be slow to disturb—there is no independency between the alleged second cause—the tuberculous state—and the first cause—the accident. Prior to the accident there was only a potestative tuberculous tendency; after it, and owing to it, there was a tuberculous condition. In other words, the accident had a double effect: it sprained the tendons and it induced the tuberculous condition. These two things acted together, and were the reason of the continuing disability; but, while they are both ingredients of the disabled condition, there has been and is, on the true construction of the policy, only one cause—namely, the accident."

In some cases the effect of the accident may be to aggravate the consequences of the disease, or the existence of the disease may aggravate the consequences of the accident. The death or disablement may not be solely due to the accident or to the disease. Both causes, though independent in their inception, may cooperate to produce a result more serious than might have been contemplated in the ordinary course as the natural consequence of either working alone. In this case there are two concurrent causes either of which may equally be regarded as the proximate cause of the death or disablement. In the absence of any exception in the policy, the death or disablement, therefore, falls within the policy, as being the natural consequence of the accident so far as the particular insured is concerned, since, but for the accident, he would not have died or been disabled. The fact that the disease is also the proximate cause of the death or disablement,

---

[1] Viscount HALDANE, Lord DUNEDIN, Lord SHAW and Sir Arthur CHANNELL.
[2] Another issue which arose in the case was whether the injury to the insured's wrist constituted a "total disablement". As to this point, see p. 33, *ante*.
[3] (1917), 117 L.T. at p. 495.
[4] I.e., the Appellate Division of the Supreme Court of Ontario and MIDDLETON, J., in the Supreme Court of Ontario.

seeing that, but for the disease, the accident would not have resulted as it did, is to be disregarded.[1]

The policy may, however, contain an exception against disease or disablement caused by the joint operation of the disease and the accident.[2]

Thus, where the exception expressly excludes death by disease, though accelerated by accident,[3] the policy does not apply if the accident is not one calculated to result in death, and it is clear that, but for the disease, the insured would not have died.[4]

Where the disease might cause the accident, but the death or disablement might be the consequence of the accident alone, the disease and the accident are successive, not concurrent, causes. The accident is the proximate cause of the death or disablement, the disease being only the remote cause, since its connection with the death or disablement is not causal, but accidental. The existence of the disease is, therefore, immaterial and the policy attaches.

Thus, the insured may be seized with a fit, whilst crossing a river,[5] or whilst bathing,[6] and be drowned; he may fall in a fit in front of a train and be killed;[7] or he may be out with a shooting party and accidentally shot while lying in a field recovering from a fit.[8] The insured does not, however, die of the fit; he is drowned or killed by "accident".

An exception in the policy, expressly excluding liability in case of death caused by disease, has no application, since the exception applies to a death actually caused by natural disease,[9] and not to a death of which the disease is not the proximate, but only the remote cause.[10]

---

[1] See *Reischer* v. *Borwick*, [1894] 2 Q.B. 548, C.A. (marine insurance), where a leak caused by a collision which had been temporarily stopped was reopened when the ship was being towed, in consequence of which the ship sank, and LINDLEY, L.J., at p. 551, pointed out that, whilst the loss was proximately caused by the collision, which was the only peril insured against in the policy, it might also be a loss by "perils of the sea" within the meaning of an ordinary policy, and that either cause was a proximate cause of the sinking.

[2] *Lawrence* v. *Accidental Insurance Co., Ltd.* (1881), 7 Q.B.D. 216, *per* WATKIN WILLIAMS, J., at p. 221: "The true meaning of this proviso (i.e. death arising from fits) is that if the death arises from a fit, then the company are not liable, even though accidental injury contributed to the death in the sense that they were both causes, which operated jointly in causing it . . . But it is essential to that construction that it should be made out that the fit was a cause in the sense of being the proximate and immediate cause of the death, before the company are exonerated, and it is nonetheless so, because you can show that another cause intervened and assisted in the causation."

[3] Presumably, an exception against disease simply, without referring to acceleration, would have the same effect, since, *ex hypothesi*, disease is equally the proximate cause.

[4] *Cawley* v. *National Employers' Accident and General Assurance Association, Ltd.* (1885), Cab. & El. 597, where it was clear that the insured would not have died from the accident, if he had not been suffering from gall-stones at the time when it happened; *McKechnie's Trustees* v. *Scottish Accident Insurance Co.* 1889, 17 R. (Ct. of Sess.) 6, where, however, the judgment of the Court below that the disease was accelerated by the accident, was affirmed on appeal on the ground that the death was not proved to have been caused by accident; *Anderson* v. *Scottish Accident Insurance Co.* 1889, 27 Sc. L.R. 20; cf. *Re Scarr and General Accident Assurance Corporation*, [1905] 1 K.B. 387, *per* BRAY, J., at p. 395.

[5] *Winspear* v. *Accident Insurance Co.* (1880), 6 Q.B.D. 42, C.A.

[6] *Reynolds* v. *Accident Insurance Co.* (1870), 22 L.T. 820; cf. *Trew* v. *Railway Passengers' Assurance Co.* (1861), 6 H. & N. 839, Ex. Ch., *per* CROMPTON, J., at p. 841.

[7] *Lawrence* v. *Accidental Insurance Co., Ltd.* (*supra*).

[8] Cf. *ibid., per* WATKIN WILLIAMS, J., at p. 222.

[9] *Winspear* v. *Accident Insurance Co.* (*supra*), *per* Lord COLERIDGE, C.J., at p. 45.

[10] *Lawrence* v. *Accidental Insurance Co., Ltd.* (*supra*), *per* WATKIN WILLIAMS, J., at p. 221.

WHERE THE DISEASE FOLLOWS THE ACCIDENT

Where the disease follows the accident in point of time,[1] the disease and the accident are not necessarily separate and independent causes so as to exclude the possibility that the natural consequences of the disease may not equally be the natural consequence of the accident. The death or disablement, though resulting directly from the disease, may, nevertheless be the natural consequence of the accident, the disease being only a link in the chain of causation, and the accident being the proximate and not the remote cause.

Where the disease is the injury caused by the accident, the death or disablement resulting from the disease results from the injury caused by the accident. It is, therefore, within the very words of the policy, and an exception within whose terms the disease in question falls is to be construed as intended to apply to the disease only when it arises in different circumstances, and not when it is the injury itself caused by the accident.

Thus, death by hernia caused by an accidental fall is death by "accident" within the meaning of the policy, notwithstanding an express exception against hernia.[2]

Where the disease is the natural consequence of the injury which is caused by the accident, the death or disablement resulting from the disease is the natural consequence of the injury, and, hence, of the accident also.[3]

The doctrine of proximate cause therefore applies, and the death or disablement, though directly caused by the disease, is proximately caused

---

[1] The length of the interval between the accident and the onset of the disease is immaterial if the relation is otherwise clear: *Shera* v. *Ocean Accident and Guarantee Corporation* (1900), 32 O.R. 411; cf. *Lawrence* v. *Accidental Insurance Co.* (*supra*), *per* WATKIN WILLIAMS, J., at p. 222. Thus, the accident may be the proximate cause, whether it results in the disease at once (*Fitton* v. *Accidental Death Insurance Co.* (1864), 17 C.B. N.S. 122) or whether the disease follows at an interval measured by hours (*Re Etherington and Lancashire and Yorkshire Accident Insurance Co.*, [1909] 1 K.B. 591, C.A.) or days (*Isitt* v. *Railway Passengers Assurance Co.* (1889), 22 Q.B.D. 504; *Mardorf* v. *Accident Insurance Co.*, [1903] 1 K.B. 584; *Accident Insurance Co. of North America* v. *Young* (1892), 20 S.C.R. 280), or even weeks (*Shera* v. *Ocean Accident and Guarantee Corporation* (1900), 32 O.R. 411). See *contra*, *Smith* v. *Accident Insurance Co.* (1870), L.R. 5 Exch. 302. The policy, may, however, impose a time limit, usually 3 months after the accident, within which the death or disablement must take place.

[2] *Fitton* v. *Accidental Death Insurance Co.* (*supra*), where leave was given to amend the pleadings for the purpose of alleging that the hernia was due to internal causes; *Claxton* v. *Travellers' Insurance Co. of Hartford* (1917), 52 Q.R.S.C. 239, where a predisposition to hernia owing to physical condition was disregarded.

[3] *Isitt* v. *Railway Passengers Assurance Co.* (*supra*), *per* WILLS, J., at pp. 511, 512: "If, as here, the assured lived for some time after injury, during this time he must live as an invalid, subject to the ordinary conditions of such a mode of life. These conditions of life are something distinct from the injury, but, when a question arises as to whether the death of the assured while subject to them was caused by the injury, it becomes essential to take into consideration these conditions of life as well as the injury, and not only these conditions, but such things as are either inseparable from them or are their natural consequences . . . Was, then, the death of the assured under the circumstances stated, the natural consequence of his injury? I think it was, I think it idle to suggest that there is anything in these circumstances which tend to show that the cold which led to his fatal attack of pneumonia was caught by the assured in some manner independent of the injury. The umpire seems to me to have found that the assured caught cold owing to his having been made an invalid by his injury and having in consequence to live as an invalid, and that the cold was due to some slight cause impossible to specify but incident to the conditions of such a life, and which would not, apart from the debility produced by the injury, have caused his death. I think that on the facts as found, there is no pretence for treating his death as less due to the injury because one step in the train of circumstances which followed was that the assured caught cold." See also *Re Etherington and Lancashire and Yorkshire Accident Insurance Co.* (*supra*).

by the accident,[1] and falls within the policy.[2] The existence of an exception within whose terms the disease in question falls is to be disregarded, if possible.[3] Any accident which does not result in death on the spot, results in the ordinary course of events in disease;[4] and if a disease so caused is to be treated as falling within the scope of the exception, the protection given by the policy is illusory.[5]

The exception is, therefore, to be construed against the insurers as intended to apply to diseases which arise independently, and not to diseases which are the mere *sequelae* of the accident.[6]

Thus, in *Re Etherington and Lancashire and Yorkshire Accident Insurance Co.*[7]

> The insured had effected a personal accident insurance policy whereby the insurers agreed to pay the sum insured if the insured sustained personal injury or death "caused by violent, accidental, external and visible means". The policy also stated: "This policy only insures against death . . . where accident . . . is the direct or proximate cause thereof . . ." The insured had a heavy fall while hunting. The ground was wet, and he was soaked through. His vitality was lowered still further by his being obliged to ride home while wet. He developed pneumonia and died. His personal representatives claimed under the the policy.
> *Held*, by he Court of Appeal,[8] that the claim succeeded. The death of the insured was "directly caused by the accident". The pneumonia arose as a direct and natural consequence from the fact that the diminution of vitality caused through the accident allowed the "pneumococca" germs to multiply and attack the lungs.

In the course of his judgment VAUGHAN WILLIAMS, L.J., said:[9]

> "I think it is impossible to limit that which is being put forward as the proximate cause to the one fact of the accident. The real truth of the matter is that the accident itself produces, and ordinarily produces, certain results, according to the nature of the accident, and the result produced according to the nature of the accident is the final step in the consequences, and it seems to me the whole transaction is really the proximate cause of the death that results . . . Here we have a fall from a horse, and a fall from a horse is undoubtedly a heavy fall, and though it caused no breakage of bones and no wound, and no obvious internal hurt, yet it involved a great shock, accompanied by a severe wetting

---

[1] *Isitt* v. *Railway Passengers Assurance Co.* (*supra*), where the insured, whilst confined to bed in consequence of an accident, caught cold and died of pneumonia, the cold and its effect being due to the lower vitality produced by the accident; *Mardorf* v. *Accident Insurance Co.*, [1903] 1 K.B. 584, C.A.; *Re Etherington and Lancashire and Yorkshire Accident Insurance Co.*, [1909] 1 K.B. 591, C.A.; *Accident Insurance Co. of North America* v. *Young* (1892), 20 S.C.R. 280; *Master of Supreme Court* v. *Reuter*, [1910] T.L. 74, where a blow on the head with a hammer was followed by cerebro-spinal meningitis; *Fidelity and Casualty Co. of New York* v. *Mitchell*, [1917] A.C. 592, P.C., where the effect of the accident was to bring out the tuberculosis which was previously latent.

[2] For the proper direction to the jury in such a case, see *Isitt* v. *Railway Passengers Assurance Co.* (1889), 22 Q.B.D. 504, *per* WILLS, J., at pp. 512, 513.

[3] *Mardorf* v. *Accident Insurance Co.* (*supra*); *Re Etherington and Lancashire and Yorkshire Accident Insurance Co.* (*supra*).

[4] *Re Etherington and Lancashire and Yorkshire Accident Insurance Co.* (*supra*), *per* FARWELL, L.J., at p. 600; cf. *Isitt* v. *Railway Passengers Assurance Co.* (*supra*), *per* WILLS, J., at p. 511.

[5] *Re Etherington and Lancashire and Yorkshire Accident Insurance Co.* (*supra*), *per* VAUGHAN WILLIAMS, L.J., at p. 597; cf. *Smith* v. *Accident Insurance Co.* (1870), L.R. 5 Exch. 302, *per* KELLY, C.B., at p. 310.

[6] *Re Etherington and Lancashire and Yorkshire Accident Insurance Co.* (*supra*), *per* KENNEDY, L.J., at p. 603; cf. *Fidelity and Casualty Co. of New York* v. *Mitchell* (*supra*), where the words of the policy were "directly, independently, and exclusively of all other causes."

[7] (1909), 100 L.T. 568, C.A.

[8] VAUGHAN WILLIAMS, FARWELL and KENNEDY, L.JJ.

[9] (1909), 100 L.T. at p. 571. See also the judgment of FARWELL, L.J., *ibid.*, at p. 572, and that of KENNEDY, L.J., *ibid.*, at p. 574.

and a ride home without any change of the wet clothes, and every case makes it palpable that the first results of such an accident would be likely to be the lowering to a great extent of the vitality of the person who had been subject to such a shock. In the second place, it seems to me beyond a doubt that such a lowering of vitality in the ordinary course of things would be likely to produce a great development of the pernicious activity of these germs which are said to exist in the respiratory organs of every human being, and that this pernicious activity of these germs would certainly produce, unless the vitality was quickened again, pneumonia, and it was from pneumonia so produced that Mr. Etherington died."

In *Mardorf* v. *Accident Insurance Co., Ltd.*[1] a personal accident insurance policy gave cover to the insured in respect of "any personal injury caused by external and accidental violence", and stated that the insurance company would pay his personal representatives £1,000 "if such injury shall be the direct and sole cause of [his] death".

The insured whilst taking off his socks found that one of them had stuck to his skin. In trying to free it he inflicted a wound with his thumb nail on the inner side of the right leg below the knee. Four days later erysipelas originating in the wound set in. This was followed by septicaemia and then by septic pneumonia, from which the insured died three weeks later. The pneumonia was the immediate cause of death. It was admitted that the septic germs were introduced into the wound at the time of the accident. The King's Bench Division held that the death was "directly and solely" caused by the accident, and judgment was given in favour of the insured's personal representative, who claimed the sum insured.[2]

WRIGHT, J. said:[3]

"The first part of the argument of Counsel for the company was that the death could not be said to have been directly and solely caused by the outward and visible means of the scratch. It seems to me that once it is agreed—as it has been agreed in this case—that the same wound broke the man's skin and introduced into the wounded surface the septic germs which eventually poisoned him, one must come to the conclusion that the condition of the lungs which proved fatal was directly and solely caused by the wound which introduced the germs which by their own powers of reproduction arrived at last at the stage when they produced the fatal disease. To take an illustration cited during the argument, let us suppose the case of a bite of a mad dog; if a person dies from hydrophobia from the bite of a mad dog, it would be introducing too great a nicety into this matter to say that the death did not result from the bite, although the actual destruction of life did not result from the bite, but from the poisoning set up by the bite. Take again, the case of a death resulting from a poisoned arrow, and the same observation would apply."

---

[1] (1903), 88 L.T. 330.

[2] The Court held that an exception stating: "This policy . . . does not apply to accidents, injuries, death or disablement caused by or arising wholly or in part from fits, disease or other intervening cause, or weakness or exhaustion, even although the disease or other intervening cause may either directly or otherwise be brought in or result from or have been aggravated by accident, or be due to weakness or exhaustion consequent on accident or the death accelerated thereby" did not apply to the present case, for the death was not caused by fits nor by disease, which was defined in the policy as meaning "typhus, scarlet or typhoid fever, smallpox, diphtheria or measles". See the judgment of WRIGHT, J., *ibid.*, at p. 333. His Lordship also held that the death had not arisen from any "other intervening cause": *ibid.*

[3] (1903), 88 L.T. at p. 333. See also *Accident Insurance Co. of North America* v. *Young (supra)*. *Cf. Smith* v. *Accident Insurance Co. (supra)*. See further, *Continental Casualty Co.* v. *Casey*, [1934] S.C.R. 541, where the insured broke a leg and infection set in and he died from uraemia, and it was held that his personal representative was entitled to the sum insured under the policy because there was no doubt that the broken leg, without which death would not have ensued, was caused by the accident.

In *Isitt* v. *Railway Passengers Assurance Co.*[1] an insurance company agreed to pay £500 to the personal representatives of an insured if "[the insured] shall sustain any injury caused by accident or violence . . . and . . . shall die from the effects of such injury within 3 calendar months from the happening thereof". The policy also stated that: "This [policy] shall not extend to any injury caused by natural disease or by any surgical operation rendered necessary by disease".

The insured fell at a railway station, and in doing so he dislocated his shoulder. He was taken home and put to bed and died from pneumonia about a month later. The pneumonia was caused by cold, and he would not have died if he had not had the fall. He had been reduced by the fall to a state of debility in which he was more susceptible to cold than he would have been. His personal representatives claimed the £500, but the insurance company maintained that it was not liable because the policy only covered death caused immediately and directly by the accident.

The Queen's Bench Division[2] held that the action succeeded, for the insured's death was due to the effects of injury caused by accident. HUDDLESTON, B., said:[3]

> "I think that the meaning of the words in the policy, 'effects of the injury', do not mean that the death must be the proximate result of the injuries, but that you must look to see whether there were serious and natural consequences leading legitimately or directly by steps from the accident to the death. What was it? There was the dislocation of the shoulder, there was pain, there was the restlessness and debility, which was such that he wanted to throw off his clothes, and such as rendered him liable to catch cold when, under ordinary circumstances, he would not have caught cold; that he did catch cold, that pneumonia followed, and that the cause of death was pneumonia. If, therefore, you are allowed to take the natural steps in order, you get a clear claim of circumstances proceeding directly from the injury to the death; injury, confinement to the house, pain, debility, cold as a consequence, pneumonia, and death. I think, therefore, if the question for us as a question of law is, whether you may take those circumstances into consideration to explain what the meaning of the words of the policy is—namely, 'the effects'—that in this case the company is liable, and that the death was the natural result of the consequences of the injury, and that the natural effect of the injury was the death."

Again, where the insured is bitten by a dog and dies of hydrophobia,[4] his death, though actually caused by the disease is the natural consequence of the accident, and an exception against death by disease has no application.

If, however, the exception shows a clear intention to exclude disease, though caused by the accident, the intention will prevail.[5]

Thus, the policy may except death arising from a particular disease e.g. erysipelas, however caused, whether by an accident or otherwise. In this

---

[1] (1889), 60 L.T. 297.
[2] HUDDLESTON, B. and WILLS, J.
[3] (1889), 60 L.T. at p. 301. See also the judgment of WILLS, J., *ibid.*, at p. 302.
[4] *Mardorf* v. *Accident Insurance Co.* (*supra*), *per* WRIGHT, J., at p. 588.
[5] If the exception relates, not to disease generally, but to certain specified diseases, a disease not specified must be disregarded; *Mardorf* v. *Accident Insurance Co.* (*supra*), where the policy was endorsed with a notice defining the word "disease" as used in the policy. *See* p. 50, footnote 2, *ante*.

case, the disease is for all purposes expressly excepted from the series of
events which create a liability in the insurers.[1]

Where the disease arises independently of the accident, the death or
disablement of the insured, if solely caused by the disease, is not within the
policy,[2] since there is no connection between them, except in point of time.[3]

If, on the other hand, the disease aggravates the consequences of the
accident, the accident is still the proximate cause of the death or disablement, and the policy, therefore, applies, unless the disease, as being equally
the proximate cause, falls within the terms of an exception.[4]

In *Jason* v. *British Traders' Insurance Co., Ltd.*[5] the insured had taken out a
personal accident insurance policy which stated that:

> "If the insured person shall sustain in any accident bodily injury resulting in
> and being—independently of all other causes—the exclusive direct and immedi-
> ate cause of the . . . injury or disablement of the insured person . . . then the
> company shall pay to the insured [certain benefits]".

The word "accident" in the policy was defined as: "An unforeseen and
undesigned casualty or mishap (not within the exceptions hereinafter
mentioned) operating by violent external and visible means". The policy
contained an exception clause stating (*inter alia*):

> "No benefit shall be payable under this policy in respect of death, injury or
> disablement directly or indirectly caused by or arising or resulting from or
> traceable to . . . (iii) (b) any physical defect or infirmity which existed prior
> to an accident."

---

[1] This illustration is given in *Smith* v. *Accident Insurance Co.* (*supra*), *per* KELLY, C.B., who
dissented from the rest of the Court, at pp. 309, 310. The majority of the Court held that
death arising from erysipelas caused by an accident fell within an exception against
death arising from "erysipelas, or any other disease or secondary cause or causes arising
within the system of the insured before or at the time of or following such accidental
injury (whether causing such death directly or jointly with such accidental injury)", and
distinguished in *Fitton* v. *Accidental Death Insurance Co.* (1864), 17 C.B. N.S. 122 partly
because of the reference to "secondary causes", and partly because the erysipelas was only
a later development and not part and parcel of the accident, as being the immediate
result of the injury in point of time. The decision of the majority in *Smith* v. *Accident
Insurance Co.* (1870), L.R. 5 Exch. 302 is, however, far from satisfactory. The object of
the exception is according to that decision, to deal with the case where it is difficult to say
whether the disease alone, or the disease jointly with the injury, was the cause of death,
and its object is carried out by precluding the necessity of inquiring into the matter:
ibid., *per* CLEASBY and CHANNELL, BB., at p. 306. At the same time, the exception must
equally apply where no difficulty arises, and its effect is, as pointed out by KELLY, C.B.,
at p. 310, to render the policy almost nugatory; *cf. Re Etherington and Lancashire and Yorkshire Accident Insurance Co.*, [1909] 1 K.B. 591, C.A., *per* VAUGHAN WILLIAMS, L.J., at p. 591.
Moreover, the erysipelas was not, in *Smith* v. *Accident Insurance Co.* (*supra*), jointly with the
accident the cause of death. The accident was not a concurrent cause; the cause of death was
the erysipelas alone. The erysipelas, however, was the direct consequence of the accident,
which was, therefore, the proximate cause of death; and the decision is, in this respect,
inconsistent with the later cases, e.g. *Isitt* v. *Railway Passengers Assurance Co.* (1889), 22
Q.B.D. 504, and *Re Etherington and Lancashire and Yorkshire Accident Insurance Co.* (*supra*).
If the decision is to be supported, it must be on the ground that a wider construction is to
be placed upon the phrase "secondary cause" than was placed upon the phrase "intervening cause" in *Re Etherington and Lancashire and Yorkshire Accident Insurance Co.* (*supra*),
in which case *Smith* v. *Accident Insurance Co.* (*supra*) does not appear to have been referred to.
[2] *Isitt* v. *Railway Passengers Assurance Co.* (*supra*), *per* WILLS, J., at p. 512.
[3] *Clidero* v. *Scottish Accident Insurance Co.* 1892, 19 R. (Ct. of Sess.) 355, *per* Lord ROBERTSON,
at p. 366.
[4] *Re Etherington and Lancashire and Yorkshire Accident Insurance Co.* (*supra*), *per* VAUGHAN
WILLIAMS, L.J., at p. 603; *cf. Smith* v. *Accident Insurance Co.* (*supra*), *per* KELLY, C.B., at
p. 311.
[5] [1969] 1 Lloyd's Rep. 281, Q.B.D.

On June 15, 1965, the insured was driving his van when the near-side rear wheel came off and the van crashed. On June 21 he suffered a coronary thrombosis. He claimed the sum insured under the policy, but the insurers denied liability on the ground that coronary thrombosis was not a bodily injury sustained in an accident, and that the claim fell with the exception mentioned above.

FISHER, J.,[1] held that the action failed. He said that there certainly was an "accident" within the meaning of the policy i.e. the coming off of the wheel and the subsequent violent motion of the vehicle until it came to rest. Counsel had contended that if an accident set in motion a train of events which caused harmful physiological changes, those changes were a bodily injury sustained in the accident; and that in the present case he would say that the accident set up anxiety which brought about a change in the blood which produced six days later a clot sufficient to occlude the coronary artery which was narrowed by a pre-existing arterial disease. In his Lordship's opinion that was a strained and unnatural use of words to call either the anxiety or the change in the blood or the clot itself "a bodily injury sustained in the accident". But even on the assumption that the argument was well-founded, the claim must fail because the bodily injury was not "independently of all other causes the exclusive . . . cause of the disablement". There were two concurrent causes i.e. the pre-existing arterial disease and the formulation of the clot. These two causes were independent of each other, and the thrombosis would not have occurred on June 21 unless both had operated. If there were any doubt about that, it would be removed by the words of the later provision in the policy. It was plain that the disablement was "directly or indirectly caused by or arising or resulting from or traceable to . . . (b) any physical defect or infirmity which existed prior to an accident", i.e. arterial disease.

The learned judge said[2] that there was no question here of an accident supervening on and following a previous event such as a fit which was within the exclusion clause. Here the arterial disease and the clotting were simultaneously present together, each a necessary condition of the thrombosis. They were both "causes which operated jointly in causing it" to use the words of WATKIN WILLIAMS, J., in *Lawrence* v. *Accidental Insurance Co., Ltd.*[3]. It would be unreal to single out one as the direct or the proximate and immediate cause rather than the other. The fact that this was a continuing condition and the other was a superimposed event did not seem to him to justify such a distinction. In fact, however, the wording of the policy in the present case made it clear that it was not only direct causes which must be looked at. If there were a number of causes, of which one (the bodily injury) could be singled out as the direct and immediate cause, the claim would nonetheless fail because there were four separate criteria which had to be satisfied, and two of them i.e. "independently of all other causes the exclusive . . . cause" would not be satisfied even though the other two were. Even if this were not so, the words "directly or indirectly" in the later provision of the policy, clearly demonstrated that no benefit was payable

---

[1] [1969] 1 Lloyd's Rep. at p. 290.
[2] *Ibid.*, at p. 291.
[3] (1881), 7 Q.B.D. 216 at p. 221.

if there was a causal relationship between the pre-existing arterial disease and the coronary thrombosis, even although it was a relationship less close than the "proximate and immediate cause" to which WATKIN WILLIAMS, J., referred.

His Lordship also held[1] that the words "physical defect or infirmity" were apt to cover any malfunctioning or departure from a healthy state of any part of the body, so the insurers were relieved from liability by the exception clause set out above. Further, he did not accept the argument of Counsel that the exception clause was solely an exclusion of certain types of accident, and that since the accident in the present case was not within any of those types, the exception clause did not apply, and observed:[2]

> "In my judgment this is not so. Plainly *one* of the things which the clause does is to exclude benefit in the case of certain types of accident (see (v) for example), but it does not follow that that is all that it does. The opening words, "no benefit shall be payable', down to the words, 'traceable to', are quite general, and in my judgment the various headings—in particular, (iii) (*b*) and (iv)— make it clear that the exclusion clause may operate even though the accident is one falling within the definition and is not *qua* accident excluded by the clause."

---

[1] [1969] 1 Lloyd's Rep. at p. 291.
[2] *Ibid.*, at p. 292.

7

THE CLAIM

The principal matters relating to the claim are the following:

1   Notice of the accident.
2   Proof of loss.
3   The amount recoverable.
4   Limitation on the amount recoverable.

1   Notice of the accident

Notice of the accident is usually required to be given to the insurers within a specified time.[1]

Whether a stipulation as to the giving of notice of injury within the required time is a condition precedent or not depends upon the intention of the parties as shown in the language of the stipulation.[2]

In *Cawley* v. *National Employers' Accident and General Assurance Association, Ltd.*[3] a condition in a personal accident insurance policy stated:

> "Notice of any accident must be given to the association within 7 days of its occurrence.   Such notice must state the date, time, place and manner of the accident, the nature of the injuries received, the extent of the disablement, the number of the policy, the name and address and the occupation of the assured, and of the person giving the notice if other than the assured."

The insured fell on some steps leading from a house on November 15, 1883, and was later admitted to hospital where he died on November 30.

---

[1] See further, Ivamy, *General Principles of Insurance Law*, 2nd Edn. 1970, pp. 348–352.

[2] See Ivamy, *General Principles of Insurance Law*, 2nd Edn., 1970, pp. 351–352. See further, *Accident Insurance Co. of North America* v. *Young* (1892), 20 S.C.R. 280; *Employers' Liability Assurance Corporation* v. *Taylor* (1898), 29 S.C.R. 104; *Warne* v. *London Guarantee and Accident Co.* (1900), 20 C.L.T. 227; *Shera* v. *Ocean Accident and Guarantee Corporation* (1900), 21 C.L.T. 138; *Evans* v. *Railway Passenger Assurance Co.* (1912), 21 O.W.R. 442; *Youlden* v. *London Guarantee and Accident Co.* (1912), 21 O.W.R. 674; *Heagle* v. *Great West Life Assurance Co.*, [1938] 1 D.L.R. 794; *Goldstein* v. *Pearl Assurance Co.*, [1940] 1 D.L.R. 810; *Glenburn Dairy, Ltd.* v. *Canadian General Insurance Co.*, [1953] 4 D.L.R. 33; *Patton* v. *Employers' Liability Assurance Corporation* (1887), 20 L.R. Ir. 93; *Hollister* v. *Accident Association of New Zealand* (1886), 5 N.Z.L.R. 49; *Haines* v. *Canadian Railway Accident Insurance Co.* (1910), 20 Man. L.R. 69, where the giving of a notice 10 days after the discovery of the insured's body was held to have complied with a condition that notice of an accident should be given within 10 days after its occurrence; *Gamble* v. *Accident Assurance Co., Ltd.* (1869), I.R. 4 C.L. 204; *Donnison* v. *Employers' Accident and Live Stock Insurance Co., Ltd.* 1897, 24 R. (Ct. of Sess.) 681; *Johnston* v. *Dominion of Canada Guarantee and Accident Insurance Co.* (1908), 17 O.L.R. 462; *Golko and W. K. G. Bulldozing, Ltd.* v. *Guardian Insurance Co. of Canada* (1963), 45 W.W.R. 378.

[3] (1885), 1 T.L.R. 255.

55

On December 1 his widow went with the policy to the insurers, who told her that it was not worth the paper it was written on because the premium had never been paid. Subsequently, however, she discovered a receipt for the premium among the insured's papers. She now brought an action against the insurers claiming the sum insured. A. L. SMITH, J., held that the action failed because no notice of the accident had been given within the time stated in the condition of the policy set out above.

Again, in *Cassel* v. *Lancashire and Yorkshire Accident Insurance Co., Ltd.*[1] a personal accident insurance policy stated that:

> "in the case of injury from accident the [insured] shall give the company notice in writing of the occurrence of the accident, and also within 14 days of the accident shall forward medical certificates of the nature and extent of the injuries received".

The insured met with an accident while paddling a canoe in July 1883. No immediate ill resulted from the accident, and whatever injury was received was not fully developed until March 1883. On March 17 he became ill, and was entirely disabled by March 26. On March 28 he gave the company notice of the accident and the injuries which he stated were the result of it. The company refused to accept the notice on the ground that it was out of time, and repudiated liability. POLLOCK, B., held that the company was entitled to do so, for the terms of the policy were perfectly clear and the condition had not been complied with.

But in *Stoneham* v. *Ocean, Railway and General Accident Insurance Co., Ltd.*[2] where the policy stated: "In case of fatal accident notice thereof must be given to the company at the head office in London within 7 days", the Queen's Bench Division[3] held that, as a matter of construction, the words did not amount to a condition precedent to the liability of the insurance company. MATHEW, J., said:[4]

> "In this case the obligation contained in the policy is that, if the assured shall die solely from the effects of an external accident within ninety days after the happening thereof, the company shall pay to the legal representatives or assigns of the assured the sum of £1000 at the expiration of three calendar months after satisfactory proof of the death of the assured shall have been given to the company. Then follows a clause to the effect that the policy shall be subject to the conditions indorsed upon the back, which are to be considered as incorporated. It does not say that they are to be considered as conditions precedent, but as 'incorporated herein.' The duty upon us is to say what the whole of these conditions mean. Some of them are referred to as terms of the policy, but not as conditions precedent. For instance, there is a clause which says that, 'For the purpose of identifying the assured, in all cases of change of residence or occupation, or change of name, whether by marriage or otherwise, due notice thereof shall be given by the assured at the company's offices in London.' Is that a condition precedent? I do not think it is intended to be, and it is not so stated to be. The next clause says that, 'If the assured shall, during the period covered by this policy, engage in any other occupation or employment involving a greater risk than is contemplated in the class of risks under which this policy is effected, he shall forthwith give notice thereof to the company, and pay such extra premiums as may be required in respect of such increased risk, and in default

---

[1] (1885), 1 T.L.R. 495.
[2] (1887), 57 L.T. 236.
[3] MATTHEW and CAVE, JJ.
[4] (1887), 57 L.T. at p. 237.

of his so doing, this policy shall become absolutely void, and the premium paid for the same shall be forfeited to the company.' The language there shows plainly that the company knew how to describe a term which was to be a condition precedent. Another term of the policy says that, 'Any question arising under, or in relation to, this policy, shall, if required by the company or the assured, or his representatives or assigns, be referred to the decision of two referees or an umpire to be appointed by the referees.' If the assured refused so to refer, would the policy be void, or, if the company refused, could they get rid of their liability? That, in my opinion, is a stipulation which must be regarded as a mere term, and not as a condition precedent. Then we come to the clause which says, that 'in case of fatal accident, notice thereof must be given to the company at the head office in London within the time of seven days.' That is intended to apply, [Counsel] argues, either to an accident which is fatal instantaneously, or to an accident which is followed at an interval by death. [Counsel] had to admit that such a construction, in many cases, would render it an honour policy, that is, one which the company could pay or not as it thought fit. Notice within seven days is not stated to be a condition of liability, nor is it stated that in default of such notice the policy shall become void. We must then consider whether the assured so understood it. If it was the intention of the company that it should be a condition precedent, it ought to have been couched in clearer language. The absence of such notice might cause the company to incur extra expense, and in such a case the assured would have to make that good. I am satisfied that such a construction as is contended for by the defendant company would be absurd. The term is not a condition precedent to the enforcement of the policy."

The payment of a claim does not of itself preclude the insured from making a further claim in respect of the same accident, if the first claim was limited to the disablement from which the insured had already suffered, and did not refer to future or prospective disablement.

Thus, in *Prosser* v. *Lancashire and Yorkshire Accident Insurance Co., Ltd.*[1] the insured, after giving a receipt in full discharge of his claim, was totally disabled for 26 weeks, and successfully made a second claim, Lord ESHER, M.R., said:[2]

"The agreement was to accept money in satisfaction of the claim; that meant the claim which had already been made, and which related solely to the disablement from which he had already suffered. It had no reference to any claim for future or prospective disablement, because none such had been made."

The policy may, however, provide that only one claim is to be made, or the payment may be made[3] "in settlement of all claims arising under the policy". In those cases no further claim is maintainable.

Where a policy covers both husband and wife, the specified sum is payable once only although both are killed in the same accident.[4]

Together with the notice of the accident particulars in respect of the following matters are usually required:

   i the date and place of the accident.

---

[1] (1890), 6 T.L.R. 285, C.A.
[2] *Ibid.*, at p. 286.
[3] *Kent* v. *Ocean, Accident and Guarantee Corporation* (1909), 20 O.L.R. 266.
[4] *Re Caire, Public Trustee* v. *Hood*, [1927] S.A.S.R. 220, where the policy stated: "Accidents to owner. This policy covers the assured and the assured's wife against personal accidents occurring to themselves while riding in mounting or dismounting from any motor car to the following extent and subject to the limits as set forth: (a) Death. The underwriters will pay to the assured's executors, administrators or assigns the sum of £1,000 in the event of death."

    ii   the nature of the injuries sustained.

    iii the cause of the accident.

In practice, a claim form is issued by the insurers, to be filled up by the insured.

2 Proof of Loss

The insured may be required to support the claim by medical certificates[1] and to give proof satisfactory to the insurers.[2]

In *Braunstein* v. *Accidental Death Insurance Co.*[3] a condition in a personal accident insurance policy stated that before the sum insured would be paid by the insurance company:

> "proof satisfactory to the directors should have been furnished by the [claimant] of the death of or accident to [the insured] together with such further evidence or information, if any, as the . . . directors shall think necessary to establish the claim."

One of the issues which arose in the case was the true interpretation of this requirement. The Court of King's Bench[4] held that it meant that the directors had no right to withhold payment by capriciously and without any reasonable ground whatever requiring further evidence perfectly immaterial to the matter in dispute, but must be construed so as to mean that the directors could ask for such further evidence as they might *reasonably* require.

In the course of his judgment WIGHTMAN, J., observed:[5]

> "Now it is said that by virtue of that clause the directors have power, if they please to exercise it, wholly to withhold payment by capriciously, and without any reasonable ground whatever, requiring further evidence perfectly immaterial to the matter in dispute, and the question is, whether, giving a reasonable construction to the intention of the parties when this clause was introduced by reference into the policy, it can be understood that the assured did agree that upon any ground whatever, however capricious or unreasonable, the directors, who are the parties to the suit, might require further evidence, though perhaps quite immaterial and impossible to obtain, or whether the clause is not to be limited to such further evidence as the directors might reasonably require. We have been referred to cases in which the parties have agreed that no payment shall be enforced by one against the other, unless a surveyor had given his certificate that the work, which was the subject-matter on which the payment was to be

---

[1] *Hollister* v. *Accident Association of New Zealand* (1886), 5 N.Z.L.R. 49. A stipulation requiring a report from the insured's medical attendant has no application where the accident results in instantaneous death and there was not, in fact, anyone medically attending the insured: *Patton* v. *Employers' Liability Assurance Corporation* (1887), 20 L.R. Ir. 93. Where the policy provides that no indemnity is to be payable unless the insured has been regularly under the care of a legally qualified medical practitioner, and the insured, who had fractured his foot put himself under the care of a competent osteopath, it was held that there had been a breach of condition and the insured could not recover under the policy: *Larouche* v. *Merchants and Employers Guarantee and Accident Co.* (1920), Q.R. 59 S.C. 376). As to the evidence sufficient to support the claim at the trial, see *Trew* v. *Railway Passengers' Assurance Co.* (1861), 6 H. & N. 839, Ex. Ch.; *A.B.* v. *Northern Accident Co.* 1896, 24 R. (Ct. of Sess.) 258.

[2] A provision that the proof must be satisfactory to the insurers means such proof as ought reasonably to satisfy them: *Trew* v. *Railway Passengers' Assurance Co.* (1860), 6 Jur. N.S. 759; *Teur* v. *London Life Insurance Co.*, [1936] 1 D.L.R. 161. Cf. *Harvey* v. *Ocean Accident and Guarantee Corporation*, [1905] 2 I.R. 1.

[3] (1862), 5 L.T. 550.

[4] WIGHTMAN, BLACKBURN and CROMPTON, JJ.

[5] (1862), 5 L.T. at p. 553. See also the judgment of CROMPTON, J., *ibid.*, at p. 554 and that of BLACKBURN, J., *ibid.*, at p. 555.

made, had been completed to his satisfaction, which certificate he might capriciously refuse to give; but there the reference is by agreement to a third person and not to the parties themselves, which would be the effect of this clause if it had the construction that [Counsel] contends for. A reasonable construction must be given to this clause, and I cannot but think that there is a good deal of weight in the observation, that after all it is rather a clause directory as between the shareholders and the directors of the company, that they shall take care that there shall be sufficient evidence brought before them, rather than to amount to a condition giving power to the directors, if they pleased, by capriciously and without reasonable ground refusing to be satisfied with the evidence brought before them, to defeat the claim of the assured. I cannot put such a construction on the deed as that—it only requires the introduction of the word 'reasonable' to remove the difficulty."

The insurers may reserve the right to have the insured medically examined from time to time, and, in the case of his death, to hold a post-mortem examination.[1]

3 Amount Recoverable

The policy invariably provides for payment of a specific sum in the event of death by accident. Where the policy covers disablement also, there is usually a table specifying the various forms of disablement and allocating compensation to each in the shape of a specific sum or of periodic payments.

If no such provision is made, the insured is entitled to recover an amount representing the expense, pain and loss immediately connected with the accident, not exceeding the amount payable in the event of death, but not compensation for loss of time or profit.[2]

In *Alder* v. *Moore*[3] a Group Personal Accident scheme had been effected with the plaintiff underwriters by the Football Players and Trainers Union for the benefit of their members. The word "member" as defined in the policy meant "a person of the male sex who is registered with the Union as a Member of the Union". By condition 8 of the policy it was provided that:

> "No claim shall be paid hereunder for permanent total disablement unless the claimant shall have given to Underwriters a signed declaration to the effect that he will take no part as a playing member of any form of professional football in the future and that in the event of infringement of this condition he will be subject to a penalty of the amount paid him in settlement of his claim."

The defendant footballer, who played for West Ham United Association Football Club, was a member of the Union, and was injured on December 26, 1955. His membership of the Union terminated on May 26, 1956. The underwriters paid him £500 in respect of his injury, and he signed the declaration required by condition 8 on August 25, 1956. He then played football professionally in December 1956 for Cambridge United Football Club. The underwriters claimed repayment of the money.

---

[1] *Donnison* v. *Employers' Accident and Live Stock Insurance Co., Ltd.* 1897, 24 R. (Ct. of Sess.) 681, where the insurers, by insisting on a post-mortem examination, were held to be precluded from asserting that the policy had been avoided by want of notice. In the absence of a special stipulation, the insurers, have, apparently, no right to demand a post-mortem examination. A stipulation requiring such information to be furnished as the insurers may require or may consider necessary or proper to elucidate the case is not sufficient: *Ballantine* v. *Employers' Insurance Co. of Great Britain* 1893, 21 R. (Ct. of Sess.) 305, *per* Lord Rutherford Clarke at p. 317.

[2] *Theobald* v. *Railway Passengers Assurance Co.* (1854), 10 Exch. 45.

[3] [1960] 2 Lloyd's Rep. 325, C.A.

It was held by the Court of Appeal[1] that the claim succeeded. The condition as to partaking in any form of professional football meant as a playing member, not as a spectator or trainer or any other capacity. It could not be read as meaning "playing member of the Union".

In the words of SELLERS, L.J.:[2]

"Apparently when the defendant commenced to play professional football again in December, 1956, he was not then a member of the Union; the club for which he played was not in the Football League and was not a club of the highest class. The defendant played first for payment of a sum for each match, and when he had established himself, he was engaged on a weekly but part-time basis. The defendant had, however, declared and agreed in consideration of the payment to him of the £500 as follows: 'I will take no part as a playing member of any form of professional football in the future', which I read as meaning, 'I will take no part in any form of professional football in the future as a playing member' (or more briefly, 'as a player'). So read I do not find it doubtful or ambiguous. The stipulation with regard to partaking in any form of professional football is as a playing member (or player), not as a spectator, or trainer or referee manager, or in any other capacity. I cannot read it as referring in any way to the defendant's membership of the Union."

SLADE, J., said:[3]

"In the light of the sole purpose for which this document was required by the underwriters, and for which it came into existence, namely, to enable them to recover their money if the 'permanent' total disablement turned out to be merely temporary, I am unable to construe the words

. . . I HEREBY DECLARE AND AGREE that I will take no part as a playing member of any form of professional football in the future . . .

as imposing a contractual obligation upon the defendant never again to play professional football. The sole concern of the underwriters, for whose protection the document alone came into existence, was not to stop the defendant from playing professional football again but to recover their £500 if he did so, and thereby established conclusively that he had never at any time been *permanently* totally disabled from doing so.

"It seems to me quite unrealistic to construe the document as imposing a *contractual* ban upon the defendant from playing professional football again. I should have thought that the underwriters would welcome his doing so, since that was their only hope of recovering their £500. They certainly could not recover it, however fit the defendant became to play professional football again, if he refrained from playing it or if he played football again but confined himself to the amateur game."

The amount recoverable may vary according to the nature of the accident. Thus, double benefits may be payable if the injury is caused by a railway accident.[4]

4 Limitation on the amount recoverable

The amount recoverable by the insured is usually made subject to the following limitations:

---

[1] SELLERS, L.J., and SLADE, J.; DEVLIN, L.J., dissenting.
[2] [1960] 2 Lloyd's Rep. at p. 329. The learned Lord Justice considered (*ibid.*, at p. 329) that there was no ground for invoking the *contra proferentem* rule. As to this rule, see Ivamy, *General Principles of Insurance Law*, 2nd Edn., 1970, pp. 318–323.
[3] [1960] 2 Lloyd's Rep. at p. 336.
[4] In *Fidelity and Casualty Co. of New York* v. *Mitchell*, [1917] A.C. 592, P.C., and in *Wallace* v. *Employers' Liability Assurance Co.* (1912), 21 O.W.R. 249, the policy provided for double benefit if the accident happened while the insured was a passenger on a public conveyance; and in *Wadsworth* v. *Canadian Railway Accident Insurance Co.* (1913), 28 O.L.R. 537, for double benefit if the injury was caused by the burning of a building, and for one-tenth benefit if the injury was caused by fits.

i *In the case of periodic payments*, the payments usually cease at the expiration of the specific period.

ii *In the case of the same accident*, if the disablement is capable of being regarded as falling under two or more heads in the table of compensation, the insured is only entitled to receive the compensation payable under one head.

iii *In the case of successive accidents*, if the insured has received payment for disablement in respect of the first accident, a deduction may have to be made from the amount recoverable in respect of the second accident, even in the event of death.

8

COUPON INSURANCE

The stress of competition in business has led to the use of insurance, and more particularly of personal accident insurance, as a means of advertisement. The purchaser of various articles, such as a newspaper, or other periodic publications, or a diary, or even a box of matches, may find himself, in consequence of his purchase,[1] insured or entitled to be insured against a variety of accidents. The rights of the purchaser in this respect are defined in a document, commonly called a "coupon", which may be annexed to or enclosed with the article purchased, or, in the case of a newspaper, may form part of it.

The liability under the coupon, is, in practice, undertaken by insurance companies carrying on accident insurance business. When coupon insurance was first introduced, the proprietors of the various articles to which the coupon was attached attempted to act as insurers themselves; but stamp difficulties intervened.[2] Certain insurance companies by private Acts of Parliament acquired power to issue unstamped policies, and it was necessary for persons wishing to use coupons for advertising purposes to arrange with such companies to undertake liability thereunder. At a later date, general powers were conferred upon all persons acting as insurers to issue unstamped policies subject to certain terms and conditions.[3] But it was still found convenient to continue the practice of arranging with insurance companies to undertake the liability under the coupon.

At the present time, the issue of coupons so far as they relate to personal accident insurance, falls within the scope of the Insurance Companies Acts, 1958 to 1967,[4] to the provisions of which the proprietors of the various articles would become subject, if they themselves undertook liability[5] under the coupon.[6]

---

[1] Prepayment of the price is not a condition precedent to enforcing the insurance; *Shanks* v. *Sun Life Assurance Co. of India* 1896, 4 S.L.T. 65, where the insured's subscription had expired, but the periodical continued to be delivered to him, no notice having been given by him to the contrary.

[2] The definition of "policy of insurance against accident" in the Stamp Act, 1891, s. 98 (1) expressly included "any notice or advertisement in a newspaper or other publication which purports to insure the payment of money upon the death of or injury to the holder or bearer of the newspaper or publication containing the notice only from accident or violence or otherwise than from a natural cause." This section has since been repealed.

[3] Stamp Act 1891, s. 116, extended by Finance Act 1895, s. 13, and Finance Act 1907, s. 8 (2).

[4] See generally, Ivamy, *General Principles of Insurance Law*, 2nd Edn., 1970, pp. 29–58.

[5] Attempts are sometimes made to exclude legal liability by providing that any benefits under the scheme are payable by way of gift. See *Woods* v. *Co-operative Insurance Society*, 1924 S.C. 692 (fire insurance).

[6] Thus, the provisions of the Life Assurance Companies Act, 1870 (which was one of the predecessors of the Insurance Companies Act, 1958) had previously been held to apply

Apart from this difficulty, businesses of the magnitude sufficient to justify the undertaking of coupon insurance on anything like an adequate scale are usually carried on by limited companies whose powers of undertaking insurance business depend upon their memorandum of association.

The coupon sometimes contains a special provision that the proprietor of the article to which it is attached, is not to be liable on the insurance. It is to be observed, however, that on the purchase of the article, there appears to be a contract between the purchaser and the proprietor by which the proprietor undertakes to the purchaser:

1 That he has entered into arrangements with the specified insurance company for insuring purchasers of the article in question; and
2 That the specified insurance company will insure the purchaser in accordance with the terms of the coupon.

The proprietor is therefore liable to the purchaser for any breach of these undertakings.[1] This liability is distinct from the liability of the insurance company as insurers.[2]

THE FORM OF THE COUPON

Two forms of coupons are in use:

1 Coupons which are intended to constitute the contract of insurance.
2 Coupons which on the face of them are an undertaking by the insurers to issue a policy of insurance to the holder of the coupon on compliance with its terms.

1   Where the Coupon is the Contract
Reduced to its simplest terms, the coupon in this form is an undertaking by the insurers to pay a specified sum to a particular person on the happening of a certain event, subject to the fulfilment of certain terms and conditions.

---

to a company selling tea under a scheme by which benefits in the nature of life insurance were provided for customers: *Re Nelson & Co.*, [1905] 1 Ch. 551 (life insurance); *Re British Widows' Assurance Co.*, [1905] 2 Ch. 40, C.A. (life insurance); *Re Nelson & Co.*, (1906) 22 T.L.R. 406 (life insurance). In the cases of insurances to which the Insurance Companies Act, 1958, does not apply, e.g. insurances of property against damage by enemy aircraft and the like, the proprietors may, if they think fit, undertake liability under the coupons themselves. Thus, during the First World War the same periodical might contain two coupons relating to aircraft risks, under one of which an insurance company undertook liability in the event of the subscriber being injured or killed, whilst, under the other, the proprietors assumed liability for damage to the subscriber's house.

[1] Cf. *De la Bere* v. *Pearson*, [1908] 1 K.B. 280, C.A. (contract), where the proprietors of a newspaper undertook to advise readers through their City editor on investments, and it was held that there was a contract with a reader who acted on their undertaking to introduce him to a good stockbroker, who was to be reasonably skilful and trustworthy, and that, by introducing him to a broker who was not a member of the Stock Exchange, and also was an undischarged bankrupt, they were guilty of a breach of contract, which rendered them liable for sums entrusted by the reader to the broker and misappropriated by him.

[2] *Law* v. *George Newnes, Ltd.* 1894, 21 R. (Ct. of Sess.) 1027 where, as pointed out by Lord RUTHERFORD CLARKE, at p. 1033, the real contract was that the insurers would pay, and the obligation of the proprietors, though, in this case, they did not raise the point but accepted the position that they were liable, if any one, was to furnish the next of kin with the means of obtaining the money from the insurers, for the breach of which obligation an action would lie. But the liability of the insurers depends upon the existence of a contract between the purchaser and the insurers; if there is no contract between them, the purchaser's remedy is against the proprietor alone: *Gould* v. *Eagle Star and British Dominions Insurance Co.* (1927), October 21 (unreported).

No further document is necessary. The coupon is itself a policy of insurance, and on fulfilment of its terms and conditions may be enforced as a policy against the insurers.[1]

2　Where the Coupon is an Undertaking to Issue a Policy

The coupon in this form contains a statement of the various benefits obtainable on payment of a specified sum, usually a registration fee, which varies according to the benefits desired, together with an application form which the holder must fill in and forward with the registration fee to the insurers.

The application form, which must be dated, asks only for the name, address, and occupation of the applicant. It may further contain a statement, to be signed by the applicant, that he agrees to accept the policy subject to its usual terms and conditions. These terms and conditions may be printed, either in full or in summary, on the coupon.

The contract of insurance is contained in the policy, when issued. But the coupon, when duly filled in and its terms and conditions fulfilled, is a contract by the insurers to issue a policy in accordance with its terms, unless they have expressly reserved the right to accept or decline any application.

The Scope of the Insurance

The protection given by coupon insurance is of a very limited kind. The scope of the insurance varies according to the language of the particular coupon policy. There is never a general insurance against accidents of all kinds, but only an insurance against certain specified accidents.

The most popular form of coupon insurance relates to accidents of transit. The accident is connected with a public vehicle of some kind, e.g. a train, a bus, an aircraft, or a passenger steamer.

The insured must be a passenger at the time of the accident. The insurance does not cover persons injured by such vehicles who are not passengers therein. Moreover, the accident contemplated is an accident to the train or other vehicle. It is not sufficient that the insured sustains an accident whilst he is travelling by the vehicle in question.[2] Thus, the insurance does not apply where the insured is injured through leaning out of the window of a train, or through being swept off the top of a bus by an overhanging branch. He must be injured by an accident itself.

The protection given by the coupon is subject to certain restrictions. The following are the usual restrictions imposed:

a The vehicle must be a public vehicle.

b The vehicle must be of the kind specified in the coupon, e.g. a train.

---

[1] *General Accident, Fire and Life Assurance Corporation* v. *Robertson (or Hunter)*, [1909] A.C. 404. For cases in which the conditions were not fulfilled, see *Hunter* v. *Hunter* 1904, 7 F. (Ct. of Sess.) 136, following *Law* v. *Newnes (George), Ltd.* 1894, 21 R. (Ct. of Sess.) 1027.
[2] The wider principle laid down in *Theobald* v. *Railway Passengers Assurance Co.* (1854), 10 Exch. 45 that there may be a "railway accident" within the meaning of the policy, although there is no accident to the train, if the accident is attributable to the insured being a passenger and arises out of an act connected with his being a passenger, is, therefore, excluded.

c The transit must take place within a prescribed area, eg.. the United Kingdom or Europe.

d An age limit may be imposed.

Other forms of coupon insurance cover street accidents and cycle accidents.[1]

In *Harper* v. *Associated Newspapers, Ltd.*[2] a personal accident insurance policy issued by the *Daily Mail* stated that £500 would be payable in case of death "if the [insured] while a pedestrian . . . in a public thoroughfare be killed by accidental impact with a moving vehicle". But there was an exception in the policy to the effect that there would be no liability on the part of the newspaper if "the insured [was] at the time of the accident in charge of any vehicle, loading, unloading, or attending to any vehicle . . ."

Another clause stated that £250 would be paid "if the [insured] shall be accidentally killed whilst riding in a public thoroughfare a bicycle . . . solely for pleasure".

The insured left his place of business and went on his bicycle to see a Mr. Walton on business. He dismounted at the foot of a hill and saw Walton coming on a footpath down the hill towards him. He stopped to talk to Walton, and was knocked down and killed by a runaway car. His personal representatives claimed under the policy. ROCHE, J., held that the claim failed and said that it was unnecessary to decide whether the insured was a pedestrian or bicyclist at the time of the accident. But if it had been necessary to do so, he would have considered that the insured was still a bicyclist, for a bicyclist was none the less a bicyclist because in the course of his journey he found it convenient to walk up a hill. If the insured was a pedestrian, he was still in charge of a vehicle within the meaning of the exception for the word "vehicle" was sufficient to include a bicycle. But in any event, assuming that the insured were a bicyclist, the personal representative could not recover the £250 because the insured was riding the bicycle for a business purpose.

A similar decision was given by ROWLATT, J., in *Hansford* v. *London Express Newspaper, Ltd.*[3], where the insured was walking home from work pushing his bicycle, and was knocked down and killed by a lorry, and it was held that his personal representatives could not recover under a similar policy containing the same exception as set out above, because the bicycle constituted a "vehicle".

THE DURATION OF THE INSURANCE

Unless the coupon provides otherwise, the period of insurance begins as soon as the acceptance is complete. The coupon may, however, prescribe a particular time for the period of insurance to begin, e.g. in the case of newspaper coupons, where the insurance may be expressed to run from 6 a.m. on the day of issue, or in the case of coupons which have to be registered or exchanged for policies, where the insurance may be expressed to run from

---

[1] A person riding a bicycle is not within an insurance covering him "whilst travelling as a passenger in a vehicle": *McMillan* v. *Sun Life Assurance Co. of India* 1896, 4 S.L.T. 66.

[2] (1927), 43 T.L.R. 331.

[3] (1928), 44 T.L.R. 349.

the date of registration or from the date of the policy or the dispatch of the receipt for the registration fee, as the case may be.

The duration of the insurance depends upon the language of the particular coupon. The period may be fixed with reference to the article to which it is attached. Thus, a newspaper or magazine coupon usually remains in force for the period during which the newspaper or magazine is current, or in the case of a permanent subscriber, for the period of his subscription. A diary coupon usually remains in force for twelve calendar months from the date of the acceptance or other date prescribed by the coupon.[1] In other cases, a definite period may be fixed. Thus, in the case of a matchbox coupon the period is usually 7 to 14 days from the date inserted by the holder. The coupon may, further, fix the hour of the day at which the insurance is to expire, e.g. in the case of a newspaper coupon which may be expressed to expire at 6 a.m. on the day following issue.[2]

THE DUTIES OF THE HOLDER OF THE COUPON

The holder of a coupon does not appear to be subject to the duty of disclosure. This follows from the fact that there are no negotiations in the proper sense of the word. The insurers issue an offer to the public which is capable of being accepted by anybody. Their attitude is not, therefore, influenced in any way by the conduct of any particular holder, since they are prepared to insure him, whoever he may be. The holder's only duty is to fill in the coupon correctly, and, in particular, not to act fraudulently by inserting a wrong date or altering the date after insertion for the purpose of prolonging the period of insurance. Even when the coupon has to be filled in and forwarded to the insurers, the holder's only duty is to fill in the coupon correctly. He is under no obligation to give any further information for which they could have asked if they had wished for it.

CLAIMS UNDER COUPONS

A claim upon a coupon insurance cannot be maintained unless the conditions prescribed by the coupon have been fulfilled. Hence, if the coupon contains an arbitration clause, a stay of an action will be granted.[3] Further, a condition often provides that the holder must, prior to the accident in respect of which the claim is made, have signed the coupon or done whatever may have been required to show his acceptance of the insurance.[4] In some cases, it is sufficient that, at the time of the accident, he is carrying on his person[5] the coupon or the article to which it is attached or both.

Where the insurance relates to accidents to vehicles, the coupon usually contains further conditions, e.g.

---

[1] Where the coupon provides that any claim must be made within twelve months of registration, the onus of proving the date of registration lies on the insurers: *General Accident, Fire and Life Assurance Corporation* v. *Robertson (or Hunter)*, [1909] A.C. 404, where, the coupon having been posted on December 25, 1905, and the claim not having been made until January 2, 1907, it was held that the insurers had not discharged the onus and the claim was in time.

[2] Or, in the case of Saturday's issue, at 6 a.m. on the following Monday.

[3] *Moore* v. *"Daily News", Ltd.* (1926), 23 Ll.L. Rep. 215, C.A.

[4] *General Accident, Fire and Life Assurance Corporation* v. *Robertson (or Hunter)*, [1909] A.C. 404.

[5] Presumably it would be sufficient, if the holder was travelling by train, that it was on the seat beside him.

1 *The holder at the time of the accident must be travelling as a passenger in the vehicle to which the accident happens*

A person travelling not as a passenger, but in the capacity of a railway servant on duty, is not protected and may, by the language of the coupon, be expressly excluded. On the other hand, a person such as a railway servant, when not on duty, may be an ordinary passenger, and may be expressly included within the insurance.

2 *The holder at the time of the accident must be a ticket- or fare-paying passenger*

It does not appear to be necessary that he should have actually procured his ticket or paid his fare before the accident.[1] But he must be a passenger for reward as opposed to a trespasser. A season ticket holder is usually included by the express language of the coupon, and the protection may be extended to persons travelling with a pass or privilege ticket and to persons in uniform travelling free of charge.

The coupon frequently provides for payment of the sum insured only in the event of death being caused by accident. There may, however, be a table of benefits varying according to the nature and effect of the injuries sustained, in the same way as in an ordinary personal accident insurance policy.[2]

Payment of the sum insured is made to the holder of the coupon or, in the case of his death, to his personal representatives. The coupon, may, however, provide that in the event of the holder's death by accident, payment may be made to a specified person, e.g. his wife.[3]

In the case of newspaper coupons the provision may be that payment is to be made to the person deemed by the editor to be the holder's next of kin. In this case the editor's decision, if *bona fide*, is final.[4] No other persons, although they may be by law the holder's next of kin, are entitled to maintain any claim, either against the insurers under the coupon or against the person deemed to be the next of kin for the whole or any part of the amount received from the insurers.[5]

---

[1] It is only in the case of railways that the fare is collected before the journey begins. In other cases, it may be collected during the journey as in the case of buses, or even after the journey is ended, as in the case of taxis.

[2] The amount payable may vary according to the nature of the vehicle to which the accident happens.

[3] But a provision that the wife of the insured should be "entitled to the benefit" of the insurance has been held to mean not that the wife was entitled to receive the insurance money on her husband's death, but that the policy covered the wife: *Re Lambert, Public Trustee* v. *Lambert* (1916), 84 L.J.Ch. 279, where, however, the question whether such an insurance covering the wife was valid was not raised.

[4] *Law* v. *George Newnes, Ltd.* (1894), 21 R. (Ct. of Sess.) 1027, where the editor decided in favour of the widow, and the action was brought by the insured's children by a former marriage.

[5] *Hunter* v. *Hunter* 1904, 7 F. (Ct. of Sess.) 136, where the action was brought by the insured's three brothers against his sister to whom the insurance money had been paid in accordance with the editor's decision. Cf. *Ashby* v. *Costin* (1888), 57 L.J.Q.B. 491, where the death allowance payable under a railway company's insurance fund was payable, with limitations, at the discretion of the committee, and it was held that the deceased's administrator could not claim payment from his sister in whose favour the committee had exercised its discretion; *Da Costa* v. *Prudential Assurance Co.* (1918), 120 L.T. 353, C.A. (life insurance), where the policy moneys were payable to the personal representatives, but the policy contained a proviso that a receipt signed by a blood relation should be a good discharge, and it was held that the insurers were accordingly discharged by a payment to a blood relation.

PART II

LIFE INSURANCE

9

INTRODUCTION

The proposer for a policy of life insurance is required to answer certain questions in the proposal form, e.g. name, date of birth, the type of policy required, the sum to be insured.[1]

He is under a duty to disclose to the insurers all material facts and not to make any misrepresentations.[2]

Of very considerable importance in life insurance is the need for the proposer to have an insurable interest in the life insured, this matter being governed by the Life Assurance Act 1774.[3]

The policy sets out the circumstances in which payment will be made, the amount of the sum insured, and the conditions precedent to the liability of the insurers.[4]

The policy may be assigned by means of a legal assignment or by an equitable one, and there are various rules to be applied in deciding the priority of the assignees where the same policy had been the subject of more than one assignment.[5]

When the event insured against takes place, the insurers are under a duty to pay the sum insured.[6]

The incidence of capital gains tax, income tax and estate duty on life insurance policies is outside the scope of this book, and the reader is referred to the standard works on these topics.[7]

---

[1] See Chapter 10, *post.*
[2] See Chapter 11, *post.*
[3] See Chapter 12, *post.*
[4] See Chapter 13, *post.*
[5] See Chapter 14, *post.*
[6] See Chapter 15, *post.*
[7] See e.g. Simon's *Taxes,* Volume E; *British Tax Encyclopaedia.*

10

THE PROPOSAL FORM

In life insurance proposal forms the questions usually asked by insurers relate to:

1 the name, residence, profession, occupation, date of birth, age next birthday, place of birth, height and weight of the proposer;
2 the description or the type of policy required, e.g. whole life policy, endowment policy, with profits policy;
3 the sum to be insured;
4 whether the policy is to be for the benefit of the insured's estate or of named beneficiaries;
5 whether a proposal has been declined or accepted at an extra premium;
6 whether a proposal has ever been made to the insurers concerned or to other insurers;
7 the name and address of the usual medical attendant;
8 details of previous illnesses and of medical advice and treatment, e.g. in the last 5 years;
9 details of any circumstances affecting the suitability of the life insured for insurance purposes.

At the end of the proposal form is a declaration to be signed by the proposer that the answers given are true and that they are to form the "basis of the contract". There may also be a declaration that he is in good health, that he authorizes the insurers to seek information from any doctor who has attended him, and that the answers given by the doctor, and any statements made to the insurers' doctor, are also to be the "basis of the contract".

If the proposal is in respect of another person whose life is to be insured, the particulars of that person, e.g. name, profession, occupation, date of birth, etc., must also be given as well as the particulars of the proposer. The proposer must also state the sum to be insured, and in what event it will be payable, and the nature and amount of the insurable interest[1] which he has in the life proposed for insurance.

---

[1] As to "insurable interest", see pp. 88–94, *post.*

II

NON-DISCLOSURE AND MISREPRESENTATION

As in other branches of insurance the insured is under a duty to disclose to the insurer all material facts and not make any material misrepresentations.

If the insured fails in such a duty, the insurer can avoid liability.

If, however, there is a "basis clause"[1] in the proposal form, the insurer may avoid liability even if the fact which is not disclosed or which is misrepresented is not a material one.

In the pages which follow examples of material and immaterial facts are given. A number of reported cases relate to the situation where the insured has given answers to questions asked by medical examiners appointed by the insurer.

EXAMPLES OF MATERIAL AND IMMATERIAL FACTS

Whether the fact not disclosed or misrepresented is material is a question of fact in each case. It is to be emphasized that a number of reported cases relative to life insurance date from the 19th century, and that by reason of the increase in medical knowledge it is not certain that they would be decided in the same way at the present time.

Age

In *Keeling* v. *Pearl Assurance Co., Ltd.*[2] the proposer was a woman effecting an insurance on her husband's life. She stated that his date of birth was November 28, 1863 and his age next birthday was 48. The proposal form was signed in October 1920. It was obvious that a mistake had been made, but the insurers issued a policy. They now sought to avoid liability on the ground that there had been a misstatement. BAILHACHE, J., held that they were not entitled to do so, and said:[3]

> "The first answer to which they object is this: The question is, the date of birth; and the date of birth is given as the November 28th, 1863. The place of birth is given as New Mills, which I understand is correct. Then the age next birthday is given as 48. Now, of course, it is obvious to anybody who does the simplest subtraction sum, that a person born in 1863 would not be 48, but would be 57, in 1920. There was no reason to suppose that time had stood still for Mr. Harry

---

[1] As to the "basis clause" see Ivamy, *General Principles of Insurance of Law*, 2nd Edn., 1970, pp. 132–133.
[2] (1923), 129 L.T. 573.
[3] *Ibid.*, at p. 574.

Keeling, and it was obvious, therefore, that there was some mistake about his age, and it turns out that, in fact, 1863 is the wrong date of the birth, and that the age next birthday, instead of being 48, ought to be 49. The insurance company had that form before them, and they saw, on the face of it, that there was a mistake somewhere about the age. Obviously, it must have hit them in the eye the moment they had the proposal form. Yet, notwithstanding that, they chose to issue a policy; and if they chose to issue a policy on a proposal form which contained a mistake, obviously, on the face of it, without further enquiry, there is no ground, in my opinion, for vitiating the policy. It is not suggested that there was any fraud in stating that the age next birthday was 48. So much for that. That, I think, gives no trouble at all."

In *Hemmings* v. *Sceptre Life Association, Ltd.*[1] the proposer for a life insurance policy on her own life stated in the proposal form that she was 41 when in fact she was 44. The sum assured was to become payable to her when she was 60. She attained that age in 1904, whereas if her statement had been correct, she would not have attained that age until 1907. The insurers discovered the mistake, and received two premiums upon the original footing, but did not notify the assignee of the policy of the discovery. The assignee claimed under the policy, but the insurers stated that they would pay only when the insured reached the age of 63. KEKEWICH, J., held that this contention failed, and that payment was due in 1904, observing:[2]

"It seems to me that it is the insurance office that is asking to make a new contract. They say in their policy that they will pay immediately after satisfactory proof has been given to the said directors of her having attained the age of sixty years; and it is impossible, as it seems to me, for anyone to say now that that means sixty years from a given date, which happens to be the date mentioned in the proposal as the date of her birth; it means the time when she actually attains sixty years. That is one of the very things which they must have considered, cannot have failed to consider, as a matter of business, when they discussed the question, and concluded the question whether they should allow the policy to remain on foot or not. As I pointed out to [Counsel] just now, it mattered not in the least to them whether they had a larger premium on the footing of the lady's being the age she really was, or the same premium to continue till she was sixty years of age, according to the date of birth as fixed in the proposal; but one way or another, no doubt, they were entitled very fairly to a larger premium, but at the risk of avoiding the policy and returning the premiums. That would have been a new contract—it was a new feature; and, of course, there was a doubt whether the representative of the assured, the assignee, would continue the policy. It was a business matter, and they must be taken to have said: 'On the whole, this policy is not so valuable as we hoped, but still it is a policy of some value, and we must continue it and we must pay'; that means, pay when the lady really attains the age of sixty years. Upon that part of the case I do not think there is really any room for doubt."

Residence

In *Huguenin* v. *Rayley*[3] Elizabeth Swayne employed an agent to arrange a life insurance policy in respect of her own life. The agent made a declaration of her state of health, and said that she was resident in the parish of Fisherton Anger. The policy contained a stipulation that it was valid only if the statement was free from all misrepresentation or reservation. The insurers called in a doctor, who found her in the county gaol there where she was

---

[1] (1905), 92 L.T. 221.
[2] *Ibid.*, at p. 223.
[3] (1815), 6 Taunt. 186.

imprisoned for debt. The Court of King's Bench said that there was nothing expressed in the terms of the policy which required the imprisonment to be stated, nor was there an omission in the statement of any matter which the insurers called for. Nevertheless, if the imprisonment were a material fact, the non-disclosure of it would be fatal. It ought to have been submitted to the jury whether the imprisonment was material, and since it had not been submitted, a new trial would be ordered.

In *Grogan* v. *London and Manchester Industrial Assurance Co.*[1] a proposer for the policy of life insurance on the life of his father stated that his father resided at "191, Great Ancots Street, Manchester", and had made a declaration that the truth of his answers should be the "basis of the contract". The father, in fact, was at the time temporarily staying at that address, and really resided in Ireland, where he returned three months later. The county court judge held that the insurers were entitled to avoid liability on the ground that the statement was untrue. The Divisional Court of the Queen's Bench Division[2] held that on its true construction, the statement was not untrue and ordered a new trial. SMITH, J., observed:[3]

> "It is not necessary for us to decide the point which would have arisen if the assured had been actually living in Ireland at the time the proposal was made and the policy effected, for the facts here are that the assured was *de facto* living at the address given at the time in question and for three months after. This brings us to the question as to what is the meaning of the term 'residence' in the document of proposal. That document, after the heading, asks, first, the name of the person proposing to effect an assurance, secondly, his profession or occupation, then his residence. Now that, in my opinion, means the place where he is living or residing at the time of making the proposal, and not where he has been residing before or where he is going to reside afterwards. If the company desired to know this, they could have asked the question in so many words in the numbered questions which follow these particulars with which the proposal opens. The assured filled up the space after 'residence' with the address where he was then residing and where he was going to reside for the next three months, and it has been argued, and the County Court judge has apparently held that that is not the true construction of the word 'residence' in this document. I am of opinion that the County Court judge was in error, and was not justified in his finding."

Acute Rheumatism

In *British Equitable Insurance Co.* v. *Musgrave*[4] the proposer failed to disclose to the insurers that nine years earlier he had had an attack of rheumatism together with heart disease which left a weakness in the mitral valve. KAY, J., held that these facts were material and ordered that the policy be cancelled.

Rupture

In *Life Association of Scotland* v. *Foster*[5] the insured had a small swelling on her groin which was a symptom of rupture. She did not disclose her condition because she did not consider it of importance. She died later from rupture from which she was suffering before and at the time of making the proposal.

---

[1] (1885), 53 L.T. 761.
[2] MANISTY and SMITH, JJ.
[3] (1885), 53 L.T. at p. 763. See also the judgment of MANISTY, J., *ibid.*, at p. 763.
[4] (1887), 3 T.L.R. 630.
[5] 1873, 11 Macph. (Ct. of Sess.) 351.

It was held that the insurers could not avoid liability on the policy on the ground of non-disclosure because she did not know nor could she have known that she had symptoms of a disease which should have been disclosed.

Lord President INGLIS said:[1]

> "My opinion is, upon consideration of the whole of the circumstances as disclosed in the evidence, that the swelling which is proved to have existed at the date of the contract of insurance has not been shown to be such a fact as a reasonable and cautious person, unskilled in medical science, and with no special knowledge of the law and practice of insurance, would believe to be of any materiality or in any way calculated to influence the insurers in considering and deciding on the risk."

Kidney Trouble

In *Godfrey* v. *Britannic Assurance Co., Ltd.*[2] a proposer for a life insurance policy in July 1961 did not disclose to the insurance company (i) that in March 1959 he had been told that he might have minor kidney trouble, and that he should lead a careful life though he need not act as an invalid; (ii) that he had been sent to hospital a month before the date of the proposal for investigation of his kidneys, and had been told that his kidney condition showed no change; (iii) that an x-ray showed a lung infection; and (iv) that he had twice in two years preceding the proposal been referred to the hospital by his own doctor for kidney trouble.

ROSKILL, J., held that these were material facts, and that even if the insured was not aware of them, he ought to have known of them. Consequently the insurance company could avoid the policy. He observed:[3]

> "I have sought to exclude from the consideration of this problem and to avoid attributing to the assured anything which could fairly only be said to be within the knowledge of a lawyer, a doctor or a man with long experience in a life office. But wherever one pauses in order to apply the standard which the law requires to be applied, I cannot think that a reasonable man with no specialist knowledge of any kind could have failed to appreciate that he was possessed of knowledge and information relating to his health . . . which were of materiality and which were calculated to influence the mind of a life office in considering and deciding on the risk."

The learned Judge considered that the facts of the case were distinguishable[4] from *Life Association of Scotland* v. *Foster*[5] and *Joel* v. *Law Union & Crown Insurance Co.*[6], for in those cases neither insured knew more than the bare existence of some physical symptoms, the swelling in the groin in the first case, and the nervous depression in the other.

Fits

In *Chattock* v. *Shawe*[7] the plaintiff had effected a policy on the life of a Colonel Greswolde, and had signed a declaration in July 1831 that the Colonel was in sound health and "had not been afflicted with nor was subject to fits." The insurers repudiated liability on the policy on the

---

[1] (1873) 11 Macph. (Ct. of Sess.) at p. 360.
[2] [1963] 2 Lloyd's Rep. 515, Q.B.
[3] *Ibid.*, at p. 532.
[4] *Ibid.*, at p. 532.
[5] *Supra.*
[6] [1908] 2 K.B. 863, C.A. For the facts of the case, see p. 86, *post*.
[7] (1835), 1 Mood. & R. 498.

ground that the statement was false. It was admitted by the plaintiff that in 1827, the Colonel had been attacked by a seizure said to be of an epileptic nature whilst stationed at Macclesfield, and by a second seizure of the same kind a few days later. The insurers attempted to show that he had been frequently afflicted with similar seizures between the occurrence at Macclesfield and the date of the policy, and from thence up to the time of his death, the immediate cause of which was stated to be a fit of some kind. As to the Macclesfield fits, the plaintiff gave evidence that they were the result of an accident which happened to the Colonel in a scuffle, in which he either fell or was thrown down some stone steps and received a very severe head injury. In summing up to the jury, Lord ABINGER, C.B., said:[1]

> "If the only fits of which proof were given had been the Macclesfield fits, I should have said, there was no breach of warranty; for the interpretation I put on a clause of this kind is, not that the party never accidentally had a fit, but that he was not, at the time of the insurance being made, a person habitually or constitutionally afflicted with fits; a person liable to fits from some peculiarity of temperament, either natural, or contracted, from some cause or other, during life. You are to say whether the evidence has satisfied you that these fits at Macclesfield were the result of accident, and did not lead to any recurrence of fits in after life, or whether you think that the defendants have shown that the Colonel was attacked by other seizures of the same kind after the Macclesfield fits; because if the evidence as to those seizures is to be depended upon, they, not being pretended to be the result of any accident, would seem to show that the party was, from the date of the Macclesfield fits, a person subject to that disorder, within the meaning of the proviso. In that case your verdict will be for the defendant."

The jury returned a verdict for the plaintiff.

Good Health

In *Yorke* v. *Yorkshire Insurance Co., Ltd.*,[2] MCCARDIE, J., said[3] that it might be that the question "are you in good health?" admitted of discussion if one embarked on subtle analogies. Yet an effort was made by Lord FULLERTON in *Hutchison* v. *National Loan Fund Life Assurance Co.*[4], where he described "good health" as "the perfect conscious enjoyment of all one's faculties and functions and the freedom from any ailment affecting them, or any symptom of ailment." MCCARDIE, J., however, said[5] that he himself ventured to think that a man might be in good health, although he lacked the full possession of that exultant and joyous vitality indicated by Lord FULLERTON. Even a pessimist might, he conceived, be a fit subject of life insurance. A jury could be relied on to know the meaning of the phrase "good health" as employed in the usual affairs of life just as they would know the meaning of the words "sober" and "temperate".

In the instant case the insured had answered "Yes", to the question "are you in good health?", and the jury found that this answer was a truthful one.[6]

---

[1] (1835), 1 Mood. & R. 500.
[2] (1918), 119 L.T. 27.
[3] *Ibid.*, at p. 29.
[4] 1845, 7 Dunl. (ct. of Sess.) 467, at p. 478.
[5] (1918), 119 L.T. at p. 29.
[6] See (1918), 119 L.T. at p. 28.

Illness

In *Yorke* v. *Yorkshire Insurance Co. Ltd.*,[1] McCardie, J., said[2] that the word "illness" must be construed in a fair business manner. It must always be a question of degree. A man might be ill without being nigh unto death. On the other hand, a man might suffer from an ailment which did not amount to an "illness". Physical or serious disorder varied in nature and gravity. One set of facts might obviously amount to a mere indisposition.

In the instant case, the insured was asked the question "What illnesses have you suffered?", and answered "None, of consequence." McCardie, J., agreed with the verdict of the jury that the answer given was untrue,[3] for in November 1911 he suffered an illness of consequence and lay in a critical condition through an overdose of veronal, and his relatives had been sent for. A doctor who had attended him gave evidence that he regarded the insured's illness as serious. The insured had warranted the truth of his statements, and the insurers were therefore entitled to avoid liability on the policy.

In *Anstey* v. *British Natural Premium Life Association, Ltd.*,[4] Bray, J., held that where the insured had answered "No" to the question "Have you had any local or other disease, personal injury, illness or infirmity?", and to the question "If you had any illness or infirmity, have you fully recovered from it?" answered "Had none", though she had had a miscarriage ten years before the date of the issue of the policy, the answer was not untrue, for the miscarriage was not an "illness or infirmity".[5]

Where a question states "Have you had any other illness, local disease or personal injury?", an insurance company can hardly expect it to be answered with strict and literal truth. It cannot reasonably expect a man of mature age to recollect and disclose every illness, however slight, or every personal injury, consisting of a contusion, or a cut, or a blow, which he might have suffered in the course of his life. It is clear that the question must be read with some limitation and qualification to render it reasonable, and that "personal injury" must be interpreted as one of a somewhat serious or severe character.[6]

Temperate Habits

In *Thomson* v. *Weems*[7] a question in a proposal form stated:—"(*a*) Are you temperate in your habits? (*b*) and have you always been strictly so?" On November 9, 1881, the proposer answered (*a*) "Temperate"; (*b*) "Yes". He died on July 29, 1882, a doctor certifying that death was due to jaundice. The House of Lords[8] held that an untrue answer had been given, and that since the policy contained a "basis clause",[9] the insurer was entitled to avoid liability.

---

[1] (1918), 119 L.T. 27.
[2] *Ibid.*, at p. 29.
[3] *Ibid.*, at p. 29.
[4] (1908), 99 L.T. 16.
[5] The decision was subsequently affirmed by the Court of Appeal: (1908), 99 L.T. 765, C.A.
[6] *Connecticut Mutual Life Insurance Co. of Hartford* v. *Moore* (1881), 6 App. Cas. 644, P.C., at p. 648 (*per* Sir Robert P. Collier).
[7] (1884), 9 App. Cas. 671, H.L.
[8] Lord Blackburn, Lord Watson and Lord Fitzgerald.
[9] As to the "basis clause", see Ivamy, *General Principles of Insurance Law*, 2nd Edn., 1970, pp. 132–133.

Lord BLACKBURN[1] said that jaundice was a disease which generally in this climate was produced by excessive drinking over a considerable period, and if it was established that the proposer had as early as March 1882 really begun to suffer from such a disease, it added greatly to the force which tended to show that he had been in the habit of drinking too much for some time before November 1881. He did not think that either class of evidence by itself would have satisfied the burden of proof which was on the insured's personal representative, but taken together they did so.

Lord WATSON[2] said that it seemed to be a fair result of the evidence that the proposer was in the habit of taking more drink than was good for him, that he was frequently affected with drink on occasions when all except himself were sober, that his indulgence to excess had become so apparent that several of his friends remonstrated with him on the subject, and that instead of repudiating the charge, he admitted it and promised amendment. That evidence was altogether inconsistent with the statement that he was at the date of the proposal a person of temperate habits.

Lord FITZGERALD said[3] that the proposer had been shown at times to have been incapable of transacting business or taking care of himself. He was elected provost of the town in the hope that the responsibilities of office might produce a reformation of his habits.

As to the meaning of the words "temperate habits" Lord WATSON said[4] that it was useless to attempt a precise definition. Men differed so much in their capacity for imbibing strong drink that quantity afforded no test. What one man might take without exceeding the bounds of moderation, another could not take without committing excess. In judging of a man's sobriety his position in life and the habits of the class to which he belonged must always be taken into account. It was the custom of men engaged in certain lines of business to take what was called "refreshment" without any imputation of excess, at times when a similar indulgence on the part of men not so engaged would be, to say the least, suspicious. But he did not think that the habits of a particular locality ought to be taken into account, or that a man, who would generally be regarded as of intemperate habits, ought to escape from that imputation because he was no worse than his neighbours. Lord FITZGERALD said[5] that the phrase "temperate habits" seemed to import abstemiousness or at least moderation. He was inclined to adopt a fair and liberal interpretation, having regard to the position of the individual, the habits of the locality, and even the peculiarities of the local municipal authorities in adjourning to neighbouring public houses "to continue the debate".

In *Southcombe* v. *Merriman*[6] the evidence as to whether the person whose life was assured was of sober and temperate habits was conflicting. The plaintiff, who had taken out the policy, proved that the person whose life was assured was of strong constitution and would sometimes spend a day or two at once at a public house, where he would drink five or six pints of ale in the

---

[1] (1884), 9 App. Cas. at p. 685.
[2] *Ibid.*, at p. 696.
[3] *Ibid.*, at p. 698.
[4] *Ibid.*, at p. 695.
[5] *Ibid.*, at p. 697. See also the speech of Lord BLACKBURN, *ibid.*, at p. 685.
[6] (1842), Car. & M. 286.

course of a day, but was not systematically intemperate, and that he never took enough to hurt him. The insurer, however, maintained that the person whose life was assured was a notorious drunkard, and that he had often been turned away from work for this reason. He had been seen to drink fifteen pints of cider before dinner, and would be away for a week or a fortnight drinking. This habit was said to have lasted up until the time of his death.

In directing the jury COLERIDGE, J., said:[1]

> "The question on the record is respecting the habits of Peter Stoneman, the deceased. You have to say whether, upon the 2nd of October, 1839, and for such a reasonable time backwards as would allow of a man evincing a habit, Stoneman was a temperate man. It is said by the plaintiff's Counsel that the question is, whether the deceased was intemperate to such a degree as to injure his health. I differ from that position: for the society has a right, from many motives of their own, to act upon what rules they please, and to stipulate, as in this case, that, even though a man's health be not impaired, every person whose life is insured at their office shall be a person of temperate habits."

His Lordship then went over the evidence, and concluded, "You ought to say, upon the weight of this evidence, whether the man, Stoneman, were of sober and temperate habits at the time of the insurance." The jury returned a verdict for the plaintiff.

In *Dennan* v. *Scottish Widows' Fund Life Assurance Society*,[2] the jury returned a verdict in favour of the defendants, who had repudiated liability on a policy on the ground that the answer to a question in the proposal form asking if the person whose life was insured was of "sober and temperate habits" was false. Evidence was given (*inter alia*) by her servants that she was in the habit of drinking spirits at times to excess so that she could walk only with difficulty. Another witness said that she had once seen her intoxicated at 4 p.m. in the street.[3]

The words "sober and temperate" must receive such an interpretation as would be placed upon them by ordinary men of normal intelligence and average knowledge of the world. So interpreted they refer only to the use or abuse of alcohol. They are not applicable to the use of veronal or other soporific or narcotic drugs. They are inappropriate to what are known as "drug habits".[4]

Disorder Tending to Shorten Life

In *Watson* v. *Mainwaring*[5] the insured stated that he had no disorder tending to shorten life. The insured died and his executors brought an action on the policy, but the insurers repudiated liability on the ground that his answer was false, for he had a disorder of the bowels. Such a disorder might proceed from a defect of the internal organs which would shorten

---

[1] (1842), Car. & M. 287.
[2] (1886), 2 T.L.R. 525. The plaintiff applied for a new trial, but the Divisional Court dismissed the motion on the ground that notice of it was given too late, and the Court's decision was upheld by the Court of Appeal: (1887), 3 T.L.R. 347, C.A.
[3] For the evidence, see (1886), 2 T.L.R. at p. 528.
[4] *Yorke* v. *Yorkshire Insurance Co., Ltd.* (1918), 119 L.T. 27 at p. 28 (*per* McCARDIE, J.). If an insurance company desires express information with regard to drug habits, a further question of a direct character should be added to the proposal form. Unless such question is expressly asked, a company must, with respect to the use of drugs by a proposer, rely on the rule which requires the disclosure of all material facts known to the proposer which might lead the insurer to refuse the risk or demand a higher premium: *ibid.*
[5] (1813), 4 Taunt. 763.

life, or it might be a mere dyspepsia which would not tend to shorten life unless it increased to an excessive degree. Several doctors stated that they had attended the insured since the policy had been effected and that he was quite free from the disorder. On the other hand, other doctors said that prior to the issue of the policy, he was a "falling man". It was left to the jury to say whether the insured's complaint was organic dyspepsia or whether the dyspepsia under which he laboured was at the time of effecting the policy of such a degree that by its excess it tended to shorten life. The jury found that it was neither excessive nor organic, and gave a verdict in favour of the plaintiff. A new trial was applied for on the ground that the fact that the insured died of the same disorder as he had before effecting the policy was conclusive proof that he was then afflicted with a disorder tending to shorten life. The Court of Common Pleas[1] refused to grant a new trial, CHAMBRE, J., observing:[2]

> "All disorders have more or less a tendency to shorten life, even the most trifling; as for instance, corns may end in a mortification; that is, not the meaning of the clause; if dyspepsia were a disorder that tended to shorten life within this exception, the lives of half the members of the profession of the law would be uninsurable."

In *Swete* v. *Fairlie*[3] the person whose life was assured in answer to the question "Are you afflicted with gout, fits, asthma, or any other disorder tending to shorten human life?" stated "Neither: occasional indigestion only." The proposal form was dated April 30, 1827. He had previously been afflicted with a disorder tending to shorten life, but the disorder was of such a character as to prevent him from being conscious of what had happened to him while suffering under it. The jury found that he was not aware of what had taken place, and consequently the fact that he had not told the insurers of the disorder was not a ground on which they could repudiate liability.[4]

In *Jones* v. *Provincial Insurance Co.*[5] the insured stated that he was "not aware of any disorder or circumstances tending to shorten his life." The policy was effected in February 1855. In 1853 and 1854, he had had two severe bilious attacks. Doctors who had attended him had differing views as to whether these attacks did tend to shorten life, but their opinions were never communicated to the insured. The insurers repudiated liability on the ground that the statement he had made was inaccurate. In directing the jury, the Judge said that:

> "if the assured honestly believed at the time he made the declaration, that the bilious attacks had no effect upon his health, and did not tend to shorten his life or to render an insurance upon it more than usually hazardous, the fact that he was aware that he had had those attacks, even though (without his knowledge) they had such a tendency would not defeat the policy."

The jury gave a verdict in favour of the insured's personal representative. The insurers applied for a new trial on the ground that the direction given

---

[1] CHAMBRE and GIBBS, JJ.
[2] (1813), 4 Taunt. at p. 764.
[3] (1833), 6 C. & P. 1.
[4] See the summing up to the jury by DENMAN, C.J., *ibid.*, at p. 7.
[5] (1857), 3 C.B.N.S. 65.

by the Judge was wrong. The Court of Common Pleas[1] refused to grant a new trial and held that the direction was a correct one.

Frequency of Medical Attendance

In *Cazenove* v. *British Equitable Assurance Co.*[2] the insured stated in answer to the question in the proposal form "How often has medical attendance been required?", "One week"., He said that on that occasion the illness was a disordered stomach, and that he was attended by a Dr. Roper. In fact, he had subsequently had a very dangerous disease for which he was attended by three other doctors. The Court of Exchequer Chamber[3] held that the insurance company was entitled to avoid liability on the policy. POLLOCK, C.B., said[4] that the answer to the question might be said to be true in one sense, for so much as was stated in it was true. But it was nevertheless an untrue statement. It was just as untrue as when a person was asked how old he was, and he stated, in answer, a number of years less than his true age. It was trifling to say that that was a true answer which required something to be added to it to make it true.

Usual Medical Attendant

Where the proposer is asked to give particulars of the "usual" medical attendant, the word "usual" implies that the medical attendant has visited him more than once.

In *Huckman* v. *Fernie*[5] a husband took out a policy on his wife's life. Acting as his agent she answered "Mr. Day" to the question "who is your usual medical attendant?" In fact, Mr. Day had attended her husband and was the usual medical attendant of the family. On one or two occasions he had not been called in to attend the wife expressly, but had accidentally called on the family, and had advised her to take something for a cold. He gave some sort of prescription, but of so little note that he had no memorandum of it in his book. In directing the jury, TINDAL, C.J., did not leave to them the question whether Mr. Day could be called her "usual medical attendant", and on this ground the Court of Exchequer[6] granted a new trial. Lord ABINGER, C.B., delivering the judgment of the Court said:[7]

> "It appears to us, therefore, that the Chief Justice would have done right if he had laid down to the jury, that if she, in answering that question, was aware that the person whose name she gave could not be the proper person to render the account that the defendant wished to have of her, it was her duty to have mentioned the circumstance, and to have stated that although Mr. Day was a person whom they might send to, he was not the usual attendant, but that the usual attendant had been Mr. Duck.[8] Let us illustrate it thus:—suppose Mr. Day had never attended her at all, but that when she married, she had ceased to have any medical attendance; what answer ought she to have given? Suppose she answered, 'I have no usual medical attendant,' that answer would have been followed up by this question: 'But had you ever any usual medical attendant?' She must have known that the question was intended to elicit from her

---

[1] COCKBURN, C.J. and CRESSWELL, J.
[2] (1860), 29 L.J.C.P. 160.
[3] POLLOCK, C.B., BRAMWELL and CHANNELL, BB., WIGHTMAN, HILL and BLACKBURN, JJ.
[4] (1860), 29 L.J.C.P. at p. 160.
[5] (1838), 3 M. & W. 505.
[6] Lord ABINGER, C.B., and ALDERSON, B.
[7] (1838), 3 M. & W. at p. 520.
[8] Her medical attendant for a number of years before her marriage.

an answer designating the person who could give the best information of the state of her constitution at that time. It appears to me, and the Court are of that opinion, that the Chief Justice should have left it to the jury to say whether, under these circumstances, Mr. Day could properly be called her medical attendant at all; and if he could not, then, as a necessary consequence, the jury have found a wrong verdict. But that is owing in some degree to the Chief Justice not assisting them by a definition of what was the real object of that inquiry, and what was the real *bona fide* sense in which this question should be answered. She must have known that the answer was intended to deceive, more especially when it is considered that she was aware that on one or two former occasions Mr. Duck's answers had prevented her effecting any policy at all."

In *Everett* v. *Desborough*[1] the person whose life was insured stated, in answer to the question "who is your usual medical attendant?" "I have never had occasion for a doctor; sometimes I have taken Harvey's quack pills, but Mr. Vicary knows as much of me as any man." Mr. Vicary was a doctor, but he had never attended him professionally, but had known him from birth and had attended the rest of the family. The Court of Common Pleas[2] non-suited the plaintiff who had effected the policy, for the statement by the life assured was untrue. BURROUGH, J., said:[3]

"Here there is beyond all question a misrepresentation of a very material fact; of the name of the person who attended the life insured. There was another person who had been used to attend him. Beyond all doubt that is a misrepresentation. At the bottom of the policy there is this phrase: 'A declaration as to all the above points will be considered as the basis of the contract between the assured and the company. If such declaration be not in all respects true, the policy will become void.' One declaration is of 'the name and place of residence of two gentlemen to be referred to respecting the present and general state of health of the life to be insured—one to be usual medical attendant of the party.' Has the plaintiff complied with that? So far from it, there has been a misrepresentation of the fact by the life insured. Vicary was not his medical attendant. There was another person who had attended, and who would have disclosed habitual intoxication. This is not complying with the terms of the policy, and I think there ought to be a nonsuit."

In *Hutton* v. *Waterloo Life Assurance*[4] the insured signed a proposal form on April 20, 1854 and stated in it "Dr. Cobb" in answer to the question "who is your usual medical attendant?" Evidence was given by the insured's widow that Dr. Cobb had been the family doctor, and that on an occasion in 1853 when the police had brought the insured home blind drunk, Dr. Clifton was called in at Dr. Cobb's request, but she could not say that Dr. Cobb had not attended her husband several times in each of the subsequent three years. But she said that if he had been seriously ill, she would have sent for Dr. Cobb. The jury at Guildhall found that the insured's statement was untrue.

Consultation of Medical Practitioner

In *Mutual Life Insurance Co. of New York* v. *Ontario Metal Products Co., Ltd.*[5] the insured was asked by question 18 of a proposal form which he signed in 1918 to "state every physician or practitioner who has prescribed for or treated

---

[1] (1829), 5 Bing. 503.
[2] BEST, C.J., PARK, BURROUGH and GASELEE, JJ.
[3] (1829), 5 Bing. at p. 519. See also the judgment of BEST, C.J., *ibid.*, at p. 517, that of PARK, J., *ibid.*, at p. 518, and that of GASELEE, J., *ibid.*, at p. 520.
[4] (1859), 1 F. & F. 735.
[5] (1924), 132 L.T. 652, P.C.

you or whom you have consulted in the past five years." He answered
"None". In 1915 his wife suffered from bronchitis, and was attended by her
doctor, Dr. Fierheller. When she had recovered, Dr. Fierheller prescribed
for her a tonic consisting of arsenic, strychnine and iron. At the time of her
illness the insured was somewhat pale and run-down, so the doctor prescribed
a hypodermic injection of the same tonic. In March, April, and May 1915,
the insured received these injections. Similar injections were given over five
months in 1916, and again in August, September and October 1917. There
were no injections for a period of about fourteen months before the policy was
issued on December 13, 1918. The Judicial Committee of the Privy Council[1]
held that the answer to the question was inaccurate, but that on the evidence,
was not a material one, and hence under the Ontario Insurance Act 1914, s. 4[2]
the insurers could not avoid liability. Lord SALVESEN said:[3]

> "There is more difficulty as to the answer to question 18. The respondents con-
> tended that this question must be read with question 17,[4] and construed as
> limited to the illnesses, diseases, &c., there referred to. It is, however, not ex-
> pressly so limited, and their Lordships see good reasons why it must be deemed
> to have a wider application. Just because a man may truthfully represent that
> he has had no illness, disease, &c., it may be important to have the means of
> testing his answer by referring to medical gentlemen who have been consulted
> or have prescribed for him. There is no reason to doubt Mr. Schuch's good faith
> in giving the answer he did. The suggestion that he should insure his life came
> from an agent of the insurance company, and it is reasonably certain that Mr.
> Schuch regarded himself as a perfectly healthy man and might well consider the
> run-down condition for which he had been treated by hypodermic injections
> as a trivial ailment. Their Lordships are, notwithstanding, of opinion that this
> answer to question 18 was, in fact, inaccurate, and that it was his duty to have
> disclosed Dr. Fierheller's name as a physician who had prescribed for or treated
> him within the five years preceding the date of the policy."

Refusal by Other Companies to Insure

The fact that another insurance company has declined to insure the
proposer has been held to be a material one which ought to have been
disclosed.

Thus, in *London Assurance* v. *Mansel*[5]

> A question in a proposal form for a life insurance policy stated: "Has a proposal
> ever been made on your life at any other office or offices? If so, when? Was it
> accepted at the ordinary premium, or at an increased premium?" The proposer
> answered: "Insured now in two offices for £16,000 at ordinary rates. Policies
> effected last year". The answer was literally true so far as it went. A policy
> was issued to him. The insurers, however, applied for a declaration that the
> policy was void on the ground of non-disclosure of a material fact *viz.*, that the
> proposer had made proposals for life insurance to a number of insurance compan-
> ies, but they had been declined.
> *Held*, by the Chancery Division, that the declaration would be granted.

JESSEL, M.R., said:[6]

---

[1] Viscount HALDANE, Lord DUNEDIN, Lord ATKINSON, Lord WRENBURY and Lord SALVESEN.
[2] Which stated:—"No contract shall be avoided by reason of the inaccuracy of any . . .
statement [i.e. in an application for a policy] unless it is material to the contract."
[3] (1924), 132 L.T. at p. 654.
[4] Which stated: "What illnesses, diseases, injuries or surgical operations have you had since
childhood?"
[5] (1879), 41 L.T. 225.
[6] *Ibid.*, at p. 227.

"We have an admission by the defendant that no less than five insurance offices had declined to accept his life. Now to suppose that any human being who knows anything about life insurance, that any decent special juryman could for a moment hesitate as to the proper answer to be given to the question, when you go to the insurance office and ask for an insurance on your life, ought you to tell them that your proposals have been declined by five other insurance offices? is, I say, quite out of the question. There can but one answer that a man is bound to say, 'My proposals have been declined by five other offices, I will give you the reasons and show that it does not affect my life,' as he admits it to be by this answer, but of that the office could judge. There can be no doubt as a proposition to be decided by a jury that such a circumstance is material. But in fact I have elements here admitted on the pleadings for deciding that question of the practice of mankind, in respect of these matters which is to be imputed to a good special juryman; because I have these two things admitted; first of all that the proposal which forms the basis[1] of the contract asks a question. 'Has a proposal been declined?' Now, of course, if it is to form the basis of the contract, it is material, because, as was said in a case in the House of Lords of *Anderson* v. *Fitzgerald*,[2] where it is part of the contract the other side cannot say it is not material, so here we have the proposal as the basis of the contract. It is impossible for the assured to say that the question asked is not a material question to be answered, and the fact which the answer would bring out is not a material fact. Secondly, we have this, that within his own knowledge the English and Scottish Law Life Assurance Office having accepted his life, which had been duly passed by their medical officer as a first-class life, after examination and merely reserving a right to decline, when they found that one other office, not five, but one, had declined the life, or rather the proposal, at once withdrew from their acceptance and declined his proposal; so that this defendant had the strongest reasons for believing from actual knowledge that the fact of a proposal having been declined was a most material circumstance, and would have the greatest effect on the mind of the proposed assurers. It seems to me, as I said before, a very plain and clear case."

In *Fowkes* v. *Manchester & London Life Assurance and Loan Association*[3] the proposer signed a declaration to the effect that the statements he had made in the proposal form were true. The policy provided that:

"If it shall hereafter appear that any fraudulent concealment or designedly untrue statement be contained [in the declaration], then all the money which shall have been paid on account of the assurance made in consequence thereof shall be forfeited, and the policy granted in respect of such assurance shall be absolutely null and void."

In answer to the question: "Has your life been proposed at any other office, and if so, has it been accepted, and at what rate?" he stated: "It has been proposed and accepted at the ordinary rate". In fact his proposal had been accepted by one insurance company but declined by another. The Court of Queen's Bench[4] held that the declaration in the proposal form and the clause in the policy set out in the policy must be read together so that it was only in the case of "designedly untrue" statements that the insurers could avoid liability. On the evidence[5], the statement was not designedly untrue, so they were liable on the policy.

---

[1] As to the "basis clause", see Ivamy, *General Principles of Insurance Law*, 2nd Edn., 1970, pp. 132–133.
[2] (1853) 4 H.L. Cas. 484.
[3] (1863), 32 L.J.Q.B. 153.
[4] COCKBURN, C.J., CROMPTON, BLACKBURN and MELLOR, JJ.
[5] As to the evidence, see the report of the case at Nisi Prius: (1862), 3 F. & F. 440.

In giving judgment BLACKBURN, J., said:[1]

> "The express mention of the design and fraud might fairly lead a lawyer to say that the effect of this was that it waived and parted with the implied tacit agreement that the misrepresentation should vitiate the policy, and confined it to the vitiating of the policy in that one case. Therefore, looking at the [*contra proferentem*] rule, and taking the whole together, it may fairly be said that upon this declaration the policy should be cut down and construed to mean that if the statement should be fraudulently and designedly untrue, then the policy should be void and the premiums forfeited, but not otherwise. If once it is made out that the declaration is to be read in that way, I agree with my brother CROMPTON that when it is brought into the policy, the word 'untrue' is to be read in the same sense as in the declaration."

ANSWERS TO QUESTIONS ASKED BY MEDICAL EXAMINERS

The proposer may by the terms of the proposal form be required to be examined by a doctor appointed by the insurers. The point then arises as to the duty of the proposer as regards the giving of answers to the questions put to him by the doctor. This will depend on whether or not there is a "basis clause".[2]

1 Where there is No "Basis Clause"

If the accuracy of the answers is not made the "basis" of the contract, the insurers are not entitled to avoid liability on the policy if the answers are inaccurate, as long as they have been given honestly by the proposer.

In *Joel* v. *Law Union and Crown Insurance Co.*[3], where the answers were not made the basis of the contract, FLETCHER MOULTON, L.J., said[4] that he entertained the strongest opinion that the replies to the doctor who examined the proposer were not contractual limitations or conditions of the contract, but were intended by both parties to be only statements made by her to the best of her knowledge for the purpose of assisting the insurers to judge the risk they were taking. The occasion and the circumstances of the statement raised a strong probability that this was so. The nature of the questions showed that they must have been regarded as relating to belief only. Considering the position of the parties at the interview, and the proposer's duty to answer fully and so to help the doctor whatever questions he put to her, it would require the strongest language in the declaration which she had made to show that she had intentionally altered her position from that of one who was bound to help the doctor to the utmost of her power to that of a contracting party entitled to view the insurers' demands with suspicion, and to hold them at arm's length in defence of her interests. There was no such language to be found in the declaration which merely went to the truth of the statements, and added little, if anything, to what the law would have implied from the fact of the statements being made. It was a case in which the

---

[1] (1863), 32 L.J.Q.B. at p. 159. See further the judgment of COCKBURN, C.J., *ibid.*, at p. 157; that of CROMPTON, J., *ibid.*, at p. 158; and that of MELLOR, J., *ibid.*, at p. 160.

[2] As to the "basis clause", see Ivamy, *General Principles of Insurance Law*, 2nd Edn., 1970, pp. 132–134.

[3] (1908), 99 L.T. 712, C.A.

[4] *Ibid.*, at p. 720. See further the judgment of BUCKLEY, L.J., *ibid.*, at p. 721.

principle of taking such a document as the present one *contra proferentem*[1] ought to be applied in the strongest way, in view of the confidential character of the interview and the relations created thereby. If such a force was to be given to what passed at a medical examination, a man ought to take a lawyer with him when he went to be examined.[2]

Again, in *Delahaye* v. *British Empire Mutual Life Assurance Co.*[3] the Court of Appeal[4] held that as a matter of construction, the proposer had warranted the truth of statements which he had made in the proposal form, but he had not done so as regards answers which he had given to the medical examiners appointed by the insurers. All that he had done was to warrant that he would tell the truth to the best of his knowledge. The jury had found that the proposer had truthfully answered the question put by the medical examiner as to whether or not he had had jaundice. Consequently the insurers could not avoid liability.

2 Where is there a "Basis Clause"

Where the accuracy of the answers is made the "basis of the contract", the insurers can avoid liability in the event of an answer being inaccurate.

Thus, in *Hambrough* v. *Mutual Life Insurance Co. of New York*[5] there was an agreement by the proposer at the foot of the proposal form that the statements which he had made in it, as well as those made by him to the insurers' medical examiner, were warranted by him to be true, and were offered to the insurers "as a consideration of the contract". The Court of Appeal[6] held that since the answers which the proposer had given to the medical examiner were untrue, the insurers could avoid liability. LOPES, L.J., said that[7] the last words of the clause set out above were equivalent to an agreement that the truth of the statements formed the "basis of the contract", or were that on which the contract was to be founded.

---

[1] As to the *contra proferentem* rule, see Ivamy, *General Principles of Insurance Law*, 2nd Edn., 1970, pp. 318–323.
[2] The learned Lord Justice went on to say ((1908) 99 L.T., at p. 720): "The members of the medical profession ought to refuse to act for [insurers] that put such an interpretation on what there passes. The duty of a medical practitioner at such a time is to work with and by the aid of the [proposer] in order to enable himself to give a reliable report to the [insurers], and not to negotiate onerous contracts woven out of the well-meant efforts of the person he is examining to assist him in his task. There is something which to my mind is repulsive in the idea of a medical man under such circumstances inducing—as he is entitled and bound to do—the [proposer] to tell him freely all that he knows about himself, with the intention of making every such statement go to increase his contractual obligations and to render the terms of the policy more onerous, and thus to give fresh chances to the [insurers] of disputing and perhaps invalidating that policy years afterwards when the man has passed away, no doubt in the confidence that the premiums he has paid through all the subsequent years of his life have secured a provision for his family."
[3] (1897), 13 T.L.R. 245, C.A.
[4] Lord ESHER, M.R., LOPES and CHITTY, L.JJ.
[5] (1895), 72 L.T. 140, C.A.
[6] Lord ESHER, LOPES and RIGBY, L.JJ.
[7] (1895), 72 L.T. at p. 141. See also the judgment of Lord ESHER, M.R., *ibid.*, at p. 141, and that of RIGBY, L.J., *ibid.*, at p. 141.

12

INSURABLE INTEREST

As in the case of other types of insurance policies it is essential for an insured to have an insurable interest.

The Life Assurance Act 1774, s. 1 states:

"From and after the passing of this Act no insurance shall be made by any person or persons, bodies politick or corporate, on the life or lives of any person or persons or on any other event or events whatsoever, wherein the person or persons for whose use, benefit, or on whose account such policy or policies shall be made, shall have no interest, or by way of gaming or wagering; and that every assurance made contrary to the true intent and meaning hereof shall be null and void to all intents and purposes whatsoever."

WHO HAS AN INSURABLE INTEREST?

Insured's Own Life

A person has an insurable interest in his own life.

In *M'Farlane* v. *Royal London Friendly Society*[1] POLLOCK, B., said[2] that there was nothing to prevent a person from insuring his own life a hundred times, paying in each instance only one premium, provided it was a *bona fide* insurance on his life, and, at the time, for his benefit. There was nothing to prevent him from dealing with such policies by assigning them to someone else, even though at the time when he effected them he had the intention of so dealing with them. There was no law against that, and it was not within the mischief of the Life Assurance Act 1774. But if *ab initio* the policy effected in the name of A. was really and substantially intended for B. alone, and that fact was concealed, a different state of facts was presented and other considerations arose. That was within the evil and mischief intended to be met by the Act of 1774.[3]

Further, in *Wainewright* v. *Bland*[4] Lord ABINGER, C.B., in directing the jury said that it had been contended by the insurers that a person effecting an insurance upon his own life for a limited time was bound to show that he had some particular interest in the continuation of life up to that period,

---

[1] (1886), 2 T.L.R. 755.
[2] *Ibid.*, at p. 756.
[3] The Divisional Court of the Queen's Bench Division directed a new trial to establish whether or not the policy had been effected for the benefit of the insured or for that of another person. See further, the judgment of CAVE, J.: *ibid.*, at p. 756.
[4] (1835), 1 Mood. & R. 481.

although it was admitted that this would not be so in the case of an insurance for the whole term of life, and observed:[1]

> "I am not aware of this distinction having been ever taken, and it does not appear to me there is any force in it. If a party has an interest in his whole life, surely he must be interested in every part of it."

The jury found that the policy was not effected *bona fide* for the benefit of the insured, but was for that of another person, and that this fact had been concealed from the insurers, who were accordingly entitled to avoid the policy. An application for a new trial was refused.[2]

Wife's Life

A husband is presumed to have an insurable interest in his wife's life, and does not have to prove that he has one.

Thus in, *Griffiths* v. *Fleming*[3]

> A husband effected an insurance on his wife's life. Counsel proceeded to prove that the husband had an insurable interest in his wife's life by showing that the wife rendered services by doing household duties and looking after the children, that these duties were a benefit to him, that they ceased on her death and that he had to pay for a servant to carry them out.
> *Held*, by the Court of Appeal, that no such evidence was necessary, for it was presumed that a husband had an insurable interest in his wife's life.

In the course of his judgment FARWELL, L. J., observed:[4]

> "In *Reed* v. *Royal Exchange Assurance Co.*[5] Lord KENYON went a step further, and held that a wife, as such, has an insurable interest in her husband's life, and he refused to allow evidence to be given by her that her late husband was entitled to a life interest of large amount. This shows that he regarded the husband and wife in the same position as the individual insured, for he would otherwise have been bound to take the evidence in order to satisfy sect. 3 of the Act.[6] If the wife's insurable interest depended on her right to necessaries at her husband's expense, or on the possession by the husband of a life interest, the Judge could not of his own motion have excluded all evidence to show the age of the spouses at the date of the insurance, and the value of the interest or necessaries according to the station in life of the parties as compared with the sum assured. The case is very shortly reported, but in my opinion Lord KENYON excluded the evidence on the same grounds on which evidence of insurable interest in the insured for his own benefit would be excluded—namely, that the case was not within the mischief of the Act. If this be so, it follows, in my opinion, that the same principle must be applied to the insurance by the husband of the wife's life; a husband is no more likely to indulge in 'mischievous gaming' on his wife's life than a wife on her husband's."

Husband's Life

A wife is presumed to have an insurable interest in her husband's life, and evidence to prove it need not be adduced.

In *Reed* v. *Royal Exchange Assurance Co.*[7]

> A wife insured her husband's life. When he died she claimed the sum insured.

---

[1] (1835), 1 M. & Rob. at p. 487.
[2] (1836), 1 M. & W. 32.
[3] (1909), 100 L.T. 765, C.A.
[4] *Ibid.*, at p. 770. See also the judgment of VAUGHAN WILLIAMS, L.J., *ibid.*, at pp. 767–768.
[5] (1795), Peake Add. Cas. 70. See *infra*.
[6] I.e. the Life Assurance Act 1774. See p. 94, *post*.
[7] (1795), Peake Add. Cas. 70.

Her counsel proceeded to prove that the husband was entitled to the interest on a large sum of money which went on his death to a third party, and that accordingly she had an insurable interest in her husband's life.
Held, by the Court of King's Bench, that it was not necessary to show an interest, for, as Lord KENYON, C.J., observed:[1] "It must be presumed that every wife had an interest in the life of her husband."

Sister's Life

A person has no insurable interest in his sister's life.[2]

Life of Parent

A son merely as such has no insurable interest in his fathers' life.

Thus, in *Howard* v. *Refuge Friendly Society*[3]

A son insured his father's life in which he had no pecuniary interest. He paid the premiums for some time but then gave the insurers notice that he was going to pay no more and claimed the return of the premiums.
Held, by the Divisional Court of the Queen's Bench Division[4], that the policies were wagering policies and that the premiums could not be recovered.

MATHEW, J., said:[5]

"I assume that the policy, on the face of it, was a policy by the plaintiff effected on the life of his father, and the contract is prohibited by reason of the want of interest on the part of the son in the father's life. He had gone on paying on the footing of these policies from 1877, as regards one, down to 1885, and from the year 1881, as regards another, down to the year 1885. The policies being wagering policies, could the assured under such circumstances repudiate the policies and recover the premiums that had been paid? According to his contention, he must admit that the policies are wagers, and therefore that the contracts come under the prohibition of the Act of Geo. 3[6] and of the more recent Act, 8 & 9 Vict. c. 109[7]. How can he bring an action in respect of such a transaction? It is said his position was that of a man who has deposited a stake in the hands of a stakeholder, and who is entitled by law to recover the stake at any time before it is paid over to the third party. It has not been, nor could it be suggested that if the money had been paid over to the other contracting party with whom the bet had been made, the money could be recovered; but it is said the true analogy here is the analogy of the stakeholder. The company were the stakeholders; they held the premiums, and until the death the assured was entitled to recover their amount. The answer is simple: they were not stakeholders; they were the other contracting parties; the company were the persons with whom the bet had been made. Now, what was the bet? The bet under the first policy was a bet of £20 to tenpence in each week that the assured would survive the week, and the tenpence was paid at the commencement of each week, and the accumulated tenpences are now sought to be recovered. It is but necessary to state the case to see that they cannot be. It appears to me the premiums in such a case can no more be recovered than the principal money could be recovered if it had been paid. If the £20 had been paid by this society on the happening of the death they could not recover it back most clearly, because there had been a wager in respect

---

[1] (1795), Peake Add. Cas. 70. It is interesting to notice that the report of the case states that the wife was afterwards indicted at Gloucester Assizes for the murder of her husband, and was acquitted.
[2] *Evanson* v. *Crooks* (1911), 106 L.T. 264.
[3] (1886), 54 L.T. 644. See further, *Greenslade* v. *London and Manchester Industrial Insurance Co., Ltd.* (1913), 48 L. Jo. 330. (Step-child insuring step-parent.)
[4] MATHEW and SMITH, JJ.
[5] (1886), 54 L.T. at p. 646.
[6] I.e. the Life Assurance Act 1774.
[7] I.e. the Gaming Act 1845.

of which they had made a payment. The same principle applies to the payment made by the other side."

Again, in *Elson* v. *Crookes*[1] where a son had insured's his mother's life in which he had no insurable interest, the premiums were held to be irrecoverable, PHILLIMORE, J., saying:[2]

> "In my opinion there is enough to show that the plaintiff paid his first premium to get an illegal thing and afterwards he knew what he was getting. Even if he did not read the policy and did not know it before, the moment he got the nomination and the questions he knew, or ought to have known, that the policy was one in which his mother was insured, and that she was the holder of the policy. That being so, the premiums having been paid in respect of an illegal policy, the plaintiff is not entitled to recover them."

Life of a Child

A father, merely as such, has no insurable interest in the life of his son. To render the policy valid under the Life Assurance Act 1774 he must have a pecuniary interest in his son's life.

Thus, in *Halford* v. *Kymer*[3]

> A father effected an insurance policy in his own name in respect of his son's life to provide against the death of his son before he reached the age of 21. The father had no pecuniary interest in the life or event insured.
> *Held*, by the Court of King's Bench,[4] that he had no insurable interest in his son's life, and the policy was void under the Life Assurance Act 1774.

In giving judgment BAYLEY, J., said:[5]

> "It is enacted by the third section,[6] 'That no greater sum shall be recovered than the amount of the value of the interest of the insured in the life or lives.' Now, what was the amount or value of the interest of the party insuring in this case?—Not one farthing certainly. It has been said that there are numerous instances in which a father has effected an insurance on the life of his son. If a father, wishing to give his son some property to dispose of, make an insurance on his son's life in his (the son's) name, not for his (the father's) own benefit, but for the benefit of his son, there is no law to prevent his doing so; but that is a transaction quite different from the present; and if a notion prevails that such an insurance as the one in question is valid, the sooner it is corrected the better."

But where the insurers pay the sum insured by the policy to the father, even though he has no insurable interest in his son's life, he is entitled to retain the money as against the son's estate.

Thus, in *Worthington* v. *Curtis*[7] a father effected a policy for his own benefit on his son's life in which he had no insurable interest. The son died intestate and the father took out letters of administration to the estate. The insurers paid the sum insured under the policy to the father as his son's administrator. Two of the son's creditors claimed that the sum paid by the insurers formed part of the son's estate. The Court of Appeal[8] held that although the policy

---

[1] (1911), 106 L.T. 462, D.C.
[2] *Ibid.*, at p. 464.
[3] (1830), 10 B. & C. 724.
[4] TENTERDEN, C.J., BAYLEY, LITTLEDALE and PARKE, JJ.
[5] (1830), 10 B. & C. at p. 729.
[6] I.e. of the Life Assurance Act 1774.
[7] (1875), 33 L.T. 828.
[8] JAMES and MELLISH, L.JJ., and BAGGALLAY, J.A.

was void under the Life Assurance Act 1774, the insurers had paid the sum insured without obligation, and the father was entitled to retain it as against all persons claiming under the son.

MELLISH, L.J., said:[1]

"The insurance company, having sufficient to call their attention to the probability of the case, acting as insurance companies generally do, never thought of raising that defence, and on administration being taken out, paid the sum without dispute. The question, then, is whether that sum really forms a portion of the assets of the son. The creditors plainly claim under the son, and can have no greater right to the policy than the son had while he was alive, and the question must therefore be determined by a consideration of the question as between the son and the father. Now, quite apart from any question of defence under the statute which might have been raised by the company, the policy clearly belongs to the father. The following test might be applied: Suppose the son had required the father to deliver up the policy, and had brought an action of detinue, the statute could not have been set up against a plea showing the father's title. Suppose, again, the father in the lifetime of the son had said he would surrender the policy to the company on obtaining the surrender value, could the son have complained, or brought an action for money had and received, or a suit in equity to prevent the father from surrendering the policy? Certainly not; because, as between the father and the son, the policy belonged to the father. The son died and the money then became payable. Assuming that one of the creditors had taken out administration, and had brought an action of detinue, he would have been in the same position as the son, and the son having no property in it, the creditors would have had no property in it. Then suppose the insurance company had chosen to pay the sum in question to the father voluntarily, and not raise the defence of the statute, could the administrator of the son have recovered it? Clearly not."

Lives of "Foster Children"

Section 9 of the Children Act 1958 states that:

"A person who maintains a foster child[2] shall be deemed for the purposes of the Life Assurance Act 1774 to have no interest in the life of the child."

Consequently any insurance taken out in respect of a foster child's life is void.

Lives of "Protected Children"

It is provided by s. 46 of the Adoption Act 1958 that:

"A person who maintains a protected child[3] shall be deemed for the purposes of the Life Assurance Act 1774 to have no interest in the life of the child."

---

[1] (1875), 33 L.T. at p. 829. See further, *Attorney-General* v. *Murray*, [1904] 1 K.B. 165, C.A., where a life policy was effected by a father on his son's life in which he had no insurable interest, and the policy was assigned to trustees of a marriage settlement and the insurers although not bound to do so, paid the sum insured to them.

[2] "Foster child" is defined by s. 2 of the Children Act 1958 and, in general, means "a child below the upper limit of the compulsory school age whose care and maintenance are undertaken for reward for a period exceeding one month by a person who is not a relative or guardian of his." See s. 2 (1).

[3] "Protected child" is defined by s. 37 of the Adoption Act 1958, which by sub-s. 1 states: "Subject to the following provisions of this section, where
   (a) arrangements are made for placing a child below the upper limit of the compulsory school age in the care and possession of a person who is not a parent, guardian or relative of his, and another person, not being a parent or guardian of his, takes part in the arrangements; or
   (b) notice of intention to apply for an adoption order in respect of a child is given under s. 3 (2) of this Act,

Any insurance effected in respect of a protected child's life is therefore void.

Life of Employer

An employee, who is under contract to serve his employer for a fixed period, has an insurable interest in his employer's life up to the amount of his salary to be paid during the period.

Thus, in *Hebdon* v. *West*[1]

> In 1855 the plaintiff was employed by a Mr. Pedder for seven years at a salary of £600 per annum. In 1857 he insured Pedder's life for £2,500 with the defendant. In 1861 Pedder died and the plaintiff sued on the policy.
> *Held*, by the Court of King's Bench, that he had an insurable interest in the employer's life to the amount of £3,000 which was sufficient to sustain the policy which was for £2,500, and that accordingly the action succeeded.

WIGHTMAN, J., observed:[2]

> "In the present case it was contended for the plaintiff that he had two kinds of insurable interest in the life of Pedder—one, on the ground of a promise that Pedder had made to him that he (Pedder) would not enforce the payment of any debt that the plaintiff might owe him during his (Pedder's) lifetime, and the other, on the ground that the plaintiff was in the employ of Pedder at a salary of £600 a year, under an agreement that the engagement should last for seven years. We do not think that the first kind of interest in the life of Pedder, namely that he had said that he would not enforce payment of debts due to him from the plaintiff during his (Pedder's) life, without any consideration or any circumstance to make such a promise in any way binding, can be considered as a pecuniary or indeed an appreciable interest in the life of Pedder. The other kind of interest, namely that which arises from the engagement by Pedder to employ the plaintiff for seven years at a salary of £600 a year, may, we think, be considered as a pecuniary interest in the life of Pedder, to the extent at least of as much of the period of seven years as would remain at the time the policy was effected, which appears to have been about five years. This, at the rate of £600 per annum, would give the plaintiff a pecuniary interest in the life of Pedder to the amount of £3,000 which would be sufficient to sustain the present policy, which is for £2,500 only."

Life of Debtor

A creditor has an insurable interest in the life of his debtor to the extent of the debt.[3]

THE TIME AT WHICH INSURABLE INTEREST MUST EXIST

The insured must have an insurable interest at the time at which the policy is effected.[4] It is immaterial whether or not he later ceases to have

---

then, while the child is in the care and possession of the person first mentioned in paragraph (*a*) of this sub-section, or, as the case may be, of the person giving the notice mentioned in paragraph (*b*) thereof, but is not a foster child within the meaning of Part I of the Children Act, 1958, he is a protected child within the meaning of this Part of this Act."

[1] (1863), 3 B. & S. 579.
[2] *Ibid.*, at p. 589.
[3] *Dalby* v. *India and London Life Assurance Co.* (1854), 15 C.B. 365.
[4] For the time at which the assured under a marine policy must have an insurable interest, see Ivamy, *Marine Insurance*, 1969, pp. 29–30.

such an interest, e.g. where before the debtor dies he pays the creditor the amount of the debt.[1]

THE SUM RECOVERABLE

Section 3 of the Life Assurance Act 1774 states:

> "And in all cases where the insured hath interest in such life or lives, event or events, no greater sum shall be recovered or received from the insurer or insurers than the amount or value of the interest of the insured in such life or lives or other event or events."

NAMING OF INTERESTED PERSONS

Section 2 of the Life Assurance Act 1774 states:

> "And . . . it shall not be lawful to make any policy or policies on the life or lives of any person or persons, or other event or events, without inserting in such policy or policies the person or persons' name or names interested therein, or for whose use, benefit, or on whose account such policy is so made or underwrote."

Group Policies

Clause 41 of the Insurance Companies Bill[2] provides that the Life Assurance Act 1774 shall not invalidate a policy for the benefit of unnamed persons from time to time falling within a specified class or description if the class or description is stated in the policy with sufficient particularity to make it possible to establish the identity of all persons who at any given time are entitled to benefit under the policy. The clause has retrospective effect.

---

[1] *Dalby* v. *India and London Life Assurance Co. (supra)*.
[2] The Bill received its Third Reading in the House of Lords on April 12, 1973.

13

THE CONTENTS OF THE POLICY

A life insurance policy sets out:

1 recitals;
2 the circumstances in which payment will be made;
3 the schedule;
4 conditions and privileges;
5 the principal place of business of the insurers.

1 Recitals

The policy states in the recitals[1] that the insurers have received a proposal and declaration which form the basis[2] upon which the insurance is granted.

2 Circumstances in which Payment will be Made

The insurers agree that on satisfactory proof of:

   i the happening of the event upon which the sum insured is payable and which is set out in the schedule;
   ii the title of the person claiming payment;
   iii the date of birth of the life insured;[3]

they will pay the sum insured as specified in the schedule to the policy.

3 Schedule

The schedule sets out the policy number, the date of commencement of the policy, the name, occupation, etc., of the life insured, the date of the proposal and declaration and the name and occupation of the insured (if not the life insured).

It states the amount of the sum insured and the event upon which it is payable, e.g.:

   i the death of the life insured; or
   ii the death of the life insured before a specified date or the survival of the life insured until that date; or
   iii the death of the life insured before the expiry date of a term insurance policy.

---

[1] As to the recitals, see Ivamy, *General Principles of Insurance Law*, 2nd Edn., 1970, p. 179, footnotes 5 and 6.
[2] As to the "basis clause", see Ivamy, *op. cit.* pp. 132–133.
[3] I.e. if age has not been previously admitted.

The person to whom the sum insured will be paid is specified.[1] The policy is expressed to be with or without participation in profits.

The amount of the first premium is stated as also are the amounts of the renewal premium, the dates when premiums are payable, and the period during which they are payable.

Finally, the date of birth is stated and whether age is or is not admitted by the insurers.

4 Conditions and Privileges

Usual conditions and privileges in life insurance policies concern the following matters:

a freedom from restrictions as to residence;
b days of grace;
c effect of understatement of age in proposal;
d effect of premium being overdue;
e surrender value;
f revival of lapsed policy;
g indesputability of policy;
h suicide.

a *Freedom from Restrictions as to Residence*

Policies usually state that they are free from all restrictions as to foreign residence, travel and occupation.

At one time there were such restrictions inserted in policies,[2] but this is not the present practice.

b *Days of Grace*[3]

The number of days' grace which are provided for in the policy depends on the interval at which the premiums are due. Thus, where they are payable quarterly or half yearly, thirty days' grace are allowed. But if they are payable monthly, the number of days of grace may be only ten.

If the insured dies during the days of grace, the unpaid premiums will be deducted from the sum insured.

c *Understatement of Age*

The policy usually states that if it is found that the insured has understated his age[4] in the proposal form, the policy will not be void, but that such sum will be payable as would have been paid at the true age for the premium actually paid.

d *Premium Overdue*

The policy sometimes states that if the premium is not received before the

---

[1] See pp. 108–112, *post*.
[2] See, e.g. *Wing* v. *Harvey* (1854), 5 De G.M. & G. 265 (restriction as to foreign residence; *Duckworth* v. *Scottish Widows' Fund Life Assurance Society* (1917), 33 T.L.R. 430 (restriction on engaging in military service.
[3] As to "days of grace", see further Ivamy, *General Principles of Insurance Law*, 2nd Edn., 1970, pp. 214–216.
[4] As to the statement of age in the proposal form, see p. 73, *ante*.

expiration of the days of grace, the policy will remain in force for one year from the date on which the first overdue premium became due, provided that two years' premiums have been received.

During this year the arrears of premium with interest at a specified rate of interest will be accepted by the company.

If at the expiration of the year the first overdue premium and interest have not been received, the balance of the surrender value of the policy will be applied to convert the policy to a paid-up policy for a reduced sum on a guaranteed basis.

e *Surrender Value*

The policy may state that after a payment of e.g. two years' premiums the policy may have a surrender value.

f *Revival of Lapsed Policy*

The policy may provide that if it lapses through non-payment of a premium, it may be revived at any time within a year from the date of lapse, provided that all overdue premiums and interest are paid. In addition, satisfactory proof of the continued eligibility of the life insured must be produced.[1]

g *Indisputability of Policy*

Some policies may state that after they have been in force for a specified period e.g. two years, provided that proof of age has been admitted by the insurers, they are to be indisputable i.e. are not liable to any ground of challenge whatever connected with the original documents proceeding on which the insurance was granted.

Thus, in *Anstey* v. *British Natural Premium Life Association, Ltd.*, the policy stated:

> "The policy, except as provided therein, will be indisputable from any cause (except fraud) after it shall have continuously been in force for two years."

A similar term may also be found in a prospectus issued by the company concerned. Thus, in the same case the prospectus said:

> "*Indisputability of policies.* After a policy has been continuously in force for two years without lapse, it is indisputable in the absence of fraud, and no *bona fide* mistakes that may have crept into the form of application or into any other document or statement made before the issue of the policy and accepted as the basis of the contract will prejudice the validity of the policy, provided always that the age has been admitted."

In that case the policy had been in force for two years, and when a claim was made under the policy, the defendants repudiated liability on the ground that some of the answers which the person whose life was insured had given were untrue, but they did not allege that there was any fraud. They contended that although they could not dispute the policy, they could say that the policy never took effect, and that the period of two years had

---

[1] As to lapse and revival of policies, see Ivamy, *General Principles of Insurance Law*, 2nd Edn. 1970, pp. 217–218.
[2] (1908), 99 L.T. 765, C.A.

never commenced. The Court of Appeal held[1] that the policy was indisputable, and that the claim succeeded, FLETCHER MOULTON, L.J., saying:[2]

> "The construction which the company seek to put upon it is that they say we cannot dispute the policy, but we can say the policy never took effect, and those two years never have commenced. That appears to me to be fraudulent nonsense. The policy has been accepted by the company, and they have received premiums under it, and the policy says that after it has been in force for two years it is indisputable except for fraud."

BUCKLEY, L.J., said[3] that the defendants had contracted that if the policy was in force for two years, they would not dispute it on the grounds which they now set up. He agreed that the words "except as provided herein" meant "except as provided in the conditions of the policy". He arrived at that from the construction of the document as a whole. If he construed it otherwise, the words at the commencement of the document would be in conflict with the later clauses.

VAUGHAN WILLIAMS, L.J., also agreeing,[4] said that the defendants' contention was wholly inconsistent with the statement in the prospectus and also inconsistent with the words of the policy, unless it were qualified by the words "except as provided herein", which might, though he did not decide the question, extend to the whole of the policy. The document was capable of two constructions, and should be construed *contra proferentem* so as to make the statement in the prospectus of some value and effect.

Even where the prospectus alone contains a term stating that the policy will be indisputable, the Court may find that the proposer has relied on such a statement in effecting the policy, and if it does so, the policy will be indisputable, for the prospectus will be deemed to have been incorporated into it.[5]

In *Anctil* v. *Manufacturers' Life Insurance Co.*[6] the plaintiff had taken out a policy on the life of a Mr. Pettigrew. He stated in the proposal that Pettigrew was his "protector" whenever he stood in need of protection. The policy stated that

> "After the policy has been in force for one year it will be incontestable for whatever cause provided that the premiums have been paid promptly and that the age of the assured has been admitted.'

Article 2590 of the Civil Code of Lower Canada stated:

> "The insured must have an insurable interest in the life upon which the assurance is effected. He has an insurable interest in the life:
> (1) of himself;

---

[1] VAUGHAN WILLIAMS, FLETCHER MOULTON and BUCKLEY, L.JJ.

[2] (1908), 99 L.T. at p. 766.

[3] *Ibid.*, at p. 767.

[4] *Ibid.*, at p. 766.

[5] *Wood* v. *Dwarris* (1856), 11 Exch. 493. See where MARTIN, B., said (*ibid.*, at p. 504): "[Counsel] has argued that this policy was effected upon the terms of the proposal, and not of the prospectus. No doubt it would be competent for the company to grant a policy upon terms which excluded the prospectus; and if that were so, the defendants would be justified in resisting this action, and might simply have traversed the replication; for the plaintiff is bound to prove not only that such a prospectus was issued, but also that the policy was made on the terms of that prospectus". Cf. *Wheelton* v. *Hardisty* (1858), 8 E. & B. 232, where the jury found that a prospectus stating that the policy was indisputable had been issued, but no express proof was given by the plaintiffs that they had seen it or were induced by it to effect the policy. See the judgment of ERLE, J., *ibid.*, at p. 263.

[6] (1899), 81 L. T. 279, P.C.

(2) of any person upon whom he depends wholly or in part for support or education;

(3) of any person under legal obligation to him for the payment of money or respecting the property or services which death or illness might defeat or prevent the performance of;

(4) of any person upon whose life any estate or interest in the insured depends."

Pettigrew died and the plaintiff claimed under the policy, but the insurers repudiated liability on the ground that he had no insurable interest. The Judicial Committee of the Privy Council[1] accepted this defence, and held that the action failed, even though the policy had been in force for a year and according to the policy was to be "incontestable". Lord WATSON observing:[2]

"The question remains whether that clause of the policy which provides that the instrument shall become 'incontestable' on the lapse of a period of a year or upwards, furnishes a good answer to the objection founded on the terms of the Code [*viz.*, that the plaintiff had no insurable interest]. Upon that point their Lordships concur in the opinion expressed by the majority of the Supreme Court [of Canada] and of the Superior Court sitting in review. The rule of the Code appears to them to be one which rests upon general principles of public policy or expediency, and which cannot be defeated by the private convention of the parties. Any other view would lead to the sanction of wager policies."

h *Suicide*

A policy sometimes provides that it is to be void in the event of the death of the life insured by his own hand within one year of the date of the policy, but that *bona fide* interests of third parties for value of which written notice has been given to the insurers before the death of the life insured are not affected.

Suicide is no longer a criminal offence,[3] so that in the absence of an express clause relating to suicide, a claim made by e.g. the personal representatives of an insured who has killed himself when sane cannot be defeated on the ground that it is against public policy to allow such a claim.[4] But the insurers are entitled to avoid liability on the ground that the insured cannot take advantage of his own intentional act.[5]

Presumably, in the absence of any express clause in the policy, the insurers would still be liable if the insured committed suicide whilst of unsound mind.

5 Principal Place of Business of Insurers

Every insurance company must specify on every policy issued by it its principal place or principal places of business at which notices of assignment may be given in pursuance of the Policies of Assurance Act 1867.[6]

---

[1] Lord WATSON, Lord MACNAGHTEN and Sir HENRY STRONG.

[2] (1899), 81 L.T. at p. 281.

[3] Suicide Act 1961, s. 1.

[4] I.e., one of the grounds in *Beresford* v. *Royal Insurance Co., Ltd.*, [1938] A.C. 586, H.L. (which was decided before the Suicide Act 1961) for holding that the claim failed.

[5] *Beresford* v. *Royal Insurance Co., Ltd.* (*supra*), where this ground for rejecting the claim succeeded, and would seem to be still applicable to cases arising after the Suicide Act 1961.

[6] Policies of Assurance Act 1867, s. 4. As to notice of assignment of a policy given in pursuance of the Act, see p. 102, *post*.

14

ASSIGNMENT

The assignment of the policy is a subject which is discussed generally else-where in this work.[1] As far as life insurance is concerned, three matters of importance require to be considered: (1) legal and equitable assignments; (2) the priority between successive assignees of the same policy; and (3) the assignee's right to sue in his own name.

LEGAL AND EQUITABLE ASSIGNMENTS

1 Legal Assignment

a *Under the Policies of Assurance Act 1867*

A legal assignment can be made under s. 5 of the Policies of Assurance Act 1867, which states that:

> "[An] assignment may be made either by endorsement on the policy or by a separate instrument in the words or to the effect set forth in the schedule[2] hereto, such endorsement being duly stamped."

To enable the assignee to sue on the policy in his own name the assignee must give notice of the date and purport of the assignment to the insurance company at its principal place of business.[3]

b *Under the Law of Property Act 1925*

A legal assignment may also be made under s. 136 of the Law of Property Act 1925 if it consists of an absolute assignment[4] by writing under the hand of the assignor[5] (not purporting to be by way of charge only). To enable the assignee to sue in his own name the assignee must give express notice in writing to the insurance company.

2 Equitable Assignment

No special form for the creation of an equitable assignment is needed. But it must be shown that the assignor had the intention of assigning.[6] Thus, to constitute an assignment it is sufficient if e.g. the policy is delivered to the

---

[1] Ivamy, *General Principles of Insurance Law*, 2nd. Edn., 1970, pp. 282–288.
[2] For the form set out in the schedule, see p. 102, *post*.
[3] Policies of Assurance Act 1867, s. 3. See p. 102, *post*.
[4] *Tancred* v. *Delagoa Bay and East Africa Rail. Co.* (1889), 23 Q.B.D. 239; *Mercantile Bank of London* v. *Evans*, [1889] 2 Q.B. 613.
[5] *Re Westerton, Public Trustee* v. *Gray*, [1919] 2 Ch. 104.
[6] *Ibid.*; *Re Williams, Williams* v. *Ball*, [1917] 1 Ch. 1; *Re King, Sewell* v. *King* (1879), 14 Ch.D. 179.

assignee, or there is an agreement to assign, or the assignor has merely signed a memorandum to assign, provided that the necessary intention to assign is shown.[1]

Property Between Successive Assignees

If the successive assignments are both legal assignments, the order of priority depends on when the notice is given to the insurers, i.e., a legal assignee whose assignment was subsequent to another assignment will gain priority over the first legal assignee by giving notice to the insurers.

If a legal assignee gives notice to the insurers, he will have priority over a prior equitable assignee provided he had no notice either actual or constructive of the existence of the earlier equitable assignment.[2]

Priority between equitable assignees depends on the date when notice was given. But by giving notice an equitable assignee cannot gain priority over another assignee if he had actual or constructive notice of the earlier equitable assignment.

Assignee's Right to Sue in Own Name

Originally the general rule was that the assignee of a life policy was not entitled to sue the insurers in his own name. He had to join the assignor as plaintiff. But if the assignor refused, then he could join the assignor as defendant.

But the assignee may now sue in his own name if he can bring himself within the provisions of:

1 The Policies of Assurance Act 1867; or
2 s. 136 (1) of the Law of Property Act 1925.

Policies of Assurance Act 1867

By this Act the assignee can sue in his own name if the following conditions are fulfilled:

a he must have the right in equity to receive and the right to give a valid discharge for the moneys assured by the policy.
b the assignment must be in the words or to the effect of the statutory form.
c notice of the assignment must have been given to the insurers.

a *Right to receive and right to give discharge for moneys assured*
Section 1 of the Act states:

"Any person or corporation now being or hereafter becoming entitled, by assignment or other derivative title, to a policy of life assurance,[3] and possessing at the time of action brought the right in equity to receive and the right to given an effectual discharge to the assurance company[4] liable under such

---

[1] *Thomas* v. *Harris*, [1947] 1 All E.R. 444.
[2] *Newman* v. *Newman* (1885), 28 Ch.D. 674. *Spencer* v. *Clarke* (1878), 9 Ch.D. 137. See further p. 103, *post*.
[3] The expression "policy of life assurance" or "policy" means "any instrument by which the payment of monies by or out of the funds of an assurance company, on the happening of any contingency depending on the duration of human life is assured or secured": Policies of Assurance Act 1867, s. 7.
[4] "Assurance company" means and includes every corporation association, society or company now or hereafter carrying on the business of assuring lives, or survivorships, either alone or in conjunction with any other object or objects: *ibid*.

policy for monies thereby assured or secured, shall be at liberty to sue at law in the name of such person or corporation to recover such monies."

In *Crossley* v. *City of Glasgow Life Assurance Co.*[1] a debtor effected two policies on his life with the defendants, and forwarded them to the creditor with a request to have a proper assignment prepared by a solicitor. No such assignment, however, was made. The creditor now claimed the sum from the defendants, but they refused to pay on the ground that the creditor had no right in equity to receive and the right to give an effectual discharge for the moneys assured or secured by the policy because there had been no valid equitable assignment. JESSEL, M.R., agreed and said[2]

> "The first point is this: It is said that that is an equitable assignment under the Act. I think it is not. It is exactly what it purports to be. The person was to instruct his solicitor to prepare an assignment. There was no agreement for assignment. It is a deposit or assignment as he thought fit. He was entitled to take either course, but he thought fit to take the second course, and allowed it to remain on deposit."

In *Spencer* v. *Clarke*[3] an agreement to execute a mortgage upon request was held not to be an equitable assignment.

In *In re Williams, Williams* v. *Ball*[4] where an insured gave a life policy to his housekeeper with an endorsement on it stating:

> "I authorize [you] to draw this insurance in the event of my predeceasing [you] this being my sole desire and intention at the time of taking this policy out."

the Court of Appeal[5] held that the purported assignment was an incomplete gift, for it was a revocable mandate which was revoked by the assignor's death, or if it took effect on death, it failed because it was a testamentary document which had not been duly executed.[6]

b *Form of Assignment*

Section 5 of the Act of 1867 states:

> "Any such assignment may be made either by endorsement on the policy or by a separate instrument in the words or to the effect set forth in the schedule hereto, such endorsement being duly stamped."

The Schedule is in the following form:

> "I *A.B.* of, *&c.*, in consideration of, *&c.*, do hereby assign unto *C.D.* of, *&c.*, his Executors, Administrators, and Assigns, the [within] Policy of Assurance granted, *&c.* [*here described the Policy*]. In witness, *&c.* . . . ."

c *Giving of Notice*

No assignment of a policy of life assurance confers on the assignee any right to sue for the amount of the policy or the moneys assured or secured

---

[1] (1876), 36 L.T. 285.
[2] *Ibid.*, at p. 286.
[3] (1878), 9 Ch.D. 137. See the judgment of HALL, V.-C., *ibid.*, at p. 141.
[4] [1917] 1 Ch. 1.
[5] Lord COZENS-HARDY, M.R., WARRINGTON and SCRUTTON, L.JJ.
[6] See the judgment of Lord COZENS-HARDY, M.R., [1917] 1 Ch. at p. 7, and that of WARRINGTON, L.J., *ibid.*, at p. 8.

by it until a written notice of the date and purport of such assignment has been given to the insurance company[1] at its principal place of business.[2]

The date on which such notice has been received regulates the priority of all claims under any assignment.[3] It is important to observe that the giving of notice does not affect the rights of persons interested in the policy *inter se*, for as NORTH, J., said in *Newman* v. *Newman*:[4]

> "[The] Act [of 1867] was passed in order to avoid the necessity of joining the assignor of the policy in actions against the insurance office, and it provides that if a certain notice is given to the office, then the assignee may sue without joining the assignor. Then these words occur 'And the date on which such notice shall be received shall regulate the priority of all claims under any assignment.' It was contended that these words went much further than was necessary for the protection of the insurance office, and affected the rights of the parties *inter se*. The argument goes as far as this, that the holder of an equitable interest having given an insufficient notice, and [the assignee] having afterwards given a statutory notice, their rights for all purposes must be governed by the terms of the statute as to priority, although the assignee had at the time notice of [the equitable interest]. In my opinion that is not the meaning of the statute, which was not intended to affect the rights of persons claiming interests in the money outside the insurance office. It was intended to give a simpler remedy against an insurance office, and also to give facilities to insurance offices in settling claims by enabling them to recognize as the first claim the claim of the person who first gave such notice as required by the statute. It was not intended in my opinion to enact that a person who had advanced money upon a second charge with notice of the first and made subject to it, should by giving statutory notice to the office exclude the person who had the prior incumbrance."

A payment *bona fide* made in respect of any policy by any insurance company before the date on which such notice is received is valid as against the assignee giving such notice.[5]

Every insurance company to whom notice has been duly given of the assignment of any policy must, upon the request in writing of any person by whom such notice was given or signed[6] and upon payment of a fee not exceeding 25p, deliver an acknowledgement in writing[7] of the receipt of such notice.[8] Every such written acknowledgement[9] is conclusive evidence of receipt of the notice.[10]

2 Under the Law of Property Act 1925, s. 136 (1)

Under s. 136 (1) of the Law of Property Act 1925 an assignor of a life policy is entitled to sue the insurers in his own name if:

1 there has been a absolute assignment of the policy by writing under the hand of the assignor (not purporting to be by way of charge only); and
2 express notice in writing has been given to the insurers.

---

[1] Policies of Assurance Act 1867, s. 3.
[2] Or if the company has two or more principal places of business, then at one of those principal places of business: *ibid.*, s. 3.
[3] *Ibid.*, s. 3.
[4] (1885), 28 Ch.D. 674, at p. 680. See further, p. 101, *ante*.
[5] Policies of Assurance Act 1867, s. 3.
[6] Or of his executors or administrators: *ibid.*, s. 6.
[7] Under the hand of the manager, secretary, treasurer or other principal officer of the company: *ibid.*, s. 6.
[8] *Ibid.*, s. 6.
[9] If signed by a person being *de jure* or *de facto* the manager, secretary, treasurer or other principal officer of the company: *ibid.*, s. 6.
[10] *Ibid.*, s. 6.

15

PROOF OF DEATH

The death of the person whose life is insured may be proved in a variety of ways including:

1 an entry in the appropriate register of deaths or a certificate of that entry;
2 evidence by a person who was present at the death or who examined the body;
3 evidence that the life insured has not been heard of for a considerable time.

1 Entry of Death in Register or Certificate of that Entry

a *Deaths in England and Wales*

An entry or a certified copy of an entry of a death in a register, or in a certified copy of a register is evidence of the death if the entry purports to be signed by some person professing to be the informant and to be such a person as might be required by law at the date of the entry to give to the registrar information concerning that death.[1]

Where more than twelve months have intervened between the date of the finding of the dead body of any person and the date of the registration of that person's death, the entry or a certified copy of the entry of the death in the register, or in a certified copy of the register, is not evidence of the death unless the entry purports to have been made with the authority of the Registrar General.[4]

A certified copy of an entry in a register or in a certified copy of a register is deemed to be a true copy notwithstanding that it is made on a form different from that on which the original entry was made if any differences in the column headings under which the particulars appear in the original entry and the copy respectively are differences of form only and not of substance.[3]

The Registrar General must cause any certified copy of an entry given in the General Register Office to be sealed or stamped with the seal of that Office.[4] Subject to what is stated above, any certified copy of an entry purporting to be sealed or stamped with the seal shall be received as evidence of the death to which it relates without any further or other proof of entry.[5]

---

[1] Births and Deaths Registration Act 1953, s. 34 (2). This sub-s. does not apply in relation to an entry of death which purports to have been made (i) upon a certificate from a coroner; or (ii) in pursuance of the enactments with respects to death at sea.
[2] *Ibid.*, s. 34 (4). [3] *Ibid.*, s. 34 (5). [4] *Ibid.*, s. 34 (6).
[5] *Ibid.*, s. 34 (6). No certified copy purporting to have been given in the General Register Office is of any force or effect unless it is sealed or stamped with the seal: *ibid.*, s. 34 (6).

b *Deaths in Scotland*

Every extract of any entry in the register books duty authenticated by the Registrar General, if the extract is from the registers kept at the General Office, Edinburgh, or by the Registrar if from any parochial or district register, is admissible as evidence without any further proof of such entry.[1]

c *Deaths in Northern Ireland*

All certified copies of entries purporting to be sealed or stamped with the seal of the General Register Office are admissible as evidence of the death to which it relates without any further or other proof of such entry.[2] No certified copy purporting to be given in the Office is of any force or effect which is not sealed or stamped.[3]

d *Deaths on H.M. Ships and Aircraft*

Her Majesty may by Order in Council[4] provide for the keeping of records:

a of deaths occurring in any part of the world on board H.M. ships;

b of deaths occurring in any part of the world on H.M. aircraft, or any other aircraft not registered in the United Kingdom but for the time being employed for the purposes of H.M. forces;

c of the death outside the United Kingdom of any person, who, being a traveller on such an aircraft, is killed on the journey in consequence of an accident.[5]

An Order in Council may provide for the transmission of certified copies of any such records to the Registrar General for England and Wales.[6]

e *Deaths on Merchant Ships*

The Department of Trade and Industry may make regulations[7]

i requiring the master of any ship registered in the United Kingdom to make a return to a superintendent or proper officer for transmission to the Registrar General of Shipping and Seamen of any death, wherever occurring outside the United Kingdom, of any person employed in the ship; and

ii requiring the master of any ship not registered in the United Kingdom which calls at a port in the United Kingdom in the course of or at the end of a voyage to make a return to a superintendent for transmission to the Registrar General of Shipping and Seamen of any death of a citizen of the United Kingdom and Colonies which has occurred in the ship during the voyage.[8]

---

[1] Registration of Births, Deaths and Marriages (Scotland) Act 1854, s. 58.
[2] Births and Deaths Registration (Ireland) Act 1863, s. 5.
[3] *Ibid.*, s. 5.
[4] See Service Departments Registers Order 1959 (S.I. 1959 No. 406) as amended by S.I. 1963 No. 1624.
[5] Registration of Births, Deaths and Marriages (Special Provisions) Act 1957, s. 2.
[6] *Ibid.*, s. 2.
[7] The regulations which have been made are the Merchant Shipping (Return of Births and Deaths) Regulations 1972 (S.I. 1972 No. 1523).
[8] Merchant Shipping Act 1970, s. 72 (1).

Regulations under this section may require the Registrar General of Shipping and Seamen to send a certified copy of any return made thereunder to the Registrar General for England and Wales.[1]

The Registrar General must record the information contained in them in the "marine register", and may also record in that register such additional information as appears to him desirable for the purpose of ensuring the completeness and correctness' of the register.[2] The enactments relating to the registration of deaths in England have effect as if the "marine register" were a register of deaths or certified copies of entries in such a register and had been transmitted to the Registrar General in accordance with those enactments.[3]

f *Deaths on Civilian Aircraft*

The Minister for Trade and Industry may by regulations[4] provide for requiring such persons as may be specified in the regulations to keep records and make returns to him:

> *i* of deaths occurring in any part of the world in any aircraft registered in Great Britain and Northern Ireland; and
>
> *ii* of the death, outside the United Kingdom of any person who, being a traveller[5] on such an aircraft, is killed on the journey in consequence of an accident.[6]

The Regulations must also provide for the transmission of certified copies of the records to the Registrar General for England and Wales.[7]

The Registrar General must cause the certified copies to be filed and preserved in the "Air Register Book of Births and Deaths".[8]

The enactments relating to the registration of deaths in England have effect as if the Air Register Book of Births and Deaths were a certified copy or duplicate register transmitted to the Registrar General in accordance with those enactments.[9]

The Minister may by regulations provide:

> *i* for the keeping in his Department of a record[10] of persons reported to him as missing, being persons with respect to whom there are reasonable grounds for believing that they have died in consequence of an accident to an aircraft registered in Great Britain and Northern Ireland;
>
> *ii* for the rectification of such a record[11]; and

---

[1] Merchant Shipping Act 1970, s. 72 (2).
[2] *Ibid.*, s. 72 (3).
[3] *Ibid.*, s. 72 (3).
[4] No regulations have yet been made, but see Civil Aviation (Births, Deaths and Missing Persons) Regulations 1948 (S.I. 1848 No. 1411).
[5] Members of the crew are included: Civil Aviation (Births, Deaths, and Missing Persons) Regulations 1948 (S.I. 1948 No. 1411) reg. 2 (6).
[6] Civil Aviation Act 1949, s. 55 (1).
[7] *Ibid.*, s. 55 (4).
[8] *Ibid.*, s. 55 (5).
[9] *Ibid.*, s. 55 (8).
[10] Civil Aviation (Births, Deaths and Missing Persons) Regulations 1948 (S.I. 1948 No. 1411) regs. 5–7.
[11] *Ibid.*, reg. 9.

iii for the transmission of information as to the matters for the time being entered on the record to the Registrar General.[1]

g *Deaths in Other Countries*

Her Majesty may provide for the registration by consular officers or other officers in the service of Her Majesty's Government in the United Kingdom of the deaths of any persons dying in a protected state or foreign country, and certificates given by such officials are evidence of the death of the person to whom they relate.[2]

Entries in the public registers of certain countries concerning deaths are also admissible in evidence.[3]

2 Evidence by Person Present at Death or who Examined Body

This evidence may be given by, e.g., a person that the assured was drowned whilst bathing or a doctor who has carried out a *post mortem* on the insured's body.

3 Evidence that the Life Insured was Not Heard of for Considerable Time

Evidence may be given by persons, who were likely to have heard from the the life insured, that nothing has been heard of by them for a considerable time, and the Court may then presume that he has died.[4]

---

[1] Civil Aviation Act 1949, s. 55 (9).

[2] British Nationality Act 1948, s. 29 (1), (2). The regulations made under this section are the Registration of Births and Deaths (Consular Officers) Regulations 1948 (S.I. 1948 No. 2837) and the Registration of Births and Deaths (High Commissioners) Regulations 1964 (S.I. 1964 No. 1967) as amended by the Registration of Births and Deaths (High Commissioners) (Amendment) Regulations 1971 (S.I. 1971, No. 608).

[3] Oaths and Evidence (Overseas Authorities and Countries) Act 1963, s. 5 (1).

[4] See, e.g. *Chard* v. *Chard*, [1956] P. 259; *Watson* v. *England* (1844) 14 Sim. 29; *Re Watkins, Watkins* v. *Watkins*, [1953] 2 All E.R. 113; *Prudential Assurance Co.* v. *Edmonds* (1877), 2 App. Cas. 487; *Willyams* v. *Scottish Widows' Fund Life Assurance Society* (1888), 4 T.L.R. 489. See generally, G. D. Nokes, *An Introduction to Evidence*, 4th Edn., 1967, pp. 72–74.

16

PAYMENT

Three matters arise in connection with payment: (*a*) when payment must be made; (*b*) to whom payment must be made; and (*c*) the sum to be paid.

A When Payment Must be Made

A life insurance policy usually states that payment will be made on satisfactory proof of:

i the happening of the event or events on which the sum insured is to become payable;

ii the title of the claimant;

iii the correctness of the date of birth of the life insured.

B To Whom Payment Must be Made

Payment may be made to various persons, depending on the circumstances:

1 the insured;

2 his personal representatives;

3 his trustee in bankruptcy;

4 his legal assignee;

5 his equitable assignee;

6 a trustee under a policy in favour of the insured's wife, husband or children;

7 a third person;

8 the Court.

1 Insured

In the case of a person insuring his own life under an endowment policy payment may be made to the insured himself on his reaching the age stated in the policy.[1]

Again, where the insured has taken out a policy on the life of another person, e.g. a debtor, it is the insured who is the person entitled to the sum insured.[2]

---

[1] As to payment to an agent of the insured, see Ivamy, *General Principles of Insurance Law*, 2nd Edn., 1970, p. 387.

[2] *Freme* v. *Brade* (1858), 2 De G. & J. 582; *Bruce* v. *Garden* (1869), 5 Ch. App. 32.

2 Insured's Personal Representatives

On the death of the insured his personal representatives are entitled to payment if the sum has not already been paid under the policy.

3 Insured's Trustee in Bankruptcy

On the insured's being made bankrupt, all his estate including the right to receive money under an insurance policy vests in his trustee in bank-ruptcy.[1]

4 Legal Assignee

Where a legal assignment has been made under the Law of Property Act 1925, s. 136 (1),[2] it is effectual[3] in law to pass and transfer from the date of the notice of assignment given to the insurers the power to give a good discharge in respect of the sum assigned without the concurrence of the assignor.[4]

If the insurers have notice:

    a that the assignment is disputed by the assignor or any person claiming under him; or

    b of any other opposing or conflicting claims to the sum assigned;

they may, if they think fit, call upon the persons making the claim to the sum insured or pay the sum insured into Court in accordance with the Trustee Act 1925, s. 63.[5]

If a legal assignment has been made under the Policies of Assurance Act 1867,[6] the assignee has power to give a valid discharge to the insurers on payment of the sum insured.

> "A payment *bona fide* made in respect of any policy by any assurance company before the date on which such notice[7] shall have been received shall be as valid against the assignee giving such notice as if this Act had not been passed."

5 Equitable Assignee

In the case of an equitable assignment, the insurers should not pay the equitable assignee without the concurrence of the assignor or his personal representatives.[8]

6 Trustee Under Policy in Favour of Wife, Husband, or Children

By the Married Women's Property Act 1882, s. 11 a policy of insurance effected by any:

    a man on his own life and expressed to be for the benefit of his wife, or his children,[9] or of his wife and children or any of them; or

---

[1] *Jackson* v. *Forster* (1860), 1 E. & E. 470, Ex. Ch.

[2] As to legal assignments made under the Law of Property Act 1925, s. 136 (1), see p. 100, *ante.*

[3] Subject to equities having priority over the rights of the assignee: Law of Property Act 1925, s. 136 (1).

[4] *Ibid.*, s. 136 (1) (*c*).

[5] *Ibid.*, s. 136 (1) proviso. See further *Re Haycock's Policy* (1876), 1 Ch.D. 611.

[6] As to legal assignments made under the Policies of Assurance Act 1867, see p. 100, *ante.*

[7] I.e., notice of the assignment.

[8] *Spencer* v. *Clarke* (1878), 9 Ch.D. 137.

[9] *Re Browne's Policy, Browne* v. *Browne*, [1903] 1 Ch. 88, where the insured married twice and it was held that the second wife and her children benefited as well as the children of the first marriage.

b by any woman on her own life and expressed to be for the benefit of her husband[1] or of her children, or of her husband and children, or any of them,

creates a trust in favour of the objects therein named.

The moneys payable under the policy do not, so long as any object of the trust remains unperformed,[2] form part of the estate of the insured nor are they subject to his or her debts.[3]

If it is proved that the policy was effected and the premiums paid with intent to defraud the creditors of the insured, they are entitled to receive, out of the moneys payable under the policy, a sum equal to the premiums so paid.[4]

The insured may by the policy, or by any memorandum under his or her hand, appoint a trustee or trustees of the moneys payable under the policy, and may make provision for the appointment of a new trustee or new trustees, and for the investment of the moneys payable under the policy.[5]

In default of any such appointment of a trustee the policy, immediately on its being effected, vests in the insured and his or her legal personal representatives in trust for the purposes stated above.[6]

If at the time of the death of the insured or at any time afterwards there is no trustee or it is expedient to appoint a new trustee or new trustees, a trustee or trustees or a new trustee or trustees may be appointed by the Court.[7]

The receipt of a trustee or trustees duly appointed, or in default of any such appointment, or in default of notice to the insurers, the receipt of the legal personal representatives of the insured is a discharge for the sum secured by the policy, or for the value thereof, in whole or in part.[8]

7   Third Person

The policy may state that payment must be made to a third person. If the payment is made to him, he can give the insurers a good discharge.[9]

The third party is not entitled to sue on the policy in his own name, for he is a stranger to it.

Exceptional circumstances, however, may arise in which the insured is to be considered as a trustee for the third party. In this case the third party can enforce payment by the insurers.[10]

---

[1] *Griffiths* v. *Fleming*, [1909] 1 K.B. 805; *Re Ioakimidis' Policy Trusts, Ioakimidis* v. *Hartcup*, [1925] 1 Ch. 403.
[2] *Cleaver* v. *Mutual Reserve Fund Life Association*, [1892] 1 Q.B. 147, where the trust created by the policy in favour of the wife became incapable of being performed because she had murdered him and so could not take under it; *Re Collier*, [1930] 2 Ch. 37; *Cousins* v. *Sun Life Assurance Society*, [1933] Ch. 126.
[3] Married Women's Property Act 1882, s. 11.
[4] *Ibid.*
[5] *Ibid.*
[6] *Ibid.*
[7] *Ibid.*
[8] *Ibid.*
[9] *Re Englbach's Estate, Tibbetts* v. *Englebach*, [1924] 2 Ch. 348.
[10] See, e.g. *Re Webb, Barclays Bank, Ltd.* v. *Webb*, [1941] 1 All E.R. 321; *Re Gordon, Lloyds Bank and Parratt* v. *Lloyd and Gordon*, [1940] Ch. 851; *Re Independent Air Travel, Ltd.*, [1961] 1 Lloyd's Rep. 604; *Re Foster's Policy, Menneer* v. *Foster*, [1966] 1 All E.R. 432; cf. *Re Engelbach's Estate, Tibbetts* v. *Engelbach*; *Re Clay's Policy of Assurance, Clay* v. *Earnshaw*, [1937] 2 All E.R. 548; *Re Sinclair's Life Policy*, [1938] 3 All E.R. 124; *Re Foster, Hudson* v. *Foster*, [1938] 3 All E.R. 357.

8 The Court

General Statutory Provisions

By s. 3[1] of the Life Assurance Companies (Payment into Court) Act 1896:

> "Subject to rules of court any life assurance company[2] may pay into [the Supreme Court] . . . any moneys payable by them under a life policy[3] in respect of which, in the opinion of the board of directors, no sufficient discharge can otherwise be obtained."

Section 4 goes on to state that

> "The receipt or certificate[4] of the proper officer shall be a sufficient discharge for the moneys so paid into court, and such moneys shall, subject to rules of court, be dealt with according to the orders of [the Supreme Court] . . ."

Rules of Court

As far as the Supreme Court is concerned, the relevant order is R.S.C. Order 92, r. 1.

This order provides that where a company wishes to make payment into Court under the Act of 1896, it must file an affidavit made by its secretary or other authorized officer.[5]

This affidavit must set out:[6]

i a short description of the policy in question and a statement of the persons entitled thereunder with their names and addresses so far as known to the company;

ii a short statement of the notices received by the company claiming an interest or title to the money assured, or withdrawing any such claim, with the dates of receipt thereof and the names and addresses of the persons by whom they were given;

iii a statement that, in the opinion of the board of directors of the company, no sufficient discharge can be obtained otherwise than by payment into Court under the Act of 1896;

iv the submission by the company to pay into Court such further sum, if any, as the Court may direct and to pay any costs order by the court to be paid by the company;

v an undertaking by the company forthwith to send to the Accountant General any notice of claim received by the company after the making of the affidavit with a letter referring to the title of the affidavit; and

vi an address where the company may be served with any summons or order, or notice of any proceeding, relating to the money to be paid into Court.

The company must not deduct from the money payable by them under the policy, any costs of or incidental to the payment into Court.[7]

---

[1] As amended by the Administration of Justice Act 1965, s. 17 (1) and Schedule 1 and the Courts Act 1971, s. 56.

[2] This expression means "any corporation, company or society carrying on the business of life assurance, not being a society registered under the Acts relating to friendly societies": Life Assurance Companes (Payment into Court) Act 1896, s. 2.

[3] This expression "includes any policy not foreign to the business of life assurance": *ibid.*

[4] For a form of certificate, see *Atkin's Court Forms*, 2nd Edn., 1968, vol. 31, p. 131.

[5] R.S.C. Order 92, r. 1 (1).

[6] *Ibid.* For a suitable form of affidavit, see *Atkin's Court Forms*, 3rd Edn., 1968), vol. 22, p. 183.

[7] R.S.C. Order 92, r. 1 (2).

No payment must be made into Court under the Act of 1896 where any action to which the company is a party is pending in relation to the policy or moneys thereby assured except with the leave of the Court to be obtained by summons in the action.[1]

Unless the Court otherwise directs, a summons by which a claim with respect to money paid into Court under the Act of 1896 is made must not, except where the summons includes an application for payment of a further sum of costs by the company which made the payment, be served on that company, but must be served on every person who appears by the affidavit on which the payment into Court was made to be entitled to or interested in the money in Court or to have a claim upon it or who has given a notice of claim which has been sent to the Accountant General in accordance with the undertaking referred to above.[2]

Exercise of the Right

A life insurance company has been held to be entitled to make use of the statutory power to pay money into Court where the policy has been lost, for, on the facts, there was a reasonable opinion that no sufficient discharge could otherwise be obtained.[3]

A company, in seeking the protection of the Act, does so at the risk of having to pay any costs to which the other party may, in consequence, be put, if its own attitude has been unreasonable.[4]

In *Re Weniger's Policy*[5] an insurance company declined to pay money into Court under the Act of 1896 unless it received an indemnity in respect of its costs. The first mortgagees of the policy gave it an indemnity and the money was paid into Court. They now contended that they were entitled to be allowed the costs of the insurance company out of the fund in Court on the ground that they were mortgagee's costs and expenses. WARRINGTON, J., held that this contention failed, and that to allow the mortgagees their costs would be to introduce a most mischievous practice. His Lordship continued:[6]

> "The insurance company claimed that they could by this process get out of the funds the costs, which the rule said they were not to get, by merely insisting on having an indemnity. If anyone chose to give an indemnity to an insurance company, he must do so at his own risk, and not with the hope of getting the costs paid out of the funds in court. The insurance company's costs could not be allowed."

C   THE SUM TO BE PAID

The sum to be paid[7] will vary according to the terms of the policy. Sometimes only the sum insured will have to be paid by the insurers. The policy may, however, state that the insured is entitled to a bonus.

---

[1] R.S.C. Order 92, r. 1 (3).
[2] *Ibid.*, r. 1 (4).
[3] *Harrison v. Alliance Assurance Co., Ltd.*, [1903] 1 K.B. 184, C.A.
[4] *Ibid.*, at p. 188 (*per* COLLINS, M.R.).
[5] [1910] W.N. 278.
[6] *Ibid.*, at p. 278.
[7] As to when interest will be payable on the sum insured, see Ivany, *General Principles of Insurance Law*, 2nd Edn., 1970, pp. 389–390. As to where the sum insured is expressed in foreign currency but is payable in English currency, see *ibid.*, p. 388.

Thus, CHANNELL, J., observed in *Prudential Insurance Co.* v. *Inland Revenue Commissioners*:[1]

"A contract of life insurance is one by which persons entitle their executors to receive a sum of money for distribution among their family in the event of their death. The objection to insurance is that, if the insured lived beyond the average period of life upon which the premiums are based, he has made a bad bargain, and he would have done better if he had saved his money and invested it at compound interest. Consequently, in order to attract insurances, it is usual for the insurance companies to give benefits to persons who live beyond the average period of life. Most of them do this by way of bonuses after the policy has been in existence for a certain period, and the giving of such a bonus, of course, does not prevent the contract from being a contract of insurance."

In addition, the policy may state that the insured is entitled to a share of the profits which have been made by the insurance company. Whether or not the company can be compelled to pay a share of the profits will depend upon the terms of the policy and of the company's memorandum of association, or of any Act of Parliament by which the company was established.

Thus, in *Baerlein* v. *Dickson*[2] a "with profits" policy had been issued by the Standard Life Assurance Company, which had been incorporated by a private Act of Parliament called the Standard Life Assurance Company's Act 1832, which by s. 51 stated that:

"It shall be in the power of the ordinary directors to appoint dividends to be made among the partners in proportion to their respective shares of the company's stock from the profits and emoluments of the company; the ordinary directors being always entitled to lay aside and accumulate such part of the profits of the company as they shall judge proper and expedient, and to dispose of the same as may appear to them best for the advantage and security of the said company, provided always that it shall be in the power of the ordinary directors to make such regulations as they shall think fit for the purpose of allowing persons who shall effect policies or transact other species of business with the company to participate in the profits arising from the class of business in which they may be respectively concerned, and that to such extent and upon such terms and conditions as the ordinary directors may from time to time think proper for encouraging the business of the company."

WALTON, J., held that a holder of a policy could not compel the company to set aside any part of its profits for the purpose of being distributed among the holders of such policies and said:[3]

"I think, therefore, that all the plaintiff is entitled to is this: that he was one of those who were to take the benefit of any distribution if distribution there were, but whether there was to be a matter entirely within the discretion of the directors: and I need not say that if they thought that there was to be a distribution how much should be distributed amongst the policy-holders. I cannot come to any other conclusion than that that must be a matter within the discretion of the directors to be dealt with by them; but, of course, to be

---

[1] [1904] 2 K.B. 658 at p. 665.
[2] (1909), 25 T.L.R. 585.
[3] *Ibid.*, at p. 588. See further, *British Equitable Assurance Co., Ltd.* v. *Baily*, [1906] A.C. 35 H.L., where it was held that the policy-holder could not prevent the insurance company from altering its practice as to the distribution of profits, for there was no contract between him and the company that it would not do so. See the speech of Lord MACNAGHTEN, *ibid.*, at p. 38.

dealt with by them in the exercise of their duties and always in good faith; in other words, honestly".[1]

The policy may contain a provision concerning its surrender value, e.g., it may state after the payment of at least two years' premiums it will have a surrender value, and that if a cash surrender value is taken, there shall be added to it the cash value of any bonus attached to the policy at the time of surrender.

---

[1] His Lordship said ((1909), 25 T.L.R. at p. 588) that there was no suggestion in the present case that the directors had not been acting according to the best of their belief in doing what they thought right and proper in the exercise of their duties.

PART III

INDUSTRIAL ASSURANCE

17

INDUSTRIAL ASSURANCE

One type of life insurance business is that of industrial assurance business[1] which is carried on by industrial assurance companies,[2] and which is strictly controlled by the Industrial Assurance Acts 1923 to 1968.[3] The Industrial Assurance Commissioner is responsible for the administration of these Acts. There are provisions in them relating to (i) the powers and restrictions on the powers of industrial assurance companies;[4] (ii) accounts, returns, inspection, valuations and meetings;[5] (iii) rights of owners of policies;[6] (iv) collectors and premium receipt books;[7] and (v) disputes.[8]

DEFINITION OF "INDUSTRIAL ASSURANCE BUSINESS"

Section 1 (2) of the Industrial Assurance Act 1923 defines "industrial assurance business" as "the business of effecting assurances upon human life premiums in respect of which are received by means of collectors."[9]

But such business does not include assurances the premiums of which are payable at intervals of two months or more.[10]

---

[1] See *infra.*
[2] See p. 118, *post.*
[3] The Acts cited by this collective title are: the Industrial Assurance Act 1923, the Industrial Assurance (Juvenile Societies) Act 1926, the Industrial Assurance and Friendly Societies Act 1948, the Industrial Assurance and Friendly Societies Act 1948 (Amendment) Act 1958, and the Friendly and Industrial and Provident Societies Act 1968.
[4] See pp. 119–121, *post.*
[5] See pp. 122–124, *post.*
[6] See pp. 124–129, *post.*
[7] See pp. 129–130, *post.*
[8] See pp. 130–131, *post.*
[9] The word "collector" includes "every person, howsoever remunerated, who, by himself or by any deputy or substitute, makes house to house visits for the purpose of receiving premiums payable on policies of insurance on human life, or holds any interest in a collecting book and includes such a deputy or substitute as aforesaid": Industrial Assurance Act 1923, s. 45 (1).
[10] *Ibid.,* s. 1 (2) (*a*). Other cases, which are of not much importance, not amounting to industrial assurance business are:
  (i) assurances effected whether before or after June 7, 1923, by a company established before that date which at that date had no assurances outstanding the premiums on which were payable at intervals of less than one month so long as the company continues not to effect any such assurances;
  (ii) assurances effected before June 7, 1923, premiums in respect of which are payable at intervals of one month or upwards, and which have up to June 7, 1923 been treated as part of the business transacted by a branch other than the industrial branch of the company;
  (iii) assurances for £25 or upwards effected after June 7, 1923, premiums in respect of which are payable at intervals of one month or upwards, and which are treated as

117

Definition of "Industrial Assurance Company"

Section 1 (1A) of the Industrial Assurance Act 1923 states that an "industrial assurance company" means "a body corporate which carries on industrial assurance business".[1]

When an industrial assurance company carries on both industrial assurance business and other business, the Act of 1923, except as otherwise expressly provided, does not apply to any of the business of the company other than the industrial assurance business.[2]

When a company has ceased to effect industrial assurances, it is, so long as it continues liable on the assurances previously effected, deemed to carry on industrial assurance business.[3]

Administration of the Acts of 1923 to 1968

Industrial Assurance Commissioner

The person who is responsible for the administration of the Acts of 1923 to 1968 is the Industrial Assurance Commissioner.[4]

Reports

The Commissioner must in every year make a report of his proceedings under the Acts.[5] The report may contain any comments he may consider desirable to make on the valuations, annual returns, or other documents or matters brought before him under the Acts, and any correspondence in relation thereto.[6] The Commissioner must include in his report a report of his proceedings under the Insurance Companies Act 1958 or under Part II of the Companies Act 1967.[7] The report must be laid before Parliament.[8]

Returns

An industrial assurance company must, as respects each year[9] as respects which it is required by the Industrial Assurance Commissioner in the prescribed form[10] so to do, send to him within such period as may be prescribed a return giving prescribed particulars as to policies of industrial assurance issued by the company which were in force at the beginning of that year, in force at the end of that year, issued during that year or discontinued or converted to free policies.[11]

---

part of the business transacted by a branch other than the industrial branch of the company, in cases where the Industrial Assurance Commissioner certifies that the terms and conditions of such assurance are on the whole not less favourable to the assured than those imposed by the Act: *ibid.*, s. 1 (2).

[1] This sub-s. was added by the Companies Act 1967, ss. 97 and 99, and Sched. 6, Part II.
[2] Industrial Assurance Act 1923, s. 1 (1).
[3] *Ibid.*, s. 1 (3).
[4] Industrial Assurance Act 1923, s. 2 (1). Anything required or authorised to be done by, to or before the Commissioner may be done by, to or before such person as he may appoint for the purpose: *ibid.*, s. 2 (2).
[5] *Ibid.*, s. 44.
[6] *Ibid.*, s. 44.
[7] Insurance Companies Act 1958, s. 21 and Sched. 2, para. 8.
[8] Industrial Assurance Act 1923, s. 44.
[9] "Year" means the financial year of the company: Industrial Assurance and Friendly Societies Act 1948, s. 13 (4).
[10] The Regulations prescribing the forms are the Industrial Assurance (Companies Forms, etc.) Regulations 1968, S.I. 1968 No. 1571.
[11] Industrial Assurance and Friendly Societies Act 1948, s. 13 (1). If a company contravenes or fails to comply with any directions given by the Commissioner, it is guilty of an offence and liable on summary conviction to a fine not exceeding £200: Companies Act 1967, s. 86 (3).

A requirement may be made generally as to all industrial assurance companies or as to any class thereof, or as to a particular company.[1] The regulations may prescribe different particulars to be given in the case of different companies or classes thereof.[2]

The Commissioner, after considering any representations made by or on behalf of the company affected, may, if it appears to him that any return sent by the company is in any particular incomplete or incorrect, reject it or give such directions as he thinks necessary for its variation.[3]

Where any direction so given entails a consequential alteration of any account sent by a company to the Department of Trade and Industry, it is the duty of the company to make such consequential alteration of it.[4]

Regulations

The Commissioner may, subject to the approval of the Treasury, make regulations for prescribing anything which under the Acts is to be prescribed and for imposing fees and generally for carrying the Acts into effect. All regulations so made must forthwith be laid before both Houses of Parliament.[5] If an address is presented to Her Majesty by either House of Parliament within the next subsequent 20 days on which that House has sat next after the regulations are laid before it praying that the regulations be annulled, they are thenceforth void, but without prejudice to the validity of anything previously done thereunder or to the making of new regulations.[6]

Offences

An industrial assurance company is guilty of an offence if it contravenes or fails to comply with the provisions of the Industrial Assurance Acts 1923 to 1968 or contravenes or fails to comply with any directions given by the Commissioner.[7]

POWERS OF INDUSTRIAL ASSURANCE COMPANIES

The powers of an industrial assurance company are to be found in its memorandum and articles of association or in the provision of a special Act of Parliament relating to it.

Life of Parent or Grandparent

An industrial assurance company is entitled to insure the life of a person's parent or grandparent for a sum which (either taken alone or when added to any sums or sums being insured to be paid to that person on that death

---

[1] Industrial Assurance and Friendly Societies Act 1948, s. 13 (2).
[2] *Ibid.*, s. 13 (2).
[3] *Ibid.*, s. 13 (3), applying the provisions of the Industrial Assurance Act 1923, s. 16. If a company contravenes or fails to comply with any directions given by the Commissioner, it is guilty of an offence under the Companies Act 1967, s. 86 (1) (*b*), and is liable on summary conviction to a fine not exceeding £200: Companies Act 1967, s. 86 (3).
[4] *Ibid.*, s. 13 (3), applying the provisions of the Industrial Assurance Act 1923, s. 16.
[5] Industrial Assurance Act 1923, s. 43. The Regulations made under this section are the Industrial Assurance (Fees) Regulations 1923, S.R. & O. 1923, No. 580.
[6] Industrial Assurance Act 1923, s. 43. If the Session of Parliament ends before the 20 days have expired, the regulations must be laid before each House of Parliament at the commencement of the next Session.
[7] Companies Act 1967, s. 86.

under any other relevant insurance or insurances taken out by him) does not exceed £30.[1]

Where any such insurance has been effected, the company must not:[2]

a pay to any person any sum which exceeds £30 when taken alone; *or*

b pay to the person by whom the insurance was taken out any sum which exceeds £30, when added to any sum or sums paid to him, on the death[3] on which money was thereby insured to be paid, by virtue of or in connection with any other relevant insurance taken out by him; *or*

c if any payment has been made on that death by virtue of or in connection with that insurance to the person by whom it was taken out and has not been repaid, pay to him on that death, by virtue of or in connection with any other relevant insurance taken out by him, any sum which exceeds £30 when added to the amount so paid and not repaid, or when added to it and to any sum or sums paid to him on that death by virtue of or in connection with any other relevant insurance or insurances taken out by him.

For the purposes of the above provisions any sum insured to be paid or paid:

a by way of bonus other than a guaranteed bonus; or

b by way of repayment of premiums

must be excluded.[4]

Where under any relevant insurance money is for the time being insured to be paid to the person by whom the insurance was taken out on the death of a grandparent of his, any assignment or charge made by him of or on all or any of the rights in respect of the insurance conferred on him by the policy or by any of the provisions of the Industrial Assurance Acts 1923 to 1968 is void.[5]

Any agreement so made by him to assign or charge all or any of those rights is void except in the case of a charge of or agreement to charge for the purpose only of securing sums paid for keeping on foot or restoring the insurance.[6]

On his bankruptcy none of those rights pass to any trustee or other person acting on behalf of his creditors.[7]

Prohibition on Issue of Illegal Policies

Any industrial assurance company which issues industrial assurance policies which are illegal or are not within the legal powers of the company

---

[1] Industrial Assurance and Friendly Societies Act 1948, s. 2 as amended by the Industrial Assurance and Friendly Societies Act 1958, s. 1 (1). The term "relevant insurance" means an insurance effected by any industrial assurance company in exercise of the power conferred by s. 2 (1): *ibid.*, s. 2 (5).

[2] Industrial Assurance and Friendly Societies Act 1948, s. 2 (2). An industrial insurance company, if it contravenes the provisions of s. 2 (2), is guilty of an offence and is liable on summary conviction to a fine not exceeding £200: Companies Act 1967, s. 86 (1) (*a*), (3). But it is not guilty of an offence under s. 2 (2) of the Act of 1948 if it is proved that, owing to any false representation on the part of the proposer, the company did not know that the insurance was in contravention of s. 2 (2): Companies Act 1967, s. 86 (2).

[3] The provisions of the First Schedule to the Act have effect as to the production of certificates of death in connection with the making payments relevant for the purposes of s. 2 (2): *ibid.*, s. 2 (3).

[4] *Ibid.*, s. 2 (2).

[5] *Ibid.*, s. 2 (4).

[6] *Ibid.*, s. 2 (4).

[7] *Ibid.*, s. 2 (4).

must be held to have made default in complying with the provisions of the Acts.[1]

Where such policy has been issued, the company is, without prejudice to any other penalty, liable to pay to the owner of the policy a sum equal to the surrender value of the policy, or a sum equal to the amount of the premiums paid, unless it is proved that owing to any false representation on the part of the proposer, the company did not know that the policy was illegal or beyond its legal powers.[2]

Prohibition of Insuring Money to be Paid on Death of Child under Ten

An industrial assurance company must not insure so as to render any sum payable under the insurance on the death of any person at any time before he or she attains the age of ten years, otherwise than by repayment of the whole or any part of premiums paid.[3]

Prohibition of Charges on Industrial Assurance Fund

An industrial assurance company must not issue any debenture or debenture stock, or raise any loan, charged or purporting to be charged on the assets of the company in which the industrial assurance fund is invested. Any such charge is void.[4]

Memorandum and Articles of Association

The provisions of the Act of 1923 have effect notwithstanding anything in the memorandum or articles of association or rules or special Act of any industrial assurance company.[5]

Restriction on Employment of Persons to Procure New Business

An industrial assurance company must not employ any person not being in its regular employment[6] to procure or endeavour to procure any person to enter into a contract of industrial assurance.[7]

---

[1] Industrial Assurance Act 1923, s. 5 (1). The company is liable on summary conviction to a fine not exceeding £200: Companies Act 1967, s. 86 (3).

[2] *Ibid.*, s. 5 (1).

[3] Industrial and Friendly Societies Act 1948, s. 6 (1). This sub-section applies only in the case of a person who at the time of the proposal is ordinarily resident in Great Britain: *ibid.*, s. 6 (1) proviso. It does not apply to a sum payable to another person who has an interest in the life of the person on whose death the sum is payable: *ibid.*, s. 6 (1) proviso. But there is power under s. 7 to extend s. 6 to persons not resident in Great Britain, and the section has been extended to the Isle of Man: Industrial Assurance and Friendly Societies Act 1948 (Northern Ireland) Order 1949, S.I. 1949 No. 598. Any industrial assurance company which contraves s. 6 (1) is guilty of an offence under the Industrial Assurance Act 1923: Industrial and Friendly Societies Act 1948, s. 16 (2). Such an offence is punishable on summary conviction by a fine not exceeding £200: Companies Act 1967, s. 86 (1) (*a*), (3).

[4] Industrial Assurance Act 1923, s. 13. This section does not apply to a temporary bank overdraft: *ibid.* If a company contravenes this section, it is guilty of an offence under the Companies Act, s. 86 (1) (*a*), 1967, and is liable on summary conviction to a fine not exceeding £200: Companies Act 1967, s. 86 (3).

[5] Industrial Assurance Act 1923, s. 14.

[6] "Regular employment" includes regular part-time as well as regular whole-time employment: *ibid.*, s. 34 (2).

[7] *Ibid.*, s. 34 (1). If a company contravenes this section, it is guilty of an offence under the Companies Act 1967 and is liable on summary conviction to a fine not exceeding £200: Companies Act 1967, s. 86 (3). A person employed by an industrial assurance company is under the same restriction as the company: Industrial Assurance Act 1923, s. 34 (1).

ACCOUNTS, RETURNS, INSPECTION, VALUATION AND MEETINGS

Annual Accounts and Returns

The Commissioner, after considering any representations made by or on behalf of the company affected, may, if it appears to him that any account, return or balance sheet sent by an industrial assurance company in pursuance of the Insurance Companies Act 1958, is in any particular incomplete or incorrect or does not comply with the requirements of that Act, reject the account, return or balance sheet or give such directions as he thinks fit necessary for its variation.[1]

Where any direction so given entails a consequential alteration of any account, return or balance sheet sent by an industrial assurance company to the Department of Trade and Industry, it is the duty of the company to make such consequential alteration of it.[2]

Inspection

If, in the case of any industrial assurance company, in the opinion of the Commissioner, there is reasonable cause to believe that an offence against the Industrial Assurance Act 1923 or the Insurance Companies Act 1958[3] has been or is likely to be committed, the Commissioner or any inspector appointed by him for the purpose has power to examine into and report on the affairs of the company.[4]

On himself holding such an inspection or on receiving the report of an inspector so appointed the Commissioner may issue such directions and take such steps as he considers necessary or proper to deal with the situation disclosed therein, and in particular may present a petition to the Court for the winding up of the company.[5]

The Commissioner may, if he considers it just, direct that all or any of the expenses of and incidental or preliminary to an inspection shall be defrayed out of the funds of the company, or by the officers or former officers or members or former members of the board of directors of the company in such proportions as the Commissioner directs.[6]

Valuations

Every valuation must be made by an actuary as defined by the Insurance Companies Act 1958, s. 33, as modified by Part II of the Second Schedule to that Act.[7]

---

[1] Industrial Assurance Act 1923, s. 16 (1).

[2] *Ibid.*, s. 16 (2). If the company contravenes or fails to comply with the directions given by the Commissioner, it is guilty of an offence under the Companies Act 1967, s. 86 (1) (*b*), and is liable on summary conviction to a fine not exceeding £200: Companies Act 1967, s. 86 (3).

[3] For the provisions of this Act, see *Ivamy, General Principles of Insurance Law*, 2nd Edn., 1970, pp. 29–58.

[4] Industrial Assurance Act 1923, s. 17 (1). An inspection may be held in public: *Hearts of Oak Assurance Co., Ltd.* v. *A.-G.*, [1932] A.C. 392.

[5] *Ibid.*, s. 17 (2).

[6] *Ibid.*, s. 17 (3). Sums directed by the Commissioner to be so paid are recoverable by him summarily as a civil debt: *ibid.* Any company or person directed to pay any part of such expenses may, with the leave of the Court, appeal against the direction to the High Court: *ibid.* See further, R.S.C. Order 93, r. 11.

[7] Industrial Assurance Act 1923, s. 18 (1) (*a*). This sub-s. was substituted by the Insurance Companies Act 1958, s. 36 (1) and Sched. 5, Part I. For the provisions of s. 33 of the Act of 1958, as modified by Part II of the Second Schedule, see Ivamy, *General Principles of*

Where the balance sheet of an industrial assurance company includes amongst its assets any sums representing expenses of organisation or extension, or the purchase of business or goodwill, and the amount of the assets exclusive of such sums (after deducting debts due by the company other than debentures and loans) is less than the amount of the industrial assurance fund,[1] the amount of the industrial assurance fund shown in the valuation balance sheet must be reduced[2] by the amount of the deficiency.[3]

Where debentures have been issued or loans raised which are charged on any of the assets of the company in which the industrial assurance fund is invested, a note giving the particulars of the charge and stating that the result shown by the valuation is subject to the liability under the charge must be inserted in the valuation balance sheet.[4]

The Commissioner, if satisfied on any valuation that any of the above provisions have not been complied with, or that the industrial assurance fund as stated in the valuation balance sheet is greater than the value of the assets available for the liabilities of that fund[5], may reject the valuation, and may direct the company to make such alteration therein as may be necessary to secure compliance with those provisions.[6]

The Commissioner may direct any industrial assurance company to furnish to him in addition to such information as it is required to furnish under the Insurance Companies Act 1958, such explanations as he may consider necessary in order to satisfy himself whether the valuation complies with the above provisions.[7]

If a valuation discloses a deficiency, the Commissioner may, if after investigation he is satisfied that the company should cease to carry on industrial assurance business, present a petition to the Court for the winding up of the company.[8]

General Meetings

At least one general meeting of every industrial assurance company must be held in every year.[9]

Except where the day, hour and place of an annual or other periodical meeting is fixed by the rules, notice of every general meeting shall either be given by the company to the members by advertisement to be published at least twice in two or more of the newspapers in general circulation in every

---

Insurance Law, 2nd Edn., 1970, pp. 537–538. For the prescribed qualifications, see Assurance Companies Rules, 1950, S.I. 1950, No. 1544, r. 13.

[1] Or of the several assurance and insurance funds as shown in that balance sheet.

[2] Industrial Assurance Act 1923, s. 18 (1) (*d*).

[3] Or by a sum bearing such proportion to that deficiency as the amount of the industrial assurance fund shown in the first-mentioned balance sheet bears to the aggregate amount of all the assurance and insurance funds so shown: *ibid.*, s. 18 (1) (*d*).

[4] *Ibid.*, s. 18 (1) (*e*).

[5] Due regard being had to the other liabilities of the company: *ibid.*, s. 18 (1) (*f*).

[6] *Ibid.*, s. 18 (1) (*f*). The company may appeal to the High Court against any decision of the Commissioner under this paragraph: *ibid.*

[7] *Ibid.*, s. 18 (1) (*g*).

[8] *Ibid.*, s. 18 (3).

[9] *Ibid.*, s. 19 (1). If a company contravenes s. 19, it is guilty of an offence under the Companies Act 1967, s. 86 (1) (*a*), and is liable on summary conviction to a fine not exceeding £200: Companies Act 1967, s. 86 (3).

county where the company carries on business, or be served on every member.[1]

The notice must specify the day, hour and place, and the objects of the meeting, and, in case any amendment of a rule[2] is intended to be proposed, must contain a copy of the amendment.[3]

The company must publish the last of the advertisements or serve the notice at least fourteen days before the day appointed for the meeting. During those fourteen days it must keep a copy of the notice in legible characters affixed in some conspicuous place in or outside every office at which the business of the company is carried on.[4]

RIGHTS OF OWNERS OF POLICIES[5]

Proposal Forms

In general, every proposal for an industrial assurance policy must contain a declaration by the person whose life is to be assured that the policy is to be taken out by him, and that the premiums are to be paid by him.[6]

This, however, is not necessary in the following three cases:[7]

 a where the policy is taken out on the life and on behalf of a child under the age of sixteen;

 b where the policy assures a payment of money on the death of a parent or grandparent and is effected in exercise of the power conferred by the Industrial Assurance and Friendly Societies Act 1948, s. 2 (1);[8]

 c where the person whose life is to be assured under the policy is a person in whom the proposer has an insurable interest.

Where the person whose life is to be assured under the policy is a person in whom the proposer has an insurable interest, the proposal must contain a statement of the nature of that interest.[9]

An industrial assurance company or any collector or agent of such a company must not issue a proposal form or accept a proposal which does not comply with the foregoing provisions.[10]

If the proposal contains a statement that the person whose life is proposed to be assured is not at the time of making the proposal a person on whose life another policy has been issued by the company, and a policy is issued in pursuance of the proposal, the company is liable under the policy, notwithstanding that the statement is not true, and the truth of the statement is made a condition of the policy.[11]

---

[1] Industrial Assurance Act 1923, s. 19 (2). The notice must be in writing, and either delivered or sent by post to the member: *ibid.*, s. 41.
[2] The expression "rules" means the memorandum and articles of association: *ibid.*, s. 45 (1).
[3] *Ibid.*, s. 19 (3).
[4] *Ibid.*, s. 19 (4).
[5] The expression "owner" in relation to any policy means "the person who is for the time being the person entitled to receive the sums payable under the policy on maturity" and in the case of an illegal policy or a policy not within the legal powers of the company which issued it means "the person who would be so entitled were the policy a legal policy or a policy within such powers": Industrial Assurance Act 1923, s. 45 (1).
[6] *Ibid.*, s. 20 (1).
[7] *Ibid.*, s. 20 (1).
[8] See pp. 119–120, *ante.*
[9] *Ibid*, s. 20 (1).
[10] *Ibid.*, s. 20 (2).
[11] *Ibid.*, s. 20 (3).

If a proposal form for an industrial assurance policy is filled in wholly or partly by a person employed by the company, the company is not, except where a fraudulent statement in some material particular has been made by the proposer, entitled to question the validity of the policy founded on the proposal on the ground of any misstatement contained in the proposal form.[1]

If the proposal form contains a misstatement as to the age of the person whose life is proposed to be assured, the company may so adjust the terms of the policy, or of any policy which may be issued in substitution or in lieu thereof, as to make them correspond with the terms which would have been applicable if the correct age of the person had been originally inserted in the policy.[2]

Where, except for the above provisions, the validity of a policy could have been questioned on the ground of any misstatement in the proposal form relating to the state of health of the person upon whose life the assurance is to be taken out at the date of the proposal, nothing prevents such a question being raised if it is raised within two years from the date of the issue of the policy founded on the proposal.[3]

Nothing in any term or condition of an industrial assurance policy issued after June 30, 1948 or in the law relating to insurance operates to except the company from liability under such a policy, or to reduce its liability under such a policy on the ground of any matter relating to the state of health of the person upon whose life the assurance is taken out, other than the ground of the prosposer's having, when making the proposal or thereafter and before the making of the contract, either:

   a made an untrue statement of his knowledge and belief as regards that matter; or

   b failed to disclose to the company something known or believed by him as regards that matter.[4]

Return of Policies and Premium Receipt Books after Inspection

If at any time an industrial assurance company, or any person employed by it, takes possession of a policy or premium receipt book or other document issued in connection with a policy, a receipt must be given, and the policy, book or document must be returned to the owner of the policy within 21 days, unless the policy has been terminated by reason of satisfaction of all claims capable of arising thereunder.[5]

Where, however, possession is taken of a policy, book or document for the purpose of legal proceedings to be taken by the company which issued the policy against a collector, the company can retain the policy, book or document so long as may be necessary for the purpose of those proceedings.[6]

---

[1] Industrial Assurance Act 1923, s. 20 (4).
[2] *Ibid.*, s. 20 (4) proviso (*a*).
[3] *Ibid.*, s. 20 (4) proviso (*b*). In relation to a policy issued after June 30, 1948, s. 20 (4) of the Act of 1923 does not apply to a statement concerning the health of the person upon whose life the assurance is taken out: Industrial Assurance and Friendly Societies Act 1948, s. 9 (2).
[4] Industrial Assurance and Friendly Societies Act 1948, s. 9 (1).
[5] Industrial Assurance Act 1923, s. 22.
[6] *Ibid.*, s. 22.

But in that case, if the policy, book or document is retained for more than 21 days, the company must supply to the owner of the policy a copy of it certified by the company to be a true copy.[1]

Notice before Forfeiture

A forfeiture cannot be incurred by any person assured by an industrial assurance company by reason of any default in paying any premium until after:

    a notice stating the amount due from him, and informing him that in case of default of payment by him within 28 days and at a place to be specified in the notice his interest or benefit will be forfeited, has been served[2] upon him by or on behalf of the company; and

    b default has been made by him in paying any premium in accordance with that notice.[3]

Provisions as to Forfeited Policies

Where notice of the forfeiture of a policy of industrial assurance by reason of default in the payment of any premium due under it has been served[4] on the owner of the policy, then if the policy:

    a is a policy for the whole term of life or for a term of 50 years or upwards, the person whose life is assured under which is a person who is at the time of such default over 15 years of age, and upon which not less than 5 years' premiums have been paid; or

    b is a policy for a term of 25 years or upwards, but less than 50 years, upon which not less than 5 years' premiums have been paid; or

    c is a policy for a term of less than 25 years upon which not less than 3 years' premiums have been paid;

the owner of the policy on making an application to the company within one year from the date of the service of the notice is entitled:

    a to a free paid-up policy for such amount as is stated in the Fourth Schedule[5] payable upon the happening of the contingency upon the happening of which the amount assured under the original policy would have been payable or of any other contingency not less favourable to the owner of the policy; or

    b if the owner of the policy is permanently resident or submits satisfactory proof of his intention to make his permanent residence outside Great Britain, the Isle of Man and the Channel Islands, or if the person whose life is assured has disappeared and his existence is in doubt, to the surrender value of the forfeited policy.[6]

---

[1] Industrial Assurance Act 1923, s. 22.
[2] The notice must be in writing and either delivered or sent by post to him or left at his last known place of abode: *ibid.*, s. 41.
[3] *Ibid.*, s. 23 (1).
[4] The notice must be in writing and either delivered or sent by post to him or left at his last known place of abode: *ibid.*, s. 41.
[5] This states that "the amount of a free paid-up policy is to be a sum bearing the same proportion to 75 per cent. of the value of the policy as the sum of £1 bears to the value of the reversion in the sum of £1 according to the contingency upon which the sum assured under the original policy was payable".
[6] Industrial Assurance Act 1923, s. 24 (1).

The amount of a free paid-up policy must be ascertained at the date when the premium following the last premium paid became due.[1] But the amount of the free paid-up policy must not exceed the difference between the amount of the forfeited policy (inclusive of any bonus added thereto) and the amount which would be assured by a corresponding policy at the same premium effected on the life of the same person according to the age of that person at his birthday next following the date of forfeiture.[2]

In every premium receipt book there must be printed a notice stating that in the event of forfeiture of any policy of industrial assurance by reason of default in the payment of premiums under it, the owner of the policy, if the policy has been in force for one of the periods stated above, is entitled to a free paid-up policy or to the surrender value of his policy, as the case may be, and that upon application to the head office of the company information as to the amount of such free paid-up policy or surrender value will be supplied.[3] It is the duty of the company to supply such information.[4]

Where the conditions of a policy are such as would confer on the owner of the policy in case of forfeiture rights more favourable to him than those conferred above, he is entitled to claim under those conditions instead if he so desires.[5]

Substitution of Policies

Where the owner of an industrial assurance policy agrees to accept a new policy in substitution for it, the company must pay him the surrender value of the old policy and must issue to him a free paid-up policy of equivalent value unless the value of the substituted policy, calculated in accordance with the rules set out in the Fourth Schedule,[6] at the date of the substitution is equal to or exceeds such surrender value.[7]

In any such case the company must furnish him with the new policy and new premium receipt book, a statement setting forth his rights stated above, and containing an account certified by the secretary of the company or other officer appointed for the purpose, showing the surrender value of the old policy and the value of the new policy.[8]

Where a substituted policy is issued and its value is equal to or exceeds the surrender value of the old policy, then, for the purpose of determining whether the owner is entitled to a free paid-up policy or surrender value, the substituted policy is deemed to have been issued at the date at which the old policy was issued, and premiums are deemed to have been paid on the substituted policy in respect of the period between that date and the date at which the substituted policy was actually issued.[9]

Transfer from One Company to Another

A person assured with an industrial assurance company, except in the case of an amalgamation or transfer of business under the Insurance Companies

---

[1] Industrial Assurance Act 1923, s. 24 (2).
[2] *Ibid.*, s. 24 (2).
[3] *Ibid.*, s. 24 (3).
[4] *Ibid.*, s. 24 (3).
[5] *Ibid.*, s. 24 (4).
[6] See p. 345. *post.*
[7] Industrial Assurance Act 1923, s. 25 (1).
[8] *Ibid.*, s. 25 (2).
[9] *Ibid.*, s. 25 (3).

Act, 1958,[1] must not be transferred from that company so as to be assured with any other company without his written consent, and in the case of a minor, without the consent of his parent or other guardian.[2]

Such consent must be in the prescribed form[3] and must have annexed to it a document in the prescribed form[4] to be furnished by the company to which the transfer is to be made setting out the terms of and rights under the existing policy, and the terms of and rights under the policy to which the assured will become entitled on transfer and the consideration (if any) which has been or is to be paid for the transfer and the person to whom such consideration has been or will be paid.[5]

The company to which the assured is sought to be transferred must furnish to the person by whom the consent is signed a copy of such consent and the document annexed to it.[6] It must also, within seven days from the date when such consent is signed, give to the company from which the assured is sought to be transferred notice[7] of the proposed transfer containing full particulars of the name and address of the assured and the number of his policy together with such consent and the document annexed to it.[8]

As from the date of the notice, the company from which the person is sought to be transferred ceases to be under any liability with respect to the policy in question, and is not required to serve any notice of forfeiture of the policy in accordance with the foregoing provisions of the Act.[9]

Payment of Claims

Where a claim arises under a policy of industrial assurance, no deduction must be made on account of any arrears of premium due under any other policy.[10]

Value of Policies

The value of a policy[11] must be calculated in accordance with the rules set out in the Fourth Schedule.[12]

The surrender value of a policy is an amount equal to 75 per cent. of the value of the policy so calculated.[13]

The rules set out in the Fourth Schedule state that the value of the policy is to be the difference between the present value of the reversion in the sum assured according to the contingency upon which it is to be payable, including any bonus added thereto, and the present value of the future net premiums.

---

[1] See Ivamy, *General Principles of Insurance Law*, 2nd Edn., 1970, pp. 47–48.

[2] Industrial Assurance Act 1923, s. 26 (1). Any company and any collector or other officer of any company concerned in such a transfer is deemed to have contravened the provisions of the Act if the provisions of this section are not complied with: *ibid.*, s. 26 (1).

[3] See Industrial Assurance (Individual Transfer) Regulations 1928, S.R. & O. 1928 No. 580.

[4] *Ibid.*

[5] Industrial Assurance Act 1923, s. 26 (2).

[6] *Ibid.*, s. 26 (3).

[7] The notice must be in writing and either delivered or sent by post: *ibid.*, s. 41.

[8] *Ibid.*, s. 26 (3).

[9] *Ibid.*, s. 26 (4). As to the provisions concerning notice of forfeiture, see p. 126, *ante.*

[10] Industrial Assurance Act 1923, s. 27.

[11] Including an illegal policy and a policy beyond the legal powers of an industrial assurance company: *ibid.*, s. 29 (1).

[12] *Ibid.*, s. 29 (1).

[13] *Ibid.*, s. 29 (2).

In general, the net premium is to be such premium as according to the assumed rate of interest and rate of mortality and the age of the person whose life is assured at his birthday next following the date of the policy is sufficient to provide for the risk incurred by the company in issuing the policy, exclusive of any addition thereto for office expenses and other charges.

But in the case of a policy other than a policy for the whole term of life issued before the person whose life is assured attained the age of ten years, the date of the policy may be assumed to be one year after the actual date, and, if it is so assumed, the term of the policy may be assumed to be one year less than the actual term.

In the case of a policy for the whole term of life issued before the person whose life is assured attained the age of ten years, no account shall be taken of any period for which the policy was in force before the anniversary of the date of the issue of the policy next preceding the date on which the age of eleven years was attained.

In the case of a substituted policy, the net premium must be calculated with reference to such sum as, according to the practice of the company for the time being, would have been assured by the premiums payable if the person upon whose life the substituted policy is issued had not been assured with the company before the issue of that policy.

Interest is to be assumed at the rate of 4 per cent. per annum.

The rate of mortality is to be assumed according to the table contained in the Sixth column of Table G in the Supplement to the 65th Annual Report of the Registrar-General.

The age of the person whose life is assured must be obtained by adding to the age attained by him at his birthday next after the date of the issue of the policy, the duration of the policy in completed years at the date as at which the value of the policy is required to be ascertained.

In the case of a policy issued for a term other than the whole term of life, the remaining term at the date at which the value of the policy is required to be ascertained must be obtained by deducting from the original term of the policy the duration of the policy in completed years at that date.

COLLECTORS AND PREMIUM RECEIPT BOOKS

Collectors

A collector of an industrial assurance company must not be a member of its board of directors or hold any other office in the company except that of superintending collectors within a specified area.[1]

He must not be present at any meeting of the company.[2]

No collector must knowingly assist in effecting a policy of industrial assurance which is illegal or not within the legal powers of the company.[3]

---

[1] Industrial Assurance Act 1923, s. 33 (1). The penalty on summary conviction is a fine not exceeding £50: *ibid.*, s. 39 (3).

[2] *Ibid.*, s. 33 (2). The penalty on summary conviction is a fine not exceeding £50: *ibid.*, s. 39 (3).

[3] *Ibid.*, s. 5 (2). The penalty on summary conviction is a fine not exceeding £50: *ibid.*, s. 39 (3).

Premium Receipt Books

An industrial assurance company must provide premium receipt books for use in respect of industrial assurance policies issued by the company, and must cause a receipt for each payment in respect of such a policy or of two or more such policies to be entered in such a book.[1]

Regulations[2] may be made by the Industrial Assurance Commissioner with respect to the form of books to be provided and to their use and the insertion of receipts in them.[3] The regulations may provide for prohibiting or restricting in any prescribed circumstances the use of a single premium receipt book for payments in respect of two or more policies.[4]

If any person wilfully makes, orders, or allows to be made any entry or erasure in, or omission from a premium receipt book, with intent to falsify that book or to evade any of the provisions of the Industrial Assurance Act 1923, he is liable on summary conviction to imprisonment for a term not exceeding 3 months or to a fine not exceeding £50 or both.[5]

An industrial assurance company must cause to be set out in every premium receipt book the matters specified in the Third Schedule to the Industrial Assurance and Friendly Societies Act 1948 relating to the provisions mentioned in that Schedule of the Industrial Assurance Act 1923, of the Act of 1948 and of regulations made for the purpose of s. 8 of the Act of 1948.[6]

The provisions[7] referred to concern provisions as to proposals for policies, return of policies and premium receipt books after inspection, notice before forfeiture, provisions as to forfeited policies, payment of claims, disputes, notices, insurances on life of parent or grandparent, premium receipt books, and restriction on liability on policies on ground of health.

DISPUTES

In all disputes between an industrial assurance company and:

 a any person assured; or

 b any person claiming through a person assured, or under or in respect of any policy, or under the Industrial Assurance Act 1923,

that person may, notwithstanding any provisions of the rules of the company to the contrary, apply to the County Court or to a Court of summary jurisdiction for the place where that person resides.[8] The Court may[9] settle the

---

[1] Industrial Assurance and Friendly Societies Act 1948, s. 8 (1).
[2] The Regulations made by the Commissioner are subject to the approval of the Treasury signified by statutory instrument which is subject to annulment in pursuance of a resolution of either House of Parliament: *ibid.*, s. 8 (2).
[3] *Ibid.*, s. 8 (2). The Regulations at present in force are the Industrial Assurance (Premium Receipt Books) Regulations 1948 (S.I. 1948 No. 2770), as amended by S.I. 1961 No. 597.
[4] Industrial Assurance and Friendly Societies Act 1948, s. 8 (2).
[5] Industrial Assurance Act 1923, s. 40.
[6] Industrial Assurance and Friendly Societies Act 1948, s. 12. If a company contravenes this section, it is guilty of an offence under the Companies Act 1967, s. 86 (1) (*a*), and is liable on summary conviction to a fine not exceeding £200: Companies Act 1967, s. 86 (3).
[7] The provisions need not be set out in full, for the Industrial Assurance Commissioner may consent to the substitution of a statement which in his opinion sufficiently sets forth their effect: Industrial Assurance and Friendly Societies Act 1948, Sched. 3.
[8] Industrial Assurance Act 1923, s. 32 (1).
[9] But in the case of a Court of summary jurisdiction only if the amount of the claim does not exceed £25 and not less than 14 days' notice of the application has been given to the company: *ibid.*, s. 32 (1).

dispute according to the provisions of the Friendly Societies Act 1896.[1] Where a dispute is settled by a Court of summary jurisdiction, the Court may make such order as to costs as it considers fair and reasonable.[2]

Any such dispute may be referred to the Industrial Assurance Commissioner:

    a by such industrial assurance company, any person assured or any person claiming through him, if the amount of the claim does not exceed £50 and the legality of the policy is not questioned, and fraud or misrepresentation is not alleged; and

    b in any case, by both parties, without restriction as to the amount of claim or the nature of the question to be decided.[3]

In any case where a doubt arises as to the continued existence of the person on whose life a policy of industrial assurance was taken out, the Commissioner may, on the application of the owner of the policy or of the company which issued the policy, award that the company shall pay to the owner of the policy the surrender value of it at the time of the award.[4] The award is a discharge for all claims by or against the company in connection with the policy.[5]

---

[1] Industrial Insurance Act 1923, s. 32 (1).
[2] *Ibid.*, s. 32 (1).
[3] *Ibid.*, s. 33 (1). Where a dispute is so referred, the Commissioner may deal with it as if it were a dispute referred to him under the provisions of the Friendly Societies Act 1896, s. 68: *ibid.*, s. 32 (1).
[4] *Ibid.*, s. 32 (2).
[5] *Ibid.*, s. 32 (2).

PART IV

PROPERTY INSURANCE

18

INTRODUCTION

Property insurance is a contract of indemnity. It differs from liability insurance, which is also a contract of indemnity, in that an indemnification against legal liability incurred by the insured is a comparatively simple matter, the only questions arising in the ordinary course being the existence of liability and its amount. An indemnification against loss of property must necessarily further take into consideration the nature and extent of the insured's interest in the property insured, and the circumstances, which, in a particular case, affect the true measure of indemnity.

WHAT CONSTITUTES A LOSS

An insurance upon property contemplates the loss of the property insured, or, where damage is covered, damage to it, caused by a peril insured against. So far as damage is concerned, to give rise to a claim, there must be actual physical damage to the property.[1] There is a loss whenever the property is destroyed;[2] but physical destruction is not essential.

In many cases as e.g., in the case of theft insurance or fidelity insurance, no question of physical destruction generally arises; and to constitute a loss, it is sufficient to show that the insured has been deprived of his property by a peril insured against.[3] The loss contemplated is, however, the loss of the property insured, and not the loss of the advantages which its continued possession might have brought to the insured.[4] Hence, the insurance does not cover consequential loss, e.g., loss of market.[5] To cover consequential loss, a special insurance must be effected.[6]

---

[1] *Moore* v. *Evans*, [1918] A.C. 185, *per* Lord ATKINSON, at p. 191.

[2] It is immaterial that the property exists in specie if it exists only in the form of a nuisance: *Cologan* v. *London Assurance Co.* (1816), 5 M. & S. 447 (marine insurance), *per* Lord ELLENBOROUGH, C.J., at p. 455.

[3] *Century Bank of City of New York* v. *Mountain* (1914), 112 L.T. 484, C.A. (insurance of securities).

[4] *Ibid.*, *per* Lord COZENS-HARDY, M.R., at p. 486: "It is a claim really, when you look at it, amounting to this, that under the policy the bank are entitled to claim an indemnity against all the banking losses which may occur to them in respect of any contracts which they may have been induced to enter into by the fraud of a third person. I cannot so read the policy. Reading it shortly, and only the material parts of it, it seems to me to contemplate only, a loss or abstraction of physical things taken away from the bank or from their branches . . . I think that the policy contemplates certain known or specific property being taken away from the plaintiffs by fraud."

[5] *Mitsui* v. *Mumford*, [1915] 2 K.B. 27; *Campbell and Phillips, Ltd.* v. *Denman* (1915), 21 Com. Cas. 357; *Moore* v. *Evans*, [1918] A.C. 185; *Molinos de Arroz* v. *Mumford* (1900), 16 T.L.R. 469.

[6] For consequential loss insurance, see generally Ivamy, *Fire and Motor Insurance*, 2nd Edn., 1973, pp. 74–78.

The doctrine of constructive total loss[1] is peculiar to marine insurance[2] and does not extend to non-marine insurance.[3]

REINSTATEMENT

The policy may contain a reinstatement clause under which the insurers may, instead of paying the insured the amount of the loss, make good the loss by reinstatement.[4]

If they do decide to exercise the option of reinstatement, they must see that the property is replaced by property of similar nature and quality.

In *Braithwaite* v. *Employers' Liability Assurance Corporation, Ltd.* (*James D. Day, Ltd., Third Parties*)[5] a burglary policy stated that the insurance company "may at their option reinstate or replace the property lost or damaged or any part thereof instead of paying the amount of the loss or damage". A diamond and sapphire floral spray brooch was stolen from the insured. Instead of paying £750, which was the sum insured under the policy, the insurance company replaced the brooch since it was cheaper to do so. For this purpose the company instructed a firm of jewellers to make a replica of the original brooch. When it was delivered to the insured, she refused to accept it, and claimed the sum insured. She said in giving evidence that the new brooch was heavy in weight, and in appearance "like an elephant's foot". It looked clumsy. When she put it on to a dress, it dragged down the material to which it was pinned. The original brooch was in the shape of a spray of the lily of the valley. The stalks of the replica were not in alignment with the stems and leaves, and the leaves were wider and thicker than on the old brooch. Further, an expert witness said that the old brooch was of superior workmanship. The leaves had a deeper build and were of livelier appearance. There was more movement in the original brooch and more life.

MacKenna, J., held that the replica was inferior to the old brooch, and had been rightly rejected by the insured. He did not think that she would have taken so strong and immediate a dislike to the replica if the appearance had been the same as the old one. The brooch was not of the high quality one was entitled to expect from a piece which cost so much. Accordingly, he gave judgment for the insured for £750. He went on to hold that the insurance company could recover from the jewellers the damages it had had to pay to the insured and the costs of the action, for their work had not been up to standard.

INDEMNIFICATION ALIUNDE

Since the insured is entitled only to an indemnity, any payment to the insured by a third party or any benefit received by the insured, which

---

[1] See generally Marine Insurance Act 1906, s. 60 and Ivamy, *Marine Insurance*, 1969, pp. 377–392.

[2] *Kaltenbach* v. *MacKenzie* (1878), 3 C.P.D. 467 (marine insurance), *per* Brett, L.J., at p. 471.

[3] *Moore* v. *Evans* (*supra*), criticising *Mitsui* v. *Mumford* (*supra*) and *Campbell and Phillips, Ltd.* v. *Denman* (*supra*). See also, *Castellain* v. *Preston* (1883), 11 Q.B.D. 380, C.A. (fire insurance), *per* Bowen, L.J., at p. 403.

[4] See Ivamy, *General Principles of Insurance Law*, 2nd Edn., 1970, pp. 405–410.

[5] [1964] 1 Lloyd's Rep. 94.

diminishes or extinguishes the loss, must be taken into account in calculating the extent of the insurers' liability.[1]

SUBROGATION

On payment of the loss, the insurers by virtue of the doctrine of subrogation are entitled to be placed in the position of the insured, and succeed to all his rights and remedies against third persons in respect of the subject-matter of insurance.[2]

TYPES OF PROPERTY INSURANCE POLICIES

In the chapters which follow, various types of insurance policies[3] are considered:

1 Burglary insurance.[4]
2 All risks insurance.[5]
3 Transit insurance.[6]
4 Livestock insurance.[7]
5 Aviation insurance.[8]
6 Plate glass insurance.[9]
7 Steam boiler insurance.[10]
8 Householder's comprehensive insurance.[11]
9 Miscellaneous insurances.[12]
10 War risks insurance.[13]

---

[1] See Ivamy, *General Principles of Insurance Law*, 2nd Edn., 1970, pp. 431–436.
[2] *Ibid.*, pp. 415–430.
[3] Other types of property insurance are considered in other volumes in this series. For fire insurance, see Ivamy, *Fire and Motor Insurance*, 2nd Edn., 1973, pp. 3–183; for motor insurance, see *ibid.*, pp. 187–351; and for marine insurance, see Ivamy, *Marine Insurance*, 1969.
[4] See Chapter 19, *post.*
[5] See Chapter 20, *post.*
[6] See Chapter 21, *post.*
[7] See Chapter 22, *post.*
[8] See Chapter 23, *post.*
[9] See Chapter 24, *post.*
[10] See Chapter 25, *post.*
[11] See Chapter 26, *post.*
[12] See Chapter 27, *post.*
[13] See Chapter 28, *post.*

19

BURGLARY INSURANCE

The loss of property by a criminal act of misappropriation may be covered by insurance. In insurance practice, a distinction is usually made,[1] as regards their form and incidents, between insurances intended to protect the insured against the criminal acts of strangers and insurances intended to protect him against criminal breaches of employees and other persons occupying towards him, positions of trust.

The risk of loss at the hands of strangers varies according as the subject-matter of insurance is contained in a building or in transit. Moreover, burglary is from its nature inseparably connected with buildings. Hence, a distinction is made, in practice, between insurances on property contained in a building and insurances on property in transit. The former class of insurance is usually called burglary insurance, although crimes other than burglary are usually included within its scope. Property in transit is usually insured against risks of transit, of which the risk of theft or pilferage is only one.[2]

GENERAL DEFINITIONS OF "BURGLARY", "THEFT" AND "ROBBERY"

The various perils insured against under a burglary policy may be summed up in the word "theft". Theft is the factor common to several crimes which differ from each other according to the circumstances in which the crime is committed.[3] Each of these crimes had its appropriate technical name, e.g., "burglary", "theft" and "robbery". If, therefore, as may be the case, technical terms are used in the policy to designate the perils insured against, it is important to consider their legal significance, since there is a presumption that they are intended to bear their technical meaning,[4] and a loss by a crime which is not, as a matter of legal definition, included in the terms used, may not be a loss by a peril insured against.[5]

At the same time technical terms cannot be given the full significance of the criminal law. They are used in a policy of insurance, not in an

---

[1] Both kinds of insurance may be combined in the same policy, See e.g. *American Surety Co. of New York* v. *Wrightson* (1910), 103 L.T. 663, where the Lloyd's policy covered not only loss by the negligence or dishonesty of servants but also loss by burglary; *Pennsylvania Co. for Insurances on Lives and Granting Annuities* v. *Mumford*, [1920] 2 K.B. 537, C.A.

[2] See pp. 181–191, *post.*

[3] See *Lake* v. *Simmons*, [1927] A.C. 487, *per* Lord SUMNER, at p. 507.

[4] See *Debenhams, Ltd.* v. *Excess Insurance Co., Ltd.* (1912), 28 T.L.R. 505, *per* HAMILTON, J., at p. 505; *Re Calf and Sun Insurance Office*, [1902] 2 K.B. 366, C.A., *per* ATKIN, L.J., at p. 380.

[5] Cf. *De Rothschild* v. *Royal Mail Steam Packet Co.* (1852), 7 Exch. 734 (bill of lading), where an exception against loss by "robbers" was held not to apply to a loss by pilferage.

indictment, and are intended to designate the causes of loss contemplated by the policy.[1]

They are therefore, on the one hand, restricted in their scope to acts capable of causing loss, whilst, on the other hand, they extend to all acts of a criminal nature to which, apart from mere technicalities, they may be reasonably taken to apply.[2]

Accordingly, it is desirable to consider the definitions of:

1 "burglary";
2 "theft";
3 "robbery".

1 "Burglary"[3]

Section 9 of the Theft Act 1968 states that:

> "(1) A person is guilty of burglary if—
> (a) he enters any building or part of a building as a trespasser and with intent to commit any such offence as is mentioned in subsection (2) below; or
> (b) having entered any building or part of a building as a trespasser, he steals or attempts to steal anything in the building or that part of it or inflicts or attempts to inflict on any person therein any grievous bodily harm.
> (2) The offences referred to in subsection (1) (a) above are offences of stealing anything in the building or part of a building in question, of inflicting on any person therein any grievous bodily harm or raping any woman therein, and of doing unlawful damage to the building or anything therein."

References to a "building" apply also to an inhabited vehicle or vessel, and apply to any such vehicle or vessel at times when the person having a habitation in it is not there as well as at times when he is.[4]

2 "Theft"[5]

Section 1 (1) of the Theft Act 1968 states that:

> "A person is guilty of theft if he dishonestly appropriates property belonging to another with the intention of permanently depriving the other of it . . ."

It is immaterial whether the appropriation is made with a view to gain, or is made for the thief's own benefit.[6]

A person's appropriation of property belonging to another is not to be regarded as dishonest:

> a if he appropriates the property in the belief that he has in law the right to deprive the other of it, on behalf of himself or of a third person; or

---

[1] But the criminal law is not to be treated as irrelevant merely because a policy is a commercial document: *Lake* v. *Simmons*, [1927] A.C. 487, *per* Lord SUMNER, at p. 509.
[2] *Saqui and Lawrence* v. *Stearns*, [1911] 1 K.B. 426, C.A., where it was unsuccessfully contended that an exception against theft, robbery or misappropriation by members of the insured's staff in a policy covering theft, robbery or burglary, did not apply where the member of the staff was only an accessory before the fact, and not the actual thief.
[3] See generally, Smith, *Law of Theft*, 2nd Edn., 1972, pp. 133–147.
[4] Theft Act 1968, s. 9 (3).
[5] See generally, Smith, *Law of Theft*, 2nd Edn., 1972, pp. 8–57.
[6] Theft Act, 1968, s. 1 (2).

   b if he appropriates the property in the belief that he would have the other's consent if the other knew of his appropriation and the circumstances of it; or

   c (except where the property came to him as trustee or personal representative) if he appropriates the property in the belief that the property to whom the property belongs cannot be discovered by taking reasonable steps.[1]

A person's appropriation of property belonging to another may be dishonest notwithstanding that he is willing to pay for the property.[2]

Any assumption by a person of the rights of an owner amounts to an appropriation.[3]

"Property" includes money and all other property, real or personal.[4]

Property is regarded as belonging to any person having possession or control of it, or having in it any proprietary right or interest (not being an equitable interest arising only from an agreement to transfer or grant an interest).[5]

A person appropriating property belonging to another without meaning the other permanently to lose the thing itself, is nevertheless to be regarded as having the intention of permanently depriving the other of it if his intention is to treat the thing as his own to dispose of regardless of the other's rights.[6] A borrowing or lending of it may amount to so treating it if, but only if, the borrowing or lending is for a period and in circumstances making it equivalent to an outright taking or disposal.[7]

3 "Robbery"

   Section 8 (1) of the Theft Act 1968 states that:

> "A person is guilty of robbery if he steals, and immediately before or at the time of doing so, and in order to do so, he uses force on any person or puts or seeks to put any person in fear of being then and there subjected to force."

MODIFICATION OF THE DEFINITIONS

   Sometimes the policy departs from the legal significance of the words used. The parties may, though using technical terms, frame their own definition, and show clearly that they do not intend to use the words by which they have defined the risk undertaken in a technical sense at all.

   Thus, in *Re George and Goldsmith and General Burglary Insurance Association, Ltd.*[8] the stock-in-trade of a jeweller was insured "against loss or damage by burglary and housebreaking[9] as hereinafter defined." The policy stated that the insurers would indemnify the insured if the property should be lost "by theft following upon actual forcible and violent entry upon the premises wherein the same is stated to be situate." Some of the jewellery was in a

---

[1] Theft Act, 1968, s. 2 (1).
[2] *Ibid.*, s. 2 (1).
[3] *Ibid.*, s. 3 (1).
[4] *Ibid.*, s. 4 (1).
[5] *Ibid.*, s. 5 (1).
[6] *Ibid.*, s. 6 (1).
[7] *Ibid.*, s. 6 (1).
[8] (1899), 80 L.T. 248, C.A.
[9] The offence of "housebreaking" was abolished by the Theft Act 1968.

glass show case in the insured's shop. The case was secured by a padlock. A thief walked into the shop through a shut but unbolted door, broke into the case and stole the jewellery. The insurers repudiated liability for the loss.

The Court of Appeal[1] held that they were entitled to do so. Lord RUSSELL, C.J., said[2] that the words "burglary" and "housebreaking" were not used in their technical sense,[3] for the controlling words in the policy were "as hereinafter defined". In his opinion the parties to the contract never intended to involve themselves in the many subtleties of the criminal law relating to the offences of burglary and housebreaking. He thought that the policy was intended to cover cases of theft following upon an entry effected by real violence as commonly understood, as distinguished from an entry effected by stealth such as had actually occurred in the present case.

He then went on to say that the entry into the shop by the thief turning the door handle was not an "actual forcible and violent entry" within the meaning of the policy, nor was an "actual forcible and violent entry" constituted by what the thief did after entering the shop. He observed:[4]

> "After entering the shop the thief proceeded to prise off an iron plate to which a locked padlock was attached, the iron plate and padlock securing an inclosure bounded by glass, and constituting as between the glass boundaries what would be called the shop front or show board. He then took out the jewellery placed in the shop front and made off with it. Now can that be said to have been an 'entry upon the premises' within the meaning of the policy? In my judgment it cannot. What is the meaning of the word 'premises' in this policy? The second condition in the policy, which I have already referred to, shows the meaning in which the word 'premises' is used in this policy. It provides that the assured shall take all due precautions for the safety of the property insured 'by securing all doors, windows, and other means of entrance'. That, I conceive, can only mean entrance into the shop from the outside. This view is corroborated by the words of the proposal which is agreed to be a part of the contract of insurance. The nature of the premises is there given as 'shop, warehouse, and dwelling', and to the question: 'How are the premises protected on basement, ground floor, and roof lights?' the answer of the assured is: 'Wood shutters and iron bars, and iron plates inside.' I therefore come to the conclusion that the plaintiff has failed to make out that his loss is covered by the policy."

To the same effect was the judgment of SMITH, L.J., who said:[5]

> "The question is, Is this act covered by the words of the policy, 'theft following upon actual forcible and violent entry upon the premises wherein the same', i.e., the property 'is herein stated to be situate'? It was argued that the glass show case was forcibly and violently entered, and that the show case constituted 'the premises' upon which the forcible and violent entry was to be made so as to create a liability in the company. But I think it is clearly not so. It is force and violence from without and not from within the premises which is covered by the policy. By the proposal which is made the basis of the contract, the nature of the premises is declared to be 'shop, warehouse, and dwelling'. That is No. 78, Strand. Then there is a question in the proposal: 'How are the premises protected on basement, ground floor, and roof lights?' The answer is: 'Wood shutters and iron bars, and iron plates inside'. How does this fit in

---

[1] Lord RUSSELL, C.J., SMITH and COLLINS, L.JJ.

[2] (1899), 80 L.T. at p. 250. See also the judgment of SMITH, L.J., *ibid.*, at p. 251 and that of COLLINS, L.J., *ibid.*, at p. 252.

[3] As to the use of words in their technical sense, see Ivamy, *General Principles of Insurance Law*, 2nd Edn., 1970, pp. 305–308.

[4] (1899), 80 L.T. at p. 251.

[5] *Ibid.*, at p. 252.

with the glass show case being the part of the premises into which the actual forcible and violent entry has to be made? Not at all."

THE PROPOSAL FORM

In connection with proposal forms in respect of burglary insurance it is convenient to consider the following topics:

1 the description of the subject-matter;
2 circumstances affecting the risk;
3 examples of non-disclosure and misrepresentation of material facts.

1   Description of Subject-Matter

The proposal form usually contains a schedule classifying under appropriate headings the various kinds of property which the insurers are prepared to insure. With certain exceptions the articles proposed to be insured are not required to be insured specifically. Each heading of the schedule operates as a general description applying to any article falling within its terms. The general description, however, is usually followed by words of particular significance, limiting the general words and indicating the particular kind of or kinds of property intended to be insured.

Hence, in *Pennsylvania Co. for Insurances on Lives and Granting Annuities* v. *Mumford*[1] where a policy covered securities "supposed or believed to be" on the insured's premises on a certain date, it was held that the policy did not cover securities which appeared in the insured's books as having been handed back to their owners before that date, although such securities had been misappropriated, since the securities were not supposed to be on the premises at the date in question, the insured, on the contrary, believing or supposing them to have been returned to the customer.

The schedule is filled in by inserting opposite each heading the sum for which the proposer wishes to insure the whole of the property falling within the description contained in the heading, and by filling in any details required as to the nature of the property. When completed, the schedule is copied into the policy or incorporated by reference.[2] It then constitutes the description of the subject-matter of insurance for the purposes of the policy.

The property to be insured is usually classified under the following headings:

a household goods;
b gold and silver articles;
c stock-in-trade;
d goods held in trust or on commission;
e articles of exceptional value;
f property of other persons.

a   *Household Goods*

The scope of this heading may be made clearer by the express exclusion or inclusion of certain specified classes of articles. Thus, gold and silver articles, watches and jewellery generally may be excluded, or the heading may be

---

[1] [1920] 2 K.B. 537, C.A.
[2] As to incorporation by reference, see Ivamy, *General Principles of Insurance Law*, 2nd Edn., 1970, pp. 179, 187.

stated to include furniture, wearing apparel, linen, cutlery, musical instruments, pictures and other classes of goods commonly found in private residences.

The governing words of the description are, however, "household goods", and the specific classes enumerated are to be construed accordingly. Thus, the word "linen" in the description does not apply to linen of any description so as to include a linen-draper's stock-in-trade. It applies only to linen used in the household.[1]

b *Gold and Silver Articles*

Also included under this heading may be watches, jewellery, trinkets and personal ornaments.

c *Stock-in-trade*

The generality of the description is necessarily controlled by the nature of the business of the proposer, which he is required to state in the proposal as part of his personal description.[2] It is, however, expressly limited in practice by requiring him to describe the subject-matter of insurance specifically as stock-in-trade of a specified trade or business, or as stock-in-trade, consisting of specified classes of goods.[3] Such a mode of description excludes goods which, although forming part of the ordinary stock-in-trade of the proposer's business, do not fall within the classes specified.

Thus, hops and malting form an ordinary part of the stock-in-trade of a corn dealer and seedsman's business, and are, therefore covered by an insurance in general terms upon the stock-in-trade of such a business.

If however, the stock-in-trade is defined for the purposes of the insurance as "consisting of corn, seed, hay, straw, fixtures and utensils in business", the hops and malting are not included, since the words "consisting of" are words of limitation, excluding everything which is not enumerated.[4] In this case it appears to be immaterial that the whole of the stock-in-trade on the premises consists of the excluded goods.[5]

d *Goods Held in Trust and on Commission*

The generality of this description also is usually limited by reference to the insured's business, or by requiring an enumeration of the classes of goods intended to be insured.

e *Articles of Exceptional Value*

In insurances upon the contents of private houses, there is usually a limit placed on the amount recoverable in respect of any one article. If the

---

[1] *Watchorn* v. *Langford* (1813), 3 Camp. 422 (fire insurance). See Ivamy, *Fire and Motor Insurance*, 2nd Edn., 1973, p. 43.

[2] Thus, where the insured is not a linen-draper, a stock of linen drapery does not fall within the words "stock-in-trade", *Watchorn* v. *Langford* (*supra*).

[3] For an example of a narrower interpretation, see *Stanton and Stanton, Ltd.* v. *Starr* (1920), 3 Ll.L. Rep. 259 (burglary insurance), where the insurance covered traveller's goods only and not general stock.

[4] *Joel* v. *Harvey* (1857), 5 W.R. 488 (fire insurance), *per* Lord CAMPBELL, C.J., at p. 488.

[5] *Ibid.*, where CROMPTON, J., disagreed with the suggestion of WIGHTMAN, J., that in such a case they might be covered.

proposer wishes to insure any article for an amount exceeding the limit, he is required to insure it specifically.[1]

f *Property of Other Persons*

In the case of a private house, the policy usually purports to cover the property of other residents in the house, whether relatives or servants[2] of the proposer. The insurance may be limited to permanent residents or may extend to visitors.

2   Circumstances affecting the Risk

The only questions in the proposal form to which special attention need be drawn are those relating to the risk and indicating what circumstances are, in the opinion of the insurers, material. The questions are necessarily more detailed in the case of an insurance upon business premises than in the case of an insurance upon a private house.

The principal circumstances affecting the risk relate to the following matters:

    a the premises containing the property insured;

    b the property to be insured;

    c the previous history of the proposer;

    d other insurance.

a   *Premises*

The risk of loss varies according to the premises[3] and the proposer is, therefore, required in the proposal not only to describe their situation, but also to give details which do not affect their identity, but which bear upon the risk and assist in defining it.

The proposer may be required to state whether the premises are, e.g., a private house, chambers, flat,[4] apartments, hotel, shop, warehouse, factory or store. Their situation as regards other buildings, e.g., whether they are detached, semi-detached, or attached, may have to be given, and the nature of the business carried on described.

The proposer may be asked to state, in the case of a private residence, whether he is the sole occupier and whether the premises are ever left unoccupied except during holidays. In the case of business premises the questions asked are more detailed, e.g., if he is not the sole occupier, he must give the number and the occupations of the other tenants, and must state whether the premises are ever left unoccupied at night.

In the case of private residences a question may be asked as to whether the doors and windows are fitted with suitable locks and fastenings.

---

[1] As to the application of the *ejusdem generis* rule, see *King* v. *Travellers' Insurance Association, Ltd.* (1931), 48 T.L.R. 53, where furs were held not to be specially valuable articles in the same sense as jewellery or watches.

[2] *Dia* v. *County Fire Office, Ltd.* (1930), 37 Ll.L. Rep. 24, where the Court declined to decide whether a doctor's assistant was his servant.

[3] See *Pearson* v. *Commercial Union Assurance Co.* (1876), 1 App. Cas. 498 (fire insurance), *per* Lord CHELMSFORD, at p. 505; *Grover and Grover, Ltd.* v. *Mathews* (1910), 15 Com. Cas. 249 (fire insurance), *per* HAMILTON, J., at p. 260.

[4] A flat occupied exclusively by an employee, although provided and furnished by the employer, is not the employer's private residence: *Dia* v. *County Fire Office, Ltd.* (1930), 37 Ll.L. Rep. 24.

In the case of business premises, he is usually required to deal specifically with all the external doors, with all the windows, front and back, on the ground floor and basement, and with trap-doors and skylights, stating how they are respectively secured and protected. He may also be required to state whether there is a caretaker on the premises.

b *Property to be Insured*

In the case of business premiums, the proposer is often required to state the estimated average value for the year of the stock-in-trade or other property insured. He may also be asked whether he keeps a stock book, and, if he does not, how he proposes to prove the amount of any loss which he may sustain. He may also be asked whether he has a safe. If so, he must describe it in detail, and state whether all valuables are placed in it when the premises are closed.

c *Previous History of Proposer*

The proposer is sometimes asked how long he has occupied the premises, and what rent, if any, he has paid. He is also required to state whether the premises have ever been entered by thieves, and, if so, how access was obtained to the premises, and what precautions have since been taken to prevent recurrence.

d *Other Insurance*

In addition to the usual questions as to other insurance, the proposer may be asked whether the property proposed to be insured is also insured against fire. If so, he is required to give the names of the insurers and to state the amount of the insurance.

3   Non-disclosure and Misrepresentation[1]

Over-valuation

In *Fournier* v. *Valentine*[2] a negative of a film on "La Grande Guerre" was valued in the policy at about £12,000. Evidence was given that it had only cost £500 to make. ROCHE, J., held that there had been a very considerable over-valuation, and that the insurers could repudiate liability under the policy on the ground that there had been non-disclosure of a material fact.

In *Trading Co. L. and J. Hoff* v. *Union Insurance Society of Canton, Ltd.*[3] some bearer shares in an Esthonian railway company were insured under a burglary policy and against theft in transit from Reval in Esthonia to Riga and then to London. The insurers denied liability for the loss of the shares on the ground that there had been non-disclosure of the real value. The value of the shares depended upon various problematical factors. The railway company had not a single railway engine or carriage or a yard of track, and was living upon the hopes of what the future might produce. It had an accrued right to a small amount of compensation from the Esthonian Government. It hoped to persuade the governments of three other

---

[1] See further Ivamy, *General Principles of Insurance Law*, 2nd Edn., 1970, pp. 90–145.
[2] (1930), 38 Ll.L. Rep. 19.
[3] (1929), 34 Ll.L. Rep. 81.

States to grant it something to which it had no legal right whatever. These facts were not disclosed to the insurers. The Court of Appeal held that the insurers were not liable.

Nationality

In *Horne* v. *Poland*[1] LUSH, J., held that in the special circumstances of the case, the insurers were entitled to repudiate liability on the ground that the insured, who had assumed an English name, had not disclosed that he was an alien born in Rumania.

Previous Losses

In *Becker* v. *Marshall*[2] the plaintiff, who carried on a furrier's business, had insured his premises against burglary and stated in the proposal form that he had never sustained a loss. In fact, his premises had been burgled on three previous occasions. The Court of Appeal held that the insurers could repudiate liability, for this fact was material and had not been disclosed.

In *Rozanes* v. *Bowen*[3] the insured's claim for an indemnity or loss under a jeweller's block policy failed, for he had failed to disclose a loss by theft in 1915, a loss through an employee in 1918 and other losses at considerably earlier dates.

In *Krantz* v. *Allan and Faber*[4] the non-disclosure of two previous losses was held to vitiate the insured's claim.

Previous Conviction

In *Schoolman* v. *Hall*[5] the insurers were held to be entitled to repudiate liability on the ground that he had not disclosed that he had a criminal record some years before a jeweller's block policy was issued to him.

In *Roselodge, Ltd.* (*formerly Rose Diamond Products, Ltd.*) v. *Castle*[6] a company was held guilty of non-disclosure of a material fact, i.e., that its sales manager had been convicted of smuggling diamonds into the United States[7], and hence the insurers were not liable on a jeweller's block policy. The Court held, however, that the fact that the principal directors of the company had bribed a police officer in 1946 and had been fined £75 was not material.[8]

Refusal to Renew Policy

The fact that another insurance company has refused to renew a policy has been held to be a material one.[9]

Refusal by other Insurers to Insure

Refusal by another insurer to issue a policy has been held to be a material fact which should be disclosed.[10]

---

[1] [1922] 2 K.B. 364. In *Becker* v. *Marshall* (1922), 12 Ll.L. Rep. 413 the Court of Appeal reserved the question whether the nationality of the insured was a material fact. See, further, *Lyons* v. *J. W. Bentley, Ltd.* (1944), 77 Ll.L. Rep. 335; *Carlton* v. *R. and J. Park, Ltd.* (1922), 12 Ll.L. Rep. 246, C.A.

[2] (1922), 12 Ll.L. Rep. 413, C.A.

[3] (1928), 32 Ll.L. Rep. 98, C.A.

[4] (1921), 9 Ll.L. Rep. 410.

[5] [1951] 1 Lloyd's Rep. 139, C.A.

[6] [1966] 2 Lloyd's Rep. 113.

[7] *Ibid.*, at p. 133.

[8] *Ibid.*, at p. 132.

[9] *Ascott* v. *Cornhill Insurance Co., Ltd.* (1937), 58 Ll.L. Rep. 41.

[10] *Glicksman* v. *Lancashire and General Assurance Co., Ltd.*, [1927] A.C. 139, H.L.

ALTERATIONS OF THE RISK

The principal alterations which may affect the risk are:

1 Removal of the insured property from the premises specified in the
    policy.
2 Change in the insured property.
3 Change of interest.
4 Change of occupancy.
5 Alteration of other circumstances.
6 Neglect of duty by the insured.

1 Removal of Property

A burglary insurance is usually connected with locality, and the removal
of the insured property from the specified locality may not be so much an
alteration of the risk as a withdrawal of the property from the operation of
the policy. If therefore, the property is insured as being in the specified
locality, the policy may only cover it while it is there; and on its removal the
policy may cease to attach, only re-attaching, if at all, on its return.

In *Leo. Rapp, Ltd.* v. *McClure*[1] a policy was issued to the insured covering the
loss of his stock of iron, steel and non-ferrous metal by burglary, housebreaking, theft or larceny "while in warehouse anywhere in the United
Kingdom". A lorry belonging to the insured, which contained a load of
metal, was stolen and was never recovered. The insured claimed for a loss
under the policy, but the underwriter refused to pay on the ground that it
had not occurred "whilst in warehouse". The lorry had been parked in a
compound consisting of a high brick wall topped with barbed wire, and
inside the yard there were two buildings, one a furniture store which was an
enclosed building, and the other a covered space consisting of a roof with no
doors, and open spaces in the yard iself. The lorry had been placed in one
of the open spaces.

DEVLIN, J., held that the action failed. He said that it was abundantly
clear that at the material time the goods were in a yard and not in a "warehouse". The ordinary natural meaning of that word was some sort of building, and that view was confirmed by the dictionary definitions to which
counsel had referred. When the insured's proposal was before him the
underwriter did not know where the goods were going to be. He had to
define in advance, and in the ordinary way if goods were "in warehouse", it
offered some sort of security which in a yard they might not have. A warehouse was generally kept locked with a warehouseman in charge who, in the
conduct of the warehouse, owed an obligation to look after the goods. In a
yard there was no such security.

There may be an express condition by which except in certain cases,
removal without the consent of the insurers is prohibited.

Removal without the consent of the insurers is usually permitted in
insurances on private residences, during the temporary absence of the insured
from the specified premises, during holidays. Notwithstanding the removal,
the policy continues to attach and the property is held covered, provided
that it is in, e.g.:

---

[1] [1955] 1 Lloyd's Rep. 292.

   a any private house or hotel in which the insured is temporarily residing at the time.

   b any private house provided that at the time the insured's premises are not occupied.

   c any bank or safe deposit to which the property is removed for safe custody.

2 Change in Property

In so far as the policy applies to specific articles, the articles specified alone are insured. If therefore the insured parts with them, they cease to be covered, since he is no longer interested in them.

New articles acquired by him are not covered since they are not described in the policy, and it is immaterial that they are intended to replace articles specifically described.

The insurance is, as a rule, however, not an insurance upon specific articles, but an insurance upon a class of articles. A change in the articles composing a particular class, whether by way of increase, decrease or substitution, does not affect the identity of the class, and, in the absence of any condition to the contrary, does not affect the validity of the policy. In the case of an insurance upon stock-in-trade, a constant change in the articles making up the class is necessarily contemplated by the parties.

Sometimes, however, there may be a condition prohibiting any material increase or decrease in the class without the consent of the insurers.

3 Change of Interest

In addition to the usual condition as to assignment, the policy may contain a further condition prohibiting the insured from changing his interest by granting a bill of sale or any other security over the insured property.

4 Change of Occupancy

It may be made a condition of the policy that the premises containing the property insured are not to be left unoccupied at night,[1] or that they are to be always occupied.[2]

The policy may provide that if the specified premises are left unoccupied[3] for more than a specified number of consecutive days or nights, the operation of the policy is to be suspended until they are again occupied. The policy may further limit the total number of days and nights during which the premises may be left unoccupied in any one period of insurance.

Premises are not "unoccupied" within the meaning of a stipulation of this

---

[1] *Winicofsky* v. *Army and Navy General Assurance Assocn., Ltd.* (1919), 35 T.L.R. 283, where the question was left open whether a statement in the proposal form that the premises were occupied at night amounted to a condition.

[2] *Simmonds* v. *Cockell*, [1920] 1 K.B. 843, where it was held that this meant, not that the premises were never to be left unattended, but that they were to be used, continuously and without interruption, i.e. as a residence, and not merely as a lock-up shop which was left unoccupied after business hours.

[3] The fact that the premises are left unoccupied without the knowledge of the insured is immaterial: *Abrahams* v. *Agricultural Mutual Assurance Association* (1876), 40 U.C.R. 175 (fire insurance).

kind merely because, owing to the temporary absence of all the inmates, there is no one on the premises at the time of the loss.[1]

If it is desired to provide for the continuous presence of someone on the premises, the wording of the stipulation must be changed, and it must be made a condition of the policy that the premises are never to be left unattended.[2]

5 Alteration of Other Circumstances

The policy sometimes provides that any alteration in the specified premises, or in any of the facts stated in the proposal, e.g., the nature of the business carried on, is to avoid the policy, unless the insurers agree to it.

6 Neglect of Duty by Insured

The declaration at the end of the proposal form signed by the proposed insured sometimes contains an undertaking by him to exercise all reasonable precautions for the safety of the insured property.

The undertaking may be amplified and defined in the policy which makes it a condition that the insured shall take all due precautions as if the property were not insured, as regards the selection and supervision of employees, the securing of all doors and windows and other means of entrance or otherwise.

Hence, if a loss takes place during the night by reason of the omission of the insured to take what a jury might think to be due precautions for the safety of the insured property, the insured cannot recover.[3] On the other hand, an omission to fasten the door of an inside show-case in a jeweller's shop is not necessarily a breach of such a condition.[4]

In *Winicofsky* v. *Army and Navy General Assurance Co.*[5] a burglary policy stated that "the assured shall take all due and proper precautions for the safety of the property insured." The insured left the insured premises in an air raid and sought refuge in an air raid shelter. One of the grounds[6] on which the insurers repudiated liability was that he was in breach of the condition set out above. BRAY, J., held[7] that this defence failed, for his act in going to the shelter and leaving the property unattended was no breach of the condition.

In *Shoot* v. *Hill*[8] a jeweller's block policy included a condition which stated:

> " . . . The assured shall keep proper stock and account books in which all sales and purchases are recorded, and . . . such books shall be available for inspection by the underwriters or their representatives."

---

[1] *Winicofsky* v. *Army and Navy General Assurance Assocn., Ltd.* (*supra*), where the inmates left the premises for an hour or two for the purpose of taking shelter during an air raid; *Simmonds* v. *Cockell* (*supra*), where the insured and his wife went out for a Sunday afternoon and evening.

[2] *Simmonds* v. *Cockell* (*supra*), *per* ROCHE, J., at p. 845.

[3] *Re George and Goldsmiths' and General Burglary Insurance Association, Ltd.*, [1899] 1 Q.B. 595, C.A. (burglary insurance), *per* Lord RUSSELL OF KILLOWEN, C.J., at p. 602.

[4] *Re George and Goldsmiths and General Burglary Insurance Association, Ltd.* (*supra*), *per* A. L. SMITH, L.J.

[5] (1919), 35 T.L.R. 283.

[6] The case also concerned the interpretation of an exception in the policy. As to this point, see p. 153, *post*.

[7] (1919), 35 T.L.R. at p. 284.

[8] (1936), 55 Ll.L. Rep. 29, K.B.

Another condition stated that it should be:

> "A condition precedent to all liability of the underwriters as regards burglary . . . that (*a*) at the time of the closing of the insured premises for business, the "Rely-a-Bell" burglar alarm shall have been put into full and proper operation, and (*b*) such alarm shall have been maintained under contract by the "Rely-a-Bell" Burglar & Fire Alarm Company Ltd."

The insured alleged that his premises had been entered and the safes opened and certain property stolen. The insurer repudiated liability on the ground (*inter alia*)[1] that the insured had not complied with the two conditions set out above. The insured's books of account were incomplete, and he was unable to produce invoices of goods stated by him to have been purchased. He said that on the night of the burglary he tested the burglar alarm, which was then in working order. A witness employed by the manufacturers of the alarm, however, examined it on the following morning, and stated that it could not have been in working order on the previous day. BRANSON, J., held that the breach of both conditions had been proved, and that the claim failed.

As to the breach of the condition concerning the keeping of books of account, his Lordship said:[2]

> "The undertaking was to 'keep proper stock and account books in which all sales and purchases are recorded.' I quite agree that it is not necessary for the fulfilment of that clause that the sheets of paper upon which his stock is kept should be bound up into a volume. In my view, it would be quite sufficient that he should keep ordinary books or even books which were not usually kept, provided that they contained the entries which he had agreed to make. According to the evidence, it is not possible to adjust his accounts unless you assume that he paid out of his cash sums of money for the purchasing of goods which were not entered in any purchase book and were not directly entered into the stock books. He says that the way that he went about it was to buy, let us say, a watch over the counter for 10s. and then to ticket it and put it aside until he had time, either by his own man or by sending it out to somebody else, to put the watch again into going order, with a polished case, ready for another sale, and then it was put into the stock book direct; so that there is nothing to show from whom it was bought, what was paid for it, how much was spent upon it in labour or the payment for labour to another firm, but there is only a sort of sudden appearance of a new watch in the stock book, priced at such a figure as Mr. Shoot thought right. That is not the kind of book which answers the description in this policy. It seems to me that it is the essence of the matter that the underwriters should, if a claim arises, be able to look at the book and see whether the man who is claiming so much for his stock has got the stock and what he paid for the stock. It is of the essence of the matter in order to enable them to check the accuracy of the value which he chooses to put on the stock. Therefore, on this ground again, I think the plaintiff fails."

With regard to the condition relating to the burglar alarm, he said:[3]

> "Mr. Tibbles[4] was a perfectly impartial witness on this matter. There was no attack upon the efficiency of his burglar alarm. On the contrary, the plaintiff's case was that the burglar alarm was in perfect condition and was working

---

[1] The insurers also contended that the claim was false and fraudulent, and BRANSON, J., held that this contention, too, succeeded: *ibid.*, at p. 38. As to fraudulent claims, see Ivamy, *General Principles of Insurance Law*, 2nd Edn., 1970, pp. 360–363.

[2] (1936), 55 Ll.L. Rep. at p. 38.

[3] *Ibid.*, at p. 36.

[4] An expert witness.

quite well on the night of the 23rd. As it is admitted that it was turned off when they went there on the morning of the 24th, it could only have been turned off if somebody had succeeded in getting hold of the only key to it which existed and had been able to make a copy of that key. It seems to me, in view of the evidence of the expert Tibbles, that, in the condition in which he found that apparatus upon the morning of Dec. 24, it could not have been left in working order on the night of the 23rd, or all the bells would have been ringing and would have continued to ring all night.

I am bound to accept the suggestion of the defendants that this burglar alarm had not been set on the night of the 23rd."

In *Jacobson* v. *Yorkshire Insurance Co., Ltd.*[1] a burglary policy taken out by a boot and shoe dealer contained a condition which stated that:

> "The insured shall keep proper books of account with a complete record of all purchases or sales, and all such books shall be regularly entered up as soon as such purchases or sales shall have taken place."

A loss took place and the insurers repudiated liability under the policy on the ground that there had been a breach of condition for, although the insured had kept a complete record of purchases, there was no record of sales.[2] The insured contended that the keeping of a record of either purchases or sales was sufficient.

HUMPHREYS, J., held that the defence succeeded. The policy must be construed in a business sense, and meant that the insured was to keep proper books of account with a complete record of all transactions, purchases or sales. His Lordship observed:[3]

> "Now, there is one line of argument by [Counsel] that I cannot follow. He said that it may be that that wording was deliberately put in by the insurance company, who may in insuring a man's stock say, 'What we require you to do is to keep a record either of your purchases or sales and we do not want you to keep a record of both.' But that is inconceivable. What they as business people want to know if they are to pay is what the stock is, and how any being can tell what the stock is if he only knows of the sales or the purchases, it is impossible to see. That is an impossible contention.
>
> But what [Counsel] also argues is that here are words, perfectly plain and unambiguous, and that as the word 'or' is used it must be assumed that the word was intended and that the company intended that there should be applied to it the ordinary English meaning. I accept that contention and I shall decide this case on the ground that in my judgment what the company required in plain terms is that he should keep proper books of account with a complete record of all transactions—because that is what proper books of account are— a complete record of all transactions, purchases or sales. That is the only possible meaning, in my view, to attach to the condition, as this is a business document drawn up by business people to protect themselves against possible false claims, though in this case there is no suggestion of fraud. This clause is drawn up to protect them against a wrong claim."

---

[1] (1933), 45 Ll.L. Rep. 281.

[2] The method of keeping records was found by the arbitrator, by whom the case was first tried, to be as follows: "All the money taken in connection with the business was placed in a tumbler which was kept in a cupboard in the living room behind the shop. Whenever money was required by the claimant in connection with the business, whether for his own requirements, casual wages, cartage, railway fares, storage or other petty cash expenses, the same was taken from the money in the tumbler; once a week the balance of money remaining in the tumbler was paid into the bank. In order to arrive at the item of monthly sales, the accountant took the amount of cash banked during the month, plus cash in hand and plus such sums as he was told had been taken out of the tumbler during the month, few only of which could be evidenced by receipts."

[3] (1933), 45 Ll.L. Rep. at p. 282.

In *Roberts* v. *Eagle Star Insurance Co., Ltd.* the insurers effected a burglary and housebreaking insurance policy in respect of his stock-in-trade at his lock-up workshop. The policy contained a condition precedent to all liability of the insurers:

> "that the Rely-a-Bell Burglar Alarm shall be put into full and proper operation whenever the premises are closed for business or are left unattended."

The premises were broken into, and some furs were stolen. The insured claimed an indemnity under the policy, but the insurers contended that he was in breach of the condition in that the burglar alarm was not in operation while the premises were left unattended.

PAULL, J., held that the action failed. There was a breaking and entering of the premises by thieves, but the insured had not put the burglar alarm into operation when he left the premises unattended.[2]

In *Bennett* v. *Yorkshire Insurance Co., Ltd.*[3] the insured was a shopkeeper, who insured his stock at his shop premises under a Traders' combined policy which included insurance cover against burglary. One of the conditions of the policy stated:

> "The insured shall keep proper books of account with a complete record of all purchases and sales and all such books shall be regularly entered up as soon as such purchases or sales have taken place."

There was a burglary at the insured's premises, and the insured claimed an indemnity in respect of the goods which had been stolen. The insurer denied liability on the ground that the insured had not kept books with a complete record of all purchases and sales. Evidence was given that wages were paid from moneys received in sales which had not been recorded.

THOMPSON, J., held that the insured's claim failed because the insurers had proved that he was in breach of the condition set out above.[4]

EXCEPTIONS

The exceptions usually contained in a burglary policy may be classified as follows:

1 exceptions excluding loss or damage from war and similar causes;
2 exceptions excluding loss or damage capable of being insured against by a policy belonging to a different species of insurance;
3 exceptions relating to the conduct of the insured;
4 exceptions relating to the conduct of other persons;
5 excepted articles.

1 War and Similar Causes

Thus, Lloyd's Burglary and Fire policy contains a clause excepting liability for:

---

[1] [1960] 1 Lloyd's Rep. 615, Q.B.D.
[2] *Ibid.*, at p. 622.
   [1962] 2 Lloyd's Rep. 270 Q.B.D.
[4] *Ibid.*, at p. 276. The evidence as to the method of recording purchases and sales is set out *ibid.*, at pp. 273–275.

"loss or damage directly or indirectly occasioned by happening through or in consequence of war, invasion, acts of foreign enemies,[1] hostilities[2] (whether war be declared or not), civil war, rebellion, revolution, insurrection,[3] military or usurped power,[4] riots,[5] civil commotion,[6] or confiscation or nationalisation or requisition or destruction of or damage to property by or under the order of any government or public or local authority."

In *Winicofsky* v. *Army and Navy General Assurance Assocn., Ltd.*[7] an exception in a burglary policy relating to a shop stated that the insurers would not be liable for "loss or damage occasioned by hostilities, riots or civil commotion, or for loot, sack, or pillage in connection therewith." The shop was burgled when the insured was in an air raid shelter in which he had sought refuge during a Zeppelin air raid on London on January 29, 1918. BRAY, J., held[8] that the insurers could not rely on the exception, and said that the burglary was not a loss by hostilities, though no doubt an air raid, which was an act of hostilities, produced a state of affairs which made things easier for the burglars. Again, he did not consider that the burglary was either loot, sack or pillage connected with hostilities. The words "loot, sack or pillage" implied something much more than a mere isolated case of burglary.

2 Loss Capable of being Insured under Different Species of Insurance

The policies specified are fire and plate glass policies. Policies covering loss by explosion may also be included.

Thus, a loss by theft in the confusion consequent on the happening of a fire is a loss by "fire" within the meaning of a fire policy,[9] and the breakage of a plate glass window is a loss within the meaning of a plate glass policy, even though the breakage is for the purpose of enabling a thief to enter the premises.[10] In neither case, therefore, has the burglary policy any application.

3 Conduct of Insured

An exception may exclude the insurers' liability if the loss is caused by the insured's wilful or negligent act. In particular a failure to take precautions for the safety of the insured property may be fatal.[11]

4 Conduct of Other Persons

In the absence of an exception it is unnecessary to consider by whom the crime causing the loss is committed.

But an express exception may be inserted excluding the liability of the insurers where the crime is committed by:

 a inmates of the insured's household or business staff;

---

[1] See Ivamy, *General Principles of Insurance Law*, 2nd Edn., 1970, p. 222.
[2] *Ibid.*, p. 225.
[3] *Ibid.*, p. 224.
[4] *Ibid.*, pp. 223–224.
[5] *Ibid.*, pp. 222–223.
[6] *Ibid.*, p. 223.
[7] (1919), 35 T.L.R. 283, K.B. The case also concerned the interpretation of a condition of the policy. As to this aspect of the case, see p. 149, *ante*.
[8] (1919), 35 T.L.R. at p. 284.
[9] See Ivamy, *Fire and Motor Insurance*, 2nd Edn., 1973, p. 146.
[10] *Marsden* v. *City and County Assurance Co.* (1865), L.R. 1 C.P. 232 (plate glass insurance).
[11] See pp. 149–152, *ante*.

b tenants or lodgers;

c persons lawfully on the premises.[1]

The exception may further extend to exclude loss or damage caused by or through their wilful or negligent acts.

Lloyd's Burglary and Fire policy excludes liability for:

"loss or damage due to burglary or any attempt thereat by, or in collusion with, any members of the assured's staff or household or inmates of that part of the premises occupied by the assured."

In *Saqui and Lawrence* v. *Stearns*[2] a burglary policy contained an exception which stated:

"Provided always that there shall be no claim on this policy . . . for loss by theft, robbery, or misappropriation by members of the assured's household, business staff, or other inmates of the assured's premises."

A porter in the insured's employment admitted one of a gang of thieves into the insured premises, which were a jeweller's shop in the Strand, so that he could hide in the coal cellar, then break through the ceiling and get at the jewellery. When the insured claimed under the policy, the insurers repudiated liability under the policy on the ground that the loss fell within the exception.

The Court of Appeal[3] held that this defence succeeded. COZENS-HARDY, M.R., observed:[4]

"I think that this is a case in which Hazel was actually guilty of theft, and that the loss has been occasioned by theft by Hazel, one of the plaintiff's staff. Then it was said that you must in some way apportion the loss; that it was not all due to Hazel; but that it was, in fact, more due to the other men who came in with their tools and carried off the jewels in sacks or other receptacles. I entirely decline to follow that. I do not think that the doctrine of asportation ought to be applied in a case of this kind. Hazel was a thief; the loss was owing to his theft; the case falls within the proviso, and the underwriters are not liable."

In *Greaves* v. *Drysdale*[5] a burglary policy relating to a jeweller's shop contained an exception which stated:

"No claim to attach to this policy when the loss is occasioned by members of the assured's staff or household or inmates of the above mentioned premises."

The burglary was discovered by two members of the insured's staff. They found that one of the shutters was loose. Later it was ascertained that the safe had been opened with a key, and had been closed and locked after cash and jewellery had been removed. The insurers repudiated liability on the ground that the loss fell within the exception in that the burglary had been perpetrated by the two members of the staff, who had staged evidence of an outside entry. The Court of Appeal[6] held that the probabilities seemed to be

---

[1] These words include tenants and members of their family or household: *Re Calf and Sun Insurance Office*, [1902] 2 K.B. 366, C.A., *per* YOUNGER, L.J., at p. 385.
[2] (1910), 103 L.T. 583, C.A.
[3] COZENS-HARDY, M.R., FLETCHER MOULTON and FARWELL, L.JJ.
[4] (1910), 103 L.T. at p. 584. See also the judgment of FLETCHER MOULTON, L.J., *ibid.*, at p. 584, and that of FARWELL, L.J., *ibid.*, at p. 584.
[5] (1936), 55 Ll.L. Rep. 95, C.A.
[6] GREER and GREENE, L.JJ., and TALBOT, J.

against rather than for the contention that the burglary had been committed by the two members of the staff, and gave judgment for the insured.

5   Excepted Articles

Certain articles are usually excepted from the scope of the policy, e.g.:

1 articles which possess a fancy value or a personal value, e.g., medals and coins, curiosities, sculptures, manuscripts and rare books, stamp collections, business books, plans, patterns, moulds, models, designs, computer system's records;

2 money and securities, title deeds;

3 articles which are usually insured under a different species of burglary policy, e.g., personal effects are excluded in the case of a policy on the contents of business premises.

PROCEEDINGS AFTER LOSS

The principal matters to be considered are:

1 Notice to the police.
2 The claim.
3 Proof of loss.

1   Notice to the Police

In addition to the ordinary notice of loss to be given to the insurers,[1] the insured is usually required to give notice to the police as soon as the loss has come to his knowledge, and to take all practicable steps to discover and punish the thief and to trace and recover the property which has been lost.[2]

2   Claim

The claim form contains a schedule in which a description of each article stolen must be inserted, together with the name of the person from whom the article was purchased or received, the date of its purchase or receipt, the amount to be deducted for depreciation the amount claimed as its present value,[3] and other relevant facts.   In addition, the insured may be asked to state the figure at which he values the total contents of the premises at the time of the loss.[4]

The insured may be required to state whether at the time of the loss the premises were occupied, and if not, he must state the date and hour when they were last occupied.

He will usually have to state the date and time when the premises were broken into, the doors or windows, if any, were forced, the rooms which were rifled, the date and time when, and the person by whom the loss was discovered, and the police station at which the police were informed.

---

[1] As to notice of loss, see Ivamy, *General Principles of Insurance Law*, 2nd Edn., 1970, pp. 348–353.

[2] If the police take possession of any property alleged to have been stolen, but found subsequently on the premises, the insured is entitled to its return, and the insurers cannot have it retained by the police until the trial of the action under R.S.C. Order 29, r. 2: *Scott* v. *Mercantile Accident Insurance Co.* (1892), 8 T.L.R. 320.

[3] As to the basis of valuation generally, see pp. 156–158, *post*. As to the effect of an excessive overvaulation, see Ivamy, *General Principles of Insurance Law*, 2nd Edn., 1970, pp. 362–363.

[4] This is for the purpose of average when the policy is "subject to average". See p. 158 *post*.

The ownership of the property must be stated, i.e., whether the insured is the sole owner of the property which has been stolen.

In addition to any other burglary policies, the insured may be required to state the sum for which the contents of the premises are insured against fire and to give the names of the fire insurers. He must also state whether he has ever sustained a previous loss by fire or burglary.

3   Proof of Loss[1]

The insured may be bound by the policy to satisfy the insurers that the property in respect of which the claim is made has been actually stolen and is not merely mislaid or missing. For this purpose the evidence of the insured and of his family or servants may not of itself be sufficient proof.[2]

In *Watts* v. *Simmons*[3] the plaintiff was the assignee of a Mr. Silverman, and claimed for a loss by burglary of about £10,000 worth of jewellery, which was alleged to have been stolen from two attache cases in Silverman's room at a hotel. LUSH, J., held that on the evidence the loss by burglary had not been proved.

In *Knoller* v. *Evans*[4] the plaintiffs were a husband and wife, who claimed an indemnity in respect of some jewellery alleged to have been stolen from their house. The jewellery was kept in a drawer of a writing desk and was found to be missing. On the previous day the husband had lost one of three keys to the front door, and on the same day a kitchen window had been left open by a maid and apparently had been open all night. BRANSON, J., held that the loss had been sufficiently proved.

In *Prudential Staff Union* v. *Hall*[5] the Union failed in its claim for an indemnity in respect of an alleged burglary at the premises of one of its members, for the evidence in support of the claim was insufficient.

In *Lek* v. *Mathews*[6] the House of Lords held that the insured had proved to its satisfaction the loss of part of his postage stamp collection which he alleged had been stolen.

CALCULATION OF THE AMOUNT RECOVERABLE

The undertaking of the insurers is usually, in express terms, to make good the loss.[7] Whatever may be the form of words used, it is clear that the insured is entitled, within the limits of the policy, to be fully indemnified against the loss in respect of the subject-matter of insurance.[8] To constitute a full indemnity, the insured must, therefore, receive a sum representing the diminution in value of the subject-matter caused by the peril insured

---

[1] See generally Ivamy, *General Principles of Insurance Law*, 2nd Edn., 1970, pp. 364–370.
[2] A statement in the proposal form that the insured intends to prove the loss by producing receipts from persons who had sold goods to him does not preclude him from proving it in some other way: *Winicofsky* v. *Army and Navy General Assurance Assocn., Ltd.* (1919), 35 T.L.R. 283.
[3] (1924), 18 Ll.L. Rep. 177.
[4] (1936), 55 Ll.L. Rep. 40.
[5] [1947] K.B. 685.
[6] (1927), 29 Ll.L. Rep. 141, H.L.
[7] *Waters* v. *Monarch Fire and Life Assurance Co.* (1856), 5 E. & B. 870 (fire insurance), *per* Lord CAMPBELL, C.J., at p. 881.
[8] *Castellain* v. *Preston* (1883), 11 Q.B.D. 380, C.A. (fire insurance), *per* BOWEN, L.J., at p. 401.

against, or, in other words, a sum representing the value which the peril has taken away.[1]

In those branches of insurance in which the amount of the loss, is, in the first instance, measurable in money, e.g., in fidelity, or solvency insurance, the insured, in fact, loses by the peril insured against a sum of money. That sum is the measure of the loss, and, therefore, no difficulty arises.

In other branches of insurance, however, where the insurance is in respect of property such as goods or choses in action other than mere money debts, the monetary value of which at any particular moment is a matter of calculation, the position is different. The loss sustained by the insured, in fact, is the loss of the property insured. But the indemnity payable to him in respect of the loss is to be measured in money, and it is therefore necessary to consider upon what basis the indemnity is to be calculated.

The basis of calculation is the value of the subject-matter of insurance.[2]

The value of the subject-matter is taken as at the time immediately preceding the loss,[3] since that is, in fact, the value which has been taken away by the peril insured against.

The value of the subject-matter is its intrinsic value,[4] which is *prima facie* to be measured by the market value, if any.[5] A difficulty arises if there is a rise in the market value between the time when the goods were bought and the time of the loss, seeing that the insured has, in a sense, made a profit. It may, therefore, be contended that by reason of the rule requiring profits to be specifically insured,[6] he cannot recover more than the prime cost, since the profit represented by the rise in value ought to have been specifically insured. This contention, however, is unsound. What the insured has lost is the value of the goods at the time of the loss, and by the terms of the policy he is entitled to be paid their value at that time and not their value at any other time.[7] As a matter of fact, the enhanced value due to the rise of the market is not profit. The profit which has to be specifically insured is of a different nature. It is purely anticipated or expected profit, i.e., profit which

---

[1] *Westminster Fire Office* v. *Glasgow Provident Investment Society* (1888), 13 App. Cas. 699 (fire insurance), *per* Lord SELBORNE, at p. 704.

[2] *Chapman* v. *Pole* (1870), 22 L.T. 306 (fire insurance), *per* COCKBURN, C.J., at p. 307.

[3] *Re Wilson and Scottish Insurance Corporation*, [1920] 2 Ch. 28, where the value had increased during the period of insurance: *Vance* v. *Forster* (1841), Ir. Cir. Rep. 47 (fire insurance); *Chapman* v. *Pole* (*supra*); *Collingridge* v. *Royal Exchange Assurance Corporation* (1877), 3 Q.B.D. 173 (fire insurance); *Glasgow Provident Investment Society* v. *Westminster Fire Office* 1887, 14 R. (Ct. of Sess.) 947 (fire insurance), *per* Lord YOUNG, at p. 989.

[4] *Hercules Insurance Co.* v. *Hunter* 1836, 14 Sh. (Ct. of Sess.) 1137 (fire insurance). The words "real and actual value" are sometimes used instead. See, e.g. *Chapman* v. *Pole* (*supra*), *per* COCKBURN, C.J., at p. 307.

[5] *Hercules Insurance Co.* v. *Hunter* (*supra*); *Glasgow Provident Investment Society* v. *Westminster Fire Office* (*supra*), *per* Lord YOUNG, at p. 989; *Rice* v. *Baxendale* (1861), 7 H. & N. 96 (carrier), *per* BRAMWELL, B., at p. 101, as explained in *O'Hanlan* v. *Great Western Rail. Co.* (1865), 6 B. & S. 484 (carrier). For a full discussion of the valuation of the subject-matter in fire insurance, see Ivamy, *Fire and Motor Insurance*, 2nd Edn., 1973, pp. 163–172.

[6] See Ivamy, *General Principles of Insurance Law*, 2nd Edn., 1970, pp. 341–342.

[7] *Re Wilson and Scottish Insurance Corporation* (*supra*) (motor insurance), where the proposal, which was made on the day on which the insured car was purchased, stated that the price paid by the insured was £250 and that the then value of the car was £250, and it was held that the insured was entitled to recover £400, the full value of the car at the time of the loss which took place during a renewal period, if the whole of the increase (which was due to an increase in the value of second-hand goods) accrued during such renewal period, the statement as to value being a continuing statement which must be accurate at the date of each renewal. Cf. *O'Hanlan* v. *Great Western Rail. Co.* (*supra*), where in an

has not been earned at the time when the value has to be ascertained for the purpose of the policy, namely, at the time of the loss, but which, if the goods had not been lost or damaged, the insured would or might have earned at a subsequent date, either by selling or using them.[1]

Where there is no market value, or where the market value is not applicable, the value of the subject-matter must be ascertained upon such materials as are available. In this case, the cost of reinstatement, after making a fair allowance of new for old, may be the most satisfactory measure of indemnity.[2]

The extrinsic value of the subject-matter, i.e., any special value due to circumstances personal to the insured, as opposed to its intrinsic value, cannot be taken into account.[3]

LIMITATIONS ON THE AMOUNT RECOVERABLE

The amount recoverable by the insured is necessarily limited by the sum insured, which fixes the maximum liability of the insurers. If, therefore, the pecuniary value of the loss exceeds the sum insured, the insurers on payment of the maximum sum payable under the policy have discharged their liability, and the insured must bear the excess himself.

Even where the amount of the loss does not exceed the sum insured, the insured is precluded from recovering his loss in full where the policy contains

    1 a contribution clause;
    2 an average clause;
    3 an excess clause.

1 Contribution Clause

The policy in insurances on property usually contains a stipulation that if, at the time of the loss, there are other subsisting policies effected by the insured, the insurers under the policy in question are not to be liable for more than a rateable proportion of the loss.[4]

2 Average Clause

The policy may contain a clause stating that it is "subject to average". The effect of such a clause is that if the sum insured is less than the value of the subject-matter, the insured in the event of a loss must bear the difference himself.[5]

3 Excess Clause

The effect of an excess clause is that the insured has no claim upon the insurers unless the loss exceeds the amount specified in it, e.g., he may have to bear the first £25.[6]

---

action against a carrier for non-delivery of drapery goods it was held, following *Rice* v. *Baxendale* (*supra*), that the measure of damages was the market value at the place and time at which the goods ought to have been delivered, or, if there was no market, the value as ascertained by taking into consideration, in addition to cost price and carriage, the reasonable profit of the importer.

[1] See Ivamy, *Fire and Motor Insurance*, 2nd Edn., 1973, p. 165.
[2] *Vance* v. *Forster* (*supra*). See further, Ivamy, *Fire and Motor Insurance*, 2nd Edn., 1973, pp. 164–165.
[3] *Hercules Insurance Co.* v. *Hunter* 1836, 14 Sh. (Ct. of Sess.) 1137 (fire insurance); *Re Egmont's (Earl) Trusts, Lefroy* v. *Egmont (Earl)*, [1908] 1 Ch. 821 (fire insurance).
[4] See generally Ivamy, *General Principles of Insurance Law*, 2nd Edn., 1970, pp. 381–383.
[5] *Ibid.*, pp. 383–384.
[6] *Ibid.*, pp. 384–385.

20

"ALL RISKS" INSURANCE

An insurance of this kind is intended to protect the insured against loss or damage generally, however caused.[2] The exact nature of the accident or casualty which causes the loss is immaterial provided that the loss is due to an accident or casualty of some kind. The policy does not cover ordinary wear and tear or deterioration.[3]

There are various forms of all risks policies, e.g., general all risks policies, contractors' all risks policies, and cash or goods in transit policies, each of which is considered in the pages which follow.

GENERAL "ALL RISKS" POLICIES

General all risks policies may be conveniently considered under the following heads:

    1 the contents of the policy;
    2 what constitutes a loss;
    3 the burden of proof;
    4 some examples from the reported decisions.

1 Contents of the Policy

The contents of a policy vary, but a typical one is the Lloyd's All Risks Policy which is composed of:

    a Recitals.
    b The perils insured against.
    c Exclusions.
    d Conditions.
    e The Schedule.

a *Recitals*

The policy states that the insured named in the Schedule has made a written proposal to the insurers and also a declaration bearing the date stated in the Schedule, and that the proposal and the declaration are to be the basis of the contract and are deemed to be incorporated into it. The receipt of the premium is also acknowledged.

---

[1] As to "all risks" policies in marine insurance, see Ivamy, *Marine Insurance* (1969), pp. 232–234.
[2] The policy is sometimes expressed to cover "loss or damage or misfortune"; but the word "misfortune" does not appear to add anything: *Moore* v. *Evans*, [1918] A.C. 185, *per* Lord ATKINSON, at p. 191.
[3] *British and Foreign Marine Insurance Co.* v. *Gaunt*, [1921] 2 A.C. 41 (marine insurance).

b *Perils Insured Against*

The insurers agree to the extent and in the manner stated below to insure against loss of or damage to the property as per the specification in the Schedule from whatsoever cause arising within the geographical limits, during the period and not exceeding the total sum insured specified in the Schedule.

c *Exclusions*

There are many exclusions from liability on the part of the insurers. They are not responsible for any loss or damage if the insured is engaged in or in any way connected with any form of professional entertaining.

Breakage of articles of a brittle nature, other than jewellery, unless such breakage is caused by burglars, thieves or fire, is not covered.

There is no liability in respect of loss or damage caused by moth or vermin or gradual deterioration, wear and tear or mechanical derangement, damage to or deterioration of any article directly caused by the actual process of dyeing, cleaning, repair or renovation. The policy does not cover loss of cash, currency or bank notes, nor loss or damage directly or indirectly caused by or contributed to by or arising from ionising radiations or contamination by radio-activity from any nuclear fuel or from any nuclear waste from the combustion of nuclear fuel.

A final exclusion clause states that the insurers will not be liable for loss or damage directly or indirectly occasioned by, happening through, or in consequence of war, invasion, acts of foreign enemies, hostilities (whether war be declared or not), civil war, rebellion, revolution, insurrection, military or usurped power or confiscation or nationalisation or requisition or destruction of or damage to property by or under the order of any Government or public or local authority.

d *Conditions*

The policy states that on each occasion on which loss of or damage to articles not separately specified occurs, the amount of the excess specified in the Schedule is to be deducted from the sum payable in respect of it. But this condition does not apply to jewellery or furs.

Any item of the specification which covers articles not separately specified is subject to average.[1]

Where any insured item consists of articles in a pair or set, the insurers are not to be liable to pay more than the value of any particular part or parts which may be lost or damaged. No notice is to be taken of any special value which such article or articles may have as part of such pair or set.

The insurers are to be entitled at their sole option to replace any article lost or damaged or to pay cash, not exceeding in any event the insured value.

In case of loss or damage, as a condition precedent to any right of indemnification, the insured must give to the insurers such information and evidence as they may reasonably require and as may be in the insured's power.

---

[4] This means that if the value of all the articles covered by such item shall at the time of any loss or damage be of greater value than the sum insured hereby in respect thereof, the insured shall be entitled to recover hereunder only such proportion of the said loss or damage as the sum insured in respect of such item bears to the total value of all articles covered by such item.

If he makes any claim knowing it to be false or fraudulent, as regards amount or otherwise, the policy is to become void and all claim under it is to be forfeited.

e *Schedule*

The Schedule states the number of the policy and the name and address of the insured. The geographical limits are set out as also is the amount of the excess applicable to articles not separately specified. The total sum insured is specified together with a statement as to the amount of the premium and the period of insurance.

2 What Constitutes a Loss

No claim attaches unless the subject-matter insured is lost or damaged.[1]

To constitute a loss the destruction of the subject-matter is not essential. It may be "lost" within the meaning of the policy, although, so far as is known, it still exists *in specie*, if the insured has been deprived of it by some accident or casualty.

It is not every deprivation, however, that amounts to a loss. The nature of the subject-matter[2] and the character and extent of the deprivation must be taken into consideration. A mere temporary deprivation does not in ordinary circumstances constitute a loss. Goods which are merely mislaid are not lost.

On the other hand, the deprivation need not be a complete deprivation, amounting to a certainty that they can never be recovered.[3] The test is uncertainty as to recovery.[4] If the probabilities are that the insured will never recover the property, and he has at the most a mere chance of recovering it, then there may be a loss within the meaning of the policy.[5]

Thus, a necklace which has been mislaid and is missing or has disappeared may be properly said to be "lost" if a reasonable time has elapsed to allow of a diligent search, and such diligent search has been made and has been fruitless.[6]

The goods are not, however, "lost" where the chances are the other way, and there is no reason to believe that they will not ultimately be recovered, although the insured may have to wait a long time. What he has lost in such a case is the advantage which he would have derived from the continued possession of the goods. But this is not what is insured.[7]

Thus, in *Moore* v. *Evans*[8], where pearls insured against all risks were

---

[1] *Moore* v. *Evans* (*supra*).
[2] In *Moore* v. *Evans*, as reported [1917] 1 K.B. 458, C.A., BANKES, L.J., at p. 471, suggested that there might be a difference between perishable goods or goods warehoused at a heavy rent, and goods such as pearls or jewellery in the hands of a customer. Cf. *Mitsui* v. *Mumford*, [1915] 2 K.B. 27, *per* BAILHACHE, J., at p. 31. But see *Moore* v. *Evans*, [1918] 2 A.C. 185, H.L., *per* Lord ATKINSON, at p. 191.
[3] *Moore* v. *Evans*, as reported [1917] 1 K.B. 458, C.A., *per* BANKES, L.J., at p. 471.
[4] *Holmes* v. *Payne*, [1930] 2 K.B. 301, *per* ROCHE, J., at p. 310.
[5] *Moore* v. *Evans* (*supra*), *per* BANKES, L.J., at p. 473, applying *Wilson* v. *Jones* (1867), L.R. 2 Exch. 139 (marine insurance), *per* BLACKBURN, J., at p. 152.
[6] *Holmes* v. *Payne* (*supra*), where the necklace subsequently fell out of an evening cloak in which it had become concealed.
[7] *Moore* v. *Evans*, [1917] 1 K.B. 458, C.A., *per* BANKES, L.J., at p. 473. Cf. *Mitsui* v. *Mumford* [1915] 2 K.B. 27 (war risks insurance); *Campbell and Phillipps, Ltd.* v. *Denman* (1915), 21 Com. Cas. 357 (war risks insurance).
[8] [1918] A.C. 185.

consigned to a customer in a foreign country "on sale or return", the mere
fact that the outbreak of the First World War rendered it impossible for
them to be lawfully returned to the insured until the end of the war was held
not to be a "loss". In the absence of any evidence to show that they had left
the proper custody[1] or that they had been lost or destroyed or damaged,
or that they had been confiscated or seized by the foreign Government, it
could not be inferred that they would not be returned in due course. The
insured had no doubt suffered a loss, but it was a loss arising out of the
failure of the transaction under which the pearls were consigned to the
customer, and was not a "loss" under the policy.

3 Burden of Proof

The burden of proving the loss lies upon the insured.[2] It is sufficient if
he proves that the loss was due to accident. He need not prove the exact
nature of the accident.[3]

Where an exception is made part of the definition of the event insured
against, so that the insurance is an insurance against any loss due to any
cause except the specified cause, the question arises as to whether the
burden of proof resting upon the insured includes the burden of proving
that the loss was not due to the excepted cause.

A policy of this kind is not like a policy against any specified peril. It is an
insurance against loss by any cause except the excepted cause. Hence, it
may be contended that the insured does not prove that the loss is covered
by the policy unless he proves at the same time that it was not caused by
the excepted cause.

Thus, in *Hurst* v. *Evans*[4], where jewellery was insured against loss arising
from any cause whatsoever, whether arising on land or water, except breakage of furniture, china, earthenware, glass and brittle articles, and except
loss by theft dishonestly committed by any servant or traveller or messenger
in the exclusive employment of the insured, it has been held that if the
jewellery is stolen, the insured cannot recover upon the mere proof of the
fact, since the insurance is an insurance against loss due to any cause except
breakage and dishonesty of servants. He must prove that the theft was not
committed by a servant in his employment.

The correctness of this decision is open to question and there does not
appear to be any sufficient reason for holding that the rule as to the burden
of proof in the case of exceptions differs from that applying in other branches
of insurance.[5]

---

[1] A mere change of bailee would not constitute a loss, even though the insured was not
consulted as to the change: *White, Child and Beney, Ltd.* v. *Eagle Star and British Dominion
Insurance Co.* (1922), 127 L.T. 571, *per* ROCHE, J., at p. 573.

[2] It is as a rule sufficient if the insured gives all the information which he has about the loss:
Arons v. *Wrightson* (1919), Times, Oct. 28.

[3] *British and Foreign Marine Insurance Co.* v. *Gaunt*, [1921] 2 A.C. 41 (marine insurance).
See generally Ivamy, *Marine Insurance* (1969), pp. 232–233.

[4] [1917] 1 K.B. 352. See further, Ivamy, *General Principles of Insurance Law*, 2nd Edn.,
1970, pp. 372–373.

[5] See the criticisms in *Munro, Brice & Co.* v. *War Risks Association*, [1918] 2 K.B.78 (marine
insurance). See also Ivamy, *General Principles of Insurance Law*, 2nd Edn., 1970, p. 373.

4   Examples from Reported Decisions

"Public Warehouse"

In *Firmin and Collins, Ltd.* v. *Allied Shippers, Ltd.* (*Alder, Third Party*)[1] the defendants, who were shipping and forwarding agents, agreed to pack and store the plaintiffs' goods pending shipment. They agreed to insure the goods, while pending shipment, in a warehouse, and effected an "all risks" policy with the third party, who was an underwriter. By the terms of the policy the goods were covered "whilst in the defendants' warehouse and/or any public warehouse". In fact, the goods were stored in premises belonging to Sumner Transport, Ltd. These premises consisted of an uncovered yard enclosed by a low corrugated iron fence.[2] The goods were damaged in a fire while in the yard. The plaintiffs claimed against the defendants on the ground that they were in breach of their contract to insure the goods. The defendants claimed against the third party alleging that the premises of Sumner Transport, Ltd. were a "public warehouse".

LYELL, J., held that the third party was not liable on the policy because Sumner Transport, Ltd., were not carrying on the business of public warehousemen and said:[3]

> "My judgment is that a public warehouseman is one whose business holds itself out to all comers to be prepared to store goods for indefinite periods; his business is to sell his accommodation for storage. It matters not to him who fills it or for how long; any given customer decides to fill it, and that seems to me to be the essence of a public warehouse. I do not attach to it the special considerations that attach to a public carrier, but it seems to me that if you purport to run a public warehouse, it is essential that you should hold yourself out to sell storage space to people, and having sold it and having been allowed to put their goods there, then, in my judgment, provided they pay the proper charges, they are entitled to say, 'I am leaving them here to rest until I desire to take them away'."

Further, their premises were not a "public warehouse" within the meaning of the policy.[4] But the defendants were liable as they had failed to keep the goods in a place where they would be covered by the policy.[5]

Loss of Manuscript

In *Frewin* v. *Poland*[6] the insured was an author and publisher, and had effected a Lloyd's Form J policy, which provided:

> "All and every risk or loss of damage. To pay up to £1,000 in the event of the destruction or loss of any manuscripts or documents, resulting in the necessity for the Assured to rewrite, including all costs of research preparation and the like."

Manuscripts of two books were lost, but the books were not rewritten. The insured claimed £860 under the policy. The parties agreed that the original cost of writing each book was £430 and the cost of rewriting would be a similar sum. The underwriter denied liability, contending that it was

---

[1] [1967] 1 Lloyd's Rep. 633, Q.B.D.
[2] The evidence concerning the layout of the premises is set out *ibid.*, at pp. 637–8.
[3] *Ibid.*, at p. 638.
[4] *Ibid.*, at p. 638.
[5] *Ibid.*, at p. 639.
[6] [1968] 1 Lloyd's Rep. 100, Q.B.D. (Commercial Court).

the actual cost of rewriting which was insured, and that no sum was payable unless and until that cost was incurred.

DONALDSON, J., held that the claim succeeded. The event insured against was "the destruction or loss of any manuscripts or documents, resulting in the necessity for the Assured to rewrite". That event had occurred, and the costs of rewriting merely quantified that loss. In the words of his Lordship:[1]

> "Has the event insured against occurred? Destruction and loss can be total or partial. If it is total, no problem arises; but a partial loss may be of comparatively minor significance or it may be so great as for practical purposes to be the equivalent of an actual total loss. Similar problems in the field of marine insurance led to the evolution of the constructive total loss. The parties have here agreed that the indemnity shall attach if the documents or manuscripts are totally lost or destroyed or are partially lost or destroyed to a degree which necessitates rewriting. This is what has happened in this case and accordingly I hold that the event insured against has occurred.
>
> This still leaves over the question of what, if anything, is payable. What is insured against is loss or damage consequent upon the event, including all costs of research, preparation and the like. The insurance is not simply against the cost of rewriting including the cost of research, etc. Had the latter been the case, the assured would have suffered no relevant loss unless and until he rewrote. As it is, the relevant loss is suffered at the moment when the manuscripts are lost and the cost of rewriting merely quantifies that loss. Accordingly, it matters not whether the assured does or does not rewrite, although the *quantum* of the loss could have been more easily proved if he had in fact rewritten."

The policy in this case contained a Mutual Assessors Clause which stated:

> "In the event of loss arising under this Policy the Underwriters and the Assured shall appoint an Assessor to be mutually agreed upon whose findings shall be binding [on] both parties."

His Lordship said (*obiter*) that this might be a most useful clause, but the insurance market might like to consider whether its general adoption would not give rise to very considerable problems. He observed:[2]

> "Nothing turns in this case upon the Mutual Assessors Clause. This may be a most useful clause, but the insurance market may like to consider whether its general adoption would not give rise to very considerable problems. For example, is the assessor to occupy a quasi-judicial position in which he is bound to disclose to the assured any information given to him by underwriters? At what stage do his findings bind the parties? It may be that the investigation at first fully supports the assured's claim and the assessor reports accordingly, but that later he obtains further information which throws a different light upon the matter. Are underwriters bound by the first report?
>
> I have illustrated my doubts with examples which may cause disquiet to underwriters; but examples could also be found which might cause an assured to doubt the wisdom of agreeing to such a clause. However, as I say, nothing turns upon the clause in the present case. There is an old adage that "claims sell insurance"; but no one has ever had the temerity to suggest that the same is true of litigation in relation to insurance claims. I mention the possible pitfalls inherent in this clause because the Judge of the Commercial Court is always deeply concerned for the well-being of the insurance market and is as much interested in avoiding the need for litigation as in presiding over it."

Loss of Diamonds

In *Roselodge, Ltd.* v. *Castle*[3] a company insured its diamonds under a Lloyd's jewellers' block policy against loss or damage "arising from any cause

---

[1] [1968] 1 Lloyd's Rep. at p. 100.

[2] *Ibid.*, at p. 103.

[3] [1966] 2 Lloyd's Rep. 113, Q.B.D.

whatsoever". One of the directors of the company was robbed with violence whilst he was carrying diamonds to the value of over £300,000. When a claim was made under the policy, the underwriters contended that they were not liable because the company had not disclosed to them that (*a*) the director concerned had been convicted of bribing a police officer in 1946 and had been fined £75; and (*b*) its sales manager had been convicted of smuggling diamonds into the United States in 1956, and one year after his release from prison had been engaged by the company.

McNAIR, J., held that the underwriters were entitled to avoid liability. He considered that the convictions of the director was not a material fact and need not have been disclosed, and observed:[1]

> "In the result I have come to the conclusion that it is not established to my satisfaction that Mr. Rosenberg's offence and conviction on a matter which has no direct relation to trading as a diamond merchant was a material fact which would have influenced a prudent underwriter. Furthermore, if the test be that laid down by FLETCHER MOULTON, L.J. in *Joel* v. *Law Union and Crown Insurance Company*[2], I am satisfied beyond any doubt that a reasonable businessman would not have imagined for a moment that this was the matter which the proposer should have disclosed as material. If any relevant question had been asked in the proposal form and untruthfully answered, the position would clearly have been quite different."

The learned Judge, however, went on to say that the conviction of the sales manager was material, and the company should have disclosed it. On this point he observed:[3]

> "After anxious consideration of the matter in all its aspects I have reached the conclusion and so find that the average reasonable businessman, though no doubt impressed by Mr. Rosenberg's charitable act in attempting and apparently succeeding in rehabilitating a man who had paid his penalty, would appreciate that [the sales manager] remained or might remain a security risk and that underwriters should have been given the opportunity to decide for themselves whether the story as a whole was one which would have influenced them in accepting the risk as offered for fixing the premium. The non-disclosure places upon the underwriters the risk that Mr. Rosenberg's estimate of [the sales manager's] rehabilitation might be wrong without their having been given an opportunity of considering it. Furthermore, if, contrary to my view, the *Joel* test is not the correct test, I would hold on balance of probabilities as a fact that the whole incident was a material fact which would have influenced the prudent underwriter."

In *Roselodge, Ltd.* v. *Castle*[4] McNAIR, J., had occasion to allude to the "moral hazard",[5] and said:[6]

> "Each of these witnesses was emphatic in the view that in a jewellery insurance of this kind the moral hazard is important. Mr. Archer[7] defined the moral hazard as the risk of honesty and integrity of the assured, and, in the case of a company the honesty and integrity of any executives or key personnel (though I think he meant the risk of dishonesty and lack of integrity). The moral hazard he considered of particular importance in the case of jewellery insurance 'because of the smallness and little weight of the jewellery and because in a

---

[1] [1966] 2 Lloyd's Rep. at p. 132, Q.B.D.
[2] [1908] 2 K.B. 863, C.A.
[3] [1966] 2 Lloyd's Rep. at p. 133.
[4] [1966] 2 Lloyd's Rep. 113, Q.B.D. (Commercial Court).
[5] See further, Ivamy, *General Principles of Insurance Law*, 2nd. Edn., 1970, pp. 101–102.
[6] [1966] 2 Lloyd's Rep. at p. 132.
[7] One of the underwriters called as witnesses.

jewellery insurance there is often a lack of adequate documentation and jewellery is very easily disposed of.' This seems to me to be a reasonable view . . ."

Loss of Jewellery

In *Jaglom* v. *Excess Insurance Co., Ltd.*[1] jewellery was insured under an "all risks" policy "whilst in the assured's bank". The "slip"[2] provided: "It is agreed to extend this policy in respect of items taken out of the bank in accordance with the rates on the attached schedule". It was amended to read: "Sub. prior advice to [the broker who negotiated the policy] only".

The insured was robbed of some of the jewellery whilst she was in a jewellers' shop where she had gone to get it repaired. She claimed an indemnity under the policy, but the insurers repudiated liability on the ground that (i) they had not come on risk until it had been taken into the custody of a bank; and (ii) if the words "taken out of the bank" were to be construed as "being out of the bank", then no prior advice had been given to the broker. DONALDSON, J., held that the claim succeeded, for it was not a requirement of the cover that there had been formal delivery of the jewellery into the bank's custody.[3] If the insurers really wanted that, they could have required a warranty that it was in the custody of the bank at some stated time or date. The use of the word "extend" in the context of the "slip" meant no more than that the insurers were accepting a second risk in addition to the first. The words "taken out of the bank" did no more than reflect the fact that the bank custody risk came first on the "slip", and that it was no doubt contemplated that the jewellery would be more in the bank that out of it. On the evidence, the broker knew that the jewellery was out of the bank.[4] The words "prior advice" in the context had no technical meaning. If the insurers wanted such formality as they claimed, they should have inserted a clause in the "slip" to read "subject to prior notice in writing by assured to [the brokers]", and this they had not done.[5]

Loss of Jerkins

In *Anglo-African Merchants, Ltd. and Exmouth Clothing Co., Ltd.* v. *Bayley*[6] the insured took out an "all risks" insurance policy[7] in respect of a quantity of Government surplus leather jerkins, which were at least twenty years old but were unused. They were described in the policy as: "New Men's Clothes in bales for export whilst at the premises of Power Packing, Ltd.. . . . including transit from the assured's premises."

Two hundred and forty-five bales were lost, and the insured claimed under the policy, but the insurers repudiated liability on the ground of non-disclosure of a material fact, *viz.*, that the goods were war surplus and at least twenty years old.

---

[1] [1971] 2 Lloyd's Rep. 171, Q.B.D, (Commercial Court).
[2] No policy was ever issued.
[3] [1971] 2 Lloyd's Rep. at p. 176.
[4] *Ibid.*, at p. 177.
[5] *Ibid.*, at p. 177.
[6] [1969] 1 Lloyd's Rep. 268, Q.B.D. (Commercial Court).
[7] The insurance was treated as being marine because, although the policy was on goods in a warehouse in England, they were there with a view to ultimate export. The policy was subscribed by syndicates concerned with the underwriting of marine risks. See *ibid.*, at p. 275.

MEGAW, J., held that these facts were material and that, since they had not been disclosed to the insurers, the claim failed. He observed:[1]

> "Having considered the whole of the evidence on this aspect, I am also satisfied that each of these matters—the fact that the goods were war surplus and their age—was a fact which was material: it would have affected the mind of a prudent underwriter in deciding whether or not to underwrite the risk at all, in deciding what limitations he might wish to impose as to the risks to be covered, in deciding what premium to quote and in deciding whether or not to require an inspection of, and report on, the goods or the place where they were being stored, or both. In particular, in relation to the fact of war surplus, I am satisfied that underwriters, rightly or wrongly, but not unreasonably, regard war surplus goods, or at any rate war surplus clothing, as being goods which they classify as 'hot': that is, involving an abnormally high risk of theft. In relation to the age of the goods, underwriters would normally and reasonably be concerned with the possibility of defects, such as staining, in respect of which claims might be made and it might be a matter of great difficulty and dispute to ascertain when the damage was in fact sustained; unless, of course, a pre-insurance inspection were to be required as a condition of accepting the risk."

His Lordship said that much evidence had been given as to the meaning of the word "new" with particular reference to the clothing trade. It was not a question of the meaning of the word in isolation, but of its meaning in the context of a request for insurance of goods which were described as being "New Men's Clothes in bales for export". The insurers contended that to describe twenty year old leather jerkins as "new" was a misdescription, a corollary of the non-disclosure that the goods were twenty years old. The insured, however, maintained that so far from being a misdescription, the use of the word "new" in the context indicated that the clothes were Government surplus, and that they were not of recent manufacture. The gist of the evidence was that in the clothing trade goods were never described as "new", e.g., in invoices, advertisements or other trade documents, unless they were Government surplus goods. If they were Government surplus goods, and were unused, they might be described as "new", despite the fact that they were not of recent manufacture. On this matter his Lordship observed:[2]

> "I accept that evidence, but I do not, on the whole of the evidence, accept the proposition that this special connotation of the word 'new', whether with or without the addition of the words 'in bales', ought to have brought it to the attention of an ordinary, prudent underwriter that the goods which he was asked to insure under the description of 'New Men's Clothes in Bales for Export' were, or might reasonably be expected to be, Government surplus clothes, or old clothes, in the sense that they were manufactured at least twenty years previously."

The insured also asserted that the insurers had waived further information about the precise nature of the goods, for a reasonable underwriter would have been put on inquiry by the description "New Men's Clothes in bales for export", and that they had made no inquiry as to their nature. The learned Judge held that the plea of waiver failed and said:[3]

> "The plaintiffs seek to assert that a reasonable underwriter would have been put on inquiry by the description 'New Men's Clothes in Bales for Export'; that such inquiry would have revealed that the goods were army surplus; that

---

[1] [1969] 1 Lloyd's Rep. 277, Q.B.D. (Commercial Court).
[2] *Ibid.*, at p. 278.
[3] *Ibid.*, at p. 278.

Mr. Gibson, though he made other inquiries, failed to make any inquiry as to the precise nature of the goods; and that the defendants thus 'waived further information upon the precise nature of the goods'. Let me assume in favour of the plaintiffs that an insurer waives his right to complain of non-disclosure, if he has received information which would put an ordinarily careful insurer on inquiry and nevertheless fails to inquire. That is put by Lord Justice SARGANT as the minimum required for a successful plea of waiver. *Greenhill* v. *Federal Insurance Co., Ltd.*[1]. Lord Justice SCRUTTON in his judgment in the same case[2] clearly regards the law on this point as much more favourable to insurers. Even on the assumption of the most lenient test, I cannot hold on the evidence that a normally prudent insurer would have been put on inquiry as to the precise nature of the goods by reason of seeing them described as 'New Men's Clothes in Bales for Export'. Some underwriters might be alerted by the word 'new' to make inquiries, because they would realize that it is an unusual adjective to apply to clothes. More underwriters, I think, would take the attitude which Mr. Gibson took: the goods are described as 'new'; they are new; they are not clothes which were manufactured years ago; they are not Government surplus, which is normally some distance away from having been newly manufactured when it is sold as surplus. I do not think that that attitude can properly be said to show any lack of care or prudence; or that failure to inquire could give rise to a valid claim of waiver."

Loss of Film

In *Richard Aubrey Film Productions, Ltd.* v. *Graham*[3] the insured took out an "all risks" insurance policy by which the insurers agreed:

"To indemnify the Insured against loss or damage from any cause whatsoever to the Raw Stock, exposed Film Negatives, Matrices, Lavenders, Positives, Working Prints, Cutting Copies and Fine Grain Prints—all mute and/or sound— the property of the Insured or for which they are responsible in respect of the Motion Picture provisionally entitled 'DICKY' . . . against all such Loss, Damage or Liability as aforesaid . . . not exceeding the sum of [£18,000] . . ."

The insured claimed under the policy for £18,000, alleging that over 40,000 feet of exposed film had been stolen. The insurers denied liability and put the insured to strict proof of loss.

WINN, J., held that the action succeeded, for the film had been stolen, and had been permanently lost to the insured.

His Lordship said[4] that it might be, though the evidence did not reveal it, that by and large, and in many cases insurers were content to deal with any claim on the footing that the insured could automatically recover from them the cost of reshooting the part of the film which had been lost, and that it worked out well enough, as a practical matter, as a basis of adjustment of a claim, but he thought that it was important that it should be appreciated that at any rate in his view of the law the cost incurred or the cost which would be incurred in re-shooting was not the measure of the amount recoverable on such a policy as the present one in the event of the destruction of the whole or part of the only copy of a cinematographic film. Policies could, of course, be negotiated for an agreed value. But the policy in the present case was not an agreed value policy. They could be negotiated, on any other basis which the contracting parties saw fit, to provide for the cost of re-shooting, with a

---

[1] [1927] 1 K.B. 65 at p. 89.
[2] *Ibid.*, at pp. 85–86.
[3] [1960] 2 Lloyd's Rep. 101, Q.B.D.
[4] *Ibid.*, at p. 105.

limit, and so on. He was not concerned with any such hypothetical different method of insuring, but only with the present policy and its specific terms. In the case of the present policy the insurers were not bound to make good the cost which had been incurred or to pay or provide the cost of remaking that which had been lost. The insured could probably have held the right to exploit the film for £20,000, and bearing in mind that the editing and final completion of the film would have cost about £3,000 and some re-shooting might have been necessary, they were entitled to £15,300 under the policy.

His Lordship observed:[1]

> "I have in mind the amount for which insurance was taken in this case, £18,000. I have in mind the fact that the editing and final completion of this film would have cost, in my judgment, £3,000 not £1,500 or £2,000, the figures that were given in evidence. I bear in mind the important factor which is not capable of monetary assessment, that in some of any re-shooting which might be necessary there would be difficulties encountered of a serious character, because the boys who figure so prominently in this comedy would have been older, and it would have been difficult to devise shooting techniques which would have effectively concealed from the viewer the fact that a different actor had been substituted, just as there were awkward difficulties to be overcome by the producer. He still had to disguise the fact that two individuals appeared as the vicar or clergyman in this film, and two as the clergyman's or vicar's wife. One of them was Mr. Aubrey himself, who was also the main character 'Dicky' in the film."

Loss of Metal

In *Atlantic Metal Co., Ltd.* v. *Hepburn*[2] some metal which was stored in a warehouse was insured under an "all risks" policy. The insured made a claim under the policy for £5,296 (based on £250 per ton which was the selling price of the metal) and alleged that about 19 tons of the metal had been lost whilst in a warehouse. The insurers repudiated liability and put the insured to strict proof. The stock cards used by the insured showed a loss, but there was evidence that they were not reliable.

PEARSON, J., held that the stock cards were not reliable, but that only about 2½ tons of the metal had been lost. The replacement value of the metal was £234 per ton, and therefore the insured were entitled to only £560 plus £56 in respect of four bags of nickel-silver which had also been stolen.

Loss of Furs

In *Simon Brooks, Ltd.* v. *Hepburn*[3] the insured were furriers who effected an insurance policy in respect of their furs. The policy stated that it covered them against:

> "All risks of loss and damage from whatoever cause arising . . . whilst anywhere in the United Kingdom including the Assured's own addresses . . . Excluding larceny and theft in respect of shop portion of Louisette Ltd."

The insured were owned by a partnership carrying on business under the name of Brown and Brown who also owned Louisette, Ltd. Both companies carried on business at the same premises in Manchester at the time the policy was effected. The partnership business carried on by Brown and Brown

---

[1] [1960] 2 Lloyd's Rep. 110, Q.B.D.
[2] [1960] 2 Lloyd's Rep. 42, Q.B.D. (Commercial Court).
[3] [1961] 2 Lloyd's Rep. 43, Q.B.D. (Commercial Court).

in Blackpool was acquired by Louisette, Ltd., and the business of Louisette, Ltd. was henceforth carried on in Blackpool. Some furs, which were the property of the insured, were sent to Louisette, Ltd. so that they could be sold. They were stolen from Louisette, Ltd.'s premises in Blackpool. The insured claimed for a loss under the policy, but the insurers contended that the risk of larceny at Louisette, Ltd.'s premises at Blackpool was excluded by the policy.

DIPLOCK, J., held that the reference in the policy to "shop portion of Louisette, Ltd." was a reference to the premises of Louisette, Ltd. at the time the policy was effected. Liability for the loss which had occurred at other premises where Louisette, Ltd., subsequently carried on trade was not excluded. He observed:[1]

> "In essence, this case turns upon whether the reference to 'shop portion of Louisette, Ltd.' is a reference to premises or a reference to persons. The point is one which is very much of first impression and the conclusions to which I have come is that it is a reference to premises; that in order to ascertain what the meaning of the expression 'shop portion of Louisette, Ltd.' is, I must look at the circumstances at the time at which the policy was entered into and see what then was the shop portion of Louisette, Ltd. At that date it was the ground floor of 36 King Street, Manchester, and, if I be right in that construction, a loss occurring at other premises where Madame Louisette, Ltd. subsequently carried on a retail trade is not excluded by that clause. As I say, the matter is one of first impression—very much of first impression—but it seems to me that one of the relevant factors is this: at the time at which the policy was entered into, retail trade was being carried on by the assured (who consisted of Simon Brooks, Ltd. and Madame Louisette, Ltd.), at two premises, namely, the ground floor at 5a St. Anne Street, Manchester, where Simon Brooks Ltd., carried on a retail trade, and the ground floor at 36 King Street, Manchester, where Madame Louisette Ltd., carried on trade. If the intention had been to exclude all loss on premises used for retail trade, then it would have been necessary to exclude also the shop portion of Simon Brooks, Ltd."

His Lordship said[2] that if one were considering that the phrase "shop portion of Louisette, Ltd." dealt with persons rather than with the premises, one would have expected to find some difference between the insurable risk involved in the personalities concerned. But both these companies, Simon Brooks, Ltd. and Madame Louisette, Ltd., were owned in the same proportion by Brown and Brown and were managed by them in exactly the same way, and, in fact, the capital of Madame Louisette, Ltd. was nearly three times as large as the capital of Simon Brooks, Ltd. Furthermore, although at that time the only respect in which either of the insured owned furs at the retail business at Blackpool, was that Simon Brooks, Ltd. supplied furs for that company, it was to be observed that the premises at Blackpool were at all material times retail premises. Again, there were facts which made the premises at 36 King Street, Manchester, a heavier risk as regards larceny from the premises than either of the other two premises, i.e., the fact that there was at the back, facing on to a narrow unfrequented street, a service door and a glass window.

CONTRACTORS' "ALL RISKS" POLICIES

Contractors' all risks policies may be considered under the following heads:

---

[1] [1961] 2 Lloyd's Rep. at p. 45.
[2] *Ibid.*, at p. 45.

1 the contents of the policy;
2 some examples from the reported decisions.

1 Contents of Policy

The contents of a policy vary, but typical clauses are to be found in the Lloyd's policy, which is composed of:

a a physical damage section;
b a public liability section;
c general exclusions;
d general conditions;
e the Schedule.

a *Physical Damage*

The underwriters agree to insure against all risks of loss or physical damage:

i the whole of the contract works;
ii temporary buildings whilst at the site or in transit;
iii contractors' plant, equipment tools and tackle whilst on the site;

for the period specified in the Schedule to the policy.

But the policy does not cover (*inter alia*) loss of or damage to aircraft or any mechanically propelled vehicle except when it is being used as a tool of the trade on the site, nor loss of cash, cheques or securities.

Further, they are not responsible for loss or damage directly or indirectly caused by fault, defect, error or omission in design, plan or specification, nor for the cost of rectifying or replacing defective material or workmanship.

Again, no liability exists in respect of loss due to wear and tear, gradual deterioration or mechanical or electrical breakdown, or in respect of any loss of use or other consequential loss.

b *Public Liability*

The underwriters agree to indemnify the insured up to the limit of liability specified in the Schedule against such sum as he shall become legally liable to pay in respect of claims made against him arising from bodily injury or disease (fatal or non-fatal) to persons or damage to property caused by any accident arising out of or happening in connection with the performance of the contract. They also agree to pay the costs and expenses incurred with their written consent of any such claim.

But this section of the policy does not cover liability for bodily injury sustained by any person arising out of and in the course of his employment by the insured, damage to property owned by the insured, damage to property directly or indirectly caused by any ship, vessel or aircraft, or by any mechanically propelled vehicle (except when such vehicle is being used as a tool of the trade on the site) and in such circumstances is not insured under a motor vehicle policy or any other insurance policy.

c *General Exclusions*

There is no liability under the policy in respect of any loss, damage or liability which is also covered by any other existing policy except in respect of any excess beyond the amount which would have been payable under such other policy if the present insurance had not been effected.

There is no cover for loss, damage or liability directly or indirectly caused by ionising radiations or contamination by radioactivity from any nuclear fuel or from any nuclear waste from the combustion of nuclear fuel.

Again there is no cover if the loss, damage or liability is directly or indirectly occasioned by or happening in consequence of war, invasion, acts of foreign enemies, hostilities (whether war be declared or not), civil war, rebellion, revolution, insurrection, military or usurped power, confiscation or nationalisation or requisition or destruction or damage to property by or under the order of any government or public or local authority.

Further, the policy does not cover penalties for non-completion or delay in completion of the contract.

d   *General Conditions*

The insured must give the underwriters immediate notice in writing of the happening of any occurrence likely to give rise to a claim under the policy.

The insured must not admit liability for or offer or agree to settle without the written consent of the underwriters any claim made against him.

In the event of partial or total cessation of work or any other occurrence whatsoever which may give rise to a claim under the policy, he must use due diligence to protect the insured property and avoid or diminish the amount of such claim.

As soon as the total contract price of the operations covered by the policy is finally determined, he must furnish the underwriters with a declaration of the price to enable the premium to be adjusted as provided in the Schedule.

If he makes any claim knowing it to be false or fraudulent as regards amount or otherwise, the policy becomes void, and all claim under it is forfeited.

e   *Schedule*

The Schedule (*inter alia*) describes the contract and the site, and states the estimated contract price, the limits of liability, the premium to be paid and the method of adjusting it in accordance with the contract price as finally determined, and the period of insurance.

2   Examples from Reported Decisions

In *Howard Farrow, Ltd.* v. *Ocean Accident and Guarantee Corporation, Ltd.*[1] the plaintiffs, who were road and sewer contractors and engineers, effected a policy with the defendants. The policy stated that the defendants would indemnify the plaintiffs in respect of:

> "Compensation which the insured shall become liable to pay for . . . accidental damage to property happening in the course of the business and occurring . . . at any place where the insured is carrying out any work."

It also stated that:

> "The indemnity contained in this policy shall not apply to or include . . . liability in respect of injury or damage caused by or in connection with or arising from . . .
> (c) . . . flood".

---

[1] (1940), 67 Ll.L. Rep. 27, K.B.D.

The plaintiffs were engaged in the construction of a culvert in and over a stream. Their workmen negligently allowed some planks to obstruct a grating in the stream, and this caused it to overflow and damage property belonging to a third party.[1] The plaintiffs paid the third party's claim against them, and now sought an indemnity from the defendants. The defendants repudiated liability on the ground that the loss fell within the exception of "flood" set out above. The plaintiffs, however, maintained that although, the damage was due to flood, the flood was the result of the negligence of their workmen and was therefore covered by the policy. MACNAGHTEN, J., held that this contention could not be accepted, and that the action failed. He observed:[2]

> "The contention that was submitted to the learned arbitrator[3] was put forward here before me. It was conceded that the damage was caused by water and that the water was in such a volume, and to such an extent, that it could properly be described as a flood; indeed, I do not know that there is any other word that could adequately describe what happened. But [Counsel] argued; Although it is true that water caused the damage, you must look further back, and since the arbitrator finds that it was the negligence of the claimants that caused the flood, then it is not true to say that the damage was caused by flood, because the damage was caused by negligence.
>
> It seems to me the damage was caused by flood and by nothing else. The flood no doubt was caused by the negligence of the claimants, and the argument of [Counsel] if I apprehend it rightly, is that since this policy indemnifies the claimants against liability brought upon them by the negligence of their servants, I ought to read these words 'injury or damage caused by or in connection with or arising from fire explosion or flood' as being qualified in this way, 'unless such fire explosion or flood is caused by the negligence of the claimants' servants.' But there is no ground on which I can add to the words of the policy the suggested limitation. If the flood had not been caused by their act, neglect or default, then they could be under no liability. Therefore the argument of [Counsel] in effect means the striking out of the policy of the very exception which it contains."

In *Jones Construction Co.* v. *Alliance Assurance Co., Ltd.*[4] the insured were contractors, who had effected an "all risks" insurance policy in respect of the construction of a dam at Derbend-I-Kahn, Iraq. The period of the policy was extended by an endorsement. Later the insurers refused to extend the policy further. The contractors applied for a declaration that the insurers were obliged to extend the period under the policy which provided:

> "The Insurers . . . will indemnify the Insured . . . for loss arising during the period stated in the Schedule or any subsequent period in respect of which the Insured shall have paid and the Insurers accepted the premium required for this extension of the terms of this Policy."

The Court of Appeal[5] held that the declaration would not be granted, for the self-extending provision had not come into operation because the required premium had not been paid and had not been accepted.

DANCKWERTS, L.J., said:[6]

> "It seems to me that on the words in the opening provisions of the policy, ' . . . or any subsequent period in respect of which the Insured shall have paid

---

[1] The evidence is set out (1940), 67 Ll. Rep. at pp. 30–31.
[2] *Ibid.*, at p. 31.
[3] Before whom the dispute between the parties was originally brought.
[4] [1961] 1 Lloyd's Rep. 121, C.A.
[5] ORMROD, DEVLIN and DANCKWERTS, L.JJ.
[6] [1961] 1 Lloyd's Rep. at p. 131.

and the insurers accepted the premium required for this extension of the terms of this Policy', it is impossible to come to any other conclusion than that the insurers were only accepting the risk, subject to their volition, for the period which was expressly mentioned, and it seems to me it would be a very strong step to take to force further risks upon the insurers, unless they had plainly, by the terms of their contract, agreed to extend the period of their risk, without further consultation with their own interests and considerations."

In *Dominion Bridge Co., Ltd.* v. *Toronto General Insurance Co.*[1] the insured had effected a "Contractor's Public Liability Policy" containing an endorsement which stated that the insurance company agreed:

> "To pay on behalf of the Insured all sums which the Insured shall become obligated to pay by reason of the liability imposed upon the Insured by law for damages because of injury to or destruction of property, caused by accident occurring within the Policy Period and while the Endorsement is in force and resulting from or while at or about the work of the Insured designated as an insured risk [in the Policy]."

The endorsement contained an exception stating that:

> "[it] shall have no application with respect to and shall not extend to nor cover any claim arising or existing by reason of any of the following matters: (1) liability or obligation assumed by the Insured under any contract or agreement . . ."

The insured entered into a contract with the British Columbia Bridge Authority to erect on masonry foundations supplied by the Authority the whole of the structural steel works for the Second Narrows Bridge at Vancouver. The contract provided (*inter alia*) that:

> "*Faulty Work.* If there is evidence of any fault, defect or injury, from any cause whatever, which may prejudicially affect the strength, durability or appearance of any section of the structure, the Contractor shall, at his own expense, satisfactorily correct such faults, or, if required, shall replace so much of said section as the Engineer may deem necesssary even to the extent of re-building the entire section."

The masonry foundations of the bridge were damaged as a result of the collapse of the steel superstructure due to the admitted negligence of the insured. The insured had the damage to the foundations repaired at a cost of $358,102, and claimed an indemnity under the policy.

The Supreme Court of Canada[2] held that the action failed, for the liability in question had been assumed by the insured under its contract with the British Columbia Bridge Authority, and it came squarely within the exclusion clause set out above. It was immaterial that such liability was tortious liability independent of contract. JUDSON, J.,[3] observed:

> " 'Liability imposed by law' and 'liability assumed under contract' were for one and the same loss. That being so, liability, even though imposed by law, was excluded from the coverage."

---

[1] [1964] 1 Lloyd's Rep. 194, Supreme Court of Canada.

[2] CARTWRIGHT, FAUTEUX, ABBOTT, MARTLAND and JUDSON, JJ.

[3] [1964] 1 Lloyd's Rep. at p. 196. The Court found it unnecessary to deal with a second exclusion clause, which stated that the insurance company was not to be liable for "injury to or destruction of (*a*) property used, owned or occupied by, or rented or leased to, or in the care, custody or control of the Insured . . .": *ibid.*, at p. 197.

In *Queensland Government Railways and Electric Power Transmission Pty., Ltd.* v. *Manufacturers' Mutual Insurance, Ltd.*[1] a railway bridge built in 1897 had been swept away by flood water. Prismatic piers were being erected by the plaintiffs when they were brought down by a flood, which was higher than any previously recorded. The plaintiffs had taken out a Contractors' All Risks policy, and claimed to be indemnified by the insurers. But the insurers repudiated liability on the ground that the loss fell within an exception which stated: "This insurance shall not apply to or include . . . loss or damage arising from faulty design and liabilities resulting therefrom."

The matter was referred to arbitration, and the arbitrator found that the design of the new piers was satisfactory, but that investigations into the cause of their failure showed that during floods they were subjected to greater transverse forces than had been realized. He made an award in favour of the insured, but the insurers applied to have it set aside on the ground that the arbitrator had misconstrued the words "faulty design", for he had said that they meant that "in the designing of the piers there was some element of personal failure or non-compliance with the standards which would be expected of designing engineers".

The High Court of Australia[2] held that the award should be set aside. The loss was due to "faulty design", and it was erroneous to confine these words to personal failure or non-compliance with the standards which would be expected of designing engineers.

BARWICK, C.J., said:[3]

> "Let it be accepted, as the arbitrator found, that the piers, as designed, failed to withstand the water force to which they were subjected because they were designed in accordance with engineering knowledge and practice which was deficient, rather than because the designer failed to take advantage of such professional knowledge as there was. Nevertheless the loss was due to 'faulty design' and the arbitrator has done no more than explain how it happened that the design was faulty. We think it was an error to confine faulty design to the 'personal failure or non-compliance with standards which would be expected of designing engineers' on the part of the designing engineers responsible for the piers. To design something that will not work simply because at the time of its designing insufficient is known about the problems involved and their solution to achieve a successful outcome is a common enough instance of faulty design. The distinction which is relevant is that between 'faulty', i.e. defective design and design free from defect. We have not found sufficient ground for reading the exclusion in this policy as not covering loss from faulty design when, as here, the piers fell because their design was defective, although according to the finding, not negligently so. The exclusion is not against loss from 'negligent designing'; it is against loss from 'faulty design', and the latter is more comprehensive than the former."

WINDEYER, J., observed:[4]

> Doubtless a faulty design can be the product of fault on the part of the designer. But a man may use skill and care, he may do all that in the circumstances may be expected of him, and yet produce something which is faulty because it will not answer the purpose for which it was intended . . . The piers failed to stand up in a flood which it might reasonably have been considered might occur and

---

[1] [1969] 1 Lloyd's Rep. 214, High Court of Australia.
[2] BARWICK, C.J., McTIERNAN, KITTO, MENZIES and WINDEYER, JJ.
[3] [1969] 1 Lloyd's Rep. at p. 217.
[4] *Ibid.*, at p. 219. See further, *ibid.*, at p. 218, where the learned Judge analysed the meaning of the word "fault".

which did occur. It seems to me that into the question whether they were of faulty design there has been intruded unnecessarily a question of whether the faults of the design were the result of fault in the designer. In other words, fault in the sense of shortcoming in the static quality and character of a thing has become involved with fault in the sense of shortcomings in conduct and action."

Floor

In *Mitchell Conveyor and Transporter Co., Ltd.* v. *Pulbrook*[1] the plaintiffs had contracted to build a new electricity generating station for Birmingham Corporation, and took out a policy with the defendant in respect of (*inter alia*):

"any loss for the cost of replacing any defective and/or faulty material or workmanship and/or design or imperfections in the original or substituted construction in the plant insured . . . together with contingent charges."

The flooring of certain buildings was to consist of an artificial stone called granolithic. The contract said that this stone was to be composed of three parts granite chippings and one part cement, but the Corporation said that the mixture was to be two parts granite chippings and one part cement. The floor was laid by sub-contractors employed by the plaintiffs, but was unsatisfactory. The Corporation claimed against the plaintiffs, who settled the claim by deducting £1,813 due to them from the Corporation under the contract. The plaintiffs now claimed this sum from the defendant.

ROCHE, J., held that the claim succeeded for the loss fell within the policy. He said[2] that the loss was due to the unsatisfactory method of laying the floor and to the fact that the plaintiffs had agreed the design or plan with the Corporation with the richer mixture of granolithic. It was part of the risk which was insured under the words:

"including any loss for the cost of replacing any defective and/or faulty material or workmanship and/or design or imperfections in the original or substituted construction of the plant insured."

"The plant insured" meant the work insured.

The learned Judge rejected[3] the contention that the risk was increased during the progress of the work by the adoption of the richer mixture. On the evidence, the richness of the mixture was not the sole cause of the trouble. But in any event the mere fact that the risk had increased did not free the defendant from liability. Again, the matter of the mixture was one which was fixed in the proportion of two to one at the time the policy was effected, or was one which was still open to be agreed pursuant to the contract between the Corporation and the plaintiffs.

---

[1] (1933), 45 Ll.L. Rep. 239, K.B.D.
[2] *Ibid.*, at p. 243.
[3] *Ibid.*, at p. 244. Another issue in the case was whether the plaintiffs were under an obligation by the terms of the contract with the Corporation to require an indemnity from the sub-contractors. ROCHE, J., held that they were under no such obligation. As to this point, see *ibid.*, p. 245.

21

TRANSIT INSURANCE

Transit insurance policies are issued in respect of (i) cash; and (ii) goods.

CASH IN TRANSIT INSURANCE

1 Contents of the Policy

The terms of "cash in transit" insurance policies vary, but a typical one is the Lloyd's form of policy which contains:

    a Recitals.
    b The perils insured against.
    c The definition clause.
    d Excepted perils.
    e Conditions.
    f The Schedule.

a *Recitals*

The policy states that the insured named in the Schedule has made to the underwriters a written proposal and declaration bearing the date specified in the Schedule, which is hereby agreed to be the basis of the contract and to be considered incorporated herein, and has paid to them the provisional premium in the Schedule.

b *Perils Insured Against*

The insurers state that they will insure against:

    i Loss of cash as provided in the Schedule from any cause whatsoever;
    ii loss of or damage to safes containing cash caused by burglars, housebreakers or thieves; and
    iii loss of or damage to the clothing of any principal or employee of the insured, not exceeding £25 each principal or employee, as a result of any persons stealing, or attempting to steal, the insured cash.

The loss or damage must occur during the period set forth in the Schedule. Further, the liability of the insurers in respect of cash shall not exceed the applicable limit or limits specified in the Schedule.

c *Definition Clause*

The word "cash" as used in the policy means:

177

1 Cash and Bank Notes	8 National Insurance stamps
2 Cheques	9 National Savings stamps
3 Securities for money	10 National Savings certificates
4 Postal Orders	11 Holiday-with-pay stamps
5 Money Orders	12 War Savings stamps
6 Postage stamps	13 War Savings certificates
7 Embossed stamps	14 Luncheon vouchers

The property, of course, must belong to the insured or be property for which he is responsible.

d *Excepted Perils*

The policy does not cover:

i Loss occasioned by dishonesty on the part of any of the insured's employees (other than messengers, or employees acting as messengers, in the course of their journeys) unless such loss is reported by the insured within 72 hours of its occurrence;

ii loss or damage directly or indirectly occasioned by, happening through or in consequence of war, invasion, acts of foreign enemies, hostilities (whether war be declared or not), civil war, rebellion, revolution, insurrection, military or usurped power or confiscation or nationalisation or requisition or destruction of or damage to property by or under the order of any government or public or local authority;

iii loss of cash (the excess of £50 covered under the Schedule) occurring at the insured's premises when they are closed, unless the cash is in a locked safe or strong-room,[1] but this exclusion does not apply to stamps affixed to National Insurance cards, National Savings cards or Holiday-with-pay cards;

iv loss or damage which at the time of the happening of such loss or damage is insured by or would, but for the existence of the policy, be insured by any other existing policy or policies, except in respect of any excess beyond the amount which would have been payable under such other policy or policies had this insurance not been effected;

v loss or damage directly or indirectly caused by or contributed to by or arising from ionising radiations or contamination by radioactivity from any nuclear fuel or from any nuclear waste from the combustion of nuclear fuel.

e *Conditions*

The Conditions state that the provisional premium is based on the estimated aggregate amounts of cash in transit during the period of the policy. This provisional premium is subject to adjustment as specified in the Schedule, for which purpose the insured must supply within 30 days after expiry or anniversary date a declaration of the actual aggregate amount of cash in transit during the period of the policy. The insured must include in that declaration:

i All drawings from the bank or post office; and

ii All sendings to the bank or post office, and transits of cash, except crossed cheques and cheques for the purpose of drawing money.

---

[1] See, e.g., *Richardson* v. *Roylance* (1933), 47 Ll.L. Rep. 173, K.B.D. (p. 179, *post*).

The insured, in case of loss or damage, must, as a condition precedent to his right to be indemnified, gives to the underwriters:

 i Notice in writing as soon as practicable and in any event within 14 days after the loss or damage has come to the knowledge of the insured;[1] and

 ii Such information and evidence as to the property lost or damaged and the circumstances of the loss or damage as the underwriters may reasonably require and as may be in the insured's power to give.

If the insured shall make any claim knowing the same to be false or fraudulent, as regards amount or otherwise, the policy is to become void and all claims thereunder shall be forfeited.

f *Schedule*

The Schedule sets out the number of the policy, the name of the insured and the address of the premises concerned.

As regards transit risks, the policy covers loss of cash drawn from the bank or post office for wages, salaries, petty cash or sundry payments, from the time of handing over at the bank or post office counter, whilst in transit until arrival at the insured's premises or other place of disbursement. As far as wages or salaries are concerned, these are covered while they are on the premises until they are paid to the employees or otherwise disbursed. As regards cash in transit to the bank or post office, this is insured from the time of leaving the insured's premises until paid in at the bank or post office.

The policy also covers loss of cash collected from customers or clients, whilst in the personal custody of the insured or authorised employees of the insured, until deposited at the insured's premises or paid in at the bank or post office on the day of receipt or next working day.

An indemnity is also provided by the policy in respect of loss of cash whilst anywhere within the insured's premises but limited to £50 unless in a locked safe or strong-room when the premises are closed. Also covered are losses of stamps affixed to National Insurance cards, National Savings cards and Holiday-with-pay cards, whilst at the insured's premises.

Another clause in the Schedule sets out the provisional premium which is payable.

The policy concludes with a statement as to the date of the written proposal and the period of insurance. It also provides for the extension of the policy for such further period or periods as may be mutually agreed upon, with 15 days' grace after expiry for renewal.

2 Examples from the Reported Decisions

In *Richardson* v. *Roylance*[2] the plaintiff was a builder, who was insured under a Lloyd's "cash in transit" policy issued by the defendant underwriter. The policy stated:

> "£20,000 on cash and/or notes from time of drawing from bank at Tooting and whilst in transit to and whilst at assured's house situated 34, Mount Ephraim Road, Streatham, S.W., overnight in locked drawer or cupboard and thence in transit to various places of disbursement in and around London including

---

[1] See, e.g., *T. H. Adamson & Sons* v. *Liverpool and London and Globe Insurance Co., Ltd.*, [1953] 2 Lloyd's Rep. 355, Q.B.D. (p. 181, *post*).

[2] (1933), 47 Ll.L. Rep. 173, K.B.D.

Staines, and whilst there until paid out . . . No claim shall attach to this policy in respect of . . . any loss occurring when the premises are closed unless the cash or notes are in a locked safe or strong room. (This clause will not apply at 34, Mount Ephraim Road, Streatham, S.W.)"

The plaintiff drew a cheque on the branch of the Midland Bank at Tooting, and was paid in cash at its branch at Winchester. Whilst at a builder's shed on some land at Winchester the cash was stolen from a padlocked wooden box. The plaintiff claimed an indemnity from the defendant.

BRANSON, J., held that the action failed. The cash which was stolen was not drawn from the bank at Tooting, although it might be said that in a loose way the money came from Tooting because the cheque was drawn on the Tooting branch.[1] Again, the loss did not fall within the policy because Winchester was not a place "in and around London".[2] Further, as the cash was stolen from closed premises, the plaintiff could not recover because it had not been kept in "a locked safe or strongroom".[3] These words could not be

"stretched to include a wooden box knocked up by a builder's carpenter for the purpose of containing plans and documents, even though it is finished off with a padlock."[4]

In *Vaughan Motors and Sheldon Motor Services, Ltd.* v. *Scottish General Insurance Co., Ltd.*[5] the plaintiffs were garage owners, who had insured money in transit and on the premises with the defendant insurance company. The policy provided (*inter alia*) that:

"The [Insurers] will indemnify the Insured against:—
    (1) Loss of Money belonging to the Insured . . .
        (c) On the Insured's premises during business hours.
        (d) In a locked safe on the Insured's premises after business hours . . .
    WARRANTED (a) that a complete record shall be kept of the Money in transit and on the premises (b) that such record shall be deposited in some place other than in the safe(s) containing the Money (c) that in the case of unoccupied premises the keys of the safe(s) shall not be left in the premises after business hours and in the case of occupied premises that the keys of the safe(s) shall not be left after business hours in or about that particular portion of the premises in which the safe(s) is/are kept and (d) all money on the premises after business hours shall be secured in a locked safe."

Money and till rolls were stolen from a safe at the garage, which was kept open all night. The plaintiffs claimed an indemnity under the policy, contending that warranty (b) set out above applied only after business hours. The defendants denied liability.

DIPLOCK, J.,[6] held that the claim failed. Warranty (b), on its true construction, meant that at all times whether during business hours or after business hours the record of the money in transit and on the premises had to be deposited in some place other than the safe, and since it had not been, the insurers were under no liability.

---

[1] (1933), 47 Ll.L. Rep. 173, K.B.D., at p. 174.
[2] *Ibid.*, at p. 174.
[3] *Ibid.*, at p. 174.
[4] *Ibid.*, at p. 174.
[5] [1960] 1 Lloyd's Rep. 479, Q.B.D.
[6] *Ibid.*, at p. 482. His Lordship also held (*ibid.*, at p. 481) that the warranty amounted to a condition precedent to the liability of the insurers.

In *T. H. Adamson & Sons* v. *Liverpool and London and Globe Insurance Co., Ltd.*[1] the plaintiffs were insured by the defendants under a "cash in transit" policy with a limit of £25 in respect of any one loss. The policy stated:

> "The insured shall, immediately upon the discovery of any loss, give notice thereof in writing to the company . . . The company shall be under no liability hereunder in respect of any loss which has not been notified to the company within fourteen days of its occurrence.

The plaintiffs gave money to an employee each week in order to purchase National Insurance stamps at a Post Office. But he systematically embezzled[2] the money over a period of two years, the total loss amounting to about £2,366. During each week the employee had retained not less than £25 per week. He disappeared on June 25, 1951. The plaintiffs became aware of the loss on June 28 and notified the defendants on June 29, and claimed an indemnity under the policy.

Lord GODDARD, C.J., held that[3] it was only the last two losses—both of them limited to £25—which came within the terms of the policy.

GOODS IN TRANSIT

1 Contents of the Policy

Typical clauses in "goods in transit" insurance policies are exemplified in the Lloyd's form, in which the principal matters are:

    a the event insured against.

    b exception clauses.

    c the average clause.

    d the due diligence clause.

    e the non-contribution clause.

    f the claims procedure.

    g the Schedule.

a *Event insured against*

The insurers agree to indemnify the insured against:

    i the insured's legal liability as a carrier for loss of the goods in transit;

    ii all risks of loss or destruction of goods which are the property of the insured or goods entrusted to him in respect of the insured's lien or other beneficial interest therein.

The words "in transit" are defined as meaning:

> "In transit per insured's vehicles and/or trailers and/or containers . . . to or from any address in the United Kingdom, including any loading and unloading[4] and packing and unpacking; and whilst in the normal course of transit the goods and/or merchandise are temporarily housed[5] on or off the vehicles and/or trailers or in containers that are on or off the vehicles and/or trailers—limit 72 hours, but extensions held covered at an additional premium to be agreed, subject to prompt advice to indemniters."

---

[1] [1953] 2 Lloyd's Rep. 355, Q.B.D.

[2] The Court was told that in certain cases he managed to get the stamps off previous cards and put them on to his employers or the cards which they had to stamp: *ibid.*, at p. 358.

[3] *Ibid.*, at p. 239.

[4] See, e.g., *Hepburn* v. *A. Tomlinson (Hauliers), Ltd.*, [1966] 1 All E.R. 418, H.L. (p. 183, *post*)

[5] See, e.g., *Crows Transport, Ltd.* v. *Phoenix Assurance Co., Ltd.*, [1965] 1 All E.R. 596 (p. 184, *post*); *Sadler Brothers Co.* v. *Meredith*, [1963] 2 Lloyd's Rep. 293 (p. 184, *post*).

b *Exceptions*

Liability is excluded (*inter alia*) in respect of mildew, vermin, inherent vice, deterioration, inefficiency of ventilation, evaporation, taint and consequential loss.[1]

In addition, the insurers are not liable for loss directly or indirectly occasioned by, happening through or in consequence of war, invasion, acts of foreign enemies, hostilities (whether war be declared or not) civil war, rebellion, insurrection, military or usurped power, or confiscation or nationalisation or requisition or destruction of or damage to property by or under the order of any government or public or local authority.

Liability for loss caused by strikes, lock-outs, ionising radiations or contamination by radioactivity from nuclear fuel is also excluded.

There is no liability if the goods are stolen from unattended vehicles unless the vehicles are garaged in a building or parked in a fully enclosed yard, the openings in the vehicle closed and securely locked, and all keys removed so far as fire regulations permit.

c *Average*

The policy is subject to the condition of average[2], i.e., if goods at the time of the loss are of greater value than the sum insured, the insured is entitled to recover only such proportion of the loss as the sum insured bears to the total value of the goods.

d *Due Diligence*

A clause states that the insured must take all reasonable precautions for the protection and safeguarding of the goods and/or merchandise and use such protective appliances as may be specified in the policy, and all vehicles, trailers, containers and protective devices must be maintained in good order.[3]

e *Non-contribution*

The policy does not cover any liability or loss or damage which is insured or would, but for the existence of the present policy, be insured by any other existing policy except in respect of any excess beyond the amount which would have been payable under such other policy had the present policy not been effected.[4]

f *Claims*

The policy states that in the event of a happening likely to give rise to a claim in respect of the goods, the insured must as soon as possible give notice of it to the insurers and furnish full particulars. In addition, the insurers are entitled to take over and conduct in the name of the insured the defence or settlement of any claim.

---

[1] See Ivamy, *General Principles of Insurance Law*, 2nd Edn., 1970, pp. 341–342.
[2] As to the condition of average, see further Ivamy, *General Principles of Insurance Law*, 2nd Edn., 1970, pp. 383–384.
[3] See, e.g., *W. and J. Lane* v. *Spratt*, [1969] 2 Lloyd's Rep. 229, Q.B.D. (Commercial Court) (p. 190, *post*).
[4] See further Ivamy, *General Principles of Insurance Law*, 2nd Edn., 1970, p. 382.

g *Schedule*

The Schedule sets out (*inter alia*) the name and address of the insured, the period of insurance, the sum insured, an excess clause,[1] and the amount of the premium.

2 Examples from Reported Decisions

Duration of transit

In *Hepburn* v. *A. Tomlinson (Hauliers), Ltd.*[2] a quantity of tobacco was insured under a "goods in transit" policy whilst being carried and/or in transit . . . including loading and unloading". The vehicles carrying the goods arrived after working hours, and were left in unloading bays at a warehouse so that they could be unloaded the next day. The goods were stolen during the night and one of the questions which arose was whether the insurers were still at risk.

The House of Lords[3] held that they were, for the period of transit was defined to include unloading, and this did not come to an end until the goods were unloaded. Lord REID observed:[4]

> "The first point taken by the [insurer] is that this is a goods in transit policy and that the cigarettes were no longer on risk when they were stolen because the transit had come to an end when the lorries were driven in to Imperial's[5] warehouse and left there for the night. The words in the policy, however, are— whilst being carried and/or in transit anywhere in the United Kingdom 'including loading and unloading'. So I need not consider what the result would be if the word 'transit' stood alone. Here it is defined as including loading and unloading. Counsel attempted to argue that there were two separate periods of risk, the period of transit and the period of loading or unloading, and that in this case the period of transit had come to an end and the period of unloading had not commenced when the theft took place. In my opinion, however, that is quite inconsistent with the wording of the policy which must mean that the period of transit during which the goods are on risk is extended so as to include unloading and only comes to an end when the unloading is completed. I am therefore clearly of opinion that the goods were still on risk when stolen."

In *Phoenix Dynamo Manufacturing Co., Ltd.* v. *Mountain*[6] the insured had effected a policy in respect of a number of flying boats under a policy which covered

> "all risks of every kind, except war risks, during construction, assembling, packing for transit, and transit of any kind, except marine to any Royal Naval Air Station in England and until handed over to the authorities."

One of the flying boats[7] had been examined on behalf of the Air Ministry at the insured's works at Bradford. It was then dismantled and the hull was put on a trolley and sent by road to Calshot. It had nearly reached

---

[1] As to "excess clauses", see Ivamy, *General Principles of Insurance Law*, 2nd Edn., 1970, pp. 384–385.
[2] [1966] 1 All E.R. 418, H.L.
[3] Lord REID, Lord HODSON, Lord GUEST, Lord PEARCE and Lord WILBERFORCE.
[4] [1966] 1 All E.R. at p. 421. See also the speech of Lord PEARCE, *ibid.*, at p. 431.
[5] I.e., Imperial Tobacco Co. (of Great Britain and Ireland), Ltd., for whom the goods were being carried.
[6] (1921), 6 Ll.L. Rep. 369, K.B.D.
[7] One hundred of these flying boats had been ordered from the insured before the Armistice, but the orders for all except 21 were cancelled later.

Calshot when the lorry drawing the trolley swung round, and the hull of the boat caught in some trees and was wrecked. The insured claimed for a loss under the policy.

ROWLATT, J., held that the action succeeded. The plaintiffs were entitled to the cost of a new hull, for, although it could be said that the damaged hull could be repaired as a matter of joinery, it could not be repaired from the point of view of the stress which a machine like this had to stand.[1]

In *Sadler Brothers Co.* v. *Meredith*[2] the insured had effected a "goods in transit" policy in respect of some cleaning machines. The policy stated that:

> "This policy is to cover all loss and/or damage from all risks of every description on goods and/or merchandise of all kinds including machinery in transit by commercial vehicles operated by the assured, and whilst being loaded or unloaded, or whilst in garage, warehouse, or depot anywhere in the United Kingdom."

The insured received instructions to clean a steamship in the London Docks, and loaded the cleaning equipment on the van of theirs which was outside the premises. On police instructions the van was moved round the corner about 70 yards away. Later the van and its contents were stolen. The insured claimed an indemnity under the policy, but the insurer denied liability on the ground that the machines were not "in transit".

ROSKILL, J., held that the action succeeded, for the goods were "in transit". His Lordship observed:[3]

> "I think here 'transit' means the passage or carriage of goods from one place to another, and I think the goods were still being carried, and therefore were still in transit from the one place to the other even though the lorry in which they were being carried was temporarily parked. Obviously an exhaustive definition of transit is impossible, and equally obviously it is undesirable, and certainly I do not propose to attempt one . . . I think it is the movement of the goods which matters and not the movement of the vehicle or other means of conveyance in which the goods are being carried . . . I have come to the conclusion that these goods were in transit within the meaning of this policy and the [assured] are entitled to recover."

In *Crow's Transport, Ltd.* v. *Phoenix Assurance Co., Ltd.*[4] the policy covered the insured, a firm of carriers, in respect of all risk of loss or damage to goods in transit per their vehicles. A clause in the policy stated that it applied in respect of all goods which belonged to or were in the custody or control of the insured.

> "whilst being loaded upon, carried by, or unloaded from the vehicles . . . and whilst temporarily housed during the course of transit whether on or off the vehicles."

A consignment of gramophone records was delivered to the carriers' London depot for carriage from London to Gateshead. The manager of the depot took them for safety down some steps to a place just outside his office door. They were to wait there until they were loaded on to a north-bound lorry. But shortly afterwards before they had been loaded, some of the

---

[1] (1921), 6 Ll.L. Rep. at p. 370.
[2] [1963] 2 Lloyd's Rep. 293, Q.B.D.
[3] *Ibid.*, at p. 307.
[4] [1965] 1 Lloyd's Rep. 139, C.A.

records were stolen. The carriers claimed against the insurance company on the ground that the loss fell within the policy.

The Court of Appeal[1] held that the action succeeded. Lord DENNING, M.R., said that the goods were clearly "temporarily housed during the course of transit" since they were housed as an incident of the transit for a few hours awaiting loading. But the question was whether they were stolen "during the course of transit" when they were off the vehicles. In his opinion they were in transit when they were awaiting loading in those vehicles. He observed:[2]

> "It seems to me that goods are 'temporarily housed during the course of transit' if they are housed as an incident of the transit, such as when they are temporarily housed for a few hours awaiting loading. [Counsel] stressed that it has got to be transit 'per INSURED's VEHICLES'. I agree. But they are in transit per the insured's vehicles when they are awaiting loading in those vehicles. Instances were put in the course of the argument. When you take a parcel to the post office or to a railway station, and you hand it over and get a receipt, the goods are in transit from the moment the post office or the railway take them. They are in transit by the post office or the railway's vehicles, as the case may be, because from that moment onwards everything that is done is incidental to that transit. So here it seems to me that from the moment that the plaintiffs accepted these goods from Decca Record Company, Ltd., and took them down the steps, they were there temporarily housed awaiting loading on the plaintiffs' own vehicles. It was an incident of the transit by those vehicles. That seems to me to be 'in transit per [the plaintiffs'] VEHICLES'."

DANCKWERTS, L.J., said.[3]

> "In my view, in a case such as the present, where the consignees . . . sent the goods in their own lorries to the plaintiffs' premises, those goods were in transit from the moment they left the premises of [the consignees]. It is true that that part of the journey was not one for which the plaintiffs were responsible and, of course, it was not covered by the terms of this policy, but the goods when they left [the consignees], then started on their journey to the north to Gateshead and they remained in my view in transit from that point until they reached their destination. When they reached the plaintiffs' premises, they had to be unloaded and, as a practical matter, it is obvious that they might occasionally be carried on one vehicle to another, but much more probably, I should have thought, in most cases, they would be put down temporarily on the ground or some place where it was convenient and kept there, it might be for minutes or it might be for hours or it might be for a day. In all those cases, it seems to me it was part of the transit and therefore plainly covered by the terms of the concluding part of the endorsement, ' . . . temporarily housed during the course of transit whether on or off the vehicles . . .'."

"Unattended"

In *Plaistow Transport, Ltd.* v. *Graham*[4] some metal ingots were stolen at night from a lorry in the course of a journey from London to Bristol. The lorry owners claimed an indemnity from the insurers under a "goods in transit" policy insuring them against all risks. The policy contained a warranty which stated: "Warranted vehicles garaged in locked garage except when employed in night journeys but then never unattended."

---

[1] Lord DENNING, M.R., DANCKWERTS and SALMON, L.JJ.
[2] [1965] 1 Lloyd's Rep. at p. 143.
[3] *Ibid.*, at p. 144.
[4] [1966] 1 Lloyd's Rep. 639, Q.B.D.

The insurers denied liability contending that the lorry was left "unattended".

NIELD, J., held that the owners' claim succeeded. The ingots were stolen whilst the driver was asleep in the vehicle[1], and it was therefore not "unattended" within the meaning of the policy, so no breach of warranty had been established. He observed:[2]

> "It is submitted on behalf of the [insurers] that when one comes to consider the passage in the policy to which I have referred, when considering the policy, what has to be decided is whether there was effective attendance; and as I understand the argument, it is submitted that, if a driver, whose job it is to attend the wagon himself, was party to the stealing of the property, that is ineffective attendance. I think this submission presents some difficulty to the [insurers], because, if the [insured] employ an ostensibly honest driver to attend the vehicle, it might be said that they discharge their duty, unless, of course, he absents himself. I do not have to determine this point, because I am satisfied that he did not leave the vehicle and that he slept throughout the theft."

In *Ingleton of Ilford, Ltd.* v. *General Accident Fire and Life Assurance Corporation, Ltd.*[3] some wines and spirits were insured under a "goods in transit" policy which stated:

> "It is hereby understood and agreed that the insurance by this Policy does not cover loss or damage by theft or pilferage whilst any vehicle within described is left unattended in any public place . . . unless such vehicle shall have been securely locked at all points of access, and unless such loss or damage follows upon forcible entry of the vehicle."

A condition of the policy also provided that: "The Insured shall cause all reasonable precautions to be taken to prevent loss or damage".

The insured's van and its contents of wines and spirits were stolen whilst their driver was in a shop at which he had delivered some goods. The ignition key was left in the van, and the van was not locked. The insured claimed for a loss under the policy, but the insurers denied liability on the ground that the van had been left "unattended". It was proved that the driver was in the shop for about fifteen minutes and did not know that the van had been stolen.

It was held by PHILLIMORE, J., that the action failed, for the van had been left "unattended". He observed:[4]

> "[The driver] went into the shop. He says that thereafter he was keeping the vehicle under observation, but not, of course, absolutely the whole time but meaning maintaining a regular observation, and he says that in the position he was in in the shop, which he marked on the plan, he could see the whole of the nearside of the vehicle and, of course, the back. I confess that I find it hard to accept that [the driver] was taking even as much in the way of precautions as he says he was, because I think it clear that he was in there for a quarter of an hour. I have no doubt that he was chatting during the time to the boy [supplied by the manager of the shop], and it seems very doubtful if he was really keeping much observation on his van in the light of the fact that it was removed and the engine presumably started without his ever observing that

---

[1] The evidence on this point is set out *ibid.*, at pp. 641–642.
[2] *Ibid.*, at p. 640.
[3] [1967] 2 Lloyd's Rep. 179, Q.B.D.
[4] *Ibid.*, at p. 181.

anything had taken place. The fact is that from where he was he could not, of course, see the far side of the van, he had no view of the driver's door, he could not see if anybody got into the driver's seat, he was not in a position to keep it under observation, that is in a position to say observe any attempt by anyone to interfere with it or so placed as to have a reasonable prospect of preventing any unauthorised interference with it . . . This van, on the facts, was quite clearly unattended, and the best proof of that is that the whole thing was removed with all its contents without its attendant even being aware of what had happened."

In *J. Lowenstein & Co., Ltd.* v. *Poplar Motor Transport (Lymm), Ltd. (Gooda, Third Party)*[1] carriers had taken out a "goods in transit" policy with the insurers. One of its clauses stated:

"3 . . . This policy does not cover liability or loss, destruction or damage in respect of or arising from or caused by . . .
   (3) Thefts of or from vehicles left unattended between 6 p.m. and 6 a.m. unless
      (i) such vehicle is locked and garaged in a building which is securely closed and locked; or
      (ii) such vehicle is locked and parked in a yard which is fully enclosed and securely closed and locked.
9 . . . If clause 3 (3) cannot be complied with then 20% co-insurance applies."

Goods were stolen from two of the carriers' lorries which were carrying them for customers, and the carriers claimed an indemnity from the insurers.

Evidence was given that in the case of the first lorry a driver named Collier had been driving for a considerable time, and at 6.25 p.m., when he left the customers' premises, had only five minutes before he was required by the Road Traffic Act 1960, s. 73, which laid down rest periods, to cease work. So he and another driver called Barlow drove in their vehicles to a fish and chip shop two miles away. The vehicles were parked out of sight of the shop, and when the drivers came out of the shop, they discovered that Collier's lorry had been stolen.

In the case of another lorry driven by a driver named Gentles, evidence was given that he was unable to load it until 6 p.m. He was unable to obtain accommodation for himself locally, so he drove to a cafe 50 minutes away and parked the lorry in an open car park where it was subsequently stolen.

NIELD, J., held that the claim in respect of the loss of the goods from both lorries failed. He considered that clause 3 (3) could not be complied with if such compliance necessitated a breach of the Road Traffic Act 1960, s. 73 or an unreasonable deviation from the direct route which it would normally take or necessitated an unbusiness-like course of conduct.[2]

His Lordship said that in the case of the first lorry, although Collier would have been in breach of the Act if he had continued to drive after 6.30 p.m., Barlow could have driven until 8 p.m., and could have remained outside the shop attending both vehicles while Collier had a meal. Further, Collier could have easily reached a secure park by 8 p.m. In any case he ought not to have left the customers' premises when he did, and both he and Barlow could have attended the vehicles outside the customers' yard until there was space for them.[3]

---

[1] [1968] 2 Lloyd's Rep. 233, Q.B.D.
[2] *Ibid.*, at p. 238.
[3] *Ibid.*, at pp. 238–239.

In the case of the lorry driven by Gentles, he ought to have made further efforts to find accommodation and should have placed the vehicle in the customers' yard, or he could have gone to a secure park and found accommodation there.[1]

Accordingly, clause 3 (3) could have been complied with without any breach of the Act and without affecting the business efficacy of the agreement between the carriers and the customers.[2]

In *A. Cohen & Co., Ltd.* v. *Plaistow Transport, Ltd.* (*Graham, Third Party*)[3] the insured were carriers, who had effected a "goods in transit" insurance policy which contained a clause stating: "Warranted vehicles garaged in locked garage at night, except when employed on night journeys, but then never left unattended."

The insured contended that some brass ingots which they were carrying for a customer were stolen, together with the lorry on which they were loaded, from a shed with a locked door in a locked yard, and claimed an indemnity from the insurers. MACKENNA, J., held that the action failed because no loss had been proved,[4] and (*obiter*) that the insurers had a good defence on the ground of breach of warranty.[5]

"In Store"

In *Wulfson* v. *Switzerland General Insurance Co., Ltd.*[6] furniture had been placed in lift vans for conveyance from Leipzig to London, and the insured wished to have it covered by insurance whilst his house in London was being prepared to receive it. The policy contained these words:

> "Leipzig via Hamburg to London and for a period of three months (or held covered at a premium to be arranged) after arrival whilst in store at Pall Mall Depositories, London, W.1."

The furniture was damaged by water, and when the insured claimed under the policy, he was met with the plea that the furniture had not been "in store", since "store" meant a covered building, and the goods had been left standing in a yard.

This contention was rejected by ATKINSON, J., who gave judgment for the insured. The learned Judge said that he thought that the words meant "whilst they are with the Pall Mall Depository for the purpose of being stored". The goods were on the premises of the depository in an enclosed yard which was locked at night, and he imagined safe from theft and fire. They were raised from the ground. They were being taken care of. The depository was intending to store them, and was being paid to store them, and he thought were "in store". If they were stored in vans negligently and damage resulted, the owner might well have a claim for damages against the depository. Any underwriter, who paid for the damage, stepped into the

---

[1] [1968] 2 Lloyd's Rep. 239, Q.B.D.

[2] *Ibid.*, at p. 239.

[3] [1968] 2 Lloyd's Rep. 587, Q.B.D.

[4] *Ibid.*, at p. 592. The evidence is set out *ibid.*, at pp. 588–592.

[5] *Ibid.*, at p. 592. His Lordship said (*ibid.*, at p. 592) that he need not decide whether it was a warranty or whether it was to be construed as an exception of liability. He thought that his strong inclination would be to hold that the words merely defined the risk. In his opinion the word "night" meant "lighting up time".

[6] [1940] 3 All E.R. 221.

shoes of the insured, and had the benefit of any claim for negligence which the insured might have. But merely because, if it were the fact, the goods were stored negligently or improperly, it did not seem to his Lordship that it followed that they were not "in store" within the meaning of the policy.

Forcible Entry

In *Princette Models, Ltd.* v. *Reliance Fire and Accident Insurance Corporation, Ltd.*[1] some ladies' dresses were insured under a "goods in transit" policy. The policy stated that:

> "It is hereby declared and agreed that the corporation will not accept liability hereunder for theft of property from unattended cars or other motor vehicles whether in the street, garage or elsewhere unless such cars or vehicles are of a fully enclosed type and unless all doors, windows, windscreens and other openings of the vehicles are left closed, securely locked and properly fastened and unless any such door, window, windscreen, opening, lock or fastener has been smashed by violent forcible means wherever entry, access or theft has been effected."

The insured's van containing dresses was stolen in a London street. The van was recovered and there were no signs of forcible entry to the driver's cab observed. But one of the two locks on the doors at the rear of the van were found to be forced. The insured claimed under the policy, but the insurers denied liability on the ground that the van was left unlocked and/or that there was no sign of "smashing" or forced entry into the van.

PEARSON, J., held that the claim failed. He said that any forcing of the driver's cab in a London street was improbable, and that the probability was that the driver's cab was not effectively locked at the time. The word "wherever" in the condition set out above referred primarily to place. His Lordship observed:[2]

> "What is the meaning of the word 'wherever'? Does it mean: 'in any case in which' which is sometimes, I think, the meaning of the word 'where' in Acts of Parliament and other places; 'where' sometimes means 'in any case in which'. Or does it mean 'wherever' in the sense of the situation of the ground? That is to say, in this case, in Dean Street or in some particular square foot of Dean Street? Or does it mean in any place on the van? In my view, the right construction is that it means on the van. It refers to some place of the van. As between 'wherever', referring to place and 'wherever' referring to any place in which, one should refer the reference to place, because that is the primary meaning. The word 'wherever' refers primarily to place and one ought to give it that meaning unless there is some reason for giving it some other meaning. It plainly can be ' at whatever place on the van entry, access or theft has been effected'."

His Lordship said that even if the driver's cab was locked, there was no forcible entry to the driver's cab when the van was stolen. Accordingly, there was no "smashing" at whatever place on the van entry, access or theft had been effected. He went on to say that:[3]

> "The other possible view is an intermediate one which, in my view, is reasonable and does give effect to the presumed intention of this clause. That is that the reference is to the first breach of the enclosure . . . because you get a requirement

---

[1] [1960] 1 Lloyd's Rep. 49, Q.B.D.
[2] *Ibid.*, at p. 56.
[3] *Ibid.*, p. 57.

that the vehicle is to be of the fully enclosed type and then the smashing is found wherever the entry, access or theft has been effected. You may get entry in this case by actually walking into the cab, and making your way into it; you may get access by somebody putting his hand in or you may get access by some other means, but the way [Counsel] put it was: Wherever the material entry or access has been effected, if at that time you have a smashing, then the condition is fulfilled, but if, when the breach in the enclosure is made, you do not get any violent smashing at that time, then the condition is unfulfilled. In my view, that argument is right."

Employee's Reference

In *W. and J. Lane* v. *Spratt*[1] the plaintiffs were haulage contractors, who had effected a "goods in transit" insurance policy with the defendant underwriter. Clause 9 of the policy stated (*inter alia*):

> "This Insured shall take all reasonable precautions for the protection and safeguarding of the goods and/or merchandise and use such protective appliances as may be specified in the Policy and all vehicles and protective devices shall be maintained in good order. Such devices shall be used at all times and shall not be varied or withdrawn without written consent by the Underwriters. It is the duty of the Insured in the event that any property of the Insured, or for which they are responsible, be lost or damaged, to take all reasonable steps to effect its recovery and/or preservation."

A man used the name of "Trout", and sought employment with the plaintiffs. He produced a Labour Exchange introduction card and a driving licence which had been stolen. He also gave the name of a previous employer. The plaintiffs telephoned them to obtain a reference from them, but were unsuccessful. The man was given employment, and collected a quantity of bacon for the plaintiffs, but neither he or the bacon were seen again. The plaintiffs claimed an indemnity from the defendant in respect of the loss, but the defendant, although admitting that the bacon was lost "in transit", repudiated liability on the ground that the clause set out above was a condition, and that the plaintiffs were in breach of it as they had taken no steps to check "Trout" or the reference.

ROSKILL, J., held that the action succeeded. He considered that the clause was not a condition, but should be construed as a warranty, and observed:[2]

> "[Counsel] argued that unless one construed Clause 9 as a condition, there was only one other clause, namely, that part of Clause 10 which I have already read, which was susceptible of being construed as a condition. That may be so, but that of itself seems to me to be no reason for forcing upon Clause 9 a construction which it does not otherwise naturally bear. If one looks at the last sentence of Clause 9, which is akin to a sue and labour clause[3] in a policy of marine insurance, that sentence is quite plainly not a condition. There is nothing in Clause 9 itself to describe it as a condition, and one is therefore left with being invited to construe this clause as a condition when there is nothing on the face of the clause to suggest that it must of necessity be so construed. I therefore see no reason for construing this Clause 9 as a condition in the sense in which I have used that term. That point, therefore, fails."

His Lordship then went on to say[4] that the clause did not impose an obligation to vet their staff with due diligence before they employed them,

---

[1] [1969] 2 Lloyd's Rep. 229, Q.B.D. (Commercial Court).
[2] *Ibid.*, at p. 236.
[3] As to the "sue and labour clause", see Ivamy, *Marine Insurance* (1969), pp. 460–468.
[4] *Ibid.*, at p. 237.

and, on the evidence, they were not at fault in demanding "Trout's" National Insurance card or photographs when they interviewed him.[1] The learned Judge observed:[2]

> "The point is not without difficulty, but I think there is force in [Counsel's] arguments, first, that this is a clause for the benefit of the underwriters and, therefore, if underwriters wish to say that it is to extend not merely to what I have called physical precautions but is to cover selection of staff, the clause ought so to state in express terms; and, secondly, that if one looks at this clause as a whole, the impression that it leaves on someone reading it is that it is not intended to cover the whole field but is limited to what, on a reasonable reading of the clause, is that which is mentioned in the clause, namely, the need to protect and safeguard the goods and merchandise. The words in the first part of the clause seem to me to be coloured by the later words in the clause and that to extend this clause so as to impose upon the assured an obligation to vet their staff with due diligence before they take them on is something which the clause does not cover. If underwriters require it, they should say so in express terms. They have not said so in express terms and, therefore, for my part, I am not prepared to stretch the language of this clause in their favour to give it a meaning which in my judgment it does not naturally bear."

He also considered that if any obligation were imposed on the plaintiffs by the clause, it would not be enough that their omission to take suitable precaution, was negligent, and it must, at least, be reckless. On the evidence, the defendant had not shown that they were reckless in failing to check "Trout's" reference.[3]

---

[1] [1969] 2 Lloyd's Rep. at p. 234.
[2] *Ibid.*, at p. 237.
[3] *Ibid.*, at pp. 230–241.

22

LIVESTOCK INSURANCE

The livestock usually insured are horses, cattle, sheep and pigs. Cattle, sheep and pigs may be insured as farming stock. Horses may be insured as farming stock or may be insured separately.

Other animals such as dogs or cats are not as a rule insured unless they possess a fancy value for show or stud purposes.

THE SUBJECT-MATTER OF INSURANCE

Where the insurance is one on specific animals, they must be described with particularity so as to place their identity beyond doubt.

For this purpose the proposed insured is usually required to state their colour, mark, species, breed,[1] name, age[2] and present market value.[3]

CIRCUMSTANCES AFFECTING THE RISK

The proposed insured is usually asked questions relating to:

1 the locality where the animals are kept;
2 the purpose for which they are used;
3 their health;
4 the possibility of infection.

1 Locality

This must be described, and, in the case of a farm, its size and character stated.

2 Purpose

In particular, the insured may be required to state whether the animals are ever let on hire.

3 Health

The insured must state whether the stock is at the time of the proposal sound and healthy,[4] and whether any of the animals proposed to be insured

---

[1] *Yorkshire Insurance Co., Ltd.* v. *Campbell,* [1917] A.C. 218, P.C. (marine insurance), where a marine policy was based on a proposal in the ordinary form, in which the horse insured was wrongly described as regards pedigree.

[2] *Clarke* v. *British Empire Insurance Co.* (1912), 22 W.L.R. 89, where the age was overstated.

[3] *Great Northern Insurance Co.* v. *Whitney* (1918), 57 S.C.R. 543, where a palpable alteration in the proposal was held to put the insurers on inquiry.

[4] It may be an express term of the contract that the policy is only to cover death from accident or disease occurring or contracted after the commencement of liability: *Sharkey* v. *Yorkshire Insurance Co.* (1916), 54 S.C.R. 92, where a policy for three months, expiring on

have previously suffered from disease. He may also be required to state the name of the veterinary surgeon usually employed by him.

4 Possibility of Infection

The insured must state whether there is, or has been, within a specified period, any contagious disease in the neighbourhood, and whether the animals insured are likely to come into contact with other animals. He may also be asked to state whether he takes in horses or cattle for grazing.

The Event Insured Against

An animal is usually insured against death from accident[1] or natural causes.[2] Mere injury not resulting in death is not, as a rule, covered.[3]

To constitute a loss, therefore, within the policy, the insured animal must die.[4] Hence, the insurance is practically an insurance on its life,[5] and not merely on insurance against its accidental death.

Exceptions

The exceptions usually found in livestock policies state that the insurers are not to be liable in the event of loss caused by:

1 intentional slaughter;[6]

September 7, contained a condition that liability was to commence on payment of the premium, and it was held that the policy did not cover the death of a horse dying from a disease contracted on the morning of June 8, before the premium was paid, although the horse did not die until the evening, by which time payment had been made. See also *Demal* v. *British American Live Stock Association* (1910), 14 W.L.R. 250, where it was a term of the contract that the horses insured should be in perfect health and condition at the time when the contract took effect, and it was held that, as regards one of the horses which had been inoculated with the disease from which it died before, although the symptoms were not noticed until the day after, the policy took effect, the insured was not entitled to recover.

[1] An insurance against death solely attributable to accidental, external, and visible injury applies although there is no external mark of injury: *Burridge & Son* v. *Haines & Sons* (1918), 118 L.T. 681, where a horse died of suffocation owing to a van falling on its neck.

[2] An insurance against "mortality" covers death from natural causes only; *St. Paul Fire and Marine Insurance Co.* v. *Morice* (1906), 11 Com. Cas. 153 (marine insurance).

[3] For an example of an insurance against "all risks", see *Jacob* v. *Gaviller* (1902), 87 L.T. 26 (marine insurance), where a dog was insured during transit from Liverpool to Lahore, "walking at Lahore to be deemed a safe arrival", and it was held that, since the dog on arrival at Lahore could only walk on three legs due to an injury suffered on the journey, there was not a "safe arrival" within the meaning of the policy.

[4] The policy may provide not only that death must take place, but that the cause of death, whether accident or disease, must arise within a specified period; *Demal* v. *British American Live Stock Association* (1910), 14 W.L.R. 250; *Sharkey* v. *Yorkshire Insurance Co.* (1916), 54 S.C.R. 92.

[5] *A.-G.* v. *Cleobury* (1849), 4 Exch. 65, where a policy of insurance on the lives of cattle was held to be chargeable with stamp duty as an insurance on lives within the meaning of the Stamp Act 1815, which dealt only with three classes of policies *viz.* marine policies, life policies and fire policies.

[6] The policy, however, often states that the insurers will not rely on this exception where they have agreed to the destruction of the animal, or where a veterinary surgeon appointed by them has given a certificate that destruction is necessary to terminate incurable suffering, or where a certificate is given by a veterinary surgeon appointed by the insured that the suffering is incurable and so excessive that immediate destruction is imperative for humane reasons without waiting for the appointment of a veterinary surgeon by the insurers. See e.g. *Shiells* v. *Scottish Assurance Corporation, Ltd.* 1889, 16 R. (Ct. of Sess.) 1014, where the horse insured, was, after the accident, destroyed on the advice of a veterinary surgeon. The onus of proving the necessity for slaughter rests upon the insured: *ibid. per* Lord MacDonald at p. 1019.

2 transport by water other than inland waterway;

3 any surgical operation unless conducted by a qualified veterinary surgeon and certified by him to have been necessitated solely by accident, disease or illness and to have been carried out in an attempt to save the animal's life;

4 Inoculation which is not of a prophylactic nature or necessitated by accident, disease or illness;

5 malicious or wilful injury by the insured or any of his servants;

6 ionising radiations or contamination by radioactivity from any nuclear fuel or from any nuclear waste from the combustion of nuclear fuel;

7 war, invasion, acts of foreign enemies, hostilities (whether war be declared or not), civil war, rebellion, revolution, insurrection or military or usurped power.

CONDITIONS

The conditions often found in livestock policies relate to:

1 change of user;

2 removal from the specified premises;

3 care of the animals;

4 proceedings after loss.

1 Change of User

It is made a condition that each animal insured must be employed only for the use stated in the Schedule.[1]

2 Removal

The policy states that it is a condition that each animal insured must remain within the geographical limits stated in the Schedule.[2]

3 Care of Animals

The insured must at all times provide proper care and attention for each animal.

In the event of any illness, lameness, accident injury or physical disability of or to any animal, the insured must immediately employ a veterinary surgeon, and if required by the insurers, allow removal for treatment.

He may also be under a duty to give notice to persons specified in the Schedule who will instruct a veterinary surgeon on the insurers' behalf if deemed necessary.

4 Proceedings after Loss

If an animal dies, similar notice must be given[3], and the insured must at his own expense have a post-mortem examination made by a veterinary

---

[1] *Stuart* v. *Horse Insurance Co.* 1893, 1 S.L.T. 91, where it was held that the insurers were not liable if the accident happened whilst the horse insured was doing work which differed from that specified in the proposal.

[2] *Gorman* v. *Hand in Hand Insurance Co.* (1877), I.R. 11 C.L. 224 (fire insurance), where the horses insured were held to be covered only whilst in the specified locality.

[3] *Gill* v. *Yorkshire Insurance Co.* (1913), 24 W.L.R. 389, where a condition requiring notice within 24 hours of illness was held to be sufficiently performed by notice within 24 hours of the time when the illness was first known, although it had commenced 3 days earlier;

surgeon. He must then forward without delay the post-mortem report and full particulars of his claim.

If the insured makes any claim knowing that it is false or fraudulent as regards amount or otherwise, the policy is to be void and all claims under it forfeited.

Shiells v. *Scottish Assurance Corporation* 1889, 16 R. (Ct. of Sess.) 1014; *Roche* v. *Roberts* (1921), 9 Ll. L. Rep. 59 where a greyhound was insured and the insured failed to recover on the policy because notice was given only to the broker by whom the policy was effected, and not to the persons stated in it.

23

AVIATION INSURANCE

Aviation insurance policies, whether issued by Lloyd's underwriters or by insurance companies, contain substantially the same provisions concerning:

1 loss of or damage to the aircraft;
2 third party liability;
3 legal liability to passengers;
4 general exclusions;
5 warranties;
6 general conditions.

1 Loss of or Damage to the Aircraft

In the Lloyd's form of policy the underwriters agree at their option to pay for, replace or make good accidental loss of or damage the aircraft stated in the Schedule[1] howsoever caused whilst it is:

a in flight;[2]   *c* on the ground;[4]
b taxying;[3]   *d* moored.[5]

---

[1] The Schedule states (a) *as to the airframe* the make, type and series number of the aircraft, its year of construction, its licensed passenger seating capacity, its declared passenger capacity for the purpose of the insurance, and identification marks; (b) *as to the engines*, the number and type; (c) *as to the value*, the value of the aircraft with standard instruments and equipment, and its value with extra equipment and accessories, and the total value; (d) *details as to the pilots;* (e) *the purposes for which the aircraft will be used;* and (f) *geographical limits.*

[2] "Flight" means from the time the aircraft moves forward in taking off or attempting to take off for the actual air transit, whilst in the air and until the aircraft completes its landing run after contact with the earth and/or water". For an example as to whether an aircraft was in flight, see *Ilford Airways, Ltd.* v. *Stevenson* (1957), 21 W.W.R. 78, where an aircraft equipped with floats was insured under a policy limited to ground risks. Flight risks were expressly excluded. The aircraft had not left the water, but a take-off was intended. She capsized in a river. It was held that an action on the policy failed, for at the time of the accident she was in "flight", since the pilot had opened the throttle, had turned into the wind, and had intended to take-off. See also *Dunn and Tarrant* v. *Campbell* (1920), 2 Ll.L. Rep. 98; affirmed (1920), 4 Ll.L. Rep. 36, C.A., as to the meaning of "first flight".

[3] "Taxying" means "when the aircraft is moving along the ground whether under its own power or momentum or in process of being towed but not in flight as defined above". In the case of aircraft whilst afloat it means "when such aircraft is not in flight or moored as defined".

[4] "On the ground" means "whilst the aircraft is not in flight or taxying as defined." For a case where the insured aircraft were destroyed on the ground at Beirut airport by members of the armed forces of Israel, and it was held that the insurers were not liable because the loss had not occurred "during the normal course of the assured's operations over Arab/Israel territory", for the word "over" meant "in the air over", see *Banque Sabbag S.A.L.* v. *Hope*, [1972] 1 Lloyd's Rep. 253, Q.B.D. (Commercial Court). See the judgment of Mocatta, J., *ibid.*, at p. 265. The decision was later affirmed by the Court of Appeal, [1973] 1 Lloyd's Rep. 233.

[5] "Moored" means "whilst the aircraft is afloat and safely secured" and includes the risks of launching and hauling up.

The underwriters, however, are not liable for the cost of making good wear and tear, gradual deterioration, structural defect, electrical or mechanical breakage or breakdown, or for loss or damage arising from such electrical or mechanical breakage or breakdown other than loss or damage caused by fire, explosion or impact of the aircraft with an external object.

The policy specifies a certain sum up to which the insured must bear liability in respect of any claim which is made.[1]

The liability of the underwriters does not exceed the value stated in the Schedule and does not extend to indemnify the insured in respect of salvage charges rendered to the aircraft,[2] general average contributions[3] or sue and labour charges.[4]

2 Third Party Liability

Under the Lloyd's policy the underwriters agree to indemnify the insured for all sums which he shall become legally liable to pay, and shall pay, as compensation including costs awarded, in respect of accidental bodily injury or accidental damage to property, provided such injury or damage is caused directly by the aircraft or by objects falling from it.

The liability of the underwriters under this section of the policy does not exceed a sum stated in it in respect of any one accident or series of accidents arising out of one event.

The cover under this section of the policy does not extend to indemnify the insured in respect of injury, damage or loss caused to or sustained by any passenger whilst entering into, being carried in, or alighting from the aircraft, or any pilot or member of the crew or any person working in, on or about the aircraft.

3 Legal Liability to Passengers

Under the Lloyd's policy the underwriters agree to indemnify the insured for all sums which he shall become legally liable to pay and shall pay as compensation including costs awarded in respect of accidental bodily injury to passengers whilst entering into, being carried in, or alighting from the aircraft.

But for the underwriters to be liable each passenger must be carried subject to the terms of a ticket issued by the insured to him before the commencement of the flight. The ticket must have printed on it in a conspicuous position a condition that the insured will not be liable for any personal injury howsoever caused except in so far as such condition is not contrary to law or to any international agreement.

---

[1] As to "excess" clauses, see Ivamy, *General Principles of Insurance Law*, 2nd Edn., 1970, pp. 384–385.

[2] "Salvage services" means "any services rendered by or in relation to the aircraft in, on or over the sea or any tidal water or on or over the shores of the sea or any tidal water in all cases in which they would have been salvage services, whether maritime or under contract, had they been rendered by or in relation to a vessel."

[3] As to general average, see Lowndes and Rudolf, *The Law of General Average* (1964) (published as Volume 7 of *British Shipping Laws*).

[4] See generally Ivamy, *Marine Insurance* (1969), pp. 460–468.

The liability of the underwriters is limited to a sum stated in the policy in respect of any one passenger and in respect of any one accident or series of accidents arising out of one event.

4   General Exclusions

Under the Lloyd's policy the underwriters are not liable under any section of the policy whilst the aircraft is being used for any illegal purpose or for any purpose or purposes other than those stated in the Schedule or whilst outside the geographical limits named therein unless due to *force majeure*.

Similarly, they are not liable whilst the aircraft is being piloted by any person or persons other than those stated in the Schedule, or whilst the aircraft is using unlicensed landing areas unless due to *force majeure* or the aircraft is covered by a special endorsement on the policy.

No liability is incurred if the loss is directly occasioned by, happening through or in consequence of war, invasion, acts of foreign enemies, hostilities[1] whether war be declared or not, civil war, rebellion, revolution, insurrection,[2] military or usurped power[3], martial law, strikes, riots,[4] civil commotions,[5] or confiscation or nationalisation or requisition or destruction of or damage to property by or under the order of any government or public or local authority.

Again, the insurers are under no liability if the total number of passengers carried in the aircraft at the time of the happening of the loss exceeds the declared passenger seating capacity stated in the Schedule. Another exception states that there is no liability on the part of the underwriters if the loss arises out of or is directly or indirectly connected with test flights after construction or reconstruction, leaving the aircraft unattended in the open without taking reasonable precautions for its safety, racing, record attempts, speed trials, aerobatics, aerial seeding or fertilization, dusting, spraying, fish spotting or any other form of flying involving abnormal hazards.

In *Alliance Aeroplane Co., Ltd.* v. *Union Insurance Society of Canton, Ltd.*[6] an aircraft was insured under a policy which excluded liability if it was lost while "racing". It crashed, and was a total loss whilst competing for a prize offered to the first aircraft to fly from Hounslow to Australia. BRAY, J., held that the insurers were not liable, for the aircraft was "racing" at the time of the loss,[7] and observed:[8]

> "Did the loss happen while the aeroplane was racing? It was undoubtedly engaged in a contest for a prize. The conditions of the contest were set forth in the prospectus put in evidence. The prize, a sum of £10,000, was to be given to the man who should first arrive at a certain place in Australia, provided he complied with the other conditions which included that he must start from Hounslow, and that the whole journey should not occupy more than 720 hours. There were seven or eight competitors, and the prize was awarded to one of them.

---

[1] See Ivamy, *General Principles of Insurance Law*, 2nd Edn., 1970, p. 225.
[2] *Ibid.*, p. 224.
[3] *Ibid.*, pp. 223–224.
[4] *Ibid.*, pp. 222–223.
[5] *Ibid.*, p. 223.
[6] (1920), 5 Ll.L. Rep. 406, K.B.D.
[7] Other issues in the case were (i) whether the policy should be rectified (see *ibid.*, at p. 407); (ii) whether the loss covered a different aircraft and not the alleged to be insured (see *ibid.*, at p. 408).
[8] *Ibid.*, at p. 407.

In my opinion, giving the word 'race' the ordinary interpretation, this contest was a 'race', and the competitors as soon as they started were 'racing'. |Speed, and not only endurance, was of importance. It was said for the |insured] that the word 'racing' means going at a racing pace, and that at the time of the loss it was not going and never would have gone at its highest speed. In my opinion, that is not the natural or ordinary meaning of the word 'racing'. I think it means engaged in a race at the time of the loss, and that the [aeroplane] was at the time of the loss 'racing'."

5 Warranties

The Lloyd's policy contains a warranty that no additional insurance on any interests on or in relation to any aircraft described in the Schedule, except such as may be required to cover personal accident and legal liability, has been or will be effected to operate during the currency of the policy by or on account of the insured, owners, managers, mortgagees or hirers except:

(i) additional insurance[1] on terms and conditions identical with those contained in the policy;

(ii) additional insurance on total loss only on any conditions other than those stated in (i) above, whether policy proof of interest, full interest admitted, or otherwise, but only to cover in respect of any one aircraft an amount not exceeding 10 per cent. of the total value of the aircraft as stated in the Schedule.

There is also a warranty that the insured will comply with all air navigation and airworthiness orders and requirements issued by any competent authority, and will take all reasonable steps to ensure that such orders and requirements are complied with by his agents and employees, and that the aircraft shall be airworthy at the commencement of each flight.

Sometimes the warranty is expressed in the form of a condition.

Thus, in *Bond Air Services, Ltd.* v. *Hill*[2] the policy contained a condition stating that:

"The insured and all persons in his employment or for whom he is responsible shall duly observe the statutory orders, regulations and directions relating to air navigation for the time being in force."

The insured aircraft was engaged on a flight from Valencia, Spain to Bovingdon Airport, and crashed into a field and became a total loss. The insurer repudiated liability on the ground that (*inter alia*) (i) the aircraft was at all material times loaded in excess of the weights permitted in the certificate of airworthiness, thus invalidating the certificate and offending against the Air Navigation Order 1923, art. 3; and (ii) the artificial horizon of the aircraft was not at all material times in fit condition for immediate use. The insurer also alleged that the burden of proving that there had been no breach of condition lay on the insured. Lord GODDARD, C.J., held that there was nothing in the policy to alter the burden of proof, and that it still lay on the insurer to prove that the condition had been broken.[3] The result of the case is not stated in the reports.

---

[1] For "other insurance", see further, Ivamy, *General Principles of Insurance Law*, 2nd Edn. 1970, pp. 279–281.

[2] [1955] 2 Q.B. 417; [1955] 2 All E.R. 476.

[3] As to this point, see Ivamy, *General Principles of Insurance Law*, 2nd Edn., 1970, p. 249.

Again, in *Obalski Chibougamau Mining Co.* v. *Aero Insurance Co.*[1] liability was denied by the insurers on the ground that the insured seaplane had been flown contrary to government regulations and was not airworthy.

Further, in *Survey Aircraft, Ltd.* v. *Stevenson and Orion Insurance Co., Ltd.* (*No. 2*)[2] an action on a policy failed because the aircraft had carried a passenger in breach of the airworthiness certificate which forbade the carriage of passengers.

6 General Conditions

The Lloyd's policy contains (*inter alia*) a condition requiring that all log books must be kept fully up to date, and must be produced to the underwriters on request in support of any claim.

The insured must use due diligence and do everything reasonably practicable to avoid or diminish any loss. He must not make any admission of liability or payment without the underwriters' written consent.

In the event of the aircraft sustaining damage he must take steps as may be necessary to ensure its safety. If he makes any claim knowing it to be false or fraudulent as regards amount or otherwise, the policy is void and all claims under it are forfeited.

If there is any change in the circumstances or nature of the risks which are the basis of the contract, the insured must give immediate notice to the underwriters.

The policy must not be assigned in whole or in part except with the consent of the underwriters verified by endorsement on it.

---

[1] [1932] S.C.R. 540.
[2] (1962), 38 W.W.R. 280.

24

PLATE GLASS INSURANCE

The special features of plate glass insurance are:
1. the subject-matter of insurance;
2. circumstances affecting the risk;
3. the event insured against;
4. the exceptions;
5. alteration of the risk;
6. proceedings after loss.

1   Subject-matter of Insurance

The subject-matter of insurance is glass only, not frames or fittings.[1] Any kind of glass may be insured, whether plate or otherwise; and the glass may be used for any purpose, not merely for the admission of light. The policy, however, contemplates glass in a fixed position. It is not intended to apply to glass vessels and similar articles.

Glass may be insured under a general description, *e.g.*, where the policy covers the glass in all the windows, doors and fanlights in a private house. In the case of business premises a more specific description is usually required.

The proposal form contains a schedule setting out the particulars of the glass proposed to be insured, including the quality and character of the glass, *e.g.*, whether it is plate glass or sheet glass, and whether it is plain or rough, or silvered, bent, stained or lettered, and the position which it occupies in the premises, *e.g.*, whether it is in a window, door or otherwise. The proposer may also be required to state whether the glass is vertical or horizontal.

Any statement of this kind, whether as to the quality, character, or position of the glass, is an essential part of the description. Glass which does not answer to the description is not insured.

2   Circumstances Affecting the Risk

To insure glass, which is already cracked or which suffers from a flaw, against breakage without disclosing the fact to the insurers entitles them to avoid liability under the policy.

The proposal form, however, usually contains an express warranty to be signed by the proposer stating that the glass is free from cracks or flaws. The policy may also provide that glass, which is already fractured, is not to be covered by the policy.

---

[1] This is usually made clear by the terms of the policy.

In the case of business premises the risk of breakage is likely to be affected by their nature and position. The proposer, therefore, is required to describe the trade or business carried on, and to state whether the premises have been recently erected or altered, and whether they are situated at a street corner.

3   Event Insured Against

The undertaking of the insurers is in express terms to make good any breakage that may happen to the glass insured during the period of insurance.

To constitute a loss, therefore, within the meaning of the policy, it is necessary that the glass should be broken. There must be an actual fracture. Mere scratching is not sufficient.[1]

The cause of the breakage is immaterial. The glass may be broken by a pure accident, *e.g.*, where a car crashes into the window and breaks it, or it may be broken by the criminal act of a third person for the purpose either of entering the premises to commit a crime or of drawing attention to a grievance.[2]

The policy is usually framed in language sufficiently wide to cover any and every cause of breakage except such as may be expressly excepted.

4   Exceptions

The insurers are usually relieved from liability by exceptions relating to:

a *Breakage falling within the scope of a fire policy*

A fire policy covers not only actual breakage by fire but also all breakage of which the fire is the proximate cause, *e.g.*, the breakage of a window for the purpose of enabling the fire brigade to enter the building.[3]

Where, however, the fire is not the proximate cause, but only the remote cause of the breakage, the exception does not apply.

Thus, where a fire upon adjacent premises causes a mob to assemble, and the mob subsequently breaks the glass insured for the purposes of gaining access to the insured's shop and plundering it, the breakage is not attributable to the fire, but to the riotous conduct of the mob, and is, therefore, covered by a plate glass policy.[4]

Sometimes the exception is made applicable only when there is in fact a fire policy in existence effected by the insured. At other times it excludes all breakage capable of being covered by a fire policy.

b *Breakage, however caused, whilst the glass is in the course of being moved.*[5]

---

[1] This may be made clear by the terms of the policy.
[2] See e.g., *London and Manchester Plate Glass Co., Ltd.* v. *Heath*, [1913] 3 K.B. 411, C.A., where the window was broken by a suffragette.
[3] *Stanley* v. *Western Insurance Co.* (1868), L.R. 3 Exch. 71 (fire insurance), *per* KELLY, C.B., at p. 74;   *Re Etherington and Lancashire and Yorkshire Accident Insurance Co.*, [1909] 1 K.B. 591, C.A. (personal accident insurance), *per* VAUGHAN WILLIAMS, L.J., at p. 599.   See further, Ivamy, *Fire and Motor Insurance*, 2nd Edn., 1973, p. 145, s. 12 of the Metropolitan Fire Brigade Act 1865 also states that any damage done by a fire brigade in the due execution of its duties is to be deemed to be damage by fire within the meaning of a fire policy.
[4] *Marsden* v. *City and County Assurance Co.* (1865), L.R. 1 C.P. 232.
[5] This form of wording avoids the difficulty in *Marsden* v. *City and County Assurance Co.* (*supra*), where the exception was against "breakage during removal", and where the Court differed as to its scope. BYLES, J., thought that it referred to removal of the glass, whilst WILLES and KEATING, JJ., excluded it to removal of the business.   All the members of the Court,

5 Alteration of the Risk

The only alterations calling for attention are:

  a the removal of the glass;

  b substitution of new glass.

a *Removal of the Glass*

The policy usually contains an express condition stating that the glass insured is only covered whilst it remains in the same position in which it was at the commencement of the insurance.

As soon as any steps are taken to remove it, whether from one part of the premises to another, or from a vertical to a horizontal position, the glass ceases to be covered.

If, however, the policy exempts the insurers from liability for breakage during removal, without indicating what kind of removal is intended, it is probable that the exception is not confined to removal of the glass, but applies to any breakage which the glass may sustain during the removal of the business or plant.[1]

b *Substitution of New Glass*

Although the policy may require a specific description of the dimensions and position of the different pieces of glass included in the insurance, it is not intended to be an insurance of the specific pieces. On the contrary, the policy usually contains provisions which make it clear that any piece of glass corresponding to the description is covered.

The policy is a contract to make good any breakage during the period of insurance. No maximum liability is specified, so that the replacing of a broken piece does not diminish the insurers' obligation. The new glass is, therefore, covered in the same way as the glass which it replaces.

In addition, there may be a special provision that glass fractured before the policy comes into force and therefore not covered is to be covered when replaced by new glass.

On the other hand, any alteration in the glass, as opposed to mere replacement, may be expressly prohibited unless the insurers consent.

6 Proceedings after Loss

The principal matters calling for attention are:

  a the duties of the insured;

  b the amount recoverable.

a *Duties of Insured*

In addition to the duties in connection with the claim, the insured is usually required to remove fittings or other impediments to replacement and to preserve the salvage.

---

however, agreed that the exception did not apply where the insured was not removing from the premises, but was merely transporting his property to a place of safety, upon the happening of a sudden emergency, i.e. a fire next door, which threatened to spread to his premises.

[1] *Marsden* v. *City and County Assurance Co.* (1865), L.R. 1 C.P. 232 where the majority of the Court took this view, only BYLES, J., thinking that "removal" was confined to removal of the glass. See footnote 5, p. 202, *ante.*

b *Amount Recoverable*

It is unusual to insert any specific amount of insurance in the policy. The undertaking of the insurers may be to make good the breakage by replacing the glass broken or they may reserve the option of paying its value.

There is usually a special provision that any salvage is to belong to the insurers.

25

STEAM BOILER INSURANCE[1]

The special features of steam boiler insurance relate to:

1 the event insured against.
2 the exceptions in the policy.

1 Event insured against

So far as the property of the insured is concerned, the policy covers loss or damage caused by the explosion or collapse of a specified boiler occasioned by pressure of steam or other fluid for which the boiler is used.[2]

A "boiler" is defined by s. 3 of the Boiler Explosions Act 1882[3] as "any closed vessel used for generating steam, or for heating water, or for heating other liquids, or into which steam is admitted for heating, steaming, boiling or similar purposes".[4] By "a closed vessel used for generating steam" is meant the whole machine in which the steam is made or produced, and where it is under pressure until it is allowed to go from the machine into something else for a different purpose.

Hence, it includes not only the boiler in which the steam is generated but also the steam pipe leading directly out of the boiler along which the steam passes, and the vessel into which it is received.[5]

---

[1] Steam boiler insurance is, in practice, confined to boilers used other than for domestic purposes. Explosions of domestic boilers are usually included within the terms of a fire policy. See Ivamy, *Fire and Motor Insurance*, 2nd Edn., 1973, pp. 71–73.

[2] A policy may be effected against the bursting of pipes and the consequent damage by leakage. See, e.g. *Canadian Casualty and Boiler Insurance Co.* v. *Hawthorne* (1907), 39 S.C.R. 558, where the policy contained an exception against damage resulting from freezing, and it was held that, where a pipe burst through the freezing of the water, damage subsequently caused by the escape of water from the pipe was not within the exception.

[3] See further *R.* v. *Boiler Explosions Act, 1882, Commissioners*, [1891] 1 Q.B. 703, C.A. (boiler explosion) *per* Lord HALSBURY, L.C., at p. 713: "The word 'boiler' is not a scientific but a popular word. It is a known instrument with reference to certain classes of machinery, and, for my own part, I should be disposed to take the popular view of a boiler, that is something to boil water in and whereby steam is made. My impression is that the nozzle of a kettle, however long, is part of the kettle, and that it is part of the instrument which generates the steam, and if the nozzle of the kettle be protracted for a considerable distance, provided the object is to keep in that vessel the steam generated by the application of heat to the water, it is just as much a boiler as if it were of different shape . . . I am by no means prepared to say that if the word 'boiler' were the only word in the Act, I should not come to the conclusion that this pipe was part of the boiler, because as I understand the facts as stated to us, this vessel, which was admitted on all hands to be generating steam, has a continuous flow of steam from the point where it rises from the water to the place at which the explosion took place."

[4] The use of boilers other than for private domestic purposes is subject to statutory restrictions and regulations, and it may therefore be assumed that the statutory definition applies.

[5] *R.* v. *Boiler Explosions Act, 1882, Commissioners*, [1891] 1 Q.B. 703, C.A. (boiler explosion), *per* Lord ESHER, M.R., at p. 716.

Thus, where steam, generated in a boiler situated above ground at a colliery and conducted under pressure down the shaft and along the working to a pumping engine in the mine, blows off a valve in the pipe, close to the pumping engine, there is a boiler explosion, since the pipe, until it reaches the valve, forms part of the boiler within the statutory definition.[1]

An "explosion" in the case of a boiler means the bursting or rupture of any part or parts by a violent and sudden tearing asunder under internal steam pressure. A "collapse" means the distortion through crushing or bending by steam pressure of the metal of the flue, firebox, tube, or any other internal part of the boiler from the form which it possessed at the time when the boiler was accepted for insurance.[2]

In addition to loss or damage to the insured's property caused by the explosion or collapse of the boiler being covered by the policy, the boiler itself is covered. The policy usually includes the insured's liability to third persons and to his employees.[3]

It does not, however, cover consequential loss arising from stoppage of works or business in consequence of the explosion or collapse, unless such loss is specifically insured against.[4]

2 Exceptions

The policy usually exempts the insurers from liability:

1 for ordinary wear and tear, cracks, defects, or deterioration due to use, unless actually resulting in explosion or collapse;

2 where at the time of the explosion or collapse the pressure or load on the safety valve or valves attached to the boiler is allowed to exceed the maximum pressure stipulated in the policy or the permissible working pressure set out in the statutory report.[5]

3 where the actual loss or damage is caused by fire whether occasioned by or resulting from explosion or collapse.

4 where the loss is caused by the wilful act or neglect of the insured.

---

[1] *R.* v. *Boiler Explosions Act, 1882 Commissioners*, [1891] 1 Q.B. 703, C.A. (boiler explosion), *per* Lord ESHER, M.R., p. 716.

[2] The terms "explosion" and "collapse" are usually defined in the policy.

[3] For employers' liability insurance, see pp. 264–275, *post.*

[4] See further Ivamy, *Fire and Motor Insurance*, 2nd Edn., 1973, pp. 74–78.

[5] For the statutory report, see the Factories Act 1961, s. 33. Certain boilers are required, to be examined thoroughly by a competent person at specified intervals *ibid.*, s. 33. (1) As a thorough examination of the insured boiler is equally beneficial to the insurers, they usually undertake, by the policy to make the statutory examination and to furnish the insured with a report of the result of the examination in the statutory form, containing the statutory particulars required by s. 33 (4) for the purpose of being entered or attached to the general register of the insured's factory. The policy further provides for the time for the examination to be arranged between the parties, and for the insured to prepare the boiler for examination by emptying it and cleaning it and rendering it accessible in every part as far as its construction will allow.

26

HOUSEHOLDER'S COMPREHENSIVE INSURANCE

Some policies effected by householders provide insurance cover against loss or damage by fire only.[1] Comprehensive insurance policies are designed to give much wider protection.

THE PERILS INSURED AGAINST

The perils insured against concern:—
1 The building.
2 The contents.
3 Miscellaneous extensions.
4 Public liability.
5 Accidents to servants.

1 Building

The policy covers the building against loss or damage caused by (*inter alia*) fire, lightning, earthquake, bursting or overflowing of water tanks, storm, tempest or flood, or impact by any road vehicle not belonging to or under the control of the insured or any member of his household.

There may be an "excess clause" whereby the insured has to bear, e.g. the first £5 of any loss or damage caused by the bursting or overflowing of water tanks or pipes, or caused by storm or tempest.

The meaning of "storm or tempest" in a householder's comprehensive insurance policy was considered in *Oddy* v. *Phoenix Assurance Co., Ltd.*[2] In this case the insured had insured a bungalow against loss or damage caused *inter alia* by storm or tempest. In November, 1963, there was heavy rain and high winds. The wind dropped on November 19 and the rain had stopped by 11 a.m. At 1.40 p.m. a wall collapsed on to the bungalow. The insured sued for its total loss, but the Court held that it did not fall within the policy because it had not been caused by storm and tempest, but only because the wall had collapsed from pressure of water which had built up behind it over a long period of persistent rain. The wind had not caused it to fall.

In the course of his judgment VEALE, J., said:[3]

---

[1] For fire insurance, see generally Ivamy, *Fire and Motor Insurance*, 2nd Edn., 1973, pp. 3, 183.
[2] [1966] 1 Lloyd's Rep. 134 (Cornwall Assizes).
[3] *Ibid.*, at p. 138. In any event the learned Judge said (*obiter*) at p. 139 that the fall was a "land-slip" which was excluded under the terms of the policy.

" 'Tempest', in my view, only means a severe storm. Therefore the operative word is 'storm'. I must approach this question much as a jury would approach it. 'Storm' means storm, and to me it connotes some sort of violent wind usually accompanied by rain or hail or snow. Storm does not mean persistent bad weather, nor does it mean heavy rain or persistent rain by itself. I do not think that any violent wind caused any part of this wall to fall. It fell . . . because of the build-up of pressure from the percolation of water through the cracks."

Again, in *S. and M. Hotels, Ltd.* v. *Legal and General Assurance Society, Ltd.*[1] the plaintiffs were the owners of a hotel in Queensborough Terrace, London, W.2, and insured it under a householder's comprehensive policy with the defendants. The perils insured against were (*inter alia*) the destruction of or damage to the building "directly caused by storm, tempest or flood". The plaintiffs employed builders to put a new floor between the existing second and third floors, and for this purpose the whole of the front of the building had to be removed. One windy night the hotel collapsed. The plaintiffs sought a declaration that the defendants were liable under the policy on the grounds that the collapse was due to a "storm".

Thesiger, J., refused to make the declaration. He said that the wind had not been a concurrent or contributing or proximate cause of the collapse,[2] and that on the evidence the collapse must have been caused by the over-stressing of the supports for the floors concerned.[3] Even if the wind had caused the collapse, the collapse was not due to a "storm" which was some-thing more prolonged and widespread than a gust of wind. In the words of his Lordship:[4]

"In my judgment a storm must be something more prolonged and widespread than a gust of wind. One swallow does not make a summer and one may have a gust without a storm although during a storm there will almost certainly be gusts. I approach the question 'Was there a storm at some time in the period of', what was originally alleged by the plaintiffs to be '24 hours or so before the collapse' by imagining myself in Hyde Park, Bayswater Road or Queensborough Terrace, at the material time. I then try to reconstruct what I would have observed from the evidence provided especially by the meteorological records as interpreted and the statements of the Australian watchman, Williams, and the inspector of police. The interpretation on the documents from Professor Scover I regard as extremely important.

I do not feel that if I had been making my way to Chelsea from Paddington Station down Queensborough Terrace on that night in May, 1968, and had turned along Bayswater Road for Notting Hill and Kensington Church Street (for Kensington Gardens would be closed at the time the collapse occurred and for some hours previously), I would have said I was out in or was caught in a 'storm'."

2 Contents

The policy covers the contents of the insured building against the perils mentioned above whilst they are in the building or deposited for safe custody

---

[1] [1972] 1 Lloyd's Rep. 157, Q.B.D. Another issue in the case was whether the plaintiffs were in breach of a condition that "the insured shall at all times maintain the building in a proper state of repair", the learned Judge holding (*obiter*) (*ibid.*, at p. 165) that even if the damage had been caused by a storm, the defendants could not rely on the condition, for it was ambiguous and the "*contra proferentem* rule" would be applied, since the condition was not in point while the building was being reconstructed. As to the "*contra proferentem* rule", see Ivamy, *General Principles of Insurance Law*, 2nd Edn., 1970, pp. 318–323.

[2] [1972] 1 Lloyd's Rep. at p. 181.

[3] *Ibid.*, at p. 181.

[4] *Ibid.*, at p. 181.

in a hotel or bank, or stored in a furniture depository. Television aerials erected on the building are similarly covered, whilst mirrors may be insured against accidental breakage.

3 Extensions to the Policy

The policy may also cover fatal injury to the insured or his wife occurring at the insured premises occasioned by thieves or by fire subject to a specified limit.

The insurers will indemnify the insured against the loss of rent which he would receive from a tenant, and also against the rent which he himself would have to pay to his landlord, whilst the premises are untenantable due to damage caused to the building by the perils mentioned above.

4 Public Liability

The policy may cover sums which the insured either as an owner or occupier of the building may become legally liable to pay in respect of claims made against him arising from bodily injury or disease to persons or damage to property caused during the currency of the policy.

In *Sturge* v. *Hackett*[1] a person was insured under a policy providing cover for "all sums to which the assured (as occupier) . . . may be held legally liable." He was the occupier of a flat in a manor house, and attempted to smoke out some birds' nests in the eaves outside the flat with the aid of a pole, to which was attached a burning paraffin soaked rag. A fire resulted, and the whole house was burnt down and the insured had to pay £51,000 by way of damages. The Court of Appeal held that he was entitled to be indemnified in respect of this sum, as he was an occupier of the premises concerned, and these included the eaves outside the flat.

As to the meaning of the words "as occupier" the Court approved the interpretation given by McNair, J., in the Commercial Court[2] where he said:[3]

" . . . The phrase 'All sums for which the Assured (as occupier . . .) may be held legally liable' in the section of the policy headed 'Liability to the Public' clearly relates, and relates only, to a well-defined group of liabilities imposed upon occupiers of premises. The words 'as occupier' connote that occupation is an essential ingredient of the liability and are not merely descriptive of the identity or status of the person to whom liability attaches. It would not be wise to attempt in this judgment to state exhaustively all the categories of liability which the law imposes upon occupiers. It is sufficient to mention one example relevant at the date of this policy,[4] namely, the occupier's liability as regards the condition of the premises vis à vis invitees and licensees. As it seems to me, the material words of the policy are words of 'legal art'[5] . . . and cover those liabilities which the law imposes upon the occupier because he is the occupier and admit of no ambiguity."

In *Mills* v. *Smith* (*Sinclair, Third party*)[6] a person was insured under a householder's comprehensive policy covering liability to the public

---

[1] [1962] 1 Lloyd's Rep. 626, C.A.
[2] [1962] 1 Lloyd's Rep. 117, Q.B.
[3] *Ibid.*, at p. 124.
[4] July 10, 1956. For the present position as to the liability of occupiers, see Occupier's Liability Act 1957.
[5] Within the principle stated by Lord Sumner in *London and Lancashire Fire Insurance Co., Ltd.* v. *Bolands, Ltd.*, [1924] A.C. 826 at p. 846.
[6] [1963] 1 Lloyd's Rep. 168, Q.B.

"for all sums which the assured . . . may be held legally liable to pay in respect of claims made by any person for damage to property caused by accident."

It was held that he was entitled to be indemnified in respect of the damages which he had had to pay to his neighbour for injury to his neighbour's house by the roots of a tree which was growing in the insured's garden. PAULL, J., held that the damage was "caused by accident" and said:[1]

"I would ask and seek to answer two questions. One: Has there been at any moment of time (or at particular moments of time) some unexpected event (or events) which has (or have) led to damage. It is true that foundations settle . . . and that that settling may be gradual. In this case, however, there has come a point of time when the movement has overstepped the safety limit, if I may use that expression, and a crack in the concrete or in the brickwork . . . of the house has started. This may have happened several times, that is, there may have been more than one crack. In humans the overstepping of movement may cause a fracture, a rupture or a haemorrhage. In a building it may cause a fracture of the concrete of the brickwork. There is no accident until the overstepping takes place. The second question is: What was the cause of the overstepping of the safety limit? My answer is that the cause was the nuisance of the roots of the tree penetrating into the [neighbour's] soil and draining away the moisture necessary to keep the movement of the house from overstepping that safety limit."

But if the brickwork of a house catches a disease from a tree, if, for instance, fungus spreads from the roots to the bricks causing a gradual eating away of them, that would not be damage "caused by accident".[2]

The insurers may also agree to indemnify the insured against liabilities to third persons in respect of death or bodily injury caused by accident, even though the accident does not arise from any liability on the part of the insured in his capacity of occupier of the premises.

Thus, in *Gray* v. *Barr* (*Prudential Assurance Co., Ltd., Third Party*)[3] the defendant's wife effected a "hearth and home" insurance policy which covered him against:

"All sums which [the defendant] shall become legally liable to pay as damages in respect of . . . bodily injury to any person . . . caused by accidents happening during the period of insurance within Great Britain."

The defendant's wife developed a liaison with a Mr. Gray. The defendant went to Gray's house with a loaded shotgun expecting to find his wife there. He deliberately fired a shot into the ceiling with the intention of frightening him. A struggle ensued, and Gray fell against the gun causing the second barrel of the gun to fire. Gray died of his injuries and his father and widow claimed damages from the defendant. The defendant admitted liability, and claimed an indemnity from the insurers under the terms of the policy set out above.

The Court of Appeal held by a majority[4] that Gray's death was not caused by "accident",[5] and therefore the claim failed. But all the Lords

---

[1] [1963] 1 Lloyd's Rep. 168, Q.B. at p. 176.
[2] *Ibid.*, at p. 175 (*per* PAULL, J.).
[3] [1971] 2 All E.R. 949, C.A.
[4] Lord DENNING, M.R., SALMON and PHILLIMORE, L.JJ.
[5] See the judgment of Lord DENNING, M.R. and PHILLIMORE, L.J., at [1971] 2 All E.R. 949 at p. 957 and p. 969 respectively, and the dissenting judgment of SALMON, L.J., on this point, *ibid.*, at p. 963.

Justices were agreed that in any event the defendant was guilty of deliberate violence, and therefore it would be against public policy to allow him to recover the sum insured. SALMON, L.J., said[1]:

> "Although public policy is rightly regarded as an unruly steed which should be cautiously ridden, I am confident that public policy requires that no one who threatens violence with a loaded gun should be allowed to enforce a claim for indemnity against any liability he may incur as a result of having so acted. I do not intend to lay down any wider proposition. In particular, I am not deciding that a man who has committed manslaughter[2] would, in any circumstances, be prevented from enforcing a contract of indemnity in respect of any liability he may have incurred for causing death or from inheriting under a will or on the intestacy of anyone whom he has killed."

5 Accidents to Servants

The policy may cover the insured's liability in respect of bodily injury by accident to his servants employed in connection with the insured premises or employed in connection with any car used by the insured or by any member of the insured's household.

EXCEPTIONS

The policy usually contains exceptions excluding the liability of the insurers for loss or damage directly or indirectly caused by or contributed to or arising from ionising radiations or contamination by radioactivity from any nuclear fuel, war, invasion, acts of foreign enemies, civil war, rebellion, insurrection, military or usurped power or confiscation or nationalisation or requisition or destruction of or damage to property by or under the order of any government or public or local authority.

CONDITIONS

The insured is usually required to give the insurers immediate notice of the happening of any occurrence likely to give rise to a claim under the policy.

He must not admit liability or offer or agree to settle any claim without their written consent. They are entitled to take over and conduct in his name any claim for indemnity against a third party, and have full discretion in the conduct of any negotiations and proceedings and the settlement of any claim.

If the insured makes a claim which he knows to be fraudulent, the policy becomes void and all claims under it are forfeited.

---

[1] [1971] 2 All E.R. 949, at p. 964. See also the judgment of Lord DENNING, M.R., *ibid.*, at p. 957, and that of PHILLIMORE, L.J., *ibid.*, at p. 970.
[2] The defendant in the present case was tried at the Central Criminal Court on a charge of murder. He was acquitted by the jury not only of murder but also of the offence of manslaughter. Lord DENNING, M.R., however, thought that there was no doubt that he was guilty of manslaughter, and that the verdict which was given was a merciful one: *ibid.*, at p. 956.

27

MISCELLANEOUS INSURANCES

Reported decisions on clauses in miscellaneous insurance policies include those on forged documents, theft,[1] consequential loss,[2] subsidence and/or collapse, water damage and strikes.

Forged Documents

In *Philadelphia National Bank* v. *Price*[3] a bank claimed against an underwriter in respect of two policies by which it was agreed that they would be indemnified for a period of 12 months from July 1930.

> "from and against all losses which [the assured bank] may sustain by reason of its having in the ordinary course of business in good faith made advances or loans against or otherwise acted upon any evidences of debt and/or any other securities or documents whatsoever which may prove to have been forged in whole or in part or invalid and/or to have other want of or defect in title."

The first policy was for $300,000 but there was an excess clause which stated:

> "Notwithstanding anything to the contrary herein contained this insurance is only to pay claims for the excess of $200,000 ultimate net loss, by each and every loss or occurrence."

The second policy was in the same form and was for $175,000 with an excess clause of $25,000.

The bank made advances to a customer on the security of invoices in respect of coal sold by him to his purchasers. The customer gave the bank a promissory note for the amount of the invoice deposited on any particular occasion.[4] In fact, during the currency of the policy the customer presented false invoices to the bank which lent him $339,331 on the strength of them. The money was not repaid so the bank claimed under the policies. The advances which were made on any one occasion never amounted to more than $25,000.

The Court of Appeal[5] held that the action failed. Each loss was a separate loss or occurrence, the excess clause applied, and the underwriter was not liable. The numerous fraudulent transactions were not so inter-related as to amount to one ultimate net loss.

---

[1] For the meaning of "theft" in the Theft Act 1968, see pp. 139–140, *ante*.
[2] The subject of consequential loss under fire insurance policies is treated in detail in Ivamy, *Fire and Motor Insurance*, 2nd Edn., 1973, pp. 74–78.
[3] (1938), 60 Ll.L. Rep. 257, C.A.
[4] The details of the arrangement made by the bank with the customer are set out *ibid.*, at pp. 263–264.
[5] Sir Wilfred GREENE, M.R., SCOTT and MacKINNON, L.JJ.

Sir Wilfrid GREENE, M.R., observed:[1]

> "In the result, in my opinion, the franchise clauses in these policies operate. There have been a number of advances made against documents, or advances or loans against or actions upon these documents. Each of those advances or loans ended in a loss and the franchise clause prevents the assured from recovering until the franchise has been worked off."

In *Equitable Trust Co. of New York* v. *Whittaker*[2] the plaintiff effected a policy with an underwriter whereby they were to be indemnified for a period of 12 months against losses up to $200,000 which they might sustain in the course of their business as bankers by taking forged or invalid documents, stolen documents or documents defective in title. The policy also stated:

> "Provided that in the event of loss this policy shall only pay claims (not exceeding the amount of this policy) the excess of an ultimate net loss of $2,500 in respect of each and every loss, such $2,500 to be borne by the assured at their own risk."

A firm named Bennett & Cummins carried on the business of loaning money in St. Pierre, South Dakota to cattlemen on promissory notes secured by chattel mortgages on the cattle, and otherwise dealing in and buying and selling cattle loan paper. The plaintiffs made an arrangement with the firm under which they opened a line of credit for the firm up to $100,000 secured by cattle paper. The firm issued a fictitious cattle paper which the plaintiffs discounted under the arrangement. This cattle paper consisted of notes which were presented once a month from July 2, 1921 to December 2, 1921. The plaintiffs discounted seven notes, all of which were forged and as a result lost $99,000. When they claimed under the policy, the underwriter contended that he was entitled to deduct $2,500 on each of the seven transactions. The plaintiffs, however, maintained that there was only one transaction and not a series of losses so that only $2,500 could be deducted from the whole of the loss.

GREER, J., held that there were seven separate transactions and that the underwriter could deduct $2,500 in respect of each of them. His Lordship observed:[3]

> "Now, it is said on the one hand that because these fraudulent documents under this arrangement were presented once a month it was one transaction, and there was only one loss, and the plaintiffs could only claim with regard to one sum of money. Mr. Miller pointed out that the original contract was to advance upon valid documents, and it seems to me each time that they came forward with their forged documents they were engaged in a fresh transaction; that it was a fraud they were committing each time, and in reference to each of these presentations of a forged document a loss occurred. There being no security, they were forged documents."

He went on to say that it had been said that the result of regarding the losses as being separate was that it produced an absurd anomaly because if the whole of the loss of $100,000 occurred with regard to forged documents each of which was under $2,500 there would be no liability under the policy at all. On this point he observed:[4]

---

[1] (1938), 60 Ll.L. Rep. at p. 267.
[2] (1923), 17 Ll.L. Rep. 153, K.B.D.
[3] *Ibid.*, at p. 155.
[4] *Ibid.*, p. 155. In *Philadelphia National Bank* v. *Price* (1938), 60 Ll.L. Rep. 257, C.A., MacKINNON, L.J., said (*ibid.*, at p. 268) that he considered that *Equitable Trust Co. of New York* v. *Whittaker* (*supra*) was rightly decided.

"I am not sure that that is not the fact, that in so far as small frauds are concerned there should be no indemnity, and that in larger frauds the liability should be with the deduction of 2,500 dollars, because in all losses on forged documents the assured would be insuring themselves up to 2,500 dollars."

Theft

In *Lim Trading Co.* v. *Haydon*[1] a firm of stockbrokers effected a Lloyd's In and Out stockbrokers' policy against the loss or deprivation of the various securities listed in it and which included shares. The policy contained a clause setting out the perils insured against. These were:

"loss by robbery, theft, fire, explosion, burglary or abstraction whether by officers, clerks or servants of the insured, or by any other person or persons or contributed to by the negligent or fraudulent conduct of the said officers, clerks or servants or other person or persons."

The stockbrokers gave shares valued at $69,346.52 to a client in exchange for three cheques which were dishonoured. They claimed against the defendant, a representative underwriter, on the ground that the loss of the shares was due to "theft" within the terms of the policy. The defendant denied liability and contended that the plaintiffs had been swindled out of their shares and that the loss did not amount to theft.

BUTTROSE, J., giving judgment in the Singapore High Court held that the transaction was one of obtaining shares by false pretences and not by "theft" with the meaning of the policy, and observed:[2]

"In essence the transaction was, in my opinion, one of obtaining the shares by false pretences and not by theft within the meaning of the policy. Under English law it would be regarded and punished as false pretences and under Singapore law as cheating and in neither case as theft either within the meaning of the policy or in the fullest sense of the term itself."

His Lordship then went on to say[3] that the inclusion of the words "fraud" and "other dishonesty" in a later part of the policy would seem to indicate that they were never intended to be included in the word "theft" when used in the earlier part of the policy where the other six perils insured against were specified, and that their omission was deliberate and intentional. It would have been a simple matter to have included them along with the six perils already enumerated or to have added to them the words "or by being taken out of their possession or control by any fraudulent means",[4] if that had been the intention.

Consequential Loss

In *Burts and Harvey, Ltd.* and *Alchemy, Ltd.* v. *Vulcan Boiler and General Insurance Co., Ltd.*[5] A consequential loss policy was effected in connection with a chemical plant which was being built for the production of maleic anhydrid the policy contained an exclusion clause which excluded the liability of the insurers for loss or damage resulting from: "Wear and tear, corrosion, erosion, failure of any part or parts the nature or functions of which necessitate their regular replacement".

---

[1] [1968] 1 Lloyd's Rep. 159, Singapore High Court.
[2] *Ibid.*, at p. 161.
[3] *Ibid.*, at p. 161.
[4] As was the case in *Pawle & Co.* v. *Bussell* (1916), 5 L.J.K.B. 1191.
[5] [1966] 1 Lloyd's Rep. 161, Q.B.D.

The plant broke down owing to a crack in a tube in a heat exchanger. Water got into the tube and mixed with the gaseous maleic-anhydrid and formed very corrosive maleic acid. The acid escaped and corroded the machinery, and the plant had to be closed down, and a consequential loss of £20,000 was incurred. The insured sued the insurers, claiming that the consequential loss was covered by the policy, and that the exclusion clause did not apply.

LAWTON, J., held that the insurers were liable. He observed:[1]

> "In any event, on my view of the construction of the exclusion clause corrosion and erosion within the meaning of that clause were never intended . . . to cover other than corrosion and erosion caused in use . . . It seems to me clear that what the [insurers] had in mind was the effect of gaseous maelic anhydrid upon the tubes through which it would pass in the ordinary process of production, and they had not in mind corrosion or erosion which was consequential upon any breakdown of the plant due to the failure of a component."

Subsidence and/or Collapse

In *J. C. Annear & Co., Ltd.* v. *Attenborough*[2] the plaintiffs were the lessees of some premises at Penryn, Cornwall, and insured them with the defendant underwriter under a policy which covered:

> "Two buildings (including quays) and store . . . £2,500. To cover subsidence and/or collapse of buildings as above including cost of repairs through above causes."

The quay was used as a coke and coal store. The floor sank and the wall bulged. The plaintiffs claimed under the policy.

Lord CALDECOTE, C.J., held that the action succeeded. There was a "subsidence" within the meaning of the policy[3] and that the damage to the floor and the wall was the result of the subsidence.[4] The cost of rebuilding the wall would in any event exceed the maximum sum payable under the policy, and the plaintiffs acordingly were entitled to claim £2,500.[5]

In *David Allen & Sons Billposting, Ltd.* v. *Drysdale*[6] the defendant underwriter had issued to the plaintiffs a policy insuring their premises, which had been built 100 or probably 200 years ago, "against loss or damage caused by subsidence and/or collapse". The local authority considered that the premises were dangerous and served a demolition notice on the plaintiffs, who in due course caused them to be demolished. They now claimed an indemnity from the defendant on the ground that the loss was caused by collapse or subsidence.

LEWIS, J., held that the action failed. He considered that the word "collapsed" did not cover the intentional demolition of the premises, for in its primary meaning it denoted "falling or shrinking together or breaking down or giving way through external pressure or loss of rigidity or support".[7] The word "subsidence" meant sinking, i.e. movement in a verticle direction as opposed to "settlement" which meant movement in a lateral direction,

---

[1] [1966] 1 Lloyd's Rep. 170, Q.D.B.
[2] (1940), 68 Ll.L. Rep. 147, K.B.D.
[3] *Ibid.*, at p. 149.
[4] *Ibid.*, at p. 151.
[5] *Ibid.*, at p. 152.
[6] (1939), 65 Ll.L. Rep. 41, K.B.D.
[7] *Ibid.*, at p. 43.

but he was of the opinion that the policy covered both subsidence in the sense in which he had defined it and also settlement.[1]   But, on the evidence, the plaintiff had not discharged the burden of showing that any subsidence occurred during the period of the policy.[2]   Even if there were any slight subsidence, such subsidence was not the proximate cause of the loss of the premises.[3]

Water Damage

In *Kündig* v. *Hepburn*[4] the owners of some sugar-beet seed insured it against "loss or damage by . . . water damage . . . whilst stored in any massive warehouse in Rotterdam." Whilst the seed was in the warehouse, Rotterdam was flooded and the insured claimed for a loss owing to water damage to the seed. The insurers repudiated liability on the ground that the warehouse was not a "massive warehouse". There was evidence that the building, which was about 50 metres by 40 metres and on a concrete foundation about 1 metre high, had walls made of planks 1⅛ in. thick and a roof covered with roofing felt.

DIPLOCK, J., rejected the argument of the insurers, and held that the warehouse was a "massive warehouse". He observed:[5]

> "[the warehouse] was built in 1916. Its dimensions are about 50 metres by 40 metres. It was erected upon a raised concrete foundation about one metre high. It was built with wooden walls made of planks, I think, of 1⅛in. thick, with a roof covered with roofing felt. What it looked like can be seen adequately, if not to excess, in a multitude of photographs which have been put before me. I am told that some 70 per cent. of the warehouses in Rotterdam are of this kind. There are larger multi-storeyed warehouses built of brick of which a photograph is also one of the exhibits in this case. [This warehouse] was not designed, or in general use, as a transit shed for goods in transit: it is used, and has been used since 1916 for the storage of goods. I have to determine whether that warehouse so constructed, so described and looking as it looks in the photographs, is a 'massive warehouse' or not. It is not suggested that the adjective 'massive' in relation to a warehouse is a term of art—it is an ordinary English word—and I have got to make up my mind whether this [warehouse] properly falls within the description 'massive warehouse' in the ordinary English sense of the term. I think it does. There may be more massive warehouses, but I think it is just sufficiently massive to come within the description. I do not think that it is a matter which calls for much elaboration."

Strikes

In *Lewis Emanuel & Son, Ltd.* v. *Hepburn*[6] the insured were fruit importers who had effected a strikes contingency insurance policy with Lloyd's underwriters. The policy provided that:

> "This insurance only to pay for physical loss or damage or deterioration caused by or arising out of Riots, Strikes, and Civil Commotions and delay consequent thereon."

The insured claimed for a loss of market caused by delay due to strikes. But the insurers refused to indemnify him on the ground that the loss did not fall within the terms of the policy.

---

[1] (1939), 65 Ll.L. Rep. at p. 43.
[2] *Ibid.*, at p. 45.
[3] *Ibid.*, at p. 45.
[4] [1959] 1 Lloyd's Rep. 183, Q.B.D. (Commercial Court).
[5] *Ibid.*, at p. 189.
[6] [1960] 1 Lloyd's Rep. 304, Q.B.D. (Commercial Court).

PEARSON, J., held that the action failed for according to the natural and ordinary meaning of the words "physical loss or damage or deterioration", and grammatically, the three possible misfortunes were of a physical kind occurring to the goods themselves, i.e. a physical loss, physical damage and physical deterioration.

His Lordship observed:[1]

"My decision, according to the natural and ordinary meaning of the words, is that all these three possible misfortunes are of the same kind: they are all of a physical kind occurring to the goods themselves. It is physical loss, physical damage and physical deterioration, and that is the conclusion at which I arrive. Further, when one construes the phrase gramatically in the one way or the other, one way is to say that the adjective 'physical' carries right through and applies to each of the three things, physical loss, physical damage and physical deterioration—that is a quite possible use of the word [counsel] gave the example of 'Tasmanian applies, pears or plums'. In that case the adjective 'Tasmanian' would qualify each of the three things, and it would be a natural use of words; but there might be other cases where the adjective would qualify only one of the three things, separated by the use of the word 'or'. But, even if it is not right on the grammatical construction, I should still hold that, in view of the subject-matter being dealt with and the way in which those words are placed in this phrase, one could understand each of the three words, 'loss', 'damage' and 'deterioration', as applying to physical happenings and not merely to financial happenings such as loss of market, and in my view, those are the decisive considerations to be taken into account here."

---

[1] [1960] 1 Lloyd's Rep. at p. 308.

28

WAR RISKS INSURANCE

The various risks arising out of war, which are in practice, excepted from a policy in the ordinary form may be specifically insured against.[1]

THE EVENT INSURED AGAINST

The event insured against may be described in general terms as loss or damage caused by war. Various phrases may be used in different policies to express the causation of the loss,[2] but their general effect is the same.

The policy may, however, be restricted to a particular kind of war risk,[3] e.g., loss or damage caused by aircraft. A policy against loss or damage caused by aircraft may expressly include British as well as hostile aircraft,[4] and may extend to loss or damage caused by bullets, cannon shells or missiles used against aircraft.

WHAT CONSTITUTES A LOSS

To constitute a loss within the meaning of the policy[5] two requirements must be fulfilled:

---

[1] See further Ivamy, *Marine Insurance* (1969), pp. 217–232 and Ivamy, *Fire and Motor Insurance*, 2nd Edn., 1973, pp. 85–87.

[2] See *Molinos de Arroz* v. *Mumford* (1900), 16 T.L.R. 469, where the policy was against all loss or damage directly caused by war, revolution, civil commotion, and/or hostilities and fire risks excluded by fire insurance companies' policies; *Curtis & Sons* v. *Mathews*, [1919] 1 K.B. 425, C.A., where the policy covered the risk of loss and/or damage, directly caused by war, bombardment, military or usurped power or by aircraft (hostile or otherwise), including bombs, shells, and/or missiles dropped or thrown therefrom, or discharged thereat, and fire and/or explosion directly caused by any of the foregoing. The term "restraint of princes" includes an act of war: *Nigel Gold Mining Co.* v. *Hoade*, [1901] 2 K.B. 849; *British and Foreign Marine Insurance Co.* v. *Samuel Sanday & Co.*, [1916] 1 A.C. 650 (marine insurance), where a declaration of war rendering a voyage illegal was held to be a restraint of princes; but it may apply although there is no war: *Janson* v. *Driefontein Consolidated Mines, Ltd.*, [1902] A.C. 484.

[3] See *Ewing & Co.* v. *Sicklemore* (1918), 35 T.L.R. 55, C.A., where the insurance covered the goods only whilst on land. For a case concerning clause 12 of the standard printed clauses approved by Lloyd's Aviation Insurance Underwriters' Association to the effect that war risk cover was automatically cancelled in the event of the outbreak of war between any of the four Great Powers, see *Banque Sabbag S.A.L.* v. *Hope* (1973), The Times, Feb. 21, C.A. (aviation insurance).

[4] If a phrase of this kind is preceded by general words, e.g. "war" or "bombardment", its use does not raise the inference that damage by British forces was not intended to be covered by such general words; *Curtis & Sons* v. *Mathews* (*supra*).

[5] As to proof of the cause of the loss, see *Nobel's Explosives Co.* v. *British Dominions General Insurance Co.*, 1918 W.C. & Ins. Rep. 106. See further, Ivamy, *General Principles of Insurance Law*, 2nd Edn., 1970, pp. 364–368.

1 A state of war must exist at the time of the loss;

2 The war must be the proximate cause of the loss.

1 Existence of State of War

There is no intermediate state between peace and war,[1] and a loss sustained before the actual outbreak of war is not within the policy even though it is the consequence of an "act of state" committed by a Government which afterwards becomes a belligerent, in contemplation of and with a view to the eventuality of war.[2]

2 War as the Proximate Cause

Any act of war is sufficient,[3] provided that it acts directly upon the subject-matter of insurance.[4]

Thus, the subject-matter of insurance may be destroyed or damaged in the course of military operations.[5] It may be captured,[6] or, being situated within the territory belonging to or occupied by a belligerent, may be seized,[7] requisitioned[8] or confiscated[9] by him. It may even be destroyed for the purpose of preventing it from falling into the hands of the enemy.[10]

On the other hand, there is no loss where the subject matter of insurance is neither destroyed nor damaged nor seized by a belligerent, the sole effect of the war being that the insured has lost the power of immediately dealing with it,[11] or selling it before it deteriorates,[12] or is prevented for the time

---

[1] *Molinos de Arroz* v. *Mumford* (*supra*) *per* BIGHAM, J., at p. 490, Cf. *Eastern Carrying Insurance Co.* v. *National Benefit Life and Property Assurance Co., Ltd.* (1919), 35 T.L.R. 292 (marine insurance).

[2] *Janson* v. *Driefontein Consolidated Mines, Ltd.* (*supra*) *per* Lord MACNAGHTEN, at p. 497.

[3] It is immaterial that the act is an illegal act: *Powell* v. *Hyde* (1855), 5 E. & B. 607 (marine insurance) *per* Lord CAMPBELL, C.J., at p. 611.

[4] *Molinos de Arroz* v. *Mumford* (*supra*) *per* BIGHAM, J., at p. 469: "In looking at the cause of the loss one must not confine oneself to the immediate physical consequence, some act of violence committed in the course of war. The proper way was to remember that there was a condition of things in existence which could be described as a state of war, and the object of the plaintiffs was to protect themselves, and of the defendant to insure the plaintiffs against the consequences of that state of things; and one of the direct consequences of that state of things was that the plaintiffs' rice was taken from them against their will"; *Curtis & Sons* v. *Mathews* (*supra*), where a fire caused by bombardment spread and destroyed the insured property; *Le Quellec et Fils* v. *Thomson* (1916), 115 L.T. 224 (marine insurance); *France (William) Fenwick & Co., Ltd.* v. *North of England Protecting and Indemnity Association*, [1917] 2 K.B. 522 (marine insurance).

[5] *Curtis & Sons* v. *Mathews* (*supra*).

[6] It is immaterial that the capture is brought about by collusion with the insured's servant in charge of the property: *Arcangelo* v. *Thompson* (1811), 2 Camp. 620 (marine insurance).

[7] *Stearns* v. *Village Main Reef Gold Mining Co., Ltd.* (1905), 10 Com. Cas. 89, C.A., where a portion of the gold seized was afterwards returned to the insured.

[8] *Molinos de Arroz* v. *Mumford* (*supra*), where rice was requisitioned by insurgents during the war in the Philippine Islands: *Curtis & Co.* v. *Head* (1902), 18 T.L.R. 771, where goods in store at Johannesburg were commandeered by the Transvaal Government in accordance with Transvaal law for the use of troops.

[9] Cf. *Sewell* v. *Royal Exchange Assurance Co.* (1813), 4 Taunt. 856 (marine insurance).

[10] *Butler* v. *Wildman* (1820), 3 B. & Ald. 398 (marine insurance), where the master of a vessel threw the money overboard just before capture.

[11] *Mitsui* v. *Mumford*, [1915] 2 K.B. 27; *Campbell and Phillips, Ltd.* v. *Denman* (1915), 21 Com. Cas. 357. Both cases arose out of the German occupation of Antwerp during the First World War.

[12] *Molinos de Arroz* v. *Mumford* (*supra*).

being from recovering possession of it from the persons to whom it was entrusted.[1]

RESTRICTIONS ON RIGHT TO RECOVER

Where the war is one in which Great Britain is a belligerent, a British subject[2] or a neutral[3] is not precluded from recovering by the fact that the loss is the consequence of military operations conducted by British forces.[4]

The subject of an enemy state, however, except where he is authorized to trade, by licence from the Crown or otherwise,[5] cannot recover, whether the loss is caused by the forces of the British[6] or their allies,[7] or by the forces of his own country.[8]

In the case of a war between two foreign countries, it is immaterial, so far as a policy effected under English law is concerned, to which of the belligerents the loss is to be attributed.[9]

EXCEPTIONS

The principal exceptions found in a policy against war risks are:

(1) *Consequential Loss or Damage*
This includes loss arising from delay, deterioration or loss of market. Thus, where goods are warehoused in a town occupied by the enemy, and the insured, is unable, in consequence, to deal with the goods in the ordinary course of business by selling them, but the enemy has not seized the goods, there is only a loss of market, not a loss of the goods, since the goods remain unharmed in the possession of the person to whom they were entrusted.[10] Similarly if an enemy aircraft falls in a field, any damage done to crops caused by spectators flocking to see it is only consequential damage, and is therefore not recoverable unless specifically insured.

(2) *Loss or damage falling within the scope of a fire policy containing the usual exception against war and riot risk.*[11]

---

[1] *Moore* v. *Evans*, [1918] A.C. 185.
[2] *Page* v. *Thompson* (1804), 1 Park on Marine Insurance (8th Edn.) 175.
[3] *Visger* v. *Prescott* (1804), 5 Esp. 184 (marine insurance).
[4] E.g., *Ewing & Co.* v. *Sicklemore* (1918), 35 T.L.R. 55, C.A.; *Curtis & Sons* v. *Mathews*, [1919] 1 K.B. 425, C.A.
[5] *Esposito* v. *Bowden* (1857), 7 E. & B. 763, Ex. Ch. (charter-party) *per* WILLES, J., at p. 793. See further Ivamy, *General Principles of Insurance Law*, 2nd Edn., 1970, pp. 519–521.
[6] *Kellner* v. *Le Mesurier* (1803), 4 East 396 (marine insurance); *Janson* v. *Driefontein Consolidated Mines, Ltd.*, [1902] A.C. 484, *per* Lord DAVEY at p. 499; *Ex parte Lee* (1806), 13 Ves. 64 (marine insurance).
[7] *Brandon* v. *Curling* (1803), 4 East 410 (marine insurance).
[8] *Janson* v. *Driefontein Consolidated Mines* (*supra*) *per* Lord BRAMPTON at p. 502.
[9] *Aubert* v. *Gray* (1862), 3 B. & S. 169, Ex. Ch. (marine insurance), where a Spanish ship was seized by the Spanish Government in order to carry troops to Morocco, where the Spanish Government was then carrying on war, and it was held that the assured, a Spanish subject was entitled to recover under a policy against loss by "restraint of princes".
[10] *Mitsui* v. *Mumford*, [1915] 2 K.B. 27; *Campbell and Phillips, Ltd.* v. *Denman* (1915), 21 Com. Cas. 357; *Moore* v. *Evans*, [1918] A.C. 185.
[11] See e.g. *Molinos de Arroz* v. *Mumford* (1900), 16 T.L.R. 469.

(3) *Breakage of glass due to concussion.*

(4) *Confiscation on destruction*[1] *by the Government*[2] *of the country where the subject matter of insurance is situated.*[3]

---

[1] This means intentional destruction. Accidental destruction by Government forces in the course of military operations is not excepted from the policy: *Curtis & Sons* v. *Mathews*, [1919] 1 K.B. 425, C.A.

[2] This means the Government in existence at the date of the loss and includes a Government such as the Bolshevist Government in Russia, which was recognized by the British Government as a *de facto* Government: *White, Child and Beney, Ltd.* v. *Eagle Star and British Dominions Insurance Co.* (1922), 127 L.T. 571, C.A.

[3] This exception applies whether the act of the Government is legal or illegal: *Powell* v. *Hyde* (1855), 5 E. & B. 607 (marine insurance) *per* Lord CAMPBELL, C.J., at p. 611.

PART V

LIABILITY INSURANCE

29

INTRODUCTION

An insurance covering property against loss by a particular peril contemplates the physical loss of the property. From the nature of a particular peril or from the circumstances of a particular accident, it happens that in many cases the loss which the insured sustains is not necessarily or exclusively the physical loss of the property itself.

He may sustain a further loss arising from the fact that in the circumstances he has become liable to make good the injury or damage caused to third persons or their property by the accident. Thus, a boiler explosion not only destroys or damages the boiler; usually it causes both injury to workmen employed by the owner of the boiler or passers-by in the street, and damage to the adjoining premises, for all of which the owner of the boiler may be legally liable. Consequently, to be adequately protected, the insured requires to be covered not only against the physical loss of the property, but also against the liabilities arising from an accident in which the property is concerned.

An insurance on property binds the insurers to make good the physical loss of the property and no more. It does not extend to liabilities.[1]

CLASSIFICATION OF LIABILITY INSURANCE

The following kinds of liability insurance are found:

1 *Public liability insurance.*[2]

This includes every kind of liability to the general public for accidental injury or damage.

One particular type of public liability insurance is in relation to the use of motor vehicles.[3] Another type relates to insurance against pollution by oil.[4] A further type is that in respect of professional negligence.[5]

2 *Employers' liability insurance.*[6]

By this type of insurance the insured is protected against his liabilities as an employer to his employees for accidental injury.

---

[1] *De Vaux* v. *Salvador* (1836), 4 Ad. & El. 420 (marine insurance). See Ivamy, *Marine Insurance* (1969), p. 203.
[2] See Chapter 30, *post.*
[3] This type of insurance is considered in Ivamy, *Fire and Motor Insurance*, 2nd Edn., 1973, pp. 187–351.
[4] See Chapter 32, *post.*
[5] See Chapter 33, *post.*
[6] See Chapter 34, *post.*

Both kinds of insurance are frequently combined with an insurance on property or an insurance against personal accident.

Thus, a motor vehicle policy combines an insurance on the vehicle with an insurance against liability for accidents caused by the vehicle. Again, a steam boiler policy covers, in the event of an explosion, not only the loss of the boiler and the damage to the insured's premises, but also the liability for the insured towards third persons and his own employees. Further, a householder's comprehensive policy usually includes a section dealing with public liability.[1]

SPECIAL FEATURES OF LIABILITY INSURANCE

There are special features of liability insurance:
1 The nature of the liability insured against.
2 The description of the subject-matter.
3 The premium.
4 Duties of the insured after loss.
5 The amount recoverable.
6 The defence of actions.

1 Nature of the Liability

The undertaking of the insurers is to indemnify the insured against sums which he becomes legally liable to pay to third persons in respect of personal injuries or damage to their property attributable to causes falling within the scope of the policy.

The right of the insured to be indemnified under the policy depends, therefore, upon the existence of a third person's right to be paid compensation by the insured. The insurers do not bind themselves to pay any sum which the insured may think fit to pay, irrespective of his liability to pay it.[2] Their contract is a contract of indemnity,[3] and the insured can claim no indemnity against a liability which he has voluntarily incurred.[4]

The policy may restrict the indemnity to sums which the insured is legally liable to pay. But this is not, strictly speaking, necessary, since, to give rise to a valid claim under the policy, the liability of the insured must be a legal liability, capable of being enforced against him by legal proceedings.[5]

It is not, however, necessary, unless the policy otherwise provides, that the question of the insured's legal liability should have been adjudicated upon by a Court of law and decided against him, or that he should actually have paid

---

[1] See Chapter 26, *ante*.

[2] Any such contract would be a wager and not a contract of indemnity. Cf. *Chippendale* v. *Holt* (1895), 1 Com. Cas. 197 (marine insurance) *per* MATHEW, J., at p. 199.

[3] *British Cash and Parcel Conveyors, Ltd.* v. *Lamson Store Service Co., Ltd.*, [1908] 1 K.B. 1006, C.A. (maintenance) *per* FLETCHER MOULTON, L.J., at p. 1014; *Weld-Blundell* v. *Stephens*, [1919] 1 K.B. 520, C.A. (agent) : (Affirmed), [1920] A.C. 956) *per* BANKES, L.J., at p. 529.

[4] Cf. *Western Assurance Co. of Toronto* v. *Poole*, [1903] 1 K.B. 376 (marine insurance); *Colonial Insurance Co. of New Zealand* v. *Adelaide Marine Insurance Co.* (1886), 12 App. Cas. 128, 135, P.C. (marine insurance); *North British and Mercantile Insurance Co.* v. *Moffatt* (1871), L.R. 7 C.P. 25 (fire insurance); *Australian Widows' Fund Life Assurance Society, Ltd.* v. *National Mutual Life Association of Australasia, Ltd.*, [1914] A.C. 634 (life insurance). But if the insured is entitled to diplomatic privilege, he may waive it without affecting his rights against the insurers: *Dickinson* v. *Del Solar* (*Mobile and General Insurance Co., Ltd., third parties*), [1930] 1 K.B. 376 (motor insurance). As to this point, see Ivamy, *Fire and Motor Insurance*, 2nd Edn., 1973, p. 283.

[5] See *Scott* v. *McIntosh* (1814), 2 Dow. 322, H.L. (militia ballot insurance); and cf. *Chippendale* v. *Holt* (*supra*).

compensation to the third person.[1] It is sufficient if the existence of legal liability is reasonably clear.[2]

In practice, the insurers usually take charge of any negotiations which may be set on foot to bring about a settlement, and, if legal proceedings are instituted, undertake the conduct of the defence on behalf of the insured.

2 Description of the Subject-matter

The subject-matter of liability insurance is the liability of the insured.[3] It is therefore important that the nature of the particular kind of liability against which he seeks protection should be described or indicated in the policy with precision.

The liability insured against is, from the nature of the insurance, a liability arising out of accident. But the insurance is not, in practice, a general insurance, conferring a universal protection against liability for all kinds of accidents. It is an indemnity against the liabilities arising out of particular kinds of accident; and therefore a description of the particular kinds of accident contemplated forms an essential part of the description of the subject-matter insured.

A description of the particular kind of liability intended to be insured against forms equally with a description of the kind of accident contemplated, an essential part of the description of the subject-matter of insurance.

To entitle the insured to an indemnity he must establish not only that the contemplated accident has happened, but also that the liability therefrom corresponds with the description in the policy. A liability which, though arising from an accident within the meaning of the policy, does not, upon the true construction of the policy, fall within its terms, is not covered.[4]

3 Premium

The practice of charging the insured a lump sum premium for his protection applies to liability insurance as well as to other kinds of insurance.

---

[1] Cf. *Liverpool Mortgage Insurance Co.'s Case*, [1914] 2 Ch. 617, C.A. (debenture insurance), approving *Re Eddystone Marine Insurance Co.*, [1892] 2 Ch. 423 (marine insurance).

[2] In *Smellie* v. *British General Insurance Co.*, [1918] W.C. & Ins. Rep. 233 the question of liability was held to be concluded by the findings in the action previously brought against the insured.

[3] *Lancashire Insurance Co.* v. *Inland Revenue Commissioners*, [1899] 1 Q.B. 353, *per* BRUCE, J., at p. 359: "The liability of the assured to compensate his workmen lies at the very root of the contract; it is the cardinal event upon which the liability of the assurer to pay the money under the policy depends." See also *Cunard Steamship Co.* v. *Marten*, [1903] 2 K.B. 511, C.A. (marine insurance) *per* ROMER, L.J., at p. 555; *Joyce* v. *Kennard* (1871), L.R. 7 Q.B. 78 (transit insurance), *per* LUSH, J., at p. 83; and cf. *Holman & Sons, Ltd.* v. *Merchants' Marine Insurance Co., Ltd.*, [1919] 1 K.B. 383 (marine insurance) *per* SANKEY, J., at p. 387.

[4] *Morrison and Mason* v. *Scottish Employers' Liability and Accident Assurance Co.* 1888, 16 R. (Ct. of Sess.) 212; *Captain Boyton's World's Water Show Syndicate* v. *Employers' Liability Assurance Corporation, Ltd.* (1895), 11 T.L.R. 384, C.A., where the insurance was against liability for personal injury caused by accidents to the boats and chutes used in the show, and it was held that, if one of the boats ran into a third person's boat and injured a passenger, there was an accident to the boat within the meaning of the policy, even though in fact the boat did not sustain any damage, in as much as it met with an accident by which a person was injured; *Smellie* v. *British General Insurance Co.*, [1918] W.C. Ins. Rep. 233, where a glazier effected an insurance against liability for accidents caused by any workman in the insured's service whilst engaged on his business as a glazier, and it was held that he was not entitled to an indemnity in respect of the conduct of his workmen not connected with their occupation as glaziers.

This practice is not, however, invariably followed. The liability arising out of a particular accident bears no relation to the value of the property concerned, whilst the chances of an accident happening depend upon the opportunities afforded by the business of the insured, and, mainly upon the number of his employees. The chances of an accident, therefore, will be according to the magnitude of his business.[1]

Accordingly, it is the practice of insurers to base the premium charged upon the number of employees or the amount paid in wages during the year of insurance. In many businesses, the number of employees, and consequently the chances of accident, varies from day to day. There is, therefore, a danger, if a lump sum premium is paid, on the one hand, that the insured may be paying for a greater protection than he required, and, on the other hand, that the insurers may be bearing a risk out of proportion to the amount which they are receiving as premium.

To meet such cases the policy usually contains a condition providing for the adjustment of the premium in accordance with the actual risk.

One type of condition states that the insured must give the insurers notice of any increase in the number of employees, and must pay the additional premium chargeable in consequence. If he fails to do so within a specified time, the policy is declared void and the premium already paid forfeited to the insurers. This method involves difficulties and inconveniences in the case of a large business, where constant changes are taking place. In any event it tends to the disadvantage of the insured, who may lose the benefit of the policy through mere inadvertence on the part of a subordinate.

Another type of condition, which is the one usually found at the present time, states that an adjustment is to be made at the end of the year of insurance. In this case the insured may be required, at the end of the year, to furnish the insurers with a statement showing the maximum number of employees for the year. If the premium is based on wages, he may be required to furnish an account of the actual wages paid during the year;[2] and, in addition, he may be required to keep a wages book,[3] in which the names of all his employees and the amounts paid to them in wages are to be entered week by week. The premium is then adjusted to correspond with the maximum number of employees or with the actual amount paid in wages, as the case may be; and the insurers receive or refund the difference between the premium as adjusted and the premium already paid.

4 Duties of Insured after Loss

The happening of an accident is at once the foundation of the insured's liability and of his right to indemnity under the policy. The insurers are the persons upon whom the consequences of the accident will ultimately fall, and it is, therefore, important that all the facts should be placed before them

---

[1] Hence, the amount of premium charged may be taken into account as showing the scope of the insurance: *Smellie* v. *British General Insurance Co.*, [1918] W.C. & Ins. Rep. 233, where the smallness of the premium supported the inference that the policy applied only to accidents on the insured's premises.

[2] *General Accident Assurance Corporation, Ltd.* v. *Day* (1904), 21 T.L.R. 88, where the obligation was held to attach, although the policy had come to an end. The insurers are not bound to supply the necessary form, unless the policy so provides: *ibid.*, *per* BUCKLEY, J., at p. 89.

[3] *Re Bradley and Essex and Suffolk Accident Indemnity Society*, [1912] 1 K.B. 415, C.A., where a stipulation to that effect was held not to be a condition precedent to liability.

as soon as possible, and that nothing should be done by the insured to their prejudice.

As the insured is relieved from liability by the terms of the policy, there is a danger that he may not take the necessary steps to protect the insurers or at least that he may not be as diligent as he would be if he had to bear the loss himself. In practice, the conduct of the defence in any action which may be brought against the insured is taken over by the insurers. But they may find that they are already prejudiced by the acts or omissions of the insured, and that the materials for the defence are scanty and imperfect. Moreover, they are not formal parties to the action, and they may be further prejudiced by the acts or omissions of the insured in the course of the litigation.

It is therefore usual for the policy to contain express conditions precedent[1] to the liability of the insurers imposing special duties upon the insured in respect of his conduct after the accident. These special duties include the following:

a the insured is required to give the insurers notice of the accident within a specified time.[2]

b he is required to obtain the names and addresses of any witnesses of the accident.

c he is required to give the insurers notice of any claim[3] made against him in respect of the accident.[4]

d he is required to give the insurers any information or assistance which they may require for the purpose of resisting or settling any claim.[5]

e he is forbidden to settle or make any payment in respect of any claim or to admit liability,[6] or make any other admission with respect to the

---

[1] Whether the stipulation is a condition precedent is a matter of construction. Contrast *Re Williams and Thomas and Lancashire and Yorkshire Accident Insurance Co.'s Arbitration* (1902), 19 T.L.R. 82 (employers' liability insurance), where a stipulation as to immediate notice was held to be a condition precedent, with *Re Coleman's Depositories, Ltd. and Life and Health Assurance Association*, [1907] 2 K.B. 798, C.A. (employers' liability insurance), where VAUGHAN WILLIAMS, L.J., at p. 804, doubted, but did not dissent from the view taken in the Court below, that a similar stipulation was not a condition precedent. See also *Re Bradley and Essex and Suffolk Accident Indemnity Society*, [1912] 1 K.B. 415, C.A. (employers' liability insurance) *per* COZENS-HARDY, M.R., at p. 421, and *Wilkinson v. Car and General Insurance Corporation, Ltd.* (1913), 110 L.T. 468, C.A. (employers' liability insurance), where it was assumed that the stipulations in question were conditions precedent. See further, Ivamy, *General Principles of Insurance Law*, 2nd Edn., 1970, pp. 236–243.

[2] *Re Williams and Thomas and Lancashire and Yorkshire Accident Insurance Co.'s Arbitration* (*supra*) (employers' liability insurance); *Re Coleman's Depositories, Ltd. and Life and Health Assurance Association* (*supra*) (employers' liability insurance); *Weir v. Accident Insurance Co.* 1908, 16 S.L.T. 141. There is no duty, however, to give notice unless it is plain that the accident is one to which the policy applies: *Smellie v. British General Insurance Co.*, [1918] W.C. & Ins. Rep. 233.

[3] This means any demand for compensation: *Wilkinson v. Car and General Insurance Corporation, Ltd.* (*supra*), where a request by a workman for arbitration was held not to be a written notice of claim within the meaning of the stipulation, but only a step in procedure.

[4] *British General Insurance Co. v. Mountain*, [1920] W.C. & Ins. Rep. 254, H.L. *per* Lord BIRKENHEAD, L.C., at p. 257. He may also be required to forward to the insurers the originals of any letters or other documents received from any claimant, within a specified time.

[5] The obligation does not arise until the insurers apply for information: *Wilkinson v. Car and General Insurance Corporation, Ltd.* (*supra*) *per* Lord READING, C.J., at p. 471.

[6] An admission of liability made by a person after an accident, even if admissible as part of the *re gestae*, is not a breach of the condition, unless he had authority to make it: *Tustin v. Arnold & Sons* (1915), 113 L.T. 95.

accident, or any claim arising therefrom, without the written consent of the insurers.[1]

5   Amount Recoverable

The insured is entitled to be indemnified against the sums which he becomes legally liable to pay during the currency of the policy in respect of accidents of the kind contemplated. This indemnity, according to the terms of the policy, may be limited or unlimited in amount. In either case, the number of accidents which actually happen during the currency of the policy may be disregarded as immaterial. Whenever an accident occurs, the insured has, subject to the limitations of the policy, if any, a right to an indemnity against its consequences.[2]

a   *Methods of Limitation*

In practice three methods of limitation are used:

   i the policy may specify the maximum amount for which the insurers are to be liable in respect of any particular accident.

   ii the policy may specify the maximum amount for which the insurers are to be liable during the currency of the policy.

   iii the policy may provide that the insured is to bear part of the liability himself.

i   *Maximum for One Accident.*—This limitation[3] applies only to the particular accident, and does not prevent the insured from claiming a further indemnity, subject in each case to the limitation, in respect of any number of accidents happening during the currency of the policy.[4]

It is to be observed that the word "accident" is ambiguous, being capable of being applied in two senses. In the case of a collision between two vehicles or other accident on a road or railway, there is in one sense only one accident, *i.e.* the accident to the vehicle or train.[5] But there is equally an accident to each person injured, and in that sense there are as many accidents as there are persons injured.[6]

Hence, where there is a limitation of liability in respect of any one accident, such limitation, in the absence of anything to show the contrary, is to be construed in accordance with the ordinary rules of construction, as applying not to one accident to the vehicle or train, but to the separate accidents to the different persons injured.

---

[1] But if the insurers decline to intervene, they cannot subsequently complain if the insured *bona fide* settles the claim: *Captain Boyton's World's Water Show Syndicate, Ltd.* v. *Employers' Liability Assurance Corporation, Ltd.* (1895), 11 T.L.R. 384, C.A., *per* Lord ESHER, M.R., at p. 384.

[2] *South Staffordshire Tramways Co.* v. *Sickness and Accident Assurance Association*, [1891] 1 Q.B. 402, C.A.; *Joyce* v. *Kennard* (1871), L.R. 7 Q.B. 78 (transit insurance) *per* LUSH, J., at p. 83. Cf. *Crowley* v. *Cohen* (1832), 3 B. & Ad. 478 (transit insurance).

[3] *McKinlay* v. *Life and Health Assurance Association* 1905, 13 S.L.T. 102, where the insured was held bound by a limitation in the policy upon which he sued, although such limitation did not appear in the proposal form when he signed it.

[4] *South Staffordshire Tramways Co.* v. *Sickness and Accident Assurance Association* (*supra*).

[5] But the accident may be described with equal propriety as an accident to either vehicle: *Captain Boyton's World's Water Show Syndicate, Ltd.* v. *Employers' Liability Assurance Corporation, Ltd.* (1895), 11 T.L.R. 384, C.A., *per* Lord ESHER, M.R., at p. 384.

[6] *South Staffordshire Tramways Co.* v. *Sickness and Accident Assurance Association* (*supra*) *per* BOWEN, L.J., at p. 407.

Accordingly, if several persons are injured, the aggregate liability of the insurers is not limited to the sum specified in the policy. But they are liable to pay damages awarded to each person injured, not exceeding in each case, the maximum specified.[1]

In order to prevent any ambiguity from arising, a different word, such as "occurrence", may be used to designate the accident to the vehicle or train, and the policy may expressly limit the liability of the insurers to a specified maximum in respect of any accident or series of accidents arising out of the same "occurrence". In this case, the aggregate liability of the insurers is measured by the specified maximum, and if there is an accident in which several persons are injured, the insured has no right to claim a larger indemnity.[2]

ii Maximum during Currency of Policy.—The effect of this is that in the event of a second or subsequent accident, all sums already paid under the policy are to be taken into account, and the insured's right of indemnity is limited to the balance, if any, remaining unpaid.[3] If therefore, the policy has been exhausted by previous accidents, the insured has no further claim.

iii Insured bearing Part of Liability.—Sometimes the liability for every accident is to be borne by the insurers and the insured in a specified proportion.

More usually, the policy specifies a certain sum, up to which the insured must bear liability, *e.g.* the first £25.[4] The effect of this is to relieve the insurers from responsibility for minor accidents altogether, and, in the case of other accidents, to give the insured a right of indemnity only in so far as the damages awarded against him exceed the specified limit.[5]

b *Costs*

An insurance against liability does not in itself necessarily carry an indemnity against the costs of proceedings brought against the insured. If the insured is held liable for the accident, the costs incurred are the consequence of his legal liability, and are therefore covered by the policy.[6] If the defence is successful, the event giving rise to the indemnity never happens; and the costs, being incurred in averting a loss under the policy, are not, strictly speaking, recoverable.[7]

---

[1] *South Staffordshire Tramways Co.* v. *Sickness and Accident Assurance Association (supra) per* BOWEN, L.J., at p. 407, where forty persons were injured owing to the overturning of a tram, and it was held that the insurers were liable for the whole amount, i.e. £833 paid in compensation, notwithstanding the limitation of "£250 in respect of any one accident."

[2] *Allen* v. *London Guarantee and Accident Co., Ltd.* (1912), 28 T.L.R. 254, where two persons knocked down by a cart, recovered £2,000 and £175 damages respectively, and it was held that the insurers were not liable for more than £300, i.e. the maximum specified in the policy.

[3] See e.g. *South Staffordshire Tramways Co.* v. *Sickness and Accident Assurance Association (supra)*, where the policy provided for a maximum liability of £1,500 in any one year; *British General Insurance Co.* v. *Mountain*, [1920] W.C. & Ins. Rep. 254, H.L., which was a case of reinsurance and the original policy provided for a maximum liability of £1,000 in respect of a single accident and a further liability of £4,500 for the year.

[4] In *British General Insurance Co.* v. *Mountain (supra)* the reinsurance policy covered the original insurers' liability in excess of £250 for any one accident.

[5] As to "excess clauses", see further, Ivamy, *General Principles of Insurance Law*, 2nd Edn., 1970, pp. 384–385.

[6] *Xenos* v. *Fox* (1869), L.R. 4 C.P. 665, Ex. Ch. (marine insurance) *per* COCKBURN, C.J., at p. 668.

[7] *Xenos* v. *Fox (supra)*, where the fact that the underwriters had consented to the action being defended was held to be immaterial.

An indemnity against costs is usually conferred by the express language of the policy, the indemnity covering not only any costs which the insured may be ordered to pay to the claimant, but also the costs incurred by the insured in defending any proceedings which may be brought against him. In this case the indemnity applies whether the insured is allowed to defend the action himself or whether, as is usually the case, the insurers undertake the conduct of the proceedings on his behalf.[1]

If the insured is allowed to conduct his defence himself, it may be made a condition precedent to liability that no costs are to be incurred by the insured without the consent of the insurers.[2]

Where there is a limitation of liability, and the damages awarded against the insured exceed the maximum specified in the policy, the policy usually contains a stipulation providing for the apportionment of the costs between the insured and the insurers in the proportion which the excess bears to such maximum.

If, however, the insurers themselves undertake the conduct of the proceedings, special considerations apply, and the right of the insured to be indemnified against costs is not necessarily governed by the stipulation.[3]

If the insurers wrongfully repudiate liability, e.g. on the ground that the insured has been guilty of a breach of condition and he is successfully sued for damages by a third party, the insurers are liable to indemnify him in respect of the costs which he has incurred, for although these costs are not within the cover expressly provided by the policy, they were recoverable as damages which reasonably flowed from the breach of contract by the insurers in repudiating liability.[4]

6 Defence of Actions

The insurers are not parties to the action brought against the insured by the person injured, and they have no independent right to intervene in the proceedings. Since, however, their contract with the insured is a contract to indemnify him against the liability which is the subject matter of the action, the insured is entitled to issue a third-party notice against the insurers, under which they may be made parties to the action.[5]

It is clear, however, that every action brought against the insured, in which the question of his liability for the accident arises, necessarily concerns the insurers, for their own liability to him is measured by the amount of damages awarded against him in the action. It is expedient, therefore, that they should have a right to see that the defence of the action is properly conducted.

---

[1] *British General Insurance Co.* v. *Mountain* (*supra*), *per* Lord BIRKENHEAD, L.C., at p. 257. See further, *Tustin* v. *Arnold & Sons* (1915), 113 L.T. 95; and cf. *"Daily Express" (1908), Ltd.* v. *Mountain* (1916), 32 T.L.R. 592, C.A., where, in an action by the insured under an insurance against the costs incurred in litigation, the bill of costs delivered in the previous action was held to be privileged; *Cornish* v. *Lynch* (1910), 3 B.W.C.C. 343, where costs were awarded to an employer, although indemnified by the insurers.

[2] *British General Insurance Co.* v. *Mountain* (*supra*). The insurers must not unreasonably withhold their consent; such consent may be implied, and the necessity for it may be waived by their conduct: *Hulton (E.) & Co., Ltd.* v. *Mountain* (1921), 37 T.L.R. 869, C.A.

[3] See p. 233, *post*.

[4] *Pictorial Machinery, Ltd.* v. *Nicholls* (1940), 67 Ll.L. Rep. 524.

[5] See e.g. *Evans* v. *Cook*, [1905] 1 K.B. 53, C.A.; *Collins* v. *Benscher* (*Balham Boiler Insurance Co., Third Parties*) (1914), Feb. 14, unreported, C.A.

Consequently, the policy usually contains a stipulation empowering the insurers to take over the conduct and control of any action or proceedings against the insured.[1] In this case, if they decline to undertake the defence of the action brought against the insured, he may settle it without consulting them, and they cannot complain of the settlement if it has been made *bona fide*.[2] If on the other hand, they defend the action, they should withdraw from the defence upon discovering that the insured has broken a condition of the policy; otherwise, by continuing the defence, they may be held to have waived the breach.[3]

The fact that the insurers take over the conduct and control of the proceedings does not affect their position as regards the person injured. They are still strangers to the action.[4]

As against the insured, however, the insurers, by intervening, may deprive themselves to some extent of the benefit of any limitation of liability contained in the policy. Having undertaken the defence, they are bound to conduct it properly. If, therefore, they are guilty of negligence in the conduct of the defence, they are liable for the consequences, and their liability is measured by the actual loss sustained by the insured, without regard to the limitation in the policy.[5]

Further, they are not entitled, merely because they choose to defend an action, to impose upon the insured an unlimited liability for costs. If, therefore, they defend the action in his name without his consent, they must indemnify him against the whole of the costs, which, as defendant, he is called upon to pay. The limitation of liability in the policy, although it still applies to the damages recovered, has no operation as regards the costs.[6] On the other hand, the position is different where the insurers undertake the defence at the insured's request. In such a case the costs are subject to apportionment in accordance with the terms of the stipulation.[7]

BANKRUPTCY OF THE INSURED

1   The Earlier Rule

The person injured is not a party to the contract of insurance. Neither at

---

[1] The solicitor conducting the defence on the instructions of the insurers stands in the relation of solicitor and client to the insured, and is liable to the insured for any negligence or default in the conduct of the action: *Walsh* v. *White and Bywaters* (1927), July 12, unreported.

[2] *Captain Boyton's World's Water Show Syndicate, Ltd.* v. *Employers' Liability Assurance Corporation. Ltd.* (1895), 11 T.L.R. 384, C.A. *per* Lord ESHER, M.R., at p. 384.

[3] *Western Canada Accident and Guarantee Insurance Co.* v. *Parrott* (1921), 61 S.C.R. 595; *Cadeddu* v. *Mount Royal Assurance Co.*, [1929] 2 W.W.R. 161.

[4] *Nairn* v. *South East Lancashire Insurance Co.*, 1930 S.C. 606, where the insurers were held not liable to the person injured for which the action had been settled.

[5] *Patteson* v. *Northern Accident Insurance Co.*, [1901] 2 I.R. 262, where the insured claimed £270, the amount of the damages awarded against him, although the policy was for £100 only, and it was held that his claim, being substantially based on negligence, fell outside the policy and was, therefore, not within the arbitration clause.

[6] *Allen* v. *London Guarantee and Accident Co., Ltd.* (1912), 28 T.L.R. 254. Cf. *Smellie* v. *British General Insurance Co.*, [1918] W.C. & Ins. Rep. 233, where the insurers were held not liable to indemnify the insured against costs, although the defence of the action brought against him was conducted by their solicitor, since the insured had employed him on his own account after they had refused to undertake the defence.

[7] In *Patteson* v. *Northern Accident Insurance Co.* (*supra*) the insurers, whilst claiming to limit their liability to £100, offered to pay the whole of the costs.

Common Law nor in Equity has he any rights against the insurers or any claim against the insured in respect of the money paid under the policy.

Consequently, prior to the Third Parties (Rights against Insurers) Act 1930, the person injured was not entitled, upon the bankruptcy of the insured, to look to the policy moneys for the payment of damages. They became part of the insured's general assets, the person injured ranking in the insolvency proceedings as an ordinary creditor only.[1] This created a position of hardship, particularly in view of the fact that in many cases the policy moneys were the only assets, seeing that the purpose of effecting the policy was to provide funds to meet the liability which had arisen.

2 The Present Position

a *Application of the Act*

In general, the Act applies to all contracts of insurance under which the insured is insured against liabilities incurred to third parties.[2] But it does not apply to contracts of reinsurance,[3] nor to any contract of insurance required to be effected under the Merchant Shipping (Oil Pollution) Act 1971.[4]

The third party's rights against the insurer arise if the insured has become bankrupt, or makes a composition or arrangement with his creditors.[5]

If the insured is a company, the third party's rights arise if a winding up order has been made, or a resolution for voluntary winding up has been passed, or a receiver or manager of the company's business or undertaking has been duly appointed, or possession has been taken by or on behalf of the holders of any debentures secured by a floating charge of any property comprised in or subject to the charge.[6]

It is immaterial whether the liability is incurred before or after any of the events stated above.[7]

Transfer of Liability

Section 1 (1) of the Act of 1930 states that

> " . . . if any such liability [to a third party] is incurred by the insured, his rights against the insurer under the contract in respect of the liability shall, notwithstanding anything in any Act or rule of law to the contrary, be transferred to and vest in the third party to whom the liability was so incurred."

Liability on the part of the insured to the third party must be established before the third party can sue the insurers under the Third Parties (Rights against Insurers) Act 1930.

In *Post Office* v. *Norwich Union Fire Insurance Society, Ltd.*[8] the insured, A. J. G. Potter & Sons, Ltd., were builders and contractors and were insured by the

---

[1] *Re Harrington Motor Co., Ex parte Chaplin*, [1928] Ch. 105, C.A.; *Hood's Trustees* v. *Southern Union General Insurance Co. of Australasia*, [1928] Ch. 793, C.A.; See generally Ivamy, *Fire and Motor Insurance*, 2nd Edn., 1973, pp. 315–317.
[2] Third Parties (Rights against Insurers) Act 1930, s. 1 (1).
[3] *Ibid.*, s. 1 (5).
[4] Merchant Shipping (Oil Pollution) Act 1971.
[5] Third Parties (Rights against Insurers) Act 1930, s. 1 (1).
[6] *Ibid.*, s. 1 (1).
[7] *Ibid.*, s. 1 (1).
[8] [1967] 1 Lloyd's Rep. 216, C.A.

defendants under a public liability policy against: "all sums which the Insured shall become legally liable to pay as compensation in respect of . . . damage to property."

Condition 3 of the policy stated:

> "No admission, offer, promise, payment or indemnity shall be made or given by or on behalf of the Insured without the written consent of the company which shall be entitled if it so desires to take over and conduct in the name of the Insured the defence or settlement of any claim . . ."

In May 1963 an underground cable belonging to the plaintiff was damaged by the insured in the course of carrying out work for a customer. The plaintiff claimed £839 10s. 3d. in respect of the cost of repairing the cable, but the insured denied liability and on June 1, 1964, went into liquidation. The plaintiff claimed against the defendants under the Third Parties (Rights Against Insurers) Act, 1930. The defendants refused to pay on the ground that the right to sue for the money did not arise until liability had been established and the amount ascertained, and that this has not been done.

The Court of Appeal[1] held, on a preliminary point of law that their refusal was justified. Lord DENNING, M.R., observed:[2]

> "It seems to me that the insured only acquires a right to sue for the money when his liability to the injured person has been established so as to give rise to a right of indemnity. His liability to the injured person must be ascertained and determined to exist, either by the judgment of the Court or by an award in an arbitration or by agreement. Until that is done, the right to an indemnity does not arise.
>
> Under the section it is clear to me that the injured person cannot sue the insurance company except in such circumstances as the insured himself could have sued the insurance company. The insured could only have sued for an indemnity when his liability to the third person was established and the amount of the loss ascertained. In some circumstances the insured might sue earlier for a declaration, *e.g.*, if the insured company were repudiating the policy for some reason. But where the policy is admittedly good, the insured cannot sue for an indemnity until his own liability to the third person is ascertained."

The learned Master of the Rolls then examined[3] the ways in which liability could be established if the insured was made bankrupt or, where the insured was a company, went into liquidation, and said that if there were an unascertained claim for damages in tort, it could not be proved in the bankruptcy nor in the liquidation of the company. But the injured person could bring an action against the wrongdoer. In the case of a company he would require the leave of the Court, but no doubt leave would automatically be given.[4] The insurers could fight the action in the name of the wrongdoer. In that way liability could be established and the injured person could then proceed against the insurers.

SALMON, L.J., said that if the Act of 1930 gave third parties the right to sue insurance companies direct, it would mean that the cause lists would

---

[1] Lord DENNING, M.R., HARMAN and SALMON, L.JJ.

[2] [1967] 1 Lloyd's Rep. at p. 219. See also the judgment of HARMAN, L.J., *ibid.*, at p. 220, and that of SALMON, L.J., *ibid.*, at p. 221.

[3] *Ibid.*, at p. 219.

[4] HARMAN, L.J., said (*ibid.*, at p. 220) that he supposed that it was possible that such leave might be refused, but he did not think that the Court need contemplate that situation until it happened, and it seemed to him to be unlikely. See further, the judgment of SALMON, L.J., *ibid.*, at p. 221.

contain the names of many defendant insurance companies, and that could
not be good for their business. If an insurance company were constantly
being sued, any customer or potential customer would or might assume,
quite wrongly, that the company was habitually repudiating liability under
its policies with its own customers.[1]

The insurers are under the same liability to the third party as they would
have been to the insured. Thus, if they can avoid liability to the insured
on the ground that he is in breach of a condition, they are under no liability
to the third party.[2]

In *Farrell* v. *Federated Employers' Insurance Association, Ltd.*[3] the plaintiff
was employed by J. O'Connor & Co., Ltd., who were building contractors,
and was injured whilst laying some pipes in a tunnel. J. O'Connor & Co.,
Ltd. had effected an employers' liability insurance policy with the defendants.
A condition of the policy stated that "Every writ served on the employer
shall be notified or forwarded to the defendants immediately". On September
8, 1964, a Mr. Pitt was appointed as a receiver of J. O'Connor & Co., Ltd.
and on January 6, 1966, a writ was served on them at their registered
office. On February 28, 1966 the plaintiff obtained judgment against them
for £14,500, but it remained unsatisfied. So he now claimed this sum from
the defendants under the Act of 1930. But they repudiated liability on the
ground that J. O'Connor & Co., Ltd. had broken the condition set out above,
for it was not until March 2, 1966 that the defendants had been notified of
the judgment, and the writ had not been forwarded to them.

The Court of Appeal[4] held that this defence succeeded, for under the Act
of 1930 the defendants were entitled to rely as against a third party on any
defence which would have been available to them as against the insured.[5]

Lord DENNING, M.R., said:[6]

> "That Act gives an injured person a direct cause of action against the insurers
> whenever the insured becomes insolvent. When the insured is a company, the
> Act applies, among other things, on a receiver being appointed: see s. 1 (1) (*b*).
> Thereupon the injured person can sue the insurers direct. But he has first to
> establish that the insured was liable to him for that amount: see *Post Office* v.
> *Norwich Union Fire Insurance Society, Ltd.*[7]; and, having done that, he stands in
> the shoes of the insured. But the insurers can avail themselves, as against him,
> of all the defences which would have been available to them as against the
> insured. So in this case the insurers said that the policy was issued subject to
> conditions on which they relied as a defence.
>
> Counsel for the plaintiff's second point was that the condition had been ful-
> filled. 'Immediate', he said, was defined by FLETCHER MOULTON, L.J., in
> *Coleman's* case.[8] It meant 'with all reasonable speed considering the circum-
> stances of the case'. He said that the writ was served here on January 7th 1966

---

[1] [1967] 1 Lloyd's Rep., at p. 221.
[2] Third Parties (Rights against Insurers) Act 1930, s. 1 (4).
[3] [1970] 3 All E.R. 632, C.A.
[4] Lord DENNING, M.R., MEGAW, L.J., and Sir Frederic SELLERS.
[5] It is to be emphasized, however, that the actual decision however would have been different
at the present time because the condition in the policy would now be void as against the
third party: Employers' Liability (Compulsory Insurance) General Regulations 1971,
reg. 2 (1) made under Employers' Liability (Compulsory Insurance) Act 1969, which came
into force on January 1, 1972. See pp. 370–373, *post.*
[6] [1970] 3 All E.R. at p. 634.
[7] [1967] 1 Lloyd's Rep. 216, C.A. See p. 234, *ante.*
[8] I.e., *Re Coleman's Depositories, Ltd. and Life and Health Assurance Association* [1904–7] All
E.R. Rep. 383, at p. 387.

and that notice was given to the insurers on March 3rd 1966, that is, some eight weeks later. That was, he said, all reasonable speed. I do not think so. I think that, in the circumstances of the case, the plaintiff's solicitors ought to have told the insurers about the writ soon after they received the letter of January 17th 1966 from the receiver. 'With all reasonable speed' would mean by the end of January 1966 at latest. Instead of doing so, the solicitors went on and signed judgment on February 28th 1966, in default of appearance. Counsel for the plaintiff said that judgment made little difference. The insurers had not been prejudiced. They could easily have got that judgment set aside and have got leave to defend. That may be. But I do not see why they should be put to that trouble. The plain fact is that the writ was not notified with all reasonable speed. The condition was not fulfilled. The insurers are entitled to rely on it."

In *Hassett* v. *Legal and General Assurance Society, Ltd.,*[1] Lilleys, Ltd. whose business was constructional work, effected a public liability policy with the defendants. Condition 4 of the policy stated: "Any communication whatever relating to the accident must be forwarded to the Society immediately."

Condition 5 stated:

"On receiving from the insured notice of any claim the Society may take upon themselves the settlement of the same . . . The Society shall if and so long as they desire have the absolute conduct and control in the name and on behalf of the insured of the defence to any proceedings that may be taken to enforce any claim covered by this policy."

The plaintiff was employed by sub-contractors engaged by Lilleys, Ltd. and was injured when some scaffolding collapsed. He brought a claim against Lilleys, Ltd., and notice of it was received in a roundabout way by the defendants. In the meanwhile, the writ was served on Lilleys, Ltd., at their registered office. No appearance was entered, and judgment was eventually signed in default. Lilleys, Ltd. was wound up, and the plaintiff claimed against the defendants under the Act of 1930. The defendants denied liability on the ground that Lilleys, Ltd. were in breach of the conditions set out above.

ATKINSON, J., held that they were entitled to do so, for it was an essential condition that they should be informed of any proceedings brought against the insured, and Lilleys, Ltd. had failed in their obligation to bring to their notice the fact that proceedings had been commenced by the plaintiff. His Lordship observed:[2]

"If there is one thing which is perfectly clear to my mind, it is that the moment any proceedings were started there was an obligation imposed upon the insured by these conditions to bring it to the notice of the insurance company, so that the insurance company would be in a position to exercise the rights which these conditions give them. Really, to argue, as has been argued, that these conditions do not impose such an obligation on the insured, seems to me to be almost arguing the impossible. At any rate, I am quite satisfied that the writ was 'a communication relating to an accident', and it is implicit in every word of Condition 5 that if proceedings are started, the insurance company must be told about them and be put into a position to exercise their rights. If it were not so, scope would be given for the exaggerated claims going through without any inquiry or testing, and insurance companies would be swindled in all directions. That condition, the performance of which was an essential condition, and as it seems to me a condition precedent to the insurance company's liability, was never performed.

---

[1] (1939), 63 Ll.L. Rep. 278, K.B.D.
[2] *Ibid.*, at p. 281. His Lordship also held (*ibid.*, at p. 282) that on the evidence the defendants had not waived the breach of the conditions. As to waiver of breach of condition, see further, Ivamy, *General Principles of Insurance Law*, 2nd Edn., 1970, pp. 251–256.

Therefore, it seems to me that the insurance company had a perfect right to say: 'Here is a judgment which has been obtained with which we have nothing whatever to do'."

In *Kearney* v. *General Accident, Fire and Life Assurance Corporation, Ltd*[1] the plaintiff was the administratrix of a workman who was killed while employed by Eric Waller, Ltd. when he fell while painting trusses of a building. She obtained judgment against Eric Waller, Ltd. but this was unsatisfied. So she claimed under the Third Parties (Rights Against Insurers) Act, 1930 against the defendants on the ground that they were liable under two employer's liability policies which had been effected by Eric Waller, Ltd.

The first insurance policy stated that:

"The [defendants] shall not be liable by virtue of this policy if at any time the Employer undertakes any work other than painting private dwellings and/or shops consisting of not more than two floors (including the ground floor) and attic, and/or single storey buildings not exceeding 25ft. in height."

The second insurance policy stated:

"It is hereby understood and agreed that any work in connection with . . .
   (h) Hangars
   (i) Roofs other than of Private Dwellings and/or Shops consisting of not more than three floors (including the ground floor and attic),
is expressly excluded from the Indemnity granted under this policy."

The insurers denied liability on the ground that the workman was engaged on work in connection with a hangar and/or in connection with a roof other than that of a private dwelling or shop. It was proved that the building was originally built as a hangar, but was being converted into a factory and storage place. The plaintiff, however, maintained that the building had ceased to be a place to house aircraft and had become a factory.

NIELD, J., held that the claim under both policies failed. He said that with regard to the first policy, the building was not a private dwelling or shop, and although it was a single storey building it exceeded 25 ft., and that, therefore, the policy did not apply. He observed:[2]

"It seems to me sufficient to say that the building here on which work was being done was not a private dwelling, it was not a shop, and although it was a single storey building it exceeded 25 ft., the highest part of the roof being 50 ft. and the lowest 20 ft."

With regard to the second insurance policy he said that although a change of user might be taken into account, what the insurers had in mind was the the physical characteristics of the building, and hangars must have been regarded by them as involving a danger of people falling down from a height. He observed:[3]

"Construing the whole of this endorsement, the exclusions clause, I reach the conclusion that [these] arguments [of the counsel for the insurers] is right, that what the insurance company had in mind was the physical characteristics of the building. It seems to me that this endorsement is setting out a number of descriptions of work which involve special hazard or danger. They are not all connected with height, but most of them are—gasometers, towers, steeples, and so on—and hangars, I think, must have been regarded by the insurers as involving danger of people falling from a height."

---

[1] [1968] 2 Lloyd's Rep. 240, Q.B.D.
[2] *Ibid.*, at p. 243.
[3] *Ibid.*, at p. 244.

The right of subrogation to which the third party is entitled under s. 1 of the Third Parties (Rights against Insurers) Act 1930 is limited in that the rights which are not referable to the particular liability of the particular insurer to the particular third party are not transferred.

Thus, in *Murray* v. *Legal and General Assurance Society, Ltd.*[1] the plaintiff was a carpenter employed by Griggs & Son, Ltd., building contractors, and was injured whilst he was working for them on some scaffolding on a building site on March 18, 1963. The company went into liquidation in July 1964. He obtained judgment for £1,936 8s. 6d. against the company, but the judgment was not satisfied. He thereupon claimed against the defendant insurance company which had issued an employers' liability insurance policy to Griggs & Son, Ltd. The insurance company, however, contended that Griggs & Son, Ltd. had not paid them £1,708 18s. by way of premiums in respect of the policy, and that this sum could be set off against the plaintiff's claim.

CUMMING-BRUCE, J., held that the plaintiff was entitled to the full sum which he claimed, and that no set-off was allowed. He considered that it was not all the rights and liabilities of the insured under the contract of insurance which were transferred to the third party, but only the particular rights in respect of the liability incurred by the insured to the third party. His Lordship observed:[2]

> "It is not all the rights and liabilities of the insured under the contract of insurance which are transferred to the third party, only the particular rights in respect of the liability incurred by the insured to the third party. When one looks at sub-s. (4) one finds the following language: 'Upon a transfer under sub-section (1) or sub-section (2) of this section, the insurer shall, subject to the provisions of section three of this Act, be under the same liability to the third party as he would have been under to the insured, but . . .' and then follows (*a*) and (*b*) which deal with the differences between the liability of the insurer to the insured and the liability of the insured to the third party; this shows that the draftsman in that sub-section was addressing his mind to problems that arise in connection with the liability of the insurer to the insured in relation to the particular liability of the insured to the third party. In my view this section had a carefully limited intention. There is no express transfer of liabilties of the insured to the insurer, as, for example, is to be found in s. 5 of the Workmen's Compensation Act, 1906, but if there is, under the policy, a defence by way of condition available against the insured that defence would be available against the third party."

He went on to say[3] that in the words used to create the statutory subrogation, the draftsman had carefully limited the subrogation to the rights under the contract in respect of the liability incurred by the insured to the third party. Rights which were not referable to the particular liability of the particular third party were not transferred. Thus, all the conditions in the policy which modified or controlled the obligations of the insurer to cover a given liability to a third party were the subject of transfer. The right to recovery of the premiums in the present case was not a term of the policy which arose in respect of the liability of the insured to the third party. The insurance company was therefore left with the same rights as the general body of creditors, *i.e.* to prove in the bankruptcy.

---

[1] [1969] 2 Lloyd's Rep. 405, Q.B.D.
[2] *Ibid.*, at p. 412.
[3] *Ibid.*, at p. 412.

If the liability of the insurers to the insured exceeds the liability of the insured to the third party, nothing in the Act of 1930 affects the rights of the insured against the insurer in respect of the excess.[1]

If the liability of the insurers to the insured is less than the liability of the insured to the third party, nothing in the Act affects the rights of the third party in respect of the balance.[2]

Void Clauses

Section 1 (3) of the Act of 1930 states that:

> "In so far as any contract of insurance . . . in respect of any liability to third parties purports, whether directly or indirectly, to avoid the contract or alter the rights of the parties upon the happening of the events specified [i.e. the insured becoming bankrupt, etc.] or upon the making of an order under s. 130 of the Bankruptcy Act 1914, in respect of his estate, the contract shall be of no effect."

Effect of Settlement between Insurer and Insured

Where the insured has become bankrupt, or where in the case of an insured being a company, a winding up order has been made or a resolution for a voluntary winding up has been passed, with respect to the company, no agreement between the insurer and the insured after liability has been incurred to a third party and after the commencement of the bankruptcy or winding up, nor any waiver, assignment, or other disposition made by, or payment made to the insured is effective to defeat or affect the rights transferred to the third party under the Act.[3]

Giving of Information to Third Parties

In the event of the insured becoming bankrupt or making a composition or arrangement with his creditors or in the event of an order being made under s. 130 of the Bankruptcy Act 1914 in respect of his estate, it is the duty of the insured or his personal representative or trustee in bankruptcy, as the case may be, to give to any person claiming that the insured is under a liability to him such information as may reasonably be required by him for the purpose of ascertaining whether any rights have been transferred and vested in him by the Act of 1930 and for the purpose of enforcing such rights, if any.[4]

Any contract of insurance in so far as it purports, whether directly or indirectly, to avoid the contract or alter the rights of the parties upon the giving of any such information or otherwise to prohibit or prevent its being given, is of no effect.[5]

If the information given to the third party discloses reasonable ground for supposing that there have or may have been transferred to him under the Act rights against any particular insurer, that insurer is under the same duty as is stated above.[6]

---

[1] Third Parties (Rights against Insurers) Act 1930, s. 1 (4).
[2] *Ibid.*, s. 1 (4).
[3] *Ibid.*, s. 3.
[4] *Ibid.*, s. 2 (1). The position is similar if a winding up order is made in respect of a company, or a resolution for a voluntary winding up has been passed, or a receiver or manager of the company's business or undertaking has been appointed, or possession has been taken by or on behalf of the holder of any debentures secured by a floating charge of any property comprised in or subject to the charge: *ibid.*, s. 2 (1).
[5] *Ibid.*, s. 2 (1).
[6] *Ibid.*, s. 2 (2).

The duty to give information includes a duty to allow all contracts of insurance, receipts for premiums and other relevant documents in the possession or power of the insured or insurer, as the case may be, to be inspected and copies taken.[1]

---

[1] Third Parties (Rights against Insurers) Act 1930, s. 2 (3).

30

PUBLIC LIABILITY INSURANCE

Public liability insurance is intended to protect the insured against liabilities to third persons other than his employees arising out of the condition or management of his property or the conduct of his business.

THE PROPOSAL FORM

The proposal form generally contains questions relating to:

1 The premises in respect of which the liability to be insured against may arise.
2 The trade or business, if any, carried on on the premises.
3 The precautions taken to guard against accident.
4 The previous history of the insured.
5 Other insurance.

1 Premises

The proposer is usually asked to state the condition of the premises as regards repairs and any special dangers existing on them, e.g., trap-doors, goods lifts, hoists or cranes.

2 Trade or Business

Questions which are asked concern the nature of the trade or business, the machinery or plant on the premises, the motive power used to drive the machinery, the number of persons employed on the premises and the nature of their work.

3 Precautions

These include the inspection or fencing of machinery and the provision of a responsible attendant.

4 Previous History of Insured

The proposed insured may be required to state whether he has been served with any notice by any public authority respecting the premises, and to give the date when they were last inspected.

5 Other Insurance

The proposed insured may be required to state whether he has effected an employers' liability insurance policy.

THE PERILS INSURED AGAINST

To give rise to a claim under the policy the personal injury, or, if covered, the damage to property, must be attributable to a cause specified in the policy.

Sometimes the policy is expressed to cover all accidents to third persons on the particular premises specified. In this case the actual cause of the accident is immaterial so long as it takes place in circumstances involving the insured in liability.

Thus, the Lloyd's Public Liability Policy states that the underwriters agree:

> "to indemnify the Assured, up to but not exceeding the amounts specified in the Schedule against such sums as the Assured shall become legally liable to pay in respect of claims made against the Assured arising from BODILY INJURY OR DISEASE (fatal or non-fatal) to persons OR DAMAGE TO PROPERTY caused by any accident occurring during the period set forth in the Schedule.
>
> (i) in or about the places specified in the Schedule, or
> (ii) elsewhere within the territorial limits specified in the Schedule in the course of any work or the performance of any duties carried out by or on behalf of the Assured in connection with the business specified in the Schedule . . ."

On the other hand, the policy may specify the causes of accident which it is intended to cover, e.g., defects in the specified premises, defects in the works,[1] machinery or plant of the insured connected with or used in his business at the specified premises, or negligence of the insured's employees on the specified premises.[2]

In *Concrete, Ltd.* v. *Attenborough*[3] the plaintiffs had effected a public liability insurance policy with the defendant underwriter:

> "against all sums which the assured shall become legally liable to pay in respect of claims made against the assured for compensation for bodily injury . . . to persons . . . resulting from any accident caused by the fault or negligence of the assured . . . whilst engaged in the assured's business as specified in the schedule hereto, and/or by any defect in the assured's premises, ways, works, machinery or plant used in the said business . . ."

A workman was employed by sub-contractors on reconstruction work at the Bodleian Library, Oxford. The plaintiffs were also sub-contractors there. The workman fell through an unprotected hole in the floor of the building which the plaintiffs had not fenced. He brought an action against the plaintiffs for negligence and/or breach of statutory duty. The plaintiffs settled the action by him, and now claimed an indemnity from the defendant.

---

[1] *Weir* v. *Accident Insurance Co.* 1908, 16 S.L.T. 141, where an accident happened in a building which the insured, who was a builder, had erected, owing to his alleged negligence in erecting it, and it was held that the building was his "works" within the meaning of the policy. Cf. *Smellie* v. *British General Insurance Co.*, [1918] W.C. & Ins. Rep. 233, where a policy effected by a glazier was held only to cover accidents on his own premises, and did not extend to premises on which he might be employed to do glazing work.

[2] A stipulation in a policy stating that the accident must happen whilst the workmen are "actually engaged" on the work of the insured does not mean that the accident must take place in their presence. Any accident occasioned by their negligence at work is covered, whether or not they are present at the time: *Smellie* v. *British General Insurance Co.* (*supra*), where the insured's workmen, whilst repairing a skylight, left a pane of glass temporarily in position on the Saturday when they left work, and the accident happened on the following Monday morning before they had returned to work.

[3] (1939), 65 Ll.L. Rep. 174, K.B.D.

BRANSON, J., held that the claim failed, for the workman, being an employee of one sub-contractor, was not an invitee of the plaintiffs and therefore they owed no duty at Common Law to him.[1] Further, although he might have succeeded against his employers for a breach of statutory duty, he could not have succeeded against the plaintiffs.[2] The plaintiffs therefore were under no legal liability to compensate him, and so the defendant was not liable to indemnify them.

In *Pictorial Machinery, Ltd.* v. *Nicolls*[3] the plaintiffs had effected a public liability policy with the defendant underwriters. The schedule of the policy described the place at which the insured's business was carried on as their business address "and/or elsewhere where insured's employees may be working". Condition 8 of the policy stated:

> "The assured shall and will at all times exercise reasonable care in seeing that the ways, implements, plant, machinery and appliances used in his (their) business are substantial and sound, and in proper order, and fit for the purposes for which they are used, and that all reasonable safeguards and precautions againt accident are provided and used."[4]

A customer of the plaintiffs ordered two glass containers of acetone, which was a very inflammable liquid, to be delivered to them at some neighbouring premises. An employee of the plaintiffs, aged 16, carried one of them under each arm. One dropped on the customer's premises causing a fire and resulting in claims against the plaintiffs. The plaintiffs claimed an indemnity under the policy, but the defendant repudiated liability on the ground that (i) the accident had not happened at a place described in the schedule; and (ii) the plaintiffs were in breach of condition 8, for they had not provided any protective covering or receptacle for the carriage of the bottles.

HUMPHREYS, J., held that the action succeeded, for the accident had occurred at a place described in the schedule,[5] and that the practice of the trade as to the method of delivery[6] indicated that there had been no breach by the plaintiffs of their obligation under condition 8. He observed:[7]

> "I find it impossible to say that on the evidence in this case I am satisfied that the plaintiffs have broken Condition 8 in that they have not used all reasonable precautions against accident, since they were following what would seem to be the ordinary and common practice in regard to the carrying of two of these things

---

[1] (1940), 65 Ll.L. Rep. at p. 178.
[2] *Ibid.*, at p. 178.
[3] (1940), 67 Ll.L. Rep. 461, K.B.D. For subsequent proceedings as to liability for costs incurred by the insured in defending the action brought by the third party, see (1940), 67 Ll.L. Rep. 524, and p. 232, *ante*.
[4] For the meaning of "provided and used", see the observations (*obiter*) of BRANSON, J., in *Concrete, Ltd.* v. *Attenborough* (1939), 65 Ll.L. Rep. at pp. 179 and 180.
[5] On this point his Lordship observed (*ibid.*, at p. 465): "I can only say that in my view the boy was working and working as the servant of his employers in delivering those goods until the moment when he had delivered them just as much as if he had been manufacturing something on behalf of his employers. Delivery was the work upon which he was engaged. In my view he was working upon the premises of [the customer] in the interests of his employers just as much as I think my servant is working for me when I tell him to go and post a letter. Until he has posted that letter I do not think I could be heard to say that he was not on my premises, and therefore he was not working at the place where he was employed, for 'the place where he was employed' is to be read as the place where he is working in my interest and on my behalf."
[6] Set out *ibid.*, at pp. 467–469.
[7] *Ibid.*, at p. 469.

upstairs (and that is all I am concerned with here) and into an office, and having regard to the fact that it has never been brought to any one's attention that there is a danger which is now known to exist, because now there has been a fire caused by the dropping of one of these bottles, and there has been the dropping of one of these bottles from the arms of a perfectly reliable and steady person."

In *Denham* v. *Midland Employers' Mutual Assurance, Ltd.*[1] Le Grand Sutcliff & Gell, Ltd., who were artesian well and civil engineering contractors, effected a public liability policy with the plaintiff underwriter

"in respect of any sums for which they might become legally liable to pay in respect of the death of persons arising in or out of the business of boring and pump engineers."

carried on by them. An exception in the policy excluded

"liability for death of . . . any person under a contract of service of apprentice- ship with [them] where such death arises out of and in the course of his employ- ment by [them]."

They also effected with the defendant insurance company an employers' liability insurance policy, which stated that:

"If any person under a contract of service or apprenticeship with the insured shall sustain any person injury by accident . . . arising out of and in the course of his employment by the insured in the business above mentioned and if the insured shall be liable to pay damages for such injury . . . [the insurance company] shall indemnify the insured against all sums for which the insured shall be so liable."

The insured had agreed to sink boreholes for Eastwoods, Ltd. under a contract which provided that Eastwoods, Ltd. would supply "the services of one labourer to assist our two skilled workmen free of charge to us". The labourer lent by Eastwoods, Ltd., was killed whilst working for the insured on premises belonging to Eastwoods, Ltd. A question arose as to whether the plaintiff underwriter or the defendant insurance company was liable to indemnify the insured in respect of the accident.

Lord GODDARD, C.J., held that the plaintiff underwriter was alone liable, for although the labourer was working under the direction of the insured, his employment was not changed to the extent that he had entered their service. The learned Lord Chief Justice observed:[2]

"I think a contract of service means a contract under which a man who is a servant agrees to serve a master for a wage. If he serves the master, then, if a wage has not been agreed between the them, he would have a right to sue his master for a reasonable amount. There are many cases in which a person who is lent by one contractor to another contractor has met with an accident, and then there comes the question as to who may be liable to pay. If the second employer has been guilty of negligence, there is no reason why he should not pay, quite apart from the relationship of master and servant, because, of course, by the very fact of the man working for him, doing a piece of work which the contractors have contracted to do, the contractor undertakes to use reasonable care towards him. I think this particular policy is indemnifying the assured for

---

[1] [1955] 1 Lloyd's Rep. 245, Q.B.D. See also *Century Insurance Co., Ltd.* v. *Northern Ireland Road Transport Board*, [1942] A.C. 509, H.L., where the question was whether a driver, who threw away a lighted match near a petrol tanker which was discharging petrol at a garage, and thereby caused an explosion, was the servant of the insured owner of the tanker or that of a company to which he had been lent.

[2] [1955] 1 Lloyd's Rep. at p. 250.

damages which he may have to pay to one of his servants who is under a contract
of service with him . . .   In this particular case [the insured] do not pay the
wages, and I cannot think that this policy which talks about a person under a
contract of service or apprenticeship is contemplating this mysterious contract
which is said to arise between a person who has been lent by his employer to
another and that other person. I very much doubt whether he can be said to be
working under a contract of service for the other person unless a good deal
more has happened than his being merely lent by his employer to that person."

In *Captain Boyton's World's Water Show Syndicate, Ltd.* v. *Employers' Liability
Assurance Corporation, Ltd.*[1] the plaintiffs had effected a liability insurance
policy with the defendants for sums not exceeding £1,000 for which the
plaintiffs might become liable "for personal injury caused to any person not
in the service of the plaintiffs by any accident to the boats and chutes" used
in a water show at Earls Court. The show consisted of a large lake upon
which were boats and a water bicycle propelled by means of paddle wheels
worked by the feet. There was also a water chute down which flat-bottomed
boats came and shot across the lake. A Mr. Jeffrey was using the water
bicycle, and while riding it he was struck by a boat which had just come down
the chute, and his leg was broken. He brought an action against the plaintiffs, who settled it for £75. The plaintiffs now claimed an indemnity under
the policy from the defendants.

The Court of Appeal[2] held that the claim succeeded. Lord EsHER, M.R.,
said that there was "an accident to the chute boat" within the meaning
of the policy, although it was not injured at all. A. L. SMITH, L.J., said that
he had come to the conclusion that the policy was not limited to something
happening to the chute boat while on the chute, and if the chute boat ran
into another boat, it was an accident to the chute boat. RIGBY, L.J., considered that the policy applied to the chute and the chute-boats, and not to
the other boats on the lake, and that although the water bicycle which
Jeffrey was using was not included in the policy, the defendants were liable
as there was an accident to the chute boat; the person injured need not be in
the chute-boat. The chute-boat had met with an accident by which a person
was injured, and so the defendants were liable.

EXCEPTED PERILS

It is usual to except liability under the policy where the accident is
attributable to causes which are specifically covered by the other kinds of
insurance, e.g., fire, explosion, vehicles, lifts or cranes. Again, liability is
included where the accident is caused by specified persons, e.g., sub-contractors or employees other than those specified in the policy. Further, the
insurers are under no liability where the accident has been brought into
operation by the insured himself, e.g., by making additions or alterations to
the specified premises, by failing to exercise due care or by permitting the
property to be used when it is known to be in a dangerous condition, or by
non-observance of statutory regulations.

The Lloyd's policy does not cover liability for bodily injury sustained by
any employee of the insured, damage to property owned by the insured or

---

[1] (1895), 11 T.L.R. 384, C.A.
[2] Lord EsHER, M.R., A. L. SMITH and RIGBY, L.JJ.

caused by the removal or weakening of support, or damage to property on which the insured or his agent or servant has been working.

It also excludes liability for bodily injury arising out of the possession or use by the insured of any power-operated lift or crane,[1] directly or indirectly caused by any mechanically propelled vehicle, ship, vessel or aircraft, or arising out of any work done thereon by the insured, arising[2] out of any goods or products manufactured, constructed, sold, supplied or distributed by the insured, arising out of food or drink poisoning, or out of the pollution of air, water or soil,[3] or directly or indirectly occasioned by, happening through or in consequence of war, invasion, act of foreign enemy,[4] hostilities[5] (whether war be declared or not), civil war, rebellion, revolution, insurrection[6] or military or usurped power.[7]

"Caused by nature of goods sold or supplied"

In *Wayne Tank and Pump Co., Ltd.* v. *Employers' Liability Assurance Corporation*[8] the plaintiffs effected a public liability insurance policy with the defendants, who agreed to indemnify them against all sums which they should be legally liable to pay consequent upon accidents happening in the course of their business of manufacturers of equipment for storage of liquids, and causing damage elsewhere than on premises owned or occupied by the plaintiffs. The policy contained an exception which stated:

> "The company will not indemnify the insured in respect of liability consequent upon . . .
>   (5) death injury or damage caused by the nature or condition of any goods or the containers thereof sold or supplied by or on behalf of the insured."

The plaintiffs installed some storage tanks at a mill where plasticine was made. Stearine[9] was to be pumped from road tankers into the storage tanks through a pipe made of plastic and called "durapipe".

Pipes then went from the storage tanks to a mixer. Some heating tape was wrapped round the pipe so that when the current was turned on, the stearine would be heated and become liquid, and could flow easily into the tanks. The plant was due to be tested on February 6, 1963. On the evening of February 5 an employee of the plaintiffs switched on the current because the weather was cold, and a blockage in the pipe had resulted. The installation was left unattended during the course of the night. The durapipe, which was quite unsuitable, caught fire and the mill was destroyed. The plaintiffs had to pay damages to the mill owners, and claimed an indemnity under the policy. The defendants repudiated liability contending that the loss fell within the exception set out above.

MOCATTA, J., gave judgment for the plaintiffs. He held[10] that, on the evidence, the loss had not been "caused by the nature or condition of the

---

[1] Unless specified in the schedule to the policy.
[2] After they have ceased to be in the possession or under the control of the insured.
[3] Unless it can be demonstrably proved to have been caused by immediate discharge consequent upon an accident.
[4] See Ivamy, *General Principles of Insurance Law*, 2nd Edn., 1970, p. 222.
[5] See *ibid.*, p. 225.
[6] See *ibid.*, p. 224.
[7] See *ibid.*, pp. 223–224.
[8] [1972] 2 Lloyd's Rep. 141, Q.B.
[9] A wax essential to the manufacture of plasticine.
[10] [1972] 1 Lloyd's Rep. 151, Q.B.

goods", but was the result of the action of the employee in turning on the current. The learned Judge also held (*obiter*)[1] that the goods had not been "sold or supplied by or on behalf of the defendants", and that these words applied to exclude indemnity when, and only when there had been completion of the activity or other business in respect of which the goods had been sold or supplied. Completion of the activity had not been shown in the present case.

ALTERATION OF RISK

Conditions referring to alteration in the risk are usually inserted in the policy and concern, e.g.

a alterations and addition to the premises;
b change of business;
c change of system;
d change of staff.

The Lloyd's Public Liability Policy contains a condition which states:

> "The Assured shall immediately give to the Underwriters full particulars in writing of any material increase in the risk, and shall pay such reasonable additional premium, if any, as may be required by the Underwriters."

DUTIES OF THE INSURED

a *During the Currency of the Policy*

The conditions of the policy often require the insured: (i) to take reasonable care to prevent accidents; (ii) to employ competent servants; (iii) to comply with any statutory requirements affecting the premises or the business or trade carried on there or any machinery or plant used there; (iv) to obey any directions of the local authority; (v) to remedy any defects, when discovered, and, until they are remedied, to take temporary precautions to prevent accidents therefrom; and (vi) to permit the insurers' representatives from time to time to inspect the premises and any machinery or plant used there.

b *After an Accident*

A condition in the policy may state that the insured must retain the premises or machinery as far as possible in the same state and condition as at the time of the accident until the insurers have had an opportunity of inspecting the scene of the accident.

A condition sets out the procedure to be followed in the event of a claim being made by a third party. Thus, the Lloyd's Public Liability Policy states:

> "The Assured shall give to the Underwriters immediate notice in writing, with full particulars, of the happening of any occurrence likely to give rise to a claim under this Policy, of the receipt by the Assured of notice of any claim and the institution of any proceedings against the Assured."

The policy usually contains a condition that the insured must not admit liability for or offer or agree to settle any claim without the written consent

---

[1] [1972] 1 Lloyd's Rep. at p. 152.

of the insurers, and that he must give them such information and assistance as they may reasonably require.

The Amount Recoverable

The amount recoverable cannot exceed the amount for which the insured is liable to the third person, including the costs of any action successfully brought by the third person to establish the insured's liability and, if the policy so provides, the insured's costs.

Thus, the Lloyd's Public Liability Policy states that the Underwriters will indemnify the insured up to but not exceeding the amounts specified in the Schedule, and in addition

> "the costs and expenses incurred with the written consent of the Underwriters in the defence of any . . . claim [by the third person], provided always that, if a payment in excess of the amount of indemnity available under this Policy has to be made to dispose of a claim, the Underwriters' liability for such costs and expenses shall be such proportion thereof as the amount of indemnity available under this Policy in respect of that claim bears to the amount paid to dispose of that claim."

The policy may provide that not more than a specified sum is to be paid in respect of liabilities during any one year of the insurance.

The policy may provide for a maximum sum to be payable in respect of any one accident.

In *South Staffordshire Tramways Co.* v. *Sickness and Accident Assurance Association*[1] the plaintiffs were insured under a liability policy effected with the defendants "against all claims for personal injuries and damage to property caused by vehicles in their possession". A clause in the policy stated:

> "So far as regards claims for personal injuries and damage to property made against the assured in respect of accidents caused by vehicles . . . and for which accidents shall be liable, the [defendants] shall pay the assured the sum of £250 in respect of any one accident . . ."

A tram belonging to the plaintiffs overturned, and 40 people were injured. The plaintiffs paid this sum and now claimed an indemnity from the defendants. The defendants, however, repudiated liability on the ground that the overturning of the vehicle and the consequent injuries to the 40 people were to be treated as "one accident" within the meaning of the policy, and that therefore only £250 was payable.

The Court of Appeal[2] held that the plaintiffs were entitled to recover £833, for the injuries suffered by each person were a separate accident within the meaning of the policy.

Bowen, L.J., said:[3]

> "But on looking at the policy we see introduced the words 'in respect of accidents'. What do those words mean? Do they mean that that is to be treated as only one accident, which has happened to a great number of persons? I should not think that anyone would suppose, looking at the first part of the agreement, that the word 'accident' was used otherwise than in the sense of injury accidentally

---

[1] (1891), 64 L.T. 279, C.A.
[2] Lord Esher, M.R., Bowen and Fry, L.JJ.
[3] (1891), 64 L.T. at p. 280. See also the judgment of Lord Esher, M.R., *ibid.*, at p. 279 and that of Fry, L.J., at p. 280.

caused to the person. The difficulty here arises from the qualification introduced afterwards; but as, until that clause is reached, the document is clearly using the word 'accident' in that meaning, I think the word must receive the same construction in the phrase limiting the liability of the defendants. I think that LAWRANCE, J.[1], was right, and that the word 'accident' is here used in the sense of mischief to an individual."

On the other hand, a different interpretation will be given if the sum payable is in respect of "any one accident or occurrence."

In *Allen* v. *London Guarantee and Accident Co., Ltd.*[2] the defendants insured the plaintiff under a policy which stated that they would indemnify the plaintiff in respect of all claims to persons injured by horses or horse-drawn vehicles in charge of the plaintiff's employees. A clause in the policy stated that there was a limit of liability of £300 in respect or arising out of "any one accident or occurrence." Two persons were injured by a horse-drawn cart in the charge of the plaintiff's employee. One of the questions which arose was whether the defendants could limit their liability to £300. PHILLIMORE, J., held that they could do so for, although in accordance with *South Staffordshire Tramways Co.* v. *Sickness and Accident Assurance Association*[3] it could be said that there were two "accidents", there was only one "occurrence."

---

[1] In the Court below: (1890), 63 L.T. 807, D.C.
[2] (1912), 28 T.L.R. 254.
[3] (1891), 64 L.T. 279, C.A.

31

NUCLEAR REACTOR INSURANCE

No person other than the United Kingdom Atomic Energy Authority must use any site for the purpose of installing or operating:

1 any nuclear reactor;[1]
2 any other installation of such class or description as may be prescribed[2] being an installation designed or adapted for

   a the production or use of atomic energy; or
   b the carrying out of any process which is preparatory or ancillary to the production or use of atomic energy and which involves or is capable of causing the emission of ionising radiations; or
   c storage, processing or disposal of nuclear fuel or of bulk quantities of other radioactive matter, being matter which has been produced, or irradiated in the production or use of nuclear fuel,

unless a "nuclear site licence" has been granted in respect of that site by the Secretary of State for Trade and Industry[3] and is for the time being in force.[4]

Where a nuclear site licence has been granted in respect of any site, the licensee must make such provision either by insurance or by some other means for sufficient funds to be available at all times to ensure that any claims which have been or may be established against the licensee are satisfied up to the aggregate amount of £5,000,000 in respect of each severally of the following periods:

   a the current cover period;
   b any cover period which ended less than 10 years before the time in question;
   c any earlier period in respect of which a claim remains to be disposed of, being a claim

      i within the relevant period within the meaning of s. 16[5] of the Nuclear Installations Act 1965; and

---

[1] Other than a reactor comprised in a means of transport whether by land, water or air: Nuclear Installations Act 1965, s. 1 (1) (i).
[2] See Nuclear Installations Regulations 1971 (S.I. 1971, No. 381).
[3] See Secretary of State for Trade and Industry Order 1970 (S.I. 1970 No. 1537).
[4] Nuclear Installations Act 1965, s. 1 (1). By s. 1 (4) anyone who contravenes this sub-section is guilty of an offence and is liable (a) on summary conviction to a fine not exceeding £100, or to imprisonment for a term not exceeding 3 months, or to both; (b) on conviction on indictment to a fine not exceeding £500 or to imprisonment for a term not exceeding 5 years, or to both.
[5] By the Nuclear Installations Act 1965, s. 16 (5) the "relevant period" is to mean the period of 10 years beginning with the relevant date within the meaning of s. 15 (1), which defines the "relevant date" as being the date of the occurrence which gave rise to the claim, or,

ii in the case of a claim such as is mentioned in s. 15 (2)[1] of that Act, also within the period of 20 years.[2]

The expression "cover period" means the period of the licensee's authority or, if the Secretary of State has given a direction that new cover shall begin in respect of the site, any of the following periods:

a the period beginning with the grant of the nuclear site licence and ending with the date specified in the first such direction;

b the period beginning with the date specified in any such direction, if any;

c the period beginning with the date specified in the last direction and ending with the end of the period of the licensee's responsibility.[3]

The "direction" referred to above is one which the Secretary of State may make if he thinks it proper to do so, on account of the gravity of any occurrence which has resulted or may result in claims against a licensee or on account of any previous occurrences, which have resulted or may result in such claims.[4] The Secretary of State can direct that a new cover shall begin in respect of the site on such date not earlier than two months after the date of the service of a notice as may be specified therein.[5]

---

where that occurrence was a continuing one, or was one of a succession of occurrences all attributable to a particular happening on a particular relevant site or to the carrying out from time to time on a particular relevant site of a particular operation, the day of the last event in the course of that occurrence or succession of occurrences to which the claim relates. For the definition of "occurrence" and "relevant site", see *ibid.*, s. 26 (1).

[1] Section 15 (2) relates to a claim in respect of injury or damage caused by an occurrence involving nuclear matter stolen from or lost, jettisoned or abandoned by (*inter alia*) the licensee of a licensed site.

[2] *Ibid.*, s. 19 (1). By s. 19 (5) a licensee who contravenes the provision of s. 19 (1) is guilty of an offence, and is liable (a) on summary conviction to a fine not exceeding £100, or to imprisonment for a term not exceeding 3 months, or to both. (b) on conviction on indictment, to a fine not exceeding £500 or to imprisonment for a term not exceeding 2 years, or to both.

[3] *Ibid.*, s. 19 (2).

[4] *Ibid.*, s. 19 (4).

[5] *Ibid.*, s. 19 (5).

32

POLLUTION BY OIL INSURANCE

The Merchant Shipping (Oil Pollution) Act 1971[1] makes it necessary for certain ships to be insured in respect of liability for pollution by oil. A certificate that they are so insured is required. There are provisions as to the rights of third parties against the insurers.

Ships to which Act is applicable

In general, the Act applies to any ship carrying in bulk a cargo of more than 2,000 tons of persistent oil of a description specified in regulations made by the Secretary of State.[2]

But it does not apply to any warship or any ship being used by the government of any State for other than commercial purposes.[3]

Necessity for Certificate

The ship must not enter a port in the United Kingdom or leave a terminal in the territorial sea of the United Kingdom, nor, if the ship is registered in the United Kingdom, a port in any other country or a terminal in the territorial sea of any other country, unless there is in force a certificate showing that there is in force in respect of the ship a contract of insurance or other security satisfying the requirements of Article VII of the International Convention on Civil Liability for Oil Pollution Damage signed in Brussels in 1969.[4]

The certificate must be

a if the ship is registered in the United Kingdom, a certificate issued by the Secretary of State;

b if the ship is registered in a Convention country other than the United Kingdom, a certificate issued by or under the authority of the government of the other Convention country;

c if the ship is registered in a country which is not a Convention country, a certificate issued by the Secretary of State or a certificate recognised by regulations made by him.[5]

---

[1] The relevant sections of the Act are set out in Appendix A, pp. 364–366, *post. The Act is not yet in force in its entirety, nor is s. 10, infra.*

[2] Merchant Shipping (Oil Pollution) Act 1971, s. 10 (1). Regulations must be made by statutory instrument, and are subject to annulment in pursuance of a resolution of either House of Parliament: *ibid.*, s. 10 (9).

[3] *Ibid.*, s. 14 (1).

[4] *Ibid.*, s. 10 (2). The International Convention is published by H.M.S.O. (Cmnd. 4403).

[5] Merchant Shipping (Oil Pollution) Act 1971, s. 10 (3).

In relation to a ship owned by a State and for the time being used for commercial purposes it is sufficient if there is in force a certificate issued by the government of that State and showing that she is owned by that State, and that any liability for pollution damage as defined in Article I of the Convention will be met up to the limit prescribed by Article V thereof.[1]

Any certificate required by the Act to be in force in respect of a ship must be carried by her, and must be produced by the master to any officer of customs of the Department of Trade and Industry, and if the ship is registered in the United Kingdom, to any "proper officer".[2]

If a ship enters or leaves, or attempts to enter or leave a port, or arrives at or leaves or attempts to arrive at or leave a terminal in contravention of the provisions of the Act as to a certificate showing that a contract of insurance is in force, the master or owner[3] is liable on conviction on indictment to a fine,[4] or on summary conviction to a fine not exceeding £35,000.[5]

If a ship fails to carry or the master fails to produce a certificate, he is liable on summary conviction to a fine not exceeding £400.[6]

If a ship attempts to leave a port in the United Kingdom in contravention of the above requirements, she can be detained.[7]

Rights of Third Parties against Insurers

Where it is alleged that the owner of a ship has incurred a liability under s. 1 of the Act[8] as a result of any discharge or escape of oil occurring while there was in force a contract of insurance or other security to which the certificate related, proceedings may be brought against the person who provided the insurance or other security, i.e. the insurer.[9]

In any proceedings brought against the insurer it is a defence (in addition to any defence affecting the owner's liability), to prove that the discharge or escape was due to the wilful misconduct of the owner himself.[10]

The insurer may limit his liability[11] in respect of claims made against him

---

[1] Merchant Shipping (Oil Pollution) Act 1971, s. 14 (2).

[2] *Ibid.*, s. 10 (5). The term "proper officer" means a consular officer appointed by Her Majesty's Government in the United Kingdom and, in relation to a port in a country outside the United Kingdom which is not a foreign country, also any officer exercising in that port functions similar to those of a superintendent: *ibid.*, s. 10 (5).

[3] The word "owner" in relation to a registered ship means the person registered as its owner, except that in relation to a ship owned by a State which is operated by a person registered as the ship's operator, it means the person registered as its operator: *ibid.*, s. 20 (1).

[4] There is no limit to the fine which may be imposed, but it must not be "excessive": Bill of Rights 1688, s. 1.

[5] Merchant Shipping (Oil Pollution) Act 1971, s. 10 (6).

[6] *Ibid.*, s. 10 (7).

[7] *Ibid.*, s. 10 (8).

[8] *I.e.*, liability (i) for any damage caused in the area of the United Kingdom by contamination resulting from the discharge or escape of persistent oil; (ii) for the cost of any measures reasonably taken after the discharge or escape for the purpose of preventing or reducing any such damage in the area of the United Kingdom; and (iii) for any damage caused in the area of the United Kingdom by any measures so taken: *ibid.*, s. 1 (1). Where a person incurs liability under s. 1 (1), he is also liable for any damage or cost for which he would be liable under that subsection if the references therein to the area of the United Kingdom included the area of any other Convention country: *ibid.*, s. 10 (2). "Damage" includes loss: *ibid.*, s. 20 (1).

[9] *Ibid.*, s. 12 (1).

[10] *Ibid.*, s. 12 (2).

[11] Under s. 4 of the Act liability can be limited to a sum not exceeding 2,000 gold francs (for each ton of the ship's tonnage or 210 million gold francs where that tonnage would result in a greater amount: *ibid.*, s. 4 (1). The tonnage of the ship is calculated in a speci-

in like manner and to the same extent as the owner may limit his liability.[1] But the insurer can do so whether or not the discharge or escape occurred without the owner's actual fault or privity.[2]

Where the owner and the insurer each apply to the Court for the limitation of his liability, any sum paid into Court in pursuance of either application must be treated as paid also in pursuance of the other.[3]

The Third Parties (Rights against Insurers) Act 1930 does not apply in relation to any contract of insurance to which the certificate required under the Act of 1971 relates.[4]

---

fied manner: *ibid.*, s. 4 (2). A gold franc means a unit of 65½ milligrams of gold of millesimal fineness 900: *ibid.*, s. 4 (3). The Secretary of State may from time to time by order made by statutory instrument specify the amounts which for the purposes of this section are to be taken as equivalent to 2,000 gold francs and 210 million gold francs respectively: *ibid.*, s. 4 (3).

[1] *Ibid.*, s. 12 (3).
[2] *Ibid.*, s. 12 (3).
[3] *Ibid.*, s. 12 (4).
[4] *Ibid.*, s. 12 (5).

33

PROFESSIONAL INDEMNITY INSURANCE

Professional indemnity insurance policies are effected by various persons, e.g. solicitors, accountants, against their liability to pay damages to their clients by reason of negligence in the performance of their professional duties.

The Proposal Form

A proposal form usually requires the proposer to state his name and address, the names of his partners (if any), the time for which his business had been conducted, his profession and the total number of his staff.

He is asked to state the risks in respect of which he requires cover (e.g. libel, legal liability arising from the negligence of himself or his employees), the amount of the indemnity required, the fees received by him for professional work over the past few years, and the details of any previous claims made against him.

In addition, he is usually required to state whether an insurer has ever refused to insure him or refused to renew his policy. He must also state whether he is aware of any negligence on his part or that of his partners which might give rise to a claim.

The Contents of the Policy

Perils Insured Against

The terms of the policy state the scope of the perils insured against, e.g. liability at law for damages and costs in respect of claims for breach of professional duty by reason of any neglect, error or omission.

Exceptions

Exceptions may exclude liability for any claim for libel and slander and for a claim brought about or contributed to by any dishonest, fraudulent or malicious act of the insured or his predecessors in business, or of persons in his employment.

Conditions

Conditions usually found in policies state that the insured must not admit liability for or settle any claim or incur any costs in connection with it without the written consent of the insurers, who are entitled to take over and conduct in the name of the insured or his firm (if any) the defence and settlement of any claim. But the insured is not bound to contest any legal proceedings unless a Queen's Counsel advises that they should be contested.[1]

Another condition may specify that the insured is to give the insurers notice of any actual claim made against him or receipt of a notice by any person of an intended claim. He must also notify them of any circumstance which is known to him and which is likely to give rise to a claim.

A further condition may state that if he makes any fraudulent claim, the policy shall become void and all claims under it shall be forfeited.

Extensions

The policy may on the payment of an additional premium be extended to cover liability for libel and slander, claims brought about by the dishonesty of the insured's employees, claims in respect of a partner's previous business, and loss of documents.

Schedule

A schedule usually sets out name of the insured or his firm, the type of business or practice, the limit of indemnity, the period of insurance, the premium payable, an excess clause, and whether extensions (as mentioned above) fall within the policy.

EXAMPLES FROM REPORTED DECISIONS

Accountant

In *Whitworth* v. *Hosken*[2] the insured, a Mr. Frith, took out an accountant's indemnity policy against loss from

> "any claim which might be made against him in respect of any act of neglect default or error on his part or that of his partners or servants in the conduct of their business as accountants."

A proposal was made to him by a Mr. Kirby that the insured should allow him to use his office for the purpose of a business as a business transfer agent, and that the insured would receive a commission on any transactions effected. The proposal was accepted. The plaintiff applied to Frith for particulars of a business advertised by Kirby as agent for a vendor and the correspondence in reply was signed "Frith & Co.". The plaintiff was induced by Kirby's fraud to pay over to him the full purchase price. An action was brought by the plaintiff against Frith and was settled by consent. Frith assigned his rights under the policy to the plaintiff, who claimed against the insurers. The insurers refused to indemnify him on the ground that Frith had not suffered any loss which arose from a claim made against him "in respect of any act of neglect or error on his part in the conduct of his business as an accountant".

Judge THOMAS held that the action failed. It had not been shown that there was any act of neglect or error by Frith, and that even if there were it was, not neglect or error "in the conduct of his business as an accountant". The learned Judge observed:[3]

---

[1] See e.g. *West Wake Price & Co.* v. *Ching*, [1956] 3 All E.R. 821. The Queen's Counsel clause has now been altered since this decision. For the facts of the case see p. 258, *post*.
[2] (1939), 65 Ll.L. Rep. 48, Mayor's and City of London Court.
[3] *Ibid.*, at p. 51.

"There is a further difficulty here in the plaintiff's way, and that is that he has got to show that, even if there was a 'neglect' or an 'error' on the part of Mr. Frith, it was a neglect or error 'in the conduct of his business as an accountant.' Now, what business was Mr. Frith doing here? He was helping Kirby in his business of a transfer agent, which Mr. Frith himself has said was an entirely separate business from the business of Mr. Frith as an accountant. It is quite true that it was hoped that Mr. Frith might get business as an accountant out of it, but that, he said himself, never transpired—and that is another fatal objection to this claim."

A professional negligence insurance policy covering claims based on negligence does not apply to a mixed claim based on negligence and fraud.

Thus, in *West Wake Price & Co.* v. *Ching*[1] a firm of accountants had effected a Lloyd's Accountants Indemnity Policy which indemnified them against claims in respect of "an act of neglect, default or error on the part of the assured or their servants in the conduct of their business as accountants". A clerk employed by the insured converted money belonging to a client to his own use. The client made a claim which was partly based on negligence and partly on dishonesty. When the insured claimed an indemnity, the insurers repudiated liability on the ground that the loss did not fall within the terms of the policy.

DEVLIN, J., held that the action failed, for the word "claim" was limited to an unmixed claim, i.e. a claim only in respect of "an act of neglect, default or error", and observed:[2]

"I have reached the conclusion that there is, in fact, a simpler and more effective test which is the correct one. It depends simply on the true construction of the policy. Businessmen often want to write into a document words which they think will amplify its meaning, but which lawyers reject as superfluous; nevertheless, the writing in of superfluities sometimes helps to clarify questions of construction. If a layman wanted a phrase such as 'claims in respect of negligence' to be altered to read 'claims in respect of negligence only' or 'claims in respect of negligence but not in respect of fraud', a lawyer would tell him that these additions were superfluous, since negligence meant negligence and nothing else and did not include fraud. That is plainly enough the effect of the decision in *Goddard and Smith* v. *Frew*.[3] If words such as these were there, however, they would serve to show that a claim in respect of negligence and in respect of fraud is excluded from the description in the policy. To come within the policy the character of the claim must be unmixed. It must be negligence alone. Applying this test, which I think is the right one, the claim in this case is outside the policy."

Estate Agent

In *Goddard and Smith* v. *Frew*[4] the plaintiffs were estate agents, who had effected a Lloyd's policy of insurance against

"all losses, costs, charges and expenses arising from all actions, proceedings, claims and demands whatsoever . . . by reason of any act, neglect, omission, mis-statement or error committed or omitted or made or written on the part of the firm . . . or any person . . . . employed by the firm."

The plaintiffs employed a collector to collect rents of property belonging to Covent Garden Properties Co., Ltd. The collector misappropriated the

---

[1] [1956] 3 All E.R. 821, Q.B.D.
[2] *Ibid.*, at p. 831.
[3] *Infra.*
[4] (1939), 65 Ll.L. Rep. 83, C.A.

rents, and the plaintiffs paid a claim by the company for the amount misappropriated. The plaintiffs now claimed an indemnity under the policy.

The Court of Appeal[1] held that the action failed, for the claim by the company was a claim for money had and received, and did not arise by reason of "any act, neglect or omission" on the part of the plaintiffs' servant.

Scott, L.J., said:[2]

> "We think that the case depends entirely on the interpretation of the words of the policy itself, and I personally am satisfied that this policy does not cover the events I have narrated. The real loss of the firm was embezzlement by their servant; that was the true proximate cause of the loss, and in my view as this is not a fidelity policy but only an indemnity policy against certain carefully described liabilities, the loss cannot be brought within this policy. If the landlords, the Covent Garden Properties Company, Ltd., instead of having their demand met at once, had had to take legal proceedings, I am sure that if [Counsel] had drawn the statement of claim or writ, he would have made it one for money had and received, and on the facts of the case I think there would have been no answer. It would have been quite immaterial to the statement of claim to put in allegations about a fraud committed by the employee, Reynolds; it would have been quite sufficient that the firm of Goddard & Smith had received the money through their employee and not accounted for it, and judgment against them would necessarily follow on that, and on nothing else."

Insurance Broker

In *Simon Warrender Pty., Ltd.* v. *Swain*[3] the plaintiffs were insurance brokers, who had effected a policy with the defendant which stated:

> "This Policy is to indemnify the Assured against all losses which the Assured may sustain . . . from errors or omissions by themselves or their employees in the conduct of their business as Insurance Brokers . . ."

The plaintiffs claimed an indemnity under the policy in respect of damages which they had paid to a third party because they had not insured a fishing boat belonging to him. The defendant repudiated liability on the ground that the loss had not been caused by "errors and omissions" within the meaning of the policy, for the employees of the plaintiffs had wilfully failed to effect the policy for the third party, and had wilfully and deliberately represented to him that the plaintiffs had authority to issue and had issued on behalf of the Switzerland and General Insurance Co. Ltd. a cover note effecting the insurance.

Else-Mitchell, J., held that the claim succeeded. The intent of the employees was not necessarily to be imputed to the plaintiffs,[4] and the defendant had not alleged a wilful and deliberate failure on the part of the plaintiffs. Accordingly, as far as the plaintiffs were concerned, the defendant's plea was that there was a mere failure by them to effect the policy. This failure was an "error or omission", and the defendant was liable.

Solicitor

In *Davies* v. *Hosken*[5] the insured, a firm of solicitors, took out a solicitors' indemnity policy which covered them against loss

---

[1] Scott, Clauson and Goddard, L.J.
[2] (1939), 65 Ll.L. Rep. at p. 85. See also the judgment of Goddard, L.J., *ibid.*, at p. 86.
[3] [1960] 2 Lloyd's Rep. 111, Supreme Court of New South Wales.
[4] *Ibid.*, at pp. 114–115.
[5] (1937), 58 Ll.L. Rep. 183, K.B.D.

"arising from any claim or claims . . . by reason of any neglect, omission or error whenever or wherever the same was or may have been committed or alleged to have been committed on the part of the firm or their predecessors in business or hereafter to be employed by the firm during the subsistence of this policy in or about the conduct of any business conducted by or on behalf of the firm or their predecessors in business in their professional capacity as solicitors."

The solicitors employed a clerk who received from their clients money for investment on mortgages. Unknown to them he fraudulently made use of the money for himself.[1] The solicitors discovered the fraud, settled the clients' claims against themselves, and sued the insurers for an indemnity under the policy.

PORTER, J., held that the action failed because the criminal act committed by the clerk did not fall within the words "neglect, omission or error". He observed:[2]

"The first problem which was raised by [Counsel] was, does this wording include fraud, and in particular, does it include the class of fraud in this case, namely, the obtaining of sums of money for pretended investment in securities which did not and were not intended to exist? *Prima facie*, I should not think the words 'neglect, omission or error' were words apt to cover a case of that kind; I should have more difficulty, I think, if the words were 'any act, neglect, omission or error.' But the word 'act' is carefully left out of the wording of the policy, and it is confined to 'neglect, omission or error.' *Prima facie* I should have thought that they do not point to a fraudulent act such as the obtaining of money; they point to an omission. Broadly speaking, if one were asked what Mr. Digby did in this case, one would have said that he concocted a scheme for obtaining money from persons with whom his previous firm had dealt and who were clients, also, of his present firm, and obtained money from them by false pretences or by fraud. But, looked at broadly, that is not neglect, omission or error; it is a positive act of fraudulently obtaining money from third parties."

In *Forney* v. *Dominion Insurance Co., Ltd.*[3] a solicitor had taken out an indemnity policy which covered him against

"any loss arising from any claim or claims which might be made upon him by reason of any neglect, omission or error committed during the period of the insurance in the conduct of his business, as a solicitor, either by him or by any person in his employment."

The policy contained a clause which limited the insurers' liability to:

"(a) in respect of any one claim or number of claims arising out of the same occurrence the sum of £3,000.
(b) in respect of all claims the sum of £15,000."

In July 1964 a Mr. Perry and his wife and a Mr. Bailey and his wife and their son Ian were travelling in a car driven by Mr. Bailey, when it was involved in an accident for which he was solely to blame. Mr. Bailey and Mr. Perry were killed, and Mrs. Perry, Mrs. Bailey and Ian suffered personal injuries. The insured was instructed on behalf of Mrs. Perry, Mrs. Bailey and Ian in connection sith their claims against Mr. Bailey's estate.

The insured's assistant obtained a grant of letters of administration for Mrs. Bailey to her husband's estate, thereby making her a potential defendant in

---

[1] The evidence as to his method of doing so is set out *ibid.*, at p. 185.
[2] *Ibid.*, at p. 185.
[3] [1969] 1 Lloyd's Rep. 502, Q.B.D. (Commercial Court).

respect of any claims which might be brought against it. This meant that Mrs. Bailey herself could not make any claim against the estate because she would be the nominal defendant. What the assistant ought to have done was to have applied for someone else to be substituted for Mrs. Bailey as administratrix.

The assistant also failed to issue the necessary writs on behalf of the clients against the estate within six months of Mr. Bailey's death as required by the Law Reform (Miscellaneous Provisions) Act 1934. In March 1966 Mr. Bailey's insurers repudiated liability in respect of the personal injuries suffered by Mrs. Perry, Mrs. Bailey and Ian on the ground that the claims were statute-barred.

Mrs. Perry, Mrs. Bailey and Ian brought claims against the insured for negligence. He admitted liability and left the assessment of damages to the Court. Mrs. Perry was awarded £2,533 for her own injuries, and £2,230 as executrix of her husband. Mrs. Bailey was awarded £2,262 in respect of her own injuries and Ian was awarded £150. The insured was also ordered to pay Mrs. Perry's costs which amounted to £766 3s. 10d., and those of Mrs. Bailey which amounted to £746 1s. 5d. So the insured's total liability came to £8,757 5s. 3d.

The insured claimed that the insurers were liable to indemnify him on the ground that he had been made liable as a result of four claims (two by Mrs. Perry in different capacities and one each by Mrs. Bailey and Ian), and that each claim arose out of a different "occurrence", and that the limit of indemnity was £3,000 in respect of each claim.

DONALDSON, J., held that there were only two "occurrences", and that the liability of the insurers was limited to £3,000 in each case. The "occurrences" were when the insured's assistant allowed Mrs. Bailey to become administratrix of her late husband's estate, and when she failed to issue writs within the six months' limitation period.

His Lordship observed:[1]

> " 'Occurrences' like accidents can be looked at from the point of view of the tortfeasor or of the victim. Ian's loss of his right to claim damages from Mr. Bailey's estate was from his point of view a different occurrence from the similar loss by Mrs. Perry. However, the provision of the policy which limits the indemnity contemplates that a number of claims may arise out of one occurrence. This seems to me to indicate that a number of persons may be injured by a single act of negligence—in other words that 'occurrence' in this context is looked at from the point of view of the insured. If this is right, I have to ask myself how often [the insured's assistant's] negligence occurred. My answer to this question is 'twice'."

Accordingly, his Lordship held that the insured was entitled to recover £3,008 1s. 5d.[2] in respect of Mrs. Bailey's claim, and £3,000 in respect of the claims of Mrs. Perry and Ian. The £3,000 limit applied to all liability whether in respect of damages or costs. On this point his Lordship observed:[3]

> "The words of the promise [set out in the policy] are quite wide enough to include a liability to a client in costs and the limitation of liability is co-extensive with and operates to restrict the whole liability, namely, liability to the client in respect of costs as well as damages."

---

[1] [1969] 1 Lloyd's Rep. at p. 508.
[2] The insurers agreed to pay this sum instead of merely £3,000. See *ibid.*, at pp. 507–508.
[3] *Ibid.*, at p. 508.

A solicitor who joins a firm may, on the true construction of a policy, be entitled to an indemnity in respect of negligent acts committed before the date of joining the partnership.

Thus, in *Maxwell* v. *Price (Halford, Third Party)*[1] the defendant was a solicitor who practised in partnership with a Mr. Ellis. They had effected a Lloyd's Solicitors' Indemnity Policy with underwriters. The policy stated that:

> "Whereas the person or persons named in the Schedule (hereinafter called 'the Firm' which expression shall include the aforesaid persons and any other person or persons who may at any time and from time to time during the subsistence of this Policy be a partner in the Firm or one of them) have made to Us . . . a written proposal . . . NOW WE THE UNDERWRITERS . . . agree to indemnify the Firm against any claim or claims for breach of professional duty as Solicitors which may be made against them during the period set forth in the . . . Schedule by reason of any negligent act, error or omission, whenever or wherever the same was or may have been committed or alleged to have been committed, on the part of the Firm of their predecessors in business or hereafter to be employed by the Firm during the subsistence of this Policy, in the conduct of any business conducted by or on behalf of the Firm or their predecessors in business in their professional capacity as Solicitors."

The plaintiff claimed damages from the defendant on the ground that he had been negligent at a time when he was not a member of the firm. Judgment was given for the plaintiff, and the defendant now sought an indemnity from the underwriters, who repudiated liability.

The High Court of Australia[2] held that the underwriters were liable. DIXON, C.J., said:[3]

> "Is there, then, any sufficient reason for implying a restriction of the indemnity to liabilities incurred since entering into the partnership, or, put another, but by no means the same, way, to liabilities incurred in the character of a partner? No one doubts that the risk of claims against the partners present and future was the central subject of the insurance; it is probably true that the nature and incidents of such liabilities made it desirable, if not necessary, to include the liability of any one partner. Counsel for the appellant underwriters went perhaps further and said that the only reason why the words 'or any one or more of them' were put in was of necessity, in view of the permutations and combinations of partners that might be liable, as distinguished from the partnership as constituted at the time of the grant of the insurance. To my mind, all this is speculation; there is just as much to be said for the hypothesis that it was desired to cover all claims made within the period upon the partners and each of them for breach by them or him at any time of professional duty.
>
> In the present case, I have failed to perceive any reason why the claim made by the plaintiff against the defendant Price should fall outside the application of the indemnity construed according to the ordinary grammatical meaning of the language it employs."

In *Webb and Hughes* v. *Bracey*[4] a solicitors' indemnity insurance policy stated that it covered the insured for losses "by reason of any neglect, omissions or errors" for the period of one year ending July 24, 1961, and allowed 15 days' grace after expiry for its renewal. It went on to provide

---

[1] [1960] 2 Lloyd's Rep. 155, High Court of Australia.
[2] DIXON, C.J., FULLAGAR. MENZIES and WINDEYER, JJ.; TAYLOR, J., dissenting.
[3] [1960] 2 Lloyd's Rep. at p. 159. See also the judgment of FULLAGAR, J., *ibid.*, at p. 162, that of MENZIES, J., *ibid.*, at p. 165, and that of WINDEYER, J., *ibid.*, at p. 166.
[4] [1964] 1 Lloyd's Rep. 465.

that "in the event of non-renewal by underwriters" any claim made against the insured during the 12 months following the expiry of the policy was deemed to have been made during the currency of the policy. The days of grace expired, and no attempt was made by the insured to renew the policy. On November 6, 1961, the insured received notice of a claim against them and sent it on to the underwriters, who declined to renew the policy. The insured maintained that the underwriters were liable because the phrase "in the event of non-renewal by underwriters" meant "in the event of underwriters not, in fact, issuing a new policy on the same terms and at the same premium as previously, for a subsequent period, irrespective of whether the underwriters had not accepted such requests as might have been made". In short the alleged meaning was "if for any reason the policy is not renewed", and it was only the underwriters who could renew a policy,

SACHS, J., however, considered that this construction ignored the meaning of the words "by underwriters". It did not accord with the meaning of the phrase as it appeared in what, after all, was a commercial document. It was a document governing the dealings between two parties, who might well expect there to be a renewal of the policy from year to year. On the one side a steady continuance of cover, on the other a steady continuance of premium income. In his view the words "by underwriters" indicated that the non-renewal must be due to some action by the underwriters. That seemed to him to be the natural meaning. This was a plain case of the non-renewal being due to the conduct of the insured in not requesting a policy, and accordingly the underwriters were not liable.

34

EMPLOYERS' LIABILITY INSURANCE

Employers' liability insurance is intended to protect the insured against his liability to pay damages for injuries sustained by persons in his employment.

Insurance against this form of liability is made compulsory by the Employers' Liability (Compulsory Insurance) Act 1969 which came into force on January 1, 1972.[1]

An insurance against employers' liability is frequently combined with insurances against other risks.

THE PROPOSAL FORM

The proposal form usually contains questions relating to:

1 the nature of the risk proposed to be insured.
2 circumstances affecting the risk.

1 Nature of Risk

The proposed insured is required to state his occupation[2] and to specify the number of employees employed by him and the nature of the work upon which they are engaged.[3]

2 Circumstances Affecting Risk

The principal circumstances shown to be material by the questions in the proposal form are:

a the character of the premises in which the employees are employed;
b the special dangers of the employment;
c the personal details of the employees to be insured;
d the amount of wages;
e whether other insurance has been effected;
f the previous history of the insured;
g other matters.

a *Character of Premises*

The proposed insured may be required to state whether the premises contribute a "factory" within the meaning of the Factories Act 1961.

---

[1] See pp. 271–275, *post.*
[2] See, e.g. *Holdsworth* v. *Lancashire and Yorkshire Insurance Co.* (1907), 23 T.L.R. 521.
[3] See, e.g. *Carlin* v. *Railway Passengers Assurance Co.* (1913), 25 W.L.R. 706, where the agent's knowledge that explosives were to be used was imputed to the insurers.

b *Special Dangers*

He is usually required to state whether machinery is used, and if so, whether it is properly guarded, whether there are lifts on the premises, and whether acids, gases, chemicals or explosives are used. If the employees are employed outside the premises, this must be stated.

c *Details of Employees*

The proposed insured may be required to state whether any of the employees are members of his family,[1] whether any of them possess any physical defects, and whether all his employees are to be included in the insurance; if not, the reason why all are not to be included is to be given.[2]

d *Amount of Wages*

He is usually required to state the amount of the wages paid, for this is one of the matters on which the premium is based.[3]

e *Other Insurance*[4]

He may be required to state whether any boilers used on the premises are insured against explosion, and if so, with whom.

f *Previous History of Insured*

He may be required to state the number of accidents to his employees during a specified period together with the amount of compensation paid in each case.

g *Other Matters*

He may be required to state whether he ever employs sub-contractors, or whether the employees are casually employed.

THE EVENT INSURED AGAINST

The event insured against is not the death or personal injury of an employee, although such death or injury is a *sine qua non*, but the liability of the employer arising therefrom.[5] The insurers, therefore, are not liable unless the insured himself is liable to pay damages.

ALTERATION OF CIRCUMSTANCES

The policy usually deals with:

---

[1] See, e.g. *Moss* v. *Norwich and London Accident Insurance Association* (1922), 10 Ll.L. Rep. 395, C.A.

[2] The fact that the insurers attempt to settle a claim by an employee does not preclude them from contending subsequently that he does not fall within the terms of the policy: *Pariseau* v. *Travellers Insurance Co.* (1920), 27 R.L.N.S. 102. The insurers may place an employee on their "black list" and object to his employment by the insured: *MacKenzie* v. *Iron Trades Employers' Insurance Association*, 1910 S.C. 79.

[3] See p. 228, *ante*.

[4] As to "other insurance", see further Ivamy, *General Principles of Insurance Law*, 2nd Edn., 1970, pp. 279–281.

[5] *Lancashire Insurance Co.* v. *Inland Revenue Commissioners*, [1899] 1 Q.B. 353, *per* BRUCE, J., distinguishing employers' liability insurance policies from life or personal accident insurance policies. Where a policy is in form a personal accident insurance policy in the name of the employee, although the premium is paid by the employer, parol evidence is not admissible to prove that it is intended only to protect the employer, against his statutory liability: *Johnston* v. *Ocean Accident and Guarantee Corporation, Ltd.* (1915), 34 N.Z.L.R. 356.

1 an increase in the number of employees;
2 the employment of sub-contractors;
3 change of business or locality.

1   Increase in Number of Employees

Any increase in the number of employees may be required to be notified to the insurers and an additional premium paid.

2   Employment of Sub-contractors

If during the currency of the policy the insured employs a sub-contractor, he may be required to notify the insurers.

3   Change of Business or Locality

The insurance is usually limited to a specified business so that the insured is not protected in respect of any other business. Where the insurance relates to a business carried on in specified premises, accidents happening elsewhere are not covered.[1]

Exceptions

Very few exceptions are set out in an employers' liability insurance policy. Thus, the Lloyd's Employers' Liability Policy contains only one exception. This states that:

> "The Underwriters shall not be liable in respect of any legal liability of whatsoever nature directly or indirectly caused by or contributed to by or arising from ionising radiations or contamination by radioactivity from any nuclear fuel or from any nuclear waste from the combustion of nuclear fuel."

Duties of the Insured

Due performance of various duties by the insured is often made a condition precedent to the insurers' liability.[2] A failure to perform them deprives the insured of protection in respect of accidents happening after the failure.[3] So far as accidents happening before the date of the failure are concerned, the right to indemnity, having vested, cannot be affected,[4] except, perhaps, where there is a clear and unambiguous stipulation to that effect.[5]

By reason of the Employers' Liability (Compulsory Insurance) Act 1969, certain conditions are void as against an employee, though if they are broken by the insured, the insurers, if they have compensated the employee, may recover from the insured the sum which they have paid to the employee.[6]

The following duties are usually imposed on the insured:

---

[1] *Pigott* v. *Employers' Liability Assurance Corporation* (1900), 31 O.R. 666. Cf. *Goulet* v. *Merchants and Employers Guarantee and Accident Co.* (1917), 51 Que.S.C. 256, where an insurance against accidents to employees engaged in the installation of electric wiring inside and outside buildings was held to cover an accident to an employee happening whilst he was taking down wires from a standard erected on a building.

[2] This is a question of construction. See, e.g. *Re Bradley and Essex and Suffolk Accident Indemnity Society*, [1912] 1 K.B. 415, C.A., which is considered at p. 269, *post*.

[3] *Daff* v. *Midland Colliery Owners' Mutual Indemnity Co.* (1913), 6 B.W.C.C. 799, H.L., *per* Lord Shaw at p. 810.

[4] *Ibid.*

[5] *Ibid.*, *per* Lord Shaw at p. 810, and Lord Dunedin at p. 815.

[6] See p. 275, *post*.

1 Duties arising before Loss

The insured may be required:

a to take reasonable precautions to prevent accidents and disease;

b to observe all statutory obligations;

c to keep a wages book.

a *Precautions to Prevent Accidents*

It is a matter of construction of the policy in each case whether a stipulation to this effect is or is not a condition.[1]

In *London Crystal Window Cleaning Co., Ltd.* v. *National Mutual Indemnity Insurance Co., Ltd.*[2] the plaintiffs were insured by the defendants under an employers' liability insurance policy, condition 4 of which stated: "The insured shall take all reasonable precautions to avoid accidents."

A window cleaner in the plaintiffs' employment received fatal injuries when he fell from a window sill on to some railings. The plaintiffs brought an action against the defendants claiming an indemnity. The defendants repudiated liability on the ground that the condition had been broken. Evidence was given that the plaintiffs supplied safety belts for the general use of their employees and that the employees were well aware that the belts were available for use. The window cleaner at the time of the accident was not in possession of a belt, and a belt could not have been used for the particular job. Lord GODDARD, C.J., held that the action succeeded, for there had been no breach of condition. The plaintiffs had carried on their business in an ordinary way and not in such a way as to invite accidents. He said that one knew perfectly well from many cases one had to try in the course of a long period of years that there was always a difficulty in getting window cleaners, for one reason or another, to use safety belts. He did not know why they would not, but one often found that they were people who disregarded their own safety. At the same time one did not suppose that when a man went out and did not take a safety belt with him, he intended to put himself, or was thinking of putting himself, into a position in which a fatal accident might easily happen. The learned Lord Chief Justice added:[3]

> "The employers here provided a safety belt for their employee, who was evidently an experienced man, and they gave him the opportunity of taking precautions for his safety. Whether he would have used the belt when he got to the club is another matter. But I do not think one could possibly say that the employers were running their business in a way that invited accidents because they did not say to the men every time they went out, or once a month, or at any time, 'There is your safety belt. We want you always to use it.'
>
> The fact that they supplied the safety belts, and that the men knew that there were safety belts there, was an intimation to the men that if they were going to a job where a safety belt was required it was there for them to use."

A condition in an employers' liability insurance policy stating that "the

---

[1] *Re Bradley and Essex and Suffolk Accident Indemnity Society*, [1912] 1 K.B. 415, C.A., *per* COZENS-HARDY, M.R., at p. 417. The contrary view was taken in *Rockhampton Corporation* v. *Yorkshire Insurance Co.* (1910), 11 C.L.R. 594, where the accident was due to the insured's negligence in running a tramcar before the tramway was completed. Cf. *Re George and Goldsmiths and General Burglary Insurance Association, Ltd.*, [1899] 1 Q.B. 595, C.A. (burglary insurance) *per* Lord RUSSELL, C.J., at p. 602, holding that a similar stipulation was a condition precedent.

[2] [1952] 2 Lloyd's Rep. 360, Q.B.D.

[3] *Ibid.*, at p. 363.

assured shall take all reasonable precautions to prevent accidents" is not broken by a negligent act on the part of a competent foreman selected by them.

Thus, in *Woolfall and Rimmer, Ltd.* v. *Moyle*[1] the insured effected an employers' liability insurance policy containing a condition that they "shall take all reasonable steps to prevent accidents". While painting the inside of the roof of a factory, some employees stood on some scaffolding which collapsed. One of them was killed and three of them were seriously injured. The work was being supervised by a competent foreman appointed by the insured, and the accident happened through his negligence. The insurers repudiated liability when a claim was made under the policy on the ground that the condition meant that the insured *and their employees* were to take reasonable steps to prevent accidents, and that it had been broken by the foreman's negligence.

The Court of Appeal[2] held that the condition had not been broken, and that the claim succeeded.

Lord GREENE, M.R., observed:[3]

> "It is conceded by counsel for the [insurers]—and quite rightly conceded in my view—that, in entrusting to this foreman the task of providing suitable and safe material for scaffolding and selecting suitable material for a particular job, the employers were taking a reasonable precaution within the meaning of condition 5. No doubt, *vis-à-vis* a workman injured through the negligence of the foreman, that would not be a sufficient answer to a claim. However, this seems to me to be irrelevant, because the question we have to answer is: 'What is meant by a "reasonable precaution" in this particular document and as between these two parties?' Counsel for the [insurers], having conceded what I have mentioned, then wished to construe the condition as importing the element of what, for shortness, I have called vicarious responsibility. He says that, notwithstanding that the selection of a competent foreman for the purposes stated is the taking of reasonable precautions, the employers are in breach of the condition if that foreman is in fact negligent in carrying out the task entrusted to him, or, in other words, that the condition has the effect, so to speak, of imposing upon the assured the burden of a guarantee of the diligence of the foreman in the performance of the task which they have reasonably entrusted to him. That seems to me to be completely inadmissible. If the delegation was reasonable, and, if, in selecting that particular foreman to perform the task, the respondents took reasonable precautions, their obligation under this condition was, in my opinion, at an end."

b *Observations of Statutory Obligations*

Thus, the insured must observe all the requirements of the Factories Act 1961, where applicable.

c *Wages Book*

The insured may be required to keep a return of all wages paid,[4] including, if necessary, wages paid by sub-contractors. This provision is important because the amount of premium payable is usually based on the amount of wages paid. A payment on account of premium is usually made when the

---

[1] [1941] 3 All E.R. 304, C.A.
[2] Lord GREENE, M.R., GODDARD and DU PARCQ, L.JJ.
[3] [1941] 3 All E.R. at p. 309. See also the judgment of GODDARD, L.J., *ibid.*, at p. 311, and that of DU PARCQ, L.J., *ibid.*, at p. 312.
[4] The insured must make this return at the stipulated time although the policy has expired: *General Accident Assurance Corporation* v. *Day* (1904), 21 T.L.R. 88.

insurance begins, and provision is made for a final adjustment at the end of the period of insurance and for payment of the balance, if any, shown to be due.

Thus, the Lloyd's Employers' Liability Policy states:

"The first premium and all renewal premiums that may be accepted are to be regulated by the amount of wages and salaries and other earnings paid to employees by the Assured during each period of insurance. The name of every employee and the amount of wages, salary and other earnings paid to him shall be duly recorded in a proper wages book. The Assured shall at all times allow the Underwriters to inspect such books and shall supply the Underwriters with the correct account of all such wages, salaries and other earnings paid during any Period of Insurance within one month from the expiry of such Period of Insurance, and if the total amount so paid shall differ from the amount on which premium has been paid, the difference in premium shall be met by a further proportionate payment to the Underwriters or by a refund by the Underwriters as the case may be."

In *Garthwaite* v. *Rowland*[1] an employers' liability insurance policy containing the stipulation set out above had been issued to the defendant by the plaintiff underwriters. The defendant had failed to supply them with a statement showing the actual amount of wages paid to all persons in his employment, and in consequence the plaintiffs were unable to ascertain whether any additional premium was payable in excess of that which had been paid or whether any rebate might be due. The plaintiffs applied for an account to be taken. The defendant contended that a statement had already been sent to the brokers as the plaintiffs' agents.

Judge THOMAS ordered that an account be taken. He considered that the brokers were the defendant's agents, and that the defendant, even if the brokers had been supplied with a statement, had not complied with the condition in the policy. His Honour observed:[2]

"In this case it is alleged that the defendant supplied an account to Messrs. Matthews, Wrightson & Co., Ltd.,[3] but although he has proved that he himself typed a letter and posted it (and produced what he says is a copy of it), which I took *de bene esse*, there is no admissible evidence of the contents of that letter and no evidence at all of the contents of the declaration which it says was included in that letter. It was sent to the agents, and not to the underwriters—as the policy requires—if it was sent; and, therefore, I think it is quite clear that the plaintiff has not received the account to which he is entitled. That being so, if he likes to take the risk of it in the present form of his particulars of claim, he is entitled to have an account, and I order that an account be taken."

In *Re Bradley and Essex and Suffolk Accident Indemnity Society, Ltd.*[4] an employers' liability insurance policy issued to a farmer whose only employee was his son, contained a condition which stated that:

"The first premium and all renewal premiums that may be accepted are to be regulated by the amount of wages and salaries and other earnings paid to employees by the insured during such period of insurance. The name of every employee and the amount of wages, salary and other earnings paid to him shall be duly recorded in a proper wages book. The insured shall at all times allow

---

[1] (1948), 81 Ll.L. Rep. 417, Mayor's and City of London Court.
[2] *Ibid.*, at p. 418.
[3] I.e., the brokers.
[4] (1911), 105 L.T. 919, C.A.

the society to inspect such books, and shall supply the society with a correct account of all such wages, salaries and other earnings paid during any period of insurance within one month from the expiry of such period of insurance."

This condition and other conditions were declared by the policy to be conditions precedent to liability. When a claim was made under the policy, the insurance company refused to indemnify him on the ground that the condition set out above had been broken, for the name and wages of every employee had not been duly recorded in a proper wages book.

The Court of Appeal[1] held that, on the true construction of the policy, the condition was not a condition precedent to liability, for the sole object of the clause was to provide for the adjustment of premiums, COZENS-HARDY, M.R., observing:[2]

> "It is perfectly clear that some of these so-called conditions are not and cannot be conditions precedent, although some of them may be and are conditions precedent. Nos. 1 and 2 dealing with notices, may be conditions precedent. No. 3, so far as any meaning can be attributed to it, seems to me not to be a condition precedent. The same remark applies to Nos. 4, 6, and 7. The question in this appeal, however, turns upon condition 5. This is obviously that which is referred to in the policy itself in the words 'subject to adjustment as hereinafter provided.' The first sentence is not a condition precedent. 'The first premium and all renewal premiums that may be accepted are to be regulated by the amount of wages and salaries and other earnings paid to employees by the insured during such period of insurance.' The third sentence also is not. 'The insured shall at all times allow the society to inspect such books, and shall supply the society with a correct account of all such wages, salaries, and other earnings paid during any period of insurance within one month from the expiry of such period of insurance, and if the total amount so paid shall differ from the amount on which premium has been paid, the differences in premium shall be met by a further proportionate payment to the society or by a refund by the society as the case may be.' The second sentence is in the following words: 'The name of every employee and the amount of wages, salary, and other earnings paid to him shall be duly recorded in a proper wages book.' . . . I think the fifth condition is one and entire, and it is to my mind unreasonable to hold that one sentence in its middle is a condition precedent while the rest of the condition cannot be so considered."

2 Duties Arising after Loss

On the happening of an accident to an employee likely to give rise to a claim under the policy, the following duties to be performed by the insured are usually made conditions of the policy:

a to give notice of the accident to the insurers;

b to forward to the insurers any notice of any claim made by the injured employee;

---

[1] COZENS-HARDY, M.R., and FARWELL, L.J.; FLETCHER MOULTON, L.J., dissenting.

[2] (1911) 105 L.T. at p. 924. See also the judgment of FARWELL, L.J., *ibid.*, at p. 927. FARWELL, L.J., also based his judgment on another ground, for he said (*ibid.*, at p. 928) that the condition was to keep a "proper wages book", and observed: "That must mean, in my opinion, 'proper under the circumstances of the case and for the business or trade of the insured'. Take the case of a lodging house keeper with one maid. I think it would be absurd to lay it down as a matter of law without evidence that it is proper or usual for such a woman to keep a wages book. And I think the same observation applies to a small farmer (even though he adds a carrier's business to his farming) who employs his son as his only servant." As to when a clause in a policy should be construed as a condition precedent to liability, see further, Ivamy, *General Principles of Insurance Law*, 2nd Edn., 1970, pp. 236–243.

c to furnish the insurers with full particulars of the circumstances giving rise to the claim;

d not to contest or settle any claim without the insurers' consent.

a   *Notice of Accident*[1]

The policy usually specifies a time within which notice of the accident must be given.

Thus, the Lloyd's Employers' Liability Policy states:

> "In the event of any occurrence which may give rise to a claim for indemnity under this Policy the Assured shall as soon as possible give notice thereof to the Underwriters in writing with full particulars . . . Notice shall also be given in writing to the Underwriters immediately the Assured shall have knowledge of any impending prosecution inquest or fatal inquiry in connection with such occurrence as aforesaid."

b   *Notice of Claim*[2]

The Lloyd's Employers' Liability Policy states: "Every letter, claim, writ, summons and process should be notified or forwarded to the Underwriters immediately on receipt."

c   *Particulars of Circumstances giving rise to Claim*[3]

These particulars may include:

i the date, place, and full details of the accident;

ii the name of the injured employee;

iii the extent of his injuries, including a statement as to whether he is still able to work or the date when he ceased to work;

iv the nature of the work on which he was engaged at the time of the accident;

v the nature of his employment, i.e., whether he was regularly or casually employed;

vi the amount of his wages.

d   *Contesting or Settling Claim*

The Lloyd's Employers' Liability Policy states:

> "No admission, offer, promise, payment or indemnity shall be made or given by or on behalf of the Assured without the written consent of the Underwriters who shall be entitled if they so desire to take over and conduct in the name of the Assured the defence or settlement of any claim or to prosecute in the name of the Assured for their own benefit any claim for indemnity or damages or otherwise and shall have full discretion in the conduct of any proceedings and in the settlement of any claim and the Assured shall give all such information and assistance as the Underwriters may require."

EMPLOYERS' LIABILITY (COMPULSORY INSURANCE) ACT 1969

The Employers' Liability (Compulsory Insurance) Act 1969 came into force on January 1, 1972,[4] and, subject to certain exceptions, makes it

---

[1] See further, Ivamy, *General Principles of Insurance Law*, 2nd Edn., 1970, pp. 348–353.

[2] The word "claim" in a condition in a policy has been held not to include a request for arbitration: *Wilkinson* v. *Car and General Insurance Corporation, Ltd.* (1913), 110 L.T. 468, C.A. But the condition may be so framed as to include it.

[3] See further, Ivamy, *General Principles of Insurance Law*, 2nd Edn., 1970, pp. 353–357.

[4] Employers' Liability (Compulsory Insurance) Act 1969 (Commencement) Order 1971 (S.I. 1971, No. 1116).

compulsory for employers to insure against liability in respect of their employees. The Act empowers the Secretary of State to make regulations under it.[1]

Which Employers must Insure

The general rule is that every employer carrying on any business[2] in Great Britain must insure, and maintain insurance, under one or more approved policies[3] with an authorized insurer[4] against liability for bodily injury sustained by his employees, and arising out of and in the course of their employment in Great Britain in that business.[5]

But the Act does not require insurance to be effected by:[6]

1 certain local authorities[7] and any police authority;
2 any body corporate established by or under any enactment for the carrying on of any industry or part of an industry or of any undertaking under national ownership or control; or
3 any employer exempted by regulations made by the Secretary of State,[8] e.g., the Government of any foreign state or Commonwealth country, London Transport Executive, a member of a mutual insurance association of shipowners.[9]

Types of Employees to be Covered

In general all employees must be covered.[10] The term "employer" means

"an individual who has entered into or works under a contract of service or apprenticeship with an employer whether by way of manual work, clerical work or otherwise, whether such contract is expressed or implied, oral or in writing."[11]

But the Act does not require an employer to insure:

i in respect of an employee of whom the employer is the husband, wife, father, mother, grandfather, grandmother, step-father, step-mother, son, daughter, grandson, grand-daughter, stepson, stepdaughter, brother, sister, half-brother or half-sister; or

---

[1] Employers' Liability (Compulsory Insurance) Act 1969, s. 6 (1). The regulations are made by statutory instrument: *ibid.* Such statutory instrument is subject to annulment in pursuance of a resolution of either House of Parliament: *ibid.*

[2] The word "business" includes a trade or profession, and includes any activity carried on by a body of persons, whether corporate or incorporate: *ibid.*, s. 1 (3) (*c*). Except as otherwise provided by regulations, an employer not having a place of business in Great Britain is deemed not to carry on business there: *ibid.*, s. 1 (3) (*d*).

[3] I.e., a policy of insurance not subject to any conditions or exceptions prohibited for those purposes by regulations made by the Secretary of State: *ibid.*, s. 1 (3) (*a*).

[4] I.e., a person or body of persons lawfully carrying on in Great Britain insurance business of any class relevant for the purposes of Part II of the Companies Act 1967 and issuing the policy or policies in the course thereof: *ibid.*, s. 1 (3) (*b*). As to Part II of the Companies Act 1967, see Ivamy, *General Principles of Insurance Law*, 2nd Edn., 1970, pp. 31–32.

[5] Employers' Liability (Compulsory Insurance) Act 1969, s. 1 (1).

[6] *Ibid.*, s. 3 (1).

[7] I.e. the Common Council of the City of London, the Greater London Council, the council of a London borough, the council of a county, county borough or county district, any joint board or joint committee which is so constituted as to include among its members representatives of any such council: *ibid.*, s. 3 (2).

[8] Employers' Liability (Compulsory Insurance) Exemption Regulations 1971 (S.I. 1971, No. 1933). See pp. 373–375, *post.*

[9] As to mutual insurance, see Ivamy, *Marine Insurance* (1969), pp. 491–495.

[10] Employers' Liability (Compulsory Insurance) Act 1969, s. 2 (1).

[11] *Ibid.*, s. 2 (2).

ii except as otherwise provided by regulations, in respect of employees not ordinarily resident in Great Britain.[1]

The present regulations made by the Secretary of State provide that the Act applies in respect of employees not ordinarily resident in Great Britain in the course of employment there for a continuous period of not less than 14 days.[2]

Certificates of Insurance

a   *The Provisions of the Act*

The Secretary of State has power to make regulations for securing that certificates of insurance in such form and containing such particulars as may be prescribed by the regulations are issued by insurers to employers entering into contracts of insurance in accordance with the requirements of the Act and for the surrender in such circumstances as may be so prescribed of certificates so issued.[3]

The employer (subject to any provisions made by the regulations as to the surrender of the certificates) must during the currency of the insurance and such further period (if any) as may be provided by regulations:

   i comply with any regulations requiring him to supply copies of the certificate of insurance for the information of his employees;

  ii produce the certificate of insurance or a copy of it to any inspector authorized by the Secretary of State for the purposes of the Act, and produce or send the certificate or a copy of it to such other persons, at such place and in such circumstances as may be prescribed by regulations;

 iii permit the policy of insurance or a copy of it to be inspected by such persons and in such circumstances as may be so prescribed.[4]

A person who fails to comply with any of the above requirements is liable on summary conviction to a fine not exceeding £50.[5]

b   *The Provisions of the Regulations*

The regulations state that every employer entering into a contract of insurance in accordance with the requirements of the Act must be issued by the insurer with whom he contracts a certificate of insurance in the form and containing the particulars specified in the Schedule to the regulations.[6] These particulars include: the name of the policy holder, the date of commencement of the insurance, and the date of expiry of the insurance.

Every certificate of insurance must be issued not later than 30 days after the date on which the insurance commences or is renewed.[7]

Where a certificate of insurance has been issued to an employer, he must display a copy or copies of it at his place of business, or where he has more

---

[1] Employers' Liability (Compulsory Insurance) Act 1969, s. 2 (2).
[2] Employers' Liability (Compulsory Insurance) General Regulations 1971 (S.I. 1971, No. 1117), reg. 4. These regulations are set out at pp. 370–373, *post.*
[3] Employers' Liability (Compulsory Insurance) Act 1969, s. 4 (1).
[4] *Ibid.*, s. 4 (2).
[5] *Ibid.*, s. 4 (3).
[6] Employers' Liability (Compulsory Insurance) General Regulations 1971, (S.I. 1971, No. 1117) reg. 5 (1). The Schedule to the Regulations is set out at p. 373, *post.*
[7] *Ibid.*, reg. 5 (2).

than one place of business, at each place of business at which he employs any person whose claims may be the subject of indemnity under the policy of insurance to which the certificate relates.[1]

Copies of any certificate of insurance must be displayed in such numbers and characters and in such positions as to be easily seen and read by every person employed whose claims may be the subject of indemnity under the policy of insurance to which the certificate relates.[2] Where the copies of the certificate are displayed in the open, they must be protected from the weather.[3] Further, they must be kept displayed until the expiration of the period of insurance stated in the certificate, or, if the policy to which the certificate relates is cancelled, until the policy is cancelled.[4] In either case, they must not be displayed thereafter.[5]

Where an employer is served with a notice issued on behalf of the Secretary of State requiring him to do so, he must produce or send to any officer of the Department of the Environment specified in the notice, at the address and within the time specified therein, the original or a copy of every certificate of insurance issued to him, which relates to a period of insurance current at the date of the notice.[6]

An employer who has entered into a contract of insurance in accordance with the requirements of the Act must, during the currency of the insurance, permit the policy or a copy of it to be inspected by any inspector duly authorized by the Secretary of State for the purposes of the Act (either in the case of a company) at the registered office or (in any case) at a place of business of the employer as the inspector requires and at a time when the inspector stipulates.[7]

Any inspector duly authorized by the Secretary of State for the purposes of the Act must, if so required when visiting any premises for those purposes, produce to any employer or his agent some duly authenticated document showing that he is so authorized.[8]

Penalty for Failure to Insure

An employer, who on any day is not insured in accordance with the Act when required to be so, is guilty of an offence and liable on summary conviction to a fine not exceeding £200.[9]

Where an offence committed by a corporation has been committed with the consent or connivance of, or facilitated by any neglect on the part of, any director, manager, secretary or other officer of the corporation, he as well as the corporation is guilty of that offence, and is liable to be proceeded against and punished accordingly.[10]

Limit of Amount of Compulsory Insurance

The amount for which an employer is required by the Act to insure and

---

[1] Employers' Liability (Compulsory Insurance) General Regulations 1971 (S.I. 1971, No. 1117).
[2] *Ibid.*, reg. 6 (2).
[3] *Ibid.*, reg. 6 (2).
[4] *Ibid.*, reg. 6 (3).
[5] *Ibid.*, reg. 6 (3).
[6] *Ibid.*, reg. 7.
[7] *Ibid.*, reg. 8.
[8] *Ibid.*, reg. 9.
[9] Employers' Liability (Compulsory Insurance) Act 1969, s. 5.
[10] *Ibid.*, s. 5.

maintain insurance is £2,000,000 in respect of claims relating to any one or more of his employees arising out of any one occurrence.[1]

Prohibition of Certain Conditions in Policies

Any condition in a policy of insurance issued or renewed in accordance with the requirements of the Act which provides (in whatever terms) that no liability (either generally or in respect of a particular claim) shall arise under the policy, or that any such liability shall cease:

 a in the event of some specified thing being done or omitted to be done after the happening of the event giving rise to a claim under the policy;

 b unless the policy holder takes reasonable care to protect his employees against the risk of bodily injury or disease in the course of their employment;

 c unless the policy holder complies with the requirements of any enactment for the protection of employees against the risk of bodily injury or disease in the course of their employment; and

 d unless the policy holder keeps specified records or provides the insurer with or makes available to him information therefrom,

is prohibited for the purposes of the Act.[2]

But nothing in the regulation which imposes these prohibitions must be taken as prejudicing any provision in a policy requiring the policy holder to pay to the insurer any sums which the insurer may have become liable to pay under the policy and which have been applied to the satisfaction of claims in respect of employees or any costs and expenses incurred in relation to such claims.[3]

---

[1] Employers' Liability (Compulsory Insurance) General Regulations 1971 (S.I. 1971 No. 1117), reg. 3.
[2] *Ibid.*, reg. 2 (1).
[3] *Ibid.*, reg. 2 (2).

PART VI

GUARANTEE INSURANCE

35

INTRODUCTION

Wherever a person in the course of his employment or in pursuance of his duties is entrusted with the collection or receipt, or with the custody or control of, money or valuable securities, or has access, by reason of his position, to the money or valuable securities of another, there is in a special degree the risk of loss by misappropriation. Such a risk can be covered by a fidelity insurance policy.

Wherever one person owes money to another there is a risk of loss, since the debtor may by reason of his insolvency or otherwise, fail to pay the debt when it falls due. This risk is equally capable of being insured against. This class of insurance, which is called solvency insurance, may cover (i) the non-payment of debts generally, whether due or to become due from a particular person or persons, e.g. the customers of the insured; or (ii) the non-payment of a particular debt, either directly where the insolvency of the debtor is insured against, or indirectly where the insurance is against the solvency of a guarantor of the debt.[1]

Differences between Guarantee and Insurance

These types of insurance bear a close analogy to each other. They are both in a sense promises to answer for the "debt, default or miscarriages" of another person, and from this point of view may be regarded as contracts of guarantee falling within s. 4 of the Statute of Frauds 1677 rather than as contracts of insurance. They have, in fact, developed in the course of business out of guarantees. The phrases "policy of guarantee" and "guarantee insurance"[2] are used in connection with them, and the word "guarantee" is used in the policy as equivalent to or in lieu of the word "insure".[3]

---

[1] An insurance of this kind is often effected where the debt is secured by mortgage or mortgage debentures to meet any deficiency in the security. This type of solvency insurance is known as mortgage or debenture insurance.

[2] The phrase "guarantee insurance" is also equivalent to reinsurance. Strictly speaking, a policy by which the insurers undertake to pay in the event of the debtor's insolvency is a solvency policy, whilst a policy by which they undertake to pay in the event of non-payment by the debtor is a guarantee policy: *Hambro* v. *Burnand*, [1904] 2 K.B. 10, C.A., *per* COLLINS, M.R., at p. 19.

[3] *American Surety Co. of New York* v. *Wrightson* (1910), 103 L.T. 663, *per* HAMILTON, J., at p. 665: "I think, although one is called a securityship bond and the other is called a guarantee, they are both essentially insurances, they both indemnify the National Park Bank of New York against losses to its property caused by certain perils insured against." See also *Parr's Bank* v. *Albert Mines Syndicate* (1900), 5 Com. Cas. 116, *per* MATHEW, J., at p. 120; *Re Law Guarantee Trust and Accident Society, Ltd., Liverpool Mortgage Insurance Co.'s Case*, [1914] 2 Ch. 617, C.A., *per* KENNEDY, L.J., at p. 636.

279

Nevertheless, the intention of the parties is to enter into a contract of insurance and not into a contract of guarantee.[1] A contract of insurance differs from a contract of guarantee in the following respects:[2]

1 The contract is usually framed in the form of a policy.

2 The contract is entered into as a matter of business.

---

[1] *Dane* v. *Mortgage Corporation*, [1894] 1 Q.B. 54, C.A., *per* Lord Esher, M.R., at p. 60: "I do not think this contract is to be looked at as one of a guarantee in the usual sense of the term, but as a contract of insurance. The defendants are incorporated as the Mortgage Insurance Corporation, Ltd. for the express purpose of insuring mortgages and other securities, and they issue policies. The contract now in question begins with the words 'This policy of insurance'. It appears to me clear that the intention was that this contract should be one of insurance, and that those who entered into it with the plaintiff should be in the position of underwriters"; *Shaw* v. *Royce, Ltd.*, [1911] 1 Ch. 138, *per* Warrington, J., at p. 147: "Now in the first place considerable discussion has taken place as to the nature of this so-called guarantee; is it or is it not an ordinary contract of suretyship, or is it not rather, although called a guarantee, a policy of insurance against the happening of certain events? If it is necessary to decide the question, in my opinion this document does not embody a mere contract of suretyship"; *Parr's Bank* v. *Albert Mines Syndicate* (*supra*) *per* Mathew, J., at p. 119.

[2] *Seaton* v. *Heath*, [1899] 1 Q.B. 782, C.A. *per* Romer, L.J., at pp. 792, 793: "I desire to make some remarks upon the question of general importance raised in this case with reference to the contract of insurance or guarantee. There are some contracts in which our Courts of law and equity require what is called *uberrima fides* to be shown by the person obtaining them; and, as that phrase is short and convenient, I will continue to use it. Of these, ordinary contracts of marine, fire and life insurance are examples, and in each of them the person desiring to be insured must, in setting forth the risk to be insured against, not conceal any material fact affecting the risk known to him. On the other hand, ordinary contracts of guarantee are not among those requiring *uberrima fides* on the part of the creditor towards the surety; and mere non-communication to the surety by the creditor of facts known to him affecting the risk to be undertaken by the surety will not vitiate the contract, unless there be fraud or misrepresentation, and misrepresentation undoubtedly might be made by concealment. But the difference between these two classes of contract does not depend upon any essential difference between the word 'insurance' and the word 'guarantee'. There is no magic in the use of those words. The words, to a great extent, have the same meaning and effect, and many contracts, like the one in the case now before us, may with equal propriety be called contracts of insurance or contracts of guarantee. Whether the contract be one requiring *uberrima fides* or not must depend upon its substantial character and how it came to be effected. There is no hard and fast line to be drawn between contracts of insurance and contracts of guarantee for the purpose which I am now considering them; and certainly the rule as to contracts of insurance is not limited, as contended, to the three forms of marine, life and fire insurance; see the observations of Jessel, M.R., in *London Assurance* v. *Mansel* (1879), 11 Ch.D. 363 (life insurance). Now when contracts of insurance are considered, it will be seen that, speaking generally, they have in common several features in their character and the way they are effected which distinguish them from ordinary contracts of guarantee. Contracts of insurance are generally matters of speculation, where the person desiring to be insured has means of knowledge as to the risk and the insurer has not the means or has not the same means. The insured generally puts the risk before the insurer as a business transaction, and the insurer on the risk stated fixes a proper price to remunerate him for the risk to be undertaken; and the insurer engages to pay the loss incurred by the insured in the event of certain contingencies occurring. On the other hand, in general, contracts of guarantee are between persons who occupy, or who ultimately assume, the positions of creditor, debtor, and surety, and thereby the surety becomes bound to pay the debt or make good the default of the debtor. In general, the creditor does not himself go to the surety, or represent, or explain to the surety, the risk to be run. The surety often takes the position from motives of friendship to the debtor, and generally not as the result of any direct bargaining between him and the creditor, or in consideration of any remuneration passing to him from the creditor. The risk undertaken is generally known to the surety, and the circumstances generally point to the view that as between the creditor and the surety it was contemplated and intended that the surety should take upon himself to ascertain exactly what risk he was taking upon himself." This statement of the law is not affected by the reversal of *Seaton* v. *Heath* (*supra*) in the House of Lords, *sub nom. Seaton* v. *Burnand*, [1900] A.C. 135: *Re Denton's Estate, Licenses Insurance Corporation and Guarantee Fund, Ltd.* v. *Denton*, [1904] 2 Ch. 178, C.A. (guarantee) *per* Vaughan Williams, L.J., at p. 188.

3 The insurers have no particular knowledge of the circumstances of the original debt or liability.

4 The insurers are not sureties.

1   Contract in Form of Policy

The contract is usually framed in the form of a policy and not in the form of a guarantee.[1] It purports on the face of it to be a contract of insurance, based upon a proposal and in consideration of a premium, in the same way as any other contract of insurance.

The nature of the contract does not, however, depend upon its form. A document which is, in form, a guarantee, may be in effect, a contract of insurance,[2] whilst, on the other hand, a document which on the face of it is called a policy of insurance, may be according to its true construction, a contract of guarantee.[3]

2   Matter of Business

The contract is entered into purely as a matter of business, the insurers agreeing to be liable for payment in the event of loss, and for no other reason. In the contract of guarantee the surety becomes bound under it often through motives of friendship for the employee or for the debtor.[4]

3   No Knowledge of Circumstances of Debt

Since the insurers have no connection with the original debt or liability, otherwise than as a matter of business, it follows that they have no particular knowledge of the circumstances.

They are, therefore, entitled, as in the case of any other contract of insurance,[5] to the fullest disclosure for the purpose of enabling them to decide whether they will accept the insurance, and to fix a premium proportionate to the risk undertaken, and, if the duty of disclosure is not fulfilled by the insured, they may avoid the contract.[6]

---

[1] *Dane* v. *Mortgage Insurance Corporation*, [1894] 1 Q.B. 54, C.A., *per* Lord ESHER, M.R., at p. 60.

[2] *Re Law Guarantee Trust and Accident Society, Liverpool Mortgage Insurance Co., Ltd.'s Case*, [1914] 2 Ch. 617, C.A., *per* BUCKLEY, L.J., at p. 631: "In arriving at the conclusion that this tripartite contract is not one of suretyship but of insurance, I have not founded myself at all upon any language in the documents. In fact, the society became bound in return for the receipt of a certain premium as the price of its obligation. This, however, does not appear in the documents to which the debenture holder was a party. The true effect of the contract is to be ascertained, I think, not upon a scrutiny of the terms used but upon an examination of its effect."

[2] *Seaton* v. *Heath* (*supra*), *per* ROMER, L.J., at p. 793; *Re Denton's Estate, Licenses Insurance Corporation and Guarantee Fund, Ltd.* v. *Denton*, [1904] 2 Ch. 178, C.A. (guarantee), where the contract, although called a policy, was held to be a guarantee, *Trade Indemnity Co., Ltd.* v. *Workington Harbour & Dock Board*, [1937] A.C. 1., where a bond was held to be a guarantee for the due completion of a contract by a third party and not a policy of insurance.

[4] *Seaton* v. *Heath*, [1899] 1 Q.B. 782, C.A., *per* ROMER, L.J., at p. 793; *Re Law Guarantee Trust and Accident Society, Ltd., Liverpool Mortgage Insurance Co., Case*, [1914] 2 Ch. 617, *per* BUCKLEY, L.J., at p. 631; *Lee* v. *Jones* (1864), 17 C.B.N.S. 482, Ex. Ch. (guarantee), *per* BLACKBURN, J., at p. 503.

[5] See Ivamy, *General Principles of Insurance Law*, 2nd Edn., 1970, pp. 90–122.

[6] *Seaton* v. *Heath* (*supra*), *per* ROMER, L.J., at p. 793. The fact that the insurers have as much means of ascertaining the nature of the risk as the creditor is an element to be taken into consideration as showing that the contract is one of guarantee; *Re Denton's Estate, Licenses Insurance Corporation and Guarantee Fund Ltd.*, v. *Denton* (*supra*), *per* VAUGHAN WILLIAMS, L.J., at p. 188. In that case, however, the knowledge seems to have been obtained from the proposal.

On the other hand, in the case of a guarantee, the duty of disclosure is not so extensive.[1] The creditor or employer need not disclose everything that is material for the surety to know.[2] The surety is put upon inquiry, and he cannot repudiate liability merely on the ground that all the facts were not disclosed to him.[3] At the same time the contract of gurantee assumes as its basis a certain state of facts,[4] and any fact inconsistent with that state of facts must, if known to the creditor or employer, be disclosed.[5]

An omission to disclose the fact is an implied representation that the fact does not exist.[6] If, therefore, the fact does exist, the guarantee is voidable on the ground of non-disclosure and it is immaterial whether such non-disclosure was fraudulent[7] or innocent.[8] To avoid the guarantee it is not sufficient to show that the fact was material merely in the sense that it might have affected the surety's judgment.[9] The fact must be one which alters the whole relationship of the parties, and makes the transaction a different one from that which the surety was prepared to undertake.[10]

Thus, where the honesty of an employee is to be guaranteed, it is assumed as the basis of the contract that he is not, to the employer's knowledge, a person who has already been guilty of dishonesty.[11]

Similarly, where payment of a debt is to be guaranteed, it is assumed that there is no contract between the creditor and the debtor which makes his position different from that which the surety would naturally expect.[12]

If, therefore, the employee is known to have been dishonest,[13] or the contract between the creditor and the debtor if of an unusual character,[14] the duty of disclosure attaches.

On the other hand, a failure on the part of the creditor to disclose the fact that the debtor is already in his debt is not necessarily a breach of duty,

---

[1] The Court expressly refused to apply the insurance rule in *North British Insurance Co.* v. *Lloyd* (1854), 10 Exch. 523 (guarantee), approved in *Lee* v. *Jones* (*supra*), *per* BLACKBURN, J., at p. 503. See also *London General Omnibus Co.* v. *Holloway*, [1912] 2 K.B. 72, C.A. (guarantee), *per* KENNEDY, L.J., at p. 86.

[2] *Hamilton* v. *Watson* (1845), 12 Cl. & Fin. 109 (guarantee), *per* Lord CAMPBELL, at p. 119; *Davies* v. *London and Provincial Marine Insurance Co.* (1878), 8 Ch.D. 469 (guarantee), *per* FRY, J., at p. 475.

[3] *Seaton* v. *Heath* (*supra*), *per* ROMER, L.J., at p. 793; *Phillips* v. *Foxall* (1872), L.R. 7 Q.B. 666 (guarantee), where the earlier cases are reviewed.

[4] *London General Omnibus Co.* v. *Holloway* (*supra*), *per* VAUGHAN WILLIAMS, L.J., at p. 77.

[5] *Hamilton* v. *Watson* (*supra*), *per* Lord CAMPBELL, at p. 119; *London General Omnibus Co.* v. *Holloway* (*supra*).

[6] *Lee* v. *Jones* (*supra*), *per* BLACKBURN, J., at p. 503; *Phillips* v. *Foxall* (*supra*), *per* BLACKBURN, J., at p. 679; *London General Omnibus Co.* v. *Holloway* (*supra*), *per* VAUGHAN WILLIAMS, L.J., at p. 77.

[7] *Lee* v. *Jones* (*supra*).

[8] *Railton* v. *Mathews* (1844), 10 Cl. & Fin. 934 (guarantee), *per* Lord COTTENHAM, L.C., at p. 941; *London General Omnibus Co.* v. *Holloway* (*supra*). Cf. *Seaton* v. *Heath* (*supra*), *per* ROMER, L.J., at p. 792.

[9] *London General Omnibus Co.* v. *Holloway* (*supra*), *per* KENNEDY, L.J., at p. 87. Cf. *Hamilton* v. *Watson* (*supra*), *per* Lord CAMPBELL at p. 119; *Lee* v. *Jones* (*supra*), *per* BLACKBURN, J., at p. 503.

[10] *London General Omnibus Co.* v. *Holloway* (*supra*), *per* FARWELL, L.J., at p. 82.

[11] *Ibid.*, *per* VAUGHAN WILLIAMS, L.J., at p. 77.

[12] *Hamilton* v. *Watson* (1845), 12 Cl. & Fin. 109 (guarantee), *per* Lord CAMPBELL at p. 119.

[13] *Smith* v. *Bank of Scotland* (1813), 1 Dow. 272 (guarantee); *Railton* v. *Mathews* (1844), 10 Cl. & Fin. (guarantee); *Phillips* v. *Foxall* (1872), L.R. 7 Q.B. 666 (guarantee); *London General Omnibus Co.* v. *Holloway* (*supra*).

[14] *Pidcock* v. *Bishop* (1825), 3 B. & C. 605 (guarantee); *Hamilton* v. *Watson* (*supra*), *per* Lord CAMPBELL at p. 119.

since it may be that the surety ought to have inferred it from the nature of the transaction.[1]

Thus, a surety who guarantees a customer's account with a bank, may naturally be expected to assume that the customer may be overdrawn already,[2] and the bank, therefore, need not disclose the fact that he is overdrawn.[3]

4 Insurers not Sureties

The insurers are not sureties. They merely undertake to pay a sum of money in a certain event.[4] The contract is one of indemnity.[5] They do not guarantee that the employee will be honest or that the debtor will be able to pay the debt, but contract that if the employee proves dishonest, or if the debtor does not pay the debt by a given date, they will pay the loss.[6] Their obligation, although in a sense collateral to the principal debt, is not an obligation to pay the principal debt by way of suretyship. It is rather an independent obligation to pay a new debt, which arises under the contract of insurance on the happening of a specified event, and which may, therefore, differ both in amount and as regards the time of payment from the original debt.[7]

Hence, the insurers of a debt already guaranteed by sureties are not, on being called on to pay the debt, co-sureties with the original sureties and

---

[1] This, in the case of a guarantee to secure due payment of balances by a *del credere* agent, the duty to disclose the existing debt depends upon the amount already due and the period during which accounts have been left unsettled: *Lee* v. *Jones* (1864), 17 C.B.N.S. 482, Ex. Ch. (guarantee), *per* BLACKBURN, J., at p. 506.

[2] *Hamilton* v. *Watson* (*supra*), as explained in *Lee* v. *Jones* (*supra*), and in *London General Omnibus Co.* v. *Holloway* (*supra*).

[3] *Hamilton* v. *Watson* (*supra*); *National Provincial Bank of England, Ltd.* v. *Glanusk*, [1913] 3 K.B. 335, (guarantee).

[4] *Dane* v. *Mortgage Insurance Corporation, Ltd.*, [1894] 1 Q.B. 45, C.A., *per* Lord ESHER, M.R., at p. 60: "An underwriter is not a surety. He is a person who undertakes to pay money in a certain event. The form of a policy is not that of a guarantee. A policy on a ship, for instance, is not an undertaking to pay the amount insured, if somebody else, e.g. the owner of another ship which has caused the loss, does not, but to pay such amount on the loss of the ship. Here the policy recites that the plaintiff is the holder of a deposit receipt for £1,000 of the Commercial Bank of Australia and is desirous of being 'insured' as hereinafter appearing, and the defendants thereby in effect promise to pay the assured the principal sum if the debtors have made default in so doing. What the defendants have done, as it appears to me, is to insure payment of the deposit receipt according to the contract made between the depositor and the bank, i.e., that the bank will pay the amount at the date fixed by that contract for payment"; *Finlay* v. *Mexican Investment Corporation*, [1897] 1 Q.B. 517, *per* CHARLES, J., at p. 522: "The contract appears to me to be really one of insurance against a particular event, namely, the default by the Capitol Company to pay the plaintiff the amount of his debenture on November 4, 1895"; *Seaton* v. *Heath*, [1899] 1 Q.B. 782, C.A., *per* ROMER, L.J., at p. 793; *Parr's Bank* v. *Albert Mines Syndicate* (1900), 5 Com. Cas. 116, *per* MATHEW, J., at p. 120; *Shaw* v. *Royce, Ltd.*, [1911] 1 Ch. 138.

[5] *Finlay* v. *Mexican Investment Corporation* (*supra*), *per* CHARLES, J., at p. 522; *Meacock* v. *Bryant & Co.*, [1942] 2 All E.R. 661.

[6] *Dane* v. *Mortgage Insurance Corporation* (*supra*), *per* Lord ESHER, M.R., at p. 61: "The policy is not a guarantee that the bank will be able to pay; it is a positive direct contract that, if the bank does not pay a certain amount on a fixed day, the insurance company will pay that amount. By the law of insurance, though the underwriter directly promises to pay on a certain event, the contract is treated as one of indemnity; and it follows, that, if the assured, who has been indemnified by the underwriters as on a total loss, saves anything upon the loss, that salvage must go to the underwriter; otherwise the assured would be more than indemnified." See also *Re Law Guarantee Trust and Accident Society, Ltd.* (1913), 108 L.T. 830, *per* NEVILLE, J., at p. 832.

[7] *Laird* v. *Securities Insurance Co.* 1895, 22 R. (Ct. of Sess.) 452, *per* Lord MACLAREN at p. 459; *Re Law Guarantee Trust and Accident Society, Ltd., Liverpool Insurance Co.'s Case*, [1914] 2 Ch. 617, C.A., *per* BUCKLEY, L.J., at p. 630.

liable to bear the loss in rateable proportion with them.[1] They are subrogated[2] as insurers to the rights of the creditor and may enforce payment of the whole debt and interest from the principal debtor and the sureties.[3]

At the same time, the line of distinction between the two classes of contract is a very fine one. Many contracts may with equal propriety be called contracts of insurance or contracts of guarantee,[4] and in many cases it is immaterial whether the particular contract is one of suretyship or one of guarantee.[5]

---

[1] The policy may, however, provide that it is to operate merely as a co-security with the other securities held by the creditor. See p. 301, *post.*

[2] As to "subrogation", see Ivamy, *General Principles of Insurance Law*, 2nd Edn., 1970, pp. 415–430. See further, *Meacock* v. *Bryant & Co.*, [1942] 2 All E.R. 661.

[3] See p. 302, *post.* A contract which although in form a policy, is in effect a guarantee, will, in the same circumstances, have the same effect, if it is to be construed not as making the insurers co-sureties with the other sureties, but as guaranteeing both the principal debtor and the other sureties: *Re Denton's Estate, Licenses Insurance Corporation and Guarantee Fund, Ltd.* v. *Denton*, [1904] 2 Ch. 178, C.A. (guarantee).

[4] *Seaton* v. *Heath*, [1899] 1 Q.B. 782, C.A., *per* ROMER, L.J., at p. 792.

[5] *Dane* v. *Mortgage Insurance Corporation, Ltd.*, [1894] 1 Q.B. 54, C.A., *per* KAY, L.J., at p. 62, followed in *Re Law Guarantee Trust and Accident Society, Ltd., Liverpool Mortgage Insurance Co.'s Case (supra)*, *per* KENNEDY, L.J., at p. 636; *Seaton* v. *Burnand*, [1900] A.C. 135, *per* Lord ROBERTSON at p. 148. Cf. *Anglo-Californian Bank* v. *London and Provincial Marine and General Insurance Co. Ltd.* (1904), 10 Com. Cas. 1, *per* WALTON, J., at p. 9; *Shaw* v. *Royce, Ltd.*, [1911] 1 Ch. 138, *per* WARRINGTON, J., at p. 147.

36

FIDELITY INSURANCE

The principal matters to be considered in fidelity insurance are:

1 The subject-matter of the insurance.
2 The contents of the proposal form.
3 The form of the policy.
4 The perils insured against.
5 The exceptions in the policy.
6 Alteration of the risk.
7 The loss.
8 Matters arising after loss.

1 Subject-matter of Insurance

The subject-matter of this class of insurance is money; the employer does not insure against the misappropriation of specific coins or securities, but against the pecuniary loss which he will sustain if his employee proves dishonest. It is therefore unnecessary to insert in the policy any specific description of the subject-matter. It is sufficiently implied in the description of the loss as "pecuniary".

The scope of the policy is, however, modified by the circumstances to which it is intended to refer. It is an insurance against the acts or defaults of a particular person, or class of persons, occupying a particular position, and the risk contemplated is that he will avail himself of the opportunities which his position gives him to be dishonest. The subject-matter of insurance is, therefore, restricted to the money to which he has access in the course of his employment. This is invariably made clear by the policy, which includes or incorporates by reference[1] a statement as to the precise nature of the employee's duties, and further provides that the insurers are to be liable only if the loss is in connection with such duties. Money, therefore, to which the employee has access in any other capacity is not insured by the policy, and the employer has no claim in the event of its misappropriation.[2]

---

[1] *Hay* v. *Employers' Liability Assurance Corporation* (1905), 6 O.W.R. 459, followed in *Elgin Loan and Savings Co.* v. *London Guarantee and Accident Co.* (1906), 11 O.L.R. 330.

[2] See *Cosford Union* v. *Poor Law, etc., Officers' Mutual Guarantee Association, Ltd.* (1910), 103 L.T. 463, where the defalcations were committed by the employee in his capacity as clerk to the parish council, and it was held that, as the insurance related only to his acts as assistant overseer, they were not covered, notwithstanding the fact that the two offices were usually united in the same person.

2 Contents of Proposal Form

The proposal may be made and the proposal form filled in either by the employer or by the employee. If the proposal is made by the employee, his statements are not necessarily binding on the employer. The employer is not bound unless he has concurred in the proposal and thus made himself responsible for the statements in it, or unless he has authorised it to be made on his behalf, in which case the employee who fills it up is his agent for the purpose of doing so, and, therefore, binds him by his signature to the declaration, To meet this difficulty, the policy usually incorporates the proposal, with a recital that the employer concurred in making it or that it was made on his behalf in which case the employer cannot enforce the policy without admitting responsibility for the proposal.

The proposal form indicates the circumstances which are, in the opinion of the insurers, material to the risk. The principal matters which require consideration are the following:

    i the duties of the employee;

    ii the temptation to dishonesty;

    iii the employee's character.

i Duties of Employee

As the risk of loss depends, so far as the insurance is concerned, upon the opportunities for misappropriation afforded by the employee's position, a statement of the capacity in which he is employed, and, if necessary, of the precise nature of his duties, is required.[1]

ii Temptation to Dishonesty

As a badly paid employee is more likely to be tempted to be dishonest than one who is well paid, the employee's total remuneration, after deducting any expenses or other sums chargeable to him, must be stated. If he receives commission as well as salary, the amount must be included in the total.

Sometimes a statement is required of the safeguards proposed to be adopted by the employer, including the system to be followed in checking the accounts.[2] The employer may further be asked whether he has suffered any losses on his part through the acts of employees filling a similar position.

iii Employee's Character

The "moral hazard"[3] of this insurance depends upon the character of the employee. The employer, if the proposal proceeds from him, is, therefore, guilty of a breach of good faith if he knows that the employee is dishonest and does not disclose the fact to the insurers.[4] Probably it is his duty to disclose even his suspicions.[5]

---

[1] A statement of this kind is also important, in the event of any change of duties taking place, as defining the exact risk undertaken by the insurers. See p. 290, *post.*

[2] *Annprior Corporation* v. *United States Fidelity and Guaranty Co.* (1914), 51 S.C.R. 94; *Railway Passengers' Assurance Co.* v. *Standard Life Assurance Co.* (1921), 63 S.C.R. 79. As to departures from the system mentioned, see p. 290, *post.*

[3] As to the "moral hazard", see Ivamy, *General Principles of Insurance Law*, 2nd Edn., 1970, pp. 101–102.

[4] *Mayfield* v. *London and Lancashire Guaranty and Accident Co. of Canada*, [1927] 1 W.W.R. 67, where the employee had, to the knowledge of the employer, been guilty of dishonesty in a previous situation.

[5] *Fertile Valley (Municipality)* v. *Union Casualty Co.* (1921), 14 Sask. L.R. 413, where the employee's conduct had been so unsatisfactory as to bring him to the verge of dismissal.

In practice, a question may be put requiring the employer to state whether he received satisfactory references as to character at the time of engaging the employee, and whether he has always been satisfied with the employee's honesty and general conduct.

If the proposal proceeds from the employee, he is required to state how and with whom he has been employed during a specified period before the proposal, stating the capacity in which he was employed and the duration of his employment with each employer. He is also required to give references, who are not to be relatives or former employers.

3 Form of Policy

A fidelity policy may be framed on the same general lines as any ordinary policy of insurance, in which case it is unilateral in form, or it may bear a close resemblance to a contract of guarantee, in which case it may be a contract *inter partes*, purporting to be made between the insurers of the first part, the employer of the second part, and the employee of the third part. In this case, the premium is usually paid in the first instance by the employee, and, in the event of his failure to pay it, power is reserved to the employer to do so, in order to prevent a lapse,[1] the insurers being required to give the employer notice of the non-payment by the employee.[2]

The policy may be (i) in respect of one individual, or (ii) a "collective" policy specifying in a schedule the names of all employees in an organization whose fidelity is to be insured with a statement of the amount insured in respect of each; or (iii) a "floating" policy in respect of employees whose fidelity is to be guaranteed, but not stating the amount insured in respect of each.[3]

4 Perils Insured Against

The perils insured against in a fidelity policy may be described in general terms as the acts or defaults of the employee resulting in loss to the employer,[4] or, more definitely, as his fraud or dishonesty,[5] or his want of integrity, honesty, or fidelity.[6] Sometimes they are defined with more precision.

---

[1] As to "lapse" of a policy, see Ivamy, *General Principles of Insurance Law*, 2nd Edn., 1970, pp. 217–218.

[2] See, *e.g. Re Economic Fire Office, Ltd.* (1896), 12 T.L.R. 142, where the form of receipt used contemplated that it would be shown to the employer, and it was held that after giving a receipt on the faith of which the employer continued to employ the employee, the insurers could not rely upon the non-payment of the premium in fact. Cf. *Towle v. National Guardian Assurance Society* (1861), 30 L.J. Ch. 900, C.A., where the receipt was in an unauthorised form.

[3] Persons holding certain offices or engaged in certain employments may be required either by statute or as a matter of administrative practice to give security for the due performance of their duties or obligations. Strictly speaking such security is to be given by bond with securities. But in practice a bond issued by an approved insurance company is accepted by the authorities concerned. Thus, there are (a) Government Bonds, e.g. (i) bankruptcy bonds given to the Department of Trade and Industry by trustees in bankruptcy; (ii) deeds of arrangement bonds given to the Senior Registrar in Bankruptcy; (iii) bonds given to the Department of Trade and Industry by liquidators of companies; and (b) Court Bonds, e.g. (i) administration bonds given to the High Court of Justice by a deceased's administrator; (ii) Court of Protection bonds; and (iii) Chancery Guarantees given to the Chancery Division of the High Court of Justice by a receiver or manager appointed by that Division. A discussion of Government and Court Bonds is outside the scope of this work.

[4] *Walker v. British Guarantee Association* (1852), 21 L.J. Q.B. 257.

[5] *Ravenscroft v. Provident Clerks' and General and Guarantee Association* (1888), 5 T.L.R. 3.

[6] *American Surety Co. of New York v. Wrightson* (1910), 103 L.T. 663, *per* HAMILTON, J., at p. 665.

If the technical terms of the criminal law are alone used to designate the
perils insured against, they are to be given the same meaning as in an indictment,[1] and the employer cannot recover against the insurers unless the specific
crime described in the policy has been committed.[2] A less strict rule of construction is, perhaps, to be applied where the technical terms are combined
with words of a more general nature, in which case the word may be used
in its popular and not in its technical meaning.[3]

5 Exceptions

A fidelity policy frequently contains no express exceptions. Since, however,
by the terms of the policy the insurers are only liable if the act or default
causing the loss is connected with the employee's employment or duties
as specified in the policy, it follows that any act or default committed outside
such employment or in the performance of different duties does not fall
within the scope of the policy.[4]

If, however, the act or default is covered by the policy, it is immaterial that
the employer[5] or person employed for the purpose failed[6] to exercise proper
supervision over the employee.

The policy may, however, provide that the omission or neglect to observe
the precautions specified in the policy shall relieve the insurers from liability.[7]
Moreover, if the policy covers acts or defaults which are not criminal, there
may be an express exception applying to acts or defaults committed in
obedience to superior orders.[8]

6 Alteration of Risk

A fidelity policy is not intended to protect the employer against any loss
attributable to the conduct of the employee named in the policy. The
protection only exists whilst the employee is employed in the specified
capacity or engaged in the specified duties. If, therefore, after the commencement of the risk, he is employed in a different capacity or required to perform

---

[1] *Debenhams, Ltd.* v. *Excess Insurance Co., Ltd.* (1912), 28 T.L.R. 505, *per* HAMILTON, J., at
p. 505: "The term 'embezzlement' in this policy meant the same thing as it meant in an
indictment. There was no reason for giving it any less strict meaning in the policy by
which the plaintiffs were insured than if a direct charge was being made."

[2] *Debenhams, Ltd.* v. *Excess Insurance Co., Ltd.* (*supra*), where the jury disagreed. The fact
that the employee has already been acquitted on the criminal charge does not debar the
employer from recovering: *Protestant Board of School Commissioners* v. *Guarantee Co. of North
America* (1887), 31 L.C.J. 254. Cf. *London Guarantie Co.* v. *Fearnley* (1880), 5 App. Cas. 911,
per Lord SELBORNE, L.C., at p. 921.

[3] *London Guarantee and Accident Co.* v. *Hochelaga Bank* (1893), 3 Que. Q.B. 25, where the
misappropriation was carried out, partly by substituting notes of a lower denomination
for notes of a higher denomination after they had been signed by the employee and brought
back to the bank, and partly by procuring cheques to be certified by the bank, the employee
having no account there. But see *London Guarantee Co.* v. *Fearnley* (*supra*), where the same
words were used and it was assumed that the policy covered only loss by embezzlement
(see *ibid.*, *per* Lord BLACKBURN, at p. 916).

[4] See p. 289, *post*.

[5] *London Guarantee and Accident Co.* v. *Hochelaga Bank* (1893), 3 Que. Q.B. 25, where the cashier
of a bank was allowed to take bundles of notes home for the purpose of signing them on
behalf of the bank.

[6] *Dougharty* v. *London Guarantee and Accident Co., Ltd.* (1880), 6 V.L.R. 376, where the instructions of the employer were disregarded.

[7] See p. 289, *post*.

[8] *Crown Bank* v. *London Guarantee and Accident Co.* (1908), 17 O.L.R. 95.

different duties, there is an alteration in the identity of the risk and the policy ceases to apply.[1]

On the other hand, an alteration of circumstances not affecting the identity of the risk, such as, for instance, a mere change of routine or the abandonment of the precautions and checks previously used, does not, unless prohibited by a condition of the policy, preclude the employer from recovering, even though the loss is facilitated by the alteration.[2]

A statement in the proposal as to the routine proposed to be followed, or the precautions and checks proposed to be used, is a mere representation of intention and does not prohibit the employer from altering them.[3] For this purpose there must be a condition of the policy clearly prohibiting alteration.[4]

In practice, the policy usually contains conditions prohibiting certain kinds of alterations and avoiding the policy if any such alteration is made.[5] The conditions in use relate to the following matters:

a the contract of employment;

b the methods of business;

c other securities; and

d the conduct of the employee.

a Contract of Employment

The conditions of the employee's employment as described in the proposal must remain unchanged.[6] His duties or responsibilities must not be increased or varied in any material particular.[7] Any change affecting the remuneration is usually prohibited, except an increase of salary.[8]

---

[1] *Wembley Urban District Council* v. *Poor Law and Local Government Officers' Mutal Guarantee Association, Ltd.* (1901), 17 T.L.R. 516; *Hay* v. *Employers' Liability Assurance Corporation* (1905), 6 O.W.R. 459; *Cosford Union* v. *Poor Law and Local Government Officers' Mutual Guarantee Association* (1910), 103 L.T. 463.

[2] *Benham* v. *United Guarantee and Life Assurance Co.* (1852), 7 Exch. 744, where it was held to be immaterial that the alteration of circumstances was brought about by the negligence of the employer; *R.* v. *National Insurance Co.* (1887), 13 V.L.R. 914. But see *Globe Savings and Loan Co.* v. *Employers' Liability Assurance Corporation* (1901), 13 Man. L.R. 531.

[3] *Benham* v. *United Guarantee and Life Assurance Co.* (*supra*), distinguished in *Towle* v. *National Guardian Assurance Society* (1861), 30 L.J.Ch. 900, C.A.

[4] A statement of intention which is, to a material extent, departed from, especially when coupled with untrue statements as to the past, may be construed as a misrepresentation of fact falling within a condition avoiding the policy in the event of misrepresentation: *Towle* v. *National Guardian Assurance Society* (*supra*). Cf. *Elgin Loan and Savings Co.* v. *London Guarantee and Accident Co.* (1906), 11 O.L.R. 330. See further, Ivamy, *General Principles of Insurance Law*, 2nd Edn., 1970, p. 124.

[5] *American Surety Co. of New York* v. *Wrightson* (1910), 103 L.T. 663.

[6] *Hay* v. *Employers' Liability Assurance Corporation* (*supra*). In the case of a partnership a condition requiring notice of any default does not require notice to be given of dissolution of partnership: *Catholic School Commission of Montreal* v. *Provident Accident Co.* (1913), 44 Q. S.C. 97.

[7] *Wembley Urban Council* v. *Poor Law and Local Government Officers' Mutual Guarantee Association, Ltd. supra*, where a clerk was subsequently entrusted with the duty of paying the employees of the council, and the loss arose from his failure to account. Cf. *Cosford Union* v. *Poor Law etc. Officers' Mutual Guarantee Association, Ltd.*, *supra*, where an assistant overseer, acting also as parish clerk, was guilty of defalcations in his capacity of parish clerk.

[8] Cf. *North Western Rail Co.* v. *Whinray* (1854), 10 Exch. 77 (guarantee), where a surety was held to be discharged by the substitution of payment by commission for a salary, though the commission earned exceeded the previous salary.

b   *Methods of Business*

The employer must continue to conduct his business in the manner described in the proposal. He must take the specified precautions and check the employee's accounts according to the specified methods.[1] The policy is equally avoided whether he adopts a new and less efficient methods of checking accounts,[2] or whether he merely fails to exercise proper supervision over the employee.[3]

c   *Other Securities*

The employer may be prohibited from releasing or varying without the consent of the insurers any guarantees or securities held by him which cover the loss insured against.

d   *Conduct of the Employee*

If the employee is found to be dishonest, the employer should not continue to employ him.[4] Sometimes the employer is required to notify the insurers if he has reasonable cause for suspecting the employee's honesty, or if the employee has been guilty of any improper conduct.[5]

7   Loss

To constitute a loss within the meaning of a fidelity policy, the employer[6]

---

[1] *Towle* v. *National Guardian Assurance Society* (*supra*); *Haworth & Co.* v. *Sickness and Accident Assurance Association, Ltd.* 1891, 18 R. (Ct. of Sess.) 563; *Elgin Loan and Savings Co.* v. *London Guarantee and Accident Co.* (1906), 11 O.L.R. 330; *Globe Savings and Loan Co.* v. *Employers' Liability Assurance Corporation*) 1901), 13 Man. L.R. 531; *Annprior Corporation* v. *United States Fidelity Co.* (1916), 51 S.C.R. 94; *St. Edouard School Commissioners* v. *Employers' Liability Assurance Corporation* (1907), 16 Que. K.B. 402, where it was held that the employer's duty extended to seeing that the employee duly conformed to any legal requirement as to the keeping or audit of his accounts. An act substantially amounting to a breach of the condition is sufficient: *Macdonald* v. *London Guarantee and Accident Insurance Co.* (1911), 19 O.W.R. 807, where the policy provided that the clerk should not be empowered to draw cheques, and his employer entrusted him with cheques signed in blank. In the absence of an express condition, it is a question of construction whether a statement as to methods of business is contractual or not.

[2] *Towle* v. *National Guardian Assurance Society* (1861), 30 L.J.Ch. 900, C.A.; *Haworth* v. *Sickness and Accident Assurance Association, Ltd.* (1891), 18 R. (Ct. of Sess.) 563.

[3] *Montreal Harbour Commissioners* v. *Guarantee Co. of North America* (1893), 22 S.C.R. 542; *St. Edouard School Commissioners* v. *Employers' Liability Assurance Corporation, supra.* But if the employer gives proper instructions, which his subordinates fail to carry out, the loss is within the policy, being caused, not by any breach of the condition on the part of the employer, but by the negligence of the employee employed to carry them out: *Dougharty* v. *London Guarantee and Accident Co., Ltd.* (1880), 6 V.L.R. 376. Cf. *Crown Bank* v. *London Guarantee and Accident Co.* (1908), 17 O.L.R. 95, where the policy expressly covered disobedience to instructions.

[4] Compare *Snaddon* v. *London, Edinburgh and Glasgow Assurance Co.* 1902, 5 F. (Ct. of Sess.) 182; and contrast *Byrne* v. *Muzio* (1881), 8 L.R. Ir. 396, where the insured had no power to dismiss, but only suspend the defaulting rate collector.

[5] *Montreal Harbour Commissioners* v. *Guarantee Co. of North America* (*supra*), where the condition required immediate notice, and notice a week after discovery of the employee's defalcations was held too late; *Globe Savings and Loan Co.* v. *Employers' Liability Assurance Co.* (*supra*), where there was a waiver. A condition requiring notice if liability is incurred, does not apply to a case of mere suspicion, however well founded; the employer is entitled to wait until he has ascertained that the employee has in fact incurred criminal liability: *Ward* v. *Law Property Assurance and Trust Society* (1856), 4 W.R. 605; *Quebec Fire Insurance Co.* v. *La Prévoyance* (1916), 50 Que. C. 300, where it was held that the employer was entitled to give the employee an opportunity of furnishing accounts.

[6] Where the same person is in the employment at the same time of two different employers, a policy effected on behalf of one employer does not necessarily cover a loss sustained by the other employer: *Cosford Union* v. *Poor Law etc. Officers' Mutual Guarantee Association, Ltd.* (1910), 103 L.T. 463, *per* PHILLIMORE, J., at p. 465.

must have sustained an actual pecuniary loss during the period of insurance.[1]

The loss is sustained when the act of causing it is committed, not when the loss is discovered.[2] The insurers are not liable, therefore, where the act is committed before the policy comes into force, even though the loss is only discovered during its currency.[3]

On the other hand, the fact that the loss is not discovered until after the policy has expired does not take away the liability of the insurers, if the act causing it was committed during the period of insurance.[4]

The policy may, however, provide that the loss must be discovered within a specified period after the expiration of the policy or the determination of the employee's employment, or even that it must be discovered during the currency of the policy, in which case the insurers are not liable if the loss is not discovered until after the lapse of the policy.[5]

8 Matters arising after Loss

The rights and duties of the parties after loss are for the most part the same and subject to the same rules as under any other contract of insurance of the same class. The principal points to be noted are the following:

   a the claim;

   b proof of loss;

   c the amount recoverable;

   d payment of the loss;

   e prosecution of the employee.

a *The Claim*[6]

The employer is by the terms of the policy usually allowed to make one claim only in respect of a particular employee.[7] If he chooses to continue to employ the employee after discovering his dishonesty, he must do so at his own risk.

---

[1] *Allis-Chalmers Co.* v. *Maryland Fidelity and Deposit Co.* (1916), 114 L.T. 433, H.L., where the loss took place before the contract was concluded.

[2] *New Zealand University* v. *Standard Fire and Marine Insurance Co.*, [1916] N.Z.L.R. 509, where the policy covered losses incurred within twelve months prior to notice of claim, and it was held that time ran from the date of the embezzlement by which the assets of the insured were diminished, and not from the date of later fraudulent acts committed for the purpose of concealment. But the policy may in express terms cover losses discovered within the period of insurance: *Pennsylvania Co. for Insurances on Lives and Granting Annuities* v. *Mumford*, [1920] 2 K.B. 537, C.A. where the policy, issued in 1916, covered all losses which the insured, during its currency, might discover that they had sustained since 1909.

[3] *Banque Nationale* v. *Lesperance* (1881), 4 L.N. 147, where the defalcations extended over a period of years, and it was held that the insurers were liable only for the amount actually misappropriated whilst the policy was in force. Cf. *Pennsylvania Co. for Insurances on Lives and Granting Annuities* v. *Mumford (supra)*; *London Guarantee and Accident Co.* v. *Cornish* (1905), 17 Man. L.R. 148, where a former policy had been cancelled and replaced by the current policy; *Allis-Chalmers Co.* v. *Maryland Fidelity and Deposit Co. (supra)*. The policy may further stipulate that the insurers are not to be liable for any loss sustained before the policy has been in force for a specified period. See *Solvency Mutual Guarantee Co.* v. *Froane* (1861), 7 H. & N. 5.

[4] *Ward* v. *Law Property Assurance and Trust Society* (1856), 4 W.R. 605.

[5] *Fanning* v. *London Guarantee and Accident Co.* (1884), 10 V.L.R. 8; *Commercial Mutual Building Society* v. *London Guarantee and Accident Co.* (1891), M.L.R. 7 Q.B. 307.

[6] See further Ivamy, *General Principles of Insurance Law*, 2nd Edn., 1970, pp. 348–363.

[7] *I.e.* in respect of the same employee. The position is different where the insurance is in respect of the staff generally.

The employer may be required to state in the claim whether there have been any previous irregularities.

b   *Proofs of Loss*[1]

Where the accounts of the employee are subject to audit by a public official, as may be the case where he is the employee of a local authority, the policy may provide that no further proof of the loss is to be required than the certificate of the auditor as to the amount of the loss, and that, for the purpose of fixing the amount recoverable, such certificate is to be final.[2]

c   *Amount Recoverable*

In estimating the amount to be paid by the insurers any salary or commission, which, but for his dishonesty, would have been payable to the employee, and any money belonging to the employee in the hands of the employer, must be deducted. If the amount of the loss exceeds the sum insured, the deduction is made from the amount of the loss and the insurers are liable for the balance up to the full sum insured.[3]

All other securities or guarantees held by the employer may have to be taken into account.[4]

By the terms of the policy, the liability of the insurers may be limited to a rateable proportion of the loss[5] in which case the loss must be apportioned in the first instance amongst the different securities, including the policy, and the employer cannot claim from the insurers more than the amount for which they are liable as co-securities or co-insurers, according to the nature of the other securities; or the insurers may be liable only for such portion of the loss as cannot be recovered from the other securities, in which case no claim arises under the policy unless the other securities have first made default, and then only to the extent of the deficiency.

Unless, however, the policy provides to the contrary, the insurers are liable in the first instance for the whole of the loss, upon payment of which they become entitled, according to circumstances, either to apportion the loss amongst the various co-securities and, as co-sureties or co-insurers, to claim contribution,[6] or to enforce by subrogation the rights of the employer against any prior securities.[7]

d   *Payment of the loss*[8]

Since the object of the insurance is the protection of the employer, the policy, even where it is effected by the employee, provides for payment

---

[1] See further Ivamy, *ibid.*, pp. 357–360.

[2] The certificate is, therefore, proof of the capacity in which the servant received the money: *Cosford Union* v. *Poor Law, etc. Officers' Mutual Guarantee Association, Ltd.* (1910), 103 L.T. 463, *per* PHILLIMORE, L.J., at p. 465.

[3] *Fifth Liverpool Starr-Bowkett Building Society* v. *Travellers Accident Insurance Co., Ltd.* (1893), 9 T.L.R. 221. But see *Board of Trade* v. *Guarantee Society* (1896), [1910] 1 K.B. 408 n. (guarantee). The same principle applies to sums recovered from the employee (*London Guarantee and Accident Co.* v. *Hochelata Bank* (1893), 3 Que.Q.B. 25).

[4] The employer may be required to state in his claim what securities he holds.

[5] As to such a limitation on the amount recoverable see Ivamy, *ibid.*, pp. 381–383.

[6] *American Surety Co. of New York* v. *Wrightson* (1910), 103 L.T. 663. As to "contribution", see further Ivamy, *ibid.*, pp. 437–457.

[7] *Employers' Liability Assurance Corporation* v. *Skipper and East* (1887), 4 T.L.R. 55. As to "subrogation", see Ivamy, *ibid.*, pp. 415–430.

[8] See further, Ivamy, *ibid.*, pp. 378–393.

to the employer. Sometimes there is an express stipulation that his receipt is to be a sufficient discharge to the insurers.

e *Prosecution of Employee*

It may be made a condition precedent to the liability of the insurers[1] that the employer must, if required by the insurers, prosecute the employee for the fraud or dishonesty giving rise to the claim.[2]

The insurers usually bind themselves to pay the costs of the employer, if the prosecution results in a conviction.[3] If the prosecution proves unsuccessful,[4] or, where the policy contains no appropriate stipulation, even if the prosecution proves successful, the employer cannot, it is submitted, recover the costs of the prosecution as falling within the scope of the policy.[5] If, however, in consequence of the proceedings, he recovers a portion of the property misappropriated, he is entitled to deduct his costs from the amount so recovered, and to credit the insurers with the balance only in diminution of the amount payable under the policy.[6]

---

[1] This must be distinguished from a stipulation requiring the employer to assist the insurers in any proceedings taken to obtain reimbursment from his employee; such a stipulation, the performance of which is postponed till after payment, is not a condition precedent to liability: *London Guarantie Co.* v. *Fearnley* (1880), 5 App. Cas. 911, *per* Lord, BLACKBURN at p. 916.

[2] *Ibid., Canada Life Assurance Co.* v. *London Guarantee and Accident Co.* (1900), 9 Que.Q.B. 183. Such a condition does not, where the employee absconds and is arrested outside the jurisdiction, require the employers to bear the expense of bringing him back: *Dougharty* v. *London Guarantee and Accident Co., Ltd.* (1880), 6 V.L.R. 376.

[3] *London Guarantie Co.* v. *Fearnley* (*supra*).

[4] For a case in which payment was made upon the express terms that the insured should supply the necessary proof for the then pending prosecution of the employee, and that, if such proofs were not supplied, the money should be repaid, see *La Prevoyance* v. *La Caisse Nationale d'Economie* (1921), 59 Que.S.C. 161, where it was held that the insurers were not entitled to claim repayment merely because the proofs supplied failed to secure the employee's conviction.

[5] See *Re Law Guarantee Trust and Accident Society, Ltd.* (1913), 108 L.T. 830, *per* NEVILLE, J., at p. 832; and cf. *Cunard Steamship Co., Ltd.* v. *Marten*, [1903] 2 K.B. 511, C.A. (marine insurance), where the printed "suing and labouring" clause was rejected as inapplicable to the particular insurance. But if the insurers have the right to require, and do require, the employers to prosecute, it is their duty to reimburse him: *Globe Savings and Loan Co.* v. *Employers' Liability Assurance Corporation* (1901), 13 Man. L.R. 531. Cf. *Hoole Urban District Council* v. *Fidelity and Deposit Co. of Maryland*, [1916] 1 K.B. 25 (affirmed on other grounds, [1916] 2 K.B. 568, C.A.), where a policy covering the due performance of a contract by the contractor was held not to cover the costs of an action brought against the contractor, which the contractor had been ordered to pay, there being no express or implied request from the insurers.

[6] See *Hatch, Mansfield & Co., Ltd.* v. *Weingott* (1906), 22 T.L.R. 366 (guarantee), where it was held to have been reasonable, in the circumstances, to prosecute, followed in *Crown Bank* v. *London Guarantee and Accident Co.*, (1908), 17 O.L.R. 95.

37

SOLVENCY INSURANCE

Special features relating to solvency insurance may be classified as follows:

1 The subject-matter of insurance.
2 Circumstances affecting the risk.
3 The premium.
4 The form of the policy.
5 The perils insured against.
6 Exceptions.
7 Alteration of the risk.
8 What constitutes a loss.
9 The amount recoverable.
10 Contribution between securities.

1 Subject-matter of Insurance

The subject-matter of solvency insurance is also money. The insurance may be:

> *i* a general insurance of all debts due or to become due from a particular person or class of persons, in which case a general description is sufficient[1]; or
>
> *ii* an insurance upon a specific debt, in which case the debt must be specifically described.

Any kind of debt may be insured, e.g., an ordinary loan,[2] the discounting of acceptances,[3] a loan secured by a mortgage[4] or a debenture[5], a deposit at a bank,[6] or a sum payable under a hire-purchase agreement.[7]

---

[1] Such as, e.g. "loss or damage in respect of goods sold": *Solvency Mutual Guarantee Co.* v. *York* (1858), 3 H. & N. 588; *Solvency Mutual Guarantee Co.* v. *Froane* (1861), 7 H. & N. 5.
[2] *Parr's Bank* v. *Albert Mines Syndicate* (1900), 5 Com. Cas. 116.
[3] *Anglo-Californian Bank, Ltd.* v. *London and Provincial Marine and General Insurance Co., Ltd.* (1904), 10 Com. Cas. 1.
[4] *Re Birkbeck Permanent Benefit Building Society, Official Receiver* v. *Licenses Insurance Corporation*, [1913] 2 Ch. 34; *Re Law Guarantee Trust and Accident Society, Ltd.* (1913), 108 L.T. 830.
[5] *Shaw* v. *Royce, Ltd.*, [1911] 1 Ch. 138; *Finlay* v. *Mexican Investment Corporation*, [1897] 1 Q.B. 517; *Re Law Guarantee Trust and Accident Society, Ltd., Liverpool Mortgage Insurance Co.'s Case*, [1914] 2 Ch. 617, C.A.
[6] *Young* v. *Assets and Investment Insurance Co.'s Trustee* (1893), 21 R. (Ct. of Sess.) 222; *Laird* v. *Securities Insurance Co., Ltd.* 1895, 22 R. (Ct. of Sess.) 452; *Dane* v. *Mortgage Insurance Corporation*, [1894] 1 Q.B. 45, C.A.; *Murdock* v. *Heath* (1899), 80 L.T. 50; *Waterkeyn* v. *Eagle Star and British Dominions Insurance Co. Ltd.* (1920), 5 Ll.L. Rep. 42.
[7] *Constructive Finance Co., Ltd.* v. *English Insurance Co., Ltd.* (1924), 19 Ll.L. Rep. 144, H.L. Cf. *Blakey* v. *Pendlebury (Trustees of Property)*, [1931] 2 Ch. 255, C.A.

Even a contingent liability arising on the default of the principal debtor, e.g., the liability of a surety to pay the debt guaranteed,[1] or on the default of other insurers to pay the amount of the loss,[2] may be the subject-matter of insurance.

2 Circumstances Affecting the Risk

The principal matters affecting the risk in the case of solvency insurance are:

   a the nature of the debt; and

   b the possibility of loss.

a *Nature of the Debt*

The proposed insured is required in the proposal form to give full particulars of the debt or debts proposed to be insured, including the name, address and occupation of the debtor.

If the debt proposed to be insured is to be insured as a secured debt, he is usually required to describe the nature of the security in detail. Thus, in the case of a mortgage debt, he may be required to give particulars of the mortgage deed, including a statement as to the tenure of the property subject to the mortgage, and, if the property is leasehold, particulars of the lease under which it is held. The property itself must also be described in detail.

b *Possibility of Loss*

As the risk of loss depends entirely upon the solvency of the debtor, there is a breach of good faith on the part of the proposed insured to effect an insurance at a time when he knows or suspects the debtor to be insolvent, unless he discloses to the insurers his knowledge or suspicions, or unless the insurers are themselves acquainted with the facts[3] or put on inquiry. Specific questions are usually asked in the proposal form as to the solvency of the debtor.[4]

When the debt is insured as a secured debt, the risk of loss depends upon the sufficiency of the security, and therefore all facts relevant to the security must be disclosed. Specific questions may be asked in the proposal form for the purpose of ascertaining the sufficiency of the security. Thus, in the case of a debt secured by a mortgage, the proposed insured may be required to deal with the following matters:

   i the age and condition of the mortgaged property;

   ii subsisting tenancies of the property;

---

[1] *Seaton* v. *Burnand* (*supra*). Cf. *Hambro* v. *Burnand*, [1904] 2 K.B. 10, C.A., where the policy covered the failure of the drawer to put the acceptor in funds to meet the bill.

[2] *MacVicar* v. *Poland* (1894), 10 T.L.R. 566; *Anglo-Californian Bank, Ltd.* v. *London and Provincial Marine and General Insurance Co., Ltd.* (*supra*).

[3] *Anglo-Californian Bank* v. *London and Provincial Marine and General Insurance Co. Ltd.*, (1904), 10 Com. Cas. 1, where the insurers knew that the debtors were in serious financial embarrassment. For the effect of the actual knowledge of the insurer on the duty to disclose material facts, see Ivamy, *General Principles of Insurance Law*, 2nd Edn., 1970, pp. 104–105.

[4] *Seaton* v. *Burnand*, [1900] A.C. 135, *per* Lord SHAND at p. 147. As to the effect of the insurer's constructive knowledge of material facts on the duty of disclosure, see Ivamy, *ibid.*, p. 206.

iii the valuation of the property for the purposes of the mortgage, and also its rateable value;

iv restrictive covenants affecting the property;

v prior incumbrances on the property;

vi special provisions in the mortgage deed modifying the usual power of sale.

In addition, the proposed insured is usually asked questions relating to the solvency of the mortgagor. In particular, he may be required to state whether the interest on the mortgage has been regularly paid, and, if not, to state the amount of the arrears and how long the interest has been in arrear. He may also be asked to give references as to the mortgagor.

Where the solvency of a surety is insured, all material facts relating to the solvency of the surety must be disclosed.[1] But the rate of interest and the circumstances of the original loan have been held to be not material facts.[2]

3 Premium

Where a specific debt is insured, a lump sum premium is usually paid and the policy remains in force until the day fixed for the repayment.[3]

Sometimes the policy provides for the payment of annual premiums. In this case the policy is still to be regarded as a continuing contract, the annual payments being in the nature of instalments of premium. No question of renewal, therefore, arises, and the insurers cannot refuse to accept an annual premium, when tendered, or determine the insurance before the date fixed for repayment of the debt.[4]

Even a failure to pay an annual premium does not, in the absence of any stipulation in the policy to that effect, produce a lapse[5] and entitle the insurers to repudiate liability.[6] Thus, where the policy is issued by an arrangement between the debtor and the insurers as part of the consideration for the debt, the premiums being payable by the debtor, the non-payment of a particular premium by the debtor does not preclude the creditor from enforcing the policy.[7]

The policy may, however, by an express stipulation, make payment of the annual premiums within the days of grace[8] a condition precedent to

---

[1] In *Seaton* v. *Burnand* (*supra*) questions as to the solvency of the surety were asked and truly answered. In *Anglo-Californian Bank* v. *London and Provincial Marine and General Insurance Co. Ltd.*, (*supra*) the jury found that the solvency of the principal debtors was also a material fact.

[2] *Seaton* v. *Burnand* (*supra*). But see *Anglo-Californian Bank* v. *London and Provincial Marine and General Insurance Co.* (*supra*), where, however, the insurers had knowledge.

[3] *Finlay* v. *Mexican Investment Corporation*, [1897] 1 Q.B. 517, where, in considering the question whether the rights of the insured under the policy were affected by a special resolution postponing the date of payment of the debentures insured, importance was attached to the fact that the policy was to continue only until the original date of payment.

[4] See Ivamy, *General Principles of Insurance Law*, 2nd Edn., 1970, p. 209.

[5] As to the lapse of a policy, see Ivamy, *ibid.*, pp. 217–218.

[6] This is probably the case, in the absence of any stipulation to the contrary, even though the premium is payable by the creditor, since there is no implied condition excusing the insurers in the event of the premium not being paid.

[7] *Shaw* v. *Royce, Ltd.*, [1911] 1 Ch. 138, *per* WARRINGTON, J., at p. 148.

[8] As to the "days of grace", see Ivamy, *ibid.*, pp. 214–216.

liability.[1] If therefore an annual premium is unpaid, the policy lapses and the insurers cease to be liable.[2]

4 Form of Policy

The policy may be framed in the usual form as a unilateral undertaking by the insurers,[3] or it may be a contract framed on the lines of a guarantee. In this case it may not be contained in a separate document, but may be indorsed on the instrument evidencing the debt which is intended to be insured.[4]

5 Perils Insured Against

In the case of solvency insurance the peril insured against may be described as default in making payment[5] in which case the mere non-payment of the debt insured as and when it falls due,[6] or within a specified time afterwards,[7] as the case may be, is sufficient to make the insurers liable, the cause of the non-payment being immaterial.[8]

In some cases, however, non-payment of the debt is not by itself sufficient.[9] The debtor must become actually insolvent.[10] The policy may further provide that the insurers are not to be liable unless the debtor's insolvency is evidenced in one of the following ways:

   i by the making of a receiving order against the debtor, or, in the case of a limited company, of a winding-up order;

  ii by the calling of a meeting of creditors, or, in the case of a limited company, by the passing of a resolution for voluntary winding up;

 iii in the event of the debtor dying before payment, by the making of an order by the Court for the administration of his estate.

---

[1] *Re Law Guarantee Trust and Accident Society, Ltd., Liverpool Mortgage Insurance Co.'s Case,* [1914] 2 Ch. 617. Cf. *Bamberger* v. *Commercial Credit Mutual Assurance Society* (1855), 15 C.B. 676 (solvency insurance).

[2] *Employers' Insurance Co. of Great Britain* v. *Benton* 1897, 24 R. (Ct. of Sess.) 908, where it was held that the fact that the risk had become a certainty long before the time fixed for the payment of the debt insured did not relieve the insured from the obligation to continue payment of the premiums.

[3] *Dane* v. *Mortgage Insurance Corporation,* [1894] 1 Q.B. 54, C.A., *Finlay* v. *Mexican Investment Corporation,* [1897] 1 Q.B. 517; *Seaton* v. *Burnand,* [1900] A.C. 135; *Anglo-Californian Bank* v. *London and Provincial Marine and General Insurance Co. Ltd.,* (1904), 10 Com. Cas. 1.

[4] *Shaw* v. *Royce, Ltd.,* [1911] 1 Ch. 138; *Re Law Guarantee Trust and Accident Society, Ltd., Liverpool Mortgage Insurance Co.'s Case (supra).*

[5] *Dane* v. *Mortgage Insurance Corporation (supra) per* Lord ESHER at p. 61; *Finlay* v. *Mexican Investment Corporation (supra), per* CHARLES, J., at p. 522; *Law Guarantee Trust and Accident Society* v. *Munich Re-Insurance Co.,* [1912] 1 Ch. 138, *per* WARRINGTON, J., at p. 154.

[6] *Young* v. *Assets and Investment Insurance Co.'s Trustee* (1893), 21 R. (Ct. of Sess.) 222; *Anglo-Californian Bank, Ltd.* v. *London and Provincial Marine and General Insurance Co., Ltd. (supra);* *Shaw* v. *Royce, Ltd. (supra).*

[7] *Laird* v. *Securities Insurance Co., Ltd.* 1895, 22 R. (Ct. of Sess.) 452; *Dane* v. *Mortgage Insurance Corporation (supra);* *Finlay* v. *Mexican Investment Corporation (supra).*

[8] *Mortgage Insurance Corporation, Ltd.* v. *Inland Revenue Commissioners* (1887), 57 L.J.Q.B. 174, *per* HAWKINS, J., at p. 181. Hence, there is equally a loss within the policy whether the debtor fails to pay through inability or refuses to pay, although he is solvent, or is prevented from paying by the effect of subsequent legislation; *Laird* v. *Securities Insurance Co., Ltd. (supra), per* Lord MACLAREN at p. 459.

[9] *Seaton* v. *Heath,* [1899] 1 Q.B. 782, C.A., *per* A. L. SMITH, L.J., at p. 789.

[10] *Murdock* v. *Heath* (1899), 80 L.T. 50. The policy may only cover insolvency due to a particular cause. See, e.g. *Waterkeyn* v. *Eagle Star and British Dominions Insurance Co., Ltd.* (1920), 5 Ll.L. Rep. 42, where the policy covered loss arising from the insolvency of a Russian bank directly due to damage or destruction of its premises or contents through riot or civil commotion, and it was held that the policy contemplated insolvency due to damage or destruction of premises or contents, and not insolvency due to inability to carry on business through Bolshevik action.

If the debtor is actually insolvent, it is immaterial that he refused to pay the debt on other grounds and not on the ground of his insolvency.[1]

Occasionally the policy is framed in still more stringent terms. The insurers may undertake liability only for such loss as is caused by the bankruptcy of the debtor or its equivalent, and their liability may be postponed until after the declaration of a final dividend.[2]

6   Exceptions

In the case of a solvency policy, the cause of the non-payment of the debt may as a rule be disregarded.

A mortgage policy may, however, contain an exception providing for a reduction in the amount payable if the security of the mortgage debt proves insufficient by reason of:

i a defect in the title to the property comprised in the mortgage; or

ii damage to the mortgaged property caused by fire or other external cause, e.g. explosion, hurricane, earthquake and invasion.[3]

In these cases the amount payable is to be reduced by the amount of any deficiency attributable to the excepted cause.

7   Alteration of Risk[4]

The policy usually contains an express condition avoiding the policy if time is given to the debtor or any alteration made in the contract modifying the rights and remedies of the creditor without the consent of the insurers.[5]

The making of an alteration which was within the contemplation of the parties at the time when they entered into the contract has, however, no effect on the validity of the policy. Thus, where the insurance covers such deficiency as there may be in a particular security after realisation by the creditor at his discretion, the mode of realisation and the circumstances in which the realisation is to take place are immaterial to the risk, and consequently any alteration or change may be disregarded.[6]

Where in the case of debentures, power is reserved to a general meeting of debenture holders to sanction by special resolution any compromise of the rights of the debenture holders against the company or its property, and the date of payment is, accordingly, by special resolution, postponed, the postponement of payment, does not, so far as the insurers are concerned, bind the insured, unless he actually consents to it. He may, therefore, enforce the policy against the insurers when the original date of payment arrives, if the debenture remains unpaid, and the insurers on payment by them of the

---

[1] *MacVicar* v. *Poland* (1894), 10 T.L.R. 566, where the policy insured the solvency of other insurers.

[2] *Murdoch* v. *Heath* (1899), 80 L.T. 50. A final dividend has been declared within the meaning of the policy when, by reason of a reconstruction, no further dividends in the liquidation can be declared: *ibid., per* BIGHAM, J., at p. 51.

[3] See further, Ivamy, *Fire and Motor Insurance*, 2nd Edn., 1973, pp. 82–85.

[4] See further, Ivamy, *General Principles of Insurance Law*, 2nd Edn., 1970, pp. 258–271.

[5] *Finlay* v. *Mexican Investment Corporation*, [1897] 1 Q.B. 517.

[6] *Law Guarantee Trust and Accident Society* v. *Munich Re-Insurance Co.*, [1912] 1 Ch. 138, *per* WARRINGTON, J., at pp. 154, 156.

insured sum are subrogated[1] to his rights as modified by the special resolution.[2]

The same principle applies where the company makes a scheme of arrangement which is binding on its creditors by statute.[3]

If, however, by special resolution of the debenture holders the insurers are released from their liability and fresh debentures which are not insured are substituted for the insured debentures, the holder loses his rights against the insurers, irrespective of whether he consents or not. He is bound to accept the fresh debentures, and any loss which takes place will be a loss under the fresh debentures, which are not insured by the policy.[4]

In the case of mortgage insurance the policy may be avoided under a special condition if the insured sells or concurs in selling the mortgaged property for less than the sum insured without the consent of the insurers,[5] or if any part of the mortgaged property ceases to be subject to the mortgage by reason of the exercise of any power of re-entry or forfeiture.

A policy insuring against trade debts may contain a condition avoiding the policy in the event of a creditor dying or retiring from business. Where, therefore, such a policy is issued to a partnership, the death of one of the partners or his retirement from the firm determines the policy, except as regards debts already in existence.[6]

8 Loss

There is a loss under a solvency policy when the debt insured is not paid on or before the date specified in the policy,[7] which may be later than the date when the debt falls due,[8] or if the non-payment must be attributable to a particular cause, when the cause comes into operation.[9]

9 Amount Recoverable

As a general rule the creditor is not bound to attempt to obtain payment

---

[1] As to "subrogation", see Ivamy, *General Principles of Insurance Law*, 2nd Edn., 1970, pp. 415–430.

[2] *Finlay* v. *Mexican Investment Corporation (supra), per* CHARLES, J., at p. 522: "The contract appears to me to be really one of insurance against a particular event, namely, the default by the Capitol Company to pay the plaintiff the amount of his debenture on November 4, 1895. That event has happened, and the defendants must therefore pay, and cannot rely upon the terms of the special resolution postponing the date of payment as exonerating them from liability. The contract, however, being one of indemnity, they are entitled on payment to be subrogated to the plaintiff's rights as modified by the special resolution if it be valid."

[3] *Dane* v. *Mortgage Insurance Corporation*, [1894] 1 Q.B. 54, C.A.; *Laird* v. *Securities Insurance Co., Ltd.* 1895, 22 R. (Ct. of Sess.) 452, where it was pointed out that the alteration of the debtor's obligation was one of the risks insured against.

[4] *Shaw* v. *Royce, Ltd.*, [1911] 1 Ch. 138. Cf. *Nepean* v. *Marten* (1895), 11 T.L.R. 480, C.A.

[5] *Re Law Guarantee Trust and Accident Society, Ltd.* (1913), 108 L.T. 830, *per* NEVILLE, J., at p. 832. A condition of this kind must be distinguished from a condition against assigning the mortgage debt. See *Re Birkbeck Permanent Benefit Building Society, Official Receiver* v. *Licenses Insurance Corporation*, [1913] 2 Ch. 34.

[6] *Solvency Mutual Guarantee Co.* v. *Freeman* (1861), 7 H. & N. 17, where it was held that the remaining partner was not liable for premiums which had been claimed by the insurers on the assumption that the policy was still in force.,

[7] *Dane* v. *Mortgage Insurance Corporation*, [1894] 1 Q.B. 54, C.A., *per* Lord ESHER, M.R., at p. 61.

[8] *Finlay* v. *Mexican Investment Corporation*, [1897] 1 Q.B. 517.

[9] *Waterkeyn* v. *Eagle Star and British Dominions Insurance Co.* (1920), 5 Ll.L. Rep. 42 where the particular cause, i.e. destruction of the premises through riot or civil commotion, etc., never came into operation.

from the debtor before calling upon the insurers to make good the loss. As soon as there is a default within the meaning of the policy,[1] he is entitled to claim payment of the whole amount insured from the insurers.[2]

On payment, the insurers are subrogated to the rights of the creditor against the debtor,[3] and, if the creditor afterwards obtains anything by way of salvage from the debtor, he must account for it to the insurers.[4]

The fact that the debt is secured, or insured elsewhere, does not, apart from any special provision in the policy, preclude the creditor from claiming the whole amount, or compel him to have recourse first to the securities or other insurances. If, however, payment in full is made under the policy, the insurers are entitled, according to circumstances, either to enforce the creditor's rights against the securities or other insurances by subrogation, or to claim contribution in their own right. Further, the policy may contain a stipulation that upon a claim being made, the insurers may require the creditor to transfer to them the insured debt or security, together with all his rights in respect thereof,[5] in which case it is sufficient if the creditor transfers such rights as he has.[6]

The right of the creditor to claim payment in full from the insurers may be restricted by the terms of the policy;[7] and the insurers may only be liable for the deficiency remaining after the creditor has exhausted his remedies against the debtor,[8] or, where the debt is secured, against the securities held

---

[1] As to "default", see p. 297, *ante*.

[2] *Laird* v. *Securities Insurance Co., Ltd., supra*; *Dane* v. *Mortgage Insurance Corporation*, [1894] 1 Q.B. 54, C.A., *per* Lord ESHER, M.R., at p. 61. Hence, unless the policy so provides, the creditor is not entitled to add any costs incurred, such as mortgagee's costs, to the amount recoverable under the policy: *Re Law Guarantee Trust and Accident Society, Ltd.* (1913), 108 L.T. 130. The writ may be specially indorsed and proceedings for judgment taken under R.S.C., Ord. 14; see *Dane* v. *Mortgage Insurance Corporation*, [1894] 1 Q.B. 54, C.A.; *Harrison* v. *Mortgage Insurance Corporation* (1893), 10 T.L.R. 141.

[3] *Laird* v. *Securities Insurance Co., Ltd. (supra)*; *Dane* v. *Mortgage Insurance Corporation (supra) per* Lord ESHER, M.R., at p. 61; *Finlay* v. *Mexican Investment Corporation*, [1897] 1 Q.B. 517; *per* CHARLES, J., at p. 522; *Parr's Bank* v. *Albert Mines Syndicate* (1900), 5 Com. Cas. 116.

[4] *Dane* v. *Mortgage Insurance Corporation (supra), per* Lord ESHER, M.R., at p. 61; "For instance, in the present case, if the bank had not failed, but had remained in perfect credit, and it had on some untenable ground refused to pay the plaintiff at the time when, according to the deposit note, payment was due, the plaintiff would not be bound first to sue the bank; the policy is made for the very purpose among others of preserving her from that necessity; she would be entitled to receive payment from the defendants, the insurers; but then, if, after they had paid her, the bank, discovering their mistake, were to pay her the amount of the deposit, she would be bound to account for it to the defendants, or on the other hand, if the bank still refused to pay, she would be bound to allow the defendants to sue in her name." See also *Murdock* v. *Heath* (1899), 80 L.T. 50, *per* BIGHAM, J., at p. 51. As to "subrogation", see further, Ivamy, *General Principles of Insurance Law*, 2nd Edn., 1970, pp. 415–430.

[5] *Re Law Guarantee Trust and Accident Society, Ltd.* (1913), 108 L.T. 830, *per* NEVILLE, J., at p. 832.

[6] *Laird* v. *Securities Insurance Co.* 1895, 22 R. (Ct. of Sess.) 452.

[7] *Re Law Guarantee Trust and Accident Society, Ltd., Liverpool Mortgage Insurance Co.'s Case*, [1914] 2 Ch. 617, C.A., *per* BUCKLEY, L.J., at p. 630, distinguishing *Dane* v. *Mortgage Insurance Corporation (supra)*.

[8] *Murdock* v. *Heath (supra)*, where the policy provided for payment of the debt insured, "less any portion previously received from the bank when the final dividend in bankruptcy or liquidation is declared"; *Re Law Guarantee Trust and Accident Society, Ltd., Liverpool Mortgage Insurance Co.'s Case (supra)*, where in certain events, the liability of the insurers was only to pay the differential sum left undischarged by the distribution of the proceeds of sale of the mortgaged properties.

by him,[1] or in the case of double insurance, for their rateable proportion of the loss.[2]

The creditor has no claim against the proceeds of a reinsurance policy effected by the insurers.[3]

10 Contribution between Securities

Where the debt insured by the policy is also secured or insured elsewhere, the existence of the securities or other insurances and the fact that the creditor has become entitled to enforce them, cannot be disregarded. The debt which is the subject-matter of insurance under the policy, is at the same time the subject-matter of the securities or other insurances. The securities or other insurances are intended to operate as co-securities with the policy, seeing that they relate to the same debt, and any loss must be apportioned between them. Except where the policy provides otherwise, the insurers are not entitled, as against the creditor, to insist upon the loss being apportioned before they have paid him, but, by the fact of payment, they acquire the right to claim contribution from their co-securities.[4]

In so far as the co-securities are not policies of insurance, the loss is apportioned in accordance with the rules of contribution applicable to contracts of guarantee, namely, in proportion to the respective amounts for which each has undertaken to be liable.[5]

If the co-securities are policies of insurance, the rules of contribution applicable to policies of insurance[6] govern the apportionment, and the loss is apportioned between them in proportion to the respective amounts for which, in the circumstances, each is independently liable.[7]

The position is different where the other securities or insurances are intended to be primarily liable for the loss. There is then no common subject-matter. The subject-matter of insurance under the policy is not the debt which is the subject-matter of the other securities or insurances, namely, the debt due from the principal debtor, but a different debt, namely, the debt as secured or insured.[8]

---

[1] Cf. *MacVicar* v. *Poland* (1894), 10 T.L.R. 566; *Anglo-Californian Bank, Ltd.* v. *London and Provincial Marine and General Insurance Co., Ltd.* (1904), 10 Com. Cas. 1.

[2] As to the right of "contribution" and "double insurance", see Ivamy, *General Principles of Insurance Law*, 2nd Edn., 1970, pp. 437–457.

[3] *Re Law Guarantee Trust and Accident Society, Ltd., Godson's Claim*, [1915] 1 Ch. 340.

[4] *Anglo-Californian Bank, Ltd.* v. *London and Provincial Marine and General Insurance Co., Ltd.* (1904), 10 Com. Cas. 1.

[5] *Pendlebury* v. *Walker* (1841), 4 Y. & C. Ex. 424 (guarantee), *per* ALDERSON, B., at p. 441: "Where the same default of the principal renders all the co-securities responsible, all are to contribute and the law superadds that which is not only the principle, but the equitable mode of applying the principle, that they should all contribute equally, if each is a surety to an equal amount; and if not equally, then proportionately to the amount for which each is a surety". See also *Deering* v. *Winchelsea (Earl)* (1787), 2 Bos. & P. 270 (guarantee), *per* EYRE, C.B., at p. 273; *Ellesmere Brewery Co.* v. *Cooper*, [1896] 1 Q.B. 75 (guarantee), *per* Lord RUSSELL OF KILLOWEN, C.J., at p. 81.

[6] See Ivamy, *General Principles of Insurance Law*, 2nd Edn., 1970, pp. 437–457.

[7] *American Surety Co. of New York* v. *Wrightson* (1910), 103 L.T. 663.

[8] *Seaton* v. *Burnand*, [1900] A.C. 135, *per* Lord MORRIS, at p. 143; *Parr's Bank* v. *Albert Mines Syndicate* (1900), 5 Com. Cas. 116, *per* MATHEW, J., at p. 119; *Mortgage Insurance Corporation, Ltd.* v. *Pound* (1895), 65 L.J.Q.B. 129, H.L., where certain persons had agreed to repay to the insurers all sums paid under the policy, and it was held that sums paid by the insurers under a scheme of arrangement were not paid under the policy, and therefore did not fall within the agreement.

Thus, in the case of a policy against the insolvency of sureties,[1] or other insurers,[2] the non-payment of the original debt, though entitling the creditor to call upon the sureties or other insurers, does not give rise to any claim under the policy. The creditor cannot enforce the policy unless the sureties or other insurers have in their turn made default.

The sureties or other insurers are not, therefore, co-sureties or co-insurers with the insurers under the policy, and no case of contribution arises. On the contrary, the insurers succeed by subrogation to the rights of the creditor against the sureties or other insurers who are, therefore, liable to the insurers for the full amount for which, under their respective contracts, they are liable to the creditor.[3]

---

[1] *Seaton* v. *Burnand* (*supra*); *Parr's Bank* v. *Albert Mines Syndicate* (*supra*).

[2] *MacVicar* v. *Poland* (1894), 10 T.L.R. 566; *Anglo-Californian Bank, Ltd.* v. *London and Provincial Marine and General Insurance Co., Ltd.* (1904), 10 Com. Cas. 1.

[3] *Parr's Bank* v. *Albert Mines Syndicate* (*supra*). As to "subrogation", see Ivamy, *ibid.*, pp. 415–430.

PART VII

REINSURANCE

38

REINSURANCE[1]

The business of insurance is not restricted to the making of contracts of insurance between the insurers and the outside world.

Both of the contracting parties may be insurers by profession, the object of the contract being to indemnify the insurers taking the place of the assured in an ordinary contract against loss which they may themselves sustain in their capacity as insurers under another contract of insurance.[2]

Where this is the case, the contract is termed a contract of re-insurance.[3]

CLASSIFICATION OF REINSURANCE

Reinsurance is of two kinds:

1 Facultative reinsurance, i.e. reinsurance against the liability on a particular policy.

2 Treaty reinsurance, i.e. reinsurance against liabilities on policies generally.

1 Facultative Reinsurance

A contract of reinsurance in the strict sense of the term is a contract by which certain insurers, called in this connection "reinsurers", undertake to indemnify other insurers, called the "reassured", against the whole or a portion of the liability which the reassured have in their turn undertaken upon a particular policy of insurance towards the insured under that policy.[4]

It is a contract by which the reassured are insured, not against direct loss, but against the liability which they have undertaken under their own contract of insurance with the insured.[5]

---

[1] For reinsurance in the case of marine insurance, see Ivamy, *Marine Insurance* (1969), pp. 481–488.

[2] Such contract is not offensive to the law as being maintenance: *British Cash and Parcel Conveyors, Ltd.* v. *Lamson Store Service Co., Ltd.*, [1908] 1 K.B. 1006, C.A. (maintenance), *per* FLETCHER MOULTON, L.J., at p. 1015.

[3] It is sometimes referred to as "guarantee business". In *Re National Benefit Assurance Co., Ltd.*, [1932] 2 Ch. 184 (marine insurance) the insurers were estopped from denying that they had guaranteed the liabilities of other insurers when they had permitted statements to that effect to be placed on the policies.

[4] *Home Insurance Co. of New York* v. *Victoria-Montreal Fire Insurance Co.*, [1907] A.C. 59, 63, P.C. The identity of the policy may be established by extrinsic evidence: *Janson* v. *Poole* (1915), 84 L.J.K.B. 1543; 31 T.L.R. 336 (marine insurance).

[5] *Joyce* v. *Realm Marine Insurance Co.* (1872), L.R. 7 Q.B. 580 (marine insurance), *per* LUSH, J., at p. 586.

Such a contract may be entered into because the reassured discover that they have entered into an improvident contract, and seek in consequence to relieve themselves from the whole, or some portion of, the liability which may eventually arise, or because the amount of the insurance exceeds the limit which they consider it prudent to place upon any one of their insurances, and they wish, therefore, to minimise their possible loss, without at the same time declining a transaction which they otherwise regard as satisfactory.[1]

Facultative reinsurance may be carried out by means of a policy. In practice, however, a policy is frequently dispensed with. The insurers wishing to effect a reinsurance submit to the proposed reinsurers a "request note", which contains particulars of the policy intended to be reinsured and certifies the period and the amount of the reinsurance. There is also a statement as to the amount, if any, retained by the insurers. The reinsurers if they decide to accept the reinsurance, issue a "take note", accepting the request and stating the amount of reinsurance undertaken.

2   Treaty Reinsurance

It is not necessary that the contract of reinsurance should be identified with any existing policy, and it is possible to make an antecedent contract with the reinsurers that they shall undertake to hold the reassured indemnified in respect of risks to be undertaken by the latter in a given period, provided that the language used by the parties is clear.[2] A contract of this kind, when reduced to writing, is known as a treaty of reinsurance, or participating agreement.

Reinsurance by treaty has developed largely in recent years and is now practically universal. By its means, especially where, as is usually the case, the risk reinsured is simultaneously covered by a number of treaties with different insurers, losses are distributed and do not fall exclusively upon the original insurers.

The rights and liabilities of the parties are regulated by the terms of the particular treaty.[3] The treaty may be applicable to all risks undertaken by the original insurers or only to particular classes, and in either case may, and usually does, extend to risks upon which they themselves are reinsurers.[4] The proportion of risk to be ceded, as it is called, to the insurers, is defined and provision is made for the periodic settlement of accounts,[5] and for the retention of a portion of the reinsurance premiums payable by the original insurers to the reinsurers for the purpose of establishing a fund, usually

---

[1] *Re Norwich Equitable Fire Assurance Society, Royal Insurance Co.'s Claim*, (1887), 57 L.T. 241, *per* KAY, J., at p. 243: "Every fire insurance company—so far as I know, every one—has a limit to its risks; *i.e.* upon a single risk it will not take more than a limited amount unless it obtains reinsurance."

[2] *Lower Rhine and Würtemberg Insurance Association* v. *Sedgwick*, [1899] 1 Q.B. 179, C.A. (marine insurance), *per* A. L. SMITH, L.J., at p. 186.

[3] *General Accident, Fire and Life Assurance Co., Ltd.* v. *National British and Irish Millers' Insurance Co., Ltd.*, [1914] C.P.D. 586. An agreement by which the net monthly premiums are to be paid to trustees to secure the reinsurers does not require registration under the Companies Act, 1948, s. 95 as being a mortgage of book debts: *Re Law Car and General Insurance Corporation*, [1911] W.N. 101, C.A. (marine insurance).

[4] Treaties confined to further reinsurance of risks already reinsured are sometimes called "retrocession agreements".

[5] *New Fenix Compagnie Anonyme d'Assurances de Madrid* v. *General Accident, Fire and Life Assurance Corporation, Ltd.*, [1911] 2 K.B. 619, C.A.

called the Premium Reserve Fund, to be held by the original insurers until the termination of the treaty, as security for the due fulfilment of their obligations by the reinsurers.[1]

There are two classes of treaty:

i *Treaties under which the insurers are given the option of taking a share upon any risk of which they may approve.*[2] This class of reinsurance is in practice little used.

ii *Treaties of obligatory reinsurance* under which the reinsurers are bound to take the agreed share upon all risks put forward for their acceptance.[3]

In the case of a treaty of obligatory reinsurance the reinsurers have no option to accept or refuse;[4] they are bound, as long as the treaty is in force, to accept all risks falling within its scope.[5] Likewise, the original insurers, are generally bound to cede the agreed share of all risks falling within the scope of the treaty, and are not at liberty to select the risks to be ceded.

A treaty of obligatory reinsurance does not constitute an amalgamation between the two companies,[6] nor are they partners[7] or principal and agent[8] either as between themselves or as regards third persons; the treaty is merely a contract of reinsurance,[9] in which the reinsurers place a greater reliance upon the judgment of the re-assured than is usual in facultative reinsurance.[10]

A fire insurance company may enter into such a treaty with a marine insurance company for the purpose of reinsuring the latter against loss or damage by fire sustained by the ships which it may insure; in this case the contract of the reinsurers, though it is a contract of fire insurance is a contract of fire insurance in respect of a marine risk,[11] and it is therefore subject to the incidents which attach to insurances of such risks.[12]

---

[1] Upon the liquidation of the reinsurers, the original insurers are not entitled to set off any balance of the fund payable to the reinsurers against moneys due from the reinsurers under other treaties, though the interest payable upon the fund may be set off: *Re City Equitable Fire Insurance Co., Ltd. (No. 2),* [1930] 2 Ch. 293, C.A.

[2] *Re Norwich Equitable Fire Assurance Society* (1887), 57 L.T. 241, *per* KAY, J., at p. 244; *Prince of Wales Assurance Co.* v. *Harding* (1858), E.B. & E. 183 (life assurance).

[3] *Re Norwich Equitable Fire Assurance Society (supra)*; *Imperial Marine Insurance Co.* v. *Fire Insurance Corporation, Ltd.* (1879), 4 C.P.D. 166.

[4] *Law Guarantee Trust and Accident Society* v. *Munich Reinsurance Co.,* [1912] 1 Ch. 138 (debenture insurance), *per* WARRINGTON, J., at p. 150.

[5] The treaty will not be applied to risks current at the date when it is effected, unless the intention is clear: *Law Guarantee Trust and Accident Society, Ltd.* v. *Munich Re-Insurance Co.* (1915), 31 T.L.R. 572 (mortgage insurance). It may by terms be applied only to insurances of a particular kind.

[6] *Re Lancashire Plate Glass, Fire and Burglary Insurance Co., Ltd.,* [1912] 1 Ch. 35.

[7] *English Insurance Co.* v. *National Benefit Assurance Co. (Official Receiver),* [1929] A.C. 114 (marine insurance).

[8] *Motor Union Insurance Co., Ltd.* v. *Mannheimer Versicherungs Gesellschaft,* [1933] 1 K.B. 812 (marine insurance).

[9] An undertaking to indemnify against risks not already undertaken is not, strictly speaking, reinsurance: *Lower Rhine and Würtemberg Insurance Association* v. *Sedgwick,* [1899] 1 Q.B. 179, C.A. (marine insurance) *per* COLLINS, L.J., at p. 189; but in practice this class of business is treated as reinsurance.

[10] *Re Norwich Equitable Fire Assurance Society (supra)*; *Glasgow Assurance Corporation* v. *Symondson* (1911), 16 Com. Cas. 109 (marine insurance); *Eastern Carrying Insurance Co.* v. *National Benefit Life and Property Assurance Co., Ltd.* (1919), 35 T.L.R. 292, (marine insurance) *per* BAILHACHE, J., at p. 294.

[11] *North British Fishing Boat Co.* v. *Starr* (1922), November 10.

[12] *Imperial Marine Insurance Co.* v. *Fire Insurance Corporation, Ltd.* (1879), 4 C.P.D. 166, where it was held, following *Stephens* v. *Australasian Insurance Co.* (1872), L.R. 8 C.P. 18 (marine insurance), that the policy attached to the goods intended to be covered in order of shipment, and that an incorrect declaration could be rectified even after loss.

The reinsurance may be expressed in the form of a policy, specifying the amount and subject-matter of reinsurance in each particular case.[1]   A formal policy is not, however, required; the treaty itself, though not embodied in a formal policy, is in effect a policy of insurance.[2]

Reinsurance under a treaty is not so much a reinsurance of particular policies as a reinsurance of business. The policies are, therefore, dealt with in bulk, by means of a document known as a "bordereau".[3] The bordereau is in the form of a table, in which are inserted the particulars of all the policies dealt with at the same time, including a statement of the amount ceded and of the amount retained in respect of each.

The entering into contracts of reinsurance, including treaty business of both kinds, is within the powers of every company formed for the purpose of carrying on the business of fire insurance, unless expressly prohibited by its memorandum of association.[4]

Sometimes a treaty of reinsurance provides that disputes or differences between the parties are to be settled by arbitration without regard to the strict rule of law and even without recourse to the Court in any event[5]. But such a clause will be held to purport to oust the jurisdiction of the Court and will therefore be void, and the treaty as a whole would not be considered to be a contract, for the parties to it would not consider it to have legal effect and any award under it would be unenforceable.

Thus, in *Orion Compania Espanola de Seguros* v. *Belfort Maatschappij Voor Algemene Verzekgringeen*[6]

> A clause in a non-marine reinsurance treaty provided that any dispute arising under it was to be referred to arbitration. It went on to state: "The arbitrators and umpire are relieved from judicial formalities and may abstain from following the strict rules of the law. They shall settle any dispute under this agreement according to any equitable rather than a strictly legal interpretation of its terms and their decision shall be final and not subject to appeal."
> *Held*, (*obiter*) that this clause was unenforceable.
> MEGAW, J., said:[7]
> "It is the policy of the law in this country that, in the conduct of arbitrations, arbitrators must in general apply a fixed and recognisable system of law, which primarily and normally would be the law of England, and that they cannot be allowed to apply some different criterion such as the view of the individual arbitrator or umpire on abstract justice or equitable principles . . .   If the parties choose to provide in their contract that the rights and obligations shall not be decided in accordance with law but in accordance with some other criterion, such as   what the arbitrators consider to be fair and reasonable,

---

[1] *Imperial Marine Insurance Co.* v. *Fire Insurance Corporation, Ltd.* (*supra*). The policy may be described in terms as a reinsurance and may make a special provision for renewal.

[2] *Forsikringsaktieselskabet National (of Copenhagen)* v. *A.-G.*, [1925] A.C. 639, *per* Lord CAVE, L.C., at p. 642;   *First Russian Insurance Co.* v. *London and Lancashire Insurance Co.*, [1928] Ch. 922, *per* ROMER, J., at p. 937; *Re Norwich Equitable Fire Assurance Society* (1887), 57 L.T. 241, *per* KAY, J., at p. 246.

[3] In practice, two bordereaux are used, the first a preliminary bordereau containing a statement as to each risk and the term of the reinsurance, the second called the definitive bordereau which gives full particulars, including details as to the premium for the risk.

[4] *Re Norwich Equitable Fire Assurance Society* (*supra*); *Re Athenaeum Life Assurance Co.*, Ex parte *Eagle Insurance Co.* (1858), 4 K. & J. 549 (life insurance).

[5] *Re Home and Colonial Insurance Co., Ltd.*, [1930] 1 Ch. 102 (marine insurance) at p. 104; *First Russian Insurance Co.* v. *London and Lancashire Insurance Co.*, [1928] Ch. 922, at p. 945.

[6] [1962] 2 Lloyd's Rep. 257.

[7] *Ibid.*, at p. 264.

whether or not in accordance with law, then, if that provision has any effect at all, its effect, as I see it, would be that there would be no contract, because the parties did not intend the contract to have legal effect—to affect their legal relations. If there were no contract, there would be no legally binding arbitration clause, and an 'award' would not be an award which the law would recognise."

CHARACTERISTICS OF REINSURANCE

A contract of reinsurance is an independent contract of insurance and not a mere contract of indemnity.[1] The rules, therefore, which govern the validity and effect of an ordinary contract of insurance apply, with the necessary modifications to a contract of reinsurance. It may be convenient, however, to show in detail how the various rules are modified in their application.[2]

The principal matters to be discussed are:

1 The insurable interest of the reinsured.

2 The amount of reinsurance.

3 The duty of disclosure.

4 The duration of the reinsurance.

5 The liability of the reinsurers.

6 The incorporation of the original policy.

7 The position of the original insured.

1   Insurable Interest of Reinsured

The reassured have no proprietary interest in the subject-matter of the original insurance; but they may be said to be interested in its safety, by reason of the liability which they have undertaken under the policy issued by them.[3]

This liability, therefore, constitutes the insurable interest upon which the validity of the reinsurance depends.[4] If they are under no liability to the insured under their policy, the foundation of the reinsurance is gone, and they cannot enforce it against the reinsurers.[5] Thus, they have no insurable interest, where it appears that the insured had himself no insurable interest,[6] or where the original contract is void by reason of his fraud or breach of duty.

The fact that the contract is one of reinsurance, and that the reassured's interest depends solely upon their liability to the original insured, does not

---

[1] *Australian Widows' Fund Life Assurance Society, Ltd.* v. *National Mutual Life Association of Australasia, Ltd.*, [1914] A.C. 634, 641 P.C. (life insurance); *Nelson* v. *Empress Assurance Corporation, Ltd.*, [1905] 2 K.B. 281, C.A. (marine insurance), *per* MATHEW, L.J., at p. 285.

[2] It may be observed that the rules do not apply in their entirety to obligatory reinsurance, but only to facultative reinsurance.

[3] *Forsikringsaktieselskabet National (of Copenhagen)* v. *A.-G.*, [1925] A.C. 639; *Nelson* v. *Empress Assurance Corporation, Ltd.* (*supra*) (marine insurance), *per* MATHEW, L.J., at p. 285.

[4] *Uzielli* v. *Boston Marine Insurance Co.* (1884), 15 Q.B.D. 11, C.A., (marine insurance), *per* BRETT, M.R., at p. 16: "What was the interest of the real plaintiffs, the reinsurers, in the ship? They were not owners, and therefore had none as owners. But they had an insurable interest of some kind, and that insurable interest is the loss which they might or would suffer under the policy upon which they themselves were liable." See also *Bradford* v. *Symondson* (1881), 7 Q.B.D. 456, C.A. (marine insurance), *per* BRETT, L.J., at p. 463; *Liverpool Mortgage Insurance Co.'s case*, [1914] 2 Ch. 617, C.A. (debenture insurance), *per* BUCKLEY, L.J., at p. 631.

[5] *Chippendale* v. *Holt* (1895), 1 Com. Cas. 197 (marine insurance), *per* MATHEW, L.J., at p. 199.

[6] *Colonial Insurance Co. of New Zealand* v. *Adelaide Marine Insurance Co.* (1886), 12 App. Cas. 128, 135, P.C. (marine insurance).

in any way affect the risk to be run by the reinsurers, since the subject-matter and the peril insured against are the same as in the original policy.[1] It is, therefore, unecessary in effecting a reinsurance, to describe it as a reinsurance,[2] or indeed to disclose the nature of the reassured's interest.

2 Amount of Reinsurance

The value of the reassured's interest is clearly the amount of liability which they have themselves undertaken to the original insured. They cannot therefore effect a reinsurance for an amount in excess of the amount of their own insurance.

There is no reason why the reassured should not, if they think fit, reinsure themselves against the whole of the liability which they have undertaken to the original insured, and thus secure that no portion of any loss which may happen shall ultimately fall upon themselves.

It is sometimes made a term of the reinsurance, however, that a definite amount of liability shall be retained by them.[3] In this case the reassured are prohibited from reducing their own liability below the specified limit by effecting further reinsurances,[4] and if they do so, they cannot claim in the event of a loss to be indemnified by the reinsurers.[5]

Similarly, where the reassured, during the negotiation for the reinsurance, represent to the reinsurers that they intend to retain a certain proportion of the risk, this representation of their intention must be regarded as a representation of a material fact, in that the reinsurers are induced thereby to abstain from making a fuller investigation into the nature of the risk, and its untruth therefore avoids the reinsurance.[6]

On the other hand, a statement that the property proposed to be reinsured is insured for a specified sum is to be construed as a statement of the amount insured by the original policy in respect of which the reinsurance is sought, and not as a representation of the total amount of insurances which may have been effected upon the same property.[7]

3 Duty of Disclosure

It is the duty of the reassured, at the time of effecting a facultative reinsurance, to disclose to the reinsurers all the material facts which are or which

---

[1] *Bradford* v. *Symondson* (*supra*).

[2] *Mackenzie* v. *Whitworth* (1875), 1 Ex.D., 36, C.A. (marine insurance).

[3] *South British Fire and Marine Insurance Co. of New Zealand* v. *Da Costa*, [1906] 1 K.B. 456 (marine insurance), where a policy of reinsurance for "£1,000, in excess of £500" was held to mean that if the liability of the reassured under the original policy should turn out to exceed £500, the reinsurers were to relieve them from the amount of the excess up to £1,000; see *Traill* v. *Baring* (1864), 4 De G.J. & Sm. 318 (life insurance), where evidence was given as to the practice of insurance offices to insist on a substantial portion of the risk being retained.

[4] The fact that the liability of the reassured has been diminished by reason of the original insured permitting certain policies to lapse which related to other portions of the property not covered by the reinsurance, and which the reassured had contracted with their reinsurers to retain, has been held not to affect the liability of the latter: *Canada Fire Marine Insurance Co.* v. *Northern Insurance Co.* (1878), 2 O.A.R. 373, C.A.

[5] In the case of reinsurance by treaty, power is frequently reserved to the original insurers to vary at their discretion the amount retained by them upon a particular insurance.

[6] *Traill* v. *Baring* (*supra*) where the reassured, after stating that they intended to retain a certain portion of the risk, changed their minds during the negotiations and reinsured the balance without informing the insurers.

[7] *Anderson* v. *Pacific Fire and Marine Insurance Co.* (1869), 21 L.T. 408, P.C. (marine insurance).

ought to have been within their knowledge[1], and if they fail to discharge this duty, the reinsurance is voidable.

It is, therefore, their duty to communicate to the reinsurers all facts disclosed to them by their insured during the negotiations for the original policy. This is usually done by submitting to the reinsurers the proposal signed by them.[2] They must further disclose all material facts which, though not communicated to them by the insured, were known to them at the time of the original insurance, together with all material facts which have come to their knowledge since that date.[3]

Thus, where it is material, they must disclose to the reinsurers the information which they may possess as to the character of the original insured. As in the case of an original insurance, this duty does not merely apply to facts within their actual knowledge, but extends to all facts which they must be presumed to have known, as being within the knowledge of their agents.[4]

The reassured need not, however, disclose the fact that the contract is one of reinsurance, since that is not a fact bearing on the risk.[5] Nor, where the contract is known to one of reinsurance, need they disclose the fact that the premium to be paid is higher than that which they are receiving under the original contract of insurance.[6] It is also unnecessary to disclose the facts which may be fairly presumed to be known to the reinsurers. Thus, the reasssured need not disclose the existence of a particular clause in the original policy, where the clause is so usual that the reinsurers should have known that it was there.[7]

The duty of disclosure does not arise where the reinsurance is effected under a treaty of obligatory reinsurance[8] but the treaty is itself a contract *uberrimae fidei*,[9] except in so far as the duty is expressly negatived.[10]

---

[1] *Blackburn, Low & Co.* v. *Vigors* (1887), 12 App. Cas. 531 (marine insurance); *Blackburn* v. *Haslam* (1888), 21 Q.B.D. 144 (marine insurance), both cases of reinsurance.

[2] *Foster* v. *Mentor Life Assurance Co.* (1854), 3 E. & B. 48 (life insurance); *Australian Widows' Fund Life Assurance Society, Ltd.* v. *National Mutual Life Association of Australasia*, [1914] A.C. 634, P.C. (life insurance), where the original proposal was expressly made the basis of the reinsurance.

[3] *Federal Insurance Co. of New Jersey* v. *Westchester Fire Insurance Co.*, [1929] 3 W.W.R. 646, where the reasured failed to disclose to the reinsurers that the crops of the insured had already been visited by hailstorms during the same season.

[4] *Blackburn* v. *Haslam* (1888), 21 Q.B.D. 144 (marine insurance); *London General Insurance Co.* v. *General Marine Underwriters' Association*, [1921] 1 K.B. 104, C.A. (marine insurance).

[5] *London and North Western Rail. Co.* v. *Glyn* (1859), 1 E. & E. 652, *per* CROMPTON, J., at p. 664; *Mackenzie* v. *Whitworth* (1875), 1 Ex.D. 36, C.A. (marine insurance), *per* BLACKBURN, J., at p. 42; *Crowley* v. *Cohen* (1832), 3 B. & Ad. 478 (insurance on canal boats), *per* PATTESON, J., at p. 488.

[6] *Glasgow Assurance Corporation, Ltd.* v. *Symondson* (1911), 16 Com. Cas. 109 (marine insurance), *per* SCRUTTON, J., at p. 119.

[7] *Marten* v. *Nippon Sea and Land Insurance Co., Ltd.* (1898), 3 Com. Cas. 164 (marine insurance). Though an unusual clause should, as a rule, be disclosed, disclosure may be dispensed with by the terms of the reinsurance policy: *Property Insurance Co., Ltd.* v. *National Protector Insurance Co., Ltd.* (1913), 108 L.T. 104 (marine insurance), where the reinsurance was "subject without notice to the same clauses and the conditions as the original policy."

[8] *Law Guarantee Trust and Accident Society, Ltd.* v. *Munich Reinsurance Co.* (1915), 31 T.L.R. 572 (mortgage insurance).

[9] *Glasgow Assurance Corporation* v. *Symondson* (*supra*), *per* SCRUTTON, J., at p. 121; cf. *General Accident, Fire and Life Assurance Corporation* v. *Campbell* (1925), 21 Ll. L. Rep. 151 (accident insurance), where a statement made during the negotiations that the outstanding claims were not serious, when in fact they were, was held to invalidate the re-insurance.

[10] *English Insurance Co., Ltd.* v. *National Benefit Assurance Co., Ltd.* (*Official Receiver and Liquidator*), [1929] A.C. 114 (marine insurance), *per* Lord SUMNER at p. 123.

4 Duration of Reinsurance

A facultative reinsurance cannot remain in force for a period exceeding the duration of the original policy intended to be reinsured, since it is a contract of indemnity against the liability to be incurred under that policy and that policy only.[1]

If the original policy is allowed to lapse, or otherwise it is to exist, the re-insurance comes to an end, even though the period fixed for its duration has not expired, and it does not, if the original policy expires and is renewed during its currency, necessarily attach to the renewed policy, since it was a reinsurance of a particular policy which no longer exists.[2] The reinsurance may, however, be framed in terms sufficiently wide to apply equally to the renewed policy.[3]

Where the reinsurance is effected at a later date than the original policy, a question may arise as to whether it relates back so as to cover a liability which has, unknown to both parties, already accrued under the original policy. The answer to this question seems to depend upon the intention of the parties as shown in their contract, and if it is clear that they intended the reinsurance to relate back the antecedent liability will be covered.[4]

A treaty of reinsurance is in practice made for a period of years, which is either fixed or determinable on notice. As a rule the treaty is expressed to include not only new insurances, but also the renewals during the period of policies effected before the commencement of the treaty. The determination of the treaty does not in the ordinary course put an end to all liability of the reinsurers; they remain liable upon the risks then current until their exploration.[5] Occasionally, special provisions are made by which the reinsurers undertake liability upon the risks current at the commencement of the treaty, and are released as from the termination of the treaty from further liability upon the risks then current.

5 Liability of Reinsurers

The event which gives rise to the liability of the reinsurers under the reinsurance is the happening of a loss covered by the original policy. The liability of the reinsurers to the reassured is, therefore, dependent upon the liability of the latter under their policy to the original insured;[6] and the

---

[1] *Lower Rhine and Würtemberg Insurance Association* v. *Sedgwick*, [1899] 1 Q.B. 179, C.A.(marine insurance) where, during the currency of a reinsurance, expressed to be a "reinsurance of of policy or policies, and subject to the same terms, conditions and clauses as original policy or policies, whether reinsurance or otherwise, and to pay as may be paid thereon", the original policies came to an end, and were replaced by a new policy differing as to valuation and in other respects from the original policies, and it was held that the "original policy or policies" referred to were the policies in existence at the date of the reinsurance, and that the reinsurers were not liable for losses which might be incurred under a policy not containing the same terms, conditions and clauses as the original policy.

[2] *Lower Rhine and Würtemberg Insurance Association* v. *Sedgwick* (*supra*) (marine insurance).

[3] *General Accident, Fire and Life Assurance Co., Ltd.* v. *National British and Irish Millers' Insurance Co.*, [1914] C.P.D. 586.

[4] *Joyce* v. *Realm Marine Insurance Co.* (1872), L.R. 7 Q.B. 580 (marine insurance) *per* LUSH, J., at p. 586. A statement that the reinsurance is to be subject to all the clauses and conditions of the original policy is a sufficient indication of their intention: *ibid*.

[5] This is usually dealt with by an express provision in the treaty which may give the original insurers an option to withdraw current risks.

[6] *Home Insurance Co. of New York* v. *Victoria-Montreal Fire Insurance Co.*, [1907] A.C. 59, 63, P.C.

reinsurers cannot be called upon to indemnify the reassured unless and until such liability is established by proof or admission.[1]

It is not necessary even where the reinsurance policy contains the words "to pay as may be paid thereon" that a payment should actually have been made under the original policy, since to require the reassured to pay the amount due under their policy before allowing them to claim the benefit of the reinsurance would, in many cases, defeat the very object with which the reinsurance was effected by compelling them to bear in the first instance the full burden of the loss.[2]

The reassured, therefore, as soon as their liability under the original policy is admitted or ascertained, may enforce payment of the amount payable under the reinsurance without showing that they have paid the amount due to the original assured.[3] This amount is only material in fixing the measure of the reinsurers' liability. Where, therefore, the reassured are insolvent, they are nevertheless entitled to claim payment in full from the reinsurers, although they have not paid their own insured the full amount of loss, and although it is clear that they will never be in a position to do so.[4]

The reinsurers may, however, by an express term of the contract of reinsurance, stipulate that, in the event of the reassured becoming insolvent, and failing to pay the whole or part of any claim covered by the reinsurance, the reinsurers are only to pay in the same proportion.[5]

In order to render the reinsurers liable under a facultative reinsurance the liability of the reassured under the original policy must be a legal one,[6] unless the reinsurance policy otherwise provides.[7] The assumption of a

---

[1] *Chippendale* v. *Holt* (1895), 1 Com. Cas. 197 (marine insurance), *per* MATHEW, J., at p. 199; *St. Paul Fire and Marine Insurance Co.* v. *Morice* (1906), 11 Com. Cas. 153 (marine insurance), *per* KENNEDY, J., at p. 164. This is the relevant date when payment by reinsurers has to be converted into foreign currency: *Versicherungs Und Transport A.G. Daugava* v. *Henderson* (1934), 151 L.T. 392, C.A.

[2] *Re Eddystone Marine Insurance Co., Ex parte Western Insurance Co.*, [1892] 2 Ch. 423 (marine insurance), where the reinsurance policy was expressed to be "subject to the same terms and conditions as the original policy or policies, and to pay as may be paid thereon"; and STIRLING, J., said at p. 427: "The words, 'to pay as may be paid thereon' do not stand in strict grammatical connection with those which immediately precede; but the effect of them is to impose an obligation as to payment on the reinsurers. The contention on behalf of the official liquidator comes to this—that those words make payment by the reinsured a condition precedent to payment by the reinsurer. Now, a main object of insurance is to relieve the reinsured from a portion of the risk previously undertaken by him; and the result of giving effect to the liquidator's contention would be that, before the reinsured obtains the benefit of his reinsurance, he must himself have paid on the original insurance, even though bankruptcy might be the result. I think that this could not be intended, and that such a construction ought not to be put on the language of the policy unless it is clearly called for. In my opinion, the words do not clearly require to be so construed. They would be satisfied if they were held to amount simply to this—that the payment to be made on the reinsurance policy is to be regulated by that to be made on the original policy of insurance."

[3] They must have complied, however, with all conditions precedent to liability affecting the reinsurance: *British General Insurance Co.* v. *Mountain* (1919), 36 T.L.R. 171, H.L. (liability insurance).

[4] *Re Eddystone Marine Insurance Co., Ex parte Western Insurance Co. (supra)*; *Liverpool Mortgage Insurance Co.'s case*, [1914] 2 Ch. 617, C.A. (debenture insurance).

[5] *Nepean* v. *Marten* (1895), 11 T.L.R. 480 (solvency insurance), where the reconstruction of the reassured company did not, in the circumstances, absolve the reinsurers from liability.

[6] *Excess Insurance Co.* v. *Mathews* (1925), 31 Com. Cas. 43, where the legality of the original policy was restored under a treaty of peace; *Re London County Commercial Reinsurance Office, Ltd.*, [1922] 2 Ch. 67 (peace insurance).

[7] *Firemen's Fund Insurance Co.* v. *Western Australian Insurance Co., Ltd.* (1927), 138 L.T. 108 (marine insurance), *per* BATESON, J., at p. 113.

voluntary liability is not sufficient.[1] If, therefore, they make a payment to their insured, which they are not legally justified in making, such as, for instance, an *ex gratia* payment,[2] or if they admit liability where they have an available defence upon their policy,[3] the reinsurance has no application. The reinsurers in such a case are not only entitled to avail themselves of any defence which may exist in connection with their own contract, but may, in addition, make use of any defence which the reassured might have used against the original insured.[4]

The reassured must not, therefore, without the consent of the reinsurers compromise the original claim;[5] and a failure on the part of the latter to object to a proposed payment to the insured is not sufficient to make them liable.[6] The reassured are, however, entitled to bring in the reinsurers as third parties, and thus bind them to abide by the result of an action brought upon the original policy by the insured.[7]

A reinsurance policy frequently contains a further provision that the reinsurers are "to pay as may be paid" on the original policy. The provision does not bind them to pay such an amount as the reassured might in their turn choose to pay, whether liable or not, since, if that were the effect of the contract, it would be a wager and not a reinsurance.[8] It assumes the

---

[1] *Chippendale* v. *Holt* (1895), 1 Com. Cas. 197 (marine insurance). Where the reassured pay under the original policy in the belief that they are legally liable, and are paid in their turn by their reinsurers, a subsequent recovery of damages from the original insured on the grounds that he had induced his insurers to pay him his claim by fraudulent representations is the enforcement of a right diminishing the reassured's loss, and the reinsurers are therefore entitled to be repaid the sum paid by them by way of reinsurance, after deducting the costs properly attributable to the recovery of the damages: *Assicurazioni Generali de Trieste* v. *Empress Assurance Corporation, Ltd.*, [1907] 2 K.B. 814 (marine insurance), following *Castellain* v. *Preston* (1883), 11 Q.B.D. 380, C.A. (fire insurance).

[2] Cf. *Colonial Insurance Co. of New Zealand* v. *Adelaide Marine Insurance Co.* (1886), 12 App. Cas. 128, 135, P.C. (marine insurance).

[3] *Australian Widows' Fund Life Assurance Society, Ltd.* v. *National Mutual Life Association of Australasia, Ltd.*, [1914] A.C. 634, P.C. (life insurance).

[4] *Re London County Commercial Reinsurance Office*, [1922] 2 Ch. 67 (peace insurance), *per* LAWRENCE, J., at p. 80.

[5] But if there is found to be a legal liability, the compromise, if reasonable, is binding: *Traders and General Assurance Association* v. *Bankers and General Insurance Co., Ltd.* (1921), 38 T.L.R. 94 (marine insurance). The reinsurers are not liable in any event beyond the amount of the compromise: *British Dominions General Insurance Co., Ltd.* v. *Duder*, [1915] 2 K.B. 394, C.A. (marine insurance).

[6] *National Marine Insurance Co. of Australasia* v. *Halfey* (1879), 5 V.L.R. 226 (marine insurance), where the reassured gave notice to the reinsurers of their intention to pay the claim, to which the reinsurers made no response.

[7] R.S.C. Ord. 16, thus altering the law laid down in *Nelson* v. *Empress Assurance Corporation, Ltd.*, [1905] 2 K.B. 281, C.A. (marine insurance) unless, perhaps, there is an arbitration clause in the reinsurance contract making an award a condition precedent: *Jones* v. *Birch Brothers, Ltd.*, [1933] 2 K.B. 597, C.A. (accident insurance).

[8] *Chippendale* v. *Holt* (1895), 1 Com. Cas. 197 (marine insurance), *per* MATHEW, J., at p. 199; "It was argued for the defendant that he was only bound to indemnify the plaintiffs against a loss for which the plaintiffs were liable on their policy. It was said for the plaintiffs that the policy that a fraudulent use might be made of the plaintiffs' option to pay would not enter into the contemplation of either party, and that it was not unreasonable that the reinsurers should trust to the honour and sound judgment of those whose liabilities they had taken upon themselves. But the contention of the plaintiffs would involve this result, that the clause must be read as if it ran 'to pay such an amount as the insurers might choose to pay whether liable or not'. This seems to me altogether unreasonable. Such a contract would be a wager, not a reinsurance. It was said that, unless the interpretation contended for were put upon the clause, no effect would be given to the final words 'to pay as may be paid thereon'; for the identity of obligation was differently provided for by the words 'subject to the same clauses and conditions as the original policy'. But those

existence of a liability, proved or admitted, on the part of the reassured, and the reinsurers cannot, therefore, be required to pay unless the reassured are themselves under a legal liability to the original insured.[1]

This liability, however, arises as soon as the reassured have taken all proper and businesslike steps to have the amount payable under the original policy fairly and carefully ascertained.[2] They are not entitled to insist upon the reassured first making payment under original policy;[3] nor can they claim to reopen the settlement between the original parties, except on the ground that it is dishonest or has been arrived at carelessly.[4]

If the reinsurance policy further contains an undertaking "to follow the settlements" of the reassured, the reinsurers are bound by a compromise honestly and properly made.[5]

Under a treaty of reinsurance the original insurers are usually given a free hand to deal with claims arising under the original policies without consulting the reinsurers, and all settlements made by the original insurers, including compromises and *ex gratia* payments, are made binding upon the reinsurers.

The amount of liability under the reinsurance cannot exceed the amount of liability under the original policy, inasmuch as the contract is one of indemnity.[6]

The precise amount to be paid, however, depends upon the terms of the particular contract, which may provide either for the payment of a certain proportion of the original loss or for a small indemnity up to the amount of insurance.[7] Where the reassured have unsuccessfully defended an action upon the original policy, they cannot, it seems, claim the costs of the action against the reinsurers,[8] unless such indemnity is specifically within the terms of the

---

words standing alone would not be applicable to a policy reinsurance, and might give rise to difficulties of construction while the final words show clearly what was meant . . . I see no ground for supposing that the form of the clause was meant to create a liability outside the limits of the original policy. The words 'to pay as may be paid thereon' would seem to assume the existence of liability proved or admitted in respect of the loss reinsured." See also *Re Eddystone Marine Insurance Co., Ex parte Western Insurance Co.,* [1892] 2 Ch. 423 (marine insurance).

[1] *Marten v. Steamship Owners' Underwriting Association* (1902), 87 L.T. 208 (marine insurance), *per* BIGHAM, J., at p. 210; *Firemen's Fund Insurance Co.* v. *Western Australian Insurance Co.* (1927), 138 L.T. 108 (marine insurance).

[2] *Western Assurance Co. of Toronto v. Poole,* [1903] 1 K.B. 376 (marine insurance), *per* BIGHAM, J., at p. 386.

[3] *Re Eddystone Marine Insurance Co., Ex parte Western Insurance Co.,* [1892] 2 Ch. 423 (marine insurance).

[4] *Western Assurance Co. of Toronto* v. *Poole (supra), per* BIGHAM, J., at p. 386; but this *dictum* has been questioned by SCRUTTON, L.J., as importing a false distinction between the right of the reinsurer to dispute liability and his rights as regards the amounts of liability: *Versicherungs Und Transport A.G. Daugava* v. *Henderson* (1934), 151 L.T. 392, C.A., at p. 393.

[5] *Excess Insurance Co.* v. *Mathews* (1925), 31 Com. Cas. 43. The reinsurance policy may expressly provide that the reinsurance is to follow a compromise on the original policy: *Street* v. *Royal Exchange Assurance* (1914), 111 L.T. 235, C.A. (marine insurance). Another phrase sometimes used is "follow the fortunes": *English Insurance Co., Ltd.* v. *National Benefit Assurance Co., Ltd. (Official Receiver),* [1929] A.C. 114 (marine insurance) at p. 117.

[6] If the reassured are legally liable for interest, the reinsurers must bear their proportion: *Excess Insurance Co., Ltd.* v. *Mathews (supra).*

[7] A contribution clause in a reinsurance policy does not become operative unless there are other reinsurance policies covering the same risk.

[8] *Nelson* v. *Empress Assurance Corporation, Ltd.,* [1905] 2 K.B. 281, C.A. (marine insurance), *per* MATHEW, J., at p. 285; *Scottish Metropolitan Assurance Co., Ltd.* v. *Groom* (1924), 41 T.L.R. 35, C.A. (marine insurance).

reinsurance.[1] If payment by the reinsurers is to be made in foreign currency, the relevant rate for calculation of the rate of exchange is when the liability of the reinsured has been ascertained.[2]

Under a treaty, the amount for which the reinsurers are liable is a rateable proportion of the loss under the original policy, fixed by the amount of cession. They are usually further made liable for their rateable proportion of expenses incurred by the original insurers in investigating and settling any claims, where substantiated or not.

6 Incorporation of Original Policy

A facultative reinsurance when expressed in a policy frequently contains a clause to the effect that the reinsurance is to be subject to the same clauses and conditions as the original policy.[3] In this case the clauses and conditions of the original policy, with the necessary modifications,[4] are incorporated into the reinsurance policy, and form part of it,[5] except insofar as they are inconsistent with its express terms.[6]

Sometimes the reinsurance policy does not expressly refer to the original policy, but is written upon a form of policy which is more appropriate to an original insurance. In this case the use of the form is merely for the purpose of identifying the original insurance,[7] and the terms contained in it are not incorporated into the reinsurance policy except in so far as they are fairly applicable to a reinsurance.[8]

Terms which are more appropriate to an original insurance, and in particular, terms which relate to matters over which the reassured cannot reasonably be expected to have control, are to be disregarded.[9]

In *Home Insurance Co. of New York* v. *Victoria-Montreal Fire Insurance Co.*[10] a reinsurance was effected by fixing a typewritten slip, which set out the terms of the reinsurance to a printed form of a fire insurance policy and incorporated all its terms. One of the conditions in the printed form stated that

> "No suit or action on this policy for the recovery of any claim shall be sustainable in any court of law or equity . . . unless commenced within 12 months next after the fire."

On March 16, 1901 the reassured indemnified the original insured whose property had been destroyed in a fire on April 26, 1900. On May 21, 1901

---

[1] *Glasgow Assurance Corporation, Ltd. (Liquidators)* v. *Welsh Insurance Corporation, Ltd.*, 1914 S.C. 320.

[2] *Versicherungs Und Transport A.G. Daugava* v. *Henderson* (1934), 151 L.T. 392, C.A.

[3] Sometimes the phrase used is "subject without notice".

[4] *Re Athenaeum Life Assurance Co.* (1858), 4 K. & J. 549 (life insurance), *per* WOOD, V.-C., at p. 555; *Chippendale* v. *Holt* (1895), 1 Com. Cas. 197 (marine insurance), *per* MATHEW, J., at p. 199.

[5] *Excess Insurance Co., Ltd.* v. *Mathews* (1925), 31 Com. Cas. 43.

[6] *Australian Widows' Fund Life Assurance Society, Ltd.* v. *National Mutual Life Association of Australasia, Ltd.*, [1914] A.C. 634, 642, P.C. (life insurance).

[7] *Home Insurance Co. of New York* v. *Victoria-Montreal Fire Insurance Co.*, [1907] A.C. 59, 64, P.C. Apart from incorporation, reference may always be made to the original policy for the purpose of discovering the scope of the reinsurance: *Crocker* v. *General Insurance Co., Ltd.* (1897), 3 Com. Cas. 22, C.A. (marine insurance), *per* COLLINS, J., at p. 28.

[8] *Home Insurance Co. of New York* v. *Victoria-Montreal Fire Insurance Co.*, [1907] A.C. 59, P.C. at pp. 63, 64: *South British Fire and Marine Insurance Co. of New Zealand* v. *Da Costa*, [1906] 1 K.B. 456 (marine insurance), *per* BIGHAM, J., at p. 460.

[9] *Home Insurance Co. of New York* v. *Victoria-Montreal Fire Insurance Co.* (*supra*); *Foster* v. *Mentor Life Assurance Co.* (1854), 3 E. & B. 48 (life insurance), *per* Lord CAMPBELL, C.J., at p. 82.

[10] (1907), 95 L.T. 627, P.C.

the reassured forwarded to the reinsurers their calculation of the amount for which they regarded the reinsurers as liable. On May 23 the reinsurers repudiated liability on the ground that the claim was out of time. The Judicial Committee of the Privy Council[1] held that the reassured were entitled to an indemnity, for on the true construction of the policy the clause as to the time limit should be ignored, since the typewritten slip carelessly purported to include many conditions inapplicable to reinsurance of which this clause was one. Such a clause was reasonable in the policy effected by the original insured, but could not apply where the reassured was unable to sue until the direct loss had been ascertained between persons over whom he had no control. Lord MACNAGHTEN observed:[2]

> "A clause prescribing legal proceedings after a limited period is a reasonable provision in a policy of insurance against direct loss to specific property. In such a case the insured is master of the situation. He can bring his action immediately. In a case of reinsurance against liability the insured is helpless. He cannot move until the direct loss is ascertained between parties over whom he has no control, and in proceedings in which he cannot intervene. If the respondents are right, an honest claim might be defeated in such a case as this without any default or delay on the part of the insured owing to unavoidable difficulties or complications, or possibly in consequence of some dilatory proceeding prompted by the very person in whose favour time is running. It is difficult to suppose that the contract of reinsurance was engrafted on an ordinary printed form of policy for any purpose beyond the purpose of indicating the origin of the direct liability on which the indirect liability, the subject of the reinsurance, would depend, and setting forth the conditions attached to it. In the result their Lordships have come to the conclusion that according to the true construction of this instrument, so awkwardly patched and so carelessly put together, the condition in question is not to be regarded as applying to the contract of reinsurance. To hold otherwise would, in their opinion, be to adhere to the letter, without paying due attention to the spirit and intention of the contract. The question does not seem to have been raised before this in Canada. In the United States, though the point has not been brought before the Supreme Court, the universally accepted opinion appears to be that a clause such as that in question in this case is not applicable to a reinsurance policy, and there are several decisions to that effect."[3]

Whether the original policy is expressly incorporated or not, the obligations of the reinsurers are necessarily defined by reference to it. Consequently, any material variation in its terms destroys the basis of reinsurance, and, if it is made without their consent, releases the reinsurers from liability.[4] On the other hand, the mere waiver of a condition of the original policy without the consent of the reinsurers probably affects the reinsurance, at least if the waiver is made in good faith and does not increase the burden of the reinsurers.[5]

---

[1] Lord MACNAGHTEN, Lord DUNEDIN, Lord ATKINSON, Sir Arthur WILSON and Sir Alfred WILLIS.

[2] (1907), 95 L.T. at p. 629.

[3] See the following cases, which were cited in the Court below: *Jackson* v. *St. Paul Fire Insurance Company*, 99 N.Y. 124; *Manufacturers' Fire and Marine Insurance Company* v. *Western Assurance Company*, 145 Mass. 419; *Faneuil Hall Insurance Company* v. *Liverpool, London, and Globe Insurance Company*, 153 Mass. 63; *Imperial Fire Insurance Company of London* v. *Home Insurance Company of New Orleans*, 68 Fed. Rep. 698; *Insurance Company of State of New York* v. *Associated Manufacturers' Mutual Fire Insurance Corporation*, 70 App. Div. Rep. N.Y. 69; *Alker* v. *Rhoades*, 73 App. Div. Rep. N.Y. 158.

[4] *Norwich Union Fire Insurance Society* v. *Colonial Mutual Fire Insurance Co.*, [1922] 2 K.B. 461 (marine insurance).

[5] *Fire Insurance Association, Ltd.*, v. *Canada Fire and Marine Insurance Co.* (1883), 2 O.R. 481.

Further, an assignment of the original policy with the consent of the re-assured, given *bona fide* and reasonably, apparently binds the reinsurers even though their consent was never obtained or even asked.[1] They cannot contend that such an assignment avoids the original policy, since it is made in accordance with the terms of the policy, and there is, therefore, no defence available to the reassured themselves on the ground that a condition has been broken. Nor can it be said that the reinsurance is itself avoided, since the reinsurers must be presumed to have known of the existence of the condition by which it is allowed.

Every cession under a treaty is usually expressed to be subject to the terms and conditions of the original policy. The original insurers are given power at their discretion to vary or waive them, and any variation or waiver is made binding upon the reinsurers.

7 Position of Original Insured

The contract of reinsurance and the original policy are two independent contracts. There is, therefore, no contractual relation between the original insured and the reinsurers, and he cannot, on account of the existence of the contract of reinsurance, assert any claim against them.[2] His position is not affected by the insolvency of the reassured;[3] he cannot proceed directly against the reinsurers, nor where they have paid the reassured the amount due, can he claim to have it handed over to him, since it forms part of the general assets of the reassured.[4] He is only an ordinary creditor and must, therefore, prove against their estate for the amount of his loss along with the other creditors.[5]

---

[1] Cf. *Fire Insurance Association, Ltd.* v. *Canada Fire and Marine Insurance Co.* (*supra*), where it was held that an assent by the reassured to a chattel mortgage by the insured on some of the insured goods, though give without the knowledge of the reinsurers, did not release them.

[2] *Forsikringsaktieselskabet National (of Copenhagen)* v. *A.-G.*, [1925] A.C. 639, *per* Lord CAVE, L.C., at p. 642; *Re Norwich Equitable Fire Assurance Society* (1887), 57 L.T. 241, *per* KAY, J., at p. 246; *English Insurance Co.* v. *National Benefit Assurance Co.*, [1929] A.C. 114 (marine insurance), *per* Lord ATKIN, at p. 125; *Liverpool Mortgage Insurance Co.'s Case*, [1914] 2 Ch. 617, C.A. (mortgage inxurance), *per* SCRUTTON, J., at p. 647.

[3] *Re Eddystone Marine Insurance Co., Ex parte Western Insurance Co.*, [1892] 2 Ch. 243 (marine insurance). See further, Marine Insurance Act 1906, s. 9 (2) which states: "Unless the policy otherwise provides, the original assured has no right or interest in respect of [the] reinsurance." Nor can the insured claim under the Third Parties (Rights Against Insurers) Act 1930, for s. 1 (5) states that for the purpose of the Act the expression "liabilities to third parties" in relation to a person insured under any contract of insurance "shall not include any liability of that person in the capacity of insurer under some other contract of insurance."

[4] Nor can the reinsurers insist on the money being paid to him: *Liverpool Mortgage Insurance Co.'s Case* (*supra*), *per* KENNEDY, L.J., at p. 641.

[5] *Re Eddystone Marine Insurance Co., Ex parte Western Insurance Co.* (*supra*); *Re Law Guarantee Trust and Accident Society, Ltd., Godson's Claim*, [1915] 1 Ch. 340 (debenture insurance). But he may be given a first charge upon the proceeds of the reinsurance: *General Insurance Co. of Trieste* v. *Miller* (1896), 1 Com. Cas. 379, C.A. (marine insurance).

APPENDICES

(A) STATUTES

THE LIFE ASSURANCE ACT 1774[1]

(14 Geo. 3 c. 48)

An Act for regulating Insurances upon Lives, and for prohibiting all such Insurances except in cases where the Persons insuring shall have an Interest in the Life or Death of the Persons insured.

Whereas it hath been found by experience that the making insurances on lives or other events wherein the assured shall have no interest hath introduced a mischievous kind of gaming:

1. No insurance to be made on lives, etc., by persons having no interest, etc.—From and after the passing of this Act no insurance shall be made by any person or persons, bodies politick or corporate, on the life or lives of any person or persons, or on any other event or events whatsoever, wherein the person or persons for whose use, benefit, or on whose account such policy or policies shall be made, shall have no interest, or by way of gaming or wagering; and that every assurance made contrary to the true intent and meaning hereof shall be null and void to all intents and purposes whatsoever.

2. No policies on lives without inserting the names of persons interested, etc.—And . . . it shall not be lawful to make any policy or policies on the life or lives of any person or persons, or other event or events, without inserting in such policy or policies the person or persons name or names interested therein, or for whose use, benefit, or on whose account such policy is so made or underwrote.[2]

3. How much may be recovered where the insured hath interest in lives.—And . . . in all cases where the insured hath interest in such life or lives, event or events, no greater sum shall be recovered or received from the insurer or insurers than the amount of value of the interest of the insured in such life or lives, or other event or events.[3]

4. Not to extend to insurances on ships, goods, etc.—Provided, always, that nothing herein contained shall extend or be construed to extend to insurances bona fide made by any person or persons on ships, goods, or merchandises, but every such insurance shall be as valid and effectual in the law as if this Act had not been made.

---

[1] The short title was given to this Act by the Short Titles Act 1896. The Act is also known as the Gambling Act 1774.

[2] The words omitted were repealed by the Statute Law Revision Act 1888.

[3] *Ibid.*

POLICIES OF ASSURANCE ACT 1867

(30 & 31 Vict. c. 144)

An Act to enable Assignees of Policies of Life Assurance to sue thereon in their own names. [20th August 1867]

1. Assignees of life policies, empowered to sue.—Any person or corporation now being or hereafter becoming entitled, by assignment or other derivative title, to a policy of life assurance, and possessing at the time of action brought the right in equity to receive and the right to give an effectual discharge to the assurance company liable under such policy for moneys thereby assured or secured, shall be at liberty to sue at law in the name of such person or corporation to recover such moneys.

2. Defence or reply on equitable grounds.—In any action on a policy of life assurance, a defence on equitable grounds, or a reply to such defence on similar grounds, may be respectively pleaded and relied upon in the same manner and to the same extent as in any other personal action.

3. Notice of assignment.—No assignment made after the passing of this Act of a policy of life assurance shall confer on the assignee therein named, his executors, administrators, or assigns, any right to sue for the amount of such policy, or the monies assured or secured thereby, until a written notice of the date and purport of such assignment shall have been given to the assurance company liable under such policy at their principal place of business for the time being, or in case they have two or more principal places of business, then at some one of such principal places of business, either in England or Scotland or Ireland; and the date on which such notice shall be received shall regulate the priority of all claims under any assignment; and a payment bona fide made in respect of any policy by any assurance company before the date on which such notice shall have been received shall be as valid against the assignee giving such notice as if this Act had not been passed.

4. Principal place of business to be specified on policies.—Every assurance company shall, on every policy issued by them after the thirtieth day of September one thousand eight hundred and sixty-seven, specify their principal place or principal places of business at which notices of assignment may be given in pursuance of this Act.

5. Mode of assignment.—Any such assignment may be made either by endorsement on the policy or by a separate instrument in the words or to the effect set forth in the schedule hereto, such endorsement or separate instrument being duly stamped.

6. Receipt of notice of assignment.—Every assurance company to whom notice shall have been duly given of the assignment of any policy under which they are liable shall, upon the request in writing of any person by whom any such notice was given or signed, or of his executors or administrators, and upon payment in each case of a fee not exceeding five shillings, deliver an acknowledgment in writing, under the hand of the manager, secretary, treasurer, or other principal officer of the assurance company, of their receipt of such notice; and every such written acknowledgment, if signed by a person being de jure or de facto the manager, secretary, treasurer, or other principal officer of the assurance company whose acknowledgment the same purports to be, shall be conclusive evidence as against such assurance company of their having duly received the notice to which such acknowledgment relates.

7. Interpretation.—In the construction and for the purposes of this Act the expression "policy of life assurance" or "policy" shall mean any instrument by which the payment of moneys by or out of the funds of any assurance company, on the happening of any contingency depending on the duration of human life, is assured or secured; and the expression "assurance company" shall mean and include every corporation, association, society, or company now or hereafter carrying on the business of assuring lives, or survivorships, either alone or in conjunction with any other object or objects.

8. Saving of contracts under 16 & 17 Vict. c. 45, or 27 & 28 Vict. c. 43, and of engagements by friendly societies.—Provided always, that this Act shall not apply to any policy of assurance granted or to be granted or to any contract for a payment on death entered into or to be entered into in pursuance of the provisions of the Government Annuities Act, 1853, and the Government Annuities Act, 1864, or either of those Acts, or to any engagement for payment on death by any friendly society.

9. Short title.—For all purposes this Act may be cited as "The Policies of Assurance Act, 1867."

Section 5   SCHEDULE

I *A.B.*, of, *&c.*, in consideration of, *&c.*, do hereby assign unto *C.D.*, of, *&c.*, his executors, administrators, and assigns, the [within] policy of assurance granted, *&c.* [*here describe the policy*]. In witness, *&c.*

MARRIED WOMEN'S PROPERTY ACT 1882

(45 & 46 Vict. c. 75)

11. Moneys payable under policy of assurance not to form part of estate of the insured.—A married woman may . . . effect a policy upon her own life or the life of her husband for her [own benefit][1]; and the same and all benefit thereof shall enure accordingly.

A policy of assurance effected by any man on his own life, and expressed to be for the benefit of his wife, or of his children, or of his wife and children, or any of them, or by any woman on her own life, and expressed to be for the benefit of her husband, or of her children, or of her husband and children, or any of them, shall create a trust in favour of the objects therein named, and the moneys payable under any such policy shall not, so long as any object of the trust remains unperformed, form part of the estate of the insured, or be subject to his or her debts: Provided, that if it shall be proved that the policy was effected and the premiums paid with intent to defraud the creditors of the insured, they shall be entitled to receive, out of the moneys payable under the policy, a sum equal to the premiums so paid. The insured may by the policy, or by any memorandum under his or her hand, appoint a trustee or trustees of the moneys payable under the policy, and from time to time appoint a new trustee or new trustees thereof, and may make provision for the appointment of a new trustee or new trustees thereof, and for the investment of the moneys payable under such policy. In default of any such appointment of a trustee, such policy, immediately on its being effected, shall vest in the insured and his or her legal personal representatives, in trust for the purposes aforesaid. If, at the time of the death of the insured, or at any time afterwards, there shall be no trustee, or it shall be expedient to appoint a new trustee or new trustees, a trustee or trustees or a new trustee or new trustees may be appointed by any court having jurisdiction under the provisions of the Trustee Act, 1850, or the Acts amending and extending the same. The receipt of a trustee or trustees duly appointed, or in default of any such appointment, or in default of notice to the insurance office, the receipt of the legal personal representatives of the insured shall be a discharge to the office for the sum secured by the policy, or for the value thereof, in whole or in part.

---

[1] The words in square brackets were substituted by the Law Reform (Married Women and Tortfeasors) Act 1935, ss. 5 (1), 8 (2) and Sch. 1, and the words omitted were repealed by ss. 5 (2), 8 (2) and Sch. 2 to that Act.

INDUSTRIAL ASSURANCE ACT 1923[1]

(13 & 14 Geo. 5 c. 8)

An Act to consolidate and amend the law relating to Industrial Assurance, and to make provision with respect to war bond policies and policies to which the Courts (Emergency Powers) Act, 1914, applies, and bond investment business.

[7th June 1923]

Industrial Assurance Business

1. Industrial assurance business.—(1) . . . where an industrial assurance company carries on both industrial assurance business and other business, nothing in this Act shall, save as otherwise expressly provided, apply to any of the business of the company other than the industrial assurance business.

(1A) In this Act "industrial assurance company" means a body corporate which carries on industrial assurance business and "collecting society" means a society registered under the Friendly Societies Act 1896 which carries on such business, being a friendly society within the meaning of that Act.

(2) For the purposes of this Act, "industrial assurance business" means the business of effecting assurances upon human life premiums in respect of which are received by means of collectors:

Provided that such business shall not include—

    (*a*) assurances the premiums in respect of which are payable at intervals of two months or more;

    (*b*) assurances effected whether before or after the passing of this Act by a society or company established before the date of the passing of this Act which at that date had no assurances outstanding the premiums on which were payable at intervals of less than one month so long as the society or company continues not to effect any such assurances;

    (*c*) assurances effected before the passing of this Act, premiums in respect of which are payable at intervals of one month or upwards, and which have up to the commencement of this Act been treated as part of the business transacted by a branch other than the industrial branch of the society or company;

    (*d*) assurances for twenty-five pounds or upwards effected after the passing of this Act, premiums in respect of which are payable at intervals of one month or upwards, and which are treated as part of the business transacted by a branch other than the industrial branch of the society or company, in cases where the Commissioner hereinafter mentioned certifies that the terms and conditions of such assurances are on the whole not less favourable to the assured than those imposed by this Act.

---

[1] Printed as amended.

(3) When a society or company has ceased to effect industial assurances, it shall, so long as it continues liable on the assurances previously effected, be deemed to carry on industrial assurance business.

2. Industrial Assurance Commissioner.—(1) The Chief Registrar of Friendly Societies shall be the authority charged with such powers and duties in relation to industrial assurance as are conferred and imposed upon him by this Act, and in that capacity and in the exercise and performance of the powers and duties of the Chief Registrar of Friendly Societies under the Friendly Societies Acts, 1896 and 1908, in relation to collecting societies he shall, as from the passing of this Act, be known as and styled the Industrial Assurance Commissioner, and is in this Act referred to as the Commissioner, and anything which under the Friendly Societies Acts, 1896 and 1908, is authorised or required to be done by, to or before the central office or the registrar or an assistant registrar shall, where the society is a collecting society, be done by, or to before the Commissioner.

(2) Anything which under this Act is required or authorised to be done by, to or before the Commissioner may be done by, to or before such person as he may appoint for the purpose.

3. Purposes for which policies may be issued.—Subject to the provisions of sections one and two of the Industrial Assurance and Friendly Societies Act, 1948, as amended by the Industrial Assurance and Friendly Societies Act 1948 (Amendment) Act 1958 amongst the purposes for which collecting societies and industrial assurance companies may issue policies of assurance there shall be included insuring money to be paid for the funeral expenses of a parent, child, grandparent, grandchild, brother, or sister, and the issuing of such policies shall be treated as part of the industrial assurance business of the society or company.

4. Assurances on children's lives.—(1) The provisions of sections sixty-two and sixty-four to sixty-seven of the Friendly Societies Act, 1896, relating to payments on the death of children shall extend to industrial assurance companies as if those provisions were herein re-enacted, and in terms made applicable to industrial assurance companies . . .

(2) A collecting society or an industrial assurance company shall not pay any sum on the death of a child under ten years of age . . . except upon production by the person claiming payment of a certificate of death issued by the registrar of deaths, or other person having the care of the register of deaths, containing the particulars mentioned in section sixty-four of the Friendly Societies Act, 1896 . . .

(3) The provisions of this section shall extend to assurances by industrial assurance companies premiums in respect of which are payable at intervals of two months or more.

(4) [*repealed.*]

5. Prohibition on issue of illegal policies.—(1) Any collecting society or industrial assurance company which issues policies of industrial assurance which are illegal or are not within the legal powers of the society or company shall be held to have made default in complying with the provisions of this Act, and, where any such policy has been issued, the society or company shall, without prejudice to any other penalty, be liable to pay to the owner of the policy a sum equal to the surrender value of the policy (to be ascertained in manner hereinafter provided), or, if the policy was issued after the commencement of this Act, a sum equal to the amount of the premiums paid, unless it is proved that owing to any false representation on the part of the proposer, the society or company did not know that the policy was illegal or beyond their legal powers.

(2) No collector of, or person employed by, a society or company shall knowingly assist in effecting a policy of industrial assurance which is illegal or not within the legal powers of the society or company.

Special Provisions as to Collecting Societies

6. Name of collecting societies.—In the case of any collecting society registered after the thirty-first day of December, eighteen hundred and ninety-five, or of a society which becomes a collecting society after the passing of this Act, the last words in the name of the society shall be "collecting society". and the society shall use its registered name on all documents issued by it and no other name.

7. Deposits by collecting societies.—(1) Every collecting society shall be under obligation to deposit with the Accountant General of the Supreme Court the sum of £20,000 and to keep that sum so deposited while it carries on industrial assurance business, and the following provisions shall have effect with respect to deposits under this section, namely,—

(*a*) the provisions substituted by the Administration of Justice Act 1965 for sections 19 (1) and 20 (1) of the Insurance Companies Act 1958 shall apply for the purposes of this section subject to the modifications that, in the provision so substituted for section 19 (1), for the references to a company there shall be substituted references to a collecting society and for the references to section 2 of the Assurance Companies Act 1909 and paragraph 1 of Schedule 2 to the Insurance Companies Act 1958 there shall be substituted a reference to this section and that regulations under the provisions so substituted for section 20 (1) shall be made by the Industrial Assurance Commissioner;

(*b*) a deposit under this section shall not be accepted except on a warrant of that Commissioner:

(*c*) In the case of a society registered and carrying on industrial assurance business at the passing of this Act, the deposit shall be made before the commencement of this Act; but in any particular case the Commissioner shall, if satisfied as to the financial position of the society at the time of the passing of this Act, postpone the time for making the deposit to some time within five years after the commencement of this Act, and shall, on the application of the society from time to time, further postpone the time for making the deposit if he is still satisfied as to the financial position of the society, but not for more than five years at any one time:

(d) . . . the deposit shall be made before the society commences to carry on such business:

(e) In the case of a society applying . . . for registry under the Friendly Societies Act, 1896, or for the registry of amendments of its rules, if the proposed rules of the society or the proposed amendments are such as will enable the society to carry on industrial assurance business, the Commissioner shall not issue to the society an acknowledgment of registry of the society or of amendment of rules, as the case may be, until the deposit has been made:

(f) . . .

(2) If a society feel aggrieved at a refusal of the Commissioner to allow further time for making a deposit under paragraph (c) of subsection (1) of this section, the society may, with the leave of the court, appeal to the High Court or, in the case of a society registered in Scotland, to the Court of Session.

(3) If the Commissioner is satisfied that a collecting society has made default in complying with the provisions of this section, the Commissioner may award that the society be dissolved and its affairs wound up.

(4) [*repealed.*]

(5) Where the rules of a collecting society (hereinafter in this subsection referred to as a subsidiary society), whether registered before or after the passing of this Act, provide that the management of that society shall be vested in the committee of management of some other friendly society (hereinafter in this subsection referred to as the principal society) which was registered before the fourth day of August, nineteen hundred and twenty-one, then—

(a) the principal society may make on behalf of the subsidiary society the deposit required to be made by this section and may apply any of its funds for that purpose, and in that case the interest on the deposit, or the securities in which the deposit is for the time being invested, shall be paid to the principal society and not to the subsidiary society; or

(b) the principal society may guarantee the liabilities of the industrial assurance fund of the subsidiary society to the extent of twenty thousand pounds in such manner and subject to such amendment of rules as the Commissioner may require, and the principal society may amend its rules accordingly; and if the Commissioner is satisfied with such guarantee he may accept the guarantee in lieu of the deposit required by this section.

Where the principal society is a society with branches, the rules of the society may provide for the central body of the society borrowing from the branches and the branches lending to the central body funds required for making such a deposit as aforesaid.

8. Provisions to be contained in rules.—(1) The rules of a collecting society shall provide—

(*a*) for a separate account being kept of all receipts in respect of the industrial assurance business transacted by the society, and for those receipts being carried to and forming a separate fund under the name of the industrial assurance fund; but nothing in this provision shall be construed as requiring the investments of the industrial assurance fund to be kept separate from the other investments of the society;

(*b*) for the industrial assurance fund being as absolutely the security of the owners of the industrial assurance policies as though it belonged to a society carrying on no business other than industrial assurance business, and not being liable for any contracts of the society for which it would not have been liable had the business of the society been only that of industrial assurance, and not being applied directly or indirectly for any purposes other than those of the industrial assurance business of the society, so however as not to affect the liability of that fund to the prejudice of persons interested in contracts entered into by the society before the fourteenth day of February, nineteen hundred and twenty-three;

(*c*) for separate valuations being made of the industrial assurance business of the society.

(2) Save as otherwise provided by the rules of a collecting society, being rules registered before the fourth day of August, nineteen hundred and twenty-one—

(*a*) the rules of a collecting society shall contain the tables in accordance with which policies of industrial assurance are issued by the society; and

(*b*) no policy shall be issued by a collecting society otherwise than in accordance with the rules of the society and with the tables for the time being in force as set forth in those rules.

(3) Such of the provisions of this Act as are mentioned in the First Schedule to this Act shall be set forth in the rules of every collecting society.

9. [*repealed.*]

10. Exemptions, total and partial.—(1) The Commissioner may, on the application of a society registered or applying for registry, grant to the society a certificate of exemption from all or any of the provisions of this Act, in any case where he is satisfied that the society does not or will not carry on the business of effecting assurances upon human life, premiums in respect of which are received by means of collectors at a greater distance than ten miles from the registered office of the society, and where he is of opinion that the society is not one to which those provisions ought to apply.

(2) A certificate of exemption under this section shall be granted subject to the condition that the society will not employ collectors to receive premiums on policies issued by the society at a greater distance than ten miles

from the registered office of the society, and, if in the case of any society to which a certificate of exemption has been so granted, the said condition is at any time not complied with, the society and any collector so employed shall be deemed to have contravened the provisions of this Act, and this Act shall be deemed as from the date of such non-compliance to have applied to the society as if no such certificate of exemption had been granted to it.

(3) The certificate shall be subject to revocation by the Commissioner, but shall remain in force until so revoked, and until notice of the revocation has been advertised in the Gazette and in some newspaper in general circulation in the neighbourhood of the registered office of the society, and also transmitted by registered letter to the society.

(4) Where at the commencement of this Act there is in force a certificate of exemption issued under section eleven of the Collecting Societies and Industrial Assurance Companies Act, 1896, or the corresponding provision of any Act repealed by that Act, the certificate shall after the commencement of this Act, continue in force until revoked and have effect as if it were a certificate issued under this section exempting the society from all the provisions of this Act.

11. Exemption of certain juvenile societies.—(1) This Act shall not apply to a juvenile society within the meaning of this section notwithstanding that premiums of the juvenile members of the society are received by means of collectors, if and so long as no premiums of any members of the society who are not juvenile members are so received.

(2) For the purposes of this section the expression "juvenile society" means a registered friendly society or branch which consists wholly or in part of juvenile members, and which is a branch of, or is shown to the satisfaction of the Commissioner to be connected with, a friendly society registered before the seventh day of June, nineteen hundred and twenty-three, and the expression "juvenile member" means a member under the age of eighteen years.

Special Provisions as to Industrial Assurance Companies

12. [*repealed.*]

13. Prohibition of charges on industrial assurance fund.—An industrial assurance company shall not, after the commencement of this Act, issue any debentures or debenture stock, or raise any loan, charged or purporting to be charged on any assets of the company in which the industrial assurance fund is invested, and any such charge shall be void:

Provided that this section shall not apply to a temporary bank overdraft.

14. Act to have effect notwithstanding memorandum, articles or special Act.—The provisions of this Act shall have effect notwithstanding anything in the memorandum or articles of association or rules or special Act of any industrial assurance company:

Provided that nothing in this Act shall affect the liability of the industrial assurance fund or of the life assurance fund in the case of a company established before the commencement of this Act to the prejudice of persons interested in contracts entered into by the company before that date.

Accounts, Returns, Inspection, Valuations, Meetings

15. Balance sheets and audit.—(1) A copy of every balance sheet of a collecting society shall, during the seven days next preceding the meeting at which the balance sheet is to be presented, be kept open by the society for inspection at every office at which the business of the society is carried on, and shall be delivered or sent by post to any member or person interested in the funds of the society, on demand.

(2) [*repealed.*]

16. Annual accounts and returns.—(1) The Commissioner, after considering any representations made by or on behalf of the society or company affected, may, if it appears to him that any account, return, or balance sheet sent by a collecting society or an industrial assurance company in pursuance of the Friendly Societies Act, 1896, or the Assurance Companies Act, 1909, is in any particular incomplete or incorrect, or does not comply with the requirements of the Act applicable to the case, reject the account, return or balance sheet and give such directions as he thinks necessary for the variation thereof.

(2) Where any direction so given entails a consequential alteration of any account, return, or balance sheet sent by an industrial assurance company to the Board of Trade, it shall be the duty of the company to make such consequential alteration therein.

17. Inspection.—(1) If, in the case of any . . . industrial assurance company, in the opinion of the Commissioner there is reasonable cause to believe that an offence against this Act or against . . . the Assurance Companies Act, 1909, has been, or is likely to be committed, the Commissioner or any inspector appointed by him for the purpose shall have power to examine into and report on the affairs of the . . . company, and for that purpose may exercise in respect of the . . . company all or any of the powers given by subsection (5) of section seventy-six of the Friendly Societies Act, 1896, to an inspector appointed under that section.

(2) On himself holding such an inspection or on receiving the report of an inspector so appointed the Commissioner may issue such directions and take such steps as he considers necessary or proper to deal with the situation disclosed therein and in particular may . . . present a petition to the court for the winding up of the company.

(3) The Commissioner may, if he considers it just, direct that all or any of the expenses of and incidental or preliminary to an inspection under this section shall be defrayed out of the funds of the society or company, or by the officers or former officers, or members, or former members of the committee

of management or board of directors of the society or company, or any of them in such proportions as the Commissioner directs and sums directed by him to be so paid shall be recoverable by him summarily as a civil debt: Provided that any society or company or person directed to pay any part of such expenses may, with the leave of the court, appeal against the direction to the High Court, or in the case of a society or company registered in Scotland to the Court of Session.

(4) [*repealed.*]

18. Provisions as to valuations.—(1) In the case of a collecting society or industrial assurance company, the following provisions shall have effect with regard to every valuation . . .

(a) The valuation shall be made by an actuary as defined by section thirty-three of the Insurance Companies Act 1958, as modified by Part II of the Second Schedule, thereto;

(b) . . .

(c) The report containing the abstract of the result of the valuation required by section twenty-eight of the Friendly Societies Act, 1896, to be sent shall be sent by a collecting society to the Commissioner within twelve months after the close of the period to which the valuation relates, and shall contain a statement as to how the values of stock exchange securities (if any) included in the balance sheet are arrived at, and a certificate, signed by the same persons as sign the balance sheet, to the effect that in their belief the assets set forth in the balance sheet are in the aggregate fully of the value stated therein less any investment reserve fund taken into account;

(d) Where the balance sheet of a society or company includes amongst the assets thereof any sums representing expenses of organisation or extension, or the purchase of business or good will, and the amount of the assets, exclusive of such sums (after deducting debts due by the society or company other than debentures and loans), is less than the amount of the industrial assurance fund, or, as the case may be, of the several assurance and insurance funds as shown in that balance sheet, the amount of the industrial assurance fund shown in the valuation balance sheet shall be reduced by the amount of the deficiency, or, as the case may be, by a sum bearing such proportion to that deficiency as the amount of the industrial assurance fund shown in the first-mentioned balance sheet bears to the aggregate amount of all the assurance and insurance funds so shown:

(e) Where debentures have been issued or loans raised which are charged on any of the assets of the company in which the industrial assurance fund is invested, there shall be inserted in the valuation balance sheet a note giving the particulars of the charge and stating that the result shown by the valuation is subject to the liability under the charge;

(*f*) The Commissioner, if satisfied on any valuation that any of the foregoing provisions of this section have not been complied with, or that the industrial assurance fund as stated in the valuation balance sheet is greater than the value of the assets available for the liabilities of that fund, due regard being had to the other liabilities of the society or company and to the foregoing provisions of this section, may reject the valuation, and may direct the society or company to make such alteration therein as may be necessary to secure compliance with those provisions:

Provided that the society or company may appeal to the High Court, or in the case of a society or company registered in Scotland to the Court of Session, against any decision of the Commissioner under this paragraph;

(*g*) The Commissioner may direct any collecting society or industrial assurance company to furnish to him, in addition to such information as the society is required to furnish under section twenty-eight of the Friendly Societies Act, 1896, or the company is required to furnish under the Assurance Companies Act, 1909 . . . . such explanations as he may consider necessary in order to satisfy himself whether the valuation complies with the provisions of this section.

(2) [*repealed.*]

(3) If in the case of a collecting society or industrial assurance company a valuation . . . discloses a deficiency, the Commissioner may, if after investigation he is satisfied that the society or company should cease to carry on industrial assurance business, award that the society be dissolved and its affairs wound up, or, in the case of a company, present a petition to the court for the winding-up of the company.

19. General meetings.—(1) At least one general meeting of every collecting society and industrial assurance company shall be held in every year.

(2) Except where the day, hour, and place of an annual or other periodical meeting is fixed by the rules, notice of every general meeting shall either be given by the society or company to the members by advertisement to be published at least twice in two or more of the newspapers in general circulation in every county where the society or company carries on business, or be served upon every member.

(3) The notice shall specify the day, hour, and place, and the objects of the meeting, and, in case any amendment of a rule is intended to be proposed, shall in respect of each amendment contain either—

(*a*) a copy of that amendment, or

(*b*) (in the case of an amendment proposed to the rules of a collecting society) an explanation of its purpose, together with a notification that a copy of the amendment may be obtained by any member on application to the society.

(4) The society or company shall publish the last of such advertisements, or serve such notice as aforesaid, at least fourteen days before the day

appointed for the meeting, and shall, during those fourteen days, keep a copy of the notice in legible characters affixed in some conspicious place in or outside every office at which the business of the society or company is carried on.

Rights of Owners of Policies

20. Provisions as to proposals for policies.—(1) Every proposal for an industrial assurance policy shall, except—

(a) where the policy is taken out on the life and on behalf of a child under the age of sixteen; or

(b) where the policy assures a payment of money on the death of a parent or grandparent and is effected in exercise of the power conferred by subsection (1) of section two of the Industrial Assurance and Friendly Societies Act, 1948; or

(c) where the person whose life is to be assured under the policy is a person in whom the proposer has an insurable interest;

contain a declaration by the person whose life is to be assured that the policy is to be taken out by him, and that the premiums thereon are to be paid by him.

Where the person whose life is to be assured under the policy is a person in whom the proposer has an insurable interest, the proposal shall contain a statement of the nature of that interest.

(2) A collecting society or industrial insurance company shall not, nor shall any collector or agent of such a society or company, issue a proposal form or accept a proposal which does not comply with the foregoing provisions of this section.

(3) If the proposal contains a statement that the person whose life is proposed to be assured is not at the time of making the proposal a person on whose life another policy has been issued by the society or company, and a policy is issued in pursuance of the proposal, the society or company shall be liable under the policy, notwithstanding that the statement is not true, and the truth of the statement is made a condition of the policy.

(4) If a proposal form for an industrial assurance policy is filled in wholly or partly by a person employed by the society or company, the society or company shall not, except where a fraudulent statement in some material particular has been made by the proposer, be entitled to question the validity of the policy founded on the proposal on the ground of any misstatement contained in the proposal form:

Provided that—

(a) if the proposal form contains a misstatement as to the age of the person whose life is proposed to be assured, the society or company may so adjust the terms of the policy, or of any policy which may be issued in substitution or in lieu thereof, as to make them correspond with the terms which would have been applicable if the correct age of the person had been originally inserted in the proposal;

(*b*) where but for this subsection the validity of a policy could have been questioned on the ground of any misstatement in the proposal form relating to the state of health of the person upon whose life the assurance is to be taken out at the date of the proposal, nothing in this subsection shall prevent such a question being raised, if raised within two years from the date of the issue of the policy founded on the proposal.

21. [*repealed.*]

22. Return of policies and premium receipt books after inspection.—If at any time a collecting society or industrial assurance company, or any person employed by such a society or company, take possession of a policy or premium receipt book or other document issued in connection with a policy, a receipt shall be given, and the policy book or document shall be returned to the owner of the policy within twenty-one days, unless the policy has been terminated by reason of satisfaction of all claims capable of arising thereunder:

Provided that, where possession is taken of a policy, book or document for the purpose of legal proceedings to be taken by the society or company that issued the policy against a collector, it shall be lawful for the society or company to retain the policy, book or document so long as may be necessary for the purposes of those proceedings, but in that case if the policy, book or document is retained for more than twenty-one days, the society or company shall supply to the owner of the policy, a copy thereof certified by the society or company to be a true copy.

23. Notice before forfeiture.—(1) A forfeiture shall not be incurred by any member or person assured in a collecting society or industrial assurance company by reason of any default in paying any premium until after—

(*a*) notice stating the amount due from him, and informing him that in case of default of payment by him within twenty-eight days and at a place to be specified in the notice his interest or benefit will be forfeited, has been served upon him by or on behalf of the society or company; and

(*b*) default has been made by him in paying any premium in accordance with that notice.

(2) This section shall extend to contracts of assurance effected by a collecting society before the commencement of this Act which are not contracts of industrial assurance within the meaning of this Act.

24. Provisions as to forfeited policies.—(1) Where notice of the forfeiture of a policy of industrial assurance by reason of default in the payment of any premium thereunder has been served on the owner of the policy, then if the policy—

(*a*) is a policy for the whole term of life or for a term of fifty years or upwards, the person whose life is assured under which is a person who is at the time of such default over fifteen years of age, and upon which not less than five years' premiums have been paid; or (*b*) is a policy for a term of twenty-five years or upwards, but less than fifty years, upon which not less than five years' premiums have been paid; or

(*c*) is a policy for a term of less than twenty-five years upon which not less than three years' premiums have been paid:

the owner of the policy shall, on making application for the purpose to the collecting society or industrial assurance company within one year from the date of the service of the notice, be entitled—

(i) to a free paid-up policy for such amount as is hereinafter mentioned payable upon the happening of the contingency upon the happening of which the amount assured under the original policy would have been payable or of any other contingency not less favourable to the owner of the policy; or

(ii) if the owner of the policy is permanently resident or submits satisfactory proof of his intention to make his permanent residence outside Great Britain, the Isle of Man and the Channel Islands, or if the person whose life is assured has disappeared and his existence is in doubt, to the surrender value of the forfeited policy ascertained in manner hereinafter provided.

(2) The amount of a free paid-up policy so issued as aforesaid shall not be less than such as may be determined in accordance with the rules contained in the Fourth Schedule to this Act, and shall be ascertained at the date when the premium following the last premium paid became due:

Provided that the amount of the free paid-up policy shall not exceed the difference between the amount of the forfeited policy (inclusive of any bonus added thereto) and the amount which would be assured by a corresponding policy at the same premium effected on the life of the same person according to the age of that person at his birthday next following the date of forfeiture.

(3) In every premium receipt book issued after the commencement of this Act there shall be printed a notice stating that in the event of the forfeiture, . . . of any policy of industrial assurance by reason of default in the payment of premiums thereunder, the owner of the policy shall, if the policy has been in force a sufficient period as provided by this section, be entitled to a free paid-up policy or, if the conditions mentioned in paragraph (ii) of subsection (1) of this section are fulfilled, to the surrender value of his policy, and that upon application to the head office of the society or company information as to the amount of such free paid-up policy or surrender value will be supplied, and it shall be the duty of the society or company to supply such information.

(4) Where the rules of a society or the conditions of a policy are such as would confer on the owner of the policy in case or forfeiture rights more favourable to the owner of the policy than those conferred by this section, nothing in this section shall prevent the owner of the policy from claiming under those rules or conditions instead of under this section.

(5) [*repealed.*]

25. Substitution of policies.—(1) Where the owner of an industrial assurance policy agrees to accept a new policy in substitution therefor, the collecting society or industrial assurance company shall pay to the owner of the policy the surrender value (to be ascertained in manner hereinafter provided) of the old policy or shall issue to him a free paid-up policy of equivalent value, unless the value of the substituted policy, calculated in accordance with the rules set out in the Fourth Schedule to this Act, at the date of the substitution is equal to or exceeds such surrender value.

(2) In any such case the society or company shall furnish to the owner of the policy, with the new policy and new premium receipt book, a statement setting forth the rights of the owner under this section, and containing an account certified by the secretary of the society or company, or other officer appointed for the purpose, showing the surrender value of the old policy and the value of the new policy.

(3) Where a substituted policy is so issued and the value thereof is equal to or exceeds the surrender value of the old policy, then, for the purpose of determining whether the owner is entitled to a free paid-up policy or surrender value under the provisions of this Act relating to forfeited policies, the substituted policy shall be deemed to have been issued at the date at which the old policy was issued, and premiums shall be deemed to have been paid on the substituted policy in respect of the period between that date and the date at which the substituted policy was actually issued.

26. Transfers from one society or company to another.—(1) A member of or person assured with a collecting society or industrial assurance company shall not, except in the case of—

> (*a*) as respects a collecting society, an amalgamation, transfer of engagements or conversion into a company under the Friendly Societies Act, 1896, or this Act; or
>
> (*b*) as respects an industrial assurance company, an amalgamation or transfer of business under the Assurance Companies Act, 1909, or this Act,

be transferred from the society or company in which he was so assured so as to become or be made a member of or be assured with any other such society or company without his written consent, or, in the case of an infant, without the like consent of his parent or other guardian, and any society or company and any collector or other officer of any society or company concerned in such a transfer shall, if the provisions of this section are not complied with, be deemed to have contravened the provisions of this Act.

(2) Such consent as aforesaid shall be in the prescribed form and shall have annexed thereto a document in the prescribed form to be furnished by the society or company to which the transfer is to be made setting out the terms of and rights under the existing policy, and the terms of and rights under the policy to which the assured will become entitled on transfer and the consideration (if any) which has been or is to be paid for the transfer and the person to whom such consideration has been or will be paid.

(3) The society or company to which the assured is sought to be transferred shall furnish to the person by whom such consent as aforesaid is signed a copy of such consent and of the document annexed thereto, and shall, within seven days from the date when such consent is signed, give to the society or company from which the assured is sought to be transferred notice of the proposed

transfer containing full particulars of the name and address of the assured and the number of his policy, together with such consent as aforesaid, and the document annexed thereto.

(4) As from the date of the said notice, the society or company from which the person is sought to be transferred shall cease to be under any liability with respect to the policy in question and shall not be required to serve any notice of forfeiture of the policy in accordance with the foregoing provisions of this Act.

27. Payment of claims.—Where a claim arising under a policy of industrial assurance is paid, no deductions shall be made on account of any arrears of premiums due under any other policy.

28. [*repealed.*]

29. Value of policies.—(1) When for the purposes of this Act the value of a policy (including an illegal policy and a policy beyond the legal powers of a collecting society or industrial assurance company) has to be ascertained, the value of the policy shall be calculated in accordance with the rules set out in the Fourth Schedule to this Act.

(2) The surrender value of such a policy shall be an amount equal to seventy-five per cent. of the value of the policy so calculated.

30. [*repealed.*]

31. Saving for certain policies issued before 3rd December, 1909.— No policy effected before the third day of December, nineteen hundred and nine, with a collecting society or an industrial assurance company shall be deemed to be void by reason only that—

(a)　the person effecting the policy had not, at the time the policy was effected, an insurable interest in the life of the person upon whose life the policy is taken out; or

(b)　the name of the person interested, or for whose benefit or on whose account the policy was effected, was not inserted in the policy; or

(c)　the assurance was not one authorised by the Acts relating to friendly societies;

if the policy was effected by or on account of a person who had at the time a bona fide expectation that he would incur expenses in connection with the death or funeral of the person whose life is insured, and if the sum assured is not unreasonable for the purpose of covering those expenses, and any such policy shall enure for the benefit of the person for whose benefit it was effected or his assigns.

Disputes

32. Disputes.—(1) In all disputes between a collecting society or industrial assurance company, and

(a)　any member or person assured; or

(b)　any person claiming through a member or person assured, or under or in respect of any policy, or under the rules, or under this Act; or

(c) any person aggrieved who has ceased to be a member or any person claiming through such person aggrieved,

that member or person may, notwithstanding any provisions of the rules of the society or company to the contrary, apply to the county court, or to a court of summary jurisdiction for the place where that member or person resides, and the court may (but in the case of a court of summary jurisdiction only if the amount of the claim does not exceed twenty-five pounds and not less than fourteen days' notice of the application has been given to the society or company) settle that dispute according to the provisions of the Friendly Societies Act, 1896, and, where a dispute is settled under this section by a court of summary jurisdiction, the court may make such order as to costs as it considers fair and reasonable:

Provided that any such dispute may be referred to the Commissioner—

(a) by such collecting society, industrial assurance company, member or person as aforesaid, if the amount of the claim does not exceed fifty pounds and the legality of the policy is not questioned, and fraud or misrepresentation is not alleged; and

(b) any any case, by both parties, without restriction as to the amount of claim or the nature of the question to be decided;

and, where a dispute is so referred, the Commissioner may deal with the dispute as if it were a dispute referred to him under the provisions of section sixty-eight of the Friendly Societies Act, 1896, . . .

(2) In any case where a doubt arises as to the continued existence of the person on whose life a policy of industrial assurance was taken out, the Commissioner may, on the application of the owner of the policy or of the society or company which issued the policy, award that the society or company shall pay to the owner of the policy the surrender value thereof at the time of the award, and the award shall be a discharge for all claims by or against the society or company in connection with the policy.

Provisions as to Collectors, etc.

33. Disabilities of collectors, etc.—(1) A collector of a collecting society or industrial assurance company shall not be a member of the committee of management, or in the case of a company of the board of directors, or hold any other office in the society or company except that of superintending collectors within a specified area.

(2) A collector or superintendent shall not be present at any meeting of the society or company.

34. Restriction on employment of persons to procure new business.—(1) A collecting society or industrial assurance company shall not, nor shall any person employed by such a society or company, employ any person not being a person in the regular employment of the society or company to procure or endeavour to procure any person to enter into a contract of industrial assurance, and no person not regularly in the employment of such a society or company shall procure or endeavour to procure any person to enter into such a contract.

(2) For the purposes of this section, references to regular employment shall include regular part-time as well as regular whole-time employment.

35. Notification of appointments of secretary and members of committee of management.—(1) Every collecting society registered before the passing of this Act shall, within one month after the passing of this Act, and every collecting society registered after the passing of this Act or society which becomes a collecting society after the passing of this Act shall, within one month of the date when it is so registered or so becomes a collecting society, send to the Commissioner in such form as he may direct, the names of its secretary and of the members of its committee of management, and every such society shall, within fourteen days after the appointment of a new secretary or a new member of the committee of management, send to the Commissioner in such form as he may direct the name of the person so appointed, together with such particulars in each case as he may require.

(2) [*repealed.*]

Amalgamations, Transfers and Conversions

36. Transfer of engagements of collecting societies.—(1) Section seventy of the Friendly Societies Act, 1896, in its application to an amalgamation and transfer of engagements of collecting societies shall have effect subject to the following modifications:—

    (i) [*repealed.*]

    (ii) An amalgamation or transfer shall not become effective unless sanctioned by the Commissioner, and the Commissioner, before sanctioning any such amalgamation or transfer, shall hear any representations made on behalf of any class of persons (including the employees of any society concerned) who allege that they are adversely affected by the amalgamation or transfer, and may require as a condition of his sanction that the terms of the amalgamation or transfer shall be modified in such manner as he may consider just.

(2) The said section as so modified shall apply to the transfer by a collecting society of its engagements to an industrial assurance company as if in subsection (2) thereof for the words "any other registered society" there were substituted the words "an industrial assurance company"; and section seventy-one of the Friendly Societies Act, 1896, so far as it enables a registered friendly society to . . . transfer its engagements to a company, shall not apply to a collecting society.

37. Transfer of business from company to society.—The provisions of the Assurance Companies Act, 1909, as amended by this Act relating to the transfer of industrial assurance business or liabilities arising in respect of industrial assurance business from one industrial assurance company to another, shall, with the necessary modifications, apply to the transfer of such business or liabilities from an industrial assurance company to a collecting society.

38. Conversion of collecting society into company.—(1) Section seventy-one of the Friendly Societies Act, 1896, so far as it relates to the conversion of a society into a company shall, in its application to a collecting society, have effect subject to the following modifications:—

(a) A copy of the special resolution shall be sent to the Commissioner;

(b) If within one month after the copy of the special resolution is so sent to him the Commissioner gives notice in writing to the society that he objects to the conversion, the conversion shall not be effected without the sanction of the High Court or in the case of a society registered in Scotland of the Court of Session;

(c) On the application to the court for such sanction the Commissioner shall be entitled to appear and be heard.

(2) Without prejudice to the powers conferred by section seventy-one of the Friendly Societies Act, 1896, as so amended, the committee of management of a collecting society having more than one hundred thousand members may petition the court to make an order for the conversion of the society into a mutual company under the Companies Acts, 1908 to 1917, and the court may make such an order if, after hearing the Commissioner if he desires to be heard, and the committee of management, and other persons whom the court considers entitled to be heard on the petition, the court is satisfied, on a poll being taken, that fifty-five per cent. at least of the members of the society over sixteen years of age agree to the conversion:

Provided that, before any such petition is presented to the court, notice of intention to present the petition shall be published in the Gazette, and in such newspapers as the court may direct.

(3) The court may give such directions as it thinks fit for settling a proper memorandum and articles of association of the company.

(4) When a collecting society converts itself into a company in accordance with the provisions of this section, subsection (3) of section seventy-one of the Friendly Societies Act, 1896, shall apply in like manner as if the conversion were effected under that section.

Offences, Notices, etc.

39. Offences.—(1) Any collecting society which contravenes or fails to comply with any of the provisions of this Act, or any directions by the Commissioner given thereunder, shall be guilty of an offence under this Act and the provisions of the Friendly Societies Act, 1896, with respect to offences thereunder and to proceedings in respect of such offences shall apply to offences by societies under this Act:

Provided that the maximum penalty that may be inflicted for an offence under this Act shall be a fine not exceeding £200.

(2) Any industrial assurance company which contravenes or fails to comply with any of the provisions of this Act, or any directions given by the Commissioner thereunder shall be guilty of an offence under this Act, and a company guilty of such an offence shall be liable to the like penalties, recoverable in the same manner, as in the case of a default in complying with any of the requirements of the Assurance Companies Act 1909 and section twenty-three of that Act shall apply accordingly.[1]

(3) If any collector of a collecting society or industrial assurance company, or any other person, contravenes or fails to comply with any of the provisions of this Act affecting such collector or other person, he shall be guilty of an offence under this Act and liable on summary conviction to a fine not exceeding fifty pounds.

(4) . . .

Any such body of persons as aforesaid shall also, without prejudice to any other penalty, be liable to pay to the owner of any policy of industrial assurance issued by them such sum as an industrial assurance company which has knowingly issued an illegal policy is under this Act liable to pay to the owner of such illegal policy.

(5) Notwithstanding any limitations on the time for the taking of proceedings contained in any Act, summary proceedings for offences under this Act, or for offences under the Friendly Societies Act, 1896, where the society by or in respect of which, or the person by or in respect of whom, the offence is alleged to have been committed is a collecting society or an officer of such a society, may be commenced at any time within one year of the first discovery thereof by the Commissioner, but not in any case after more than three years from the commission of the offence.

(6) The court by which a fine is imposed in pursuance of this Act may direct that the whole or any part thereof shall be applied in or towards the payment of the costs of the proceedings and subject to any such direction and, subject in England to section four of the Criminal Justice Administration Act, 1914, all such fines shall, notwithstanding anything in any other Act, be paid into the Exchequer.

40. Penalities for falsification.—If any person wilfully makes, orders, or allows to be made any entry or erasure in, or omission from a collecting book or premium receipt book, with intent to falsify that book, or to evade any of the provisions of this Act, he shall be liable on summary conviction to imprisonment . . . for a term not exceeding three months or to a fine not exceeding fifty pounds or to both such imprisonment and fine.

41. Notices.—Where any notice is required by this Act to be served upon any member or other person, the notice shall be in writing, and either

---

[1] Section 39 (2) is repealed by the Companies Act 1967, s. 130 (4) (*a*) and Sched. 8, Part I, except in relation to contraventions or failures occurring before the passing of the 1967 Act.

delivered or sent by post to him, or, in the case of a notice of default, so delivered or sent or left at his last known place of abode.

42. [*repealed.*]

General

43. Regulations.—The Commissioner may, subject to the approval of the Treasury, make regulations for prescribing anything which under this Act is to be prescribed and for imposing fees and generally for carrying this Act into effect and all regulations so made shall forthwith be laid before both Houses of Parliament, and, if an address is presented to His Majesty by either House of Parliament within the next subsequent twenty days on which that House has sat next after the regulations are laid before it praying that the regulations may be annulled, they shall thenceforth be void but without prejudice to the validity of anything previously done thereunder or to the making of new regulations. If the Session of Parliament ends before such twenty days as aforesaid have expired, the regulations shall be laid before each House of Parliament at the commencement of the next Session as if they had not previously been laid:

Provided that the regulations so made shall not be deemed to be statutory rules to which section one of the Rules Publication Act, 1893, applies.

44. Report of Commissioner.—The Commissioner in every year shall make a report of his proceedings under this Act, which may contain any comments he may consider desirable to make on the valuations, annual returns, or other documents or matters brought before him under this Act, and any correspondence in relation thereto, and the report shall be laid before Parliament.

45. Interpretation.—(1) In this Act, unless the context otherwise requires—

The expression "collector" shall include every person, howsoever remunerated, who, by himself or by any deputy or substitute, makes house to house visits for the purpose of receiving premiums payable on policies of insurance on human life, or holds any interest in a collecting book and includes such a deputy or substitute as aforesaid:

The expression "premium" includes contribution:

The expression "collecting book" includes any book or document held by a collector in which payments of premiums are recorded:

The expression "premium receipt book" includes any book or document held by the owner of a policy in which acknowledgments of receipts of premiums payable in respect of the policy are entered:

The expression "owner" in relation to any policy means the person who is for the time being the person entitled to receive the sums payable under the policy on maturity, and in the case of an illegal policy or a policy not within the legal powers of the society or company which issued it means the person who would be so entitled were the policy a legal policy or a policy within such powers:

The expression "rules" in relation to a company means the memorandum and articles of association of the company:

The expression "the Companies Acts" means the Companies Acts, 1908 to 1917, and any Acts repealed by the Companies (Consolidation) Act, 1908.

Other expressions have the same meaning as in the Friendly Societies Act, 1896.

(2) Where under this Act the Commissioner awards that a collecting society be dissolved and its affairs wound up, the award shall be made in the like manner and have the like consequences as if it were an award made under section eighty of the Friendly Societies Act, 1896, and may direct in what manner the assets are to be divided or appropriated:

Provided that the society may appeal against the award to the High Court or in the case of a society registered in Scotland to the Court of Session.

(3) The application of this Act to Scotland, the Isle of Man, and the Channel Islands shall be subject to the same modifications as are expressed in the Friendly Societies Act, 1896, with respect to the application of that Act, and for the purposes of this Act the Isle of Man and the several Channel Islands shall be deemed to be counties.

46. Short title, extent, commencement, and repeal.—(1) This Act may be cited as the Industrial Assurance Act, 1923.

(2) This Act shall extend to Great Britain, the Isle of Man, and the Channel Islands.

(3), (4) [*repealed.*]

SCHEDULES

Section 8   FIRST SCHEDULE

SECTIONS OF ACT TO BE CONTAINED IN THE RULES OF COLLECTING SOCIETIES
Section 5.   Prohibition on issue of illegal policies.

．　　　．　　　．　　　．　　　．

Section 15.   Balance sheets and audit.
Section 18.   Provisions as to valuations.
Section 19.   General meetings.
Section 20.   Provisions as to proposals for policies.

．　　　．　　　．　　　．　　　．

Section 22.   Return of policies and premium receipt books after inspection.
Section 23.   Notice before forfeiture.
Section 24.   Provisions as to forfeited policies.
Section 25.   Substitution of policies.
Section 26.   Transfers from one society or company to another.
Section 27.   Payment of claims.

．　　　．　　　．　　　．　　　．

Section 31.   Savings for certain policies issued before 3rd December 1909.
Section 32.   Disputes.
Section 34.   Restriction on employment of persons to procure new business.
Section 40.   Penalities for falsification.
Section 41.   Notices.

[*Schedules 2, 3 and 6 repealed.*]

FOURTH SCHEDULE

RULES FOR VALUING POLICIES

1. The value of the policy is to be the difference between the present value of the reversion in the sum assured according to the contingency upon which it is payable, including any bonus added thereto, and the present value of the future net premiums.

2. The net premium is to be such premium as according to the assumed rate of interest and rate of mortality and the age of the person whose life is assured at his birthday next following the date of the policy is sufficient to provide for the risk incurred by the company or society in issuing the policy, exclusive of any addition thereto for office expenses and other charges:

Provided that—

(a) In the case of a policy other than a policy for the whole term of life issued before the person whose life is assured attained the age of ten years, the date of the policy may be assumed to be one year after the actual date, and, if it so assumed, the term of the policy may be assumed to be one year less than the actual term:

(b) In the case of a policy for the whole term of life issued before the person whose life is assured attained the age of ten years, no account shall be taken of any period for which the policy was in force before the anniversary of the date of the issue of the policy next preceding the date on which the age of eleven years was attained;

(c) In the case of a substituted policy, the net premium shall be calculated with reference to such sum as, according to the practice of the society or company for the time being, would have been assured by the premiums payable if the person upon whose life the substituted policy is issued had not been assured with the society or company before the issue of that policy.

RULE FOR ASCERTAINING THE AMOUNT OF A FREE PAID-UP POLICY

The amount of a free paid-up policy is to be a sum bearing the same proportion to seventy-five per cent. of the value of the policy as the sum of one pound bears to the value of the reversion in the sum of one pound according to the contingency upon which the sum assured under the original policy was payable.

GENERAL RULES APPLICABLE BOTH FOR VALUING POLICIES AND FOR ASCERTAINING THE AMOUNT OF A FREE PAID-UP POLICY.

1. Interest is to be assumed at the rate of four per centum per annum.

2. The rate of mortality is to be assumed according to the table contained in the Sixth column of Table G in the Supplement to the Sixty-fifth Annual Report of the Registrar-General.

3. The age of the person whose life is assured shall be obtained by adding to the age attained by him at his birthday next after the date of the issue of the policy, the duration of the policy in completed years at the date as at which the value of the policy is required to be ascertained.

4. In the case of a policy issued for a term other than the whole term of life, the remaining term at the date at which the value of the policy is required to be ascertained shall be obtained by deducting from the original term of the policy the duration of the policy in completed years at that date.

THIRD PARTIES (RIGHTS AGAINST INSURERS) ACT 1930

(20 & 21 Geo. 5 c. 25)

An Act to confer on third parties rights against insurers of third-party risks in the event of the insured becoming insolvent, and in certain other events. [10th July 1930.]

Be it enacted by the King's most Excellent Majesty, by and with the advice and consent of the Lords Spiritual and Temporal, and Commons, in this present Parliament assembled, and by the authority of the same, as follows:

1. Rights of third parties against insurers on bankruptcy &c. of the insured.—(1) Where under any contract of insurance a person (hereinafter referred to as the insured) is insured against liabilities to third parties which he may incur, then—

(a) in the event of the insured becoming bankrupt or making a composition or arrangement with his creditors; or

(b) in the case of the insured being a company, in the event of a winding-up order being made, or a resolution for a voluntary winding-up being passed, with respect to the company, or of a receiver or manager of the company's business or undertaking being duly appointed, or of possession being taken, by or on behalf of the holders of any debentures secured by a floating charge, of any property comprised in or subject to the charge;

if, either before or after that event, any such liability as aforesaid is incurred by the insured, his rights against the insurer under the contract in respect of the liability shall, notwithstanding anything in any Act or rule of law to the contrary, be transferred to and vest in the third party to whom the liability was so incurred.

(2) Where an order is made under section one hundred and thirty of the Bankruptcy Act 1914, for the administration of the estate of a deceased debtor according to the law of bankruptcy, then, if any debt provable in bankruptcy is owing by the deceased in respect of a liability against which he was insured under a contract of insurance as being a liability to a third party, the deceased debtor's rights against the insurer under the contract in respect of that liability shall, notwithstanding anything in the said Act, be transferred to and vest in the person to whom the debt is owing.

(3) In so far as any contract of insurance made after the commencement of this Act in respect of any liability of the insured to third parties purports, whether directly or indirectly, to avoid the contract or to alter the rights of the parties thereunder upon the happening to the insured of any of the events specified in paragraph (a) or paragraph (b) of subsection (1) of this section or upon the making of an order under section one hundred and thirty of the Bankruptcy Act 1914, in respect of his estate, the contract shall be of no effect.

(4) Upon a transfer under subsection (1) or subsection (2) of this section, the insurer shall, subject to the provisions of section three of this Act, be under the same liability to the third party as he would have been under to the insured, but—

    (a) if the liability of the insurer to the insured exceeds the liability of the insured to the third party, nothing in this Act shall affect the the rights of the insured against the insurer in respect of the excess; and

    (b) if the liability of the insurer to the insured is less than the liability of the insured to the third party, nothing in this Act shall affect the rights of the third party against the insured in respect of the balance.

(5) For the purposes of this Act, the expression "liabilities to third parties", in relation to a person insured under any contract of insurance, shall not include any liability of that person in the capacity of insurer under some other contract of insurance.

(6) This Act shall not apply—

    (a) where a company is wound up voluntarily merely for the purposes of reconstruction or of amalgamation with another company; or

    (b) to any case to which subsections (1) and (2) of section seven of the Workmen's Compensation Act 1925, applies.

2. Duty to give necessary information to third parties.—(1) In the event of any person becoming bankrupt or making a composition or arrangement with his creditors, or in the event of an order being made under section one hundred and thirty of the Bankruptcy Act 1914, in respect of the estate of any person, or in the event of a winding-up order being made, or a resolution for a voluntary winding-up being passed, with respect to any company or of a receiver or manager of the company's business or undertaking being duly appointed or of possession being taken by or on behalf of the holders of any debentures secured by a floating charge of any property comprised in or subject to the charge it shall be the duty of the bankrupt, debtor, personal representative of the deceased debtor or company, and, as the case may be, of the trustee in bankruptcy, trustee, liquidator, receiver, or manager, or person in possession of the property to give at the request of any person claiming that the bankrupt, debtor, deceased debtor, or company is under a liability to him such information as may reasonably be required by him for the purpose of ascertaining whether any rights have been transferred to and vested in him by this Act and for the purpose of enforcing such rights, if any, and any contract of insurance, in so far as it purports, whether directly or indirectly, to avoid the contract or to alter the rights of the parties thereunder upon the giving of any such information in the events aforesaid or otherwise to prohibit or prevent the giving thereof in the said events shall be of no effect.

(2) If the information given to any person in pursuance of subsection (1) of this section discloses reasonable ground for supposing that there have or may have been transferred to him under this Act rights against any particular insurer, that insurer shall be subject to the same duty as is imposed by the said subsection on the persons therein mentioned.

(3) The duty to give information imposed by this section shall include a duty to allow all contracts of insurance, receipts for premiums, and other relevant documents in the possession or power of the person on whom the duty is so imposed to be inspected and copies thereof to be taken.

3. Settlement between insurers and insured persons.—Where the insured has become bankrupt or where in the case of the insured being a company, a winding-up order has been made or a resolution for a voluntary winding-up has been passed, with respect to the company, no agreement made between the insurer and the insured after liability has been incurred to a third party and after the commencement of the bankruptcy or winding-up, as the case may be, nor any waiver, assignment, or other disposition made by, or payment made to the insured after the commencement aforesaid shall be effective to defeat or affect the rights transferred to the third party under this Act, but those rights shall be the same as if no such agreement, waiver, assignment, disposition or payment had been made.

[**4.** This section applies to Scotland only.]

5. Short title. This Act may be cited as the Third Parties (Rights against Insurers) Act 1930.

INDUSTRIAL ASSURANCE AND FRIENDLY SOCIETIES ACT 1948

(11 & 12 Geo. 6, c. 39)

An Act to amend the Friendly Societies Acts, 1896 to 1929, and the Industrial Assurance Acts, 1923 to 1929, and to amend provisions corresponding or relating to provisions of those Acts contained in the Industrial and Provident Societies Acts, 1893 to 1928, and other enactments, as to payments on deaths of children, payments on deaths where no grant of probate or administration has been made, investment in savings banks, the designation of auditors appointed thereunder, the mode of determination of disputes and interpretation.   [30th June 1948]

Amendments as to insurances authorised, and as to alienation of insurance benefits

1. Cesser of powers to insure for funeral expenses.—The powers to insure conferred on registered friendly societies and on industrial assurance companies by the following enactments in the Friendly Societies Act, 1896, the Industrial Assurance Act, 1923, and the Industrial Assurance and Friendly Societies Act, 1929 (in this Act referred to respectively as the Act of 1896, the Act of 1923, and the Act of 1929) shall cease to be exercisable at the expiration of one year from the day appointed for the coming into operation of section twenty-two of the National Insurance Act, 1946, that is to say—

    (*a*)   so much of paragraph (*b*) of subsection (1) of section eight of the Act of 1896 as relates to insuring money for funeral expenses;

    (*b*)   section three of the Act of 1923 (which relates to insuring money for funeral expenses); and

(c) section one of the Act of 1929 (which relates to insuring money to be paid on the duration of a life for a specified period, either with or without provision for a payment in the event of a death before the expiration of the period but subject to a limitation of any payment at death to an amount reasonable for funeral expenses):

Provided that—

(a) this section shall apply only to insurances where the funeral expenses in question are those, or the life in question is that, of a person who at the time of the proposal is ordinarily resident in Great Britain; and

(b) nothing in this section shall prejudice any insurance effected in exercise of any of the said powers before the expiration of one year from the day appointed as aforesaid, or any rights or liabilities in respect of any such insurance.

2. Power to insure life of parent or grandparent for not more than £30; and prohibition of alienation of such insurances.—(1) Amongst the purposes for which registered friendly societies and industrial assurance companies may insure shall be included insuring money to be paid to the member (in the case of such a society) or to the person insured (in the case of such a company) on the death of a parent or grandparent of his:

Provided that this subsection shall apply only where the death in question is that of a person who at the time of the proposal is ordinarily resident in Great Britain.

(2) Such a society or company shall not, in effecting an insurance at any time in exercise of the power conferred by the preceding subsection, insure to be paid to any person on the death of any one of his parents or grandparents any sum which (either taken alone or when added to any sum or sums for the time being insured to be paid to that person on that death under any other relevant insurance or insurances taken out by him) exceeds [thirty pounds], and, where an insurance has been effected in exercise of that power, shall not—

(a) by virtue of or in connection with that insurance, pay to any person any sum which exceeds [thirty pounds] when taken alone, or

(b) by virtue of or in connection with that insurance, pay to the person by whom that insurance was taken out any sum which exceeds thirty pounds when added to any sum or sums paid to him, on the death on which money was thereby insured to be paid, by virtue of or in connection with any other relevant insurance taken out by him, or

(c) if any payment has been made on that death by virtue of or in connection with that insurance to the person by whom it was taken out and has not been repaid, pay to him on that death, by virtue of or in connection with any other relevant insurance taken out by him, any sum which exceeds thirty pounds when added to the amount so paid and not repaid, or when added to it and to any sum or sums paid to him on that death by virtue of or in connection with any other relevant insurance or insurances taken out by him:

Provided that there shall be excluded for the purposes of this subsection any sum insured to be paid, or paid,—

    (i)   by way of bonus other than a guaranteed bonus;

    (ii) by way of repayment of premiums; or

    (iii) under a free paid-up policy which is in force as such at, or has been applied for or claimed before, the passing of this Act.

(3) The provisions of the First Schedule to this Act shall have effect . . . as to the production of certificates of death in connection with the making of payments relevant for the purposes of the last preceding subsection.

(4) Where under any relevant insurance money is for the time being insured to be paid to the person by whom the insurance was taken out on the death of a parent or grandparent of his, any assignment or charge made by him after the passing of this Act of or on all or any of the rights in respect of the insurance conferred on him by the policy or by any provision of the Industrial Assurance Acts, 1923 to 1929, or of this Act, and any agreement so made by him to assign or charge all or any of those rights, shall (except in the case of a charge or agreement to charge for the purpose only of securing sums paid for keeping on foot or restoring the insurance) be void, and on any bankruptcy of his where the receiving order or the award of sequestration of his estate was made after the passing of this Act none of those rights shall pass to any trustee or other person acting on behalf of his creditors.

(5) In this section and in the said Schedule the expression "relevant insurance" means an insurance effected by any registered friendly society or industrial assurance company in exercise either of the power conferred by subsection (1) of this section or of any power conferred by section three of the Act of 1923 or section one of the Act of 1929, and references to a payment on a person's death include references to a payment for his funeral expenses.

3. Power of friendly society to insure life of spouse of member.— There shall be added to the objects mentioned in subsection (1) of section eight of the Act of 1896 (which specifies the objects of societies which may be registered as friendly societies) the insuring of money to be paid to the member—

    (*a*) on the death of the husband or wife of the member; or

    (*b*) on the duration for a specified period of the life of the husband or wife of the member, either with or without provision for the payment of money in the event of his or her death before the expiration of that period.

4. Amendments consequential on preceding sections.—There shall be made in the Acts of 1896, 1923 and 1929, the amendments, consequential on the provisions of the three preceding sections, which are set out in the Second Schedule to this Act.

5. [*repealed*].

6. Prohibition of insuring money to be paid on death of a child under ten.—(1) A society (whether registered or unregistered), an industrial assurance company, an organisation of workers within the meaning of the

Industrial Relations Act 1971, or an organisation of employers within the meaning of the Act, shall not insure so as to render any sum payable under the insurance on the death of any person at any time before he or she attains the age of ten years, otherwise than by repayment of the whole or any part of premiums paid:

Provided that—

(*a*) . . .

(*b*) . . .

(*c*) this subsection shall apply only in the case of a person who at the time of the proposal is ordinarily resident in Great Britain;

and this subsection shall not apply to a sum payable to another person who has an interest in the life of the person on whose death the sum is payable.

(2) The preceding subsection shall have effect in substitution for section sixty-two of the Act of 1896 (which limits amounts that may be insured or paid on the death of a person under ten years of age), both as it applies to societies and as it applies, by virtue of subsection (1) of section four of the Act of 1933, to industrial assurance companies, and, by virtue of section two of the Trade Union Act Amendment Act, 1876, to trade unions; and sections sixty-three to sixty-six of the Act of 1896 and subsection (2) of section four of the Act of 1923 (which relate to persons to whom, and to conditions on which, payments may be made on the death of a person under ten years of age) shall cease to have effect:

Provided that those enactments (other than the provisions thereof as to the persons to whom payment may be made) shall continue to apply as respects insurances effected before the passing of this Act, or effected thereafter by virtue of paragraph (*a*), (*b*) or (*c*) of the proviso to the preceding subsection, and as respects payments under such insurances.

(3) [*repealed*].

7. Power to extend application of preceding provisions of this Act which are limited to persons resident in Great Britain.—If provision for the payment of death grants corresponding to the provision therefor made by or under the National Insurance Act, 1946, is made by or under the law of a country or place outside Great Britain, His Majesty shall have power, exercisable by Order in Council a draft whereof shall be laid before Parliament, to provide for extending the application of section one of this Act, subsection (1) of section two thereof, and subsection (1) of section six thereof, subject to any modifications necessitated by differences between any provision made by or under the said Act of 1946 and the corresponding provision, to insurances where the funeral expenses in question are those, or the life or death in question is that, of a person who at the time of the proposal is ordinarily resident in that country or place, and for consequential amendments of provisions of this Act.

Amendments as to procedure and administration

8. Premium receipt books.—(1) A collecting society, and an industrial assurance company, shall provide premium receipt books for use in respect of policies of industrial assurance issued by the society or company, and shall cause a receipt for each payment in respect of such a policy or of two or more such policies to be inserted in such a book.

(2) Regulations may be made by the Commissioner, subject to the approval of the Treasury signified by statutory instrument which shall be subject to annulment in pursuance of resolution of either House of Parliament, with respect to the form of books to be provided as aforesaid and to the use thereof and the insertion of receipts therein, and, without prejudice to the generality of this subsection, regulations made for the purposes thereof may provide for prohibiting or restricting in any prescribed circumstances the use of a single premium receipt book for payments in respect of two or more policies.

9. Liability on policies not to be restricted on grounds of health if proposer's knowledge and belief is properly disclosed.—(1) Nothing in any term or condition of an industrial assurance policy issued after the passing of this Act or in the law relating to insurance shall operate to except the society or company from liability under such a policy, or to reduce the liability of the society or company under such a policy, on the ground of any matter relating to the state of health of the person upon whose life the assurance is taken out, other than the ground of the proposer's having, when making the proposal or thereafter and before the making of the contract, either—

(a) made an untrue statement of his knowledge and belief as regards that matter; or

(b) failed to disclose to the society or company something known or believed by him as regards that matter.

(2) In relation to a policy issued after the passing of this Act, subsection (4) of section twenty of the Act of 1923 (which relates to misstatements contained in certain proposal forms for industrial assurance policies) shall not apply to a misstatement concerning the state of health of the person upon whose life the assurance is to be taken out.

10. Obligations as to delivery of policies and of copies of rules and amendments thereof.—(1) A collecting society shall supply a member, free of charge, with the following, that is to say—

(a) on his insuring with the society, with a printed policy signed by two of the committee of management and by the secretary, or, if the society has been granted a certificate under section ten of the Act of 1923 exempting it from the requirement imposed by this paragraph to supply a policy, with a copy of the rules of the society;

(b) on written demand by him if a copy of the rules of the society has not previously been supplied to him, with a copy of the rules of the society;

(c) on written demand by him if the rules of the society have been amended since he has been supplied with a copy thereof and a copy of the amendment has not previously been supplied to him, with a copy of the amendment;

and shall, on demand by him and on payment by him of such sum not exceeding [two shillings] as the society may require, supply a member to whom a copy of the rules of the society has been supplied with a further copy thereof.

(2) Where an amendment of the rules of a collecting society modifies the terms or conditions of any insurance issued by the society by way of increase of premiums or reduction of benefit, the society shall, within two months from the date on which the amendment is registered pursuant to section thirteen of the Act of 1896, either—

(*a*) serve every member of the society with a notice containing a statement which, in the opinion of the Commissioner, sufficiently sets forth the effect of the amendment; or

(*b*) publish such a statement by advertisement in two or more of the newspapers in general circulation in every county where the society carries on business.

A member served with a notice under paragraph (*a*) of this subsection shall be regarded for the purpose of the preceding subsection as if he had been supplied with a copy of the amendment in question.

(3) For the purposes of this section, a policy shall be deemed to be signed by a person if it bears a stamped, printed or lithographed reproduction of his signature placed thereon with his authority.

(4) [*repealed*].

11. Matters to be set out in rules of collecting societies.—(1) Subsection (3) of section eight of the Act of 1923 (which requires the provisions of that Act mentioned in the First Schedule thereto to be set forth in the rules of collecting societies) shall extend to the following provisions, that is to say—

Subsections (2), (4) and (5) of section two of this Act	—Insurances on life of parent or grand-parent: limit on amount, and prohibition of assignment or charge
Section eight of this Act	—Premium receipt books
Section nine of this Act	—Restriction of liability on policies on ground of health
Subsections (1) and (2) of section ten of this Act	—Obligations as to delivery of policies, and of copies of rules and amendments thereof
The First Schedule to this Act	—Death certificates in connection with payments referred to in section two (2) of this Act,

and shall have effect, both as regards those provisions and as regards the relevant provisions of the Act of 1923, subject to the modification that the rules may, if the Commissioner consents, in any case, and shall in the case of the provisions of the First Schedule to this Act, in lieu of setting out the provisions in question, contain a statement which, in the opinion of the Commissioner, sufficiently sets forth the effect thereof.

(2) References to the above-mentioned provisions of this Act shall accordingly be inserted in the First Schedule to the Act of 1923.

(3) The requirement imposed by subsection (3) of section eight of the Act of 1923 to set out provisions of that Act in rules shall, in the case of a provision

which is amended by this Act, be construed as relating to that provision as so amended.

(4) [*repealed*].

12. Matters to be set out in premium receipt books, and to be published.—(1) [*repealed*].

(2) A collecting society, and an industrial assurance company, shall cause to be set out, in every premium receipt book provided by them after the coming into operation of this subsection for use in respect of policies of industrial assurance, the matters specified in the Third Schedule to this Act relating to the provisions mentioned in that Schedule of the Act of 1896, of the Act of 1923 and of this Act and of regulations made for the purposes of section eight of this Act.

(3) . . . the last preceding subsection shall not come into operation as respects any regulations made under section eight of this Act until the expiration of six months from the date on which the regulations come into operation.

(4) [*repealed*].

13. Returns as to industrial assurances.—(1) A collecting society and an industrial assurance company shall, as respects each year as respects which they are required by the Commissioner in the prescribed manner so to do, send to him within such period as may be prescribed a return giving prescribed particulars as to policies of industrial assurance issued by the society or company which were in force at the beginning of that year, in force at the end of that year, issued during that year or discontinued or converted to free policies during that year.

(2) A requirement under this section may be made either generally as to all such societies or companies, or as to any class thereof, or as to a particular society or company, and the regulations may prescribe different particulars to be given in the case of different societies or companies or classes thereof.

(3) Section sixteen of the Act of 1923 (which authorises the Commissioner to reject returns under the Act of 1896 or the Assurance Companies Act, 1909, which are incomplete or incorrect or do not comply with the requirements of the Act applicable, and to give directions for the variation thereof) shall apply to returns under this section.

(4) In this section the expression "year" means, in relation to a collecting society, a year ending on a thirty-first day of December, and, in relation to an industrial assurance company, a financial year of the company.

14. [*repealed*].

15. Amendments of registered societies' rules consequential on this Act.—(1) The rules of a registered society shall be amended for the purpose of bringing them into conformity with the provisions of this Act, and amendments made for that purpose shall be sent to the registrar within one year from the day appointed for the coming into operation of section twenty-two of the National Insurance Act, 1946.

(2) If the registrar is satisfied, and certifies, that amendments sent to him within the period required by virtue of the preceding subsection, or within such further time as the registrar may in special circumstances allow, are for the purpose of bringing the rules of a registered society into conformity with the provisions of this Act or for the purpose of enabling the society to exercise any power conferred by this Act, and have been approved by the committee, he may register the amendments notwithstanding that the provisions of the rules of the society as to the alterations of rules or the making of new rules have not been complied with, or (in the case of a friendly society formed and established before the fifteenth day of August, eighteen hundred and fifty) that the rules of the society do not make provision for the alteration thereof, and an amendment registered under this section, shall, unless it is for some other reason invalid, be valid notwithstanding as aforesaid.

16. Provisions as to offences.—(1) Any registered society not being a collecting society which contravenes or fails to comply with any of the provisions of this Act, or of a direction given under section fourteen of this Act, shall be guilty of an offence under the Act of 1896, and, in the case of a contravention of subsection (2) of section two of this Act or of subsection (1) of section six thereof, shall be liable to a fine not exceeding one hundred pounds:

Provided that such a society shall not be guilty of an offence under the Act of 1896 by reason of its insuring in contravention of subsection (2) of section two of this Act if it is proved that, owing to any false representation on the part of the proposer, the society did not know that the insurance was in contravention of that subsection.

(2) Any collecting society or industrial assurance company which contravenes or fails to comply with any of the provisions of this Act, or of regulations made for the purposes of section eight thereof, shall be guilty of an offence under the Act of 1923:

Provided that such a society or company shall not be guilty of an offence under the Act of 1923 by reason of its insuring in contravention of subsection (2) of section two of this Act if it is proved that, owing to any false representation on the part of the proposer, the society or company did not know that the insurance was in contravention of that subsection.

(3) Any collector of a collecting society or industrial assurance company, or any other person, who contravenes or fails to comply with any of the provisions or regulations made for the purposes of section eight of this Act affecting such collector or other person shall be guilty of an offence under the Act of 1923.

(4) Any society not being a registered society, and any organisation of workers or organisation of employers, which contravenes subsection (1) of section six of this Act shall be guilty of an offence under the Act of 1896 and shall be liable to a fine not exceeding fifty pounds.

(5) Notwithstanding any limitation on the time for the taking of proceedings contained in any Act, summary proceedings for offences under the Act of 1896 may be commenced at any time within one year of the first discovery thereof by the registrar, but not in any case after more than three years from the commission of the offence:

Provided that this subsection shall not apply where the society by or in respect of which, or the person by or in respect of whom, the offence is alleged to have been committed is a collecting society or an officer of such a society (for which cases corresponding provision is made by subsection (5) of section thirty-nine of the Act of 1923).

Miscellaneous and general

17. Protection for members of registered societies joining the forces.—(1) Any provision in the rules of a registered society which purports to deprive persons of membership of the society or of any interest therein by reason of their service in any of the naval, military or air forces of the Crown (which expression shall for the purposes of this section be treated in the case of a woman as including service in any of the capacities mentioned in the Fourth Schedule to this Act) shall be of no effect, and no person shall be fined for failure to attend any meeting of the society or otherwise to comply with the rules thereof if the failure was due to his or her service as aforesaid.

(2) [*repealed.*]

(3) Notwithstanding anything in the Government of Ireland Act, 1920, the Parliament of Northern Ireland shall have power to make laws for purposes similar to any of the purposes of this section.

18. Provisions as to payments on deaths in certain circumstances.—(1) The powers to determine questions of title conferred on a majority of the trustees of a registered society by section fifty-eight of the Act of 1896 (which relates to payment of small sums to which members of registered societies are entitled on the death intestate of such a member) shall be exercisable by the committee of the society in lieu of by a majority of the trustees, and accordingly a reference to the committee shall be substituted for each reference to a majority of the trustees in that section and for the reference thereto in section sixty of the Act of 1896 (which refers to the said section fifty-eight).

(2), (3) [*repealed.*]

19. Provisions as to investment by registered societies and certain other bodies.—(1)–(4) [*repealed.*]　(5) It is hereby declared that nothing in section forty-four of the Act of 1896 (which enacts that the trustees of a registered society may invest its funds to any amount in the ways therein mentioned, including investment in the Post Office Savings Bank or in any savings bank certified under the Trustee Savings Banks Act, 1863), . . . is to be construed as imposing any obligation on any savings bank authority as respects their or his receiving any such funds, money or capital.

In this subsection the expression "savings bank authority" has the meaning assigned to it by subsection (3) of section ten of the Savings Banks Act, 1920.

(6) This section shall extend to Northern Ireland.

20-22. [*repealed.*]

23. Interpretation.—(1) In this Act, except where the context otherwise requires,—

(*a*) the expression "society" means a society for any of the purposes specified in section eight of the Act of 1896, the expression "registered society" means a society registered under that Act, and references to a society or to a registered society or to a registered friendly society include references to a branch of such a society;

(*b*) the expression "policy" includes any contract of assurance, and for the purposes of this Act the date of the making of any such contract shall be deemed to be the date of the issue of a policy;

(*c*) the expression "proposal" in relation to an insurance, includes an application for an insurance, and the expression "proposer" shall be construed accordingly; and

(*d*) . . .

(2) In this Act the expression "parent" includes a stepfather and a stepmother.

(3) [*repealed.*]

24. Extent.—(1) This Act shall extend to Great Britain, the Isle of Man and the Channel Islands.

(2) Except as regards subsection (3) of section seventeen thereof and section nineteen thereof, this Act shall not extend to Northern Ireland.

25. Short title, citation, construction and repeal.—(1) This Act may be cited as the Industrial Assurance and Friendly Societies Act, 1948.

(2) This Act and the Industrial Assurance Acts, 1923 to 1929, may be cited together as the Industrial Assurance Acts, 1923 to 1948, and this Act and the Friendly Societies Acts, 1896 to 1929, may be cited together as the Friendly Societies Acts, 1896 to 1948.

(3) References in this Act to any other enactment shall, except so far as the context otherwise requires, be construed as references to that enactment as amended by or under any other enactment, including this Act.

(4) This Act, in its application to collecting societies and industrial assurance companies, shall be construed as one with the Industrial Assurance Acts, 1923 to 1929, and in its application to friendly societies, not being collecting societies, shall be construed as one with the Friendly Societies Acts, 1896 to 1929.

(5) [*repealed.*]

SCHEDULES

FIRST SCHEDULE   Section 2

DEATH CERTIFICATES IN CONNECTION WITH PAYMENTS REFERRED TO IN
SUBSECTION (2) OF SECTION TWO

1. A registered friendly society or industrial assurance company shall not, by virtue of or in connection with any relevant insurance of money to be paid on the death of a parent or grandparent of the person by whom the insurance was taken out, pay to that person on the death any sum not excluded for the purposes of subsection (2) of section two of this Act by the proviso thereto, except upon production of a certificate of the death for the purposes of this Schedule stated therein to be issued to the person to whom the payment is made, unless the death occurred outside Great Britain.

2. On so making payment of any such sum the society or company shall cause to be indorsed on the certificate a statement showing—

(a) the name of the society or company;

(b) the amount of any such sum paid; and

(c) the date of the contract for the insurance;

and on receiving any repayment of a sum so paid by virtue of or in connection with an insurance effected in exercise of the power conferred by subsection (1) of section two of this Act the society or company shall cause to be indorsed on the certificate a statement showing the repayment.

3. Where such a society or company is charged with a contravention of subsection (2) of section two of this Act in respect of the payment by the society or company of a sum which exceeded the limit of [thirty pounds] imposed by paragraph (b) or (c) of that subsection in consequence of the addition as thereby required of another sum paid by another such society or company, or of two or more other sums so paid, and which would not have exceeded that limit apart from such addition, it shall be a defence for the society or company charged to prove—

(a) that the sum in respect of which they are charged was paid in accordance with paragraph 1 of this Schedule; and

(b) that the certificate produced disclosed no payment by any other society or company of any sum or sums required by the said paragraph (b) or (c) to be added, or disclosed such payment but only to an amount insufficient to cause the sum in respect of which they are charged to exceed the said limit;

subject however in the case of a certificate which is a duplicate to the provisions of paragraph 6 of this Schedule.

4. Certificates of death for the purposes of this Schedule, and applications for the issue thereof, shall be in such form as may from time to time be specified by the Registrar General, including, in the case of such a certificate, a statement that it is issued for the purposes of this Schedule, and particulars of the name and address of the person to whom the certificate is issued, and of his relationship (whether child, grandchild or stepchild) to the deceased, as stated in the application.

5.—(1) Regulations shall be made by the Registrar General by statutory instrument as to the issue of certificates for the purposes of this Schedule, and the regulations shall provide for securing that, except as mentioned in subparagraph (2) of this paragraph, more than one certificate for the purposes of this Schedule of the same death shall not be issued to the same person.

(2) The said regulations shall provide for the issue to a person to whom a certificate of a death for the purposes of this Schedule has been issued of a duplicate thereof in the event of the loss or destruction of the certificate which it replaces, subject to conditions for requiring—

(a) the making by that person of a statutory declaration stating that the certificate which the duplicate replaces has been lost or destroyed, and stating whether any indorsement had been made on that certificate, and, if so, by what society or company;

(b) if it is so stated that an indorsement had been made on that certificate by any society or company, the recording on the duplicate of a requirement that it is to be produced to that society or company for having the indorsement repeated on the duplicate; and

(c) the surrender for destruction of the certificate which the duplicate replaces in the event of its being recovered.

6. On production to a society or company of a duplicate which records a requirement for an indorsement made by them to be repeated as mentioned in the last preceding paragraph, the society or company shall cause the duplicate to be indorsed accordingly, and paragraph 3 of this Schedule shall not apply in the case of a certificate which is a duplicate whereon such a requirement is recorded unless the duplicate has been indorsed by the society or company in question.

7. The fee payable on the issue of a certificate of a death for the purposes of this Schedule shall be two shillings.

8. The Statutory Instruments Act, 1946, shall apply to a statutory instrument containing regulations made for the purposes of this Schedule in like manner as if it had been made by a Minister of the Crown.

9. In this Schedule the expression "Registrar General" means the Registrar General of births, deaths and marriages:

Provided that in the application of this Schedule to Scotland the said expression means the Registrar General of births, deaths and marriages in Scotland.

[*Sched.* 2 *amends the Friendly Societies Act* 1896, *s.* 8 (1); *the Industrial Assurance Act* 1923, *ss.* 3, 20 (1); *and the Industrial and Friendly Societies Act* 1929, *s.* 1 (1).]

THIRD SCHEDULE Section 12

MATTERS TO BE SET OUT IN PREMIUM RECEIPT BOOKS

The matters to be set out in premium receipt books under section twelve of this Act are the following, that is to say—

(a) As to the following provisions of the Act of 1923, either those provisions (as amended by this Act in the case of a provision which is amended thereby), or, as to any of them as to which the Commissioner consents to the substitution of a statement which in his opinion sufficiently sets forth the effect thereof, such a statement—

Subsection (4) of section 20.	Provisions as to proposals for policies.
Section 22	Return of policies and premium receipt books after inspection.
Section 23	Notice before forfeiture.
Section 24	Provisions as to forfeited policies.
Section 27	Payment of claims.
Section 32	Disputes.
Section 41	Notices.

(b) As to the following provisions of this Act and of regulations, either those provisions, or, as to any of them as to which the Commissioner consents to the substitution of a statement which in his opinion sufficiently sets forth the effect thereof, such a statement—

Subsections (2), (4) and (5) of section 2.	Insurances on life of parent or grandparent: limit on amount, and prohibition or assignment or charge.
Section 8 and regulations made for the purposes thereof.	Premium receipt books.
Section 9	Restriction of liability on policies on ground of health.
Subsections (1) and (2) of section 10 (in the case of collecting societies only).	Obligations as to delivery of policies, and of copies of rules and amendments thereof.

(c) As to the following provisions of the Act of 1896 and of this Act, a statement which in the opinion of the Commissioner sufficiently sets forth the effect thereof—

Subsections (1) and (2) of section 6 of this Act and section 62 of the Act of 1896 taken together.	Payments on death of children under ten years of age.
The First Schedule to this Act.	Death certificates in connection with payments referred to in section 2 (2) of this Act.

　　　　　　FOURTH SCHEDULE

WOMEN'S AUXILIARY SERVICES

1. Member of Queen Alexandra's Royal Naval Nursing Service or any reserve thereof.

2. Member of the Women's Royal Naval Service.

3. Woman medical or dental practitioner serving in the Royal Navy or any naval reserve.

4. Member of Queen Alexandra's Imperial Military Nursing Service or any reserve thereof.

5. Member of the Territorial Army Nursing Service or any reserve thereof.

6. Member of the Auxiliary Territorial Service.

7. Woman employed with the Royal Army Medical Corps or the Army Dental Corps with relative rank as an officer.

8. Member of Princess Mary's Royal Air Force Nursing Service or any reserve thereof.

9. Member of the Women's Auxiliary Air Force.

10. Woman employed with the Medical Branch or the Dental Branch of the Royal Air Force with relative rank as an officer.

11. Member of the Voluntary Aid Detachments employed under the Admiralty, Army Council or Air Council.

[*Scheds. 5 and 6 repealed.*]

NUCLEAR INSTALLATIONS ACT 1965

(1965 c. 57)

19. Special cover for licensee's liability.—(1) Subject to section 3 (5) of this Act and to subsection (3) of this section, where a nuclear site licence has been granted in respect of any site, the licensee shall make such provision (either by insurance or by some other means) as the Minister may with the consent of the Treasury approve for sufficient funds to be available at all times to ensure that any claims which have been or may be duly established against the licensee as licensee of that site by virtue of section 7 of this Act or any relevant foreign law made for purposes correspondingly to those of section 10 of this Act (excluding, but without prejudice to, any claim in respect of interest or costs) are satisfied up to an aggregate amount of five million pounds in respect of each severally of the following periods, that is to say—

　　(*a*)　the current cover period, if any;

　　(*b*)　any cover period which ended less than ten years before the time in question;

　　(*c*)　any earlier cover period in respect of which a claim remains to be disposed of, being a claim made—

　　　　(i) within the relevant period within the meaning of section 16 of this Act; and

　　　　(ii) In the case of a claim such as is mentioned in section 15 (2) of this Act, also within the period of twenty years so mentioned;

and for the purposes of this section the cover period in respect of which any claim is to be treated as being made shall be that in which the beginning of the relevant period aforesaid fell.

(2) In this Act, the expression "cover period" means the period of the licensee's responsibility or, if a direction has been given in respect of the site under subsection (4) of this section, any of the following periods, that is to say—

(a) the period beginning with the grant of the nuclear site licence and ending with the date specified in the first such direction;

(b) the period beginning with the date specified in any such direction and ending with the date specified in the next such direction, if any;

(c) the period beginning with the date specified in the last such direction and ending with the ending of the period of the licensee's responsibility;

and for the purposes of this definition the period of the licensee's responsibility shall be deemed to include any time after the expiration of that period during which it remains possible for the licensee to incur any liability by virtue of section 7 (2) (b) or (c) of this Act, or by virtue of any relevant foreign law made for purposes corresponding to those of section 10 of this Act.

(3) Where in the case of any licensed site the provision required by subsection (1) of this section is to be made otherwise than by insurance and, apart from this subsection, provision would also fall to be so made by the same person in respect of two or more other sites, the requirements of that subsection shall be deemed to be satisfied in respect of each of those sites if funds are available to meet such claims as are mentioned in that subsection in respect of all the sites collectively, and those funds would for the time being be sufficient to satisfy the requirements of that subsection in respect of those two of the sites in respect of which those requirements are highest:

Provided that the Minister may in any particular case at any time direct either that this subsection shall not apply or that the funds available as aforesaid shall be of such amount higher than that provided for by the foregoing provisions of this subsection, but lower than that necessary to satisfy the requirements of the said subsection (1) in respect of all the sites severally, as may be required by the direction.

(4) Where, by reason of the gravity of any occurrence which has resulted or may result in claims such as are mentioned in subsection (1) of this section against a licensee as licensee of a particular licensed site, or having regard to any previous occurrences which have resulted or may result in such claims against the licensee, the Minister thinks it proper so to do, he shall by notice in writing to the licensee direct that a new cover period for the purposes of the said subsection (1) shall begin in respect of that site on such date not earlier than two months after the date of the service of the note as may be specified therein.

(5) If at any time while subsection (1) of this section applies in relation to any licensed site the provisions of that subsection are not complied with in respect of that site, the licensee shall be guilty of an offence and be liable—

(*a*)   on summary conviction to a fine not exceeding one hundred pounds, or to imprisonment for a term not exceeding three months, or to both;

(*b*)   on conviction on indictment, to a fine not exceeding five hundred pounds, or to imprisonment for a term not exceeding two years, or to both.

EMPLOYERS' LIABILITY (COMPULSORY INSURANCE) ACT 1969

(1969 c. 57)

An Act to require employers to insure against their liability for personal injury to their employees; and for purposes connected with the matter aforesaid.

[22nd October 1969]

BE IT ENACTED by the Queen's most Excellent Majesty, by and with the advice and consent of the Lords Spiritual and Temporal, and Commons, in this present Parliament assembled, and by the authority of the same, as follows:

1.   Insurance against liability for employees.—(1) Except as otherwise provided by this Act, every employer carrying on any business in Great Britain shall insure, and maintain insurance, under one or more approved policies with an authorised insurer or insurers against liability for bodily injury or disease sustained by his employees, and arising out of and in the course of their employment in Great Britain in that business, but except in so far as regulations otherwise provide not including injury or disease suffered or contracted outside Great Britain.

(2) Regulations may provide that the amount for which an employer is required by this Act to insure and maintain insurance shall, either generally or in such cases or classes of case as may be prescribed by the regulations, be limited in such manner as may be so prescribed.

(3) For the purposes of this Act—

(*a*)   "approved policy" means a policy of insurance not subject to any conditions or exceptions prohibited for those purposes by regulations;

(*b*)   "authorised insurer" means a person or body of persons lawfully carrying on in Great Britain insurance business of any class relevant for the purposes of Part II of the Companies Act 1967 and issuing the policy or policies in the course thereof;

(*c*)   "business" includes a trade or profession, and includes any activity carried on by a body of persons, whether corporate or unincorporate;

(*d*)   except as otherwise provided by regulations, an employer not having a place of business in Great Britain shall be deemed not to carry on business there.

2. Employees to be covered.—(1) For the purposes of this Act the term "employee" means an individual who has entered into or works under a contract of service or apprenticeship with an employer whether by way of manual labour, clerical work or otherwise, whether such contract is expressed or implied, oral or in writing.

(2) This Act shall not require an employer to insure—

    (*a*) in respect of an employee of whom the employer is the husband, wife, father, mother, grandfather, grandmother, step-father, step-mother, son, daughter, grandson, granddaughter, stepson, step-daughter, brother, sister, half-brother or half-sister; or

    (*b*) except as otherwise provided by regulations, in respect of employees not ordinarily resident in Great Britain.

3. Employers exempted from insurance.—(1) This Act shall not require any insurance to be effected by—

    (*a*) any such authority as is mentioned in subsection (2) below; or

    (*b*) any body corporate established by or under any enactment for the carrying on of any industry or part of an industry, or of any undertaking, under national ownership or control; or

    (*c*) in relation to any such cases as may be specified in the regulations, any employer exempted by regulations.

(2) The authorities referred to in subsection (1) (*a*) above are the Common Council of the City of London, the Greater London Council, the council of a London borough, the council of a county, county borough or county district in England or Wales, a county, town or district council in Scotland, any joint board or joint committee in England and Wales or joint committee in Scotland which is so constituted as to include among its members representatives of any such council, and any police authority.

4. Certificates of insurance.—(1) Provision may be made by regulations for securing that certificates of insurance in such form and containing such particulars as may be prescribed by the regulations, are issued by insurers to employers entering into contracts of insurance in accordance with the requirements of this Act and for the surrender in such circumstances as may be so prescribed of certificates so issued.

(2) Where a certificate of insurance is required to be issued to an employer in accordance with regulations under subsection (1) above, the employer (subject to any provision made by the regulations as to the surrender of the certificate) shall during the currency of the insurance and such further period (if any) as may be provided by regulations—

    (*a*) comply with any regulations requiring him to display copies of the certificate of insurance for the information of his employees;

    (*b*) produce the certificate of insurance or a copy thereof on demand to any inspector duly authorised by the Secretary of State for the purposes of this Act and produce or send the certificate or a copy thereof to such other persons, at such place and in such circumstances as may be prescribed by regulations;

(c) permit the policy of insurance or a copy thereof to be inspected by such persons and in such circumstances as may be so prescribed.

(3) A person who fails to comply with a requirement imposed by or under this section shall be liable on summary conviction to a fine not exceeding £50.

5. Penalty for failure to insure.—An employer who on any day is not insured in accordance with this Act when required to be so shall be guilty of an offence and shall be liable on summary conviction to a fine not exceeding two hundred pounds; and where an offence under this section committed by a corporation has been committed with the consent or connivance of, or facilitated by any neglect on the part of, any director, manager, secretary or other officer of the corporation, he, as well as the corporation shall be deemed to be guilty of that offence and shall be liable to be proceeded against and punished accordingly.

6. Regulations.—(1) The Secretary of State may by statutory instrument make regulations for any purpose for which regulations are authorised to be made by this Act, but any such statutory instrument shall be subject to annulment in pursuance of a resolution of either House of Parliament.

(2) Any regulations under this Act may make different provision for different cases or classes of case, and may contain such incidental and supplementary provisions as appear to the Secretary of State to be necessary or expedient for the purposes of the regulations.

7. Short title, extent and commencement.—(1) This Act may be cited as the Employers' Liability (Compulsory Insurance) Act 1969.

(2) This Act shall not extend to Northern Ireland.

(3) This Act shall come into force for any purpose on such date as the Secretary of State may by order contained in a statutory instrument appoint, and the purposes for which this Act is to come into force at any time may be defined by reference to the nature of an employer's business, or to that of an employee's work, or in any other way.

MERCHANT SHIPPING (OIL POLLUTION) ACT 1971

(1971 c. 59)

An Act to make provision with respect to civil liability for oil pollution by merchant ships, and for connected purposes.   [27th July 1971]

Be it enacted by the Queen's most Excellent Majesty, by and with the advice and consent of the Lords Spiritual and Temporal, and Commons, in this present Parliament assembled, and by the authority of the same, as follows:

*   *   *   *   *

10. Compulsory insurance against liability for pollution.—(1) Subject to the provisions of this Act relating to Government ships, subsection (2) of this section shall apply to any ship carrying in bulk a cargo of more than 2,000 tons of persistent oil of a description specified in regulations made by the Secretary of State.

(2) The ship shall not enter or leave a port in the United Kingdom or arrive at or leave a terminal in the territorial sea of the United Kingdom nor, if the ship is registered in the United Kingdom, a port in any other country or a terminal in the territorial sea of any other country, unless there is in force a certificate complying with the provisions of subsection (3) of this section and showing that there is in force in respect of the ship a contract of insurance or other security satisfying the requirements of Article VII of the Convention (cover for owner's liability).

(3) The certificate must be—

(a) if the ship is registered in the United Kingdom, a certificate issued by the Secretary of State;

(b) if the ship is registered in a Convention country other than the United Kingdom, a certificate issued by or under the authority of the government of the other Convention country; and

(c) if the ship is registered in a country which is not a Convention country, a certificate issued by the Secretary of State or a certificate recognised for the purposes of this paragraph by regulations made under this section.

(4) The Secretary of State may by regulations provide that certificates in respect of ships registered in any, or any specified, country which is not a Convention country shall, in such circumstances as may be specified in the regulations, be recognised for the purposes of subsection (3) (c) of this section if issued by or under the authority of the government of the country designated in the regulations in that behalf; and the country that may be so designated may be either or both of the following, that is to say—

(a) the country in which the ship is registered; and

(b) any country specified in the regulations for the purposes of this paragraph.

(5) Any certificate required by this section to be in force in respect of a ship shall be carried in the ship and shall, on demand, be produced by the master to any officer of customs or of the Department of Trade and Industry and, if the ship is registered in the United Kingdom, to any proper officer within the meaning of section 97 (1) of the Merchant Shipping Act 1970.

(6) If a ship enters or leaves, or attempts to enter or leave, a port or arrives at or leaves, or attempts to arrive at or leave, a terminal in contravention of subsection (2) of this section, the master or owner shall be liable on conviction on indictment to a fine, or on summary conviction to a fine not exceeding £35,000.

(7) If a ship fails to carry, or the master of a ship fails to produce, a certificate as required by subsection (5) of this section the master shall be liable on summary conviction to a fine not exceeding £400.

(8) If a ship attempts to leave a port in the United Kingdom in contravention of this section the ship may be detained.

(9) Regulations under this section shall be made by statutory instrument, which shall be subject to annulment in pursuance of a resolution of either House of Parliament.

12. Rights of third parties against insurers.—(1) Where it is alleged that the owner of a ship has incurred a liability under section 1 of this Act as a result of any discharge or escape of oil occurring while there was in force a contract of insurance or other security to which such a certificate as is mentioned in section 10 of this Act related, proceedings to enforce a claim in respect of the liability may be brought against the person who provided the insurance or other security (in the following provisions of this section referred to as "the insurer").

(2) In any proceedings brought against the insurer by virtue of this section it shall be a defence (in addition to any defence affecting the owner's liability) to prove that the discharge or escape was due to the wilful misconduct of the owner himself.

(3) The insurer may limit his liability in respect of claims made against him by virtue of this section in like manner and to the same extent as the owner may limit his liability but the insurer may do so whether or not the discharge or escape occurred without the owner's actual fault or privity.

(4) Where the owner and the insurer each apply to the court for the limitation of his liability any sum paid into court in pursuance of either application shall be treated as paid also in pursuance of the other.

(5) The Third Parties (Rights against Insurers) Act 1930 and the Third Parties (Rights against Insurers) Act (Northern Ireland) 1930 shall not apply in relation to any contract of insurance to which such a certificate as is mentioned in section 10 of this Act relates.

14. Government ships.—(1) Nothing in the preceding provisions of this Act applies in relation to any warship or any ship for the time being used by the government of any State for other than commercial purposes.

(2) In relation to a ship owned by a State and for the time being used for commercial purposes it shall be a sufficient compliance with subsection (2) of section 10 of this Act if there is in force a certificate issued by the government of that State and showing that the ship is owned by that State and that any liability for pollution damage as defined in Article I of the Convention will be met up to the limit prescribed by Article V thereof.

(3) Every Convention State shall, for the purposes of any proceedings brought in a court in the United Kingdom to enforce a claim in respect of a liability incurred under section 1 of this Act, be deemed to have submitted to the jurisdiction of that court, and accordingly rules of court may provide for the manner in which such proceedings are to be commenced and carried on; but nothing in this subsection shall authorise the issue of execution, or in Scotland the execution of diligence, against the property of any State.

(B) STATUTORY INSTRUMENTS

INDUSTRIAL ASSURANCE (PREMIUM RECEIPT BOOKS) REGULATIONS 1948[1]

(S.I. 1948 No. 2770)

1. A premium receipt book provided for use in respect of any policy or policies effected on or after the 5th day of July, 1949, shall contain the following particulars in respect of each such policy to which the book relates:

(*a*) the number (if any) and date of the policy;

(*b*) the name of the life assured as stated in the proposal or the life assured's present name, and his age as stated in the proposal or such corrected age as may have been entered in the book with the authority of the owner of the policy;

(*c*) the name of the proposer as stated in the proposal or the proposer's present name; and

(*d*) the amount of the premium and the interval at which it is payable.

2. An entry relating to a policy proposed by any person and effected on or after the 5th day of July, 1949, shall not be made in any book containing an entry (other than an entry made in accordance with the proviso to this Regulation) relating to any policy not proposed by that person:

Provided that this Regulation shall not prohibit the making in a book in respect of any policy proposed by that person of an entry relating to a policy the proposer of which is a child, stepchild or grandchild of that person and is under sixteen years of age when the entry is made, or is the spouse of that person.

3. Any collector who receives a payment in respect of a policy or policies shall enter in the appropriate book the amount of the payment and shall initial the entry.

4.—(1) An entry relating to a policy on which none of the premium payments is in arrear shall not be made in a book relating to a policy on which a premium payment is in arrear, unless the book contains a previous entry relating to the first-mentioned policy.

(2) An entry relating to a policy on which a premium payment is in arrear shall not be made in a book relating to a policy or policies on none of which a premium payment is in arrear, unless the book contains a previous entry relating to the first-mentioned policy.

(3) For the purposes of this Regulation two books, one of which has been

---

[1] The regulations are printed as amended by the Industrial Assurance (Premium Receipt Books) (Amendment) Regulations, 1961, S.I. 1961, No. 597.

provided to replace or continue the other, shall be deemed to be the same book, and in the case of any books divided into sections containing separate entries in respect of one or more policies, each such section shall be deemed to be a separate book.

5. A society or a company or a collector shall not cause or permit a premium receipt book to be provided or any entry to be made therein which does not comply with any of the provisions of these Regulations.

6.—(1) The Interpretation Act, 1889, shall apply to the interpretation of these Regulations as it applies to the interpretation of an Act of Parliament.

(2) In these Regulations—

    (*a*) "premium receipt book" or "book" means a premium receipt book provided for the purposes of section 8 (1) of the Industrial Assurance and Friendly Societies Act, 1948;

    (*b*) "policy" means a policy of industrial assurance;

    (*c*) "society" and "company" mean a collecting society and an industrial assurance company respectively;

    (*d*) "proposer" includes a person on whose behalf a policy has been proposed and does not include a person who has proposed a policy on behalf of another, and the word "proposed" shall be construed accordingly; and

    (*e*) "name" means surname together with the initial letter or letters of any christian name or names.

(3) These Regulations may be cited as the Industrial Assurance (Premium Receipt Books) Regulations, 1948, and shall come into operation on the 5th day of January 1949.

INDUSTRIAL ASSURANCE (PREMIUM RECEIPT BOOKS) (DECIMAL CURRENCY) REGULATIONS 1970
(S.I. 1970 No. 1012)

The Industrial Assurance Commissioner, with the approval of the Treasury, pursuant to section 8 (2) of the Industrial Assurance and Friendly Societies Act 1948, section 7 (5) of the Decimal Currency Act 1969 and of all other powers enabling him in that behalf, hereby makes the following Regulations:

1.—(1) These Regulations may be cited as the Industrial Assurance (Premium Receipt Books) (Decimal Currency) Regulations, 1970, and shall come into operation on 1st September 1970.

(2) In these Regulations—

"principal Regulations" means the Industrial Assurance (Premium Receipt Books) Regulations 1948[1] as amended by the Industrial Assurance Premium Receipt Books) (Amendment) Regulations, 1961;[2]

---

[1] S.I. 1948, No. 2770.
[2] S.I. 1961, No. 597.

"policy" and "premium receipt book" have the meanings assigned by regulation 6 of the principal Regulations;

"new currency" and "old currency" have the meanings assigned by section 16 (1) of the Decimal Currency Act 1969;

"prescribed scheme" means the scheme prescribed in Schedule 4 to the Industrial Assurance (Decimal Currency) Regulations 1970;[1]

"approved scheme" means a special scheme approved in pursuance of section 6 (3) of the Decimal Currency Act 1969;

"collector" has the meaning assigned by section 45 (1) of the Industrial Assurance Act 1923;

"industrial assurance company" and "collecting society" have the meanings assigned by section 1 of the Industrial Assurance Act 1923 as amended by Schedule 6 to the Companies Act 1967.

(3) The Interpretation Act 1889 shall apply to the interpretation of these Regulations as it applies to the interpretation of an Act of Parliament.

2.—(1) A premium receipt book provided for use in respect of a policy effected before 15th February 1971 under which premiums are payable weekly or fortnightly may on and after that date, if the condition specified in paragraph (2) of this regulation is fulfilled, contain particulars of the total amount in the new currency of four successive weekly or, as the case may be, of two successive fortnightly premiums payable under the policy instead of the particulars of the premiums as required by subparagraph (*d*) of regulation 1 of the principal Regulations.

(2) The condition referred to in paragraph (1) of this regulation is that the amounts in the new currency payable in respect of premiums payable under the policy are determined under—

(*a*) paragraphs 1 or 2 of Schedule 3 to the Industrial Assurance (Decimal Currency) Regulations 1970, or

(*b*) the provisions of an approved scheme under which the amount in the new currency payable in respect of all or any part of each of four successive weekly or each of two successive fortnightly premiums is separately provided for.

3. A collector who on or after 15th February 1971 receives in respect of a policy a payment in the old currency which is not a whole number of pounds may instead of entering so much of that amount as is in shillings and pence in the appropriate premium receipt book in accordance with regulation 3 of the principal Regulations enter therein the corresponding amount in the new currency calculated in accordance with the provisions of the Schedule to these Regulations.

4. A premium receipt book provided for use in respect of a policy effected before 15th February 1971 shall on and after that date contain—

(*a*) a statement approved by the Industrial Assurance Commissioner explaining the effect of the provisions of the Industrial Assurance (Decimal Currency) Regulations 1970, being Regulations made

---

[1] S.I. 1970, No. 931.

under section 6 of the Decimal Currency Act 1969, relating to the determination of the amounts in the new currency payable in respect of premiums payable under the policy that fall due on or after that date, or,

(b) if the policy is one to which the prescribed or an approved scheme applies, information explaining the effect of the scheme on that policy including:—

   (i) how the amounts in the new currency payable in respect of premiums payable under the policy that fall due on or after 15th February 1971 are determined,

   (ii) if increased benefit is payable under the policy by virtue of the scheme, that the owner of the policy will be notified at his request of its amount, and

   (iii) in the case of a policy to which the prescribed scheme applies, the conditions under which the owner of the policy may appeal to the Industrial Assurance Commissioner if he considers that the increased benefit payable under the policy by virtue of the scheme is unfair in relation to any increased payable payments by him.

S. D. Musson,

Date 3rd July 1970.   Industrial Assurance Commissioner.

We approve these Regulations.

Reginald Eyre,
Bernard Weatherill,
Two of the Lords Commissioners of
Her Majesty's Treasury.

Date 7th July 1970.

EMPLOYERS LIABILITY (COMPULSORY INSURANCE) GENERAL REGULATIONS 1971

(S.I. 1971 No. 1117)

The Secretary of State, in exercise of his powers under sections 1 (2) and (3) (*a*), 2 (2), 4 (1) and (2) and 6 of the Employers' Liability (Compulsory Insurance) Act 1969 (hereinafter referred to as "the Act") and of all other powers enabling him in that behalf, hereby makes the following Regulations:—

Commencement, citation and interpretation

   1.—(1) These Regulations may be cited as the Employers' Liability, Compulsory Insurance) General Regulations 1971 and shall come into operation on 1st January 1972, with the exception of Regulations 6 and 7 which shall come into operation on 1st January 1973.

   (2) The Interpretation Act 1889 shall apply to the interpretation of these Regulations as it applies to the interpretation of an Act of Parliament.

Prohibition of certain conditions in policies of insurance

2.—(1) Any condition in a policy of insurance issued or renewed in accordance with the requirements of the Act after the coming into operation of this Regulation which provides (in whatever terms) that no liability (either generally or in respect of a particular claim) shall arise under the policy, or that any such liability so arising shall cease—

(a) in the event of some specified thing being done or omitted to be done after the happening of the event giving rise to a claim under the policy;

(b) unless the policy holder takes reasonable care to protect his employees against the risk of bodily injury or disease in the course of their employment;

(c) unless the policy holder complies with the requirements of any enactment for the protection of employees against the risk of bodily injury or disease in the course of their employment; and

(d) unless the policy holder keeps specified records or provides the insurer with or makes available to him information therefrom,

is hereby prohibited for the purposes of the Act.

(2) Nothing in this Regulation shall be taken as prejudicing any provision in a policy requiring the policy holder to pay to the insurer any sums which the latter may have become liable to pay under the policy and which have been applied to the satisfaction of claims in respect of employees or any costs and expenses incurred in relation to such claims.

Limit of amount of compulsory insurance

3.   The amount for which an employer is required by the Act to insure and maintain insurance shall be two million pounds in respect of claims relating to any one or more of his employees arising out of any one occurrence.

Employees not ordinarily resident in Great Britain

4.   The requirements of the Act and regulations thereunder shall apply in respect of employees not ordinarily resident in Great Britain who are present in Great Britain in the course of employment there for a continuous period of not less than fourteen days, as they apply in respect of employees ordinarily resident in Great Britain.

Issue of certificates of insurance

5.—(1) Every employer entering into a contract of insurance in accordance with the requirements of the Act shall be issued by the insurer with whom he contracts, in respect of the policy of insurance expressing the contract, with a certificate of insurance in the form and containing the particular specified in the Schedule to these Regulations.

(2) Every such certificate of insurance shall be issued not later than thirty days after the date on which the insurance commences or is renewed.

Display of copies of certificates of insurance

6.—(1) Where a certificate of insurance has been issued to an employer in accordance with Regulation 5 he shall display a copy or copies of that certificate at his place of business or, where he has more than one place of business, at each place of business at which he employs any person whose claims may be the subject of indemnity under the policy of insurance to which that certificate relates.

(2) Copies of any certificate of insurance issued in accordance with Regulation 5 shall be displayed in such numbers and characters and in such positions as to be easily seen and read by every person employed whose claims may be the subject of indemnity under the policy of insurance to which the certificate relates, and, where displayed in the open, shall be protected from the weather.

(3) Copies of any certificate of insurance issued in accordance with Regulation 5 shall be kept displayed until the expiration of the period of insurance stated in the certificate or if the policy of insurance to which the certificate relates is cancelled before that time, until the policy is cancelled and, in either case, shall not be displayed thereafter.

Production of certificates of insurance

7. Where an employer is served with a notice issued on behalf of the Secretary of State requiring him to do so, he shall produce or send to any officer of the Department of Employment specified in the notice, at the address and within the time specified therein, the original or a copy of every certificate of insurance issued to him in accordance with Regulation 5, which relates to a period of insurance current at the date of the notice.

Inspection of policies of insurance

8. An employer who has entered into a contract of insurance in accordance with the requirements of the Act shall during the currency of the insurance permit the policy of insurance expressing the contract or a copy of the policy to be inspected by any inspector duly authorised by the Secretary of State for the purposes of the Act either (in the case of a company) at the registered office or (in any case) at a place of business of the employer as the inspector requires and at a time when the inspector requires it to be produced for inspection, being a time of which reasonable notice has been given.

Production by inspectors of evidence of authority

9. Any inspector duly authorised by the Secretary of State for the purposes of the Act shall, if so required when visiting any premises for those purposes, produce to an employer or his agent some duly authenticated document showing that he is so authorised.

9th July 1971.

Robert Carr,
Secretary of State for Employment.

SCHEDULE   Regulation 5

CERTIFICATE OF INSURANCE

EMPLOYERS' LIABILITY (COMPULSORY INSURANCE) ACT 1969

(A copy or copies of this certificate must be displayed at each place of business at which the policy holder employs persons covered by the policy.)

Policy No.................

1. Name of policy holder.
2. Date of commencement of insurance.
3. Date of expiry of insurance.

We hereby certify that the policy to which this certificate relates is issued in accordance with the requirements of the Employers' Liability (Compulsory Insurance) Act 1969 and regulations thereunder.

Signed on behalf of.............................(Authorised Insurer)

.... (Signature)

EMPLOYERS' LIABILITY (COMPULSORY INSURANCE) EXEMPTION REGULATIONS 1971

(S.I. 1971 No. 1933)

The Secretary of State, in exercise of his powers under section 3 (1) (*c*) of the Employers' Liability (Compulsory Insurance) Act 1969 and of all other powers enabling him in that behalf, hereby makes the following Regulations:—

Commencement and citation

1. These Regulations may be cited as the Employers' Liability (Compulsory Insurance) Exemption Regulations 1971 and shall come into operation on 1st January 1972.

Interpretation

2.—(1) The Interpretation Act 1889 shall apply to the interpretation of these Regulations as it applies to the interpretation of an Act of Parliament.

(2) In these Regulations—

"the Act" means the Employers' Liability (Compulsory Insurance) Act 1969;

"joint subsidiary" has the same meaning as in section 51 (5) of the Transport Act 1968; and

"subsidiary" has the same meaning as in section 154 of the Companies Act 1948 (taking references in that section to a company as being references to any body corporate).

Exemptions

3. The following employers are hereby exempted from the requirement of the Act to insure and maintain insurance:—

(*a*) any body which is for the time being a body holding a certificate issued by a government department (not being a certificate which has been revoked) stating that claims established against that body in respect of any liability of the kind mentioned in section 1 (1) of the Act will, to any extent to which they are incapable of being satisfied by that body, be satisfied out of moneys provided by Parliament;

(*b*) the Government of any foreign state or Commonwealth country;

(*c*) any inter-governmental organisation which by virtue of any statute or Order in Council has the legal capacities of a body corporate;

(*d*) any subsidiary of any such body as is mentioned in section 3 (1) (*b*) of the Act (which exempts any body corporate established by or under any enactment for the carrying on of any industry or part of an industry, or of any undertaking, under national owner-ship or control) and any company of which two or more such bodies are members and which would, if those bodies were a single body corporate, be a subsidiary of that body corporate;

(*e*) any passenger transport executive established under the Transport Act 1968 and any subsidiary thereof;

(*f*) the London Transport Executive, any subsidiary and any joint subsidiary thereof;

(*g*) Cable and Wireless Limited;

(*h*) companies which are statutory water undertakers within the mean-ing of the Water Acts 1945 and 1948;

(*i*) the Metropolitan Water Board;

(*j*) the Lee Conservancy Catchment Board;

(*k*) the Conservators of the River Thames;

(*l*) any regional water board and any water development board within the meaning of the Water (Scotland) Act 1967;

(*m*) any river authority established under the Water Resources Act 1963;

(*n*) any river purification board within the meaning of the Rivers (Prevention of Pollution) (Scotland) Act 1951;

(*o*) any development corporation within the meaning of the New Towns Act 1965 or the New Towns (Scotland) Act 1968;

(*p*) the Commission for the New Towns;

(*q*) the Letchworth Garden City Corporation;

(*r*) the Schools Council for Curriculum and Examinations;

(*s*) the Scottish Certificate of Education Examination Board;

(*t*) any managing committee of an approved probation home or an approved probation hostel within the meaning of the Criminal Justice Act 1948;

(*u*) any licensing compensation committee appointed under section 16 of the Licensing Act 1964;

(*v*) any magistrates' courts committee and the Committee of Magistrates for inner London established under the Justices of the Peace Act 1949;

(*w*) any probation and after-care committee established under the Criminal Justice Act 1948;

(*x*) any employer who is a member of a mutual insurance association of shipowners or of shipowners and others, in respect of any liability to an employee of the kind mentioned in section 1 (1) of the Act against which the employer is insured for the time being with that association for an amount not less than that required by the Act and regulations thereunder, being an employer who holds a certificate issued by that association to the effect that he is so insured in relation to that employee;

(*y*) any licensee within the meaning of the Nuclear Installations Act 1965, in respect of any liability to pay compensation under that Act to any of his employees in respect of a breach of duty imposed on him by virtue of section 7 of that Act.

26th November 1971.

Robert Carr,
Secretary of State for Employment.

INDEX